D1475062

AQUINAS

TLS
11/29/05

'This is by far the best book we have on Aquinas's philosophy as a whole, and it will undoubtedly become a standard point of reference for anyone interested in his work' **Robert Pasnau**, *Mind*

'This book is an astounding achievement. It will not be superseded for decades. It will surely remain on the bibliography for as long as Thomas Aquinas is regarded as a major thinker, for as long then as there is Western philosophy' **Fergus Kerr**, *Ars Disputandi*

"a massive work of bridge-building that is *triply* impressive. Not only does she have a very comprehensive knowledge of Aquinas's texts to take off from, but she is well read in the contemporary Anglo-American analytic philosophy where she will land, and she has an acute and lucid critical mind with which to test the load-bearing capacity of the bridges she builds." **Timothy McDermott**, *Times Literary Supplement*

Eleonore Stump is the Robert J. Henle, S.J., Professor of Philosophy at Saint Louis University. Her previous books include *Boethius's De topicis differentiis* (1978; reprinted 1989); *Boethius's In Ciceronis Topica* (1988); *Dialectic and Its Place in the Development of Medieval Logic* (1980); *The Cambridge Companion to Aquinas* (ed. with Norman Kretzmann) (1993); *Aquinas's Moral Theory: Essays in Honor of Norman Kretzmann* (ed. with Scott MacDonald) (1999); and The Cambridge Companion to Augustine (ed. with Norman Kratzmann) (2001).

ARGUMENTS OF THE PHILOSOPHERS

The purpose of this series is to provide a contemporary assessment and history of the entire course of philosophical thought. Each book contains a detailed, critical introduction to the work of a philosopher or school of major influence and significance.

Also available in the series:

*Aquinas	Eleonore Stump
*Descartes	Margaret D. Wilson
*Hegel	M. J. Inwood
*Hume	Barry Stroud
*Kant	Ralph C. S. Walker
*Kierkegaard	Alastair Hannay
*Locke	Michael Ayers
*Karl Marx	Allen Wood
Malebranche	Andrew Pyle
*Merleau-Ponty	Stephen Priest
*Nietzsche	Richard Schacht
*Plato	Justin Gosling
*Plotinus	Lloyd P. Gerson
*Rousseau	Timothy O'Hagan
*The Presocratic Philosophers	Jonathan Barnes
*Santayana	Timothy L. S. Sprigge
*Sceptics	R. J. Hankinson
*Wittgenstein, 2nd edition	Robert Fogelin

* also available in paperback

AQUINAS

Eleonore Stump

Routledge
Taylor & Francis Group

LONDON AND NEW YORK

First published 2003
by Routledge
2 Park Square, Milton Park, Abingdon, OX14 4RN

Simultaneously published in the USA and Canada
by Routledge
270 Madison Ave, New York, NY 10016

First published in paperback 2005

Routledge is an imprint of the Taylor & Francis Group

© 2003, 2005 Eleonore Stump

Typeset in Garamond by Taylor & Francis Books Ltd
Printed and bound in Great Britain by
TJ International Ltd, Padstow, Cornwall

All rights reserved. No part of this book may be reprinted or reproduced or
utilised in any form or by any electronic, mechanical, or other means, now
known or hereafter invented, including photocopying and recording, or in any
information storage or retrieval system, without permission in writing from the
publishers.

British Library Cataloguing in Publication Data
A catalogue record for this book is available from the British Library

Library of Congress Cataloging in Publication Data

ISBN 0–415–02960–0 (hbk)
ISBN 0–415–37898–2 (pbk)

FOR MY DEARLY LOVED CHILDREN

We have also a more sure word of prophecy, whereunto you do well that ye take heed, as unto a light that shineth in a dark place, until the day dawn, and the day star arise in your hearts.

He that overcometh and keepeth my works unto the end ... I will give him the morning star ... I am Alpha and Omega, the beginning and the end, the first and the last ... I am the root and the offspring of David, the bright and morning star.

CONTENTS

CONTENTS

PREFACE

There are some books which only a young and inexperienced scholar would undertake to write but which only a senior scholar who knows enough to shrink from the task might conceivably be able to write. This is one of those books. Its explicit purpose is to explicate the views of Aquinas with some historical accuracy and to bring them into dialogue with the corresponding discussions in contemporary philosophy. On the face of it, of course, this sort of twinned investigation should be the aim of any philosophical study of the texts of a thinker from some previous age. If such a study is not carried out with historical accuracy, the result may be philosophically interesting, but it will not count as a study of the thought of that historical figure. On the other hand, if the views of preceding periods are presented in such a way that they make no contribution to current philosophical discussion, then the historical views are preserved only as museum specimens, and not as living interlocutors still able to influence philosophical thought. The explicit aim of this book is therefore a good one. The problem comes in the attempt to execute it. Aquinas wrote on a very broad range of issues, in highly technical and sophisticated ways, so that understanding and presenting his thought is a daunting undertaking. Connecting it with related discussions in contemporary philosophy is a Herculean task.

In one way or another, I have been engaged in this task for more years than I care to acknowledge. In the process, I have learned a great deal, including lessons about the need for compromise. The compromise is what some readers may notice first.

Readers familiar with Aquinas will find that some part of Aquinas's thought – or, perhaps more offensively, some standard explication of it – which strikes them as particularly important is not represented in this book at all. The list of things I have left out of this book is at least as long as its table of contents. So, to take just one of many things which could be given as an example, I have said virtually nothing about the relationship of Aquinas's views to the views of preceding thinkers, either those in the ancient Greek and Hellenistic world or those in the earlier Latin-speaking medieval period or about the way in which Aquinas's thought was influenced by the

Islamic and Jewish philosophy and theology of his own milieu. With very few exceptions, I have also not discussed the development of his thought from his early works to his mature writings. And I have only briefly touched on or omitted completely certain topics frequently discussed in general studies of Aquinas's thought, including, for example, the relation of philosophy to theology, the distinction between essence and existence, the metaphysical notion of participation, real relations between God and creatures, and many others. My reason for not treating these issues and topics is that it is not possible to do everything in one volume, even a fat volume, and that the things I have omitted are regularly discussed in standard reference works on Aquinas. At any rate, it is abundantly clear that some compromise is necessary between the ideal plan of presenting all of Aquinas's thought and any practicable plan for one book. I have tried to pick those issues and topics that allow a reader to see Aquinas's whole worldview in broad outline and to appropriate in particular some of its richest and most powerful parts.

On the other hand, but still on the same point, readers coming to this volume from contemporary philosophy may find that in many places where they might have wanted or expected a bridge between Aquinas's thought and contemporary philosophy, Aquinas's thought is presented alone, without reference to current work in the field. Here, too, compromise has been necessary if the volume was to be kept within any reasonable bounds. In effect, I concentrated bridge-building efforts on those topics where, by the vagaries of academic interests and trends, there is some special confluence of Aquinas's views and current philosophical debate, so that either Aquinas's thought is particularly illuminated by something in the contemporary discussion or has something particularly interesting to contribute to it. But even within these constraints, I have had, in the end, to leave unexplored topics that might have been profitably pursued, including, for example, the nature of causation, the role of final causes in explanation, the notion of truth, the notion of beauty, human emotions, divine impassibility, the persons of the Trinity, and many others. The bridge-building of this volume is thus only a contribution to an on-going process, which requires many scholars with various skills and interests, of handing on Aquinas's thought in all its richness and power.

Some readers may also wonder at the way in which the subjects are grouped in the table of contents, which is not simply a list of the main areas in contemporary philosophy, such as metaphysics, epistemology, philosophy of mind, and so on, and at the mix of theology and philosophy in this volume. It would be possible to extract, for example, Aquinas's metaphysics or epistemology from various parts of his work and present his thought in a form more familiar to contemporary philosophy. But Aquinas himself does not present his views in this form in his systematic treatments. After experimenting with different approaches, I have decided that there is merit in following *roughly* Aquinas's categorization and ordering, and thus the order of the table of contents for this volume largely (but not entirely) reflects the order of Aquinas's *Summa theologiae*. At any rate, it seemed to me in the end that Aquinas's own view of the world emerges more clearly in this way, and the mix of what we now would clearly count as philosophy with theology is unquestionably representative of his own mode of writing. And, clearly, no bridge-building between his thought and contemporary philosophy is possible without beginning with *his* thought; his voice is not brought into current debate if it is not *his* voice which is being heard. On the other hand, readers interested in knowing Aquinas's positions primarily as they relate to some area of contemporary philosophy will have no trouble finding them even with this arrangement. His epistemology, for example, can be found in Chapters 7 and 8, on the nature of human knowledge and the mechanisms of human cognition.

The one regret I have with my decision to arrange the material in this way is that some readers who begin at the beginning and read through from there will perhaps never get past the opening chapters, where some of the densest and most technical discussion occurs. I encourage readers who might get bogged down in the section on the ultimate foundation of reality to read the chapters in any order that interests them. Although there is certainly something that is lost if the chapters are not read in order, I have nonetheless tried to make it possible to read each chapter on its own; and there are ample cross-references to show a reader who reads in this way where he or she might profitably turn to other chapters for further discussion of the same issues.

A word of explanation is also in order as regards secondary literature. The secondary literature on Aquinas is vast and of uneven quality; an attempt to canvass and evaluate all of it would be bulky and often tedious to one or another group of readers in the audience at which this book is aimed. In the time I was working on this book, I read and profited from much of this literature, but in the book itself, I have cited and discussed only those secondary sources that make a direct and immediate contribution of an especially valuable sort to a particular subject as I discuss it in a given chapter. The bibliography of the book reflects this practice, and so many helpful, interesting secondary sources on Aquinas's thought are omitted from the bibliography; this book is intended as a philosophical study of Aquinas, rather than as a textbook survey of his thought. In addition to the standard Thomistic bibliographies, readers interested in a reference bibliography, or in a survey approach to Aquinas's work, can find it, for example, in *The Cambridge Companion to Aquinas* (Cambridge University Press, 1993), edited by Norman Kretzmann and me. Finally, in the time in which I was doing what I firmly intended to be the last revisions on this manuscript, some excellent new books on Aquinas appeared, and some others were delivered to their publishers; they will undoubtedly be in print before this book is. If I had stopped to digest those books and to include comments on them here, the last revisions would have been delayed even longer; and so, although I look forward to learning from and commenting on that newly appeared literature, I have not engaged it here.

Acknowledgements

Then there is the matter of acknowledgements. In the course of writing this book, I have accumulated a great number of debts to people whose help – of one kind or another – has contributed to bringing this book to fruition and has made it better than it would otherwise have been.

The most important acknowledgement and the one needing the most explanation is my debt to Norman Kretzmann. When I was originally approached about writing this book, I agreed to undertake it only if Norman would write it with me, and he and the Press both agreed to my request. Norman and I realized that this book would be a long, slow project, and we planned some of our joint papers as preparation for it. In the event, however, Norman became ill with what he knew was a terminal disease; and we decided together that his remaining energies ought to go into trying to finish the projected three-volume study of Aquinas's *Summa contra gentiles* which he had in progress. As it was, I am sad to say, he succeeded in finishing only two of those volumes: *The Metaphysics of Theism* (Oxford University Press, 1997) and *The Metaphysics of Creation* (Oxford University Press, 1999). (What work he did do on the third volume has also been published, in a special issue of *Medieval Philosophy and Theology* edited by my friend Scott MacDonald, who sorrowed with me at Norman's death.)

Nonetheless, the joint work Norman and I did in preparation for this book is reflected here. In addition to an overview of Aquinas's life and work, we wrote together three papers on divine eternity, and one each on God's knowledge, God's goodness and God's simplicity. All of that work is ancestral to the chapters on those topics in this book. One piece – our introduction to Aquinas's life and work – is reproduced here with only small changes, but I have reworked extensively all the rest of our joint articles. The chapter on divine simplicity is the most radically altered. Our original attempt to defend Aquinas's account of divine simplicity, I now see, was seriously incomplete; and although I do not suppose that even now I am able to give a complete and successful exposition and defense of this part of Aquinas's thought, I do think I can take the defense a significant step further than Norman and I were originally able to do.

In addition to the chapters which bear some greater or lesser resemblance to the papers we did together, all the rest of this book reflects Norman's thought as well. He was my teacher, mentor and friend; and his extensive, helpful, critical comments on all my work have informed the thought underlying every part of this book. Or, what is more nearly true to say, over our many years of working together, my way of thinking about things became so entangled with his that it is not possible to make a sharp division between what is mine and what is his. I have no words to express what a loss his death was for me.

I should perhaps add here that, in addition to the papers jointly authored by Norman and me, other papers of mine (listed in the bibliography) are the ancestors of many of the chapters in this book. All of these papers are revised, most of them heavily. In some cases, such as the chapter on faith, the revisions are drastic enough to make the connection to the earlier paper hard to recognize.

I also need to acknowledge the help of many other scholars and philosophers. The following people gave me helpful comments on larger or smaller parts of the manuscript or on a paper that was a precursor to a chapter in it: Marilyn Adams, Robert Adams, William Alston, William Anglin, Richard Bernstein, James Bohman, David Burrell, Terry Christlieb, Bowman Clarke, Norris Clarke, Richard Creel, Richard Cross, Fred Crosson, Brian Davies, Stephen Davis, Lawrence Dewan, Therese Druart, Ronald Feenstra, Fred Feldman, Thomas Flint, Shawn Floyd, Harry Frankfurt, Leon Galis, John Greco, William Hasker, Joshua Hoffman, Al Howsepian, Christopher Hughes, James Keller, James Klagge, Brian Leftow, David Lewis, Howard Louthan, Scott MacDonald, Steven Maitzen, William Mann, George Mavrodes, Deborah Mayo, Ralph McInerny, Alan McMichael, Ernan McMullin, Harlan Miller, Gerald O'Collins, Timothy O'Connor, Robert Pasnau, Derk Pereboom, Alvin Plantinga, Cornelius Plantinga, Jr., Chris Pliatska, Philip Quinn, Gary Rosenkrantz, James Ross, Michael Rota, William Rowe, Joseph Runzo, Bruce Russell, Brian Shanley, Christopher Shields, Sydney Shoemaker, Richard Sorabji, Robert Stalnaker, James Stone, Nicholas Sturgeon, Richard Swinburne, Charles Taliaferro, Kevin Timpe, Thomas Tracy, John van Engen, Bas van Fraassen, Peter van Inwagen, Theodore Vitali, Edward Wierenga, John Wippel, Nicholas Wolterstorff. At the stage at which I was preparing to enjoy the relief of sending the manuscript off in the post, Jim Stone gave me extensive and helpful comments on virtually all of it; I owe him a great debt for this labor of his, which has made the final product more careful and polished than it otherwise would have been. The final stage of the revisions has also profited significantly from the labors of my two exemplary research assistants, Chris Pliatska and Kevin Timpe, who ferreted out and fixed many, but no doubt not all, of the instances of sloppiness that tend, miserably enough, to creep into a work of this size.

I also need to acknowledge the superb facilities and pleasant personnel of the National Humanities Center, where some of the work for this book was done. I am grateful as well to the Religion Program of the Pew Charitable Trusts for a year of leave, during which I made considerable progress on the manuscript. I also want to express my heartfelt thanks to Father Michael McGarry, C.S.P., and the Tantur Ecumenical Institute in Jerusalem, of which Father McGarry is Rector. The sad events in the Middle East notwithstanding, Tantur is one of the best places for contemplative academic work.

The beauty of the Institute and its location, the excellence of its library, and the dedicated commitment of the staff and Rector of Tantur make it wonderful to work there; I remember with gratitude my weeks at Tantur working on this book.

Finally, I need to express gratitude of a more personal sort. The period in which I finished this manuscript was marked for me by a firestorm of grief, and I owe more than I can say, certainly in any conventional form, to Father Theodore Vitali, C.P., whose wise counsel and great-hearted willingness to suffer with me walked me through the storm. The Jesuit and Dominican communities at Saint Louis University have also been an unparalleled blessing to me in this time. Married female Protestant that I am, I have found in those communities deeply comforting company for the road. The Dominican Prior has pronounced me the world's most improbable Thomist and with exemplary patience has welcomed me into his fold. The Jesuits I am grateful to call my friends have made 'consolation' a word in my working vocabulary.

I also owe a great debt of gratitude to my husband Donald. In over thirty years of marriage, he has gone with me through all the battles that come with starting out poor, overworked and off-balance (in the way only the tumults of child-raising can produce), and yet trying to do one's best anyway for those whom one loves. If the world gave medals for such things, he would be the world's most decorated veteran. And finally I am grateful to my children, whom I have loved to distraction all the years this book was in progress. Loving them and wishing fervently for their flourishing has given me whatever insight I possess into the idea of the mothering love of God that animates Aquinas's whole worldview. This book is dedicated to them.

LIST OF ABBREVIATIONS

CT	*Compendium theologiae*
DEE	*De ente et essentia*
DPN	*De principiis naturae*
DRJ	*De regimine Judaeorum ad Ducissam Brabantiae*
DRP	*De regimine principum*
DSS	*De substantiis separatis*
DUI	*De unitate intellectus contra Averroistas*
In BDT	*Expositio super librum Boethii De trinitate*
In I Cor	*Commentarium super Epistolam I ad Corinthios*
In II Cor	*Commentarium super Epistolam II ad Corinthios*
In DA	*Sententia libri De anima*
In DC	*Sententia super librum De caelo et mundo*
In DDN	*Expositio super Dionysium De divinis Nominibus*
In Gal	*Reportatio super Epistolam ad Galatas*
In Heb	*Expositio super Epistolam ad Hebraeos*
In Meta	*Sententia super Metaphysicam*
In NE	*Sententia libri Ethicorum*
In PA	*Sententia super Posteriora analytica*
In Phil	*Reportatio super Epistolam ad Philippenses*
In Rom	*Commentarium super Epistolam ad Romanos*
In Sent	*Scriptum super libros Sententiarum*
In I Thess	*Reportatio super Epistolam Primam ad Thessalonienses*
QDA	*Quaestio disputata de anima*
QDM	*Quaestiones disputatae de malo*
QDP	*Quaestiones disputatae de potentia*
QDSC	*Quaestio disputata de spiritualibus creaturis*
QDV	*Quaestiones disputatae de veritate*
QDVC	*Quaestiones disputatae de virtutibus in communi*
QQ	*Quaestiones quodlibetales*
SCG	*Summa contra gentiles*
ST	*Summa theologiae*

LIST OF AQUINAS'S WORKS

Not all of Aquinas's works exist in critical editions, but the many volumes of the Leonine edition ordinarily provide the best available Latin texts. Most volumes of the Marietti editions reproduce the Leonine text in handier form with useful aids to research. There are many translations into English and other modern languages, but by no means all the works have been translated. For detailed lists of editions and translations of each work see Torrell (1993), Weisheipl (1983) or Gilson (1956). Ingardia (1993) is an indispensable bibliography. Deferrari and Barry (1948) is an indispensable lexicon. Busa (1974–80) provides an exhaustive but somewhat unwieldy resource for research in Aquinas. The following is an approximately chronological list of works, excluding letters and liturgies.

Aquinas, Thomas (1248–73) *Opera Omnia* (Complete Works), ed. Leonine Commission, S. Thomae Aquinatis Doctoris Angelici. *Opera Omnia*. Iussu Leonis XIII, P.M. edita, Rome: Vatican Polyglot Press, 1882–. (Many of the editions in this series are repeated in the Marietti Editions.)
Aquinas, Thomas (1248–52 or 1252–6) *De principiis naturae, ad fratrem Sylvestrum* (On the Principles of Nature, for Brother Sylvester). (Written either at Cologne, 1248–52, or Paris, 1252–6.)
Aquinas, Thomas (1251/2) *Expositio super Isaiam ad litteram* (Literal Commentary on Isaiah). (Written at Cologne.)
Aquinas, Thomas (1251/2) *Postilla super Ieremiam* (Commentary on Jeremiah). (Written at Cologne.)
Aquinas, Thomas (1251/2) *Postilla super Threnos* (Commentary on Lamentations). (Written at Cologne.)
Aquinas, Thomas (1252/3? or 1273?) *Postilla super Psalmos* (Commentary on Psalms). (Written either at Paris, 1252/3, or Naples, 1273. Incomplete, covers Psalms 1–54.)
Aquinas, Thomas (1252–6) *De ente et essentia, ad fratres et socios suos* (On Being and Essence, For His Brothers and Companions). (Written at Paris.)
Aquinas, Thomas (1253–6) *Scriptum super libros Sententiarum* (Commentary on the Sentences). (Written at Paris.)

Aquinas, Thomas (1256) *Principia: 'Hic est liber mandatorum Dei' et 'Rigans montes de superioribus suis'* (Inaugural Lectures: 'This Is the Book of God's Commandments' and 'Watering the Hills from His Places Above'). (Written at Paris.)

Aquinas, Thomas (1256) *Contra impugnantes Dei cultum et religionem* (Against Those Who Assail the Worship of God and Religion). (Written at Paris, a refutation of William of Saint-Amour's *De periculis novissimorum temporum*.)

Aquinas, Thomas (1256–9) *Quaestiones disputatae de veritate* (Disputed Questions on Truth). (Written at Paris.)

Aquinas, Thomas (1256–9) *Quaestiones quodlibetales* VII–XI (*Quodlibetal Questions* VII–XII). (Written at Paris.)

Aquinas, Thomas (1257/8) *Expositio super librum Boethii De trinitate* (Commentary on Boethius's *De trinitate*). (Written at Paris; incomplete.)

Aquinas, Thomas (1259?) *Expositio super librum Boethii De hebdomadibus* (Commentary on Boethius's *De hebdomadibus*). (Written at Paris; incomplete.)

Aquinas, Thomas (1259–65) *Summa contra gentiles* (Synopsis [of Christian Doctrine] Directed Against Unbelievers). (Written at Paris, Naples and Orvieto.)

Aquinas, Thomas (1261–5) *Expositio super Iob ad litteram* (Literal Commentary on Job). (Written at Orvieto.)

Aquinas, Thomas (1261–5 or 1265–8) *Expositio super librum Dionysii De divinis nominibus* (Commentary on Dionysius's *De divinis nominibus*). (Written at Orvieto, 1261–5, or Rome, 1265–8.)

Aquinas, Thomas (1262–8) *Glossa continua super Evangelia* (*Catena aurea*) [A Continuous Gloss on the Four Gospels (The Golden Chain)]. (Written at Orvieto and Rome.)

Aquinas, Thomas (1263/4) *Contra errores Graecorum, ad Urbanem IV Pontificem Maximum* (Against Mistakes of the Greek [Fathers of the Church], for Pope Urban IV). (Written at Orvieto, on an anonymous treatise, *De fide sanctae trinitatis contra errores Graecorum*.)

Aquinas, Thomas (1264) *De rationibus fidei contra Saracenos, Graecos, et Armenos, ad cantorem Antiochiae* (On Arguments for the Faith Directed against Mohammedans, Greek Orthodox Christians and Armenians, for the Cantor of Antioch).

Aquinas, Thomas (1265–6) *Quaestiones disputatae de potentia* (Disputed Questions on Power). (Written at Rome.)

Aquinas, Thomas (1265–6) *Quaestio disputata de anima* (Disputed Question on the Soul). (Twenty-one articles, written at Rome.)

Aquinas, Thomas (1265–7) *Responsio ad fr. Ioannem Vercellensem de articulis 108 sumptis ex opere Petri de Tarentasia* (Reply to Brother John of Vercelli Regarding 108 Articles Drawn from the Work of Peter of Tarentaise [on the Sentences]). (Written at Rome.)

Aquinas, Thomas (1265–7) *Compendium theologiae, ad fratrem Reginaldum socium suum* (A Compendium of Theology, for Brother Reginald, his Companion). (Written at Rome; incomplete.)

Aquinas, Thomas (1266–72) *Quaestiones disputatae de malo* (Disputed Questions on Evil). (Written at Rome and Paris.)

Aquinas, Thomas (1266–68) *Summa theologiae* Ia (Synopsis of Theology, First Part). (Written at Rome. See below for IaIIae, IIaIIae and IIIa. The whole of the *Summa theologiae* can be found in the Leonine edition, vols 4–12.)

Aquinas, Thomas (1267) *De regno* [or *De regimine principum*], *ad regem Cypri* (On Kingship [or On the Governance of Rulers], for the King of Cyprus). (Written at Rome. Authentic only through Book II, c. 4.)

Aquinas, Thomas (1267–8) *Sententia super De anima* (Commentary on Aristotle's *On the Soul*). (Written at Rome.)

Aquinas, Thomas (1267–8) *Quaestio disputata de spiritualibus creaturis* (Disputed Question on Spiritual Creatures [Angels]). (Eleven articles, written at Rome.)

Aquinas, Thomas (1268–9) *Sententia super Physicam* (Commentary on Aristotle's *Physics*). (Written at Paris.)

Aquinas, Thomas (1268–9) *Sententia super Meteora* (Commentary on Aristotle's *Meteora*). (Written at Paris; incomplete.)

Aquinas, Thomas (1268–70) *Sententia super De sensu et sensato* (Commentary on Aristotle's *De sensu et sensato*). (Written at Paris.)

Aquinas, Thomas (1268–71) *Summa theologiae* IaIIae (Synopsis of Theology, First Part of the Second Part). (Written at Rome and Paris.)

Aquinas, Thomas (1268–72) *Quaestiones quodlibetales* I–VI, XII (Quodlibetal Questions I–VI, XII). (Written at Paris.)

Aquinas, Thomas (1269) *De forma absolutionis sacramentalis, ad generalem magistrum Ordinis* (On the Form of Sacramental Absolution, for the Master General of the Order [John Vercelli]). (Written at Paris.)

Aquinas, Thomas (1269) *De secreto* (On Secret Testimony). (Written at Paris. A committee report in which Aquinas is the lone dissenter, supporting the right of a religious superior to compel a subject to reveal a secret even under the seal of confession.)

Aquinas, Thomas (1269–70) *Lectura super Matthaeum* (Lectures on the Gospel of Matthew). (Written at Paris.)

Aquinas, Thomas (1269–70) *De perfectione spiritualis vitae* (On the Perfecting of the Spiritual Life). (Written at Paris, directed against Gérard d'Abbeville's *Contra adversarium perfectionis christianae*.)

Aquinas, Thomas (1269–72) *Sententia libri Politicorum* (Commentary on Aristotle's *Politics*). (Written probably at Paris; incomplete.)

Aquinas, Thomas (1270?) *Sententia super De memoria et reminiscentia* (Commentary on Aristotle's *De memoria et reminiscentia*). (Written probably at Paris.)

Aquinas, Thomas (1270) *Tabula libri Ethicorum* (An Analytical Table of Aristotle's *Ethics*). (Written at Paris; incomplete.)

Aquinas, Thomas (1270) *De unitate intellectus, contra Averroistas* (On the Unicity of Intellect, Against the Averroists). (Written at Paris.)

Aquinas, Thomas (1270–1) *Sententia super Peri hermenias* (Commentary on Aristotle's *De Interpretatione*). (Written at Paris; incomplete.)

Aquinas, Thomas (1270–2) *Lectura super Ioannem* (Lectures on the Gospel of John). (Written at Paris.)

Aquinas, Thomas (1270–3) *Sententia super Metaphysicam* (Commentary on Aristotle's *Metaphysics*). (Written at Paris and Naples.)

Aquinas, Thomas (1270–3) *Expositio et lectura super Epistolas Pauli Apostoli* (Commentary and Lectures on the Epistles of Paul the Apostle). (Written at Paris and Naples.)

Aquinas, Thomas (1271) *De aeternitate mundi, contra murmurantes* (On the Eternity of the World, Against Grumblers). (Written at Paris.)

Aquinas, Thomas (1271) *Responsio ad magistrum Ioannem de Vercellis de articulis 42* (Reply to Master John Vercelli Regarding 42 Articles). (Written at Paris. Aquinas's answers to doctrinal questions which Vercelli submitted also to Albert the Great and Robert Kilwardby.)

Aquinas, Thomas (1271–2) *Summa theologiae IIaIIae* (Synopsis of Theology, Second Part of the Second Part). (Written at Paris.)

Aquinas, Thomas (1271–2) *Contra doctrinam retrahentium a religione* (Against the Teaching of Those who Dissuade [Boys] from Entering the Religious Life). (Written at Paris, opposing the work of Gérard d'Abbeville.)

Aquinas, Thomas (1271–2) *Sententia libri Ethicorum* (Commentary on Aristotle's *Nicomachean Ethics*). (Written at Paris.)

Aquinas, Thomas (1271–2) *Sententia super Posteriora analytica* (Commentary on Aristotle's *Posterior Analytics*). (Written at Paris.)

Aquinas, Thomas (1271–2) *Quaestio disputata de virtutibus in communi* (Disputed Question on the Virtues in General). (Thirteen articles, written at Paris.)

Aquinas, Thomas (1271–2) *Quaestio disputata de caritate* (Disputed Question on Charity). (Thirteen articles, written at Paris.)

Aquinas, Thomas (1271–2) *Quaestio disputata de correctione fraterna* (Disputed Question on Fraternal Correction). (Two articles, written at Paris.)

Aquinas, Thomas (1271–2) *Quaestio disputata de spe* (Disputed Question on Hope). (Four articles, written at Paris.)

Aquinas, Thomas (1271–2) *Quaestio disputata de virtutibus cardinalibus* (Disputed Question on the Cardinal Virtues). (Four articles, written at Paris.)

Aquinas, Thomas (1271–3) *De substantiis separatis, ad fratrem Reginaldum socium suum* (On Separated Substances [Angels], for Brother Reginald, his Companion). (Written at Paris or Naples, incomplete.)

Aquinas, Thomas (1272) *Quaestio disputata de unione verbi incarnati* (Disputed Question on the Unity of the Incarnate Word). (Five articles, written at Paris.)

Aquinas, Thomas (1272) *Expositio super librum De causis* (Commentary on the *Liber de causis*). (Written at Paris.)

Aquinas, Thomas (1272–3) *Summa theologiae IIIa* (Synopsis of Theology, Third Part). (Written at Paris and Naples, incomplete.)

Aquinas, Thomas (1272–3) *Sententia super libros De caelo et mundo* (Commentary on Aristotle's *On Heaven and Earth*). (Written at Naples; incomplete.)

Aquinas, Thomas (1272–3) *Sententia super libros De generatione et corruptione* (Commentary on Aristotle's *On Generation and Corruption*). (Written at Naples, incomplete.)

Aquinas, Thomas (1273, or 1261–8?) *Collationes in decem praecepta* (Sermon Commentaries on the Ten Commandments). (Written at Naples, 1273, or possibly at Orvieto and Rome, 1261–8.)

Aquinas, Thomas (1273, or 1268–72?) *Collationes super Ave Maria* (Sermon Commentaries on the Ave Maria). (Written at Naples, 1273, or possibly at Paris, 1268–72.)

Aquinas, Thomas (1273) *Collationes super Credo in Deum* (Sermon Commentaries on the Apostles' Creed). (Written at Naples.)

Aquinas, Thomas (1273) *Collationes super Pater Noster* (Sermon Commentaries on the Lord's Prayer). (Written at Naples.)

INTRODUCTION
Life and overview of Aquinas's thought

Introduction

Thomas Aquinas (1224/6–1274) lived an active, demanding academic and ecclesiastical life that ended while he was still in his forties. He nonetheless produced many works, varying in length from a few pages to a few volumes. Because his writings grew out of his activities as a teacher in the Dominican order and a member of the theology faculty of the University of Paris, most are concerned with what he and his contemporaries thought of as theology. However, much of academic theology in the Middle Ages consisted in a rational investigation of the most fundamental aspects of reality in general and of human nature and behavior in particular. That vast domain obviously includes much of what is now considered to be philosophy, and is reflected in the broad subject matter of Aquinas's theological writings.

The scope and philosophical character of medieval theology as practised by Aquinas can easily be seen in his two most important works, *Summa contra gentiles* (*SCG*) (*Synopsis [of Christian Doctrine] Directed Against Unbelievers*) and *Summa theologiae* (*ST*) (*Synopsis of Theology*). However, many of the hundreds of topics covered in those two large works are also investigated in more detail in the smaller works resulting from Aquinas's numerous academic disputations (something like a cross between formal debates and twentieth-century graduate seminars), which he conducted in his various academic posts. Some of those topics are taken up differently again in his commentaries on books of the Bible and/or works by Aristotle and other authors. Although Aquinas is remarkably consistent in his several discussions of the same topic, it is often helpful to examine parallel passages in his writings when fully assessing his views on any issue.

Aquinas's most obvious philosophical connection is with Aristotle. Besides producing commentaries on Aristotle's works, he often cites Aristotle in support of a thesis he is defending, even when commenting on Scripture. There are also, in Aquinas's writings, many implicit Aristotelian elements, which he had thoroughly absorbed into his own thought. As a convinced Aristotelian, he often adopts Aristotle's critical attitude towards theories associated with Plato, especially the account of ordinary substantial forms as separately existing entities. However, although Aquinas, like other medieval scholars of western Europe, had almost no access to Plato's works, he was influenced by the writings of Augustine and the pseudo-Dionysius. Through them he absorbed a good deal of Platonism as well; more than he was in a position to recognize as such.

On the other hand, Aquinas is the paradigmatic Christian philosopher–theologian, fully aware of his intellectual debt to religious doctrine. He was convinced, however, that Christian thinkers should be ready to dispute rationally on any topic, especially theological issues, not only among themselves but also with non-Christians of all sorts. Since, in his view, Jews accept the Old Testament and heretics the New Testament, he thought Christians could argue some issues with both groups on the basis of commonly accepted religious authority. However, because other non-Christians,

> for instance, Mohammedans and pagans – do not agree with us about the authority of any scripture on the basis of which they can be convinced … it is necessary to have recourse to natural reason, to which everyone is compelled to assent – although where theological issues are concerned it cannot do the whole job[1]

(since some of the data of theology are initially accessible only in Scripture). Moreover, Aquinas differed from most of his thirteenth-century Christian colleagues in the breadth and depth of his respect for Islamic and Jewish philosopher–theologians, especially Avicenna and Maimonides. He saw them as valued co-workers in the vast project of philosophical theology, clarifying and supporting religious doctrine by philosophical analysis and argumentation. His own commitment to that project involved him in contributing to almost all the areas of philosophy recognized since antiquity, omitting only natural philosophy (the precursor of natural science).

A line of thought with such strong connections to powerful antecedents might have resulted in no more than a pious amalgam. However, Aquinas's philosophy avoids eclecticism because of his own innovative approach to organizing and reasoning about all the topics included under the overarching medieval conception of philosophical Christian theology, and because of his special talents for systematic synthesis and for identifying and skillfully defending, on almost every issue he considers, the most sensible available position.

Early years

Thomas Aquinas was born at Roccasecca, near Naples, the youngest son of a large Italian aristocratic family. As is generally true of even prominent medieval people, it is hard to determine exactly when he was born; plausible arguments have been offered for 1224, 1225 and 1226. He began his schooling in the great Benedictine abbey at Monte Cassino (1231–9), and from 1239–44 he was a student at the University of Naples. In 1244 he joined the Dominican friars, a relatively new religious order devoted to study and preaching; by doing so he antagonized his family, who seem to have been counting on his becoming abbot of Monte Cassino. When the Dominicans ordered Aquinas to go to Paris for further study, his family had him abducted en route and brought home, where he was kept for almost two years. Near the end of that time, his brothers hired a prostitute to try to seduce him, but Aquinas angrily chased her from his room. Having impressed his family with his high-minded determination, in 1245 Aquinas was allowed to return to the Dominicans, who again sent him to Paris, this time successfully.

At the University of Paris, Aquinas first encountered Albert the Great, who quickly became his most influential teacher and eventually his friend and mentor. When Albert moved on to the University of Cologne in 1248, Aquinas followed him there, having declined Pope Innocent IV's extraordinary offer to appoint him abbot of Monte Cassino while allowing him to remain a Dominican.

Aquinas seems to have been unusually large and extremely modest and quiet. When during his four years at Cologne, his special gifts began to be apparent, despite his reticence and humility, Albert assigned the still-reluctant Aquinas his first active part in an academic disputation. Having failed in his efforts to shake his best student's arguments on this occasion, Albert declared, "We call him the dumb ox, but in his teaching he will one day produce such a bellowing that it will be heard throughout the world."

In 1252 Aquinas returned to Paris for the course of study leading to the degree of master in theology, roughly the equivalent of a twentieth-century PhD. During the first academic year, he studied and lectured on the Bible; the final three years were devoted to commenting on Peter Lombard's *Sentences*, a standard requirement for the degree at that time. Produced in 1253–6, Aquinas's massive commentary (often referred to as the *Scriptum super libros Sententiarum* (*Commentary on the Sentences*) is the first of his four theological syntheses (*SCG*, *ST*, and the *Compendium theologiae* being the others). It contains much valuable material, but because it is superseded in many respects by his great *Summa contra gentiles* and *Summa theologiae* the *Scriptum* has not yet been studied as much as it should be.

During that same four-year period, Aquinas produced *De ente et essentia* (*On Being and Essence*), a short philosophical treatise written for his fellow Dominicans at Paris. Although it is indebted to Avicenna's *Metaphysics*, *De ente* is distinctively Aquinas's own, expounding many of the concepts and theses that remained fundamental to his thought throughout his career.

First Paris regency

In the spring of 1256, Aquinas was appointed regent master in theology at Paris, a position he held until the end of the academic year 1258–9. *Quaestiones disputatae de veritate* (QDV) (*Disputed Questions on Truth*) is the first of his sets of disputed questions and the most important work he produced during those three years. It grew out of his professorship, which obliged him to conduct several formal public disputations each year. QDV consists of twenty-nine widely ranging Questions, each devoted to some general topic such as conscience, God's knowledge, faith, goodness, free will, human emotions and truth (the first Question, from which the treatise gets its name). Each Question is divided into several Articles, and the 253 articles are the work's topically specific units: for example, q. 1, a. 9 is "Is there truth in the senses [*in sensu*]?"

The elaborate structure of each of those articles, like much of Aquinas's writing, reflects the "scholastic method", which, like medieval disputations in the classroom, had its ultimate source in Aristotle's recommendations in his *Topics* regarding dialectical inquiry. Aquinas's philosophical discussions in that form typically begin with a yes/no question. Each article then develops as a kind of debate. It begins with arguments for an answer opposed to Aquinas's own position; these arguments are commonly, if somewhat misleadingly, called 'objections'. Next come the arguments *sed contra* (but, on the other hand); in later works, these arguments are often reduced to a single citation of some generally accepted authority that Aquinas construes as on his side of the issue. The *sed contra* is followed by Aquinas's reasoned presentation and defense of his own position. This is the master's "determination" of the question, called the '*corpus*' or 'body' of the article. An article normally concludes with Aquinas's rejoinders to each of the objections (indicated by 'ad 1', and so on, in references).

Conducting "disputed questions" was one of the duties of a regent master in theology, but the theology faculty also provided regular opportunities for "quodlibetal questions", occasions on which a master could, if he wished, undertake to provide replies to any and all questions proposed by members of the academic audience. These occasions were scheduled, for the master's own good, during the two penitential seasons of the church year. Aquinas seems to have accepted this challenge on at least five of the six such occasions occurring during his first regency at Paris, producing *Quaestiones quodlibetales* (*Quodlibetal Questions*) in which he offers his considered judgment on issues ranging from whether the soul is to be identified with its powers to whether the damned behold the saints in glory.

Aquinas's commentaries on Boethius's *De trinitate* (*On the Trinity*) and *De hebdomadibus* (sometimes referred to as '*How Substances are Good*') are his other philosophically important writings from this period of his first regency. Although several philosophers had commented on those Boethian treatises in the twelfth century, the subsequent influx of Aristotelian works had left them almost universally disregarded by the time Aquinas wrote his commentaries. No one knows for certain why or for whom Aquinas wrote them, but he might well have undertaken these studies for his own edification on topics that were then becoming important to his thought.

The *De trinitate* commentary (*Expositio super librum Boethii De trinitate*) presents Aquinas's views on the relationship of faith and reason and on the methods and inter-relations of all the recognized bodies of organized knowledge, or "sciences". Boethius's *De hebdomadibus* is the *locus classicus* for the medieval consideration of the relation between being and goodness. Dealing with this topic in his commentary on that treatise, Aquinas also produced his first systematic account of metaphysical participation, one of the important Platonist elements in his thought. Participation, he claims, obtains when the metaphysical composition of something A includes some X as one of A's metaphysical components, when X also belongs to something else B that is X in its own right and when X's belonging to B in this way is presupposed by A's having X. For example, an effect participates in its cause in this way, on Aquinas's view, and creatures participate in various ways in their Creator.

Naples and Orvieto: *Summa contra gentiles* and biblical commentary

Aquinas's activities between 1259 and 1265 are not well documented, but he seems definitely to have left his professorship at Paris at the end of the academic year 1258–9. He probably spent the next two years at a Dominican priory in Naples, working on the *Summa contra gentiles*, which he had begun in Paris and which he subsequently finished in Orvieto where, as lector, he was in charge of studies at the Dominican priory until 1265.

Summa contra gentiles is unlike Aquinas's three other theological syntheses in more than one respect. Stylistically, it is unlike the earlier *Scriptum* and the later *Summa theologiae* in not following the scholastic method; instead, it is written in ordinary prose divided into chapters, like his *Compendium theologiae* (*Compendium of Theology*) which he seems to have written immediately afterwards (1265–7). More importantly, the *Scriptum*, *Summa theologiae* and the *Compendium* are all contributions to revealed theology, which essentially includes the data of revelation among the starting points of its theorizing. In *Summa contra gentiles*, on the other hand, Aquinas postpones revealed theology to the last (fourth) book, in which he deals with the "mysteries", the few doctrinal propositions that, on his view, cannot be arrived at by natural reason alone and that have their sources in revelation only; and he takes these up with the aim of showing that even those propositions "are not opposed to natural reason".[2] He devotes the first three books of *SCG* to fully developing a natural theology, dependent on natural reason and independent of revelation. As developed in Books I–III of *SCG*, this natural theology is able to accomplish a very large part of theology's job, from establishing the existence of God through working out details of human morality.

Discussions important for understanding Aquinas's positions in many areas of philosophy are also scattered, not always predictably, among interpretations of the text in his biblical commentaries. During Aquinas's stay in Orvieto and around the time he was writing Book III of *Summa contra gentiles*, on providence and God's relations with human beings, he also produced his *Expositio super Iob ad litteram (Literal Commentary on Job)*, one of the most fully developed and philosophical of his biblical commentaries, rivaled in those respects only by his later commentary on Romans. The body of the Book of Job consists mainly of the speeches of Job and his "comforters". Aquinas sees those speeches as constituting a genuine debate, almost a medieval academic disputation (determined in the end by God himself), in which the thought develops subtly, advanced by arguments. His construal of the argumentation is ingenious, the more so because twentieth-century readers have tended to devalue the speeches as tedious reiterations of misconceived accusations countered by Job's slight variations on the theme of his innocence.

Aquinas's focus is also at variance with the modern view, which supposes the book to cast doubts on God's goodness (and so to cast doubts on the existence of an omnipotent, omniscient, perfectly good God) insofar as it presents the problem of evil, raised by the horrible suffering of an innocent person. Aquinas's main interest in the book is in its implications for the doctrine of providence. As Aquinas interprets it, the book explains the nature and operations of divine providence, which he understands as compatible with permitting bad things to happen to good people. As Aquinas sees it:

> If in this life people are rewarded by God for good deeds and punished for bad, as Eliphaz [one of the comforters] was trying to establish, it apparently follows that the ultimate goal for human beings is in this life. But Job means to rebut this opinion, and he wants to show that the present life of human beings does not contain the ultimate goal, but is related to it as motion is related to rest, and a road to its destination.[3]

The things that happen to a person in this life can be explained in terms of divine providence only by reference to the possibility of that person's achieving the ultimate goal of perfect happiness; the enjoyment of union with God in the afterlife.

In discussing Job's lament that God does not hear his prayers, Aquinas says that Job has that impression because God sometimes

> attends not to a person's pleas but rather to his advantage. A doctor does not attend to the pleas of the invalid who asks that the bitter

medicine be taken away (supposing that the doctor doesn't take it away because he knows that it contributes to health). Instead, the doctor attends to the patient's advantage; for by doing so he produces health, which the sick person wants most of all.[4]

In the same way, God sometimes permits a person to suffer despite prayers for deliverance, because God knows that those sufferings are helping that person achieve what he wants most of all.

Rome: disputed questions, Dionysius and the *Compendium*

In 1265 Aquinas went from Orvieto to Rome, having been appointed to establish a Dominican studium and to serve as regent master there. This Roman period of his career, which lasted until 1268, was particularly productive. Some of his major works dating from 1265–8 are just what would have been expected of a regent master in theology, in particular, three sets of disputed questions, *Quaestiones disputatae de potentia* (*Disputed Questions on {God's} Power*), *Quaestio disputata de anima* (*Disputed Question on the Soul*) and *Quaestio disputata de spiritualibus creaturis* (*Disputed Question on Spiritual Creatures*). In the earliest of these, *Quaestiones disputatae de potentia*, there are eighty-three Articles grouped under ten Questions; the first six questions are on divine power, while the final four are on problems associated with combining the doctrine of Trinity with God's absolute simplicity. The much shorter *De anima* is concerned mainly with metaphysical aspects of the soul, concluding with some special problems associated with the nature and capacities of souls separated from bodies (Articles 14–21). The eleven articles of *De spiritualibus creaturis* again address many of those same concerns but also go on to some consideration of angels as another order of spiritual creatures besides human beings, whose natures are only partly spiritual.

During this same period, or perhaps while he was still at Orvieto, Aquinas wrote a commentary on the pseudo-Dionysian treatise *De divinis Nominibus* (*On the Divine Names*), a deeply Neoplatonist account of Christian theology dating probably from the sixth century. Aquinas, like everyone else at the time, believed that it had been written in the apostolic period by the Dionysius who had been converted by St Paul. For that reason, and perhaps also because he had first studied the book under Albert at Cologne, it had a powerful influence on Aquinas's thought. Very early in his career, while he was writing his *Scriptum*, he thought Dionysius was an Aristotelian,[5] but while writing the commentary on this text he realized that its author must have been a Platonist.[6] His commentary, which makes clear sense of a text that is often obscure, may, like his commentaries on Boethius, have been written for his own purposes rather than growing out of a course of lectures.

In any case, his study of Dionysius is one of the most important routes by which Platonism became an essential ingredient in his own thought.

The *Compendium theologiae* (*Compendium of Theology*), already mentioned in connection with *Summa contra gentiles*, was once thought to have been written much later and to have been left incomplete because of Aquinas's death. However, its similarity to *Summa contra gentiles* not only in style but also in content has lately led many scholars to assign it to 1265–7. Among Aquinas's four theological syntheses, the *Compendium theologiae* is unique in the brevity of its discussions and in having been organized around the theological virtues of faith, hope and charity. Had it been completed, it might have provided a novel reorientation of the vast subject matter of medieval theology, but Aquinas wrote only ten short chapters of the second section, on Hope, and none at all of the third section, on Charity. He did complete the first section on Faith, but since most of the 246 chapters in the section simply provide much briefer treatments of almost all the theological topics Aquinas had already dealt with in *Summa contra gentiles*, the *Compendium* as he left it seems important mainly as a précis of material that is developed more fully in the other work (and in *Summa theologiae*).

Rome: Aristotelian commentary

While some of Aquinas's prodigious output in Rome from 1265–8 is, broadly speaking, similar to work he had already done, it also includes two important innovations, one of which is the first of his twelve commentaries on works of Aristotle. At the beginning of his commentary on *De anima* (*Sententia super De anima*), his approach is still a little tentative and (for Aquinas) unusually concerned with technical details. These features of the work once led scholars to describe the commentary on the first book of *De anima* as a *"reportatio"* (an unedited set of notes taken at his lectures), or even to ascribe this first third of Aquinas's commentary to another author. However, René Gauthier has argued persuasively that the difference between the commentary's treatments of Book I and of Books II and III of *De anima* is explained by differences between the books themselves, and that in fact none of Aquinas's commentaries on Aristotle resulted from lectures he gave on those books.[7] Discrepancies within this work, the first of Aquinas's Aristotelian commentaries, are likely to be at least in part a consequence of the fact that he was finding his way into this new sort of enterprise, at which he quickly became very adept. In a recent volume of essays on Aristotle's *De anima*, Martha Nussbaum describes Aquinas's work as "one of the very greatest commentaries on the work" and "very insightful".[8] T.H. Irwin, a leading interpreter of Aristotle, acknowledges that at one point in the *Sententia libri Ethicorum* (*Commentary on Aristotle's Nicomachean Ethics*), Aquinas "actually explains Aristotle's intention more clearly than Aristotle explains it himself".[9] Such judgments apply pretty generally to Aquinas's

Aristotelian commentaries, all of which are marked by his extraordinary ability as a philosophical commentator to discern a logical structure in almost every passage he examines in every sort of text: not only Aristotle's but also those of others, from Boethius to St Paul.

Since commenting on Aristotle was a regular feature of life for a member of a medieval arts faculty but never part of the duties of an academic theologian, Aquinas's many Aristotelian commentaries were technically extracurricular and therefore an especially impressive accomplishment for someone who was already extremely busy. Some scholars, admiring Aquinas's achievements in general but focusing on the fact that his professional career was entirely in the theology faculty, have insisted on classifying only the Aristotelian commentaries as philosophical works. Certainly these commentaries are philosophical, as purely philosophical as the Aristotelian works they elucidate. However, Aquinas wrote these commentaries not only to make good philosophical sense of Aristotle's very difficult texts but also, and more importantly, to enhance his own understanding of the topics Aristotle had dealt with. As he remarks in his commentary on *De caelo*, "the study of philosophy has as its purpose to know not what people have thought, but rather the truth about the way things are",[10] and he believed that the theologian's attempt to understand God and everything else in relation to God was the fundamental instance of the universal human drive to know the truth about the way things are. On the other hand, his view of the best way of making intellectual progress in general looks very much like the age-old method of philosophy:

> But if any people want to write back against what I have said, I will be very gratified, because there is no better way of uncovering the truth and keeping falsity in check than by arguing with people who disagree with you.[11]

Rome: *Summa theologiae*

The other important innovation from Aquinas's three-year regency in Rome is *Summa theologiae*, his greatest and most characteristic work, begun in Rome and continued through the rest of his life. *Summa theologiae*, left incomplete at his death, consists of three large Parts. The First Part (Ia) is concerned with the existence and nature of God (Questions 1–43), creation (44–9), angels (50–64), the six days of creation (65–74), human nature (75–102) and divine government (103–19). The Second Part deals with morality, and in such detail that it is itself divided into two parts. The first part of the Second Part (IaIIae) takes up human happiness (Questions 1–5), human action (6–17), the goodness and badness of human acts (18–21), passions (22–48) and the sources of human acts: intrinsic (49–89) and extrinsic (90–114). The second part of the Second Part (IIaIIae) begins with the three theological virtues and corresponding vices (Questions 1–46), goes on through the four "cardinal virtues" and corresponding vices (47–170) and ends with special issues associated with the religious life (171–89). In the Third Part, Aquinas deals with the incarnation (Questions 1–59) and the sacraments (60–90), breaking off in the middle of his discussion of penance.

Aquinas thought of *Summa theologiae* as a new kind of textbook of theology, and its most important pedagogical innovation, as he sees it, is in its organization. He says he has noticed that students new to theology have been held back in their studies by several features of the standard teaching materials, especially "because the things they have to know are not imparted in an order appropriate to a method of teaching", an order he proposes to introduce (*ST prooemium*). It may well have been his enthusiasm for this new approach that led him to abandon work on his quite differently organized *Compendium theologiae*, and his natural preoccupation during this period with the writing of *Summa theologiae* Ia may also help to account for the fact that his other work of that time shows a special interest in the nature and operations of the human soul, the subject matter of Questions 75–89 of Ia.

Second Paris regency

In 1268 the Dominican Order again assigned Aquinas to the University of Paris, where he was regent master for a second time until, in the spring of 1272, all lectures at the university were canceled because of a dispute with the Bishop of Paris. The Dominicans then ordered Aquinas to return to Italy.

Among the astounding number of works Aquinas produced in those four years is the huge Second Part of *Summa theologiae* (*ST* IaIIae and IIaIIae), nine Aristotelian commentaries, a commentary on the pseudo-Aristotelian *Liber de causis* (which, as Aquinas was among the first to realize, is actually a compilation of Neoplatonic material drawn from Proclus), sixteen biblical commentaries and seven sets of disputed questions (including the set of sixteen *Quaestiones disputatae de malo* [*Disputed Questions On Evil}*, the sixth of which provides a detailed discussion of free choice). His literary productivity during this second regency is the more amazing because he was at the same time embroiled in various controversies.

Sending Aquinas back to Paris in 1268 seems to have been, at least in part, his order's response to the worrisome movement of "Latin Averroism" or "radical Aristotelianism", then gaining ground among members of the arts faculty who were attracted to interpretations of Aristotle found in the commentaries of Averroes. However, only two of his many writings from these years seem to have obvious connections with the Averroist controversy. One of these, his treatise *De unitate intellectus, contra Averroistas* (*On {the Theory of} the Unicity of Intellect, against the Averroists*) is an explicit critique and rejection of a view distinctive of the movement. As Aquinas describes it, that view holds that the aspect of the human mind which

Aristotle calls the possible intellect ... is some sort of substance separate in its being from the body and not united to it in any way as its form; and, what is more, that this possible intellect is one for all human beings.[12]

After briefly noting that this view's incompatibility with Christian doctrine is too obvious to warrant discussion at any length, Aquinas devotes the entire treatise to showing that "this position is no less contrary to the principles of philosophy than it is to the teachings of the Faith", and that it is even "entirely incompatible with the words and views" of Aristotle himself.[13]

Besides the unicity of intellect, the other controversial theory most often associated with thirteenth-century Averroism is the beginninglessness of the universe. In many of his works, Aquinas had already considered the possibility that the world had always existed, skillfully developing and defending the bold position that revelation alone provides the basis for believing that the world began to exist, that one cannot prove either that the universe must or that it could not have begun, and that a world both beginningless and created is possible (although, of course, not actual). The second of Aquinas's Parisian treatises that is plainly relevant to Averroism is *De aeternitate mundi, contra murmurantes* (*On the Eternity of the World, against Grumblers*), a very short, uncharacteristically indignant summary of his position.

Aquinas, however, could not complain that Aristotle had been misinterpreted regarding the eternity of the world; after initially supposing this to be the case, he had become convinced that Aristotle really did think he had proved that the world must have existed forever. For this reason, Aquinas's position on this issue did not distance him enough from the Averroists in the view of their contemporary "Augustinian" opponents, most notably the Franciscans Bonaventure and Pecham. In fact, the "Grumblers" against whom Aquinas directed his treatise were probably not so much the Averroists in the arts faculty as those Franciscan theologians who maintained that they had demonstrated the impossibility of a beginningless world.

Aquinas's principled dissociation from some important Franciscans on this point must have helped to make his second Paris regency much more troubled than his first. In disputations conducted in Paris in 1266–7, the Franciscan master William of Baglione implicated Aquinas's views in the propositions he attacked, claiming that things Aquinas was saying encouraged the two heretical Averroist theses denounced by Bonaventure, namely the eternity of the world and the unicity of the intellect. "The 'blind leaders of the blind' decried by William evidently include Thomas as their chief."[14] It has also been persuasively argued that Aquinas's *De aeternitate mundi* was directed in particular against his Franciscan colleague in theology, John

Pecham.[15] It seems, then, that Aquinas's development of a distinctly philosophical theology — which, like Albert's, was more Aristotelian than Augustinian — was dividing him from his colleagues in the Paris faculty of theology during these years. It may also have been bringing him closer to the philosophers in the arts faculty.

Last days

In June 1272 the Dominicans ordered Aquinas to leave Paris and go to Naples, where he was to establish another studium for the order and to serve as its regent master. Except for some interesting collections of sermons (originally preached in his native Italian dialect), the works dating from this period — two Aristotelian commentaries and the Third Part of *Summa theologiae* — were left unfinished. On or about 6 December 1273, while he was saying mass, something happened to Aquinas that left him unable to go on writing or dictating. He himself saw the occasion as a special revelation. When Reginald of Piperno, his principal secretary and long-time friend, pressed him to know what had happened, Aquinas explained to him that everything he had written seemed like straw to him by comparison with what he had seen and what had been revealed to him. He believed that he had at last clearly seen what he had devoted his life to figuring out and, by comparison, all he had written seemed pale and dry. Now that he could no longer write, he told Reginald, he wanted to die.[16] Soon afterwards he did die, on 7 March 1274 at Fossanuova, Italy, on his way to the Council of Lyons, which he had been ordered to attend.

Metaphysics

Every part of Aquinas's philosophy is imbued with metaphysical principles, many of which are recognizably Aristotelian. Consequently, concepts such as potentiality and actuality, matter and form, substance, essence, accident and the four causes — all of which are fundamental in Aquinas's metaphysics — have an Aristotelian context. Aquinas invokes such principles often, and he employs them implicitly even more often. Two of his earliest writings — *De principiis naturae* (*On the Principles of Nature*) and especially *De ente et essentia* (*On Being and Essence*) — outline much of his metaphysics. Perhaps the most important thesis argued in *De ente et essentia* is the one that became known as "the real distinction", Aquinas's view that the essence of any created thing is really, not just conceptually, distinct from its existence. Metaphysically speaking, corporeal beings are composites of form and matter, but all creatures, even incorporeal ones, are composites of essence and existence. Only the first, uncreated cause, God, whose essence is existence, is absolutely simple.

Except for his commentary on Aristotle's *Metaphysics*, Aquinas devoted no mature treatise to metaphysics itself. However, since he considers metaphysics to be the science of being considered generally (*ens commune*), and since he argues that being itself is first of all God himself and that all being depends on God, his philosophy does begin with metaphysics insofar as the most systematic presentations of his thought (in *Summa contra gentiles* and *Summa theologiae*) start with the investigation of God-in-himself considered as the foundation of the nature and existence of everything.[17]

Being, Aquinas says, is intellect's most fundamental conception,

> inherently its most intelligible object and the one in which it finds the basis of all conceptions ... Consequently all of intellect's other conceptions must be arrived at by adding to being ... insofar as they express a mode of being which is not expressed by the term "being" itself.[18]

There are, he claims, just two legitimate ways of making such additions. The first results in the ten Aristotelian Categories, each of which is a "specified [or specific] mode of being" – substance, quantity, quality and the rest. The results of "adding to being" in the second way are less familiar. Aquinas takes them to be five modes of being that are entirely general, characterizing absolutely every being. That is, being, wherever and however instantiated, exhibits these five modes, which transcend the Categories because they are necessary modes of all specified being: thing (*res*), one, something (*aliquid*), good, true. These five, together with being itself, are the transcendentals, predicable correctly of absolutely anything that is. *Good* and *true* are the philosophically interesting cases, because some beings are obviously not good and because *true* seems applicable only to propositions.

The claim that all beings are true depends on taking 'true' in the sense of 'genuine', as in 'true friend', a sense that had been explored in detail by Anselm of Canterbury. In Anselm's view, any being is true in this sense to the extent to which it agrees with the divine idea of such a thing (and is false to the extent that it does not agree). Absolutely every thing that is agrees at least to some extent with the divine idea that is an ingredient in its causal explanation. Propositions are true if they correspond to the way things are in the world; things in the world are true if they correspond to what is in the mind, God's mind first, ours derivatively. So, Aquinas says:

> in the soul there is a cognitive and an appetitive power. The word 'good', then, expresses the conformity of a being to appetite (as is said at the beginning of the Ethics: 'The good is what all desire'). The word 'true', however, expresses the conformity of a being to intellect.[19]

The central thesis of Aquinas's meta-ethics grows out of the theory of the transcendentals. The thesis is the metaphysical principle that the terms

13

'being' and 'good' are the same in reference, differing only in sense.[20] What all desire is what they take to be the good, and what is desired is at least perceived as desirable.[21] Desirability is thus an essential aspect of goodness. If a thing of a certain kind is genuinely desirable as a thing of that kind, it is desirable to the extent to which it is perfect of that kind: a complete specimen, free from relevant defect. But a thing is perfect of its kind to the extent to which it has actualized its specifying potentialities, the potentialities that differentiate its species from other species in the same genus. So, Aquinas says, a thing is desirable as a thing of its kind and hence good of that kind to the extent to which it is actualized and in being.[22] Generally, then, 'being' and 'goodness' have the same referent: all being, including the actualization of specifying potentialities. The actualization of a thing's specifying potentialities to at least some extent is on the one hand its existence as such a thing; it is in this sense that the thing is said to have being. On the other hand, however, the actualization of a thing's specifying potentialities is, to the extent of the actualization, that thing's being whole, complete, free from defect: the state all things are naturally aimed at. It is in this sense that the thing is said to have goodness.[23]

Aquinas's concept of analogy is important to his thought. It is often presented, correctly, in terms of analogical predication. However, his concept of analogy can be explained at a more fundamental level in connection with causation. Setting aside "accidental" causation – for example, a gardener's uncovering buried treasure – Aquinas thinks that efficient causation always involves an agent (A), a patient (P) and a form (f). In non-accidental efficient causation, A antecedently has f, somehow. A's exercising causal power on P brings about f in P, somehow. Thus the efficient cause is A's acting (or exercising a power it has), and the effect is P's having f. The fact that A and P can have f in several different ways is what is brought out in 'somehow'. The paradigm – straightforward efficient causation – is the kind that Aquinas calls univocal: cases in which first A and then P have f in just the same way, and in which f can therefore be predicated truly of each in just the same sense. The metal hotplate and the metal kettle bottom resting on it are both called hot univocally: the form *heat* in these two causally related objects is the same specifically and differs only numerically.

However, Aquinas also recognizes two kinds of non-univocal efficient causation. The first, equivocal causation, characterizes cases in which there is no obvious respect in which to say that the f effected in P is found antecedently in A, and yet there is a natural causal connection (as there standardly is an etymological explanation for equivocal predication). If A is solar power and its effect is the hardening (f) of some clay (P), then obviously the sun's power is not itself hard, as the clay is. To say what it is about solar power that hardens clay will not be as easy as explaining the heating of the kettle, and yet the hardening of the clay must, somehow, be brought about by that power. In such a case, A has f only in the sense that A has the power to bring about f in P.

Second, analogical causation occurs when, for instance, a blood sample (P) is correctly labeled 'anemic', although of course the blood itself does not have anemia and cannot literally be anemic. The physiology of the sample's donor (A) brings about a condition (f) in the sample that is an unmistakeable sign of anemia in A, thus justifying that (analogical) labeling of the sample.

For theological purposes, Aquinas is interested not in natural analogical causation but rather in the artificial kind: the kind that involves ideas and volitions, the artisan's kind.

> In other agents [the form of what is to be brought about occurs antecedently] in keeping with intelligible being, as in those agents that act through intellect – the way a likeness of the house exists antecedently in the builder's mind.[24]

Since the status of entirely univocal causation depends on there being a merely numerical difference between the f in A and the f in P, an intellective agent effecting its ideas is obviously not a univocal cause. But nor is this difference between the antecedent f and the consequent f so wide as to constitute equivocal causation. In fact, the kind of association between the idea and its external manifestation is closer than the kind found in natural analogical causation; and since, in Aquinas's view, "the world was brought about not by chance but by God acting through intellect ... it is necessary that there be a form in the divine mind, a form in the likeness of which the world was made".[25] God, then, is the non-univocal, non-equivocal, intellectively analogical efficient cause of the world.

Philosophy of mind

Aquinas's philosophy of mind is part of his more general theory of soul, which naturally makes use of his metaphysics. Obviously he is not a materialist – most obviously because God, the absolutely fundamental reality in his metaphysics, is in no way material. Aquinas classifies every thing other than God as either corporeal or incorporeal (spiritual); he sometimes calls purely spiritual creatures – such as angels – 'separated substances' because of their essential detachment from body of any sort. However, this exhaustive division is not perfectly exclusive because human beings, simply by virtue of the human soul, must be classified not as simply corporeal but also as spiritual in a certain respect.

Merely having a soul of some sort is not enough to give a creature a spiritual component, however. Every animate creature has a soul (*anima*) – "soul is what we call the first principle of life in things that live among us"[26] – but neither plants nor non-human animals are in any respect spiritual. Aquinas holds that even the merely nutritive soul of a plant, or the nutritive + sensory soul of a beast, is like the soul of a human being in being the form of a body. No soul, no first principle of life, can be matter. On the other hand, any vegetable or animal body has the life it has only in virtue of being a body whose special organization confers on it natural potentialities: that is, in virtue of the substantial form that makes it actually be such a body. Therefore, the first principle of life in a living non-human body, its soul, is no bodily part of that body but is rather its form, one of the two metaphysical components of the composite of matter and form that every body is. For plants and beasts, unlike humans, the form that is the soul goes out of existence when the composite dies, and it is in that sense that the souls of plants and beasts are not spiritual.

Only the soul of a human being is analysed as nutritive + sensory + rational. Aquinas thinks of this soul not as three nested, cooperating forms, but as the single substantial form that gives a human being its specifically human mode of existence. (In defending this thesis of the unicity of substantial form, Aquinas differed from many of his contemporaries.) He often designates this entire substantial form by its distinctively human aspect of rationality. He also thinks that the human soul, unlike the souls of plants and beasts, is subsistent: that is, it continues to exist after separating from the body in death. He says, for example: "It is necessary to say that that which is the principle of intellective activity, what we call the soul of a human being, is an incorporeal, subsistent principle."[27] The human soul, just because it is distinctively mind (the principle of intellective activity), must therefore be described not only as incorporeal but also as subsistent.

It may seem impossible for Aquinas's account to accommodate the theological doctrine that souls persist and engage in mental acts after the death of the body. If the separated soul is a form, what is it a form of? Aquinas is not a universal hylomorphist; unlike some of his contemporaries, he does not think that there is "spiritual matter" that angels or disembodied souls have as one of their components, but rather that they are separated forms that configure no matter at all. Thus when he claims that the soul exists apart from the body, he seems to be holding the view that there can be a form with nothing of which it is the form. Moreover, Aquinas thinks that an angel or the soul separated from the body engages in mental activity. However, a form seems not to be the sort of thing that engages in acts of any sort, and so it appears that even if there were some way to explain the existence of the soul apart from the body, its acting could not be explained.

In this connection, it is helpful to examine Aquinas's broader view of form. The world is ordered metaphysically in such a way that at the top of the universal hierarchy there are forms – God and angels – that are not forms of anything. Near the bottom of the hierarchy are forms that configure matter but cannot exist in their own right, apart from the corporeal composites they inform. The forms of inanimate things and of animate, non-rational things are of that sort. Those forms inform matter, but when the resultant composites cease to exist, those forms also cease to exist. In the middle – "on the borderline between corporeal and separated [that is, purely spiritual] substances" – are human souls, the metaphysical amphibians.[28] Like angels, human souls are subsistent, able to exist on their own; but, like the forms of inanimate things, human souls configure matter.

Seeing the soul in this light helps to explain some of what is initially puzzling in Aquinas's account. The human soul has a double character. On the one hand, unlike the forms of other material things, it is created by God as an individual entity in its own right, able to exist by itself as do purely immaterial angels. On the other hand, like the form of any corporeal thing, it exists in the composite it configures, and it comes into existence only with that composite, not before it.

Theory of knowledge

Nature, Aquinas thinks, must be arranged so as to enable human beings in general to satisfy their natural desire to know.[29] His view of the arrangement actually provided seems at first too tight to be true, involving some sort of formal identity between the extramental object (O) and the cognizing faculty (F) in its actually cognizing O. However, Aquinas takes that (Aristotelian) identity claim to mean only that the form of O is somehow in F.[30] O's form comes to be in F when F receives species, either sensory or intellective, of O. These species may be thought of as encodings of O's form. If O is a particular corporeal object – an iron hoop, for instance – then in O itself, O's form informs matter to produce an iron hoop of just those dimensions at just that spatio-temporal location. (In Aquinas's account of individuation, it is matter that is 'signate' that individuates O's form.) But when the appropriately encoded form is received in an external sense faculty F (which uses a bodily organ), then, even though it is received materially in F's matter, it is nonetheless received differently from its reception in the matter of the hoop. The imposition of the form on the matter of the sense organ constitutes an "intentional" or "spiritual" reception of the form, contributing to a cognition of the hoop rather than metaphysically constituting a new, individuated matter-form composite.

Sensory species received in external senses are standardly transmitted to "internal senses", the organs for which, Aquinas thought, must be located in the brain. Among the most important of these for purposes of cognition are phantasia and imagination (although Aquinas usually treats imagination as part of the power of phantasia). Phantasia and imagination produce and preserve phantasms, the sensory data that are necessary preconditions for intellectual cognition. Imagination and phantasia are also indispensable to conscious sensory cognition. In Aquinas's view, sensible species themselves

17

are not the objects of cognition, and what he says about phantasia suggests that having sensible species is not sufficient for having sensory cognition. O itself, currently having a natural effect on the external senses, is consciously sensed because phantasia has processed O's sensible species into phantasms.

The form presented in a phantasm has of course been stripped of its original, individuating matter, but a phantasm of O remains particularized as a phantasm in virtue of having been received in the different matter of phantasia's organ, while remaining recognizably the form of O because of the details of O that are preserved in it. However, cognition of O as an iron hoop is conceptual, intellective cognition, for which phantasms are only the raw material.

In intellect itself, Aquinas distinguishes two Aristotelian "powers". The first is agent intellect, the essentially active or productive aspect of intellect, which acts on phantasms in a way that produces "intelligible species". These constitute the primary contents of intellect, stored in possible intellect, intellect's essentially receptive aspect.

> Through intellect it is natural for us to have cognition of natures. Of course, [as universals] natures do not have existence except in individuating matter. It is natural for us to have cognition of them, however, not as they are in individuating matter but as they are abstracted from it by intellect's consideration.[31]

This is the work of agent intellect, producing intelligible species. The intelligible species of O are unlike sensory species of it in that they are only universals, which occur as such only in possible intellect: for example, round, metallic, iron hoop. These "universal natures" are not only received in the intellective faculty F, the possible intellect, but are also of course used regularly as the devices indispensable for intellective cognition of corporeal reality:

> Our intellect both abstracts intelligible species from phantasms, insofar as it considers the natures of things universally, and yet also has intellective cognition of them [the things] in the phantasms, since without attending to phantasms it cannot have intellective cognition of even those things whose [intelligible] species it abstracts.[32]

It is in this way that "in intellection we can have cognition of such [particular, corporeal, composite] things in universality, which is beyond the faculty of sense".[33]

Thus both sense and intellect have cognition of O, a particular corporeal thing. However, sense has cognition of O only in its particularity.[34] Further, an individual intellect that happened to have the concept *iron hoop* would have cognition only of a universal nature that happened to be instantiated in O, and not also of any instantiation of that nature – unless that intellect were also attending to phantasms of O. It is as a result of this attending that intellect also cognizes O itself, but as exemplifying a universal, for example, as an iron hoop.[35]

Although intellect regularly has cognition of a corporeal particular in the way described, its proper object, Aquinas says, is that particular's universal nature, or "quiddity". Intellect's "first operation", then, is its cognition of a universal, its proper object (although as we have seen, agent intellect's abstracting of intelligible species is a necessary step on the way to the cognition of the quiddities of things). Aquinas sometimes calls this first operation "understanding". However, *scientia*, which is one of the last operations of intellect (the operation of discursive reasoning) and which is a pinnacle of intellective cognition, also has the natures of things as its objects. Universal natures, the proper objects of intellect's first operation and the objects of the culminating theoretical knowledge of nature, must then be thought of as proper objects of both the beginning and the culmination of intellective cognition. What is cognized in an unanalyzed way in the first operation of the intellect – for example, *animal* – is in scientific cognition analyzed into the essential parts of its nature – *sensitive animate corporeality* – which are themselves comprehended in terms of all their characters and capacities. In theory, in potentiality, the culminating cognitive state is all that could be hoped for: "if the human intellect comprehends the substance of any thing – a rock, for example, or a triangle – none of the intelligible aspects of that thing exceeds the capacity of human reason."[36]

Intellect's "second operation" includes the making of judgments, affirming by propositionally "compounding" with one another concepts acquired in the first operation, or denying by "dividing" them from one another. At every stage past initial acquisition, the cognition of quiddities will partially depend on this second operation, and on reasoning as well:

> the human intellect does not immediately, in its first apprehension, acquire a complete cognition of the thing. Instead, it first apprehends something about it – that is, its quiddity, which is a first and proper object of intellect; and then it acquires intellective cognition of the properties, accidents, and dispositions associated with the thing's essence. In doing so it has to compound one apprehended aspect with another, or divide one from another, and proceed from one composition or division to another, which is reasoning.[37]

Reasoning is sometimes called intellect's third operation.

The framing of propositions and the construction of inferences involving them are necessary preconditions of the culminating intellective cognition Aquinas recognizes as *scientia*, which he discusses in greatest detail in his

Sententia super Posteriora analytica (*Commentary on Aristotle's Posterior Analytics*). The interpretation of his account of *scientia* is controversial, but one helpful way to view it is as follows. To cognize a proposition with *scientia* is, strictly speaking, to accept it as the conclusion of a "demonstration". Of course, many premises in demonstrations may themselves be conclusions of other demonstrations; some, however, must be accepted not on the basis of demonstration but *per se*.[38]

Such propositions, knowable *per se* (although not always *per se* knowable by us) are Aquinas's first principles. Like Aristotle, he thinks of them as immediate propositions; that is, they cannot themselves be the conclusions of demonstrations, and their truth is evident to anyone who fully understands their terms, who not merely grasps their ordinary meaning but also comprehends the real nature of their referents. The predicate of an immediate proposition belongs to the *ratio* of the proposition's subject, and the *ratio* is the formulation of the subject's real nature.[39] Thus, for example, Aquinas considers 'God exists' to be self-evident, since according to the doctrine of simplicity, God's nature is God's existence. 'God exists' is a good example of a proposition knowable *per se* but, as Aquinas insists, not knowable *per se* by us. It is for that reason that he develops a number of *a posteriori* arguments for God's existence, among which the most famous are the "Five Ways", found in *ST* Ia.2.3.

Anyone who has a developed concept of the subject's real nature is certain of the truth of such an immediate proposition:

> but there are some immediate propositions the terms of which not everyone knows. That is why although the predicate of such a proposition does belong to the ratio of its subject, the proposition need not be granted by everyone, just because its subject's [metaphysical] definition is not known to everyone.[40]

Because proper demonstrations are isomorphic with metaphysical reality, the facts expressed in their premises are regularly to be construed as causes, of the facts in their conclusions,[41] although in some cases demonstrative reasoning goes the other way, from effects to causes. So, having *scientia* with respect to some proposition is the fullest possible human cognition, by which one situates the fact expressed by a conclusion in an explanatory theory that accurately maps metaphysical or physical reality.

According to Aquinas, then, what demonstration provides is not so much knowledge, as it has been conceived of by classical foundationalists such as Descartes, as it is depth of understanding and explanatory insight. In general, Aquinas does not begin with self-evident principles and derive conclusions from them deductively; "rather [he begins] with a statement to be justified (it will become the 'conclusion' only in a formal restatement of the argument) and 'reduce[s]' it back to its ultimate explanatory principles."[42] When

20

Aquinas himself describes his project generally, he says that there are two different processes in which human reason engages: discovery (or invention) and judgment. When we engage in discovery, we proceed from first principles, reasoning from them to other things; in judgment we reason to first principles on the basis of a kind of analysis. In his view, it is judgment's reasoning process, not that of discovery, that leads to *scientia*, and judgment is the subject of the *Posterior Analytics*: "Judgment goes with the certitude of *scientia*. And it is because we cannot have certain judgment about effects except by analysis leading to first principles that this part of human reasoning is called 'analytics'."[43]

Sceptical worries seldom intrude on Aquinas's scattered development of his systematically unified theory of knowledge, largely because it is based on a metaphysics in which the first principle of existence is an omniscient, omnipotent, perfectly good God, whose rational creatures could not have been made so as to be standardly mistaken about the rest of creation.

Will and action

Philosophy of mind is obviously relevant to epistemology in its account of the mechanisms of cognition, especially of intellect. In its account of will, it is just as obviously relevant to action theory and to ethics. Aquinas's concern with moral issues is even greater than his considerable interest in epistemological issues, and his ethics is so fully developed that he integrates his systematic treatment of acts of will into it rather than including such a treatment in his philosophy of mind.

As intellect is the cognitive faculty of the distinctively human rational soul, so will is its appetitive faculty. As a kind of natural inclination, will's metaphysical provenance is more primitive than intellect's, because will is the most subtle terrestrial instantiation of an utterly universal aspect of creation. Not only every sort of soul but absolutely every form, Aquinas maintains, has some sort of inclination essentially associated with it; and so every hylomorphic thing, even if inanimate, has at least one natural inclination: "on the basis of its form, fire, for instance, is inclined toward a higher place, and toward generating its like."[44] Inclination is the genus of appetite, and appetite is the genus of will. The human soul of course involves natural appetites (for example, for food), but its sensory and intellective modes of cognition bring with them sensory appetites, or passions (for example, for seafood), and rational appetites, or volitions (for example, for food low in fat content).

In human beings, sensory appetite is a cluster of inclinations (passions) to which we are subject (passive) by animal nature. Following an Aristotelian line, Aquinas thinks of sensory appetite as sorted into two complementary powers: the concupiscible (that is, pursuit/avoidance appetite) and the irascible (that is, competition/aggression/defense appetite). With the former are associated the passions of joy and sadness, love and hate, desire and repugnance; with the latter, daring and fear, hope and despair, anger.

For philosophy of mind and for ethics, one important issue is the manner and extent of the rational faculties' control of sensory appetite; a control without which the harmony of the human soul is threatened and morality is impossible, especially in Aquinas's reason-centered ethics with its focus on virtues and vices. A human being who is not aberrantly behaving like a non-rational animal "is not immediately moved in accordance with the irascible and concupiscible appetite but waits for the command of will, which is the higher appetite".[45] But the kind of control exercised by a cognitive rational faculty standardly identified in this role as "practical reason" rather than the broader "intellect" is less obvious, and is particularly interesting in view of Aquinas's account of intellective cognition.

The rational faculties can direct the attention of the external senses and compensate to some extent for their malfunctioning, but they cannot directly control what the external senses initially perceive on any occasion. On the other hand, sensory appetite and the internal senses are not directly related to mind-independent external things, and so to some extent "they are subject to reason's command", although they too can fight against reason.[46] Elaborating an Aristotelian theme,[47] Aquinas observes that the soul's rule over the body is "despotic": in a normal body, any bodily part that can be moved by an act of will in fact will be moved immediately when and as will commands. But the rational faculties rule sensory appetite "politically", because the powers and passions that are the intended subjects of this rational governance are also moved by imagination and sense, and so are no slaves to reason. "That is why we experience the irascible or the concupiscible fighting against reason when we sense or imagine something pleasant that reason forbids, or something unpleasant that reason commands."[48]

According to Aquinas, the volition for happiness in general is an ineluctable part of human nature. Nonetheless, "the movement of a creature's will is not determined in particular to seeking happiness in this, or in that".[49] This sort of freedom of will is freedom of specification or "freedom as regards the object", the freedom in the "determining" aspect of volition. It is distinguished from freedom of exercise or "freedom as regards the act", the freedom associated with will's "executive" capacity, for either acting or not acting to achieve something apprehended as good.

The interpretation of Aquinas's account of freedom of will is controversial. The very phrase 'freedom of will' is part of the difficulty. Aquinas often speaks of *liberum arbitrium* (free decision or judgment); and although this Latin phrase is often translated as 'free will', *liberum arbitrium* cannot be attributed to will alone. It is a power that inheres in the system of intellect and will as a whole and emerges from their interaction. However, it is perhaps safe to say that, since Aquinas emphatically denies that any volition caused by something extrinsic to the agent can be free, his account of freedom of will is not a version of compatibilism.[50] The one apparent exception has to do with God's acting on a human will. Aquinas holds that among extrinsic forces, God alone can act directly on some other person's will without violating the will's nature, that is, without undermining its freedom.[51] On this basis, some interpreters characterize Aquinas as a theological compatibilist; however, the subtle complexities of his account of God's action on human wills leads others to claim that a full appreciation of those complexities would show that Aquinas is not in any sense a compatibilist.

Aquinas's analysis of human action, built on his account of will and intellect, is complicated and not readily summarized. Generally speaking, he finds elaborately ordered mental components in even simple acts. For instance, in a case of raising one's hand to attract attention we are likely to suppose that the mental antecedents of the bodily movement are just the agent's combined beliefs and desires, whether or not the agent is fully conscious of them. Aquinas would of course agree that the agent need not be completely aware of the overt action's mental antecedents, but he sees them as having a complex, hierarchical structure. Although this structure can look deterministic, it is not on Aquinas's view because at almost any point in the interaction between intellect and will, will could direct intellect to reconsider, to direct attention in some other way, or even just to direct intellect to stop thinking about the issue.[52]

Ethics, law and politics

Aquinas's moral theory is developed most extensively and systematically in the Second Part of *Summa theologiae*. (Broadly speaking, the general theory is in IaIIae and the detailed consideration of particular issues is in IIaIIae.) Like almost all his predecessors, medieval and ancient, Aquinas sees ethics as having two principal topics: first, the ultimate goal of human existence, and second, how that goal is to be won, or lost. Of the 303 Questions making up *Summa theologiae*'s Second Part, 298 are concerned in one way or another with the second topic, and only the first 5 are concerned directly with the first (although in *SCG* III he devotes Chapters 25–40 to a detailed examination of it).

Summa theologiae IaIIae.1–5, sometimes called 'the Treatise on Happiness', develops an argument to establish the existence and nature of a single ultimate end for all human action, or, more strictly, the kind of behavior over which a person has "control". First, "all actions that proceed from a power are caused by that power in accordance with the nature of its object. But the object of will is an end and a good", that is, an end perceived as good by the willer's intellect.[53] From this starting point, Aquinas develops an argument designed to show that a human being necessarily (though not always consciously) seeks everything it seeks for its own ultimate end, happiness.

Aquinas argues that the often unrecognized genuine ultimate end for which human beings exist (their "object") is God, perfect goodness personified; and perfect happiness, the ultimate end with which they may exist (their "use" of that object), is the enjoyment of the end for which they exist. That enjoyment is fully achieved only in the beatific vision, which Aquinas conceives of as an activity. Since the beatific vision involves the contemplation of the ultimate (first) cause of everything, it is, whatever else it may be, also the perfection of all knowledge and understanding.[54]

Aquinas devotes just four questions of *ST* IaIIae (18–21) to "the goodness and badness of human acts in general". Although considerations of rightness and wrongness occupy only a fraction of the discussion in Questions 18–21, Aquinas nonetheless appears to think of rightness and wrongness as the practical, distinctively moral evaluations of actions. His emphasis on the broader notions of goodness and badness reveals the root of his moral evaluation of actions in his metaphysical identification of being and goodness.

What makes an action morally bad is its moving the agent not towards, but away from, the agent's ultimate goal. Such a deviation is patently irrational, and Aquinas's analysis of the moral badness of human action identifies it fundamentally as irrationality, since irrationality is an obstacle to the actualization of a human being's specifying potentialities, those that make *rational* the differentia of the human species. In this as in every other respect, Aquinas's ethics is reason-centered:

> In connection with human acts the words 'good' and 'bad' are applied on the basis of a comparison to reason, because ... a human being's good is existing in accordance with reason, while what is bad for a human being is whatever is contrary to reason. For what is good for any thing is what goes together with it in keeping with its form, and what is bad for it is whatever is contrary to the order associated with its form.[55]

It would be a mistake, however, to suppose that Aquinas takes moral evil to consist in intellective error. Because of the very close relationship he sees between intellect and will, the irrationality of moral wrongdoing will be a function of will as well, not just of intellect. In Aquinas's view, the moral evaluation of a human action attaches primarily to the "internal act", the volition from which the external act derives. Since "will is inclined toward reason's good [the good presented to will by intellect] by the very nature of the power of will", bad volition stems from defective deliberation.[56] As intellect and will continually influence each other, so bad deliberation can also be an effect of bad volition. Moreover, practical intellect's mistakes in identifying the best available course of action may also have the passions of the sensory soul as sources.

Furthermore, "because the good [presented by intellect] is varied in many ways, it is necessary that will be inclined through some habit toward some determinate good presented by reason so that [will's determining] activity may follow more promptly".[57] Habits of will are conditions necessary for our carrying out our volitions in particularly good or particularly bad ways, as regards both the "executive" and the "determining" aspects of volition; and the habits that play these crucial roles in Aquinas's moral theory are the virtues and the vices.

The four cardinal virtues can be understood as habits of this sort. Reason's habit of good governance generally is prudence; reason's restraint which wards off self-serving concupiscence is temperance; reason's persevering rather than giving in to self-serving irascible passions such as fear is courage; reason's governance of one's relations with others is justice. Aquinas's normative ethics is based on virtues; it is concerned with dispositions and then with actions stemming from those dispositions.

In addition to the moral virtues in all their various manifestations, Aquinas also recognizes intellectual virtues that, like the moral virtues, can be acquired by human effort. On the other hand, the supreme theological virtues of faith, hope and charity cannot be acquired but must be directly infused by God. Aquinas introduces these virtues and others in *Summa theologiae* IaIIae. 49–88 and examines them in detail throughout IIaIIae.

Passions, virtues and vices are all intrinsic principles, or sources, of human acts. However, there are extrinsic principles as well, among which is law in all its varieties. Consequently, Aquinas moves on in *Summa theologiae* IaIIae.90–108 to his Treatise on Law, a famous and original treatment of the subject. The best-known feature of the treatise is Aquinas's concept of natural law. Law in general is "a kind of rational ordering for the common good, promulgated by the one who takes care of the community",[58] and

> the precepts of natural law are to practical reasoning what the first principles of demonstrations are to theoretical reasoning ... All things to be done or to be avoided pertain to the precepts of natural law, which practical reasoning apprehends naturally as being human goods.[59]

Human laws of all kinds derive, or should derive, from natural law, which might be construed as the naturally knowable rational principles underlying morality in general:

> From the precepts of natural law, as from general, indemonstrable principles, it is necessary that human reason proceed to making more particular arrangements ... [which] are called human laws, provided that they pertain to the definition (*ratio*) of law already stated.[60]

As a consequence of this hierarchy of laws, Aquinas unhesitatingly rejects some kinds and some particular instances of human law, for example: "A tyrannical law, since it is not in accord with reason, is not unconditionally a law but is, rather, a perversion of law."[61] Even natural law rests on the more fundamental "eternal law", which Aquinas identifies as divine providence, "the very nature of the governance of things on the part of God as ruler of the universe".[62]

In *De regimine principum* (*The Governance of Rulers*), his most important political work, Aquinas begins by sounding the familiar medieval theme: monarchy is the best form of government. He is careful, however, to distinguish a monarch from a tyrant; the first wields his power primarily for the well-being of his people, and the second wields his power first and foremost for his own well-being. Aquinas also realizes that a single ruler is easily corrupted and that monarchy therefore has a tendency to turn into tyranny. He countenances disobedience and even revolution against a monarch who has become a tyrant only in special circumstances, but he does maintain that in those circumstances radical means, including tyrannicide, may be justified (*De regimine principium* 6). Perhaps because he appreciates the dangers in monarchy, he works republican elements into his theory of good government. His later commentary on Aristotle's *Politics* emphasizes the citizen as one who rules and is ruled in turn. There is also a strongly egalitarian element in his theory of political justice.

Theology: natural, revealed and philosophical

Because Aquinas developed most of his thought within the formal confines of thirteenth-century theology, and because this has in turn affected his place in the history of philosophy and the assessment of his work, some attention must be paid to the ways in which much of what we recognize as philosophy was an essential component of what he thought of as theology.

Aquinas devotes the first three books of *Summa contra gentiles* to a systematic development of natural theology, which he saw as part of philosophy (cf. *ST* Ia.1.1 ad 2). As part of philosophy, natural theology must of course be based entirely on "principles known by the natural light of intellect",[63] principles of the sort that underlie Aristotle's metaphysics, which Aristotle himself thought of as culminating in theology (see Aquinas's interpretation of that thought in the prooemium to his *Sententia super Metaphysicam* (*Commentary on Aristotle's Metaphysics*)). In fact, the way Aquinas works in *SCG* I–III strongly suggests that he may have thought of natural theology as a science subordinate to metaphysics, somewhat as he would have understood optics to be subordinate to geometry.

However, there is something odd about that project of his. By Aquinas's day, the churchmen governing universities had overcome most of their initial misgivings about the recently recovered works of the pagan Aristotle, and had acknowledged officially that the study of Aristotelian physics and metaphysics (with their integrated minor component of natural theology) was compatible with the then universally recognized availability of revealed truths about God. Medieval Christians had come to appreciate the ancient philosophers' attempts to uncover truths about God on the basis of observation and reasoning alone as having been justified, even commendable, given their total ignorance of revelation. However, no philosopher in Aquinas's circumstances could have justifiably undertaken a new project of natural theology heuristically.

Still, no opprobrium would attach to natural theology taken up expositionally. The aim of such an enterprise would be not to develop theology from scratch but rather to show, in the spirit of Romans 1:20, the extent to which what had been supernaturally revealed could, in theory, have been naturally discovered. Such an enterprise is what *SCG* I–III seems to represent.

Evidence from a chronicle written about seventy years after Aquinas began *Summa contra gentiles* once led scholars to suppose that he had written it as a manual for the use of Dominican missionaries to Muslims and Jews. If that were so, then the work's presentation of natural instead of revealed theology in its first three books would have been dictated by the practical purpose of rationally deriving the truth about God, and about God's relation to everything else, for people who would not have acknowledged the revealed texts that Aquinas would otherwise have cited as the source of that truth. But nobody, and certainly not Aquinas, could have supposed that Muslims or Jews needed to be argued into perfect-being monotheism of the sort developed in those first three books, which contain nothing that he would have taken to be contrary to Judaism or Islam. If Aquinas had intended *Summa contra gentiles* as a manual for missionaries to educated Muslims, Jews or Christian heretics, he would have wasted the enormous effort represented in the 366 copiously argued chapters of Books I–III (see Gauthier 1961, 1993, for a persuasive rejection of the earlier account).

What Aquinas himself says about his purpose in writing *Summa contra gentiles* suggests that what he wrote had at least its formal cause not in an attempt to aid missionary activities, but instead in his consideration of the inter-relation of philosophy and Christianity. He begins by writing about the concerns of a wise person, one of those "who give things an appropriate order and direction and govern them well".[64] Obviously, such a person has to be concerned with goals and sources, and so the wisest person will be "one whose attention is turned toward the universal goal, which is also the universal source", which Aquinas takes to be God.[65] Because this natural theology is oriented as it is, "it must be called the greatest wisdom itself, as considering the absolutely highest cause of all".[66] Therefore, the highest, most universal explanatory truth must be wisdom's concern.

Anyone aspiring to wisdom will attend to metaphysics, since, Aquinas reports, Aristotle rightly identified metaphysics as "the science of truth – not

27

of just any truth, but of the truth that is the origin of all truth, the truth that pertains to the first principle of being for all things".[67] And, as he says in an observation that suits his own enterprise, "sometimes divine wisdom proceeds from human philosophy's starting points".[68] However, since it is the business of one and the same science

> to pursue one of two contraries and to repel the other ... the role of the wise person is to meditate on the truth, especially the truth regarding the first principle, and to discuss it with others, but also to fight against the falsity that is its contrary.[69]

The truth regarding the first principle will be the truth about God, supposing natural theology can show that God exists; and so the explanatory truth associated here with metaphysics is the truth associated also with theology.

No one knows what title, if any, Aquinas himself gave to this work. In some of its medieval manuscripts, it is entitled *Liber de veritate catholicae fidei contra errores* (*A Book About the Truth of the Catholic Faith, Directed Against Mistakes*), a title that comes closer to accurately representing the book's aim and contents than the more pugnacious, traditional *Summa contra gentiles* (*Synopsis [of Christian Doctrine] Directed Against Unbelievers*). During the nineteenth century, when *Summa theologiae* was instead normally referred to as *Summa theologica* (*Theological Synopsis*), *Summa contra gentiles* was sometimes published under the deliberately contrasting title *Summa philosophica* (*Philosophical Synopsis*). That contrast, although potentially misleading, has some truth in it, as may be seen in Aquinas's plan for *SCG* I–III:

> Since we intend to pursue by way of reason the things about God that human reason can investigate, the first consideration is of matters associated with God considered in himself [Book I]; second, of the emergence of created things from him [Book II]; third, of the ordering and directing of created things toward him as their goal [Book III].[70]

In this pursuit by way of reason, Aquinas must and does shun "authoritative arguments" of any sort, but he shows good sense in not restricting himself to "demonstrative arguments" in developing natural theology. He does, of course, use demonstrative arguments when he thinks he has them, but, like almost all philosophers of any period, he recognizes philosophy's need for "probable arguments" as well. A demonstrative argument takes as its premises propositions that explain the fact in the argument's conclusion by elucidating its causes (or, sometimes, its effects), and so it produces, or presents, scientific understanding. A probable argument, the sort that has always been most prevalent in philosophy, is one based on premises of any sort that are accepted widely or by experts in the relevant field; and so one group may be convinced by a probable argument that another group rejects. Of course, Aquinas has to make use of authoritative arguments in the fourth (and last) book, where he turns from natural to revealed theology, and his tolerance of them there is part of what distinguishes Book IV's argumentation from the sort that characterizes Books I–III.

In *SCG* IV, Aquinas engages in what has come to be called philosophical theology, the application of reason to revelation. Philosophical theology shares the methods of natural theology broadly conceived – in other words, analysis and argumentation of all the sorts accepted in philosophy – but it lifts natural theology's restriction on premises, accepting as assumptions revealed propositions. This includes those that are initially inaccessible to unaided reason, such as the "mysteries" of Christian doctrine. In his many works of philosophical theology, Aquinas tests the coherence of doctrinal propositions (including the mysteries), attempts explanations of them, uncovers their logical connections with other doctrinal propositions and so on, in order to bear out his conviction that the doctrines themselves are eminently understandable and acceptable, and that the apparent incoherence of some of them is only a feature of our initial, superficial view of them.

Summa theologiae is the paradigm of philosophical theology. The very first Article of the very first Question makes it clear at once that it is not natural theology that *Summa theologiae* is a *summa* of, since it begins by asking whether we need any "other teaching, besides philosophical studies", which in Aquinas's usage means the studies that medieval beginners in theology would have just completed in the arts faculty. The question arises because philosophical studies are characterized not only as dealing with "the things that are subject to reason", but also as encompassing "all beings, including God", as a consequence of which there is a part of philosophy that is theology.

Although Aquinas accepts this characterization of philosophy's subject matter as universal and as including a part that is properly called theology, he offers several arguments to support his claim that revealed theology is nonetheless not superfluous. In one of those arguments, he claims that a thing's "capacity for being cognized in various ways brings about a difference between sciences". By this he means that different sciences can reason to some of the same conclusions on the basis of different premises or evidence. In his example, he points out that in order to support the proposition that the earth is round, a naturalist uses empirical observations, while a cosmologist might support that same conclusion on a strictly formal basis. He concludes:

> And for that reason, nothing prevents the same things from being treated by philosophical studies insofar as they can be cognized by the light of natural reason, and also by another science insofar as they are cognized by the light of divine revelation. That is why the

theology that pertains to *sacra doctrina* [in other words, revealed theology] differs in kind from the theology that is considered a part of philosophy.[71]

In this argument, Aquinas might appear willing to concede that revealed and natural theology differ only in this methodological respect, that they simply constitute two radically different ways of approaching the very same propositions about God and everything else. However, he would not actually concede this. There are propositions that belong uniquely to revealed theology's subject matter, simply because the different premises with which revealed theology begins can also lead to conclusions not available to unaided reason. And, of course, no doctrinal proposition that is initially available to human beings only in virtue of having been revealed by God can be part of natural theology's subject matter.

On the other hand, no propositions appropriate to natural theology are excluded from *ST*'s subject matter. The propositions that belong to natural theology form a proper subset of those that belong to revealed theology:

> It was necessary that human beings be instructed by divine revelation even as regards the things about God that human reason can explore. For the truth about God investigated by a few on the basis of reason [without relying on revelation] would emerge for people [only] after a long time and tainted with many mistakes. And yet all human well-being, which has to do with God, depends on the cognition of that truth. Therefore, it was necessary for human beings to be instructed about divine matters through divine revelation so that [the nature of human] well-being might emerge for people more conveniently and with greater certainty.[72]

When he sums up his examination of *sacra doctrina*, or revealed theology, Aquinas says that its "main aim ... is to transmit a cognition of God, and not only as he is in himself, but also as he is the source of things and their goal, especially of the rational creature".[73] Thus the subject matter of *sacra doctrina*, the theology presented in this *summa* of theology, is the most basic truths about everything, with two provisos: first, it is about God and about things other than God as they relate to God as their source and goal; second, among the things other than God with which it deals, it is especially about human beings, whose study of theology should be motivated by the fact that their well-being depends specially on their grasp of certain theological truths. And, Aquinas insists, universal scope is just what one should expect in a rational investigation of the truth about God:

> All things are considered in *sacra doctrina* under the concept of God, either because they are God, or because they have an ordered rela-

tionship to God as to their source and goal. It follows from this that
the subject of this science is really God

even though the intended explanatory scope of the science is universal.[74]

In referring to *sacra doctrina* as a 'science', Aquinas means to characterize
it as a systematic, reasoned presentation of an organized body of knowledge
consisting of general truths about some reasonably unified subject matter. In
that broadly Aristotelian sense, it is not obviously wrong to think of
theology as a science (as it would be in the narrower, twentieth-century
sense of 'science'). It is in that sense that the science of theology as Aquinas
develops it in *ST* would now be called philosophical theology; the enterprise
of employing the techniques and devices of philosophy in clarifying,
supporting and extending the propositions that are supposed to have been
revealed for theology's starting points. Thus, some of the work of philosophical theology is an attempt to explain revealed propositions and
systematically work out their implications.

Like natural theology, which is subordinate to metaphysics, philosophical
theology is a subordinate science. However, because it begins its work on
divinely revealed propositions, Aquinas identifies the science to which it is
subordinate as God's knowledge of himself and everything else, available to
human beings directly only in the afterlife.[75] As he says earlier:

> For us, the goal of faith is to arrive at an understanding of what we
> believe – [which is] as if a practitioner of a subordinate science were
> to acquire in addition the knowledge possessed by a practitioner of
> the higher science. In that case the things that were only believed
> before would come to be known, or understood.[76]

Not even the doctrinal mysteries are impervious to rational investigation,
although unaided reason could never have discovered them. Regarding one
central mystery, for example, Aquinas says: "It is impossible to arrive at a
cognition of the Trinity of the divine persons by means of natural
reason."[77] However, he says this in the twenty-second of a series of seventy-
seven articles of *ST* devoted to analysing and arguing about the details of
Trinity, in other words, in the midst of subjecting this mystery to philosophical theology. As he explains in the very Article in which he rules out
the possibility of rationally discovering that there are three divine persons:

> There are two ways in which reason is employed regarding any matter
> ... in one way to provide sufficient proof of something fundamental
> ... in the other way to show that consequent effects are suited to some-
> thing fundamental that has already been posited ... It is in the first
> way, then, that reason can be employed to prove that God is one, and
> things of that sort. But it is in the second way that reason is employed

in a clarification of Trinity. For once Trinity has been posited, reasonings of that sort are suitable, although not so as to provide a sufficient
proof of the Trinity of persons by those reasonings.[78]

Aquinas is also careful to point out that it isn't mere intellectual curiosity or
even a defense of the faith that is served by a rational clarification of Trinity.
In his view, this application of philosophical theology – confirming faith by
reason, showing that Trinity is not after all irrational, exposing the intricate
connections between these and other doctrinal propositions – aids one's
understanding of creation and salvation.

Part I

THE ULTIMATE
FOUNDATION OF REALITY

1

METAPHYSICS
A theory of things

Introduction

Obviously, one cannot do justice even to a few parts of Aquinas's meta-physics in a single chapter,[1] but I want to lay out roughly here the main elements of what might be called 'Aquinas's theory of things'. This is not the same as his ontology or his theory of what there is in the world, since he supposes that being – what there *is* – is spread over all the ten Aristotelian categories and not just the category of substance, which includes things. It is not the same as his theory of substance either, however, since it is arguable that not everything he recognizes as a thing counts for him as a substance.[2] For the purposes of this chapter, I will take things to include not only substances and artifacts but also at least some of the parts of which substances are constituted. By 'parts' in this context, I mean both what Aquinas called 'integral parts', such as the hand of a human being or the roof of a house, and also metaphysical parts, such as matter and form, which constitute material things in a way different from the way they are constituted by their integral parts.[3] In order to understand Aquinas's basic worldview, it is important to understand his theory of things, and especially his view of what it is for something to be *one* thing.

Aside from the fact that it is complicated and technical, Aquinas's theory of things is difficult to understand for at least two reasons. First, it makes use of Latin terms whose English equivalents are common terms in contemporary philosophy; but the meanings of the Latin terms and their English equivalents are not invariably identical.[4] Special care is therefore necessary with the technical terminology if confusion is not to be introduced into the interpretation of Aquinas. Second, on many of the key issues of Aquinas's metaphysics, contemporary metaphysics is itself at least contentious. (A cursory review of the contemporary literature on the nature of the constitution relation, for example, or on the nature of persistence through time illustrates the point.) We are accustomed, however, to explaining something by transposing what is obscure in it into something that is clearer to us; and we often clarify obscure views from other historical periods by mapping them on to something in contemporary views which we feel we understand better. But so much in contemporary metaphysics is not clear, at least not clear to those other than the proponents of the contemporary view in question, that this ordinary method of introducing clarity into the interpretation of historical philosophical positions is not readily available for medieval metaphysics.

For these reasons, even if there were no difficulties in Aquinas's metaphysics itself, an insistence on a complete and consistent explanation of Aquinas's theory of things would be likely to yield a position that is unfaithful to Aquinas's thought, and an attempt to be faithful to his thought is likely to yield a theory that strikes us as unsatisfactory with regard to completeness or consistency. Perhaps the best that can be done in these circumstances is to narrow the gap between his way of understanding metaphysics and our own.

Matter and form

Aquinas thinks that some things are made out of matter and other things (such as angels) are not. It is easiest to approach his theory of things by beginning with his views about things made out of matter. A macro-level material thing is matter organized or configured in some way, where the organization or configuration is dynamic rather than static. That is, the organization of the matter includes causal relations among the material components of the thing as well as such static features as shape and spatial location. This dynamic configuration or organization is what Aquinas calls 'form'.[5] A thing has the properties it has, including its causal powers, in virtue of having the configuration it does; the proper operations and functions of a thing derive from its form.[6] (I am here thus making a conceptual distinction between the organization of a thing and the properties the thing has in virtue of being organized in that way, and in what follows I will sometimes speak of a form's conferring certain properties on the whole it configures.)

Like many contemporary philosophers, Aquinas recognizes levels of organization. What counts as matter for a macro-level object may itself be organized or configured in a certain way; that is, the matter of a thing may itself be constituted of matter and form.[7]

A typical medieval example given to illustrate the matter/form distinction is a bronze statue, but for our purposes here it will be more helpful to take a contemporary example. So consider the protein called 'CAT/Enhancer-Binding Protein' (C/EBP), one of the proteins known to play an important role in regulating gene expression.[8] In its active form, the molecule is a dimer with an alpha helix coil. On Aquinas's way of thinking about material objects, the form of C/EBP is the configuration of the dimer, including the alpha helix coil; and the dimer subunits constitute the matter. Of course, each dimer subunit is itself a composite. The form of the subunit is the configuration of its amino acids, in which, for example, in one region every seventh spot must be occupied by leucine; and the amino acids composing the subunit are its matter. Amino acids themselves are also clearly composites, however. The matter of an amino acid such as leucine is the carbon, hydrogen, nitrogen and oxygen of which it is composed, and the form is the way that material is combined, including the characteristic NH_2 configuration common to all the amino acids and the sequence of carbon and hydrogen peculiar to leucine. We can evidently go on in this way until we come, for example, to the proton of a hydrogen atom. The quarks that compose it are its matter, and their configuration – the right combination of and interactions between up and down quarks – is the form of the proton. But at some point this process of moving down the levels of organization of a macro-level thing must come to a halt. For Aquinas, the lowest-level material component which counts as matter organized in a certain way is an element.[9] An element is constituted of matter and form, but if we conceptually strip away the form or configuration of an element, all that remains is prime matter; matter which cannot itself be decomposed further into matter and form.

Prime matter is thus matter without any form at all, "materiality" (as it were) apart from configuration. When it is a component in a matter-form composite, prime matter is the component of the configured composite which makes it the case that the configured thing can be extended in three dimensions and can occupy a particular place at a particular time. But by itself, apart from form, prime matter exists just potentially; it exists in actuality only as an ingredient in something configured.[10] So we can remove form from prime matter only in thought; everything which exists in reality is configured in some way. For this reason, Aquinas sometimes says that form is the actuality of anything.[11] Configuration or organization is necessary for the existence of anything at all; without form, nothing is actual.

This point holds also for immaterial things. For Aquinas, there are things that exist and are organized in a certain way, but the organization is not an organization of matter. An angel, a certain kind of intelligence, is an example. An angel has no matter to configure, but it is nonetheless configured in a certain way. It has certain properties, such as being a knower, and not others, such as weighing two hundred pounds. And so there is a kind of organization in an angel, too, which we can think of as an organization of properties. An angel has one constellation of properties rather than another, and in virtue of these properties it also has one set of causal powers rather than another.[12]

Consequently, although matter is not necessary for the existence of a thing, on Aquinas's view, form is. For Aquinas, to be is to be configured.

Substantial and accidental forms

Aquinas takes it that the forms of material objects can be divided into two sorts, substantial forms (that is, the substantial forms of primary substances) and accidental forms. (Immaterial things can also have both substantial and accidental forms, but in the discussion which follows, for the sake of simplicity, my focus will be just on that part of Aquinas's theory of things which has to do with things made of matter.[13]) For present purposes we can understand his distinction between these two sorts of forms roughly in this way. The difference between the substantial and the accidental forms of material objects is a function of three things: (1) what the form organizes or configures; (2) what the configuration effects; and (3) what kind of change is produced by the advent of the configuration.

Regarding (1): a substantial form of a material thing configures prime matter. An accidental form, on the other hand, configures something which is an actually existing complete thing, a matter-form composite.[14] Or to put the same point in a different way, if we conceptually strip away a substantial form from a material thing (and don't immediately replace it with another substantial form of some sort), what is left cannot exist in actuality. Nothing that is actual consists only of prime matter plus accidental properties. But if we strip away any particular accidental form, what is left is still an actually existing complete thing, and it remains the same complete thing it was before the accidental form was stripped away. (On the other hand, it is not possible to strip away all accidental forms from a material thing. It is necessary to a material thing that it have accidental forms, even if it is not necessary that it have one rather than another accidental form.)

Regarding (2): for this reason, configuration by a substantial form brings it about that a thing which was not already in existence comes into existence. Since any thing that comes into existence exists as a member of a kind, the substantial form of a thing is thus also responsible for a thing's belonging to a particular primary kind or lowest species. On Aquinas's views, every substance is a member of exactly one lowest species or primary kind, although species can be ordered hierarchically under genera, which can themselves be ordered hierarchically under higher genera until one comes to the highest genus, which is *substance*. Configuration by an accidental form, on the other hand, brings it about only that an already existing thing comes to have a certain property, without ceasing to be the thing (or the kind of thing) it was.[15] Accidental forms are thus responsible for the non-essential properties of a thing; the addition or removal of an accidental form does not alter the species to which the whole belongs or the identity of the whole.[16]

Regarding (3): the change produced by the advent of a substantial form is therefore a generation of a thing. The change produced by the advent of an accidental form, by contrast, is only an alteration of one and the same thing.[17]

It is clear from these claims that any material thing which exists has a substantial form. But Aquinas's claims about substantial form also imply that no existing material thing has more than one substantial form.[18] A composite which consists of prime matter configured by a substantial form could not itself be one component among others of a larger whole configured by yet another substantial form. That is because a substantial form of a material thing configures prime matter; but if a substantial form were to configure what is already configured by a substantial form, then it would be configuring a matter-form composite, not prime matter. (Of course, the new substantial form might simply replace the previous one, but in that case the composite would still be configured by only one substantial form.)

Furthermore, Aquinas's claims about substantial forms limit the way in which already existing things can be combined into a composite substance. Barnacles have a substantial form, and so do starfish. If a barnacle attaches itself very firmly to the back of a starfish, that attaching will not constitute a generation of a substance. If it did, there would be one thing – the barnacle–starfish composite – which had more than one substantial form, the form of the barnacle and the form of the starfish.[19] So what the attachment of the barnacle to the starfish effects, on Aquinas's views, is just that two complete things come to have a property or properties which they did not have before, as, for example, the property of being fastened together. The new configuration of the barnacle attached to the starfish will thus be an accidental one. Any case in which two already existing material things come together into some kind of composite without ceasing to exist as the things they were before they came together will similarly be a case of alteration rather than generation, and the new composite will be configured with an accidental, rather than a substantial, form.[20]

Any ordinary artifact is configured only with an accidental form. The production of an artifact, such as an axe with a metal blade attached to a wooden handle, brings together already existing things – a metal thing and a wooden thing – which in the new composite still remain the things they were before being conjoined. An artifact is thus a composite of things configured together into a whole but not by a substantial form.[21] Since only something configured by a substantial form is a substance, no artifact is a substance.

Substances and artifacts

Elements – earth, air, fire and water – are substances, and so is a material made of one element.[22] Furthermore, different elements can combine to form a compound which is itself a substance.[23] So, for example, earth and fire can combine to form flesh. But they can do so only when the substantial form of each combining element is lost in the composite and is replaced by the one substantial form of the whole compound.[24] Furthermore, the substances which are compounds of elements, such as flesh or blood, can combine into one thing, such as an animal, only when they also are not substances in their own right in the newly composed whole.[25] On Aquinas's view, the parts of a whole are actual (rather than potential) things existing in their own right only when the composite of which they are parts is decomposed.[26] If this were not so, says Aquinas, then there would be as many substances in one thing such as a human being as there are parts in him, a conclusion Aquinas clearly regards as absurd.[27]

An objector might suppose here that, for example, flesh in an animal is the same as flesh existing on its own. Since Aquinas is willing to grant that flesh existing on its own is a substance, it seems that it must be a substance when it is in an animal as well. Consequently, the objector might maintain, Aquinas's principle that there cannot be more than one substantial form in a thing is violated. In an animal, there will be at least both the substantial form of the flesh and the substantial form of the animal.

But this objection to Aquinas fails to take into proper consideration his understanding of form. On his view, flesh existing on its own does not have the same form as flesh in an animal. That is because flesh in an animal can perform the functions proper to that flesh, as flesh existing on its own cannot.[28] The proper function of flesh (or any other constituent of the whole) is given by the substantial form of the whole. When it exists on its own, without being configured by the form of the whole animal, no part of an animal functions as it does when it is in the whole. And so flesh in an animal, unlike flesh which exists on its own, is configured by the one substantial form of the animal and not by the substantial form of flesh.[29]

In the context of his philosophical theology, Aquinas gives a helpful summary of his views of composition.[30] A composite can be constituted of two or more constituents in three ways, he says. (i) It can be constituted of complete things which in the composite remain as the complete things they were before being conjoined; their conjoining is thus effected by an accidental form such as order or figure. Artifacts such as heaps and houses are composites of this sort; substances are not. (ii) It can be constituted of complete things that do not remain complete things in their own right but lose their own substantial forms in the resulting composite. A mixture composed of diverse elements is an example of this sort of whole. Mixtures of this sort are substances if they exist on their own,[31] but not if they are themselves components of a substance. (iii) It can be constituted of things which are not complete things or substances in their own right but which make one complete substance by their union. The coming together of prime matter and substantial form to constitute a substance is his example here.[32]

One implication of these views of Aquinas is that no part of a substance counts as a substance in its own right as long as it is a component of a larger whole that is a substance. That is because the substantial form which such a part would have if it existed on its own is lost when it becomes part of a composite substance and is replaced by the one substantial form of the composite.[33]

Aquinas's claims about substance here can perhaps be understood by a contemporary analogy. Hydrogen and oxygen are the components of water, and we can decompose a water molecule into hydrogen and oxygen. But when water exists as a whole, as water, we do not actually have hydrogen or oxygen; we have water. Furthermore, the substantial form of water informs prime matter and not oxygen and hydrogen. That is, the configuration of a water molecule is a configuration of the materiality of the whole molecule; it is not a configuration of hydrogen added to a configuration of oxygen. If oxygen and hydrogen each kept precisely the configuration they had in their isolated state and were just somehow pushed together, the resulting composite would not be water. In order to get water, the configuration that oxygen had and the configuration that hydrogen had before oxygen and hydrogen conjoined into a water molecule are replaced by a new configuration that includes, for example, the polar covalent bond between hydrogen and oxygen. Furthermore, the emerging thing – the water – has characteristics and causal powers different from either hydrogen or oxygen because of that configuration of the whole.[34] Aquinas explains the idea in this way:

> the nobler a form is the more it dominates corporeal matter and the less it is submerged in it and the more it exceeds it in its operation or power. And so we see that the form of a mixed body has a certain operation which is not caused from the qualities of the elements [of which that body is composed].[35]

We can put the general point at issue here the other way around: if we divide a composite substance into its parts, we may turn what was one substance into several substances.[36] For example, according to Aquinas, there are simple living things (such as certain worms) which can be cut in half to form two living things of the same sort.[37] During the time that the parts were parts of the composite substance and did not exist on their own, they were not actual substances themselves.[38] There were not actually two worms in the one worm before it was cut in two.

Furthermore, the whole worm ceases to exist when it is divided and the two new worms come into existence.[39] In the case of fission involving animals which are not human, then, Aquinas's view implies that the career of the whole substance lasts only as long as the whole is intact; and so for him, each of the fissioned substances is a different substance from the whole existing before the fission. (What he would say about the thought experiments of contemporary philosophy in which a human person is fissioned into two persons cannot be inferred from this part of his metaphysics alone because there are special characteristics of the form which is the human soul that complicate the case.)

So a material substance comes into existence when prime matter is configured by a substantial form. The constituent things that existed before being woven together by that configuration (if there were previously existing things) cease to exist as things in their own right,[40] and a new thing is generated. Elements are the most fundamental composites of matter and form, and all other material substances are composed of them. But when different elements come together to form a compound, their substantial forms are replaced by a new substantial form which configures the newly generated whole. An artifact, on the other hand, comes into existence when things which already exist as things in their own right are rearranged in such a way that each of the rearranged parts remains the thing it was, and the whole composite is united by an accidental, rather than a substantial, form. The resulting composite is thus *one* thing in some weaker sense than is at issue in the case of a substance.

Finally, things include substances and artifacts, but these do not exhaust the class of things. That is because a severed hand or a disembodied soul, for example, is also a thing, although not a thing which is itself a substance or an artifact.[41]

Hands and souls are parts of substances, although they represent different sorts of parts. A hand is an integral part, a matter-form composite which contributes to the quantity – the spatial extension – of the whole substance of which it is a part.[42] A soul, on the other hand, is not itself a matter-form composite, and the spatial extension of a whole human being does not derive from the immaterial soul itself.[43] A soul is thus not an integral part, but a metaphysical part.[44] What keeps each sort of part from counting as a substance, for Aquinas, is that it is not a complete thing in its own right, and it can be defined only with some mention of the whole in its definition. A hand, for example, is an appendage of a human being; a (rational) soul is the substantial form of a human being.

People sometimes suppose that Aquinas defines a substance as something which can exist on its own; but, as the list of things in the preceding paragraph makes clear, this definition of substance cannot be Aquinas's. In Aquinas's view, there are things that can exist on their own, such as severed hands, disembodied souls and artifacts, which nonetheless are not substances.[45] So, at best, for Aquinas, the ability to exist on its own is a necessary but not a sufficient condition for something's being a substance.

It would be helpful to be able to say here with some precision just what a substance is for Aquinas, in order to shed light on his view of the nature of the difference between substances and other sorts of things. But it is difficult to give a non-circular analysis of Aquinas's concept of substance or substantial form, in my view.

When Aquinas himself gives a careful characterization of substance,[46] he tends to describe a substance as a thing which has a nature such that the thing can exist on its own.[47] But, of course, one wants to know why this description cannot apply to a severed hand. If the answer is that natures are the sort of thing had only by substances, not by parts of substances, then 'nature' is a technical term defined in terms of substance, and so the description of substance is circular.

One might take a clue from the preceding description of Aquinas's views of parts and try adding a conjunct to Aquinas's characterization of substance in this way: a substance is something (i) which has a nature such that the thing can exist on its own, *and* (ii) which is a complete thing in its own right. But this also is not sufficient to give a non-circular way of differentiating substances from artifacts. There seems to be no reason why we should not think that an artifact is a complete thing unless we have some understanding of complete things such that only substances can be complete things.

Given Aquinas's understanding of artifacts as a collection of substances conjoined by an accidental form, we might try adding yet a third conjunct: (iii) which does not include mention of another complete thing (that is, a primary substance or a whole artifact) in its definition.

But it is not at all clear that even this formula is adequate. An axe, for example, apparently has a nature such that it can exist on its own, and it does seem to be a complete thing; so if it is excluded by this conjunctive definition of substance, it must be in virtue of the third conjunct. But it is hard to see why an axe cannot be defined without mention of the substances which compose it. Why couldn't an axe be defined in terms of its function, for example, rather than in terms of its material components?

Finally, one might try excluding artifacts from the category of substances on the grounds that there is a close connection between being a complete thing and having a substantial form, such that only composites configured by substantial forms are complete things. In that case, artifacts will in fact be excluded. But now the characterization of substance is circular again, since complete things are defined in terms of substantial forms, which only substances have.[48]

It may be that the best clue for finding a non-circular distinction between substance and artifact lies in Aquinas's insistence that substantial forms configure prime matter, but that the parts of an artifact retain their own substantial forms within the larger whole they compose. There are various notions of emergence in the literature, and they are usually restricted to properties. But for present purposes we can understand the emergence of a whole W roughly in this way: W is an emergent thing if and only if the properties and causal powers of W are not simply the sum of the properties and causal powers of the constituents of W when those constituents are taken singillatim, outside the configuration of W. On Aquinas's account of substance and with this rough understanding of the notion of an emergent thing, a substance is an emergent thing with respect to its parts, which lose their own substantial form in constituting the whole. By contrast, it is much easier to see an artifact such as an axe just as the sum of its parts, and to see the causal powers and the properties of an axe as the sum of the causal powers and properties of the constituents of the axe. Even philosophers who are willing to countenance the notion of emergent things might balk at considering an axe emergent with regard to its parts.

But the promise of this way of distinguishing substance and artifact is considerably diminished by considering, say, styrofoam. On the face of it, styrofoam appears to be an artifact insofar as it is the product of human design, but it seems closer to water than to axes as regards emergence. It may be that if Aquinas had known some of the products of contemporary technology, he would have found the distinction between substance and artifact much harder to make crisp and clear. Alternatively, it may be that he would have thought that not all products of human design count as artifacts. Maybe styrofoam is a substance, but one that human beings help bring into existence, in much the same way that human design goes into the production of new breeds of dogs, without its being the case that a dog is an artifact. If Aquinas were willing to countenance such things as styrofoam as substances, then perhaps the notion of an emergent thing could be used as the basis for a distinction between substances and artifacts.

Individuation and identity

From the fact that Aquinas thinks an angel or a disembodied human soul, each of which is a form, can exist on its own, we can see that he thinks a form can be a particular.[49] In fact, for Aquinas, everything that exists in reality is a particular; universals exist only in the mind.[50]

A form that is an angel, an immaterial intelligence, always exists on its own. One immaterial intelligence is differentiated from another by the features of the form itself.[51] The properties that make up the nature or species of one angel, which are conferred by the substantial form of the angel, are different from the properties that make up the nature or species of every other angel; and Aquinas thinks that there can be no more than one angel for every species of angel. Consequently, an angel is individuated in virtue of its substantial form, which is unique to it.[52] What is necessary and sufficient for something to be *this* angel is that it have *this* substantial form.

Much more needs to be said to clarify the notion of an individuating substantial form, but it is worth noticing at the outset the implications of Aquinas's views as regards change over time.

According to the medieval metaphysics Aquinas accepts, any composite substance,[53] even an immaterial substance, has accidental forms as well as a substantial form, and accidental forms are forms a thing can gain or lose while remaining one and the same thing. Now on a commonsensical view of change over time, change is a matter of one and the same thing's having a property at one time which it lacks at another time. Medieval metaphysics, including Aquinas's, begins with a commitment to this commonsensical notion of change and then works to provide an explanation of something's remaining numerically one and the same through the change.

Contemporary metaphysics, by contrast, begins with a commitment to the law of the indiscernibility of identicals:

> (LII) For any x and y, x is identical to y only if x and y have all and only the same properties.

On the contemporary commitment to (LII), what needs explaining is change over time, and it is often explained in ways which are complicated, if not counter-intuitive.[54]

If Aquinas accepts a principle like (LII), it is this:

> (Aquinas's Principle) (AP): For any x and y, x is identical to y only if, for any time t, x exists at t if and only if y exists at t, and if x exists at t, x has at t all and only the properties y has at t.

According to (AP), it need not be true that x has just the same properties as y in order to be identical to y, as long as the properties x has at a time are the same as the properties y has at that time, and neither x nor y exists at any time the other does not. For Aquinas, x and y can differ in some of their accidental properties and still be numerically identical, provided that the differing accidental properties in question are ones that x has at t_n and that y has at t_m.

(AP) gives only a necessary condition for identity and not also a sufficient one; for Aquinas, x and y can meet the condition in (AP) without being identical. Indiscernibility of properties at a time and coincident existence are not sufficient for identity, on his views. To see that this is so, consider two men, Aaron David and Nathan Daniel. Let it be the case that the thing referred to by 'Aaron' exists only from t1 to t2; these, then, are also the only times at which the thing referred to by 'David' exists. Similarly, let it be the case that the thing referred to by 'Nathan' exists only from t3 to t4, so that these are also the only times at which the thing referred to by 'Daniel' exists. It will be the case as well that at any time in the interval t1–t2, Aaron has all and only the properties that David has at that time. Similarly, at any time in the interval t3–t4, Nathan has all and only the properties that Daniel has at that time. Now let 'Cicero' be an abbreviation for 'Aaron and Nathan', and let 'Tully' be an abbreviation for 'David and Daniel'. Then what is referred to by 'Cicero' and what is referred to by 'Tully' meet the condition in (AP). But neither Cicero nor Tully is a thing at all, on Aquinas's view, let alone one and the same thing. So the condition in (AP) is insufficient for identity. What else, then, is needed, on Aquinas's view?[55]

As I explained just above, Aquinas thinks that an immaterial substance is always individuated by the substantial form unique to it. So, for Aquinas, the following principle is true:

(AP1) For any immaterial substances x and y, x is identical to y if and only if the substantial form of x is identical to the substantial form of y.

In contrast to (AP), (AP1) needs no temporal indicators because, unlike accidental forms, a substantial form cannot be gained and lost by a thing over time; if a substantial form goes out of existence, the thing configured by that form ceases to exist as well. On the other hand, since the substantial forms of immaterial substances are individuated by their species-specific properties, (AP1) implies an analogue to (LII):

(AP2) For any immaterial substances x and y, x is identical to y only if x has all and only the species-specific properties that y has.

(LII) is the law of the indiscernibility of identicals; but, in fact, because Aquinas thinks that the substantial form of any species of immaterial substance necessarily belongs to just one individual, and because these forms are differentiated by differences in the configurations themselves, in this special case an analogue to the law of the identity of indiscernibles also holds:

(AP3) For any immaterial substances x and y, x is identical to y if x has all and only the species-specific properties that y has.

Even for the special case of immaterial substances, however, Aquinas will not accept (LII) itself because of his views about accidents. An angel, too, has accidents, and one and the same angel can gain or lose an accidental property without ceasing to be the thing it was.

Finally, for Aquinas, the view that finds expression in (AP1) can be generalized. Any thing is *this* thing just in virtue of the fact that the form which conjoins the parts of it into one whole is *this* form. For example, a material substance such as Socrates is this human being in virtue of having *this* substantial form. What is necessary and sufficient for something to be identical to Socrates is that its substantial form be identical to the substantial form of Socrates.[56] So Aquinas accepts this more general principle:

(AP4) For any substances x and y, x is identical to y if and only if the substantial form of x is identical to the substantial form of y.

Matter as the principle of individuation

But what makes something *this* substantial form rather than some other? Since on Aquinas's views there cannot be more than one individual for any species of immaterial thing, in the case of an immaterial substance, the substantial form is individuated just by the properties of that form itself; that configuration cannot be shared by any other individual. For any species of material thing, however, there are many individuals within a species, and the species-specific properties conferred by the substantial form of each member of the species will therefore be the same. Aquinas designates the collection of these species-specific properties with the Latin term translated 'nature'; the nature of a thing is what is signified by the species name of the thing, and a thing's nature is given by its substantial form.[57] The species-specific properties conferred by the substantial form of Plato − that is, the nature of a human being − are the same as the species-specific properties conferred by the substantial form of Socrates. How, then, are the substantial forms of material objects such as human beings individuated?

We might be inclined to think that, on the contrary, such forms *cannot* be individuated. The configuration or the form of a human being is a universal, we might suppose. It is the same in every human being; that is why there is a human nature which is in every human being. One substantial form of a human being cannot therefore be distinguished from that of another human being. *A fortiori*, a substantial form can't be what individuates a human being.

Aquinas's response to this sort of objection is expressed succinctly in his well-known line that matter individuates.[58] It is easier, however, to repeat the line than to see what he meant by it. The difficulty has to do at least in part with the notion of matter at issue in the line.

A substantial form of a material substance configures prime matter; but prime matter is matter devoid of any form, without any configuration, something which exists only potentially and not actually, since anything that actually exists is configured. Prime matter can thus hardly be what individuates a form.

On the other hand, any actually existing material substance has a determinate quantity of matter. At any given time, it occupies a particular amount of space; it is extended to a determinate degree in each of the three dimensions of space. If this particular chunk of matter were somehow responsible for individuating forms (or material things), then a form (or a material thing) would go out of existence when the quantity of matter in the material thing in question changed. Some metaphysicians might not mind such a conclusion, but Aquinas is not among them. The particular quantity of something is an accident, and an accident is a property which a thing can gain and lose while remaining one and the same, on Aquinas's view.

The notion of matter at issue in Aquinas's account of the individuation of material things is thus neither prime matter nor matter configured as it is in an actually existing thing.

When Aquinas attempts to explain the concept of matter relevant to individuation, he tends to speak of it as matter under indeterminate dimen- sions,[59] that is, matter which is extended in three dimensions but where the degree of extension in any dimension is not specified. Now any actually existing matter has determinate dimensions. But the particular degree of extension in a dimension is one thing; the materiality, as it were, of matter is another thing. The determinate dimensions of a material thing have to do with exactly what space that thing occupies; the materiality of the matter is responsible for the space-occupying feature itself. Matter is the sort of thing which is *here* now, in a way that numbers, for example, are not. This feature of matter, however, can be considered without specifying the precise spatial locations that the matter occupies. When Aquinas talks of matter under indeterminate dimensions, he is calling attention to this feature of matter. It is not a feature which is ever had by any actually existing matter in isolation from that matter's having some determinate dimensions. Nonetheless, any actually existing matter with determinate dimensions has this space-occupying feature, which can be considered independently of that matter's determinate dimensions.

In his commentary on Boethius's *De trinitate*,[60] Aquinas raises the question whether form individuates. Given his oft-repeated line that matter individuates, one would expect him to answer the question in the negative; but, in fact, the answer is affirmative. Matter is *this* matter in virtue of having spatial extension; but spatial extension, even if the dimensions of that extension are indeterminate, is a quantity, and quantity is an accident. So, there is at least a sense in which an accidental form individuates. Or, to put the same point in another way, prime matter, which lacks all form, is not matter under indeterminate dimensions and does not individuate.

On this way of understanding matter under indeterminate dimensions, *this* matter under indeterminate dimensions is distinguished from any other by spatial continuity.[61] Between this matter and that matter there will have to be a spatial discontinuity or gap. It also seems reasonable to assume that temporal continuity is required to distinguish this matter from that matter over time. A gap of either space or time thus entails that there is no longer the same matter.

No doubt, one could wish for a great deal more clarity and precision with regard to the notion of matter Aquinas has in mind when he claims that matter individuates. But perhaps this is enough to point us roughly in the right direction for making sense of his concept of substantial forms that are individual rather than universal.

Consider, for example, two molecules of water. Each one has the properties of water, the nature of water, which is conferred by the water-specific configuration, the substantial form, of the molecule. But the configuration of water molecule A inheres in *this* matter, and the configuration of water molecule B inheres in *that* matter. Because matter has an irreducible space-occupying feature, we can distinguish one substantial form from another by its association with matter. This substantial form is the configuration of this matter, and that one is the configuration of that matter.[62]

In the case of human beings, Aquinas's idea is the same. What individuates Socrates? For Aquinas, it is not that Socrates has a set of essential properties unique to him, as an angel does. It is also not that, in addition to his having the usual set of properties essential to all human beings, a human nature, Socrates also has a collection of accidental properties such that the conjunction of them is not shareable by anything else. Rather, what individuates Socrates is *this* substantial form of a human being; and a substantial form of a material substance such as a human being is *this* substantial form in virtue of the fact that it configures *this* matter.

Consequently, it is clear why Aquinas thinks that properties other than those which are part of the nature of a thing are accidents. Only the nature is conferred by the substantial form, but since *this* substantial form is sufficient for the existence of *this* thing, any other properties are such that the thing can gain or lose them and remain the same thing.[63] On the other hand, it is also clear that anything which has a substantial form necessarily has accidents, as a quick survey of the nine Aristotelian categories of accidents makes evident; nothing that has a substantial form can be without any accidents at all.[64]

A variation on the principle in (AP4) can also be formulated about material things which are not substances, such as artifacts. What gives an artifact such unity as it has, what makes it the one thing it is, is an accidental form that configures the whole. But accidental forms can also be individuated by their connection with matter. Aquinas's attitude towards substantial forms extends to the forms that are in the nine Aristotelian categories other than substance. Any actually existing quality, such as redness, for example, is a particular. It is *this* redness, distinguished from every other redness of the same hue and intensity by being the redness that configures *this* material thing rather than some other.

For Aquinas, a universal is the concept a knower has when he abstracts, for example, redness from a material thing in which the particular form (*this* redness) is and considers it just as redness, apart from its association with the particular matter it configures.[65] What actually exists in reality, however, is just a particular form in a particular thing. So, for artifacts, which are configured by accidental rather than substantial forms, a thing will be *this* artifact if and only if it is configured by *this* accidental form.

Someone might wonder at this point whether (AP4) does not entail some analogue to (LII), just as (AP1) did. On (AP4) a substance x is identical to a substance y if and only if the substantial form of x is identical to the substantial form of y; and, for material substances, something will be identical to the substantial form of x if and only if it configures *this* matter, the matter under indeterminate dimensions which is one of x's constituents. So it seems that from (AP4) we can derive an analogue to (LII) formulated in this way:

> (AP5) For any substances x and y, x is identical to y only if (i) x has all and only the species-specific properties that y has, and (ii) x has the property of being constituted by this matter if and only if y has the property of being constituted by this very same matter.

But whatever else one may think about a property characterized as *the property of being constituted by this matter*, it is clear that nothing could have it which was not constituted by this matter. And so what ultimately individuates material things will be matter, as Aquinas maintains, and not forms or properties.

Constitution and identity

A further conclusion from these views of Aquinas is that constitution is not identity,[66] and a whole is something more than the sum of its parts. It is especially clear that this conclusion holds for substances.

The general designation Aquinas uses for a thing which has a particular substantial form is the Latin term transliterated 'supposit' or the Greek term transliterated into Latin as '*hypostasis*'.[67] Since he recognizes particulars in categories other than substance, he tends to use the Latin terms translated 'particular', 'singular' and 'individual' more broadly than 'supposit' or 'hypostasis'. *This* redness, for example, is an individual or a particular in the category of quality. A supposit is a particular or individual just in the category of substance.[68] The Latin term translated 'person' is Aquinas's technical term for an individual substance of a rational nature.[69]

On Aquinas's views, although the existence of a particular substantial form is necessary and sufficient for the existence of a supposit, a supposit is not identical to its substantial form alone. A substantial form is only a constituent of a supposit.

To begin with, any thing which has a substantial form necessarily also has accidents, even though it is not necessary that it have one accident rather than another. So a substantial form is not the only metaphysical constituent of a thing; any thing will also have accidental forms as metaphysical constituents. In addition, for material substances, the matter that makes the substantial form of a material supposit a particular is also a constituent of the supposit.[70] So any supposit has more metaphysical constituents than just a substantial form. Insofar as all these constituents compose the supposit, the supposit is not identical to some subset of them.

Furthermore, as I explained above, it is also the case for Aquinas that a substantial form configures prime matter, rather than integral parts that are themselves matter-form composites; and so a supposit is not identical to the collection of its integral parts either. A material substance, for example, is composed of elements but is not identical to the collection of elements that make it up. The integral components of a whole by themselves do not include the substantial form of the whole; and when one integral component is combined with others by the substantial form that conjoins the whole, the part loses whatever substantial form it may have had before merging into the composite. The collection of the particular bits of earth, air, fire and water that come together to compose a material substance on Aquinas's view are thus not identical to the substance they compose. A substantial form is also needed to conjoin the parts into a whole. And although we can decompose a whole substance into its integral components in such a way that they exist as actual substances in their own right, in the whole the substantial form configures prime matter, not the integral matter-form composites into which the whole can be decomposed.

Aquinas's views clearly entail, then, that for substances constitution is not identity, for constituents of either a metaphysical or an integral sort.

Finally, there is also a sense in which, even for artifacts, constitution is not identity. An artifact is composed of material substances, but they are substances conjoined into some whole by means of a form; the substances do not comprise an artifact without the configuring of the form. So even though the form is an accidental form, it remains the case that the material components of an artifact are not all there is to the whole. (An accidental form is thus essential to an artifact, even though it is not essential to the existence of the substances of which the artifact is composed. A clear, non-circular definition of substance, if there were one, would no doubt help explain why the forms of artifacts are not to be counted as substantial forms, even though the form of an artifact is essential to the existence of the artifact and gives the artifact its species and proper function.)

Constitution and identity: the special case of the soul

That constitution is not identity on Aquinas's view helps explain what he means by his claim that the substantial form of a human being, the soul, can persist in a disembodied condition.

Since a material supposit is composed of matter and form as its constituents, if constitution were identity, then the loss of either matter or form would be enough to entail the loss of the whole supposit. In that case, any supposit would cease to exist when it lost either its substantial form or the matter configured by that form. But because constitution is not identity for Aquinas, it is possible for him to suppose that a supposit survives the loss of some of its constituents, provided that the remaining constituents can exist on their own and are sufficient for the existence of the supposit.

That constitution is not identity in the case of human beings is clear when it comes to integral parts, on either the macroscopic or the microscopic level. A human being can survive the loss of some of his elemental bits (or molecular constituents) or even the loss of some of his larger integral parts, such as a hand.

But Aquinas thinks the point about constitution and identity holds also for metaphysical parts in the special case of a human being, whose substantial form can exist on its own. Normally, the integral parts of a human being include two hands, but a human being can exist without being in the normal condition. Analogously, the metaphysical constituents of a human being normally include matter and substantial form, but Aquinas thinks that a human being can exist without being in the normal condition in this way either.

It is easy to become confused about Aquinas's position here. In his commentary on I Corinthians,[71] Aquinas says, "Since a soul is part of a body of a human being, it is not the whole human being, and my soul is not me."[72] Passages such as this one suggest to some scholars that for Aquinas, a human person ceases to exist with the death of the body. We can put the point here in this way. If my soul is not *me*, but my soul is all that continues to exist after the death of my body, then it seems that *I* do not survive bodily death. Whatever else can be said about what persists after bodily death, it is not me.

A second, closely related[73] objection arises from Aquinas's insistence that the soul alone is not a human being.[74] On the interpretation I have been arguing for here, a substantial form is sufficient for the existence of the supposit whose form it is, and so the existence of a human soul is sufficient for the existence of a human being. But if the existence of a soul is sufficient for the existence of a human being, then since for Aquinas the soul sometimes exists in a disembodied condition, it seems that on my interpretation, the soul in that condition must *be* a human being, contrary to Aquinas's own oft-repeated claim.

But the passages in which Aquinas denies that a soul is a person or a human being need to be read in the context of Aquinas's other views. So, for example, Aquinas thinks that after death a human soul either enjoys the rewards of heaven or suffers the pains of hell.[75] He maintains that the separated soul is capable of understanding and choosing.[76] He also holds that after death a human being can appear to the living; for example, speaking of the disembodied soul of a martyr Felix, Aquinas says that Felix – not a simulacrum but the human being Felix – appeared to the people of Nola.[77] He claims that the holy Fathers in hell – who are separated souls – were waiting for Christ and were delivered by Christ's descent into hell.[78] In these passages and many others, Aquinas attributes to disembodied souls properties which he and we take to be most characteristic of human persons, including intellectual understanding and love.

These passages are compatible with the passages in which Aquinas claims that a soul is not a person if we give proper weight to the distinction between constitution and identity in his thought. A human person is not identical to his soul; rather, a human person is identical to a particular in the species *rational animal*. A particular of that sort is normally, naturally, constituted of an array of bodily parts and is composed of form and matter. Because constitution is not identity for Aquinas, however, a particular can exist with less than the normal, natural complement of constituents. It can, for example, exist when it is constituted only by one of its main metaphysical parts, namely the soul. And so although a person is not identical to his soul, the existence of the soul is sufficient for the existence of a person.

Similarly, it *is* true that on Aquinas's account a soul is not *identical* to a human being, but a human being can exist when he is composed of nothing more than one of his metaphysical constituents, namely his form or soul. For Aquinas, in the case of human beings, the persistence of one metaphysical part of the whole thing is sufficient for the existence of that thing. Because constitution is not identity, however, it does not follow from this claim that the part is identical to the whole, or that a soul by itself is identical to a human being.

It may help in this connection to consider a roughly analogous position regarding bodily parts and wholes. Some contemporary philosophers suppose that a human being is identical to a living biological organism; but they also hold that, although this organism is ordinarily composed of a complete human body, it is capable of persisting even when the body has been reduced to nothing more than a living brain or part of a brain.[79] On this view, a human being is capable of existing when she is composed only of a brain part, but she is not identical to the brain part that composes her in that unusual condition. In the same way, for Aquinas, a human being is capable of existing when she is composed of nothing more than a metaphysical part, without its being the case that she is identical to that metaphysical part.

It is also worth noticing that if this interpretation were not correct, if Aquinas supposed a human being to be identical to her constituents so that she ceased to exist as a human being when she ceased to be embodied, then there would be an incoherence in his position. That is because he could not hold such a view of a human being consistently with his view of the nature of change. On the Aristotelian understanding of change Aquinas inherits and accepts, a thing which gains or loses an accidental form undergoes change while remaining one and the same thing. Quantities, including quantity of matter, are accidents, however. So, on Aquinas's position, a human being who loses a quantity of matter, such as a hand or a leg, for instance, remains one and the same thing while undergoing change. If, however, constitution were identity for Aquinas, then a human being whose material constituents changed would cease to be the thing she was and become some other thing instead.[80] In that case, contrary to Aquinas's position, the gain or loss of an accident such as quantity of matter would not be a change in a human being; it would be the destruction of one thing and the generation of another. The fact that Aquinas holds the view of change he does, then, supports the interpretation I have been arguing for here.

So for Aquinas, constitution is not identity. Consequently, contrary to the objections, the claim that the existence of a soul is sufficient for the existence of a person or a human being is compatible with Aquinas's claim that a soul by itself is not a person or a human being.

A different worry can arise in this connection based on the fact that for Aquinas, substantial forms are individuated by matter. Separated souls are substantial forms that do not inform matter. So it seems that, on Aquinas's views, either such souls are not individuals or else matter does not individuate the substantial forms of human beings. But this worry is misplaced. It is possible for one separated soul to be distinguished from another on the basis of its *past* connection with matter, rather than on the basis of a present connection with matter. The disembodied soul of Socrates is the substantial human form which at some time in the past configured *this* matter, the matter that was part of Socrates in his embodied state. The disembodied soul of Plato is the substantial human form which at some time in the past configured the matter that was part of Plato in *his* embodied state. It remains the case, then, that matter individuates, even in the case of disembodied souls. Matter individuates a disembodied form in virtue of its past connection to matter. And, of course, it will also be true that this history carries with it other differences as well, including differences of memories, desires, understanding, and so on.

If this is right, then for Aquinas spatio-temporal continuity of material constituents is not necessary for the existence of a human person. A human person can persist in a disembodied condition, so that there are spatio-temporal gaps in the existence of the material parts of a human person. Temporal continuity of a substantial form, however, is always necessary. If a human soul existed in an embodied human person (say, Socrates) from t1–t2, failed to exist from t2–t3, and then existed again in a disembodied condition from t3–t4, the explanation I gave for the individuation of disembodied souls by matter would fail. On what basis would one say that the disembodied soul which exists from t3–t4 is the soul which from t1–t2 configured the matter that was part of Socrates?[81]

The relation of a composite to its parts

If constitution is not identity, then we need to consider what the relation of a composite whole to its constituent parts is.

Perhaps the first point to note is that, on Aquinas's understanding of substantial forms, there cannot be two material supposits, two whole material substances, in the same place at the same time.[82] I have already explained that any thing can have only one substantial form on Aquinas's views. Since any given matter occupying a particular place at a time can be configured by only one substantial form and since only a thing configured by a substantial form is a supposit, it is clear that there cannot be two whole material supposits coincident in place and time.

The general point here holds also for artifacts. Suppose, for example, that at t1 there is a lump of bronze which a sculptor fashions into a bronze statue that comes into existence at t2. On Aquinas's view, the lump of bronze is a thing whose matter is bronze and whose form is the configuration that makes the bronze a lump. When the sculptor makes the lump into a statue, the matter which is the bronze is preserved; but the configuration which made that matter a lump is lost and is replaced by a new configuration which makes the matter a statue. If the statue is melted down, then the matter of the bronze is preserved, and it may again acquire the configuration of a lump; but the configuration of the statue will be lost, and so the statue will cease to exist. Thus, although they are composed of the same matter, in virtue of having different forms the lump and the statue are not the same thing.

On the other hand, the lump and the statue cannot exist at the same time and place as separate things, because one and the same matter cannot at one and the same time have the configuration of a lump and the configuration of a statue. (Aquinas therefore subscribes to a dictum also argued for in contemporary philosophy: one thing cannot be itself and another thing.[83])

One might object that in the space occupied by the statue, or the place occupied by the lump, there is bronze as well as a statue or a lump, so that there are after all two material things in one place, whether the bronze is a lump or a statue. But for Aquinas, the bronze considered in itself, apart from the configuration of the statue or the configuration of the lump (or some other configuration), is not a thing at all. To be a thing requires having a form of a whole of some sort. If the bronze has the form of a statue, the thing that exists is a statue; if it has the form of a lump, the thing that exists is a lump. Without *any* form of a whole, the bronze is not a thing.

So, for Aquinas, the bronze and the statue are not identical, and yet they are not separate things either. Instead, the statue is a composite material thing which has the bronze as its material constituent. Lynne Rudder Baker summarizes positions which distinguish constitution from identity by saying:

For a long time, philosophers have distinguished the 'is' of predication ... from the 'is' of identity ... If the constitution view is correct, then there is a third sense of 'is', distinct from the other

two. The third sense of 'is' is the 'is' of constitution (as in 'is (constituted by) a piece of marble').[84]

An additional complexity stems from the fact that, for Aquinas, there can
also be composition within a constituent of a whole.[85] In fact, Aquinas
thinks that there is even composition within the nature a thing has in virtue
of its substantial form. For any actually existing thing, that nature is
compounded of more than one property.[86] So, for example, a human being
has human nature in virtue of the substantial form that is the human soul,
and human nature is compounded of the properties of rationality and
animality. Human nature is nonetheless a unity. Although on Aquinas's view
nothing is identical to its constituents, the constitution relation is nonetheless a unity relation.

Aquinas distinguishes among different sorts of unity relations. Perhaps
most important is his distinction between a union in nature and a union in
supposit. When *rationality* and *animality* are conjoined into one nature in
virtue of the one substantial form of a human being, there is a union of *rationality* and *animality* which is a union in nature. But there is also the unity
brought about by the constitution relation of the whole matter-form
composite. The constituents of a whole thing are united in the whole they
compose. In the case of individual substances, Aquinas speaks of this as a
union in supposit. So in the case of a material substance, the accidental forms,
the substantial form and the matter of a thing are conjoined into one whole
thing, and their conjunction is a union in supposit.

Finally, a union in person is a special sort of union in supposit; it is a union
in supposit when the supposit in question is a person.[87] For example, *rationality* (which is included in the nature of a human person such as Socrates)
and *snub-nosedness* (which is an accident of Socrates's) are conjoined in Socrates.
They are thus conjoined with a union of person, in Aquinas's terms. Union of
person is particularly important in Aquinas's philosophical theology, in
particular in his interpretation of the doctrine of the incarnation.

Because the constitution relation is a unity relation, even if a property
or causal power is conferred on a thing just in virtue of its having one
constituent or another, the property or causal power is a property or causal
power of the whole thing. For example, on Aquinas's views, the substantial
form of a supposit is responsible for the fact that that supposit has a
certain nature and certain causal powers associated with that nature.[88]
Socrates has the power to reason in virtue of having a human substantial
form. Nonetheless, the thing to which the operation of those powers is
attributed is the supposit – Socrates, for example – and not his particular
substantial form.[89] In consequence, *rationality* is predicated of Socrates
simpliciter. [90]

In fact, the constitution relation lets us make a distinction among the
properties of a composite.[91] The whole can have a property either in its own

right or else derivatively, in virtue of the fact that one of its constituents has that property in its own right; and the same point applies, *mutatis mutandis*, to the parts of a whole.[92]

So, for example, the molecule C/EBP, described above, has the property of being coiled in the alpha helix manner, but it has that property in virtue of the fact that it has parts which are coiled in that way. The whole molecule "borrows"[93] these properties from its constituents, and it has them only in virtue of the fact that the alpha helix subunits of the molecule have in their own right the property of being coiled in that way. On the other hand, C/EBP has the property of regulating DNA transcription, and this property it has in its own right, in consequence of the shape of the molecule as a whole, which allows it to fit into one of the grooves of DNA. Similarly, in addition to having a property in its own right, a constituent of a whole can also have a property in virtue of the fact that the whole has that property in its own right. The alpha helix coil in C/EBP has the property of regulating DNA transcription in virtue of the fact that the whole molecule has in its own right the property of regulating DNA transcription.

Baker emphasizes the fact that in cases in which a whole borrows a property from its parts, the property in question is nonetheless genuinely to be attributed to the whole. She says:

> Borrowing walks a fine line. On the one hand, if *x* borrows *H* from *y*, then *x* really has *H* – piggyback, so to speak … [I]f I cut my hand, then *I* really bleed … I borrow the property of bleeding from my body, but I really bleed. But the fact that I am bleeding is none other than the fact that I am constituted by a body that is bleeding. So, not only does *x* really have *H* by borrowing it, but also – and this is the other hand – if *x* borrows *H* from *y*, there are not two independent instances of *H*: if *x* borrows *H*, then *x*'s having *H* is entirely a matter of *x*'s having constitution relations to something that has *H* non-derivatively.[94]

Although Aquinas does not draw this distinction among properties explicitly, his metaphysical views about constitution provide for it, and he relies on it in one place after another. So, for example, he argues that whatever follows naturally on the accidents or the parts of a suppositum is predicated of the whole suppositum on account of the accident or part in question. As he puts it in a discussion of the actions of parts and wholes:

> the action of a part is attributed to the whole, as the action of an eye is attributed to a [whole] human being but never to another part [of a human being], except perhaps *per accidens*, for we do not say that a hand sees because of the fact that the eye sees.[95]

And in another place, he explains that a man is said to be curly on account of his hair or seeing on account of the function of the eye.[96] Similarly, in discussing the powers of the soul, the substantial form of a human being, Aquinas says:

> We *can* say that the soul understands in the same way that we can say that the eye sees; but it would be more appropriate to say that *a human being* understands *by means of* the soul.[97]

Here a property (understanding) of a metaphysical part, the soul, and a property (seeing) of an integral part, the eye, are transferred to the whole, the person, which in effect borrows these properties from its parts.

Alteration and replacement

For all material things other than human beings, Aquinas thinks that the form of the whole comes into existence with the whole and goes out of existence when the material composite ceases to exist. Although the substantial form of a human being also comes into existence just with the existence of the whole human being, including the whole human body, in Aquinas's view the soul can exist on its own even after the composite as a whole has ceased to exist. But human substantial forms are the only exception to the general rule for the forms of material things. There are no disembodied forms of cows or axes.

Since the forms that conjoin such things as cows and axes are also individuated by matter, however, one might wonder to what extent a change in the matter constituting a material thing is compatible with the persistence of the form of that thing and thus with the persistence of the thing itself, for forms which cannot exist apart from the material composite they configure.

In the case of material composites which are substances, the form that conjoins the whole configures prime matter. So any matter coming into the composite loses its own substantial form and is configured by the one substantial form of the whole. Furthermore, the form is individuated by matter under indeterminate dimensions, so that a change in a particular quantity or quality of matter does not affect the identity of the form. It seems therefore that considerable change in matter is compatible with the persistence of the individual substantial form, provided that there is spatio-temporal continuity of matter in the changing material composite configured by that form, for the reasons I gave above in the discussion of matter under indeterminate dimensions.[98] It is important also to emphasize in this connection that the change in matter has to be a change that is compatible with the matter's continuing to be configured by one and the same substantial form. If the change in matter were such that, for example, a cow were gradually turned into an axe, then the change in matter would no longer be compatible with the matter's being configured by the substantial form of a cow.

The case of artifacts is somewhat different, however. In the case of artifacts, the individual form conjoining the whole is also individuated by its matter; but it is an accidental form, and it configures complete material things, rather than prime matter. The composite whole is thus a collection of substances, and these substances are the matter of the whole. Furthermore, new matter coming into the whole is not given its substantial form by the form of the whole; it keeps whatever substantial form it had before it became part of the composite. Finally, like the forms of all material composites except human beings, the accidental form uniting an artifact comes into existence with the existence of the collection of substances it configures and goes out of existence when the collection ceases to exist. For these reasons, there is some reason to think that, for Aquinas, if all the substances comprising the artifact were removed and replaced by other substances, the original artifact would cease to exist. But if that is right, then the persistence of the form of an artifact, and so the persistence of the artifact, is not compatible with the replacement of all the material parts of the thing it configures.

How many of the material parts of an artifact can be replaced compatible with the persistence of the particular accidental form configuring the artifact as a whole is much less clear.[99] One would, of course, like to have some principled way of drawing the line between a change of matter which is just an alteration in the artifact, and a change of matter which changes the identity of the form of the whole, so that the original form, and consequently the original artifact, no longer exist. As far as I can see, however, nothing in Aquinas's metaphysics mandates a particular way of drawing this distinction.

But perhaps this result is not such a bad one. The heap of stones which is an Egyptian pyramid can survive the replacement of one old stone with a new one. It cannot survive the replacement of all the old stones with a whole set of new ones; in that case, we have a replica of that pyramid, and not the original pyramid itself. But perhaps there is no definite answer to the question when in the process of putting a new stone for an old one we have crossed the line from repairing the old pyramid to constructing a replica of it.

Conclusion

I have looked briefly here just at the key elements in that part of Aquinas's metaphysics which might be called 'a theory of things'. Fully to do justice to Aquinas's metaphysics would require a large volume just on this topic, and even then there would no doubt be readers who would find that their own candidates for the most important parts of Aquinas's metaphysics had been left out. Nonetheless, in this quick survey of Aquinas's views of matter and form, substance and artifact, individuation, identity, change and constitution, I have tried to shed some light on those parts of Aquinas's metaphysics most likely to be obscure or alien to contemporary readers. These parts of his metaphysics also strike me as among his most fundamental philosophical views, which structure his way of thinking about many other things. Together with his theology of the nature of God, this part of his metaphysics forms the basis of his worldview, on which his other positions rest. In what follows I will look at his treatment of several divine attributes in order to provide an exposition of the fundamentals of his theological views. Given the importance of his account of these attributes in the rest of his work, in everything from ethics to epistemology, it is important to consider these attributes in some detail.

2

GOODNESS

Introduction

As Aquinas's treatment of ethics in his *Summa theologiae* and other works makes clear, his is a virtue-based ethics. He does sometimes discuss moral principles or rules. So, for example, in *ST* he devotes one question each to the precepts of justice and of fortitude.[1] But the precepts of justice turn out to be simply the Ten Commandments, and the precept of fortitude seems to be only the biblical commandment to be afraid of God rather than human beings. On the other hand, in 170 questions in the second part of the second part of *ST* (as well as in various other works), Aquinas lays out his account of the virtues for human beings. These include not only the cardinal or moral virtues (prudence, justice, courage, and temperance) and the virtues connected to these, but also the theological virtues (faith, hope, and charity) and the intellectual virtues (wisdom, knowledge, and understanding).

Aquinas's account of the virtues is rich and complex, and his discussion of them is situated in an intricate network of medieval lore.[2] This lore includes the seven gifts of the Holy Spirit, at least three of which are twins of the intellectual virtues: courage, piety, fear, counsel (*consilium*), wisdom, *scientia* (generally translated as 'knowledge'), and understanding. In addition, Aquinas also weaves into his account the twelve fruits of the Holy Spirit (faith, charity, joy, peace, patience, long-suffering, goodness, benevolence, meekness, moderation, continence, and chastity) and the seven beatitudes: Blessed are they that hunger and thirst after justice; blessed are the peacemakers, the meek, the poor in spirit, the mourners, the merciful, and the pure in heart. Finally, Aquinas completes his account of the virtues by contrasting them with their opposed vices, focusing in particular on the list the medievals knew as the seven deadly sins, a list at least as old as Cassian and given particular form by Gregory the Great. In order from worst to least, these are pride, envy, wrath, sloth, avarice, gluttony, and lust.

In Part III of this book, I try to give some idea of the depth and power of this ethical system by picking one representative virtue from each of the three kinds of virtue Aquinas recognizes – moral, intellectual, and theological – and devoting a chapter to the examination of each one. In this chapter,

I want to examine the metaphysics of goodness that underlies all of Aquinas's ethics. This metaphysics supplies for his virtue-based ethics the sort of meta-ethical foundation that some contemporary virtue-centered ethics has been criticized for lacking,[3] and it grounds an ethical naturalism of some philosophical sophistication. Moreover, it complements Aquinas's Aristotelian emphasis on rationality as a moral standard by supplying a method of determining ethically relevant degrees of rationality. Finally, when Aquinas's naturalism is combined with his account of God as absolutely simple, it effects a connection between morality and theology that offers an attractive alternative to divine-command morality, construing morality not merely as a dictate of God's will, but as an expression of his nature.

Aquinas's central meta-ethical thesis

The central thesis of Aquinas's meta-ethics is that:

> (T) 'being' and 'goodness' are the same in reference (*idem secundum rem*), but differ only in sense (*differunt secundum rationem tantum*).[4]

What does Aquinas mean by this claim,[5] and what are his grounds for it? He himself begins his support for the claim by citing and supporting the connection Aristotle sees between goodness and desirability. He says: "The formula of the good consists in this, that something is desirable, and so the Philosopher (*Ethics* I) says that the good is what all desire."[6] It is important to understand this claim in the right way. Although all things desire goodness, not all things capable of pursuing goodness with understanding understand what really is good; it is possible for creatures with intellect and will to desire an apparent good as a real one.[7] According to Aquinas:

> Something is desired in two ways, either because it is good or because it appears good. Of these, the first is what is good, for an apparent good does not move by itself but insofar as it has some appearance (*species*) of good; but the good moves by itself.[8]

For Aquinas, then, desirability is one way or another an essential aspect of goodness.

Now if a thing is desirable as a thing of a certain kind, then, on Aquinas's views, it is desirable to the extent to which it is perfect of that kind, i.e., to the extent to which it is a whole, complete specimen, free from relevant defect. For Aquinas:

> That by which anything is said to be good is its proper virtue ...
> but a virtue is a kind of perfection, for we say that anything is

perfect when it attains its proper virtue, as is clear in *Physics* VII. And so everything is good from the fact that it is perfect. And that is why everything desires its own perfection as its proper good.[9]

But, then, in Aquinas's terms, a thing is perfect (good of its kind) and hence desirable insofar as it is in being. That is, a thing is perfect of its kind to the extent to which it is fully realized. According to Aquinas: "the perfection of anything is its goodness",[10] but "a thing is perfect to the extent to which it is in actuality".[11] Or, as he puts it in another place: "As regards nature (*naturaliter*) the good of anything is its actuality and perfection."[12]

In another gloss on Aristotle's dictum, Aquinas takes the sense of 'goodness' to be brought out in the notion of that in which desire culminates:

> The end is that in which the desire of the thing acting or moving rests ... But this is part of the formula of the good, [namely,] that it fulfills desire, for the good is what all desire. And so every action and every motion is for the sake of the good.[13]

Now what is desired is desired for the sake of something else, for the sake of something else and for its own sake, or solely for its own sake. What is desired solely for its own sake is what the desirer perceives as the desirer's final good, that for the sake of which it desires all the other things it desires, that in which the hierarchy of its desires culminates. Aquinas says: "Since anything desires its own perfection, a thing desires as its ultimate end that which it desires as the good perfecting and completing of itself."[14]

But what each desirer desires in that way is the fulfillment of its own nature, or at least that which the desirer perceives as the very best for the desirer to have or be. On Aquinas's views, each thing aims above all at being as complete, whole, and free from defect as it can be.[15] The state of its being complete and whole, however, just is that thing's being fully actual, whether or not the desirer recognizes it as such. Therefore, full actualization is equivalent to final goodness, aimed at or desired by every thing. Speaking of human beings, Aquinas says:

> necessarily, everything which a human being desires, he desires for the sake of the ultimate end ... [Now] whatever a human being desires he desires under the aspect of the good. And if the good is not desired as the perfect good, which is the ultimate end, it must be desired as instrumental to the perfect good.[16]

On his view, however,

> as far as the formula of the ultimate end is concerned, all [human beings] agree in the desire of the ultimate end, because all

[human beings] desire the fulfillment of their perfection, which is the formula of the ultimate end.[17]

And so Aquinas maintains that every action is ordered toward being, toward preserving or enhancing being in some respect either in the individual or in its species; in acting, all things aim at being. As Aquinas puts it in one place:

every action and every motion is apparently ordered in some way to being, either that being might be conserved in the species or the individual, or that it might be newly acquired. For what being is is the good. And so everything desires to be. Therefore, every action and every motion is for the sake of the good.[18]

Now, on Aquinas's view, "everything desires to be in actuality in accordance with its mode. And this is clear from the fact that everything in accordance with its nature resists corruption."[19] He spells out this element of his view more clearly in his interpretation of Augustine's dictum that the formula of the good consists in mode, species and order. He says:

Everything is said to be good insofar as it is perfect, for in this way it is desirable ... But a thing is said to be perfect if it lacks nothing in accordance with the mode of its perfection. Now everything is what it is by means of its form; and there are certain things presupposed by the form and other things that necessarily follow from the form. Consequently, for something to be perfect and good, it must have a form, as well as those things that precede and follow from the form ... Now the form is what is meant by 'species' [in Augustine's dictum] because everything is constituted in its species by means of [its] form ... But an inclination to an end, either an action or something of this sort, follows from the form, because everything insofar as it is in actuality acts and aims at that which is appropriate for it in accordance with its form.[20]

And in another place he says: "The form by means of which something is in actuality is a certain perfection and a certain good, and in this way every being in actuality is a certain good."[21]

Aquinas summarizes this part of his position by saying: "the form and being of a thing is its good and perfection, insofar as its nature is concerned."[22] Or, as he puts it when he is thinking of the nature of a thing conferred by its form:

everything is completed insofar as it is in actuality, for actuality is the perfection of a thing ... Now every nature is completed by means of the fact that it has being in actuality, and thus, since being good is desirable by all, every nature is completed by means of participation in the good.[23]

For all these reasons, then, Aquinas accepts the view, already well established by his time,[24] that goodness and being are correlative, that 'goodness' and 'being' are the same in reference.

Full actuality and substantial form

In those passages cited above which make a connection between goodness and form, the form in question must be the substantial form of a thing, since only the substantial form of a thing makes it be in actuality. An accidental form makes a thing be something-or-other, but the substantial form of a thing makes it be in actuality as a thing of a certain kind or species with a particular nature.[25] As Aquinas puts it in one place: "every being and every good depends on a form, from which it takes its species."[26]

Furthermore, for Aquinas, the nature of a thing consists in the properties that thing has in virtue of being informed by its substantial form. So to have a better idea of what Aquinas means by the notion of *being* in the passages above, we need to consider very briefly his understanding of a thing's substantial form and nature.

On Aquinas's view, every substance has a substantial form.[27] The substantial form of a thing is the configuration of the thing which gives it those characteristics that place the thing in its species. But, for Aquinas, any species is analyzable into a genus plus a differentia.[28] The species *human being*, for example, is analyzable into *animal*, which is the genus in question, and *rational*, which is the differentia separating human beings from all other species within the genus *animal*. The nature or essence of a thing consists in those properties that place it in its species. Aquinas says:

> A nature or essence ... can be understood in two ways. In one way, in accordance with the proper formula of that nature, and this is the consideration of the nature itself, strictly speaking. In this way, there is nothing true of the nature except what belongs to the nature insofar as it is of such-and-such a sort ... For example, being rational and animal (and the other things in the definition [of a human being]) belong to a human being insofar as he is a human being.[29]

Now the nature or essence conferred by the substantial form invariably includes at least one power, capacity or potentiality, which is its differentia, or species-specifying property, because every substantial form is a source of some activity or operation.[30] Aquinas says:

anything which has an essence either is itself a form or has a form, for anything is classified in a genus or species by means of [its] form. But a form ... has the formula of goodness, since it is a source of action.[31]

And elsewhere he says:

There are two kinds of powers, namely, power with respect to being and power with respect to acting; and the perfection of either kind of power is called a virtue ... Power with regard to acting stems from the form [of a thing], which is the source of action, since anything acts insofar as it is in actuality.[32]

So, according to Aquinas, a thing's differentia, which is a characteristic of the thing constituting it in its species, also needs to be understood as the power for an activity or operation peculiar to that species and essential to every member of the species. On Aquinas's views, the nature of a thing – that is, the nature the thing has as a member of a particular species – includes the power to engage in an operation determining of that thing as a member of that species. So, for example, the differentia for the species *human being* is *rational*, and the power to engage in reasoning is determining of and essential to a human being as a member of the species *human being*.[33] We can call the operative power that is the differentia of a thing its 'specifying (that is, species-specific) potentiality'.

The actuality of a thing can thus be understood in two ways, according to Aquinas. On the one hand, there is the actuality which a thing has just in virtue of existing as a thing of a certain sort, with a particular substantial form that confers on it the specifying potentiality characteristic of its species. On the other hand, that particular potentiality is part of the essence of the thing in question; and so as that potentiality becomes actualized, there is a sense in which the thing in question becomes actualized also, because a part of its nature that was only potential becomes actual. Aquinas puts the point this way:

principally and *per se* [the good] consists in perfection and in actuality. But actuality is of two kinds: first [actuality] and second [actuality]. First actuality is the form and integrity of a thing; but second actuality is an operation.[34]

And somewhat later he says: "the good, absolutely considered, consists in actuality and not in potentiality; but the final actuality is an operation."[35]

So a thing is perfected when and to the extent to which the thing performs instances of its specific operation and thereby actualizes its specifying potentiality. A thing's operation in accord with its specifying potentiality brings into actuality what was not actual but merely potential in that thing's nature as conferred by its substantial form. In Aquinas's sense of 'perfect', therefore, a thing is perfect of its kind to the extent to which it actualizes the specifying potentiality conferred by its form. As Aquinas explains when human beings are at issue:

> Happiness is the final perfection of a human being. But everything is perfect to the extent to which it is in actuality, for potentiality is imperfect without actuality. Consequently, happiness must consist in the final actuality of a human being. Now it is evident that an operation is the final actuality of a thing that operates; for this reason it is also called 'the second actuality' by the Philosopher (*De anima* II), for something having a form can be operating in potentiality [only].[36]

Or, as he puts it more generally,

> the nature of a thing is perfected by means of [its] form ... But the form itself is ordered finally to an operation, which either is the end [for that thing] or else is a means to [that] end. [37]

The same in referent but different in sense

The evaluative sense of 'perfect' is then explained by the connection between actuality and goodness: for something to be actual is for it to be in being, and 'being' and 'goodness' are the same in reference. A thing is good to the extent to which it is actual;[38] it is good of its kind or perfect to the extent to which its specifying potentiality is actualized, and bad of its kind or imperfect to the extent to which its specifying potentiality remains unactualized.[39]

According to Aquinas's view, therefore, when the terms 'being' and 'goodness' are associated with any particular sort of thing, both terms refer to the being of that thing. It is in this way that 'being' and 'goodness' have the same referent. On the other hand, the preceding considerations put us in a better position to understand Aquinas's notion that there is a difference in sense between 'being' and 'goodness'. It should be clear by now that being is to be considered both absolutely and in a certain respect. Considered *absolutely*, being is the instantiation of a thing which has (or is) a certain substantial form; this is the mere existence of a thing of some sort. But since each substantial form also includes a specifying potentiality, when that potentiality is actualized, the thing actualizing it is more fully a thing of that sort, a better specimen. When being is considered in this second way, it is correct to say that *in a certain respect* there is an increase of being for that thing. The ordinary sense of 'being' is being considered absolutely, that is, a thing's mere existence as the instantiation of a thing with a substantial form conferring a nature that includes a specifying potentiality. On the other hand, the actualization of a thing's specifying potentiality is also the being of a thing, and the general sense of 'goodness' is being understood in this way, what Aquinas, following Aristotle, calls 'second actuality'. This is the state each thing naturally aims at, and it is in this state that the thing is said to have goodness.

It is an important consequence of this account of being and goodness that no thing that exists can be completely without goodness, a view that Aquinas accepts and associates particularly with Augustine.[40] Because the referent of both 'being' and 'goodness' is *being*, according to Aquinas's view it is true, strictly speaking, that every thing that has being is good, to some extent. This consequence can be inferred directly from the central thesis about being and goodness,[41] but some of its moral and theological implications are worth pointing out. Evil is always and only a defect in some respect to some extent; evil can have no essence of its own. Nor can there be a highest evil, an ultimate source of all other evils, because a *summum malum*, an evil devoid of all good, would be nothing at all.[42] On the other hand, because the senses of 'being' and 'goodness' are different, Aquinas can also say that a thing which falls far short of the actualization of its specifying potentiality is not good simpliciter. A human being is defective, bad or evil not because of certain positive attributes but because of privations of being appropriate to his or her nature, in particular, those that consist in failing to actualize the human specifying potentiality for reason.[43] And, in general, the extent to which a thing is not good of its kind is the extent to which it has not actualized, or cultivated dispositions for actualizing, the potentiality associated with its nature.[44]

From meta-ethics to normative ethics

So because the differentia for *human being* is *rational*, a good human being is one who has actualized his capacity for rationality. Since, for Aquinas, a good human being is a moral human being, normative ethics is then a matter of applying the general metaphysics of goodness to human beings. The *moral* good is a matter of the being and the goodness of human persons. Aquinas says:

> anything is naturally inclined to an operation appropriate for it in accordance with its form ... And so since the rational soul is the proper form of a human being, every human being has a natural inclination to act in accordance with reason. And this is to act in accordance with virtue.[45]

In another place, he puts the point this way:

in human actions good and evil are predicated in relation to reason, because ... the good for a human being is to be in accordance with reason, and evil is what is against reason. For the good of any thing is what is appropriate for it in accordance with its form, and evil is what is outside the order of its form. Consequently, it is clear that the differentia of good and evil, considered with respect to the object [of an action], is in itself related to reason ... [So] certain actions are called human or moral insofar as they proceed from reason.[46]

And he goes on to say:

evil implies a privation – not an absolute privation but rather one following a certain potentiality. For an act is said to be evil in its species not from the fact that it has no object but rather because it has an object which is not in accordance with reason.[47]

Now, for Aquinas, the specifying potentiality of a human being, namely, the capacity for reason, is located in the cognitive and appetitive rational powers, intellect and will. The actualization or perfection of these powers produces human virtues. According to his view:

virtue designates a certain perfection of a power (*potentia*). But the perfection of anything consists precisely in relation to its end. Now the end of a power is an act. And so a power is said to be perfected insofar as it is determined to its end ... There are certain powers which in themselves are determined to their acts, such as natural active powers ... Rational powers, however, which are proper to a human being, are not determined to one thing but are related indeterminately to many things; nonetheless, they are determined to an act by means of a habit ... And so human virtues are habits.[48]

And somewhat later he says:

everything derives [its] species from its form ... but the form of a human being is the rational soul ... Consequently, what belongs to a human being in accordance with the rational soul is natural to him in accordance with the formula of [his] species ... Now in accordance with the nature of the species [virtue is naturally in a human being in an inchoate way] insofar as there are naturally in the reason of a human being certain naturally known principles, both about things that can be known and about things that are to be done, ... and insofar as there is in the will a natural desire for the good which is in accordance with reason.[49]

Elsewhere, Aquinas puts the point this way:

> in human beings there are only two principles of human action, namely the intellect or reason and the appetite [or will], for these two are [principles of] movement in a human being, as is said in *De anima* III. Consequently, every human virtue must perfect one of these principles. If it perfects the speculative or practical intellect to yield a good human act, it will be an intellectual virtue. But if it perfects the appetitive part, it will be a moral virtue.[50]

So, for Aquinas, the operation deriving directly from the substantial form conferring human nature is acting in accordance with reason. Actions of that sort actualize the specifying potentiality of human beings; a human being acting in accordance with reason makes actual what would otherwise have been merely potential in the nature conferred by his substantial form. By converting the specific potentiality of a human being into actuality, an agent's actions in accordance with reason increase the extent to which the agent has being as a human being; and so, given the connection between being and goodness, such actions increase the extent to which the agent has goodness as a human being. And this is moral goodness. Human or moral goodness, then, like any other goodness appropriate to one species, is acquired in performing instances of the operation specific to that species, and in the case of humanity this is the rational employment of the rational powers, intellect and will.

Furthermore, because whatever actualizes a thing's specifying potentiality thereby also perfects the nature of the thing, what is good for a thing is what is natural to it, and what is unnatural to a thing is bad for it;[51] in fact, on Aquinas's views of the metaphysics of goodness, what is evil cannot be natural to anything.[52] As for human nature, since it is characterized essentially by a capacity for rationality, what is irrational is contrary to nature where human beings are concerned. Aquinas says:

> The virtue of anything consists in its being well disposed in a manner suited to its nature; and so it must [also] be the case that whatever in anything is disposed contrary to what suits its nature is called 'vice'. But we need to consider that the nature of anything is chiefly the form in accordance with which the thing is classified into its species. Now a human being is put in his species by means of the rational soul. And so what is contrary to the order of reason is, strictly speaking, contrary to the nature of a human being insofar as he is a human being; but what is in accordance with reason is in accordance with the nature of a human being insofar as he is a human being ... Consequently, a human virtue, which makes a human being good and renders his work good, is in accordance with

human nature to the extent to which it agrees with reason; but a vice is contrary to human nature to the extent to which it is contrary to the order of reason.[53]

Finally, because of its association with the intellect, a human will is inclined towards goodness not just naturally (like the appetitive aspect of every other being below the level of human beings in the metaphysical order of creation) but also "along with an awareness of the nature of the good – a condition that is a distinguishing characteristic of intellect".[54] Rational beings are "inclined toward goodness itself considered universally" rather than naturally directed towards one particular sort of goodness.[55] Consequently, the actions that contribute to a human agent's moral goodness will be acts of free will in accordance with reason.[56]

Supervenience

On Aquinas's views, an object a has goodness (to any extent) as an A if and only if a has the property of having actualized its specifying potentiality (to that extent). In particular, moral goodness supervenes on rationality in such a way that if any human being is morally good (to any extent), that person has the property of having actualized his or her capacity for reason (to that extent); and if any human being has that property (to any extent), he or she is morally good (to that extent). One way to understand Aquinas's position, then, is to take it as a kind of supervenience theory.[57] Goodness supervenes on the natural property of the actualization of a specifying potentiality; moral goodness supervenes on the actualization of rationality, which is the specifying potentiality for human beings.

The relationship Aquinas sees between goodness and natural properties is complex and can be shown most easily by analogy. Fragility supervenes on certain natural properties without being reducible to any one of them.[58] A thing x is fragile in virtue of chemical bonding A a thing y in virtue of chemical bonding B, and a thing z in virtue of chemical bonding C. Fragility cannot be reduced to or identified with bonding A, B or C, but it supervenes on each of them. It may be that what is common to x, y and z is that each has weak chemical bonds in crucial spots, but those weak bonds are chemically quite distinct in connection with A, B and C. In that case it can be said that the characteristic of being fragile and the characteristic of having weak chemical bonds in crucial spots are coextensive, and that fragility supervenes on natural characteristics, and yet it must also be denied that fragility can be identified with any one of those characteristics.

The relationship between fragility and other characteristics in that analysis is like the relationship between goodness and natural characteristics in Aquinas's metaphysics of goodness. A thing's goodness and the actualization of the thing's specifying potentiality are coextensive. Goodness in general is not to be identified with a particular natural characteristic, however, because the natural characteristic that is the actualization of a specifying potentiality will vary from one species of thing to another. And the same observation holds regarding *being*: what is required to be a fully actualized member of species X is different from what is required to be a fully actualized member of species Y. The degree of actualization of the specifying potentiality for an X is the degree of being as an X, and this is also the degree of goodness as an X. But the specifying potentiality for an X differs from the specifying potentiality for a Y. So being and goodness are correlative, but neither is to be identified with any one particular natural characteristic on which it supervenes.

But is moral goodness in particular identical with the natural characteristic of actualized rationality? The question is complicated for Aquinas because, on the face of it, he recognizes other species of things – angels, for example – which are, apparently, rational[59] and to which attributions of moral praise or blame are appropriate. Since human beings are rational animals, human moral goodness is coextensive with actualized rationality. But a specifying potentiality is specific to a species; and so, whatever exactly the specifying potentiality of an angel might be, it will not be rationality. Nonetheless, (some sort of) moral goodness (or badness) is a characteristic of all beings whose nature involves freedom of choice, whether or not they are human. And so not even moral goodness is necessarily coextensive with the actualization of reason, the specifying potentiality for human beings. Goodness as an X will, for every X, consist in the actualization of an X's specifying potentialities, but there is no natural characteristic such that goodness (or even moral goodness) is identical with it (where identity of properties is taken to require at least necessary coextension).

Objections to the central meta-ethical thesis

On the basis of this exposition of Aquinas's central meta-ethical thesis against its metaphysical background, we are in a position to consider some of the objections the thesis is certain to generate. The first two of those are in fact considered and argued against by Aquinas himself.

> *Objection 1*: A thing's being and its being good are clearly not the same; many things that are, are not good. Consequently, being and goodness are clearly not coextensive. But if the terms are identical in reference, as Aquinas claims they are, being and goodness would have to be coextensive.[60]

This first objection trades on the apparently counter-intuitive character of a corollary of the central thesis, namely, everything is good insofar as it is in being; as I've shown above, this is a corollary that Aquinas accepts. But the corollary cannot be reduced to an absurdity simply by observing that there are things that are not good. It is true that in accordance with the central thesis, a thing has goodness in a certain respect and to a certain extent simply by virtue of possessing a substantial form and thus existing as a thing of a certain sort. The *sense* of 'goodness', however, is not simply the possession of some substantial form but, in particular, the actualization of the specifying potentiality of the nature conferred by that form. Only to the extent to which a thing has actualized that potentiality is it true to say unqualifiedly that the thing is good. For instance, to call Hitler good (without identifying some special respect, such as demagoguery) is to imply that he was good as a human being, or as a moral agent; but this is false in ways that Aquinas's practical morality could detail by indicating how Hitler failed to actualize the capacity for reason.[61]

> *Objection 2*: Goodness admits of degrees, but being is all or nothing. No rock, desk, or dog is in being just a little; no dog is in being more than another dog. On the other hand, things clearly can increase or decrease in goodness, and one thing can be better or worse than another thing of the same kind. Therefore, 'goodness' and 'being' cannot have the same referent.[62]

It may be right to say of existence that it is all or nothing; and, for Aquinas, the ordinary sense of 'being' is existence simpliciter. But every instance of existence is existence *as* something or other, and existence as something or other typically admits of degrees. A thing can be a more or less fully developed actualized specimen of its kind; it can have actualized its specifying potentiality to a greater or lesser degree. The ordinary sense of 'goodness', however, has to do with this actualization of the specifying potentiality. And so it is by no means clear that being in general is all or nothing. On Aquinas's views, there is more to being than just existence; the actualization of the specifying potentiality of a thing is also being of a sort. Furthermore, unlike mere existence as a thing of a kind, the actualization of a specifying potentiality can be gradual, so that the being of the thing whose specifying potentiality is being actualized can admit of degrees. Consequently, although on Aquinas's account 'being' and 'goodness' both refer to being, because their senses are different, it can still be true that there are things which are not good.

> *Objection 3*: According to Aquinas's central meta-ethical thesis, the more being, the more goodness. Now consider the biblical story of Ahasuerus, who had very many wives and concubines. If Ahasuerus fathered, say, 150 children, he was partially responsible for the existence of 150 human beings and, consequently, for the goodness supervening on the being that constituted their existence. In that

case, however, his unrestrained procreation would in and of itself be a clear instance of promoting goodness, since the increase of human beings is an increase of being and consequently of goodness. But, intuitively considered, that consequence is absurd.

Human beings who bring another human being into existence have not in virtue of that fact alone produced any goodness, on Aquinas's views of the sense of 'goodness'. Since Aquinas takes the sense of 'goodness' to be the actualization of a thing's specifying potentiality, then a human being produces goodness to the extent to which he actualizes his own or something else's specifying potentiality. Considered in itself, bringing children into the world does nothing to actualize any human being's specifying potentiality.[63] On the contrary, a man who fathered exceedingly many children, as in my example above, would probably contribute to a *decrease* of goodness. He would be unable to have much parenting influence on the lives of his children or to give them the care they needed just because there were so very many of them, and therefore it is at least a probable consequence of his unrestrained procreation that there would be more people whose chances of actualizing their specifying potentialities were less than they would be have been had he not had so many wives and so numerous a progeny.

But *Objection 3* is more complicated than the preceding objections just because goodness does supervene on being, for Aquinas. Consequently, whenever a thing has being in any respect, it also has goodness in some respect to some extent. And so it can still look as if Aquinas is stuck with the counter-intuitive conclusion the objection wants to foist on him; but neither we nor Aquinas would count a man such as Ahasuerus a moral hero or even morally praiseworthy just because he fathered such a large number of children. The rejoinder to *Objection 1* will help here. The small amount of goodness that must supervene on even the mere existence of a thing is not enough to call that thing good. In fact, if the thing falls too far short of the full actualization of its specifying potentiality, it is bad (or evil) considered as an instance of its kind, even though there is goodness in it. So insofar as Ahasuerus could not do what he ought to have done to help his children develop into good human beings, his unrestrained procreation could not count as the production of goodness; and to the extent to which his fathering so many children would be a factor in diminishing or preventing his care of them, it counts as producing badness.

Objection 4: According to Aquinas, loss of being is loss of goodness: badness (or evil) is the privation of goodness, which is a privation of being. In that case, taking penicillin to cure strep throat would be a bad thing to do, since it would result in the destruction of countless bacteria. But that consequence is absurd.

Objection 4 gains a special strength from the fact that it forces a defender of Aquinas's position to take on the task of ranking natural kinds. The task may seem not just uncongenial but impossible for anyone who understands goodness as supervenient on being itself. In Jack London's story "To Build a Fire", either a man will save his life by killing his dog or the dog will continue to live but the man will die. Since in either case one being is left, it may look as if Aquinas's theory must be neutral on the question of which of those beings should survive. But a widely shared moral intuition would consider the case in which the dog dies and the man survives to be highly preferable.

Far from offending that intuition, Aquinas's theory can explain and support it because his metaphysics provides a systematic basis on which to rank natural kinds: the Porphyrian Tree, a standard device of medieval metaphysics inherited from Hellenistic philosophy. A Porphyrian Tree begins with an Aristotelian category (*substance* is the standard medieval example) and moves via a series of dichotomous differentiae from that most general genus through its species. (In theory, all its possible species can be uncovered by this means.) The dichotomies produce progressively more specific species by the application of a pair of complementary differentiae to a less specific species or subordinate genus already in the tree. In this way, for example, *substance* yields *corporeal substance* and *incorporeal substance* to begin the tree. Corporeal substances can in turn be divided into those capable and those incapable of growth and reproduction and other life processes; and corporeal substances capable of life processes can be divided into those capable and those incapable of perception – roughly speaking, animals and plants, respectively. Finally, those animate corporeal substances capable of perception can be divided into those capable and those incapable of reason – human beings, on the one hand, and all other animals, on the other. In this schema, then, human beings are corporeal substances capable of life processes, perception, and reason.

Since each dichotomy in the tree is generated by the application of complementary differentiae, and since (setting aside the complicated case of the first dichotomy) all the differentiae applied involve capacities, one of the species (or genera) encountered in any pair after the first is characterized by a capacity its counterpart lacks. But, given Aquinas's views of being and actuality, an increment in capacity or potentiality constitutes an increment in being; and, because of the supervenience of goodness on being, a species or genus with more capacities of the sort that show up in the differentiae will have potentially more goodness than one with fewer. So, other things being equal, the goodness of a human life is greater than that of a dog's just because of rationality, the incremental capacity.[64]

We do not have to accept the universal applicability of the Porphyrian Tree in order to see that in it Aquinas does have a method for ranking at least some natural kinds relative to one another, and that the method is entirely consistent with his central thesis. Moreover, the method yields results that elucidate and support the intuitive reaction to the Jack London story: other things being equal, we value a human being more than a dog (or a colony of bacteria) because there is more to a human being than there is to a dog (or a colony of bacteria). Finally, although Aquinas subordinates all other species of animals to the human species, this feature of his theory cannot be interpreted as sanctioning wanton cruelty towards non-human animals or their gratuitous destruction. It is another corollary of his central meta-ethical thesis that any destruction of being is always *prima facie* bad in some respect and to some extent. Because some destruction may be less bad than the only available alternative, it may be rationally chosen. But unless there is some greater good, that is, some enhancement of being, that can be achieved only by means of destruction, an agent who chooses to destroy something will choose irrationally.

Rationality and the cardinal virtues

For Aquinas, then, moral goodness is the kind of goodness attainable by human beings, who are rational; and, on his views, a human being is good to the extent to which she actualizes her rationality, her specifying potentiality. A moral virtue is a habit of the will disposing the will to choose in accordance with reason.[65] The particular nature of the virtue, however, depends on the relation between reason and the disposition of the will. Aquinas says:

> The formal principle of virtue ... is the good of reason, and this can be considered in two ways. [It can be considered] in one way insofar as it consists in the very act (*consideratio*) of reason; and in this way there will be one cardinal virtue, which is called 'prudence'. [It is considered] in another way insofar as the order of reason is applied to something else. And this [can occur in two ways]. Either [the order of reason is applied] to operations, and then [the virtue is] justice. Or [it is applied] to passions, and then there must be two virtues. For the order of reason must be applied to the passions when they are opposed to reason, and this can happen in two ways. [It happens] in one way when passion drives [someone] to something contrary to reason, and then the passion needs a restraint, which is called 'temperance'. [It happens] in another way when a passion, such as fear of dangers or toil, holds [a person] back from something which reason commands; and then, in order not to draw back, a human being must be anchored in what comes from reason, and this [virtue] is courage.[66]

As he makes clearer in other passages,[67] for Aquinas, prudence links moral virtues with intellectual virtues. He understands prudence as the habit of skillfully choosing means appropriate for the attaining of ends; in this way, prudence is concerned with directing actions. So, for example, Aquinas says:

> prudence is a virtue most necessary to a human life, for living well consists in acting well. But in order for someone to act well, it matters not only what he does but also how he does it, so that he acts in accordance with a right choice, and not only out of impulse or passion. But choice has to do with things ordered to an end, and so two things matter for the rightness of a choice, namely, the appropriate end and what is suitably ordered to the appropriate end.[68]

As for the cardinal virtues concerned with controlling passions, if the passions are of a sort that need to be controlled in order to keep them from thwarting rationality, the relevant habit is temperance; but if the passions are the sort that need to be controlled in order to keep them from deterring the agent from an action to which reason prompts him, the relevant habit is courage.[69] Finally, if what is at stake in the exercise of rationality is not the agent's governance of himself but his actions affecting other people, then the relevant habit is justice.[70]

And so, unlike the intellectual virtues, which are habits in the intellect, the moral virtues are habits in the appetitive faculty or will. For Aquinas,

> every act of virtue can be done by choice, but only that virtue which is in the appetitive part of the soul yields a right choice, for ... choosing is an act of the appetitive part. And so a habit of choice, which is the principle of choice, is only that habit which perfects the appetitive power.[71]

The evaluation of actions

Because the virtues and vices, which constitute the central structure of Aquinas's theory of ethics, are conceived of as habitual inclinations or dispositions towards certain sorts of actions, it will also be helpful to look briefly at his analysis and evaluation of human actions.[72]

A human action, strictly speaking, is one in which a human agent exercises the specifically human rational faculties of intellect and will.[73] Absent-minded gestures, consequently, are not human actions even though they are "actions associated with a human being".[74] Understood in this way, every human action has an object, an end, and certain circumstances in which it is done.

An action's object, as Aquinas conceives of it, is fundamentally the state of affairs that the agent intends to bring about as a direct effect of the action.[75] We might characterize the object as the immediate aim or purpose of the action. So, for example, when in the biblical story Esther goes uninvited into the court of King Ahasuerus's palace, the object of her action is an audience with the king. Aquinas puts the point in scholastic terms; he says:

> every action takes [its] species from its object ... And so a difference in the object [of an action] has to produce a difference in species in actions ... [Now] nothing which is *per accidens* constitutes a species but only that which is *per se*.[76]

And a little later in the same article, he gives an example having to do with sex: "the conjugal act and an act of adultery differ in species in their relation to reason."[77]

Now, in Aquinas's analysis of action, an action's object is distinguished from the action's end.[78] As Aquinas says in one place:

> it is possible that an action which is one as regards [its] natural species is ordered to different ends of the will. For example, [the act of] killing a human being, which is one and the same as regards [its] natural species, can be ordered to either the preservation of justice or the satisfaction of wrath as its end.[79]

It is not possible here to do justice to Aquinas's complicated account of the difference between an action's object and its end, but we might provisionally think of an action's end as the agent's motive for performing the action.[80] So the end of Esther's action of coming to the palace is to persuade Ahasuerus to rescind his decree mandating the death of all the Jews in his kingdom. Seen in this way, the *object* of an action is *what* the agent intends to accomplish as a direct result of her action, while its *end* is *why* she intends to accomplish it. (A little later we will see some reasons for nuancing this interpretation somewhat.)

On his view, the end of an action, as well as the action's object, have to be taken into account in determining the action's species, that is, in determining what the action essentially is.[81] Given this view of his, together with the central meta-ethical thesis regarding being and goodness, it is not surprising to find him maintaining that the goodness or badness of any action is to be decided on the basis of an assessment of both the action's object and end. If the contemplated states of affairs that the action aims at and that motivate the agent are good, the action is good; if either the object or the end is not good, the action is not good.

So far, this account of the goodness of actions seems to ignore the fact that certain types of actions are morally neutral. The object of pitching horseshoes is to get them to fall around a stake, a state of affairs that certainly seems to be neither morally good nor morally bad. Suppose the end of such an action on a particular occasion is to entertain a sick child, which we may suppose is morally good. Then it might seem that the action itself, pitching horseshoes to entertain a sick child, would have to be evaluated by Aquinas as not good; although its end is good, its object is only neutral and so not good.

This counter-intuitive evaluation can be dispelled by taking into account Aquinas's concept of the *circumstances* of an action: when was the action done? where? by whom? how? etc.[82] An action's circumstances are obviously not essential features of a *type* of action; but they are what might be called *particularizing* characteristics, because any broadly conceived type of action is particularized or recognized as the particular action it is by attending to its circumstances. So, for example, part of what makes Esther's action the particular action it is, is its circumstances. She comes uninvited to the court of the king's palace at a time when Ahasuerus has decreed death for anyone who comes into the court of the palace without having been called by the king, unless the intruder "finds favor with the king". Furthermore, because it has been a month since the king last sent for her, Esther has reason to believe she is out of favor with the king. Finally, she comes there at a time when Ahasuerus has decreed the death of all the Jews in his kingdom, and Esther's intention is to speak for her people. It is on the basis of a consideration of these circumstances that the action of coming uninvited to the king, which seems morally neutral in its type, is particularized as Esther's act of courage and altruism.[83]

The importance of a consideration of circumstances in Aquinas's evaluation of actions can be seen in the fact that he takes any and every action particularized by its circumstances to be either good or bad, even though the type of the action broadly conceived of may be morally neutral. (His paradigms of morally neutral types of actions are picking a straw off the ground or taking a walk.[84])

Not all of an action's characteristics are included among its circumstances. So, for example, Esther's action has the properties of contributing to the death of Haman and of being commemorated in a book of the Bible. But, according to Aquinas's theory, neither of those properties can or should make any difference to an evaluation of Esther's action. An action's circumstances, he says, are those properties of it that are related *per se* to the action being evaluated; all its other properties are related to it only *per accidens*.[85]

By this distinction he seems to mean that the circumstances of Esther's particular action, the action being evaluated in our example, are features accidental to the *type* of action she performs – coming uninvited to the king – but not accidental to her particular action on that particular occasion. On the contrary, even our understanding of the object and end of her particular action is heavily influenced by what we know of its circumstances. In light of that knowledge we might want to revise our original broad assessment and say, more precisely, that the object of her action is a *dangerous and difficult* audience with the king, and that its end is a *resolute and self-sacrificial* attempt to get the king to rescind his edict.

The action's circumstances may be called its *intrinsic* accidents, the others its *extrinsic* accidents. The intrinsic accidents of Esther's action clarify and redefine our understanding of *what she does*, what she is responsible for; its extrinsic accidents – such as its being commemorated in a book of the Bible – obviously contribute nothing to such an understanding. Even the extrinsically accidental fact that her action has some causal relationship with Haman's death is not in any way a feature of what *she* does, because the connection between her action and his death is an unforeseeable and partly fortuitous chain of events, something she could not be held responsible for.

So Aquinas's evaluation of actions is based entirely on a consideration of *what* those actions *are* and not on a consideration of their extrinsic accidents. In that way, it is a natural outgrowth of his central meta-ethical thesis. The object and end of an action determine the action's type and so, broadly speaking, they determine the being of the action. The action's circumstances determine the being of the particular action that is actually performed, and in doing so they clarify and refine our understanding of the particular action's object and end. A particular (actually performed) action, then, is good only in case both its object and its end as informed by its circumstances are good; otherwise the particular action is bad. The goodness of the action's object or end depends, in turn, on whether the contemplated state of affairs motivating or aimed at by the agent is good, as judged by the central meta-ethical thesis. The end of Esther's action, for example, is to persuade the king to rescind his decree of death for all the kingdom's Jews. But the king's decree was irrational, on Aquinas's view, since it would have resulted in a great loss of being and hence of goodness without any greater good to justify that loss. Helping to bring about the rescinding of an irrational decree, however, is rational, other things being equal, and therefore morally good.[86] (Analogous things can be said about the object of Esther's action.)

Problems for application of the thesis

In the story of Esther, her attempt to save her people involves her knowingly risking her life; as she says, in the story: "and if I perish, I perish". How, if at all, is the evaluation of her action in terms of its object and end affected by that circumstance of the action? Aquinas would, not surprisingly, find that aspect of her action praiseworthy. In discussing courage, he praises risking one's life in the defense of the common good as a prime example of that virtue.[87] But suppose (revising the story in the biblical book of Esther) that Esther succeeds in saving her people and dies in the attempt. Would Aquinas's theory still evaluate her action as good in that case?

There is a simple-minded application of Aquinas's central meta-ethical theory to that question which is an emphatic affirmative: of course Esther's action is good even if it costs her her life; it saves thousands of lives at the expense of one. On balance, there is a great surplus of being and consequently of goodness.

Although the affirmative reply seems right, the reason given for it is repugnant. If this simple-minded book-keeping approach were what Aquinas's thesis about being and goodness required, the thesis would lead to results that are egregiously inconsistent with the rest of Aquinas's moral theory as well as repugnant to moral intuitions shared by most people in his time and ours. That this is so can be shown by considering applications of the simple-minded approach to three cases more complicated than the revised version of Esther's story. The first of these is a version of one of Aquinas's own examples.

> *The heaven case*: Johnson is a murderer, and Williams is his innocent victim. But when Johnson murders him, Williams (unbeknownst to Johnson) is in a state of grace and so goes to heaven. The ultimate end of human existence is union with God in heaven, and so by bringing it about that Williams achieves that ultimate end, Johnson brings about an increase of being (and consequently of goodness). In reality, then, Johnson's murder of Williams is morally good.

Aquinas considers his version of the heaven case as an objection to his own claim that the deliberate killing of an innocent person is never morally justified. In the body of the article arguing for this claim, before he turns to the objection, Aquinas says:

> if we consider a human being in himself, it is not permissible to kill anyone, because we ought to love in any [human being], even a sinner, the nature which God has made; but this nature is destroyed by killing ... The killing of a sinner becomes permissible, however, in relation to the common good, which is destroyed by sin. Now the life of righteous human beings maintains and promotes the common good ... And so it is in no way permissible to kill an innocent [human being].[88]

One objection to this position which Aquinas considers is an *a fortiori* argument. Since it is sometimes permissible to kill a sinful person, the objection runs, it must all the more so be the case that it is sometimes permissible to kill an innocent person, since no injury is done to an innocent person, who at death goes straight to heaven.[89] In his rejoinder to this objection, Aquinas holds that the fact that Williams goes to heaven, the good that is supposed to justify Johnson's murder of Williams, is a characteristic of Johnson's action that is related to it only *per accidens*. That is, Williams going to heaven is an extrinsic accident of Johnson's action.

Aquinas is apparently thinking along these lines: Williams's spiritual condition and not Johnson's action is what causes Williams to go to heaven, and it is an extrinsic accident of Johnson's action that Williams was in that condition at the time of the murder. Since it is a feature of Aquinas's theory that an action is to be evaluated solely on the basis of what it *is* and not on the basis of any of its extrinsic accidents, his evaluation of Johnson's action would not take any account of the fact that Williams goes to heaven. What Johnson's action *is*, as far as the story goes, is simply the murder of an innocent person, which is of course not morally justifiable in Aquinas's theory.

Aquinas's treatment of the heaven case seems generally right, but his conclusion that sending Williams to heaven is only an extrinsic accident of Johnson's action appears to depend on the fact that Johnson does not (presumably cannot) know that Williams is in a state of grace. If Johnson knew that killing Williams would result in Williams going to heaven, it would at least be harder to deny that achieving that result was part of the end of Johnson's action and thus part of what Johnson's action was. In order to see the way in which Aquinas's theory avoids simply endorsing a maximizing of being, we need to consider some cases relevantly like the heaven case but in which there is no similar ignorance on the part of the agent.

> *The hostage case*: A madman takes five people hostage and threatens to kill them all unless Brown kills Robinson, an innocent bystander. Brown decides that killing Robinson is morally justified by the surplus of being (and consequently of goodness) that will result from using Robinson's death to save the lives of the five hostages.

In the hostage case, the object of Brown's action is Robinson's death, and its end appears to be the saving of five lives. Aquinas's way of dismissing the counter-intuitive moral assessment in the heaven case is clearly unavailable as a way of dealing with the hostage case. The good that appears to justify Brown's action is in fact the end of Brown's action, and this must therefore be taken into account in evaluating the action. In considering how Aquinas would deal with the hostage case, it will be helpful to look somewhat more closely at his conception of the end of an action.

Since it is Aquinas's view that actions should be evaluated only on the basis of what they are and not on the basis of their extrinsic accidents, and since it is also his view that actions are to be evaluated on the basis of their ends, the state of affairs sought after as the end of the action must be in some sense intrinsic to the action itself. For that reason it seems clear that the notion of motive, although it is in certain respects close to Aquinas's notion of end, is not completely interchangeable with it. For Aquinas, a state of affairs counts as the end of an action if and only if the agent performs the action for the sake of establishing that state of affairs, *and* the agent *can* in fact establish that state of affairs by performing that action. That is why

Aquinas says, for example, that "the end of human acts is their terminus, for that in which a human act terminates is that which the will [of the agent] intends as an end".[90] And he goes on to explain, "the end [of an act] is not something altogether extrinsic to the act, because the end is related to the act as its principle or terminus".[91]

In the hostage case, the good that is supposed to justify Brown's killing the innocent Robinson is the saving of five lives. But that good cannot be the end of Brown's action because it is not a state of affairs he can establish by killing Robinson. The survival of the hostages depends not on Brown's action but on the action of the madman, who can of course kill them all even if Brown meets his demand. Therefore, the survival of the hostages is not a state of affairs Brown himself can be said to establish by killing Robinson. Once the more precise notion of the end of an action has been introduced, the hostage case can be assimilated to the heaven case after all. In both cases, the good that is supposed to justify the killing of an innocent person turns out not to be an intrinsic part of the action being evaluated but rather only an extrinsic accident of it; and for that reason it must be left out of account in the evaluation of the action. When Brown's action in the hostage case is evaluated in that way, it is evaluated simply as the deliberate killing of an innocent person; and since that state of affairs is unquestionably bad, the action itself is bad.

But even if this attempt to defend Aquinas's evaluation of actions were successful in the hostage case, it will apparently fail if we alter the form of the counter-example in one crucial respect.

> *The hospital case*: Five patients in a hospital are waiting for donors to be found so that they can undergo transplant operations. One of them needs a heart, the second, a liver, the third, lungs, and the fourth and fifth each need a kidney. Every one of the five patients will be able to lead a normal life if, but only if, an organ donor can be found. Each of them will die very soon without a transplant operation. Jones, the skilled transplant specialist in charge of these patients, decides that killing Smith, a healthy, innocent person, is morally justified by the surplus of being (and consequently of goodness) that will result from using Smith's organs to save the five critically ill patients.[92]

The end of Jones's action, even on the more precise interpretation of 'end', is the saving of five lives. In the hospital case, unlike the hostage case, no other agent's action is needed to establish the state of affairs Jones aims to establish, because he is a relevantly skilled specialist in charge of the five patients. And if the saving of their lives can in this case count as the end of Jones's action, then it must be taken into account in evaluating the action. For that reason, the tactic that was effective in defending Aquinas's evaluation of actions against the hostage case will not work against the hospital case.

But Aquinas's evaluation of actions requires taking into account the action's object as well as its end. Since the object and the end together make the action what it *is*, and since the goodness of anything is a function of its being, both object and end must be good if the action is to be good. The object of Jones's action in the hospital case, however, is the death of the innocent Smith and the removal of his organs, which is unquestionably morally bad, on Aquinas's views. As he puts it, "it is never permissible to kill an innocent person".[93] But the sacrifice of one to save many in the hospital case is formally like the revised version of Esther's story. In order to understand Aquinas's evaluation of the hospital case and to see whether it applies also to Esther's courageous act of altruism, we need to look briefly at Aquinas's account of justice.

Justice and its place in the scheme of the virtues

Unlike the other cardinal virtues of prudence, temperance, and courage, justice is the virtue in Aquinas's scheme of the virtues which has to do with a person's relations to others in a society and to the society itself. In Aquinas's view, a society has a being of its own. Some things contribute to the being of a society, and others to its dissolution. That is why Aquinas takes the stand he does, for example, with regard to capital punishment. He says:

> every part is ordered to the whole as imperfect to perfect, and for this reason every part is naturally for the sake of the whole. And because of this, we see that if the removal of some member is advantageous for the health of the whole body, for example because that member is decayed and capable of corrupting the other [members of the body], then it is praiseworthy and health-giving to cut it away. Now every individual person is related to the whole community as a part to a whole. And for this reason if a human being is dangerous to the community and capable of corrupting it because of some sin [on his part], then it is praiseworthy and health-giving to kill him so that the communal good may be preserved.[94]

Aquinas's ready acceptance of capital punishment in particular and his privileging of the state over the individual in general will strike many readers as chilling;[95] later, in the chapter on justice, I will examine in detail concerns about Aquinas's political theory. Here I want to consider just enough of Aquinas's understanding of justice to enable us to see the resources his theory of ethics has for handling apparent counter-examples such as the hospital case.

In accordance with Aquinas's meta-ethics, the things that contribute to a society's being are part of the society's good, and the virtue of justice generally in the members of the society is directed towards establishing and preserving that common good. Aquinas, who follows Aristotle closely here, distinguishes distributive from commutative justice.[96] Distributive justice is the rational regulation of the distribution of the society's worldly goods, aiming at a rational relationship in that respect between the society as a whole and any individual member of it.[97] Commutative justice, on the other hand, is the rational regulation of relationships among individuals or subgroups within the society. The basis of commutative justice in Aquinas's treatment of it is the view that human beings considered just as persons are equals, and that it is therefore rational for them, considered just as persons, to treat one another as equals, and irrational for them to treat one another unequally, considered just as persons.[98]

A used-car dealer and his customer, considered just as persons, are equals. If the dealer deceives the customer about the defects of a car and so cheats him out of much of the purchase price, then in that particular exchange the dealer gets a greater share than the customer. But this is contrary to reason, on Aquinas's view, because the dealer and the customer are equals in all relevant respects. The inequality of the trade is part of what makes it an instance of cheating, and so cheating is morally bad because it contravenes the principles of commutative justice.[99]

According to Aquinas, then, whenever one person takes something away from another, the action will be just only if it is rational. A necessary (though not also sufficient) condition of its being rational is its involving an even trade, in an extended sense of 'trade' in many cases. A slanderer, for instance, takes away the victim's reputation and gives nothing in return; slander is thus an injustice.[100] Murder is a particularly great injustice,[101] since in depriving the victim of life, one of the greatest of goods on Aquinas's view, the murderer is not only providing no compensation but also rendering the victim incapable of receiving any such compensation.[102]

In the hospital case, the object of Jones's action is characterized by exactly that sort of injustice. His taking of Smith's life and vital organs involves considerable benefit for his five patients, but great harm to Smith, and harm for which there can be no compensatory good for Smith. Jones's action of killing Smith is thus an injustice towards Smith; and this injustice is a sufficient condition for evaluating Jones's action as morally bad, on Aquinas's views, regardless of the beneficial aspects of the end of that action. Aquinas puts the point this way:

> the disposition of things as regards goodness is the same as their disposition as regards being ... Now just as the being of a thing depends on the agent and the form, so the goodness of a thing depends on the end ... Now human actions ... have the formula of goodness from the end on which they depend, in addition to the unconditional good that is in them. And consequently the goodness in a human action can be considered in four ways. In one way with regard to the genus [of the

action], that is, insofar as it is an action, because it has goodness to the extent to which it is an action and in being ... In another way with regard to the species [of the action], which the action gets from its appropriate object. In a third way with regards to the circumstances, which are a kind of accident [of the action]. And in a fourth way with regard to the end [of the action].[103]

And he goes on to say:

> nothing keeps an action from having goodness in one of the afore-said [four] ways but lacking it in another. As far as this goes, an action which is good as regards its species or circumstances can be ordered to a bad end, and conversely. Nonetheless, it is not a good action simpliciter unless all [four kinds of] goodness come together [in it].[104]

Consequently, Aquinas can give a negative evaluation of Jones sacrificing Smith in the hospital case without also having to give a negative evaluation of an act of self-sacrifice such as Esther's. Esther would not be guilty of any injustice if she gave up her own life for her people, although of course Ahasuerus would be guilty of injustice if he took her life in those circumstances. In fact, according to Aquinas's account of commutative justice, it is impossible for Esther to be unjust to herself, because a person cannot take for herself an unfair share of goods from herself. The reasons for disapproving of Jones's action in the hospital case thus do not apply to Esther's hypothetical self-sacrifice, and approval of Esther's sort of self-sacrifice need not and should not be based on the simple-minded book-keeping application of Aquinas's central meta-ethical thesis.[105]

Agent-centered restrictions in Aquinas's ethics

These considerations give some reason to think that Aquinas's ethics is a deontological theory of morality that can handle the problem of agent-centered restrictions. Samuel Scheffler has described these restrictions as rendering "typical deontological views ... apparently paradoxical". He says:

> An agent-centred restriction is, roughly, a restriction which it is at least sometimes impermissible to violate in circumstances where a violation would serve to minimize total overall violations of the very same restriction, and would have no other morally relevant consequences. Thus, for example, a prohibition against killing one innocent person even in order to minimize the total number of innocent people killed would ordinarily count as an agent-centred restriction. The inclusion of agent-centred restrictions gives traditional deontological

views considerable anti-consequentialist force, and also considerable intuitive appeal. Despite their congeniality to moral common sense, however, agent-centred restrictions are puzzling. For how can it be rational to forbid the performance of a morally objectionable action that would have the effect of minimizing the total number of comparably objectionable actions that were performed and would have no other morally relevant consequences? How can the minimization of morally objectionable conduct be morally unacceptable?[106]

While Aquinas's theory certainly endorses the truism that the good is to be maximized, it also interprets the nature of goodness in general and of good actions in particular in such a way that no action whose object is characterized by injustice can be rationally performed, no matter how great a good is incorporated in the action's end. On this basis, a generalization of agent-centered restrictions can be endorsed and accommodated in Aquinas's ethical theory.

The generalized version of Scheffler's example is a prohibition against perpetrating or permitting one injustice of uncompensatable suffering even in order to minimize the total number of such injustices, and at this level of generality "the very same restriction" is the restriction against perpetrating or permitting injustice. On Aquinas's views, especially his views about justice and the place of justice in the scheme of the virtues, agent-centered restrictions that prohibit agents from perpetrating or permitting actions that constitute an injustice are rational for that very reason, regardless of the good to be achieved by performing those actions.

A brief word on natural law

Aquinas's account of natural law has been the subject of extensive discussion,[107] and it cannot be treated here in passing in any detail, but it does need to be considered, even if only briefly.

It is not always clear what natural law is, on Aquinas's views, and different characterizations of it are given, sometimes even by the same interpreter. So, for example, sometimes natural law is described as if it were a matter of innate and incorruptible knowledge of moral truths. Ralph McInerny explains it this way: "natural law is reason's natural grasp of certain common principles which should direct our acts."[108]

Elsewhere, however, McInerny's descriptions of natural law make it look more as if natural law is itself a set of moral principles of some especially fundamental sort. So, for example, he says, "natural law is a dictate of reason"; and a little later he remarks that there is a way in which "natural law is a claim that there are moral absolutes".[109]

On the other hand, natural law is also sometimes described as a matter of the metaphysics, rather than the epistemology, of morality, as something which grounds morality. So, for instance, in a discussion of the relation of rights and law, John Finnis says, "if I have a natural – as we would say, human – right I have it by virtue of natural law".[110]

Aquinas's characterization of the natural law is complicated enough to justify these different descriptions. He himself explains the natural law as a certain participation on the part of a rational creature in God's eternal law,[111] and he explains the divine eternal law as the ordering in God's mind of created things in the world.[112] For a rational creature to participate in the eternal law is for it to have a share of the eternal divine reason and to have a natural inclination to its own proper end. But to have a share in the divine reason is to have the light of human reason which enables human beings to discern what is good and what is evil.[113] Somewhat later, he maintains that a human being can be subject to the eternal law in two ways, first, by partaking of the eternal law by way of knowledge and, second, by partaking of it by way of an inward principle which moves to action; and he goes on to remark that both ways are diminished in the wicked because their knowledge of the good and their inclination to it are imperfect.[114]

Elsewhere he argues that although we do not know the eternal law as it is in the divine mind, it can be made known to us either by reason or by revelation.[115] And he goes on to remark that we can know in a general way what God wills because we know that God wills what is good. And so he says, "whoever wills something under some description (*ratio*) of the good has a will conformed to the divine will as far as the description of what is willed [is concerned]".[116]

Aquinas describes law in general as an ordinance of reason for the common good which is made by someone who has the care of the community and which is promulgated. So the question arises for him whether natural law is also promulgated. To this question, he replies that the natural law is promulgated just in virtue of God's instilling it into a person's mind as a matter of natural knowledge.[117] But the natural knowledge in question consists in very general moral precepts, the precepts of the natural law, such as that the good is to be done and the bad is to be avoided.[118]

Although these very general precepts cannot be completely wiped out even in evil people, secondary precepts derived from these can be blotted out; and even the application of the most general precepts to particular actions can be hindered by the effects of moral evil on a person's intellect.[119]

Aquinas makes an analogous point as regards the natural inclination to act in accordance with the good. He says:

> all acts of virtue pertain to the natural law ... for everything to which a human being is inclined in accordance with his nature pertains to the natural law. Now everything is naturally inclined to

an operation appropriate to it in accordance with its form ... And so since the rational soul is the proper form of a human being, there is in every human being a natural inclination to act in accordance with reason. But this is to act in accordance with virtue.[120]

But, as he goes on to explain:

if we are talking about virtuous acts in themselves, that is, insofar as they are considered in their proper species, then in this way not all virtuous acts belong to the natural law. For many things are done virtuously to which nature at first does not incline; rather human beings come to find them by the investigation of reason, as useful for living well.[121]

And in another text, he argues that even the natural inclination to the good can be undermined by moral evil. In the wicked, not only is the natural knowledge of the good corrupted by passions and morally evil habits, but also "the natural inclination to virtue is corrupted by habits of vice".[122]

In an extensive discussion of synderesis, which Aquinas explains as an innate habit of knowledge in the practical reason, Aquinas puts his account of natural law in a broader context, which is helpful in understanding the complexities of his position.[123] On Aquinas's theory of angels, angels, unlike human beings, simply know things, without having to reason their way to conclusions on the basis of other things they know. The foundation of this angelic knowledge is an innate understanding of certain things implanted in them by God at their creation.[124] Human beings share so much of angelic nature that God has also implanted in their rational faculties certain habits which are innate to them. Now for human beings, the rational faculties are both intellect and will, and the intellect itself can be understood both as speculative and as practical reason. The innate habit of knowledge of speculative reason has to do with fundamental principles of abstract reason, such as the law of non-contradiction. We just find ourselves strongly inclined to believe this and other basic laws of reason. The innate habit of knowledge in the practical reason, on the other hand, has to do with things that are to be done, such as the precept of the natural law mentioned above. In the will, however, what is implanted in the rational faculty is not a habit of knowledge but rather an innate inclination to act. The will is a hunger for the good, and by God's design of it it is naturally inclined to will the good, as perceived by reason. So one way to understand natural law on Aquinas's views is as the pair of innate, divinely implanted habits in the practical reason and the will. Synderesis is then the name for the habit in the practical reason.

Aquinas goes on to distinguish synderesis from conscience, which is a matter of making use of the innate habit in the practical reason, both in considering what to do in particular circumstances and in evaluating past actions one has done.[125] Synderesis is incapable of error, on his account, and cannot be extinguished by sin;[126] but conscience can err.[127] Aquinas takes the stern position that an erring conscience binds. Acting against one's conscience is always a moral evil; but if one acts in accordance with an erring conscience, what one does will also be a moral evil.[128]

The theological interpretation of Aquinas's central meta-ethical thesis

Aquinas's central meta-ethical thesis has a theological interpretation more fundamental than any of its other applications to ethics, and it is appropriate to end a consideration of his account of the metaphysics of goodness and the meta-ethical foundation of morality with this theological position.

Since Aquinas takes God to be essentially and uniquely "being itself" (*ipsum esse*), then on Aquinas's central meta-ethical thesis God alone is also essentially goodness itself.[129] Aquinas says, "for God alone, [his] essence is his being ... And so he alone is good through his essence".[130]

And on the question on God's simplicity, he says, "God is identical with (*idem quod*) his essence or nature ... God is his own deity, his own life, and whatever else is predicated in this way of God."[131]

Aquinas's central meta-ethical thesis regarding being and goodness together with his view of divine simplicity thus entails a relationship between God and morality that avoids the embarrassments of both theological subjectivism and theological objectivism, and provides a basis for an account of religious morality different in important ways from the more commonly known divine command morality discussed by contemporary philosophers of religion. Because this part of Aquinas's meta-ethics depends on the doctrine of simplicity, I will postpone discussion of it to Chapter 3 on simplicity. What needs to be pointed out here, however, is that on Aquinas's meta-ethical views, the goodness for the sake of which and in accordance with which God wills whatever he wills regarding human morality is identical with his nature.

Conclusion

Aquinas's central meta-ethical thesis, worked out in the context of his general metaphysics, provides a sophisticated metaphysical grounding for his virtue-based ethics. It constitutes, as it were, a grand unified theory of goodness, within which his account of human morality is situated, as a particular application of the general theory. And when the central meta-ethical thesis is combined with Aquinas's theological views, especially his understanding of the doctrine of divine simplicity, then the theological interpretation of the central meta-ethical thesis constitutes the basis for a religious ethics that makes God essential to human morality but without tying morality to God's will. The result is a metaphysically grounded, objective normative virtue ethics which is theological at least in this sense that it is ultimately based on God's nature.

3

GOD'S SIMPLICITY

Introduction

Aquinas puts a discussion of God's simplicity near the beginning of his treatment of the nature of God in *Summa theologiae*. The medieval account of the divine attribute of simplicity is perhaps the most difficult and controversial piece of medieval philosophical theology but also one of the most important.[1]

The doctrine that God is absolutely simple derives from the metaphysical considerations that have led philosophers and theologians to maintain that God is a being whose existence is self-explanatory, an absolutely perfect being, or pure actuality.[2] I am not concerned here with the foundations of the doctrine, however; for present purposes the doctrine can be taken as a datum,[3] having its most influential formulations in Augustine, Anselm, and, of course, Aquinas.[4]

Because the doctrine is notoriously difficult, and because the treatment of it in this chapter will emphasize its difficulties, it is worth noting at the outset that simplicity also offers impressive advantages for constructive rational theology. For instance, it provides a way out of a dilemma for religious morality and a way of strengthening the cosmological argument, as the last section of this chapter will show. It is also fundamental to the Thomistic worldview. It is foundational for everything in Aquinas's thought from his metaphysics to his ethics.

Despite its metaphysical credentials, its long-established position at the center of orthodox Christianity's doctrine of God, and its advantages for rational theology, the doctrine of simplicity is not viewed with much favor in contemporary philosophy of religion, primarily because it seems outrageously counter-intuitive or even incoherent. In attributing a radical unity to God, and to God alone, it rules out the possibility of there being in God any of the real distinctions on the basis of which we make sense of other real things. Consequently, it has seemed to many philosophers and theologians to give rise to paradoxical or flatly inconsistent conclusions.

A large part of the difficulty in dealing with the doctrine of divine simplicity, in my view, has to do just with understanding what the doctrine is and is not claiming. Medieval modalities are one source of the confusion. Aquinas formulates the claims of the doctrine of divine simplicity using terms whose English translations are in common use in contemporary metaphysics, but, as is widely recognized among scholars of medieval logic,[5] it is perilous to assume that medieval and contemporary modal terms have the same meaning.

I will therefore begin by laying out the claims that comprise the doctrine of divine simplicity as Aquinas presents those claims, and then I will show that the meaning contemporary metaphysics would assign to at least some of those claims cannot be the meaning Aquinas had in mind. Without being able to give a detailed analysis of Aquinas's theory of modality, I will nonetheless suggest what seems to me a more nearly accurate interpretation of the claims in which Aquinas sees the doctrine of simplicity comprised. With so much clarification, I will then turn to the problems the doctrine has been thought to raise. Some of these are easily handled by a better understanding of the claims of the doctrine, but there are others that remain difficult to treat. In my view, the most troublesome problem arises from the distinction between what God can and cannot freely choose. I will attempt to shed some light on Aquinas's reasons for supposing that this distinction does not threaten the doctrine of simplicity. In the process, I will consider what some scholars have taken to be the religiously untoward consequences of the doctrine, including the apparent consequence that God, as pure actuality, is unable to be responsive to created things and contingent events. I will argue that, properly understood, the doctrine has no such implications. Furthermore, it is true that the doctrine has serious implications for our ability to know and talk about God; but, as I will argue, Aquinas's interpretation of the doctrine is nonetheless meant to keep it from reducing us to the sort of agnosticism to which, in Aquinas's view, Maimonides's espousal of divine simplicity led him. Finally, in the last section I will conclude with a brief consideration of some of the advantages of the doctrine for philosophical theology.

Simplicity and agnosticism about God's nature

Aquinas begins his discussion of the doctrine of divine simplicity in *ST* Ia.3 with a short prologue. He says:

> When we know with regard to something *that* it is, we still need to ask what it is like (*quomodo sit*), in order to know with regard to it what it is (*quid sit*). But because we are not able to know with regard to God what he is, but [rather] what he is not, we cannot consider with regard to God what he is like but rather what he is not like ... It can be shown with regard to God what

he is not like by removing from him those things not appropriate to him, such as composition and motion and other things of this sort.

This passage and others like it have sometimes been pressed into service as evidence for an agnosticism on Aquinas's part with regard to the nature of God. But caution is warranted here. It is true that Aquinas explains divine simplicity only in terms of what God is not – not a body, not composed of matter and form, and so on. But in the course of showing what God is not, Aquinas relies heavily on positive claims about God. So, for example, he argues that God is not a body on the basis of these claims among others: God is the first mover; God is pure actuality; God is the first being; God is the most noble of beings. In arguing that God is not composed of matter and form, Aquinas in fact makes a huge, substantial, positive metaphysical claim about the nature of God. He says:

a form which is not able to be received in matter but is subsistent by itself (*per se subsistens*) is individuated in virtue of the fact that it cannot be received in something else. And God is a form of this sort.[6]

And, of course, if there were really *nothing* we could know about God's nature, then it is difficult to see how Aquinas could suppose he had proved that God exists. It is not possible to prove the existence of something with regard to which one knows *only* what it is not and nothing at all about what it is. As far as that goes, knowing that something exists is knowing something more about it than what it is not.

Furthermore, in *ST* Ia.13, the question about the names of God, Aquinas explicitly repudiates the sort of agnosticism some scholars in effect attribute to him; Aquinas himself associates such a position with Moses Maimonides and rejects it emphatically. The text in question is worth quoting at length here. Aquinas says:

with regard to the names of God which are said negatively or which signify some relation of God to a creature, it is evident that they do not in any way signify the substance of God. Rather they signify the separation of something from God or the relation of God to something else or rather of something else to him. But with regard to names which are said absolutely and affirmatively of God, such as 'good', 'wise', and the like, people have many opinions.

For some have said that although all these names are said affirmatively of God, nonetheless, they have been crafted more to separate something from God than to posit something in him. And so these people say that when we say that God is living, we signify that God does not exist in the manner of an inanimate thing, and so on for other such names. And this is the position of Rabbi Moses.

Others say that these names are imposed to signify a relationship of God to created things, so that, for example, when we say 'God is good', the sense is 'God is the cause of goodness in things'. And the same point applies in other such cases.

But both of these opinions appear unsuitable, for three reasons. First, because neither of these positions can give a reason why some names should be said of God rather than others. For God is a cause of bodies in the same way he is a cause of goodness. And so if when we say 'God is good', nothing is signified other than that God is the cause of goodness in things, in the same way it should be possible to say that God is a body because he is the cause of bodies. Similarly, in saying that God is a body, one separates [from God] that he is only a being in potentiality, as prime matter is ... Thirdly, because this is against the intention of those speaking about God. For when they say that God is living, they intend to say something other than that God is the cause of our life or that he differs from inanimate bodies.

And so we need to say something else, namely, that names of this sort signify the divine substance and are predicated of God substantially, but they fall short in their representation of him ... Therefore, when one says 'God is good', the sense is not 'God is the cause of goodness' or 'God is not evil'. But this is the sense: 'what we call goodness in creatures pre-exists in God and in a higher mode'. And so it does not follow from this that being good belongs to God insofar as he causes goodness. Rather the converse is the case: because he is good, he diffuses goodness in things.[7]

In this same question, Aquinas considers an objection someone could read out of Damascene, which is very like a position sometimes attributed by scholars to Aquinas himself; in fact, at first glance, it seems to be just the position Aquinas outlines in the prologue to the question on simplicity. Aquinas cites Damascene to this effect: "Any [name] said of God cannot signify what God is with regard to substance; rather, it can show [only] what God is not."[8] In repudiating this objection, Aquinas says: "Damascene says that these names do not signify what God is because none of these names expresses perfectly what God is, but each of them signifies God imperfectly."[9] These passages and others like them strongly suggest that it is a mistake to read the prologue to *ST* Ia.3 as implying agnosticism about God's nature.

How, then, are we to understand that prologue? I am inclined to think that part of the problem in interpreting Aquinas's remarks in the prologue correctly has to do with the expression '*quid est*'.[10] The expression *quid est* ("what it is") is a technical term of medieval logic. Peter of Spain, for example, gives the standard medieval formula for a genus as "that which is predicated of many things differing in species in respect of what they are (*in eo quod quid est*)"; a differentia, on the other hand, is defined as "that which is predicated of many things differing in species in respect of what they are like (*in eo quod quale*)".[11] Now the essence of anything is comprised of both genus and differentia, and genus differs from differentia only in virtue of the fact that genus, unlike differentia, is predicated *in eo quod quid est*. It is therefore possible, in the terms of medieval logic, for someone who does not know the *quid est* of a thing nonetheless to know a great deal about the essence of that thing in virtue of knowing the differentia of it, which is not predicated *in eo quod quid est*. So whatever exactly '*quid est*' means in Aquinas's thought, in the terms of medieval logic Aquinas's claim that we cannot know with regard to God *quid est* does not *by itself* imply that we can know nothing positive about God. On the contrary, as I showed above, the claim that we cannot know the *quid est* of God is apparently compatible in Aquinas's own mind with the many positive claims he makes about God.

In examining Aquinas's understanding of the doctrine of divine simplicity, therefore, we should not simply assume on the basis of the prologue that he has adopted a thorough-going agnosticism as regards our knowledge of God's nature.

The claims of the doctrine of divine simplicity

The doctrine of simplicity, as Aquinas understands it, can be sorted into several specific theses, the most important of which can be summarized in three claims.

The first distinguishes God from material objects:

(1) It is impossible that God have any spatial or temporal parts that could be distinguished from one another as here rather than there or as now rather than then, and so God cannot be a physical entity.

Aquinas denies that there is any matter in God or that God has any dimensions,[12] and so he rules out spatial parts in God. In addition, Aquinas derives divine eternality, which includes God's being outside of time, from divine immutability,[13] which he derives in turn from divine simplicity.[14] On Aquinas's view, then, the doctrine of simplicity also has the implication that God has no temporal parts.

Next, the standard distinction between an entity's essential and intrinsic accidental properties cannot apply to God:

(2) It is impossible that God have any accidental properties.

Aquinas says:

> there can be no accident in God. First, because a subject is related
> to an accident as potentiality to actuality, for with regard to an acci-
> dent a subject is in actuality in a certain respect. But being in
> potentiality is entirely removed from God.[15]

To ward off misunderstanding, it is important to add that the properties at
issue in this claim clearly have to be taken as what we call 'intrinsic properties', and it may be useful to say just a little here about the familiar
distinction between intrinsic and extrinsic properties, between real properties and Cambridge properties. It is not easy to come by a satisfactory
criterion for precisely distinguishing intrinsic or real properties from
extrinsic or Cambridge properties, but the distinction is widely recognized
and sometimes easy to draw. For present purposes it is perhaps enough to say
that a change in x's extrinsic properties can occur without a change in x,
while a change in x's intrinsic properties is as such a change in x.[16] My belief
that I am in Saint Louis is one of my intrinsic accidental properties; my
being mentioned in this book is an extrinsic accidental property of mine.
The intrinsic properties of numbers are all essential; numbers, like God,
cannot have intrinsic accidental properties. But no entity, not even a mathematical or a divine entity, can be exempted from having extrinsic accidental
properties.

Third, the doctrine of simplicity as Aquinas understands it rules out the
possibility of components of any kind in the essence that is the divine
nature. Even when it has been recognized that all God's intrinsic properties
must be essential to him, it must be acknowledged as well that

(3) whatever can be intrinsically attributed to God must in reality just be
the unity that is his essence.

On Aquinas's view, then, God is his own essence or nature.[17] In medieval
logic, an essence is analyzable into genus and differentia, which separates
one species from another within the genus, but Aquinas argues that God is
not in a genus or a species.[18] For Aquinas, it is impossible that there be any
real distinction between one essential property and another in God or
between God and his nature. Furthermore, for all things other than God,
there is a difference between what they are and that they are, between their
essence and their existence, but on the doctrine of simplicity the essence
which is God is not different from God's existence. Therefore, unlike all
other entities, God is his own being.

In these claims, the counter-intuitive character of absolute simplicity
emerges clearly, as can be seen from the particular problems apparently
stemming from one or another of the denials of distinctions.[19] The problems

that are the focus of this chapter are raised primarily by claims (2) and (3).[20] From those claims it seems to follow, for instance, that God's knowledge is identical with God's power and also with anything that can be considered an intrinsic property of his, such as one of God's actions – his talking to Cain, for instance. Moreover, God's talking to Cain must, it seems, be identical with God's talking to Abraham and, for that matter, with any other divine action, such as God's plaguing Pharaoh's Egypt with a hailstorm. And it is not only the drawing of distinctions among God's attributes or actions that is apparently misleading. God's talking to Cain is evidently not really an action of God's, as Cain's talking is an action of his; rather, it is part of God's essence. Even that formulation is apparently too broad: God's talking to Cain is not part of his essence; it is his essence, and God himself is that essence.

These unreasonable apparent implications of the doctrine of simplicity lead to further embarrassments for the doctrine. If God's talking to Cain is essential to God, it is apparently necessary and thus not something God could refrain from doing. Moreover, since God's talking to Cain begins at some instant, t_1, it is apparently God's-talking-to-Cain-beginning-at-t_1 that is essential and therefore necessary, so that it is not open to God even to initiate the conversation a split second earlier or later. So if in accordance with the doctrine of simplicity, each action of God's is in all its detail identical with the divine essence, the doctrine apparently entails that God could not do anything other or otherwise than he actually does. Indeed, given the doctrine of simplicity, it is not clear that God can talk to Cain at all, even under the severe restrictions just considered. Every temporal action, unless it is coextensive with all of time, begins and/or ends. If it is true that God talks to Cain, then at t_1 God is talking to Cain and sometime after t_1 God is not talking to Cain. But in that case it seems that God has an intrinsic property at one time which he lacks at another time, and no such distinction is possible under the doctrine of simplicity.

Resolving some of the difficulties

Many, but not all, of these counter-intuitive conclusions can be dispelled by clarifying the view of God's nature that gives rise to the doctrine of simplicity and by developing the distinction between intrinsic and extrinsic properties.

In virtue of being absolutely perfect, God has no unactualized potentialities but is entirely actual, or in act. No temporal entity could satisfy that description,[21] and so no temporal entity could be a perfect being. Nevertheless, the atemporal pure actuality that is God can have various manifestations and effects in time.[22] It is in that way that there is a mistake in thinking of God's talking to Cain as one of the things God does in the strict sense in which a temporal agent's action is an intrinsic property of the agent. Rather, the one thing that is God and is atemporally actual has a variety of effects in time: a conversation with Cain at t_1, a conversation with Abraham at t_2, and the production of a hailstorm in Egypt at t_3.

Of course God's talking to Cain is not the same as God's talking to Abraham, but that undoubted distinction does not compromise God's absolute simplicity because those events are to be understood as various temporal effects of the single eternal act, God's action in the strict sense. Everyone recognizes analogous characterizations of ordinary human actions: the man who flips the switch on the wall may be correctly described as doing just that one thing or he may, equally correctly, be said to do many things in doing that one thing (turning on the light, waking the dog, frightening the prowler, etc.) – a case of one action with many correct descriptions or many consequences, of one action in the strict sense and many actions in a broader sense.

But in this ordinary case there are many really distinct facts about that one action – that it results in the turning on of the light, that it results in the waking of the dog, etc. If the conversation with Cain and the hailstorm in Egypt are analogous to these, will there not be many really distinct facts about God's one action and thus, in that special case, about God himself? Yes, but not in a way that compromises simplicity. As a standard characterization of the single divine action we can use Aquinas's formulation: "God wills himself and other things in one act of will."[23] As Aquinas understands it, God's willing himself and other things consists in God's willing at once, in one action, both goodness and the manifestation of goodness;[24] and there is no special difficulty in understanding goodness to be manifested differently to different persons on different occasions (even in the form of different speeches or meteorological displays appropriate to different circumstances) in ways that must be counted among the extrinsic accidental properties of the goodness manifested. On Aquinas's view, the multiplicity of the objects of God's will is no more in tension with his simplicity than the multitude of the objects of his knowledge is.[25]

The absence of real distinctions among divine attributes such as omnipotence and omniscience is to be explained along similar lines. According to the doctrine of simplicity, what human beings call God's omnipotence or God's omniscience is the single eternal entity considered under descriptions they find variously illuminating, or recognized by them under different kinds of effects or manifestations of it. What the doctrine of simplicity requires one to understand about all the designations for the divine attributes is that they are all identical in reference but different in sense, referring in various ways to the one actual entity which is God himself or designating various manifestations of it. So Aquinas says:

> the names said of God are not synonymous. This would be easy to
> see if we were to say that names of this sort are used to separate

[attributes from God] or to designate a relation of cause with respect to creatures, for in this way there would be various meanings (*rationes*) of these names in accordance with various negations or various effects denoted. But since it was said that names of this sort signify the divine substance, although imperfectly, it is also clearly evident that ... they have different meanings.[26]

'Perfect power' and 'perfect knowledge' are thus analogues for 'the morning star' and 'the evening star': non-synonymous expressions calling to mind quite distinct manifestations of one and the same thing referred to. There is as much truth and as much potential misinformation in 'Perfect power is identical with perfect knowledge' as there is in 'The morning star is identical with the evening star'. And 'Perfect power is identical with perfect knowledge' does not entail that power is identical with knowledge any more than the fact that the summit of a mountain's east slope is identical with the summit of its west slope entails the identity of the slopes.[27]

Most of the problems we have so far raised about absolute simplicity are resolved or at least alleviated on the basis of these considerations. The respect in which God is utterly devoid of real distinctions does not, after all, preclude our distinguishing God's actions in the world from one another or from God himself. And insofar as an eternal being can eternally produce various temporal effects, variously timed, nothing in the doctrine of simplicity rules out God's intervention in time.[28] But these difficulties for absolute simplicity are the easy ones. The hardest one to resolve is the apparent incompatibility of God's simplicity and God's free choice. For all I have said so far, the doctrine of simplicity still seems to entail that the only things God can do are the things he does in fact.[29]

The apparent incompatibility of simplicity and free choice

Since no one whose will is bound to just one set of acts of will makes real choices among alternative acts, it looks as if accepting God's absolute simplicity as a datum leads to the conclusion that God has no alternative to doing what he does. If we begin from the other direction, by taking it for granted that God does make choices among alternatives – another central tenet of Christian theology foundational for Aquinas's thought – it seems that God cannot be absolutely simple. For the doctrine of divine free choice can be construed as the claim that some of God's properties are properties he chooses to have – such as his being the person who talks to Cain at t_1. But it makes no sense to suppose that God freely chooses all his properties, so that it is up to him, for example, whether or not the principle of non-contradiction applies to him, or whether he is omnipotent, good, eternal or simple. Considerations of this sort evidently require us to draw a distinction between two groups of characteristics attributed to God: those that are freely chosen and those regarding which God has no choice. And this distinction, it seems, cannot be explained as only a reflection of diversity in the temporal effects brought about by the single eternal activity which is God, or as no more than different manifestations of a single active goodness. Instead, this distinction appears to express a radical diversity within divine agency itself, in that some truths about God – such as that he exists – are not subject to his control, while others – presumably such as that he talks to Cain at t_1 – are consequences of his free choice.[30]

Nor can this distinction be explained away as an instance of referring to one and the same thing under different descriptions in ways suited to human minds, which can acquire only fragmentary conceptions of the absolute unity that is God. As I argued above, there is no inconsistency in the claim that an absolutely simple entity is correctly described as omnipotent regarded in one way and as omniscient regarded in another way. But recourse to the human point of view appears to be unavailable as a basis for explaining the apparent distinction between necessary and freely chosen divine acts of will. Moves in that direction would either present the necessary acts as really indeterminate or deny free choice to God, by suggesting that the appearance of free choice in God is really only a consequence of certain extrinsic accidental properties of his or by presenting the apparently freely chosen acts as not really choices on God's part.[31] So the strategy for defending Aquinas's interpretation of the doctrine of divine simplicity against imputations of inconsistency which I gave above cannot reconcile divine simplicity with divine freedom of choice.

Nonetheless, it is abundantly clear that Aquinas takes God to be possessed of choice or *liberum arbitrium*;[32] he argues for it vigorously in a variety of places. It is also clear that for Aquinas, *liberum arbitrium* is the power for choosing among alternative possibilities. In addition to the standardly cited passage in *ST* Ia.19.10, for example, Aquinas says in *QDV* 24.3, "there remains to God a free judgment [*liberum iudicium*] for willing either this or that, as there is also in us, and for this reason we must say that *liberum arbitrium* is found in God." In particular, Aquinas holds that God was free to create or not to create, that God's creating was not brought about in God by any necessity of nature.[33]

Furthermore, in his argument for God's free will in ST, Aquinas explicitly draws the distinction which raises the worry to which I have called attention here. He says: "Since God wills his own goodness of necessity but other things not of necessity ... with respect to those things which he wills not out of necessity, he has *liberum arbitrium*."[34] Here, then, Aquinas distinguishes between acts of will necessary for God, such as the will for his own goodness, and acts of will not necessary for God, such as the act of will to create. How is this distinction not a real distinction in God?

Two related apparent incompatibilities

The apparent incompatibility of freedom of choice and simplicity in God has some resemblance to two others, which are worth calling attention to in this connection. For the sake of completeness, I will discuss both of them here before returning to the apparent incompatibility of divine simplicity and free choice.

The first has to do with omnipotence and God's moral goodness. There seems to be an inconsistency in the concept of a being that is supposed to be both essentially omnipotent and essentially perfectly good.[35] An acceptable definition of omnipotence is notoriously hard to formulate,[36] but any serious candidate has at its core the idea that an omnipotent person can do anything logically possible. An essentially perfectly good person, however, cannot perform any evil action; such a person is essentially impeccable. Since evil actions are among the logical possibilities, however, there are many things an essentially perfectly good person cannot do which, on the face of it, an omnipotent person must be able to do. And so it seems that no person can be both omnipotent and essentially perfectly good, as God is said to be.

The second associated apparent incompatibility lies within the notion of essential perfect goodness itself. Some important accounts of perfect goodness have emphasized desirability, which surely is to be acknowledged as the passive, esthetic aspect of goodness; but any acceptable notion of perfect goodness must also include its active, moral aspect.[37] The notion of a morally good (or evil) person seems to entail that person's capacity to do both good and evil, however; and, on that classic understanding of moral agency, the idea of a person who is essentially morally good is inconsistent. The classic understanding might be sketched in this way:

> A person P in a world $w1$ is morally good in deciding to perform action x at time t only if there is some possible world $w2$ like $w1$ in all respects up to t, but at t in $w2$ P does not decide to perform action x but decides instead to do a different action that is evil.[38]

But a person who is essentially perfectly good is by definition a person who does only good in every possible world inhabited by that person. So it seems that one requirement for moral goodness (and hence for perfect goodness) is incompatible with one requirement for perfect goodness; and so no person can be essentially perfectly good (as God is said to be).

These two problems are associated with the problem regarding simplicity and choice because in all three of them there is an appearance of incompatibility between certain characteristics of a perfect being and God's free will. If God's will regarding his actions in time is thought to be free to choose evil, it seems God can be neither absolutely simple nor essentially good. On the other hand, if in an attempt to preserve simplicity and essential perfect

102

goodness God is conceived of as incapable of choosing evil, it seems he can be neither omnipotent nor morally good.

Will

In order to deal with these apparent incompatibilities, it is important to be clear about Aquinas's view of free will in God and of the nature of free will in general.[39] For example, one presupposition in the discussion of the apparent incoherence of the notion of essential goodness is that a free will is essentially an independent, neutral capacity for choosing among alternatives, but this is certainly not Aquinas's position. On the contrary, Aquinas takes the will to be a natural inclination towards goodness associated with the agent's understanding of goodness. A clearer view of this part of Aquinas's theory will help us see why on Aquinas's view there is no incompatibility between omnipotence and essential perfect goodness as well as no incoherence in the notion of essential perfect goodness itself. With so much clarification, we can then return to the problem of divine simplicity and God's free choice.

Although Aquinas is convinced that freedom of choice is a characteristic of human wills as well as of God's will, his general account of the nature of will presents it as fundamentally neither independent nor neutral:

> In their own way, all things are inclined by an *appetitus*[40] toward what is good, but variously ... Some things ... are inclined toward what is good along with an awareness of the nature of the good – a condition that is a distinguishing characteristic of an intellect – and these are the things most fully inclined toward what is good. Indeed, they are, so to speak, directed to the good not merely by something else (as are things that lack cognition), or directed only to some good in particular (as are things that have only sense cognition); instead, they are as if inclined toward goodness itself considered universally. And that inclination is called *will*.[41]

General and specific links between the will and goodness are built into this definition. The will is understood by Aquinas not as an equipoised capacity, but rather as falling under the genus of natural inclinations towards what is good. And what distinguishes the will from other species of that genus (such as the instincts to seek food and shelter) is the will's essential association with the intellect rather than merely with sensation (*appetitus rationalis* vs *appetitus sensitivus*). In associating the will with the intellect (as the appetitive and cognitive faculties of the rational soul), Aquinas means to claim, among other things, that the will, naturally inclined towards goodness itself considered universally, inclines the agent towards subsidiary ends which the intellect presents to the will as good. The will understood as naturally inclined towards goodness and as relying to a considerable extent on the intellect is obviously neither neutral nor independent, and such an account of its nature is bound to raise questions about its freedom and its capacity for genuine choice. But, as can be seen in the quoted passage, Aquinas also understands the will to be self-directed, and he expressly argues in various places that human beings do have free will.[42]

His conviction that all these features can be consistently and plausibly ascribed to the will is founded on an analysis of necessity that is incorporated into his theory of the will. In general, on Aquinas's view, what is necessary is what cannot not be. The species of necessity are sorted out on the basis of the four Aristotelian causal principles. Two of those principles – matter and form – are intrinsic to what is necessitated, and necessity of the sort associated with them is exemplified, Aquinas says:

> with respect to an intrinsic *material* principle when we say that it is necessary that everything with contrary components be perishable, or with respect to an intrinsic *formal* principle when we say that it is necessary that a triangle have three angles equal to two right angles.[43]

Necessity of both these sorts Aquinas calls "absolute" (or "natural"). The two *extrinsic* causal principles, on the other hand, are associated with two distinct sorts of necessity. The "necessity of the *end*, sometimes called utility" is exemplified when something is recognized as necessary in that "someone cannot attain, or cannot readily attain, some end without it – as food is necessary for life, and a horse for a journey".[44]

Finally, the necessity associated with *efficient* causation, "the necessity of coercion," occurs "whenever someone is compelled by some agent so that he cannot do the contrary of what he is compelled to do".[45]

On this basis, the obvious questions raised by the directedness and dependency of the will as understood by Aquinas can be answered. Is a will that is naturally directed towards goodness not naturally necessitated and hence unfree? The answer, on Aquinas's view, is that the will's being directed towards goodness, the ultimate end for all things, is naturally necessitated; but that natural necessity, far from threatening freedom, is a precondition of the will's making choices. Aquinas, following Aristotle, takes the will's activity of choice to depend on its inclination towards the ultimate end as the intellect's activity of reasoning depends on its grasp of the first principles.[46] Choice, as distinct from whim or chance, is motivated, and some motives are subsidiary to others, happiness being the supreme motive or highest good for human beings. So the ultimate end, recognized as a precondition of choice, lies outside the scope of choice, the objects of which are means or subsidiary ends leading more or less directly to that necessitated end or, more broadly, things willed for the end.

Still, does the end not necessitate the means? Necessity of the end in its weak, horse-for-journey variety obviously poses no threat to freedom of choice: you can walk rather than ride. Aquinas takes it to be no more threatening in its strong, food-for-life variety, presumably because even when an end such as the continuation of one's life cannot be attained without a specific means such as food, one can choose to reject the end – a presumption that is even more plausible in his other example of this variety: "from the volition to cross the sea comes the necessity in the will of wanting a ship."[47] In the strongest and most clearly relevant variety of necessity of the end, the ultimate end, happiness, is itself absolutely necessary and hence impossible to reject; but the necessity of the end appropriate to human happiness is the weak variety, allowing for choices among more or less (or equally) efficacious means to the unrejectable end.

Even if this summary account of will's involvement with necessity of the sorts associated with matter, form, and end is given the benefit of the doubts it is likely to raise, it answers only questions raised by the natural directedness of will. But what about will's dependence on intellect? Can that not be construed as involving necessity of the sort associated with efficient causation, the one sort of necessitation Aquinas admits is incompatible with freedom of will?

The plainest, most familiar evidence that the intellect, in presenting to the will what it conceives of as good, does not cause the will to will anything is that the intellect sometimes presents what it takes to be equally good alternatives. A more theory-laden but no less effective sort of evidence is available in a closer look at Aquinas's conception of the relationship between intellect and will. When the intellect presents what it takes to be good, without alternatives, the intellect does indeed move the will, but only as an end moves an agent, "because what is conceived of as good is an object of the will and moves it as an end".[48] The only necessity emanating from the intellect, then, is the necessity of the end, and we have already seen that such necessity does not preclude freedom. Even more important is the fact that the will also moves the intellect, and that this moving is carried out "in the way an agent moves something",[49] the will compelling the intellect to attend to some things and to ignore others. So if there is efficient causation anywhere in the relationship between the intellect and the will, on Aquinas's view it occurs only in the will's action on the intellect – a consideration that enhances rather than threatens the will's freedom. What the intellect comes to consider good is thus to some extent under the influence of the will, an influence that is especially powerful because almost everything that is an option for the will can be considered under different descriptions and can consequently be presented as good or as bad depending on which features of it are being attended to and which are being ignored.

On this basis, we can then sketch as much of Aquinas's account of free will and its relation to moral goodness and evil as is necessary for the discussion here. For various reasons ranging from ignorance to the complex interaction of will and intellect we have just summarized, the intellect can mistakenly present a bad thing as good or a good thing as better than it is; and in consequence of the intellect's mistaken presentation, the will, a self-directed rational wanting of the good, turns to evil. But nothing in Aquinas's theory of free will requires a free will to be able to choose evil over good. The principle much defended by some contemporary philosophers that a person acts with free will and moral responsibility only in case he could have done otherwise than he did is therefore not a principle Aquinas espouses.[50] Evil does get chosen, of course, but only because it has been presented as good in some respect. And so the possibility of moral evil in the will stems from a defect in the agent whose will it is: the agent's intellect must be mistaken in its evaluation of the options open to the will either because of some defect just in the intellect or because the intellect has been brought into such a defective condition by a will which is already morally defective.

God's will and moral evil

Since in virtue of being essentially omniscient God's intellect cannot be ignorant of anything, it cannot present a mistaken assessment of goodness. Every human will is so constituted as to have happiness as its specific natural end, regardless of its intellect's level of understanding of that goal. God's will, on the other hand, has its natural end, the universal ultimate end, simply in virtue of God's perfect understanding of the nature of goodness. Since God is omniscient, he knows himself perfectly; and, in accord with the doctrine of simplicity, he is his goodness, which is perfect goodness itself. Therefore, what God's intellect infallibly discerns as perfect goodness is God himself. And so God's will, which necessarily wills what God's intellect understands to be absolutely good and presents as such to the will, necessarily wills the divine nature. So Aquinas says: "God necessarily wills his own goodness, and he cannot will the contrary."[51]

Although God's willing perfect goodness is necessary, as is a human being's willing happiness, the differences between the divine and human wills in this respect are more significant than that similarity. The essential inclination of the human will towards happiness is part of the constitution of human beings, which they are caused to have. But God's willing of the ultimate end is self-directed in the way just described; and it also has no external cause, having its sole source in God himself. And so for Aquinas it counts as free will although it does not involve choice. Aquinas says, "in respect of its principal object, which is its own goodness, the divine will does have necessity – not, of course, the necessity of coercion, but the necessity of natural order, which is not incompatible with freedom".[52]

This necessity of natural order is the necessity of a perfect will's willing what a perfect intellect presents to it as perfectly good. It is a necessity compatible with freedom because the necessity of the willing stems only from the impossibility of any obstacle to the will's performing its self-directed function or of any defect in the functioning of either the intellect or the will. So when God's acts of will have himself as their object, they are necessary, and yet their necessity is the necessity associated with a final cause when that final cause is clearly and fully understood as such. Necessity of that sort is not incompatible with the will's freedom.

Aquinas's theory of the nature of will in general and of God's will in particular is thus enough both to resolve the apparent incompatibility of omnipotence and impeccability and to allay worries about the compatibility of the freedom of the divine will and conditionally necessitated moral divine acts such as God's keeping his promise to Abraham. God's keeping his promise to Abraham is conditionally necessitated because once the promise has been made (the condition without which there is no necessitation), God cannot fail to keep it since promise-breaking is wrong (except in circumstances inapplicable to an omniscient, omnipotent being), and it is impossible for an essentially perfectly good person to do anything wrong. This sort of conditional necessitation is, however, compatible with the freedom of the divine will in just the same way and for just the same reason as the absolute necessity of God's willing himself is not an infringement of God's freedom of choice. The necessity in each case is the necessity of the end. Since the will is by its nature a self-directed wanting of the good, which is its final cause, when the goodness of some object (such as God's nature, or the keeping of a promise) is not overridden by other considerations, and when the intellect clearly and completely recognizes it as such (as an omniscient intellect cannot fail to do), then the will necessarily wants that object, not because the will is compelled by anything outside itself to will the object, but because there is no defect or obstacle impeding the will from exercising its self-directed function. In this way, God's keeping his promise to Abraham is both freely willed and necessitated by its goodness, which is the final, not the efficient, cause of that divine act. And analogous considerations will apply to any act which is said to be impossible for God to will because it would be evil for him to do so. Consequently, the paradox of essential goodness is resolved on the basis of Aquinas's theory of will: there is no absurdity in postulating a perfectly good moral agent for whom doing evil is impossible.

Furthermore, so far from being incompatible with impeccability, omnipotence in fact entails impeccability on Aquinas's theory of will: if the will and its intellect are not defective — that is, if a being is perfect in power with respect to its will and intellect — it follows that that being is impeccable, since only a being defective in intellect or will ever wills evil.

The remaining problem

The apparent incompatibility between divine free choice and absolute simplicity is still left unresolved, however, because it is only God's nature (the perfect goodness which he is) and conditionally necessitated acts of will (such as keeping his promise) that God is said to will in such a way that he cannot will the contrary, either absolutely or conditionally. His willing of other things is said to be characterized not merely by the absence of any coercion but also by the possibility of alternative divine acts. According to Aquinas, the reason for this difference is that "the ultimate end is God himself, since he is the highest good";[53] and

> since God wills himself as the end but other things as things that are for the end, it follows that in respect of himself he has only volition, but in respect of other things he has selection [among alternatives] (*electio*).[54]

Of course, this passage must not be read as claiming that God wills his own goodness as the end and everything else he wills as *means* to that end, with the implication that perfect goodness (or God himself) is in the process of becoming fully actualized or is in need of things other than itself for its perfection. Aquinas's point is that God's goodness is the final cause for the sake of which he wills other things. So, for example, God wills that a certain sort of animal be rational in order to make a human being, he wills to make a human being in order to complete his making of the universe, and he wills to make the universe because it is good – that is, for the sake of goodness, which he is and which is the end, the final cause, of all his actions.[55] But that end can be served in various ways, and therein lie the alternatives available for divine *electio* or selection. God might have chosen to create a different universe, provided it was good and created because it was good, e.g., a universe with different physical laws, different elements, different forms of life. And there is reason to suppose that a more fundamental sort of alternative is also open to him. Since goodness, the end served by his actions, is present and perfect even if nothing else exists, because God himself is perfect goodness, it is open to God not to create at all.

So far, then, it looks as if the acts of God's will can be classified into three sorts: first, the one absolutely necessary act of willing himself; second, acts conditionally necessitated either logically or morally by some logically antecedent divine act; and, third, acts that are selected by God from among alternatives available to God. But this analysis of God's acts of will does seem incompatible with God's simplicity. If we can distinguish between necessitated divine acts and divine acts such that it is possible for God to have done otherwise, in what sense is there no distinction within God? It seems, on the face of it, that this analysis attributes contingency to some of God's acts. And if some divine acts are contingent, then it seems that God does have intrinsic accidental properties, properties such that God could exist and have properties other than these, contrary to the explicit claims of the doctrine of divine simplicity, as Aquinas expounds and defends it.

Furthermore, if God has intrinsic accidental properties, then it also looks as if the distinctions Aquinas is concerned to deny in God in fact must characterize God on Aquinas's position. For example, there will be a difference between essence and accident in God. In addition, there will be a distinction between God and his nature. In virtue of God's having accidental properties, it will be possible to distinguish between God, in whom these accidental properties inhere, and the nature of God, which is only essence and not a compound of essence and accident. Two of the three central claims of the doctrine of divine simplicity as Aquinas understands it thus still seem falsified by Aquinas's account of free choice in God.

Before trying to make progress on this problem, we will find it helpful to replace the previous, serviceable paradigms of God's free choice with a more fundamental one. There are two reasons why talking to Cain or to Abraham and subjecting Egypt to a hailstorm are not the sort of actions best suited to provide paradigms of divine free choice or most threatening to divine simplicity. In the first place, the clearest instances of God's free choice are cases of choosing between equally good contrary alternatives, and it is far from clear that *not* counseling Cain, *not* promising Abraham a glorious progeny, or *not* punishing a recalcitrant Pharaoh are alternatives as good as those God chooses. In the second place, as we have seen, all such actions in the world might seem at least *prima facie* explicable as extrinsic accidental characteristics of the unique divine action, various manifestations of the eternal diffusion of divine goodness. But there is an act of the divine will that seems (a) distinguishable from God's willing of himself; (b) representable as a choice between equally good alternatives; and (c) not even *prima facie* explicable as no more than an extrinsic accidental characteristic of God's willing of himself – and that is God's freely choosing to create. So for the remainder of this discussion, God's act of creation will serve as the paradigm of God's free choice.

God's accidental properties

It is imperative in this connection to look more closely at Aquinas's understanding of the nature of accidental properties.[56]

The first thing to notice here is that although Aquinas denies that there are any accidental properties in God,[57] he also claims that it is possible for God to do things he does not do (*possit facere quae non facit*). So, for example, in a passage that deserves quoting at length, Aquinas says:

> Some have supposed that God acts as it were from the necessity of nature, ... in such a way that from the divine operation there can

result neither other things nor another order of things, except what is now. But we have shown ... that God does not act as it were from the necessity of nature but that his will is the cause of all things and also that his will is not naturally or of necessity determined to these things. And so in no way is it the case that this course of things comes from God of necessity in such a way that other things could not come [instead].

Others, however, have said that the divine power is determined to this course of things because of the order of divine wisdom and justice, without which God does nothing. But since the power of God, which is his essence, is nothing other than the wisdom of God, it can appropriately be said that there is nothing in the power of God which is not in the order of the divine wisdom, for the divine wisdom embraces the whole potency of [divine] power. And yet the order introduced in things by the divine wisdom, in which the formula of justice consists, ... does not exhaust (*non adaequat*) the divine wisdom, so that the divine wisdom is limited to this order ... And so we must say unconditionally that God is able to do things other than those he does.[58]

Elsewhere he says, "although God does not will to do other than he does, he can will other things; and so, speaking unconditionally (*absolute*), he can do other things [than he does]".[59] Aquinas emphasizes this point in speaking of God's *liberum arbitrium* or free choice. God creates freely, on Aquinas's view, and the freedom at issue in God's willing of creation, unlike God's willing of his own goodness, does involve alternative possibilities. Aquinas says:

the divine will is related to opposites, not in such a way that he wills something and afterwards wills it not [to be], which would be incompatible with his immutability, and not that he is able to will good and evil, because [this] would suppose defect in God, but because he is able to will or not to will *this*.[60]

So, on Aquinas's view, in this world God wills, for example, to create, but it is not necessary that God create; it is possible that God not create.[61] There is therefore another possible world in which God exists and does not will to create.

Thomists have typically supposed that Aquinas's claim that God has no accidents is consistent with his claim that God could do other than he does. For example, Reginald Garrigou-Lagrange says: "God's free act of creation, although it would be possible for Him not to act, is not an accident."[62]

And later he says:

God is absolutely immutable, although it was in His power not to choose that which He freely choose from eternity. For this free choice is not even in the least degree a superadded accident in God, and it posits no new perfection in Him.[63]

But how are these positions to be reconciled? If God can do other than he does, then it is possible for God to exist as God and yet will differently from the way he actually does will. In that case, however, on our current way of thinking about modality, the way God actually wills is not necessary to him. Hence, that God wills in the way he does is a contingent fact about God and God's willing in this way is an accident of his. And yet Aquinas holds not only that God has no accidents but even that God is his own nature; and so, since the nature of God is invariable, it seems that God must be the same in all possible worlds in which he exists.

In my view, it is unreasonable to suppose that Aquinas is guilty of a large, explicit, obvious, and uncomplicated contradiction. A more reasonable explanation of this apparent conflict in his views is therefore that Aquinas's denial of accidents in God and his insistence on God's being his own nature do not mean what current notions of modality would take them to mean.

The standardly accepted medieval description of an accident gives some support to this hypothesis. According to Peter of Spain, who is handing on a well-established position, an accident is what can come to a subject and be absent from a subject without the corruption of that subject; but he sees it as a problem for this view, one requiring discussion to resolve, that there are accidents which are always found in their subjects. Although being black is an accident of crows, crows (in the actual world) are always black.[64] That this example is thought to be even a *prima facie* obstacle for the standard description of an accident strongly suggests that an accident is not being thought of simply as a property a thing has in some but not all of the possible worlds in which it exists.[65] Furthermore, corruption occurs when something that has existence ceases to exist, and so the fact that the description of an accident is framed in terms of corruption gives some added support to this hypothesis; what is at issue in Peter of Spain's description of an accident is change over time, not change across possible worlds. Finally, Aquinas himself sometimes cites this standard description of an accident, but he uses it in an argument that God can have no accidents because God cannot change over time.[66]

When Aquinas himself describes an accident, he does not categorize it as a property a thing does not have at a time but could have had at that time (or has at that time but could have not had at that time), or in any other way that suggests he is thinking of accidents in terms of synchronous possibilities across different possible worlds. Instead, he characterizes an accident entirely differently, namely, as something that has being but in an incomplete sort of way.[67] So, for example, he says:

because essence is what is signified by a definition, it must be the case that [accidents] have essence in the same way in which they have a definition. But they have an incomplete definition, because they cannot be defined unless a subject is put in their definition. And the reason for this is that they do not have being *per se*, devoid of a subject. Instead, as substantial being results from form and matter when they come together in composition, so accidental being results from a subject and an accident when an accident comes to a subject ... That to which an accident comes is a being complete in itself, subsisting in its own being, which naturally precedes the accident which comes to it. And so the conjunction of the accident coming [to a subject] with that to which the accident comes does not cause that being in which a thing subsists, by means of which a thing is a being *per se*, but it causes a certain kind of secondary being, without which a subsistent thing can be understood to be ... And so from an accident and a subject is not produced something that is one *per se* but only [something that is] one *per accidens*.[68]

It is clear from this passage that Aquinas assumes the description of an accident given by Peter of Spain, as something that can come to or be absent from a subject without the corruption of that subject. And as he himself goes on to describe an accident, he focuses on the metaphysically secondary or deficient character of an accident. He does *not* characterize an accident as any property a thing has in some but not all of the possible worlds in which it exists, so that every feature a thing fails to have in all the worlds in which it exists has to count as an accident.

But does it not seem as if Aquinas *should* have defined an accident in just this way? Of the ten Aristotelian categories, all nine other than substance count as accidents; and the category of substance is the category including individuals and their essences. So anything non-essential to a particular thing is in fact an accident. And since the essence of a thing is the same in every possible world in which it exists, any feature a thing has in some but not all the possible worlds in which it exists will apparently have to be an accident, even on Aquinas's metaphysics. It seems, then, that on Aquinas's own views an accident must be any feature of a thing which that thing could have but does not have to have – that is, any feature which a thing has in some but not all the possible worlds in which it exists.

If this were Aquinas's position, however, then he could hardly maintain that God has no accidents but that God could do other than he does.

In the passage cited above, Aquinas's account of accidents emphasizes the metaphysical incompleteness of accidents, and it may be that this emphasis points us in the right direction for understanding his position about God's accidents. On Aquinas's view, an accident is what has only incomplete being. It does not have subsistent being or being *per se*, and its addition to something produces only an accidental unity, like the unity of a heap of stones, for example, and not the unity that is produced by the conjunction of matter and substantial form, which produces a substance. An ordinary created thing can be other than it is just in those parts of it that are metaphysically insubstantial, so to speak. A created thing is metaphysically limited enough that only some of its metaphysical parts, its invariant or necessary metaphysical parts, have complete being; and so its variant features, those it has in some but not all the possible parts in which it exists, have the sort of incomplete being Aquinas attributes to accidents. That is why, for created things categorized by means of the Aristotelian categories, it is true that any feature a thing has in some but not all the possible worlds in which it exists will be an accident. God, on the other hand, is metaphysically perfect and unlimited. And so, in the case of God, Aquinas seems to be thinking, even what is variable about him across possible worlds, as distinct from across time, has complete being.

If this is right, then this is the sense in which we should understand that God has no accidents – not that God is exactly the same in all possible worlds in which he exists but that there is nothing at all incomplete or insubstantial about God in any respect, even though God is not the same in all possible worlds.

These remarks about Aquinas's understanding of the modal terms at issue in the doctrine of simplicity are only allusive and suggestive, not precise or analytically explanatory. But that they are roughly on the right track is further confirmed by the way Aquinas argues to the conclusion that God has no accidents. So, for example, as a quick and supposedly decisive argument in the *sed contra* of the relevant question in *QDP*, Aquinas says this:

> every accident is dependent on something else (*habet dependentiam ab alio*). But there can be nothing of this sort in God, because anything that depends on something else must be caused, but God is the first cause [and] in no way caused [himself].[69]

If by denying accidents of God, Aquinas were trying to argue, in effect, that God is the same in all possible worlds, then it is not at all clear that God's non-dependence would count as an acceptable argument for it, in Aquinas's own view since, as we have seen, Aquinas argues in various places that (non-dependent) God can do other than he does.

There is additional confirmation for this way of understanding Aquinas in the reply Aquinas himself makes to a putative objector who raises the very sort of worry which has been at issue here. The objector says:

> What is not necessary to be is equivalent to what is possible not to be. Therefore, if it is not necessary that God will something of the

things that he wills, it is possible that he not will this, and it is [also] possible that he will that which he does not will. And so the divine will is contingent with respect to either of these. And in this way it is [also] imperfect, because everything contingent is imperfect and mutable.[70]

In his reply, Aquinas does not deny that God can will other than he does; he denies only that God's ability to will otherwise entails that there is anything in God which is imperfect or changeable over time. He says:

sometimes a necessary cause has a non-necessary relation to an effect, and this is because of a defect in the effect, and not because of a defect in the cause ... That God does not will of necessity something of the things he wills happens not on account of a defect in the divine will but on account of a defect which belongs to what is willed in accordance with its formula (*ratio*), namely, because it is such that the perfect goodness of God can be without it. And this is a defect which accompanies every created good.[71]

Aquinas also says things which strongly suggest that angels are like God in being their own nature. And yet, for Aquinas, angels are capable even of change over time.[72] An angel moves from one place to another; it gains in knowledge over time, as what was future becomes present and is made known to the angel; it learns mysteries of grace as God chooses to reveal them; and so on. Nonetheless, Aquinas says of the angels:

nothing extraneous can be adjoined to any nature or essence of form, even if that which has the nature or form or essence can have something extraneous in itself, for humanity receives in itself nothing which is not part of the formula of humanity. This is clear from the fact that in definitions which signify the essence of things, anything added or subtracted changes the species ... In any creature at all, there is found a difference between what is had and [the creature] which has it. Now in composite creatures, there are two differences, because the very supposit or individual has the nature of the species (as a human being has humanity) and it has being besides, for a human being is not either his humanity or his being. For this reason, there can be some accident in a human being, but not in his humanity or in his being. But in simple substances there can be only one difference, namely, between essence and being. For in [the case of] angels, every supposit is its own nature ... And so in substances of this sort it is possible to find some intelligible accident, but not a material accident. But in God there is no difference between what is had and the one having it ... Rather, he himself is both his own nature and his own being. And for this reason nothing foreign or accidental can inhere in him.[73]

So whatever it is for a thing to be its own nature is compatible, on Aquinas's view, even with change in that thing over time and also across possible worlds.

I am glad to say that it is beyond the scope of this chapter to give with any depth or precision a positive account of Aquinas's understanding of the notion of having an accident or being one's nature, but the considerable evidence amassed here is enough to show clearly that Aquinas does not understand these notions as they would be understood in contemporary philosophy. In particular, he does not take any property anything has in some but not all possible worlds in which it exists as an accident of that thing; and, on his view, a thing can be its own nature without that thing's having only properties necessary to it. However exactly Aquinas does understand the notions of having an accident and being one's own nature, it is clear, then, that for him the denial that God has accidents does not entail that God is the same in all possible worlds in which he exists, and the claim that God is his own nature does not entail that God is necessarily whatever he is.

God's responsiveness

Incomplete as this exposition of Aquinas's position is, it is sufficient to undermine one widely discussed attack on Aquinas having to do with the responsiveness of a simple God.

In other parts of his work, when the doctrine of simplicity is not at issue, it is clear that Aquinas thinks God is responsive to creatures. Aquinas maintains, for example, that God answers human prayers. He cites with approval Augustine's claim that if God did not hear prayers, then the publican in the Gospel would have prayed in vain for mercy.[74] But, of course, if what God does once the publican prays is exactly the same as what God would have done in case the publican had not prayed this petitionary prayer, then there is no point to the publican's prayer; the world with the publican's petition is the same as it would have been without the petition (excepting, of course, the petition itself). And in that case, the publican's prayer would have been in vain. Since Aquinas's approval of Augustine's line clearly implies that the publican's prayer is not in vain, it is reasonable to conclude that, on Aquinas's view, God does something (e.g., giving the publican mercy) in response to something that the publican does (namely, asking for mercy).

But because on the doctrine of divine simplicity God is pure actuality, without any potentiality, and because the claims of simplicity include the claims that God is his nature and has no accidents, some interpreters of Aquinas's account argue that, whatever Aquinas himself may have supposed, the Thomistic God cannot be responsive to anything in creation. In maintaining, for example, that a simple God answers prayers, Aquinas is just being inconsistent, on this objection.

An argument of this sort has been common with process theorists. So, for instance, a representative process theorist, David Ray Griffin, argues against the possibility of a God who is both simple and responsive by highlighting the claim that God is pure actuality. Griffin says, "*actus purus* is equatable with impassibility, for it implies that God does not have passive power, the power of being acted upon".[75]

Griffin's idea seems to be this. In order to be responsive, God would have to do something that he otherwise would not do, and he would have to do it because of something that a creature does. But if God is pure actuality, then it seems that God could not do anything because of what a creature does, because responsiveness of this sort requires potentiality. That is, for God to be responsive in this way, what God does would have to depend at least in part on what creatures do; but if God has no potentiality, then it seems that nothing about God can depend on anything about creatures. The facts about God, one might say, are set, and nothing that creatures do can alter those facts.

Since facts about what God knows are among these unalterable divine facts, it seems that there can be no mutability in creation either. Thus, Griffin goes on to say:

> if event x failed to occur ... and if something else instead of x occurred, ... this would violate the divine immutability, impassibility, and nontemporality. Worse yet, since the knowledge and the essence of God are identical, God's essence would be changed – God would no longer be God, or at least not the same God.[76]

On Griffin's view, then, "The chief question to raise is whether Aquinas can self-consistently assert the reality of contingent events, given his doctrine of God",[77] and the answer Griffin gives is decidedly in the negative.

But this line of attack on Aquinas is confused in more than one respect, as the preceding examination of Aquinas's thought should make clear. It is true that a simple God cannot change over time; but, as I have been at pains to show, in Aquinas's view, nothing about this claim entails that God could not do other than he does or that God is the same in all possible worlds. Consequently, the doctrine of simplicity, as Aquinas understands it, does not rule out contingency even in God, in our sense of 'contingency' which involves differences across possible worlds, rather than change over time.

This conclusion is enough to show that God can be responsive, because responsiveness does not require change over time. In order to be responsive to creatures, God has to do something he does *because of* what a creature does; but he does not have to change something that he had been planning to do *before* the creaturely action in question. He does not even have to do what he does *after* something a creature does.[78] In order for God to be responsive, it needs to be true only that if the creature had done otherwise, God might have done otherwise as well. That is, among the worlds similar in the relevant respects to this one but in which the publican exists and yet does not ask for mercy, there has to be at least one in which God does not grant the publican mercy and in which God's motive for failing to give mercy includes the publican's failing to ask for it.[79] On Aquinas's account of divine simplicity, however, it is possible even for a simple God to fulfill this condition for responsiveness in virtue of the fact, as Aquinas sees it, that God could do other than he does. Simplicity thus does not rule out divine responsiveness.

The same point resolves other, similar worries often raised in this connection.[80] It is true, on Aquinas's interpretation of the doctrine of divine simplicity, that God's knowledge, for example, is immutable, but only in the sense that it cannot change over time,[81] not in the sense that it is the same in all possible worlds. If things in the world had been different, then God's knowledge would also have been different; in a different possible world, God would have known something different from what he knows in this world. For the same reason, nothing in God's knowledge or will prohibits there being change across possible worlds in creatures, so that divine simplicity is compatible with creatures having the ability to do other than they do, with contingency (in our sense of the term) in the created world. So, for example, on Aquinas's views, in this world, God knows and wills to permit Adam's fall, and neither God's will nor his intellect can change over time. But if Adam had willed otherwise than he did, then, since, according to Aquinas, God could do other than God does, God would have known something and willed something other than he did. Similarly, in the actual world, God wills to create with a will that cannot change over time, and he knows with a similarly unchangeable knowledge that he wills to create. But in a possible world without creatures, God does not will to create, and he knows that he does not will to create; and in that world, neither his intellect nor his will can change over time either. Divine simplicity is even compatible with there being in creatures change over time. God can know with unchangeable knowledge in the eternal present that a creature will have property A but not property B at t_1 and property B but not property A at t_2.[82]

The doctrine of simplicity thus does not preclude contingency in the created world. As Aquinas puts it:

> God wills everything that is required for a thing that he wills, as was said. But some things have a nature in accordance with which they have to be contingent, not necessary, and for that reason God wills some things to be contingent. The efficient causality of the

divine will requires not only that what God wills to exist exists, but also that it exists in the mode God wills it to exist in ... And so the efficient causality of the divine will does not preclude contingency.[83]

In the same place, Aquinas provides another way of supporting this conclusion, one that is worth adding here:

Conditional necessity in a cause cannot result in absolute necessity in the effect. But God wills something with regard to creatures not with absolute necessity but only with the necessity that comes from a condition ... Therefore, absolute necessity in created things cannot result from the divine will; but it is only absolute necessity that rules out contingency.[84]

As Aquinas sees it, then, one of the reasons why God's absolute simplicity does not entail the absence of contingency in the world created by him is just that part of what God wills with conditional necessity is that there be contingency in what he creates. As Aquinas himself explains this point, God wills to create things with components that guarantee their contingency.[85] His example involves the nature of matter, but a better example might be the free will of human beings, where free will is understood in an incompatibilist sense. By willing to create an entity with such free will, God would bring it about that there is contingency in creation.[86] In any event, then, by one means or another it seems open to a simple God to specify not just the things whose existence he brings about but also the manner in which they exist, including the mode of their existence.

God always determining and never determined

Divine simplicity has been used as the basis of one other argument to the conclusion that God cannot be responsive. That argument, surprisingly enough, has been put forward with vehemence not by attackers of Aquinas such as process theorists but rather by defenders of Aquinas, who see the conclusion of the argument as a good and important feature of Aquinas's thought. It is worth looking at this argument with some care.[87]

A representative version of the argument can be found in the work of Garrigou-Lagrange. In discussing and rejecting a Molinist interpretation of Aquinas's views of grace and free will, Garrigou-Lagrange says:

God is either *determining* or *determined*, there is no other alternative ... The knowledge of God is the CAUSE *of our free determinations*, or else it is CAUSED *by them* ... *The knowledge of God either measures things or is measured by them*. Only anthropomorphism can admit the second term of the dilemma and therefore, from sheer necessity, we must keep to the first.[88]

The argument for this conclusion is based on simplicity. Garrigou-Lagrange says:

> one of the fundamental reasons ... why every Thomist will always reject the Molinist theory [which is willing to accept "the second term of the dilemma"], is that this [Molinist] theory of necessity causes one to posit a *passivity in the pure Act*. If the divine causality is not *predetermining* with regard to our *choice*, ... the divine knowledge is fatally *determined* by it. To wish to limit the universal causality and absolute independence of God, necessarily brings one to place a passivity in Him, a passivity in the *self-subsisting Being*, in the *self-subsisting Intellect*. If, in fact, the divine motion does not infallibly assure the execution of a divine intrinsically efficacious and predetermining decree, it follows, as Molina and his disciples maintain that, *of two men equally tempted and EQUALLY HELPED by God*, it happens that one consents to co-operate with the grace and the other does not. And then the *difference*, which distinguishes the good from the bad consent and this man from that other, does not come from God, but *solely from man's free will* ... It becomes consequently quite clear for one who speaks seriously and does not wish to trifle with words, that *the foreknowledge is passive* when one positively asserts that this *difference* does not at all come from God; just as I am a *passive* spectator *when I see* that this man, independently of me, is seated, whereas that other is standing ... A new passivity has entered into the pure Act, who henceforth is no more like to God than is the false diamond like the true ... [It] is only *afterwards that God*, although He is Being itself, Intelligence itself, Goodness itself, saw and willed it determinately. There is a twofold passivity in pure Act.[89]

Garrigou-Lagrange thus postulates a dilemma: for everything, either God determines it or he is determined by it, where determination for Garrigou-Lagrange either is or is equivalent to causation, as the preceding texts make clear. And he argues for the first horn of the dilemma on the grounds that the second presupposes passivity, which cannot be in a God who is pure actuality. Garrigou-Lagrange goes so far as to apply this argument to God's knowledge. If God knows something because it exists or is the case, then there is passivity in "Intelligence itself". By the same token, if God wills something because of something creatures do, there is yet another sort of passivity in God, namely, in God's will. Therefore, since God cannot be passive, God cannot do anything in response to what creatures do. He can, presumably, do something because of something else he does; he can will that Hannah conceive because he wills that Hannah pray for a child. But, on Garrigou-Lagrange's position, God cannot will Hannah's conception because of Hannah's prayer; and he cannot know Hannah's prayer because Hannah makes it. If he did, God would know and will what he does because of something that a creature does. In that case, according to Garrigou-Lagrange, God would be determined, instead of determining, and there would be passivity in God, as there cannot be on the doctrine of simplicity.

The first thing to see about this argument of Garrigou-Lagrange's is that the dilemma with which the argument begins – God is either determining or determined – is a false one. A human intellect knows, for example, that an animal is a corporeal substance. Now clearly, for Aquinas, the human intellect does not cause it to be the case that an animal is a corporeal substance; so a human being is not determining in this case. But the human knower is not determined either. That is because, on Aquinas's views, the human intellect is not passive but active in the process of cognition. The human intellect operates on phantasms with causal efficacy to extract intelligible species, in the first operation of the intellect, on which all the other operations of the intellect depend; but neither the sensible species from which the phantasms derive nor the phantasms themselves act on the intellect with causal efficacy.[90] So the human intellect neither causes what it knows nor is caused by it.

Furthermore, even Garrigou-Lagrange must admit that at least sometimes exactly the same thing has to be said about God's intellect. So consider, for example, God's knowledge that he exists. Plainly, in this case, God's knowledge does not cause what God knows.[91] On the other hand, however, God's intellect is also active, just as the human intellect is; and so God's intellect is not caused to know God's existence by that existence. The divine intellect knows the divine existence *because* God exists; but nothing in this claim entails that the mode of cognition by which the divine intellect has this knowledge includes the causal action of anything on the divine intellect. So, for God as for human knowers, *tertium datur*, it is possible that God's knowledge neither cause nor is caused by what it knows.

But, even supposing that we are not constrained by Garrigou-Lagrange's dilemma, what about his apparently powerful claim that if God knows *afterwards* what is the case in virtue of knowing it because it is the case, then there is passivity in God's intellect?

Here, it must be said, we can dismiss as a red herring the notion that God's knowledge would have to be *after* the object of God's knowledge if God knows what he knows *because* it is the case. Since the doctrine of simplicity entails that God is outside time, there is no before and after in the life of God. God therefore must be simultaneous with the object of his knowledge.[92] But the relation of simultaneity between knower and known is sufficient for the knower's knowing what he knows *because* what he knows is the case. Your knowing that you are in pain is simultaneous with your being in pain; nonetheless, you know that you are in pain *because* you are in pain.

But we can reformulate Garrigou-Lagrange's claim without the specification that God's responsiveness would introduce succession into God's life. So suppose we focus just on the heart of his claim, namely, that if God's intellect or will are in some state because of some state in creatures, then there is passivity in God's intellect or will. Here, of course, it is important to be clear about what Aquinas takes passivity to be. In a representative explanation of passivity in the course of a discussion of God's power, Aquinas says, "Passive power is the principle of being acted on by another (*principium patiendi ab alio*)";[93] and a little later he says, "a thing is passive (*patitur*) to the extent to which it is in potentiality".[94]

As I have been at pains to show, Aquinas himself thinks that a God who is pure act can nonetheless do other than he does, and the ability to do other than one does is sufficient for responsiveness. Therefore, God does not need to change over time in order to be responsive. So we can put to one side the concern that there has to be potentiality in a responsive God. But does there have to be passivity even without potentiality? According to the first passage I cited just above, something is passive in case it is acted upon by another. If God wills what he wills or knows what he knows because of something a creature does, must we then conclude that there is passivity in God in this sense?

Now it is clear that even a human being can will to do something because of what someone or something else does, without being acted upon by that other person or thing. So, for example, the director of a new educational center might will to name it after Thomas More because of the things More said and did, but More is not acting on the director when the director wills to name the center after More. More is dead.[95] Furthermore, for the reasons I gave just above, even a human intellect is not acted upon when it knows something because that something is the case. On Aquinas's view of the way in which the intellect even of a human being functions, the intellect is always active when it knows. The intellect acts on the phantasms to abstract the intelligible species; the phantasms do not act on the intellect. So a human being can will or know something because of what something or someone else does without being acted upon. But then, in Aquinas's understanding of passivity as being acted upon, neither a human will nor a human intellect is passive in virtue of acting responsively.

A fortiori, neither God's will nor God's intellect is acted upon when God wills or knows something because of what creatures do. But consider Hannah who prayed for a child.[96] God's will is not efficiently caused to be in the state it is in when God freely wills to cause conception in Hannah because of Hannah's prayer for a child. God can therefore will what he does because of Hannah's prayer without its being the case that his will is acted upon by something outside himself. The will of a responsive God therefore need not be passive. Similarly, God's intellect is not passive when God knows what he does because what he knows is the case, since his intellect is active in the process of cognition, as I explained above.

So, for these reasons, while Aquinas's interpretation requires that there be no passivity in God, on Aquinas's views the claim that there is no passivity in God does not entail that God cannot be responsive.

I have to add here that the religiously powerful passages in Aquinas's poetry and biblical commentaries (and there are very many of them) would be unintelligible, in my view, if Aquinas really supposed that God is utterly unresponsive to creatures. So, for example, in his commentary on Philippians, Aquinas says: "When [Paul] says 'the Lord is near', he points out the cause of joy, because a person rejoices at the nearness of his friend."[97]

But it is difficult to see how a human being could have a relationship of friendship to someone who was entirely unresponsive to him or how the relationship a human being had to such an unresponsive person could cause joy.[98] On the contrary, the process theorists seem to me right in this one regard: there is something religiously pernicious about the notion of an entirely unresponsive God. Anthropomorphism is correctly repudiated for reshaping a transcendent God to human form, but what is worthy of Garrigou-Lagrange's vituperation is only the order of the relationship of likeness between God and human beings on anthropomorphic views. Destroy enough of the likeness between God and human beings, as Garrigou-Lagrange's position does, and what is left of the line, central also to Aquinas's thought, that God made human beings in his own image? It is therefore only a good thing that Aquinas's interpretation of the doctrine of divine simplicity does not have the implications Garrigou-Lagrange argues that it does.

Conditional necessity

Nonetheless, a problem seems to remain. Even if we grant Aquinas more than many interpreters at this stage will be ready to concede, namely, that Aquinas's claim that God can do other than he does can be reconciled with his claims that God has no accidents and is his own nature, there is still some question whether Aquinas is entitled to hold, as he does, that all composition in God is ruled out. On the face of it, it seems that some composition must remain. That is because we can make a distinction – an apparently *real* distinction among intrinsic characteristics of God – between those divine acts of will that are the same in all possible worlds and those that vary across possible worlds. If we can make such a distinction, if God can be responsive in virtue of not being the same in all possible worlds, then it seems that he cannot be simple. So perhaps there is something more to be said for Griffin's complaint that Aquinas's doctrine of divine simplicity leaves no room for contingency (in our sense of the term), at least within God's acts of will.

In my view, this is the most difficult form of the objection that divine simplicity and divine free choice are incompatible. What can be done to explain and defend Aquinas's position against this objection depends on his notion of conditional necessitation.

On Aquinas's view, any divine act that is an instance of free choice, such as the act of will to create, is necessitated conditionally, but not absolutely. It is not absolutely necessitated because, to put it roughly and briefly, the proposition 'God does not create' does not by itself entail a contradiction.[99] On the other hand, that God's willing to create (or any other act of divine free choice) is conditionally necessitated, in Aquinas's sense of 'conditional necessity', is a consequence of God's simplicity. If God chooses one of a pair of alternatives neither of which is absolutely necessary for him, the other member of the pair is in consequence inevitably unavailable for him. And so, (A) it is not logically possible for a simple being that creates not to create. That observation about God may seem trivial, for it may seem precisely analogous to this observation about a human being; (B) it is not logically possible for the entity that is Socrates and running *not* to be running. And Observation (B) is trivial because, of course, (C) it is logically possible for Socrates not to be running. Although it is necessary that if Socrates is running he is running, it is not necessary that Socrates is running.

Claim (C) may be made about Socrates because Socrates can be dissociated from his running. The sort of necessity with which running is connected to Socrates is just what the medievals called 'the necessity of the present'. On the supposition that Socrates is in fact running now, that present state of affairs cannot now be otherwise. And yet, we are entitled to assume, before now it was open to Socrates either to run now or not to run now, i.e., before now Socrates could have exercised (and presumably did exercise) free choice regarding his running now.

But this way of dissociating Socrates from his running in order to show the triviality of (B) cannot be used to dissociate God from his creating (or choosing to create), to show that (A) is trivial in the way (B) is. The reason why the necessity of Socrates's running while he is running does not preclude his freely choosing not to run is that before the time of his running Socrates could have brought it about that he not be running at that later time. But nothing of that sort can be said of God with regard to his creating. His act of creating is a timeless action in the eternal present, and so it is logically impossible for there to be anything before (or after) his act of creating and consequently logically impossible that before the eternal present God could do something to bring it about that he does not create in the eternal present. Aquinas's conditional necessity in God is thus like the necessity of the present, except that the present in question is the timeless present which characterizes all of God's life at once.

Whatever God wills, then, in his one timeless act of will, is ineluctable for him, in the sense that it cannot be changed. But, as I explained above, although God's acts of *liberum arbitrium* are conditionally necessary in this sense, they are not absolutely necessary for God. God's creating, for example, is not entailed by the laws of logic or by the nature of deity or by the combination of them, and it could have been the case that God willed not to create. And so God's willing to create is necessary, but only conditionally, given that he does create. Nothing in this sort of necessity impugns the freedom of his will, because which logical possibility is actualized and which logical possibility is left unactualized depends on nothing other than God's will. And yet his willing is (conditionally) necessitated since *as things are* it is not possible that not willing to create be correctly ascribed to him. In God's case, then, it seems that, for Aquinas, what is conditionally necessary for God is what cannot be changed over time in God in consequence of something God wills, whereas what is absolutely necessary is what cannot be changed across possible worlds.

Even assuming clear sense can be made of this distinction between conditional and absolute necessity, questions remain. If there are possible worlds in which God omits to do what he does in the actual world, then in such worlds does God not have unactualized potentialities, contrary to the doctrine of simplicity which takes God's simplicity to be essential to God? For example, in the possible world in which God wills not to create, would God not have an unactualized potentiality, namely, the potentiality to create? Second, no matter how we understand the notion of conditional necessity, aren't we *still* left with a distinction in God, namely, between those parts of God's act of will which are absolutely necessitated and those that are only conditionally necessitated? And will not even this distinction count as a real distinction in God?

Aquinas addresses questions of the first sort in *SCG* I.82. There he argues that a will can have open to it an option which it does not take either (a) because it is not actualizing some potentiality it has, or (b) because there is more than one way, equally good, of actualizing the same potentiality. Albert Schweitzer, for example, had open to him the options of becoming either a medical missionary or a concert pianist, and it seems unreasonable to deny that in not opting for the latter career he left unactualized a potentiality he had, an instance of type (a). On the other hand, when the family doctor cures a child's strep throat with Keflex rather than with Ampicillin, it does not seem sensible to say that he leaves some potentiality of his unactualized. Instead, this seems to be an instance of type (b): there is an alternative that is not adopted because the state of the doctor's medical art is such that there is more than one, equally good way for the doctor to actualize his potentiality for practicing medicine.

On Aquinas's view, such acts of divine will as creating are instances of type (b). God's end or aim is goodness; he wills what he wills for the sake of goodness. Since according to the doctrine of simplicity he himself is goodness, he is in this respect in the same position as the family doctor: there is more than one, equally good way in which he can achieve his aim, and one of those ways consists in willing just himself and not creating anything.[100] From this point of view, it is misleading to say that God has a potentiality for creating – even an unactualized potentiality (in the case of the God-only world) – just as it would be inaccurate to say that the family doctor has an unactualized potentiality for prescribing Ampicillin rather than Keflex. Rather, if *per impossibile* one were to ascribe a potentiality to God, then God would (as it were) have a potentiality, invariably and ineluctably actualized, for willing goodness; and *this* (as it were) potentiality would be actualized in God's willing himself, whether or not he wills anything other than himself. Therefore, on Aquinas's view, even the supposition that God does not will to create – probably the most troublesome supposition for the view that God is essentially entirely actual – would not entail that God has any unactualized potentialities.[101]

As for the second question regarding the apparent distinction between the conditionally and absolutely necessitated in God, the problem is that the distinction seems, on the face of it, to be a real distinction in God's nature, between the metaphysical "softness" of willing to create (for example) and the metaphysical "hardness" of willing goodness.[102] Willing to create characterizes God's nature in only some possible worlds, while willing goodness characterizes it in all possible worlds; therefore, it seems that there are at least two different sorts of characteristics in the divine nature, distinguished from one another by having or lacking the characteristic of obtaining in all possible worlds.

Aquinas, I think, would have supposed that this line of thought confuses a logical distinction to which we have every right with a difference in God's will for which there is no basis. On Aquinas's account of God's will, God wills himself and everything else he wills in a single simple act of will. Because some but not all of the objects of that single act of will might have been other than they are, we are warranted in drawing a logical distinction between the conditionally and the absolutely necessitated objects of that single act of will; but nothing in that warrant licenses the claim that the act of will is not entirely one, that there are two really distinct acts of will, or one act of will in two really distinct parts. Even if we should go so far as to say that with regard to some but not all of its objects, God's will itself might have been different from what it is, this counterfactual claim shows us again only a logical distinction among the objects of the willing and not a difference within the divine will itself. What the logical distinction picks out is a difference in the ways in which the single act of divine will is related to the divine nature, on the one hand, and to created things, on the other. But the mere fact that one thing is related in different ways to different things does not entail that it has distinct *intrinsic* properties, only distinct Cambridge properties. The difference between the relationship of the divine will to the divine nature and the relationship of the divine will to creatures stems not from a difference in the divine will itself but from logical differences among the diverse objects of that will.

An analogy may help clarify this part of Aquinas's position, even though it is fully suitable in only a few respects. If some woman, Monica, looks directly into a normal unobstructed mirror, then in a single glance she sees herself and other things. On any such occasion, Monica invariably sees herself, so that in the context of the example her seeing of herself is physically necessitated. But what she sees besides herself will vary from context to context and so is not physically necessitated. We might therefore draw a warrantable logical distinction between the necessitated seeing of herself and the non-necessitated seeing of other things. Still, that logical distinction provides no basis for inferring that there is a real distinction within Monica's *act* of seeing. Her *act* of seeing remains a single undivided glance in spite of its being properly subjected to our logical distinction. The basis for the logical distinction is not some division within Monica's glance but is rather the difference among the objects of her glance and the different ways in which those objects are related to Monica's one undifferentiated act of seeing.

If this line of thought is right, then Aquinas has all he wants or needs with regard to God's single act of will and its differing objects. The fact that we can distinguish conditionally from absolutely necessitated aspects of God's will shows us an appropriate logical distinction but provides no basis on which to infer a difference within the divine will itself. There is a necessary relationship between God's willing and God's nature considered as an object of his willing because his will is by definition a wanting of the good and God's nature is goodness, on Aquinas's view. But any other things God wills for the sake of goodness are such that goodness is realizable without them, and so the connection between God's will and these objects of his will is *not* necessary. Therefore, the distinction between those aspects of the divine will which could have been and those which could not have been otherwise reflects a difference in the ways in which the divine will is related to itself and to other things. And these different relationships give rise to different counterfactual truths – e.g., 'God might have willed not to create'; 'Even if God had not willed to create, he would still have willed himself'. But although the differing relationships and differing counterfactuals imply that God is not the same in all possible worlds, they do not show that in any given world God's act of will is not one single metaphysically indivisible act. They provide the basis for drawing a conceptual distinction among Cambridge properties of God's will, but because the distinction arises just from considering the different ways in which the divine will can be related to its objects, they do not constitute a metaphysical distinction among God's intrinsic properties any more than Monica's single glance is intrinsically divisible because of the different sorts of objects to which it is related. But absolute simplicity rules out only metaphysical differences within God's nature; it does not and could not provide any basis for objecting to logical or conceptual differences. And so the conceptual distinction between those aspects of the divine nature which could have been otherwise and those which could not is compatible with the doctrine of simplicity.

Implications of the doctrine of divine simplicity

Having worked to defend the coherence of Aquinas's interpretation of the doctrine of divine simplicity, I want to conclude by saying something about its usefulness. From the earlier discussion in this chapter, it is clear that the development of the doctrine and the resolution of its difficulties provide grounds on which to resolve the apparent incompatibility of omnipotence and impeccability and the seeming paradox of essential goodness (with its tension between impeccability and divine free choice). These are important subsidiary results, by-products of the effort to make sense of Aquinas's position. But what I want to bring out now is the more direct importance of the doctrine as Aquinas understands it for the consideration, first, of God's relationship to morality and, second, of the cosmological argument.

The question 'What has God to do with morality?' has typically been given either of two answers by those who take it seriously.[103] God's will is sometimes taken to create morality in the sense that whatever God wills is good just because he wills it. Consequently,

> (TS) right actions are right just because God approves of them and wrong actions are wrong just because God disapproves of them.[104]

Alternatively, morality is taken to be grounded on principles transmitted by God but independent of him, so that a perfectly good God frames his will in accordance with those independent standards of goodness. Consequently,

> (TO) God approves of right actions just because they are right and disapproves of wrong actions just because they are wrong.

The trouble with (TS) is that it constitutes a theological subjectivism in which, apparently, anything at all could be established as morally good by divine fiat. So although (TS) makes a consideration of God essential to an evaluation of actions, it does so at the cost of depriving the evaluation of its moral character. Because it cannot rule out anything as absolutely immoral, (TS) seems to be a theory of religious morality that has dropped *morality* as commonly understood out of the theory. (TO), on the other hand, obviously provides the basis for an objective morality, but it seems equally clearly not to be a theory of *religious* morality since it suggests no essential connection between God and the standards for evaluating actions. Furthermore, on

(TO), the status of the standards to which God looks for morality seems to impugn God's sovereignty.

So the familiar candidates for theories of religious morality seem either, like (TS), to be repugnant to common moral intuitions or, like (TO), to presuppose moral standards apart from God, which God may promulgate but does not produce. For different reasons, then, both these attempts at a theory of religious morality seem inadequate; neither one provides both an objective standard of morality and an essential connection between religion and morality.

The doctrine of divine simplicity entails a third alternative which provides what neither (TS) nor (TO) is capable of. Because God is simple, he is goodness; that is, the divine nature itself is perfect goodness. Thus there is an essential relationship between God and the standard by which he judges; the goodness for the sake of which and in accordance with which he acts, in accordance with which he wills only certain things to be morally good, is his nature. On the other hand, because it is God's whole nature, not just his arbitrary decision, which is said to constitute the standard for morality, only things consonant with God's nature could be morally good. According to the doctrine of simplicity, then, God's essential connection with morality provides an objective rather than a subjective moral standard.

These sketchy remarks of course suggest no more than the outline of an objective theological meta-ethics, and it is a long way from even a fully worked out meta-ethics to a set of specific moral prescriptions.[105] To progress from the meta-ethical foundations inherent in absolute simplicity to a full-fledged moral system requires expounding, defending, and developing the theory which originated in pagan antiquity and was transmitted by Augustine and Boethius – that 'goodness' and 'being' are different in sense but the same in reference.[106] But despite the effort it calls for, a religious morality of the sort that might be based on the doctrine of divine simplicity is promising and worthy of a place among its competitors.

The other set of issues in connection with which the doctrine makes a major difference has to do with the cosmological argument. Some philosophers – Leibniz, for instance – have held that unless we admit the existence of a being that exists necessarily we are reduced to pointing to a brute fact by way of answering the question why there is something rather than nothing, and the principle of sufficient reason leads such philosophers to claim that there cannot be brute facts.[107] Other philosophers, most recently Richard Swinburne,[108] have held the more modest thesis that theism provides a simpler explanation for the universe than atheism does. Swinburne thinks that God is a simpler and thus a more rational stopping-point for explanation than is the universe itself, because "there is a complexity, particularity, and finitude about the universe which cries out for explanation, which God does not have ... [The] supposition that there is a God is an extremely simple supposition".[109]

The trouble with Swinburne's thesis is that he rejects the notion of God as an entity whose existence is logically necessary, and so it is not clear why we should share his intuition that theism constitutes a more rational stopping-point for explanation than atheism does. Philosophers such as Leibniz and Clarke, who rest their versions of the cosmological argument on the principle of sufficient reason, do tend to hold that God is a necessary being. But the trouble with their position is that they seem unable to account for the necessity of God's existence even though they appear to be obliged to do so by the very nature of the principle of sufficient reason that warrants their cosmological arguments. They apparently both cannot find and must have an explanation for the necessity of God's existence. Finally, the principle of sufficient reason, which cosmological arguments depend on, has itself been called into question. William Rowe, for instance, has argued that the principle is not a metaphysically necessary truth but rather a logically impossible falsehood.[110]

The doctrine of simplicity significantly alters the discussion of all these related issues. In arguing against the principle of sufficient reason, Rowe attempts to show that it is impossible for every contingent fact to have an explanation. A crucial premise in his argument is the assumption that:

(R) "For any contingent fact C the fact which explains it cannot be a necessary fact, otherwise C would not be contingent."

And Rowe goes on to show that every other possible explanation of any contingent fact C is such that it entails at least one unexplained contingent fact. Consequently, the principle of sufficient reason must be false. The effect of the doctrine of simplicity on this intriguing argument is to call (R) into question. The doctrine of simplicity entails that God is a logically necessary being all of whose acts of will are at least conditionally necessitated, but that among those acts of will is the volition that certain things be contingent. No matter what the modal status of God's conditionally necessitated acts of will may be, if it is possible for a logically necessary, omnipotent being to will that certain entities or events be contingent, as I have been at pains to argue that it is on Aquinas's interpretation of the doctrine of simplicity, then (R) is false. Consequently, a crucial premise in Rowe's argument against the principle of sufficient reason is false, on Aquinas's views.

Furthermore, the doctrine of simplicity can supply what Clarke's version of the cosmological argument lacks, the explanation of the necessity of God's existence. The answer to the question 'Why does God exist?' is that he cannot not exist, and the reason he cannot not exist is that he is his own nature because he is simple. Since his nature is internally consistent, it exists in all possible worlds, and so God, who is his nature, exists in all possible worlds. The necessity of God's existence is not one more characteristic of God which needs an explanation of its own but is instead a logical consequence of

God's simplicity. The short answer to the further question 'Why is God simple?' is 'Because God is an absolutely perfect being, and absolute perfection entails absolute simplicity', and the fuller version of that answer is to be found in Christian rational theology as developed by Augustine, Anselm, and Aquinas, for instance.

Given the doctrine of simplicity, then, it is reasonable to claim that God is an entity whose existence – whose necessary existence – is self-explanatory in the sense that the explanation of the existence of the entity that is simple is provided entirely by the nature of the entity. And that conclusion supplies the justification, lacking in Swinburne's account, for claiming that God is a simpler stopping-point for universal explanation than the universe itself is. If we assume that God does not exist, the answer to the question 'Why is there something rather than nothing?', or the search for an explanation of all contingent facts, leaves at least one brute fact, at least one inexplicable contingent fact. But given Aquinas's view of the way in which a necessary cause could bring about contingent effects, if God exists and is absolutely simple, the causal chain of contingent facts has its ultimate explanation in a cause that is both necessary and self-explanatory.

The concept of God's absolute simplicity, then, brings with it not only metaphysical intricacy but also considerable explanatory power.

4

GOD'S ETERNITY

Introduction

Aquinas's understanding of God as eternal is foundational for very many of his theological views. The concept of eternity, as Aquinas understands it, also makes a significant difference to a variety of issues in contemporary philosophy of religion, including, for instance, the apparent incompatibility of divine omniscience with human freedom and of divine immutability with the efficacy of petitionary prayer; but because the concept has been misunderstood in the current philosophical discussion or cursorily dismissed as incoherent, for a long time it did not receive the attention it deserves from contemporary philosophers.[1] In this chapter, I expound and attempt to defend Aquinas's interpretation of the concept of divine eternity.

Sometimes, as in the case, for example, of Aquinas's views of God's knowledge, the main difficulty in expounding Aquinas's position is ferreting out just what it is Aquinas means to claim. But sometimes, as in the case of Aquinas's account of divine eternity, that difficulty seems small next to the problem of defending his account against the objections that have seemed decisive against it in the view of some philosophers and theologians. The main focus of this chapter will consequently be the defense of Aquinas's position as regards divine eternity.[2] There are, of course, also problems as regards the exposition of Aquinas's account. Eternality (the condition of having eternity as one's mode of existence) can be misunderstood in either of two ways. Sometimes it is confused with limitless duration in time – sempiternality – and sometimes it is construed simply as atemporality, eternity being understood in that case as roughly analogous to an isolated, static instant. The second misunderstanding of eternality is not so far off the mark as the first; but a careful consideration of the texts shows that atemporality alone does not exhaust eternality as Aquinas conceived of it, and that the picture of eternity as a frozen instant is a radical distortion of the concept, as Aquinas understands it.

Aquinas's interpretation of the doctrine of eternity is hardly original to him; on the contrary, it has a long and complicated history. By Aquinas's time, the *locus classicus* for discussions of eternity was Boethius's definition and description of eternity. And so I will begin with a brief exposition of the relevant Boethian texts before presenting Aquinas's interpretation.

Boethius's definition of eternity

Boethius discusses eternity in two places: *The Consolation of Philosophy*, book 5, prose 6, and *De trinitate*, Chapter 4. The immediately relevant passages are these:

> *(CP)* That God is eternal, then, is the common judgment of all who live by reason. Let us therefore consider what eternity is, for this makes plain to us both the divine nature and knowledge. Eternity, then, is the complete possession all at once (*totum simul*) of illimitable life. This becomes clearer by comparison with temporal things. For whatever lives in time proceeds as something present from the past into the future, and there is nothing placed in time that can embrace the whole extent of its life equally. Indeed, on the contrary, it does not yet grasp tomorrow but yesterday it has already lost; and even in the life of today you live no more fully than in a mobile, transitory moment ... Therefore, whatever includes and possesses the whole fullness of illimitable life at once and is such that nothing future is absent from it and nothing past has flowed away, this is rightly judged to be eternal, and of this it is necessary both that being in full possession of itself it be always present to itself and that it have the infinity of mobile time present [to it].[3]

> *(DT)* What is said of God, [namely, that] he is always, indeed signifies a unity, as if he had been in all the past, is in all the present – however that might be – [and] will be in all the future. That can be said, according to the philosophers, of the heaven and of the imperishable bodies; but it cannot be said of God in the same way. For he is always in that for him *always* has to do with present time. And there is this great difference between the present of our affairs, which is *now*, and that of the divine: our now makes time and sempiternity, as it were, running along; but the divine now, remaining, and not moving, and standing still, makes eternity. If you add '*semper*' to 'eternity', you get sempiternity, the perpetual running resulting from the flowing, tireless now.[4]

Boethius's definition of eternity, which has its sources in the Greek philosophical tradition,[5] is thus this: *Eternity is the complete possession all at once of illimitable life.*[6] Four ingredients in this definition need to be emphasized.

It is clear, first of all, that on Boethius's definition, anything that is eternal has life.[7]

The second and equally explicit element in the definition is illimitability: the life of an eternal being cannot be limited; it is impossible that there be a beginning or an end to it. The natural understanding of such a claim is that the existence in question is infinite in duration, unlimited in either 'direction'. But there is another interpretation that must be considered in this context despite its apparent unnaturalness. Conceivably, the existence of an eternal entity is said to be illimitable in the way in which a point or an instant may be said to be illimitable: what cannot be extended cannot be limited in its extent.

There are texts that can be read as suggesting that this second interpretation is what Boethius intends. In *CP* eternal existence is expressly contrasted with temporal existence described as extending from the past through the present into the future, and what is eternal is described contrastingly as possessing its entire life *at once*. Boethius's insistence in *DT* that the eternal now is unlike the temporal now in being fixed and unchanging strengthens that hint with the suggestion that the eternal present is to be understood in terms of the present instant "standing still". Nevertheless, there are good reasons for rejecting this less natural interpretation. In the first place, some of the terminology Boethius uses would be inappropriate to eternity if eternity were to be conceived as illimitable in virtue of being unextended. He speaks in *CP* more than once of the *fullness* of eternal life. In *DT,* and in *CP* immediately following the passage quoted above, he speaks of the eternal present or an eternal entity as *remaining* and *enduring*.[8] And he claims in *DT* that it is correct to say of God that he is *always*, explaining the use of 'always' in reference to God in such a way that he can scarcely have had in mind a life illimitable in virtue of being essentially durationless. The more natural reading of 'illimitable', then, also provides the more natural reading of these texts.[9] So we can understand Boethius's definition to mean that the life of an eternal entity is characterized by beginningless, endless, infinite duration.

The concept of duration that emerges in the interpretation of 'illimitable life' is the third ingredient I want to emphasize. Its importance is highlighted by the fourth ingredient, which is presented in the only phrase of the definition still to be considered: 'the complete possession all at once'. As Boethius's explanation of the definition in *CP* makes clear, he conceives of an eternal entity as atemporal, and he thinks of its atemporality as conveyed by just that phrase in the definition. What he says shows that something like the following line of thought leads to his use of those words. A living temporal entity may be said to possess a life; but since the events constituting the life of any temporal entity occur sequentially, some later than others, it cannot be said to possess all its life *at once*. And since everything in the life of a temporal entity that is not present is either past and so no longer in its possession or future and so not yet in its possession, it cannot be said to have the *complete* possession of its life.[10] So whatever has the complete possession of all its life at once cannot be temporal. The life that is the mode of an eternal entity's existence is thus characterized not only by illimitable duration but also by atemporality. (Analysis of this paradoxical combination will be the subject of extended discussion below.)

A caveat may be useful here. With the possible exception of Parmenides, none of the ancients or medievals who accepted eternity as a real, atemporal mode of existence meant thereby to deny the reality of time or to suggest that all temporal experiences are illusory. In introducing the concept of eternity, such philosophers, and Boethius in particular, were proposing two separate modes of real existence. Eternity is a mode of existence that is neither reducible to time nor incompatible with the reality of time.

Aquinas's adoption of the Boethian formula

The first article of *ST* Ia.10, which is the question on divine eternity in *ST*, uncharacteristically lacks the *sed contra*, the part of the article in which Aquinas generally quotes an authority on his side. But that lack probably stems from the fact that the issue in the article is whether Boethius's formula for eternity is a good one, and all the objections in this article are objections to one or another part of Boethius's formula. The authority in question that might have been cited in the *sed contra* is thus no doubt Boethius himself, the defense of whose definition of eternity is the subject of the article.

That Aquinas intends to adopt the Boethian formula is apparent in other places besides this discussion in *ST*. The first objection in the very next article in *ST* Ia10.2, is also focused on Boethius, for example; and although the reply to that objection does not mention Boethius by name, the reply is based on Boethius's views in the texts I presented above and is formulated in Boethius's terms. The Boethian formula, explicitly attributed to Boethius, is also the basis for Aquinas's discussion of eternity in *Compendium theologiae* cc.5–8, where Aquinas highlights the combination of being always (*semper*) and atemporality in the Boethian concept of eternity. In *QDV* 12, the question on prophecy, Aquinas cites the Boethian formula as part of his explanation of the way in which God knows future things.[11] The heart of the Boethian definition is also at issue in *SCG* I.15, where Aquinas emphasizes the same elements of eternity as those he focuses on in *CT* and distinguishes the atemporal everlastingness of God from the everlastingness of time. In this chapter of *SCG*, Aquinas says:

> God is entirely without motion ... Therefore, he is not measured by time ... not can any succession be found in his being ... [Rather, he

has] his being all at once (*totum simul*) – in which the formula of eternity consists ... And divine authority bears witness to this truth, for Psalm 101.13 [says], "Thou, Lord, endurest thoughout eternity (*in aeternum permanens*)."

And there are other places as well in which it is clear that Aquinas is using or presupposing the Boethian formula of eternity.[12] In what follows, however, I will concentrate on Aquinas's discussion of eternity in *ST*, his most mature and developed treatment of the topic.

In *ST* Ia.10.1, Aquinas makes it abundantly clear that he accepts all four parts of the Boethian definition to which I called attention above. Obj. 1 in a.1 takes issue with *illimitability* in the Boethian definition, and obj. 2 argues against the use of *life*; Aquinas defends both these parts of the Boethian definition in his replies to the objections. The reply to obj. 5 defends the part of the Boethian definition having to do with atemporality. And eternity as duration is defended in the replies to objections 2 and 6.

Because of the importance of the notion of duration in the Boethian concept of eternity, it is worth having a closer look at Aquinas's treatment of the second objection in *ST* Ia.10.1. The objection runs this way: " 'Eternity' signifies a certain duration (*quandam durationem*). But duration has to do with being more than with life. And therefore *being*, rather than *life*, ought to be put in the definition of eternity."[13]

In reply, Aquinas says:

> That which is truly eternal is not only being but living. And living includes in a certain way operation, as being does not. But the extension (*protensio*) of duration seems to go with operation, rather than with being.

It is also helpful in this connection to notice the way in which Aquinas understands the part of the Boethian definition having to do with illim-itability. So, for example, in the corpus of *ST* Ia.10.1, Aquinas cites the combination of atemporality and illimitability as the heart of the concept of eternity. As he explains there:

> Two things make eternity known: first, the fact that what is in eter-nity is interminable, that is, lacking beginning and end (since 'term' refers to both); second, the fact that eternity lacks succession, since it exists all at once.

In *ST* Ia.10.2, however, Aquinas argues that God is his own duration; and in *ST* Ia.10.2 ad 2, he explains that God endures beyond all ages (*durat ultra quodcumque saeculum*). This article, combined with the preceding text, thus makes it clear that the interminability of God's existence is to be understood as the interminability of unending duration, rather than as the interminability of a point or instant.[14]

Furthermore, in *ST* Ia.10.4, the first objection takes as a premise the claim that eternity, like time, is a measure of duration; in the reply to the objection, Aquinas disputes only the assumption that time and eternity are the same kind of measure of duration, not that eternity is a measure of duration. In *ST* Ia.10.4 ad 3, this point is developed. In that reply, Aquinas maintains that time as a measure of duration is the measure of motion, whereas eternity as a measure of duration is the measure of permanent being.

It is clear, then, from these texts and others as well that Aquinas accepts the Boethian definition of eternity in all four of its elements.[15] The concept of eternity as Aquinas accepts it is thus the concept of a life with infinite atemporal duration. This concept has seemed obviously incoherent to some contemporary philosophers.[16] To evaluate it properly, however, requires first understanding it, and so in the next sections of this chapter I consider the implications of the Boethian formula as Aquinas accepts it.

Presentness and simultaneity

Because an eternal entity is atemporal, there is no past or future, no earlier or later, *within* its life; that is, the events constituting its life[17] cannot be ordered sequentially from the standpoint of eternity. But, in addition, no temporal entity or event can be earlier or later than or past or future with respect to the whole life of an eternal entity, because otherwise such an eternal life or entity would itself be part of a temporal series. Aquinas explicitly associates succession with time and dissociates succession from God. He says:

> There is succession in every motion, and one part after another, on the basis of which we number before and after in motion. And so [this is how] we apprehend time, which is nothing but the number of before and after in motion. But in what lacks motion and is always the same, we cannot find before and after. Therefore, just as the formula for time consists in the numbering of before and after in motion, in the same way the formula for eternity consists in the apprehension of the uniformity of that which is entirely outside motion ... What is entirely immutable cannot have a beginning and an end any more than it can have succession ... And eternity is thus characterized by two things. First, by the fact that what is in eternity is illimitable ... Secondly, by the fact that eternity itself lacks succession, existing all at once.[18]

Here it should be evident that, although the stipulation that an eternal entity completely possesses its life all at once entails that it is not part of any sequence, it does not rule out the attribution of presentness or simultaneity to the life and relationships of such an entity, nor should it. Insofar as an entity *is*, or *has*, life, completely or otherwise, it is appropriate to say that it has present existence in some sense of 'present'; and unless its life consists in only one event or it is impossible to relate an event in its life to any temporal entity or event, we need to be able to consider an eternal entity or event as one of the *relata* in a simultaneity relationship.

And so Aquinas tends to emphasize presentness and simultaneity (or "all-at-onceness") in talking of eternity. He says, for example: "God's vision is measured by eternity, which is all at once; consequently, all times and everything done in them is subject to his sight."[19] Elsewhere, he claims that the eternal divine gaze views future events "presently" (*praesentialiter*).[20] In the discussion of God's knowledge in *ST*, Aquinas explains that God knows future contingent things not as future but in the same way in which he knows everything in time, namely, insofar as future contingent things are present to God from eternity; and Aquinas goes on to compare God's knowledge of things in time to the knowledge of someone who sees a road from a great height and thus sees all the travelers on it at once.[21]

I will look briefly at the applicability of presentness to something eternal and then consider in some detail the applicability of simultaneity.

If anything exists eternally, it exists. But the existing of an eternal entity is a duration without succession; and because eternity excludes succession, no eternal entity has existed or will exist. It *only* exists. It is in this sense that an eternal entity is said to have present existence. But since that present is not flanked by past and future, it is obviously not the temporal present. Furthermore, the eternal, pastless, futureless present is not instantaneous but extended, because eternity, as Aquinas understands it, includes duration. The temporal present is a durationless instant, a present that cannot be extended without falling apart entirely into past and future intervals. The eternal present, on the other hand, is by definition an infinitely extended, pastless, futureless duration.

Simultaneity is of course generally and unreflectively taken to mean existence or occurrence at one and the same time. But to attribute an eternal entity or event simultaneity with anything, we need a coherent characterization of simultaneity that does not make it altogether temporal. It is easy to provide a coherent characterization of a simultaneity relationship that is not temporal in case both the *relata* are eternal entities or events. Suppose we designate the ordinary understanding of temporal simultaneity '*T-simultaneity*':

(T) T-simultaneity = existence or occurrence at one and the same time.

Then we can easily enough construct a second species of simultaneity, a relationship between two eternal entities or events:

(E) E-simultaneity = existence or occurrence at one and the same eternal present.

For Aquinas's purposes, however, what is needed as regards species of simultaneity is not E-simultaneity so much as a simultaneity relationship between two *relata* of which one is eternal and the other temporal. It has to be possible to characterize such a relationship coherently if Aquinas is going to be able to maintain that there are connections between an eternal and a temporal entity or event. An eternal entity or event cannot be earlier or later than, or past or future with respect to, any temporal entity or event. So if there is to be any relationship between what is eternal and what is temporal, then, it must be some species of simultaneity.

Now in forming the species T-simultaneity and E-simultaneity, I have in effect been taking the genus of those species to be something like this:

(G) Simultaneity = existence or occurrence at once (i.e., together).

And I have formed those two species by giving specific content to the broad expression 'at once'. In each case, we spelled out 'at once' as meaning at one and the same *something – time*, in the case of T-simultaneity; *eternal present*, in the case of E-simultaneity. In other words, the *relata* for T-simultaneity occur together at the same time, and the *relata* for E-simultaneity occur together at the same eternal present. What we want now is a species of simultaneity – call it *ET-simultaneity* (for eternal–temporal simultaneity) – that can obtain between what is eternal and what is temporal. It is only natural to try to construct a definition for ET-simultaneity as we did for the two preceding species of simultaneity, by making the broad 'at once' in (G) more precise. Doing so requires starting with the phrase 'at one and the same _____' and filling in the blank appropriately.

To fill in that blank appropriately, however, would be to specify a single mode of existence in which the two *relata* exist or occur together, as the *relata* for T-simultaneity coexist (or co-occur) in time and the *relata* for E-simultaneity coexist (or co-occur) in eternity.[22] But, on Aquinas's view of divine eternity, it is theoretically impossible to specify a single mode of existence for two *relata* one of which is eternal and the other temporal. To do so would be to reduce what is temporal to what is eternal (thus making time illusory), or what is eternal to what is temporal (thus making eternity illusory), or both what is temporal and what is eternal to some *third* mode of existence; and all three of these alternatives are ruled out by Aquinas's interpretation of the doctrine of eternity. For Aquinas, both time and eternity are real, and there is no other mode of existence to which those two can be reduced.[23]

So, for example, Aquinas considers this objection:

It is impossible for two measures of duration to be simultaneous, unless one is a part of the other, for two days or two hours are not simultaneous, but a day and an hour are simultaneous because an hour is a part of a day. But eternity and time are simultaneous, since each implies a certain measure of duration. Therefore, since eternity is not a part of time, because eternity exceeds time and includes it, it seems that time is a part of eternity and not different from eternity.[24]

Aquinas replies to this objection not by denying that eternity is a measure of duration but by repudiating the general point about simultaneity. He says: "this argument would work if time and eternity were measures that fell within one [and the same] genus, [but] this is manifestly false."[25] Against this background, then, it is not conceptually possible to construct a definition for ET-simultaneity analogous to the definitions for the other two species of simultaneity, by spelling out 'at once' as 'at one and the same _____' and filling in the blank appropriately. What is temporal and what is eternal coexist, on Aquinas's view, but not within the same mode of existence; so there is no single mode of existence that can be referred to in filling in the blank in such a definition of ET-simultaneity.

The significance of this difficulty and its implications for a working definition of ET-simultaneity can be better appreciated by returning to the definition of T-simultaneity for a closer look.

Philosophers of physics, explaining the special theory of relativity, have taught us to be cautious even about the notion of temporal simultaneity; in fact, the claim that temporal simultaneity is relative rather than absolute is fundamental to the special theory of relativity.[26]

For all ordinary practical purposes, and also for our theoretical purposes in this chapter, time can be thought of as absolute, along Newtonian lines. But, simply in order to set the stage for our characterization of ET-simultaneity, it will be helpful to look at a standard philosophical presentation of temporal simultaneity along Einsteinian lines.[27]

[I]magine a train traveling at six-tenths ... the speed of light ... One observer (the 'ground observer') is stationed on the embankment beside the track; another observer (the 'train observer') is stationed at the middle of the train. Suppose that two lightning bolts strike the train, one at each end ... Suppose, further, that the ground observer sees these two lightning bolts simultaneously ... [The train observer also sees the two lightning bolts, but] since he is traveling toward the light ray emanating from the bolt that strikes the front of the train, and away from the bolt that strikes the rear of the train, *as viewed from the ground system*, he will see the lightning bolt strike the front of the train ... before he sees the other lightning bolt strike the rear of the train ... This, then, is the fundamental result: events occurring at different places which are simultaneous in one frame of reference will not be simultaneous in another frame of reference which is moving with respect to the first. This is known as *the relativity of simultaneity*.[28]

I am leaving to one side philosophical issues raised by this example and simply accepting it for present purposes as a standard example illustrating Einstein's notion of the relativity of temporal simultaneity. According to this example, the very same two lightning flashes are simultaneous (with respect to the reference frame of the ground observer) and not simultaneous (with respect to the reference frame of the train observer). If we interpret 'simultaneous' here in accordance with our definition of T-simultaneity, we will have to say that the same two lightning flashes occur at the same time and do not occur at the same time; that is, it will be both true and false that these two lightning flashes occur at the same time. The incoherence of this result is generated by filling in the blank for the definition of T-simultaneity with a reference to one and the same time, where time is understood as one single uniform mode of existence. The special theory of relativity takes time itself to be relative and so calls for a more complicated definition of temporal simultaneity than the common, unreflective definition given in (T), such as this relativized version of temporal simultaneity:

(RT) RT-simultaneity = existence or occurrence at the same time within the reference frame of a given observer.

This relativizing of time to the reference frame of a given observer resolves the apparent incoherence in saying that the same two lightning flashes occur and do not occur at one and the same time. They occur at the same time in the reference frame of one observer and do not occur at the same time in the reference frame of a different observer.[29]

Once this is understood, we can see that, if we persist in asking whether or not the two lightning bolts are *really* simultaneous, we are asking an incoherent question, one that cannot be answered. The question is asked about what is assumed to be a feature of reality, although in fact there is no such feature of reality; such a question is on a par with 'Is Uris Library *really* to the left of Morrill Hall?' There is no absolute state of being temporally simultaneous with, any more than there is an absolute state of being to the left of. We determine the obtaining of the one relationship as we determine the obtaining of the other, by reference to a reference frame. The two lightning flashes, then, are RT-simultaneous in virtue of occurring at the same time within the reference frame of the ground observer and not RT-simultaneous in virtue of occurring at different times within the reference frame of the train observer. And, Einstein's theory argues, there is no privileged reference frame such that with respect to it we can determine whether the two events are *really* simultaneous; simultaneity is irreducibly relative to reference frames, and so is time itself. Consequently, it would be a mistake to think that there is one single uniform mode of existence that can be referred to in specifying 'at once' in (G) in order to derive a definition of temporal simultaneity.

These difficulties in spelling out even a very crude acceptable definition for temporal simultaneity in the light of relativity theory foreshadow and are analogous to the difficulties in spelling out an acceptable definition of ET-simultaneity. More significantly, they demonstrate that the difficulties defenders of the concept of eternity encounter in formulating such a definition are by no means unique to their undertaking and cannot be assumed to be difficulties in the concepts of ET-simultaneity or of eternity themselves.

Finally, and most importantly, the way in which we cope with such difficulties in working out a definition for RT-simultaneity suggests the sort of definition needed for ET-simultaneity. Because one of the *relata* for ET-simultaneity is eternal, the definition for this relationship, like that for E-simultaneity, must refer to one and the same present rather than to one and the same time. And because in ET-simultaneity we are dealing with two equally real modes of existence, neither of which is reducible to any other mode of existence, the definition must be constructed in terms of *two* reference frames.

So we can characterize ET-simultaneity in this way. Let 'x' and 'y' range over entities and events. Then:

> (ET) For every x and every y, x and y are ET-simultaneous if and only if
>
>> (i) either x is eternal and y is temporal, or vice versa (for convenience, let x be eternal and y temporal);
>
> and
>
>> (ii) with respect to some A in the unique eternal reference frame, x and y are both present – i.e., (a) x is in the eternal present with respect to A, (b) y is in the temporal present, and (c) both x and y are situated with respect to A in such a way that A can enter into direct and immediate causal relations with each of them and (if capable of awareness) can be directly aware of each of them;
>
> and
>
>> (iii) with respect to some B in one of the infinitely many temporal reference frames, x and y are both present – i.e., (a) x is in the eternal present, (b) y is at the same time as B, and (c) both x and y are situated with respect to B in

such a way that B can enter into direct and immediate causal relations with each of them and (if capable of awareness) can be directly aware of each of them.[30]

Given the concept of eternity, condition (ii) provides that a temporal entity or event which is temporally present is ET-simultaneous with every eternal entity or event;[31] and condition (iii) provides that an eternal entity or event which is eternally present (or simply eternal) is ET-simultaneous with every temporal entity or event.

On this definition, if x and y are ET-simultaneous, then x is neither earlier nor later than, neither past nor future with respect to, y – a feature essential to any relationship that can be considered a species of simultaneity. Further, if x and y are ET-simultaneous, then x and y are not temporally simultaneous; since either x or y must be eternal, it cannot be the case that x and y both exist *at one and the same time* within a given reference frame. ET-simultaneity is symmetric, of course; but, since no temporal or eternal entity or event is ET-simultaneous with itself, the relationship is not reflexive; and the fact that there are different domains for its *relata* means that it is not transitive. The propositions

(1) x is ET-simultaneous with y;

and

(2) y is ET-simultaneous with z;

do not entail

(3) x is ET-simultaneous with z.

And even if we conjoin with (1) and (2)

(4) x and z are temporal,

(1), (2), and (4) together do not entail;

(5) x and z are temporally simultaneous.

(RT) and the Einsteinian conception of time as relative have served the only purpose there is for them in this chapter, now that they have provided an introductory analogue for the characterization of ET-simultaneity, and we can now revert to a Newtonian conception of time, which will simplify the discussion without involving any relevant loss of precision. In ordinary human circumstances, all human observers may appropriately be said to share one and the same reference frame, and distinguishing individual reference frames for the discussion of time in the rest of this chapter would be as inappropriate as taking an Einsteinian view of time in a discussion of historical chronology.

Implications of ET-simultaneity

If x and z are temporal entities, they coexist if and only if there is some time during which both x and z exist. But if anything exists eternally, its existence, although infinitely extended, is fully realized, all present at once. Thus the entire life of any eternal entity is coexistent with any temporal entity at any time at which that temporal entity exists.[32] From a temporal standpoint, the temporal present is ET-simultaneous with the whole infinite extent of an eternal entity's life. From the standpoint of eternity, every time is present, co-occurrent with the whole of infinite atemporal duration.[33]

The implications of this account of ET-simultaneity can be shown by considering the relationship between an eternal entity and a future contingent event. Medieval philosophers and theologians believed that there would be a being who was the Antichrist, but that Antichrist's existence and the events of Antichrist's life were paradigmatically future contingents. So suppose that Antichrist will be born precisely at noon on 9 August 2090. Then Antichrist's birth some years from now *will be* present to those who will be there at his entry into the world, but it *is* present to an eternal entity. It cannot be that an eternal entity has a vision of Antichrist's birth before it occurs; in that case an eternal event would be earlier than a temporal event. Instead, the actual occasion of Antichrist's birth is present to an eternal entity. It is not that the future preexists somehow, so that it can be inspected by an entity that is outside time, but rather that an eternal entity that is wholly ET-simultaneous with 9 August 1974, and with today, is wholly ET-simultaneous with 9 August 2090, as well. It is *now* true to say 'The whole of eternity is ET-simultaneous with the present'; and of course it was true to say just the same at noon of 9 August 1974, and it will be true to say it at noon of 9 August 2090. But since it is one and the same eternal present that is ET-simultaneous with each of those times, there is a sense in which it is now true to say that Antichrist at the hour of his birth is present to an eternal entity; and in that same sense it is now true to say that Christ's birth is present to an eternal entity. If we are considering an eternal entity that is omniscient, it is true to say that that entity is *at once* aware of Christ's birth and of the birth of Antichrist (although of course an omniscient entity understands that those events occur sequentially – in the nature of the case, it is not possible that there be an Antichrist before the birth of Christ – and knows the sequence and the dating of them); and it is true to say also that for such an entity both those events are present at once.[34]

Such an account of ET-simultaneity suggests at least a radical epistemological or even metaphysical relativism, and perhaps plain incoherence. On the supposition that Antichrist is born in 2090, we *know* that Antichrist is not now alive. An omniscient eternal entity *knows* that Antichrist is now alive. Still worse, there is a sense in which an omniscient eternal entity also *knows* that Antichrist is not now alive, and so Antichrist is apparently both alive and not alive at once in the eternal present.

These absurdities appear to be entailed partly because the full implications of the concept of eternity have not been taken into account. Some aspects of ET-simultaneity may be more intuitively apparent in a picture that has heuristic value although it is in some ways crude and misleading. Imagine two parallel horizontal lines, the upper one representing eternity and the lower, time; and let presentness be represented by light. Then from a temporal viewpoint the temporal present is represented by a dot of light moving steadily along the lower line, which is in this way lighted successively, while the eternal present is represented by the upper line's being entirely lighted at once. So from a temporal viewpoint the temporal present is ET-simultaneous with the infinite present of an eternal being's life. On the other hand, from the viewpoint of a being existing in the persisting eternal present, each temporal instant is ET-simultaneous with the eternal present, but only insofar as that instant is temporally present. So, from the eternal being's point of view, the entire time line is lighted at once. From an eternal viewpoint, every present time is present, co-occurrent with the infinite whole of the eternal present.

What is present to an entity depends on its mode of existence. What is present to an eternal entity may be present, past, or future with respect to some particular temporal entity, just as some building may be to the right with respect to one frame of reference but to the left with respect to another.[35] An eternal entity's mode of existence is such that its whole life is ET-simultaneous with each and every temporal entity or event. Any particular temporal event, such as the opening of the Berlin Wall or the end of the AIDS epidemic in Africa is thus, as it is occurring, ET-simultaneous with the eternal present. But, relative to us, given our location on the temporal continuum in the early twenty-first century, the first of those events is past, and the second is future.

So an eternal entity's mode of existence is such that its whole life is ET-simultaneous with each and every temporal entity or event; consequently, Antichrist's birth, like every other event involving Antichrist, is really ET-simultaneous with the whole life of an eternal entity. But when Antichrist's birth is being related to *us*, today, then, given our location in the temporal continuum, Antichrist's birth is not simultaneous (temporally or in any other way) with respect to us, but really future.[36]

These results are sufficient to dispel the appearance of either metaphysical or epistemological relativism in the doctrine of eternity.

Atemporal duration

With this much understanding of an eternal entity's mode of existence, we are in a position to consider the apparent incoherence generated by combining atemporality with duration in the definition of eternity.

One way in which to try to dispel the apparent incoherence of the notion of atemporal duration is to consider, even if only very briefly, the development of the concept of eternity. The concept can probably be found in Parmenides (although this interpretation of Parmenides is controversial),[37] but it finds its first detailed formulation in Plato, who makes use of it in working out the distinction between the realms of being and becoming; and it receives its fullest exposition in pagan antiquity in the work of Plotinus.[38] The thought that originally stimulated this Greek development of the concept of eternity was apparently something like this. Our *experience* of temporal duration gives us an impression of permanence and persistence which an analysis of time convinces us is an illusion or at least a distortion. Reflection shows us that, contrary to our familiar but superficial impression, temporal duration is only apparent duration, just what one would expect to find in the realm of becoming. The existence of a typical existent temporal entity, such as a human being, is spread over years of the past, through the present, and into years of the future; but the past is not, the future is not, and the present must be understood as no time at all, a durationless instant, a mere point at which the past is continuous with the future.[39]

Such radically evanescent existence cannot be the foundation of existence. Being, the persistent, permanent, utterly immutable actuality that seems required as the bedrock underlying the evanescence of becoming, must be characterized by genuine duration, of which temporal duration is only the flickering image. Genuine duration is fully realized duration – not only extended existence (even *that* is theoretically impossible in time) but also existence *none* of which is already gone and *none* of which is yet to come – and such fully realized duration must be atemporal duration. Whatever has atemporal duration as its mode of existence is "such that nothing future is absent from it and nothing past has flowed away", whereas of everything that has temporal duration it may be said that from it *everything* future is absent and *everything* past has flowed away. What has temporal duration "does not yet grasp tomorrow but yesterday it has already lost"; even today it exists only "in a mobile, transitory moment", the present instant. To say of something that it is future is to say that it is not (yet), and to say of something that it is past is to say that it is not (any longer). Atemporal duration, by contrast, is duration none of which is not – none of which is absent (and hence future) or flowed away (and hence past). On this way of thinking about time and eternity, eternity, not time, is the mode of existence that admits of fully realized duration.

The ancient Greek philosophers who developed the concept of eternity were thus using the word '*aiôn*', which corresponds in its original sense to our word 'duration', in a way that departed from ordinary usage in order to introduce a notion which, however counter-intuitive it may be, can reasonably be said to preserve and even to enhance the original sense of the word. It would not be out of keeping with the tradition that runs through Parmenides, Plato, and Plotinus into Augustine, Boethius, and Aquinas to claim that it is only the discovery of eternity that enables us to make genuinely literal use of words for duration, words such as 'permanence' and 'persistence', which in their ordinary, temporal application turn out to have been unintended metaphors. 'Atemporal duration', like the ancient technical use of *'aiôn'* itself, violates established usage; but an attempt to convey a new philosophical or scientific concept by adapting familiar expressions is not to be rejected on the basis of its violation of ordinary usage. The apparent incoherence in the concept is thus a consequence of continuing to think of duration only as 'persistence *through time*'.

Nonetheless, some contemporary critics[40] have argued that duration apparently carries with it the notion of extension, and extension is by its nature divisible. Consequently, either there must after all be succession in the existence of anything that has duration, so that the concept of atemporal duration is really incoherent after all, or else the terms 'duration' and 'extension' (and other relevant terms of this sort) are being used equivocally of God and of temporal things. And in that case we must either be able to give a univocal definition of atemporal duration or concede that 'atemporal duration' is an unintelligible expression.

But even if, for the sake of the argument, we accept the assumption that the existence of every enduring temporal thing is extended and therefore divisible, on Aquinas's views it does not follow that the terms 'duration' or 'extension' are used equivocally of eternal God and temporal creatures. If God is absolutely simple, as Aquinas maintains, then many terms cannot be predicated *univocally* of God and creatures. On the other hand, only a radically agnostic theism would maintain that terms ordinarily predicated of creatures can be predicated of God just in some *equivocal* sense. For Aquinas, analogical predication is the traditionally recognized solution to what otherwise would seem to be an insoluble dilemma.[41]

So, for example, Aquinas thinks that knowledge is said of God and creatures analogically, not univocally or equivocally. But precisely which features of creaturely knowledge are features of divine knowledge too, and precisely what in God takes the place of features of creaturely knowledge that are obviously inappropriate to him – these are things we could say only in case we could comprehend God's sort of knowledge better than we can, in which case we would of course be able to explain more of it in univocal terms. Where univocal accounts are theoretically unavailable and equivocal predication is worse than worthless, we may be said to be in circumstances of irreducibly analogical predication.[42] Similarly, in seeking those features of eternal extension (or duration, or presentness) that take the place of the analogous temporal features, in seeking even a list of all the features shared by temporal and atemporal duration, critics of the concept of eternity are seeking what cannot be found if, as Aquinas supposes, this, too, is a case of irreducibly analogical predication. Aquinas says:

no name is predicated univocally of God and creatures; but neither is it said purely equivocally, as some have said, because, on this view, nothing could be known or demonstrated of God. Rather, it would always fall into the fallacy of equivocation ... [We] must consequently say that such names are said of God and creatures according to analogy.[43]

And so Aquinas denies that human beings cannot develop an intelligible account of God's nature or mode of existence. To suppose that we cannot know anything about God because we cannot apply predicates univocally to him and to creatures, he says:

is as much contrary to philosophers, who have demonstratively proved many things about God, as it is contrary to the Apostle, who says that the invisible things of God are clearly seen, being understood by means of those things which are made (Romans 1:20).[44]

On the basis of analogical predication, Aquinas supposes, for example, that essentially illimitable eternal duration, like conceivably unbounded temporal duration, is a measure of existence, indicating some degree of permanence of some sort on the part of something that persists – although, of course, divine existence, permanence, and persistence will be analogous to, not identical with, temporal existence, permanence, and duration. On Aquinas's view:

we can speak about any thing in two ways: in one way, in accordance with the nature of things; in another way, in accordance with our consideration ... If we take a measure of duration in the first way, then in this way duration which is all at once belongs only to God and not to any creature.[45]

According to Aquinas, then, acknowledging the impossibility of predicating certain terms univocally of God and creatures does not drive us into using them equivocally. Analogical predication remains available, and it leaves open a way along which understanding can be developed.

Atemporal life

Since a life is a kind of duration, some of the apparent incoherence in the notion of an atemporal life may be dispelled in rendering the notion of atemporal duration less readily dismissible. But life is in addition ordinarily associated with processes of various sorts, and processes are essentially temporal; and so the notion of an atemporal entity that has life can also seem incoherent.[46]

Now what Aquinas is thinking of when he attributes life to eternal God is the doctrine that God is a mind. So, for example, in connection with the question whether life is fittingly attributed to God, he says, "that for which [it is true] that his nature is his very understanding ... this is what has the highest degree of life. And such is God. So life is in God most of all."[47] And elsewhere he says, "understanding is a sort of living ... But God is his understanding ... Therefore, God is his living and his life."[48] And he goes on to claim that "God's understanding and living is God himself ... Therefore his life does not have succession but is all at once."[49]

Since on Aquinas's views the life of God is all at once and so atemporal, the mind that is God must be different in important ways from a temporal, human mind. Considered as an atemporal mind, God cannot deliberate, anticipate, remember, or plan ahead, for instance, since all these mental activities essentially involve time, either in taking time to be performed (like deliberation) or in requiring a temporal viewpoint as a prerequisite to performance (like remembering). But it is clear that there are other mental activities that do not require a temporal interval or viewpoint. Knowing seems to be the paradigm case. Learning, reasoning, inferring take time, but knowing does not. In reply to the question 'What have you been doing for the past two hours?' it makes sense to say 'Studying logic' or 'Proving theorems', but not 'Knowing logic'. Similarly, it makes sense to say 'I'm learning logic', but not 'I'm knowing logic'.

And knowing is not the only mental activity requiring neither a temporal interval nor a temporal viewpoint. Willing, for example, unlike wishing or desiring, seems to be another. Furthermore, nothing atemporal can be material, and so the mind of God cannot be material; perceiving is therefore impossible in any literal sense for the mind that God is. But nothing in the nature of incorporeality or atemporality seems to rule out the possibility of awareness.

It is true that *feeling* angry is impossible for an atemporal entity, if feelings of anger are essentially associated, as Aquinas thinks they are, with bodily states. He says:

> Every affective passion occurs in accordance with some bodily change, such as the constriction or dilation of the heart, or something of this sort. But nothing of this sort can happen in God since he is not a body or a power in a body.[50]

As Aquinas points out, however: "there are certain passions which, although they are not fittingly attributed to God as passions, nonetheless [just] on the basis of their species do not imply anything incompatible with divine perfection."[51]

And so God can have an analogue to these passions, though without a bodily state. Joy and love are examples, according to Aquinas.[52]

Moreover, even those passions that have something in them inappropriate for deity can be attributed to God in some sense. So, with regard to being angry, Aquinas says: "God is sometimes said to be angry insofar as, in accordance with his wisdom, he wants to punish someone."[53]

Although God cannot *feel* angry, then, there is nothing, on Aquinas's views, that prevents us from supposing that God can *be* angry, a state the components of which might be, for instance, being aware of an injustice, disapproving of it, and willing its punishment.

It seems, then, that the notion of an atemporal mind is not incoherent, but that, on the contrary, such a mind can have a variety of faculties or activities. The notion of an atemporal mind is thus not *prima facie* absurd, and so neither is the notion of an atemporal life; for any entity that has or is a mind must be considered to be *ipso facto* alive, whatever characteristics of other living beings it may lack.

An eternal entity's acting in time

The difficulties considered so far have had to do with the concept of eternity itself. They are by no means all the objections to the concept which have been raised in contemporary discussions; but many of the objections not explicitly considered here involve difficulties over simultaneity, and such objections can be dealt with adequately in the light of the previous discussion of ET-simultaneity. Recognizing the necessity for a relationship of ET-simultaneity between eternal God and things in time is enough, for example, to reveal the misunderstanding underlying such attempted reductions of the concept to absurdity as this one:

> But, on St Thomas' view, my typing of this chapter is simultaneous with the whole of eternity. Again, on his view, the great fire of Rome is simultaneous with the whole of eternity. Therefore, while I type these very words, Nero fiddles heartlessly on.[54]

With so much examination of objections to the concept itself, we can now turn to apparent problems in theological applications of the concept, particularly those which arise in considering the possibility of interaction between eternal and temporal entities. Aquinas plainly supposes that God not only creates temporal things but also knows them and providentially interacts with them. So, for example, he says: "[W]e must say that everything is subject to divine providence, not only in general but also in particular ... The causality of God, who is the first agent, is extended in such a way as to include every entity."[55]

There are, however, several reasons for thinking that an eternal entity could not interact with or otherwise affect temporal entities, events, or states of affairs.[56] Just as an eternal entity cannot exist in time, so, someone might suppose,

(I) an eternal entity cannot act in time.

It might seem, furthermore, that

(II) the nature of a temporal action is such that the agent itself must be temporal.

Nelson Pike provides the following case in point:

> Let us suppose that yesterday a mountain, 17,000 feet high, came into existence on the flatlands of Illinois. One of the local theists explains this occurrence by reference to divine creative action. He claims that God produced (created, brought about) the mountain. Of course, if God is timeless, He could not have produced the mountain *yesterday*. This would require that God's creative activity and thus the individual whose activity it is have position in time. The theist's claim is that God *timelessly* brought it about that yesterday, a 17,000 feet high mountain came into existence on the flatlands of Illinois ... [But] the claim that God *timelessly* produced a temporal object (such as the mountain) is absurd.[57]

On this basis, Pike denies that God, considered as atemporal, could produce or create anything; whatever is produced or created begins to exist and so has a position in time. And it might be argued along similar lines that

(III) an atemporal entity could not preserve anything temporal in existence because to do so would require temporal duration on the part of the preserver.

If God is taken to be eternal, considerations I, II, and III are incompatible with doctrines which Aquinas certainly accepts, such as the divine creation and preservation of the world[58] and divine response to petitionary prayer,[59] and which he himself supposes to be compatible with divine eternality. Furthermore, and worse, considerations I–III militate against the central doctrine of Christianity, since the Incarnation of Christ entails that the second person of the Trinity has a temporal nature and performs temporal actions during a certain period of time.[60] If I–III have to be accepted, then there are major inconsistencies in Aquinas's views.

But, in fact, all three of these considerations are confused. In connection with consideration I, a distinction must be drawn between (a) acting in such a way that the action itself can be located in time, and (b) acting in such a way that the effect of the action can be located in time. For temporal agents, the distinction between (a) and (b) is generally nugatory; for an atemporal entity, however, (a) is impossible. An agent's action is an event in the agent's life, and there can be no temporal event in the atemporal life of God. But such an observation does not tell against (b). If an eternal God is also omnipotent, he can do anything it is not logically impossible for him to do. Even though his actions cannot be located in time, he can bring about effects in time unless doing so is logically impossible for him. Aquinas himself is clear about this distinction. For example, in discussing creation in *SCG*, he argues that the creation of things in time does not imply succession on the part of the creator.[61]

Considerations II and III may be construed as providing reasons for thinking that it is indeed logically impossible for an atemporal entity to produce temporal effects. Pike's version of consideration II, however, involves a confusion like the confusion just sorted out for consideration I. He says:

(9) [I]f God is timeless, He could not have produced the mountain *yesterday*.
(10) The claim that God *timelessly* produced a temporal object (such as the mountain) is absurd.

Both these propositions are ambiguous because of the possibility of assigning different scopes to "yesterday" and to 'timelessly' (or 'atemporally'), and the ambiguities can be sorted out in this way:

(9a)   If God is atemporal, he cannot yesterday have brought it about that a temporal object came into existence.
(9b)   If God is atemporal, he cannot (atemporally) bring it about that a temporal object came into existence yesterday.
(10a) It is absurd to claim that God atemporally brings it about that a temporal object came into existence.
(10b) It is absurd to claim that God brings it about that a temporal object came into existence atemporally.[62]

Apparently without taking account of the ambiguity of propositions (9) and (10), Pike understands them as (9a) and (10b) respectively. Propositions (9a) and (10b) are indeed true, but they do not support Pike's inference that an atemporal God cannot produce a temporal object. In drawing that inference, Pike seems to be relying on an assumption about a temporal relationship that must hold between an action and its effect. The assumption is not entirely clear; in some passages of his *God and Timelessness* it looks as if Pike thinks that an action and its effect must be simultaneous, an assumption that is plainly false in general regarding actions and their effects as ordinarily conceived of. But if we do adopt co-occurrence as a theoretically justifiable condition on causal connection between an action and its effect, we can point out that any and every action of an eternal entity is ET-simultaneous with any temporal effect ascribed to it. And, since it would simply beg the question to insist that only *temporal* simultaneity between an action and its effect can satisfy this necessary condition of causal connection, there is no reason for denying of an eternal, omnipotent entity that its atemporal act of willing could bring it about that a mountain came into existence on 14 July, 2002 (or whatever yesterday's date happens to be). Consequently, there is no reason for thinking it absurd to claim that a divine action resulting in the existence of a temporal entity is an atemporal action.

So propositions (9b) and (10a) are false, although they are legitimate senses of the ambiguous propositions (9) and (10).

Consequently, consideration II is also confused.

The reasons for rejecting the first two considerations apply as well, *mutatis mutandis*, to consideration III. If it is not impossible for an omnipotent, eternal entity to act in eternity (by atemporally willing) in such a way as to bring it about that a temporal entity begins to exist at a particular time, it is not impossible for an omnipotent, eternal entity to act in eternity (by atemporally willing) in such a way that that temporal entity continues to exist during a particular temporal interval.

Presence and prayer

An interesting variation on Pike's objection to the concept of eternity has also been raised by William Hasker. Hasker argues that if the fundamentally relevant metaphysical relationship between an eternal being and temporal beings is correctly portrayed in ET-simultaneity, then an eternal God could not be *directly aware* of temporal facts.[63] Moreover, God could not be present to human beings *directly and immediately*, in the way that Aquinas and most traditional theists believe he is. In general, Hasker thinks:

> (H) to be directly aware of or present to temporal beings requires being temporal oneself.

Now Aquinas would not accept (H). In addition to the many passages, some of which I cited above, in which Aquinas talks about God's knowledge of temporal things as gaze or sight, or some other divine analogue of a kind of direct awareness, there are many passages in which Aquinas expresses forcefully his sense that God is immediately present to human beings. For example, in his commentary on Galatians, in discussing the relation of an eternal God to human persons, Aquinas says:

> the ultimate perfection, by which a person is made perfect inwardly, is joy, which stems from the presence of what is loved. Whoever has the love of God, however, already has what he loves, as is said in 1

John 4:16: 'whoever abides in the love of God abides in God, and God abides in him.' And joy wells up from this.[64]

Aquinas develops the same idea, somewhat more soberly, in discussing the mission of an eternal divine person. In that context, Aquinas says:

> There is one general way by which God is in all things by essence, power, and presence, [namely] as a cause in the effects partici-pating in his goodness. But in addition to this way there is a special way [in which God is in a thing by essence, power, and presence] which is appropriate for a rational creature, in whom God is said to be as the thing known is in the knower and the beloved is in the lover ... In this special way, God is not only said to be in a rational creature but even to dwell in that creature as in his temple ... The Holy Spirit is possessed in the very gift of sanc-tifying grace and dwells in a human being. And so the Holy Spirit himself is given and sent.[65]

So Aquinas does not suppose that being directly aware of something temporal or being directly present to something temporal requires being temporal oneself. And, in fact, (H) seems to be false. (H) appears to depend on a more general principle:

> (GP) x can be directly aware of or present to y only if x and y share the same mode of existence.

(GP) certainly is incompatible with the concept of ET-simultaneity, which is the mode of relation between eternal God and temporal things. But neither Aquinas nor any traditional theist would be willing to accept (GP) as applied to *space*. Since God is non-spatial on the view of Aquinas and most other traditional theists, it would follow from (GP) that God cannot be directly aware of spatial beings. But if (GP) is unacceptable as applied to space, it cannot reasonably be applied to time either. If God can be directly aware of his creatures without sharing their *spatial* mode of existence,[66] why should we suppose that he cannot be directly aware of them without sharing their *temporal* mode of existence?

A different sort of difficulty arises in connection with answering prayers or punishing injustice, for instance, since in such cases it seems necessary that the eternal action occur later than the temporal action; and so the reasons for rejecting considerations I, II, and III, based on the ET-simul-taneity of eternal actions with temporal events, seem inapplicable. The problem of answering prayers is typical of difficulties of this sort. An answer to a prayer must be later than the prayer, it seems, just because

> (11) something constitutes an answer to a prayer only if it
> is done because of the prayer;[67]

and

> (12) something is done because of a prayer only if it is
> done later than the praying of the prayer.

Now (11) is true, but a little reflection makes (12) look doubtful even as applied to temporal entities. If at 3 o'clock, a mother prepares a snack for her little boy because she believes that when he gets home at 3:30 he will ask for one, it does not seem unreasonable to describe her as preparing the food because of the child's request, even though in this case the response is earlier than the request. Whatever may be true regarding temporal entities, however, if (12) is true, it would obviously rule out the possibility of an eternal entity's responding to prayers.

But consider the case of Hannah's praying on a certain day to have a child and her conceiving several days later.[68] Both the day of her prayer and the day of her conceiving are ET-simultaneous with the life of an eternal entity. If such an entity atemporally wills that Hannah conceive on a certain day after the day of her prayer, then such an entity's bringing it about that Hannah conceives on that day is clearly a response to her prayer, even though the willing is ET-simultaneous with the prayer rather than later than it. If ET-simultaneity is a sufficient condition for the possibility of a causal connection in the case of God's bringing about the existence of 2 temporal entity, it is likewise sufficient for the possibility of his acting because of a prayer prayed at a particular time.[69]

The Incarnation

The principal difficulty in the doctrine of the Incarnation seems intractable to considerations of the sort which alleviate difficulties associated with an eternal entity's willing to bring about a temporal event, because according to the doctrine of the Incarnation an eternal entity itself entered time. If we take the essence of the doctrine of the Incarnation to be expressed in

> (13) "When the fulness of the time was come, God sent
> forth his Son, born of a woman" (Galatians 4:4),

it is not difficult to see, in the light of the discussion so far, how to provide an interpretation that shows that, as regards God's sending his Son, the doctrine is compatible with God's eternality:

> (13′) God atemporally wills that his Son be born of a
> woman at the appointed time.

But the possibility of making sense of an eternal action with a temporal effect does not settle this issue, because the principal difficulty here does not lie in the nature of the relationship between an eternal agent and a temporal effect. The difficulty here is rather that an eternal entity is also (somehow) a *component* of the temporal effect – an effect which is, to put it simplistically, an eternal entity's having become temporal without having ceased (*per impossibile*) to exist eternally.

Formulating the difficulty in the doctrine of the Incarnation simplistically, however, simply exacerbates it. And whereas this formulation of it may present an insuperable difficulty for one or more of the heresies of the Patristic period that took the person of Christ to be only divine or only human, it is ineffective against the orthodox doctrine of the Incarnation that Aquinas accepts. Anything more than a sketch of this intricate doctrine is outside the scope of this chapter,[70] but we need to consider it very briefly here in order to suggest some reasons for supposing that, contrary to first appearances, the doctrine of the Incarnation is not incompatible with the doctrine of God's eternality.

The doctrine of the Trinity maintains that God, although one substance, consists in three persons, the second of which is God the Son. The doctrine of the Incarnation maintains that the second person of the Trinity has not merely one essence or nature, like every other person divine or human, but two: one, the divine nature common to all the persons of the Trinity; the other, the human nature of the incarnate Christ. One of the explicitly intended consequences of the doctrine's specifying a dual nature for Christ is that statements predicating something of Christ can be ambiguous unless they contain a phrase relativizing the predicate to one or the other or both of his two natures. So, for example, Aquinas poses the question "Is this true: Christ is a creature?"; and in answering the question he says: "We must not say without qualification 'Christ is a creature' or '[Christ is] less than the Father', but rather [we have to say this] with a determination, namely, *in accordance with his human nature*."[71]

Strictly speaking, then, the proposition

>   (14) Christ died

is ambiguous among these three readings:[72]

>   (14a) Christ with respect to his divine nature (or *qua* God) died;
>   (14b) Christ with respect to his human nature (or *qua* man) died;

and

>   (14c) Christ with respect to his divine and human natures (or *qua* both God and man) died.

From the standpoint of traditional Christianity, which Aquinas accepts, (14a) and (14c) are false, and (14b) is true. (14b) is not to be interpreted as denying that God died,[73] however – such a denial forms the basis of at least one Christian heresy – but rather as denying that God, the second person of the Trinity, died with respect to his divine nature.

This interpretation of the doctrine of the Incarnation is loaded with at least apparent paradox, and it is not part of my purposes in this chapter even to sketch an analysis of it; but, whatever its internal difficulties may be, the doctrine's specification that Christ has a dual nature provides *prima facie* grounds for denying the incompatibility of God's eternality and God's becoming man. An account of the compatibility of divine eternality and the Incarnation can be developed along these lines.[74] The divine nature of the second person of the Trinity, like the divine nature of either of the other persons of the Trinity, cannot become temporal; nor could the second person at some time acquire a human nature he does not eternally have. Instead, the second person eternally has two natures; and at some temporal instants, all of which are ET-simultaneous with the existence of each of these natures in their entirety, the human nature of the second person has been temporally actual. At those times and only in that nature, the second person directly participates in temporal events.

This is, of course, just a rudimentary outline of a defense of the compatibility of eternality and Incarnation. But it is enough to show at least that the doctrine of the Incarnation cannot be reduced to the belief that God became temporal and that, if it is understood in the traditional way in which Aquinas accepts it, the doctrine can be seen to have been constructed in just such a way as to avoid being reduced to that simple belief. And those observations are sufficient to allay the suspicion that eternality must be incompatible with the central doctrine of orthodox Christianity.

God's knowledge of the future and the past

Although there are many other issues involving the relation of an eternal God to things in time that might profitably be considered here,[75] it is perhaps fitting to conclude an examination of Aquinas's interpretation of divine eternality by examining the effect of divine eternality on issues concerning God's knowledge of the future and the past.

First, the short answer to the question whether God can change the past is 'no'. But it is misleading to say, with Agathon, that not even God can change the past.[76] God *in particular* cannot change the past. The impossibility of *God's* changing the past is a consequence, not of the fact that what is past is over and done with, but rather of the fact that the past is solely a feature of the experience of temporal entities. It is just because no event can be past with respect to an eternal entity that an eternal entity cannot alter a *past* event.[77] An omnipotent, omniscient, eternal entity can affect temporal events, but it can affect events only as they are actually occurring. As for a past event, the time at which it was actually occurring is the time at which it is present to such an entity; and so the Battle of Waterloo is present to God, and God can affect the battle. Suppose that he does so. God can bring it about that Napoleon wins, though we know that he does not do so, because whatever God does at Waterloo is over and done with as we see it. So God cannot alter the past, but he can alter the course of the Battle of Waterloo.[78]

Second, the short answer to the question whether God can foreknow contingent events is also 'no'. It is impossible that any event occur later than an eternal entity's present state of awareness, since every temporal event is ET-simultaneous with that state, and so an eternal entity cannot foreknow anything. Instead, such an entity considered as omniscient knows – is aware of – all temporal events, including those which are future with respect to our current temporal viewpoint; but, because the times at which those future events will be present events are ET-simultaneous with the whole of eternity, an omniscient eternal entity is aware of them as they are present.[79] So, Aquinas says:

> a contingent, insofar as it is *future*, cannot be known by any cognition which cannot admit of falsity. Consequently, since God's knowledge does not and cannot admit of falsity, it would be impossible that God have knowledge of future contingents if he were to know them insofar as they are future. Now something is known insofar as it is future when the relation of past to future is found between the cognition of the cognizer and the occurrence of the thing [in question]. But this relation cannot be found between the divine cognition and any contingent thing. Instead, the relation of the divine cognition to anything is always as the relation of what is present to what is present.[80]

On this basis, Aquinas supposes that something can be both contingent and future and yet also be cognized by God with infallible knowledge.[81] He goes on to say:

> although a contingent is not determinate as long as it is future, nonetheless from the point at which it is produced in the nature of things it has a determinate truth; and [only when it is in] this mode is the gaze of divine cognition brought to bear on it.[82]

The moment in time at which a contingent which is future with respect to us is temporally present is a moment ET-simultaneous with the whole of eternity. For this reason, Aquinas thinks that God knows any given future contingent but only as it is present. And so, Aquinas thinks, God's knowledge of a thing no more undermines its contingency than my seeing what you are now doing undermines the contingency of your act. According to Aquinas:

> it does not follow that [a future contingent] is said [to be] necessary unconditionally [because God knows it] or that the knowledge of God is fallible, anymore than my sight is fallible when I see Peter sitting, although this is contingent.[83]

So although God cannot know the past or foreknow the future, he can know in the one eternal present every event in time as that event is temporally present, including all those events that are past or future with respect to us.

Conclusion

As Aquinas understands it, then, God's eternality is the illimitable enduring present of the life of the mind that God is. This present is atemporal but ET-simultaneous with every moment of time as that moment is present. In the eternal present, God not only lives but also is directly aware of and directly present to everything in time. Providing that these claims are understood in the way argued for here, Aquinas's account of divine eternity is coherent, and there is no logical impossibility in the notion of an eternal being's knowing future contingents or acting in time, including acting in the ways central to certain other traditional Christian doctrines also defended by Aquinas.

5

GOD'S KNOWLEDGE

Introduction

Most people agree that any being that could count as God would have to know everything there is to know. But *how* is God supposed to know what he knows? Obviously, not by beginning with sensations, the way human beings generally do, since, as perhaps even more people agree, God is not corporeal and so cannot have sensations. Conceivably, material objects might make some other sort of cognitively effective causal impression on an incorporeal God, but it's not easy to imagine what that might be. Besides, any account of such an impression would face the apparently insuperable obstacle of the absolute impassibility that is often included among standard divine attributes.[1] Still, if a person's moving her hand from here to there cannot causally affect the mind of God, how does God know that she is moving her hand? 'He just does!' has some appeal as a response on behalf of an omnipotent being, but it's no answer.

Aquinas worked hard at providing answers to questions of this sort about God's knowledge, but the explanation he developed is in many respects perplexing. Furthermore, Aquinas's account of God's knowledge is sometimes interpreted in such a way as to exacerbate its difficulties; and so, before I turn to the puzzles in Aquinas's account, I want to say something about the problems of one common way of understanding that account.

For the sake of having an example, consider the interpretation of Leo Elders.[2] Elders says that, according to Aquinas: God knows "all things which exist at any time, whether past, present or future ... [He] knows whatever will come to be in the succession of time."[3] But "God's knowledge of things other than himself can only be based on his causality. He knows things because he is their cause and he knows them in and through his causality."[4] In discussing Aquinas's views of God's causality, Elders says:

> It is manifest that God causes things by his intellect ... [Of course,] an intelligible form alone is not a principle of action unless there is

159

an inclination to produce this effect. Hence God's intellect must be determined to precisely this effect by his will.[5]

Nonetheless, Elders holds: "God's knowledge is a *causal* knowledge so that God knows things because he makes them."[6] And Elders is not alone in interpreting Aquinas's account of God's knowledge in this way. Brian Shanley, for example, says:

> Nothing skews an account of Aquinas more than the erroneous imputation to God of a perceptual paradigm of knowledge ... God's knowledge is not effected by and dependent upon what is known, but rather is itself causative of what is known.[7]

Interpretations such as this have an unusual epistemological implication. Strictly speaking, human beings cannot know a contingent thing or state of affairs unless it first exists or obtains, but, on this interpretation of Aquinas's account, for God the converse is the case: strictly speaking, nothing can exist, occur, or obtain, unless God first knows it. Where God is concerned, on this interpretation of Aquinas's account, knowledge is logically prior to and causally efficacious of the reality of what is known.

Although, as I will explain below, this interpretation of Aquinas's account of God's knowledge seems to be based on things Aquinas says, it has very serious problems as an interpretation of his views.

In the first place, it, of course, will not do as a general account of God's knowledge. That is because, on Aquinas's view, there are many things God is said to know that no one supposes Aquinas takes God to cause. To begin with, there is God's knowledge of himself, his nature and existence, and of necessary truths; this divine knowledge cannot be causative, on anyone's interpretation of Aquinas. So, for example, Aquinas takes God to know necessary truths, but God's knowledge does not cause these truths. God knows that 1 = 1, but he does not thereby (or in any other way) cause it to be the case that 1 = 1. Additionally, and more importantly, God knows that he exists, that he is a knower, and that he has a certain nature. But it is evident that God's knowing these things does not cause them to be. God's knowing cannot be the efficient cause of God's existence or of his being a knower, since these things are logically prior to his knowing. And if God knows anything, then he at least has the nature of a knower, so that his having a nature is also logically prior to his knowing, not a causal effect of it.

In addition, there is also God's knowledge of those possible creatures that God chooses not to create and that consequently do not exist.[8] In a text that seems on the face of it to support Elders's interpretation, a passage in which Aquinas says that things depend on God as an artifact depends on its artisan, so that the existence of things depends on God's knowledge, rather than the other way around, Aquinas goes on to point out that any artisan has two sorts of knowledge of his creation; speculative and practical. Practical knowledge results in the production of the artifact, but speculative knowledge of an artifact is compatible with the artisan's never producing that artifact. For that reason, Aquinas says: "God has knowledge of things he intends never to create and that therefore never exist."[9] Clearly, this knowledge of God's is not causative either.

So it is clear that we cannot interpret Aquinas as holding that *all* God's knowledge is causative. For some of God's knowledge, a perceptual paradigm understood analogously is apparently just right: this part of God's knowledge *is* dependent on the prior existence of something, namely, God's nature and ideas, rather than the other way around.

Second, even if we restrict the discussion to God's knowledge of temporal things in the actual world, there are serious problems with interpreting Aquinas as holding that God's knowledge is the efficient cause of all he knows.

To begin with, since on Elders's sort of interpretation, God's knowledge is always the cause of what God knows, it follows that God does not know human evil if he does not cause it. Consequently, on this interpretation, Aquinas has to hold either that God causes human evil, or that he has no knowledge of it and is, therefore, not omniscient. But since Aquinas certainly takes God to be omniscient and also maintains in many places[10] that God does not cause sinful actions, this interpretation has the infelicitous consequence of attributing a fairly obvious contradiction to Aquinas.[11] Worse yet, there are passages in which Aquinas explicitly rejects the position this interpretation has to ascribe to him. So, for example, Aquinas says, "it does not follow that God is the cause of evils because he knows evils".[12]

In addition, since on this interpretation, God causes all human actions in virtue of knowing them, the interpretation appears to commit Aquinas to a determinism that leaves no room for human free will.[13] But even if there were some way to account for human freedom within the all-encompassing realm of God's efficient causality, identical with his knowledge, on this interpretation it is nonetheless God who is the ultimate efficient cause, and so the ultimate agent, of sinful human actions, just in virtue of knowing them. Here the issue is *not* whether human freedom can be reconciled with God's causal activity. It is rather whether God's being the first efficient cause of a sinful human action does not make him responsible for the occurrence of the sinful action he causes.

Finally, on this interpretation, God's knowledge of future contingents should be explainable just as God's knowledge of anything else is, namely, as a function of the causal efficacy of the divine cognition. In fact, there should be no special problem about God's knowledge of future contingents. If God's knowledge of things in time is always causative, then God's knowledge of a future free action should also be adequately explained in the same way: God knows it in virtue of causing it. But Aquinas manifestly supposes that God's knowledge of future contingents has to be explained in a very different way, in terms of God's eternality.[14] So, for example, he says:

> There is no knowledge of a contingent as future by means of any cognition that is not liable to falsity. Consequently, since there is no falsity or any liability of falsity in the divine knowledge, it would be impossible for God to have knowledge of future contingents if he were to cognize them as they are future ... [But] since the vision of God's knowledge is measured by eternity, which is all at once and nonetheless includes time as a whole ... , it follows that he sees whatever occurs in time not as future but as present ... And so God infallibly sees all contingents, whether they are present to us or past or future, because they are not future to him.[15]

Aquinas here clearly supposes that God's eternity is crucial to explaining God's knowledge of future contingents.

Elders himself reads Aquinas's explanation of God's knowledge of future contingents in this sort of way. Future contingents, he says, "can be considered ... in their causes; [but] since these are not determined to one effect, they cannot give certitudinal knowledge".[16] Instead, Elders argues, in order for God to know contingent states of affairs that are future with respect to us, they must be really present to God in eternity: "Without their being present, God cannot know them with certitude."[17] And the reason Elders gives for this claim is that God "knows these things as they exist in reality. There is no science [i.e., full-fledged, 'certitudinal' knowledge] without existing things as its object."[18]

But, of course, if Elders's interpretation of Aquinas's account of God's knowledge is correct, if for Aquinas God knows things only insofar as he causes them, then to hold that a consideration of future contingent things in their *causes* is insufficient to provide divine knowledge of them is tantamount to saying that God *cannot* have knowledge of future contingents. Furthermore, as I pointed out above, on Elders's interpretation, God's knowledge of anything other than himself is logically prior to and causative of the existence of its object because of the causative nature of divine knowledge. By Elders's own lights, then, it must count as a mistake to say, as he does, that "without their being present, God cannot know them [i.e., future contingents] with certitude" or that "[t]here is no science without existing things as its object". On the contrary, Elders's interpretation is committed to the conclusion that without God's first knowing them, future contingent things and events cannot be at all.

So, if God's all-encompassing knowledge is always and only causative, then not only is God's consideration of future contingents in their causes *sufficient* for his knowledge of them, but, in fact, knowledge of them in their causes (or in their primary, divine cause) is the *only* way God can know them. In that case, invoking the doctrine of divine eternity to explain the atemporal presence of temporal objects to God's cognition is simply irrelevant to an explanation of God's knowledge of future contingents. As the preceding paragraphs make clear, however, Aquinas certainly does hold that divine knowledge of future contingents must be explained in terms of their atemporal presence to God as objects of his cognition.[19] On the interpretation of God's knowledge as efficiently causal of all God knows, on the other hand, there is not only no need for the doctrine of eternity in an explanation of God's knowledge of future contingents, there is not even any room for it. So either Aquinas's account of God's knowledge of future contingents is inconsistent with his general account of God's knowledge, or Aquinas does not in fact suppose that God's knowledge is always causal.

To my mind, these considerations pose insuperable problems for any interpretation such as that of Elders which takes God's knowledge to be the efficient cause of whatever God knows or of all the things in time in the actual world which God knows.

Problems of Aquinas's account

It is not hard to see how the sort of interpretation represented by Elders's work arises. It draws its main support from a claim Aquinas makes repeatedly. In *Summa theologiae*, for example, Aquinas asks whether God's knowledge is the cause of things, and his answer is a resounding affirmative:

> It must be said that God's knowledge is the cause of things. For God's knowledge is related to all created things as a craftsman's knowledge is related to the things he crafts, but a craftsman's knowledge is the cause of the things he crafts.[20]

In *Summa contra gentiles*, too, Aquinas maintains that "God knows things other than himself insofar as he is the cause of them";[21] and in arguing for this claim he says that

> one has adequate cognition of an effect through the cognition of its cause ... But God himself is, through his essence, the cause of being for other things. And so, since he has the fullest possible cognition of his essence, we must hold that he has cognition of other things as well.[22]

This last passage hints at several other real perplexities in Aquinas's account of God's knowledge which have to be dealt with by any interpretation of his account. For Aquinas, all cognition requires an assimilation between the cognizer and what is cognized,[23] and for there to be such an assimilation

163

there must be in the cognizer a likeness or form of the thing being cognized.[24] And so Aquinas says that "everything that is understood is understood through some likeness (*similtudo*) of it in the one who understands"; and

> cognizers are distinguished from non-cognizing things in this respect, that non-cognizing things have only their own form, but a cognizer is naturally suited to have a form of something else as well, for a form (*species*) of what is cognized is in the cognizer.[25]

Human beings acquire the forms necessary for cognition from extramental reality. So, in a person who is cognizing a cup, who recognizes the thing she sees as a cup, the epistemically requisite form of *cup* has its immediately operative stimulus in that cup itself, present before her and causally affecting her vision. Or when a person smells bread baking or hears a car crash outside her window or feels an insect running across her arm, she normally has those cognitions because something in extramental reality is causally affecting her senses and providing her intellect with raw material from which it abstracts the requisite forms.

Things are different in the case of God. Even divine cognition requires an intelligible form, Aquinas thinks, but in God's cognition of something other than himself the requisite intelligible form is *not* drawn from the thing cognized. Instead, the form through which God cognizes any and all created things is just his own nature, so that it seems that God cognizes creatures solely in virtue of cognizing himself.

> There are two ways in which something is cognized: one, in itself; the other, in something else ... [A thing is cognized] in something else, ... for example, when a man is seen in a mirror through a form belonging to the mirror ... Now [God] sees things other than himself not in themselves but in himself, insofar as his essence contains a likeness of things other than himself.[26]

So God, unlike human cognizers, does not acquire an intelligible form of a cognized created thing from the thing cognized. Rather, he has cognition of himself and of all things other than himself through just one intelligible form, which is his own nature: "The only intelligible form by which the divine intellect has intellective cognition is God's own essence."[27]

Furthermore, the single intelligible form through which God knows is an all-encompassing, perfectly universal form. "To the extent to which an intellect is higher," Aquinas says, "it can with a single [form] cognize several things, to which a lower intellect can attain only through many [forms]."[28] Therefore, for God's intellect, which is the greatest possible, there is just one perfectly universal intelligible form, namely, the divine essence.

But if God knows things other than himself only in virtue of knowing himself, and if the intelligible form through which God knows is the most universal, then it is not easy to see how God knows individual creatures, including human beings, as they are in themselves.

Finally, Aquinas's account raises a particularly difficult form of an objection commonly leveled against dualism: how could an immaterial mind interact with matter?[29] The question has special force against Aquinas because in his discussions even of human cognition he emphatically denies that the immaterial human intellect can know material things directly. What the immaterial intellect can know directly is only immaterial universals abstracted from the particular material things that instantiate them. The human intellect does know material things, Aquinas thinks, but only in virtue of reverting to the "phantasms", immaterial likenesses acquired through corporeal external senses and processed by corporeal internal senses but accessible to incorporeal intellect.[30] Extrapolating from this feature of his account of human cognition, one can see how an entirely immaterial God might know universals or natures. But it is not clear how God could know material particulars themselves, since, among other considerations, there are no divine corporeal senses through which the divine intellect could be put in touch with particulars. These features of Aquinas's account make it seem as if it is a species of Averroism, in which God can know his own nature and all universals or creaturely natures but cannot know individuals – or at least not material individuals, such as human beings.

Of course, there are excellent reasons for being immediately skeptical about any interpretation of Aquinas's account that makes it look Averroistic – most obviously because, in expressly opposing Averroism, Aquinas claims explicitly that God does know material individuals. What's more, he insists that God knows them with "*proper* cognition". That is, God knows material individuals as individuals, and not just through the natures they instantiate or the species to which they belong. In summing up his argument to this effect in *Summa theologiae*, Aquinas says: "Consequently, we must say that God cognizes things other than himself with proper cognition: not only insofar as they share in the nature of being but insofar as each one is distinguished from another."[31] Again, he says: "God's knowledge must extend all the way to particular things that are individuated by matter."[32] Aquinas thinks that material individuals must be among the objects of God's knowledge because he takes God to be the creator of material individuals initially and to exercise direct providential governance over all of them always,[33] and it is hard to see how God could create or directly govern embodied individuals if he could not know them individually.

The problem is that as Aquinas explains his account of God's knowledge, it does seem to commit him to some species of Averroism, in virtue of his claims that God knows other things just in knowing himself and that the single intelligible form through which God knows everything is the most universal form. Furthermore, the passages in which Aquinas claims that God's knowing anything other than himself is his causing it also seems to commit Aquinas to a causal form of universal epistemic determinism by an omniscient God. But, in addition to raising serious philosophical and theological difficulties for Aquinas, epistemic determinism and an Averroistic account of God's knowledge are contrary to Aquinas's own explicit, characteristic positions on human freedom and God's knowledge of particulars. Worse yet, universal epistemic determinism and Averroism are apparently incompatible with each other.

I am convinced that the picture of Aquinas's account of God's knowledge that leaves it liable to these difficulties is distorted. And although I cannot solve all the problems his account raises, I can show that it involves neither universal epistemic determinism by God nor Averroism, without its conflicting with considerations of impassibility.

The analogy of angelic cognition

In order to construct a more accurate presentation of Aquinas's account of God's knowledge, it is helpful to work through his theory of angelic cognition. Since Aquinas takes angels to be entirely immaterial and superhuman but non-omniscient beings, and since his understanding of all superhuman cognition is to a considerable extent connected to his understanding of human cognition, his treatment of angelic cognition provides an intermediate account that illuminates what he has to say about divine cognition.

In the first place, according to Aquinas, angels, like all other intellective beings, have cognition through intelligible forms; but they are like God and unlike human beings in cognizing through forms that are *not* taken from objects of cognition. So, Aquinas says:

> The lower intellective substances, human souls, have intellective power that is not complete by nature but is completed in them successively, in virtue of the fact that they get intelligible forms from things. But intellective power in higher spiritual substances – in angels, that is – is complete by nature through intelligible forms, insofar as, along with their natures, they have intelligible forms for understanding all the things that by nature they can cognize.[34]

And elsewhere he says:

> An angel does not cognize individuals through an acquired form at all, because it does not cognize [anything] through a form it gets from a thing; for [if it did, then] in that case things would act on its intellect, which is impossible. Nor does it cognize [an individual] through some form newly infused by God, newly revealing some-

thing to the angel. For the forms an angel has in it, which were created along with it, are sufficient [for it] to cognize everything cognizable [by it].[35]

So, unlike a human being, who normally has cognition of a cup in front of her through an intelligible form of *cup* that she acquires in consequence of having been causally affected by a cup acting on her senses, an angel is supposed to cognize whatever it cognizes through intelligible forms provided at its creation along with its nature – its concreated, or innate, intelligible forms. Like God, then, an angel is said to cognize anything other than itself solely through an aspect of itself.

Second, like God and unlike human beings, angels are absolutely immaterial knowers. For that reason, angelic cognition, like divine cognition, is entirely intellective, surpassing human intellective cognition in the degree of universality and the fewness of the intelligible forms it needs in order to cognize things. Characterizing angelic knowledge, Aquinas says:

> God understands all things through his one essence. But the higher intellective substances, although they do understand through more than one form, [in comparison with lower intellective substances] they understand through fewer and more universal forms, more powerful for comprehending things, because of the efficacy of the intellective power that is in them. In the lower [intellective substances], however, there are more forms, which are less universal and less efficacious for comprehending things, to the extent to which [these lower substances] fall short of the intellective power of the higher ones.[36]

Consequently, Aquinas says that, "an angelic mind's cognition is more universal than a human mind's cognition, because it extends to more things using fewer means".[37]

So far, then, it looks as if some of the problems in Aquinas's account of divine cognition affect his account of angelic cognition as well. Since angels are absolutely immaterial cognizers, without corporeal senses, in their case, too, it is hard to see how they could cognize embodied individuals as such. And, as we've just seen, Aquinas does emphasize the universality of their knowledge. Consequently, a kind of Averroism seems to threaten his theory of angelic knowledge, too. Furthermore, angels are supposed to know things other than themselves through intelligible forms built into their natures, not through forms acquired from such things. So, like God, angels seem, mysteriously, to cognize things other than themselves solely by way of a kind of introspection. But how could beings whose cognition depends on innate intelligible forms know material particulars at all unless the existence and behavior of those particulars were predetermined?

Despite these similarities between angelic cognition and divine cognition, Aquinas of course denies that angels know what they know in virtue of knowing what they will, or that angelic cognition is causative at all.[38] So although an intelligible form in an angelic intellect functions as a means of cognition (as does a form in a human intellect or, in God's case, the divine essence itself), angelic intelligible forms do not cause the things angels cognize, anymore than they are drawn from them.

Aquinas is equally explicit in his denial of any sort of Averroism with regard to angelic cognition. Angels, he reasons, must know singular, embodied things: "no one can guard something he is not cognizant of. But angels guard individual human beings ... And therefore angels cognize individuals."[39]

But if it is a mistake to interpret Aquinas's view of angelic cognition as entailing Averroism or causal determinism of an epistemic sort, then the formal similarities between his accounts of angelic and divine cognition provide the beginning of a basis for supposing that it may also be a mistake to see either of those difficulties as entailed by his views of God's knowledge. If we can see how angelic cognition is supposed to work without running into Averroism or causal determinism, we may also gain some insight into the appropriate interpretation of Aquinas's account of God's knowledge.

In approaching problems of divine cognition via a consideration of Aquinas's account of angelic cognition, the following three questions are perhaps the most useful. First, how could an angel cognize individuals, given that angels cognize only universally? Second, how could an angel cognize individuals other than itself without acquiring forms from them? Third, and finally, how could intelligible forms built into an angel's nature at its creation enable it to cognize individuals other than itself unless the existence and behavior of those individuals were predetermined? Considering these questions will put us on the right track for interpreting Aquinas's account of God's cognition.[40]

Cognizing universally

To see how the first question should be answered, it is essential to be clear about what Aquinas means by cognizing universally. In discussing angelic cognition, Aquinas provides this explanation:

> The expression 'cognizing something universally' is used in two ways. In one way, as regards the thing cognized, as [when] one cognizes only the universal nature of a thing. And in this way cognizing something universally is cognizing it more imperfectly, for a person who knew of a human being only that it is animal would cognize it imperfectly. In the other way, as regards the medium of cognizing. And cognizing something universally in this

way is cognizing it more perfectly, for the intellect that can have proper cognition of individuals through one universal medium is more perfect than an intellect that cannot do so.[41]

In other words, when Aquinas maintains that angels cognize universally, he does not mean that *what* they cognize is always a universal, as if angels were supposed to have only common natures as objects of their cognition. But what, exactly, is the other sense of 'cognizing universally', the sense in which he does mean to claim that angels cognize universally?

We get some help towards an answer to this question when we recognize that Aquinas thinks that even the human intellect cognizes individuals universally in this other sense. In cognizing anything, the human intellect standardly and primarily apprehends the quiddity, or the *quod quid est,* of a thing.[42] (By '*quod quid est*' here Aquinas means the kind to which something belongs, considered in an unanalyzed way – that is, in medieval terms, the species as distinct from the definition.[43]) Yet, Aquinas claims, the human intellect does cognize material particulars:

> just as we could not sense the difference between sweet and white unless there were one common [internal] sensory power that had cognition of both, so, too, we could not cognize the relation of universal to particular unless there were one power that cognized them both.[44]

But, he goes on to say, the human intellect cognizes material individuals *through* their shared universal:

> Intellect, therefore, has cognition of both [the universal and the individual], but in different ways. For it has cognition of the nature of the species, or of the *quod quid est*, by extending [to it] directly; it has cognition of the individual itself, however, by a kind of reflection, insofar as it turns back to the phantasms from which the intelligible forms are abstracted.[45]

The intellect, in other words, uses an abstract intelligible form – the intellectively abstracted quiddity of a material particular – as the means by which to cognize the particular picked out by the phantasm. But when it does so, the intelligible form is only the medium through or by which the intellect knows the material particular, not *what* it knows: "the intelligible forms by which the possible intellect is actualized are not the intellect's object. For they are related to the intellect not as *what* is understood, but rather as *that by which* it understands."[46]

What Aquinas has in mind here can be elucidated by considering recent neurobiological work. As a result of neurological deficits brought about by injury or disease, certain patients manifest various kinds of agnosia. A patient who has a visual agnosia, for example, has normally functioning channels for visual input and is in possession of ordinary concepts but cannot use visual data for cognition just because he cannot associate the data with the appropriate concepts in his possession.

In Oliver Sacks's popular presentation of visual agnosia, a patient who had the concept *glove* and who could identify a glove as such if he could touch it was shown a glove by Sacks, who held it up in front of the patient and asked him, "What is this?" "A continuous surface with five outpouchings," the patient promptly replied. When Sacks asked again, "Yes, but *what is it?*", the patient made an effort, using the unreliable method of inferring from a thing's accidents to its *quod quid est* (as Aquinas would say), and guessed, "A coin dispenser?"[47] The patient could sense the material individual presented to his sight; that is why he could readily describe what was presented to his eyes as "a continuous surface with five outpouchings". But the patient could nonetheless not cognize the thing presented to his eyes as a glove precisely because he could not get at the *quod quid est* of what he saw by means of the visual data he had.

On the other hand, the patient's doctor Sacks, who has a completely normal visual system, does recognize as a glove a glove presented to his eyes; and yet, when he does so, he does not for that reason have the *quod quid est* of the glove as the *object* of his cognition. Rather, as Aquinas would say, Sacks has cognition of this material individual, he cognizes the glove as a glove, *through* the appropriate universal intelligible form, by associating the visual data with the concept *glove*.[48]

So, cognizing universally in the relevant sense in which Aquinas thinks angels and humans cognize universally is cognizing a thing by means of a common nature under which it is subsumed. And the cognition of particulars requires cognizing universally in this way; even consciously seeing a cup involves recognizing as something or other what one is being visually affected by. That is why a person with a normally functioning visual system sees a glove as a glove. To see something, for a normally functioning cognizer, is to see it *as* whatever it is, and this is to cognize it universally, in the sense at issue here.

Aquinas also thinks that more powerful intellects are able to cognize particulars as subsumed under fewer, higher universals. So, for example, a little boy may be able to cognize his mother's disposable coffee cup in virtue of being able to apply to it the universal *cup*. But (other things being equal) a chemist who knows the nature of Styrofoam, and a physicist who understands the basic constituents of matter, are equipped to have deeper, fuller cognitions of the same object. They, too, cognize through the universal *cup*, but that universal is subsumed under other universals, which are themselves subsumed under other universals, and so on until we come to the highest universal available to the cognizer in question – perhaps, in the case of the physicist, the nature of matter itself. The scientists' cognition of the particular locates it within the grand scheme of things.

This feature of cognition seems to be what Aquinas has in mind in reasoning that higher angels must know by subsuming things under fewer universals than lower angels do. He says:

> The higher the angel, the fewer the forms through which it can apprehend the whole realm of intelligible things. We can recognize a kind of instance of this among ourselves, for there are some people who cannot grasp an intelligible truth unless it is laid out for them in particulars, individual case by individual case. And this, of course, is a result of the weakness of their intellects. But there are others, whose intellects are stronger, who can grasp many things on the basis of a few.[49]

So, when we see the second of Aquinas's senses of 'cognizing universally', it is clear how an intellect that is in epistemic contact with individuals cognizes them in virtue of cognizing universally.[50]

Cognizing through concreated intelligible forms

This way of answering the first question about angelic cognition seems to make the second and third questions harder. How could an angel cognize other created things without acquiring intelligible forms from them? A human being cognizes a particular cup through the intelligible form *cup*, but human beings typically get their intelligible forms of cognized objects from the objects themselves.[51] How could intelligible forms built into an angel's nature at its creation enable it to cognize individuals other than itself without acquiring forms from them? Aquinas himself recognizes this problem and formulates it pointedly:

> if through a form concreated along with it [an angel] could cognize some particular when it is present, then [the angel] would have cognized it from the beginning of [the angel's] own existence, while the cognized thing was still future. But that could not be, because cognizing future things belongs only to God.[52]

The solution here depends, first, on recognizing, as before, that in the cognition of a particular the intelligible form is not what is cognized but rather only the medium through which cognition takes place. So, Aquinas says:

> Intelligible forms are related to intellect as sensible forms are related to sense. But a sensible form is not what is sensed; rather, it is that by which a sense senses. Consequently, an intelligible form is

not what is actually understood, but [only] that by which the intellect understands.[53]

Except in cases of introspectively attending to one's concepts themselves, the intelligible form of a particular is not the object of cognition, on Aquinas's view, but something like a representation of it by means of which the particular is cognized.[54]

It is also helpful to recognize here that, as the current neurobiological research on agnosia suggests, the direct, immediate cognition of things outside the mind involves at least three components. There is (a) just being in epistemic contact with something, as when an agnosia patient with otherwise normal vision receives and initially processes visual data from something visually presented to her. Then there is the higher processing of that visual input, which has two components: (b) possessing a concept or intelligible form[55] through which what one is in contact with can be rendered intelligible, and (c) applying the appropriate concepts or intelligible forms one possesses to that with which one is in epistemic contact. The agnosia patient in Sacks's case is characterized by components (a) and (b) but is unable to achieve (c): he cannot apply the concept *glove*, which he does possess, to the glove in front of him. That is why, although he can describe the features of the glove appropriately, he cannot recognize the glove as a glove. For that reason, his visual agnosia prevents him from having proper cognition of that glove.

The outlines of this tripartite analysis of the process of cognition show up in Aquinas's own explanation of angelic cognition. Aquinas ascribes to a putative objector the objection that angels cannot have any new cognitions just because they have all their intelligible forms or representations built into them at their creation. Aquinas replies that although angels do not acquire any new intelligible forms, they are capable of new cognitions because they can newly *apply* the intelligible forms naturally inherent in them to things that are newly present to them.[56]

So the intelligible forms, the media of angelic *or* human cognition, are something like conceptual lenses. The angelic or human intellect might be thought of as looking through them in order to cognize or render intelligible the things with which the cognizer is (by some means) in epistemic contact. On this interpretation of Aquinas's notion of intelligible forms, it does not much matter whether the conceptual lenses are acquired through experience, human-fashion, or come as part of the cognizer's original equipment. It is easy to suppose that the media of cognition must be acquired from extramental things because it is easy to conflate the different components of the cognitive process and to think of the acquisition of intelligible forms as the sole means of simultaneously making epistemic contact and rendering intelligible the things with which the cognizer is in contact. But that these are distinct components is clearly indicated by the case of the

agnosia patient. When he moves from a bizarre but acceptable general characterization (*"a continuous surface with five outpouchings"*) to an incorrect
specific characterization (*"a coin purse"*) despite his possession of the appropriate concept *glove*, he shows that he is in command of only some and not
all of those components. Although the agnosia patient has the intelligible
form of a glove (as Aquinas would say) in his intellect before the glove is
presented to him, he cannot do what Aquinas thinks that the angels do with
the intelligible forms in their minds from the time of their creation, namely,
apply it newly to something newly presented to the mind.

Aquinas's account of angelic cognition thus presupposes the sort of
distinction among the components of the process of cognition I outlined
above; but his discussion of angelic cognition is most helpfully understood
as concerned with only components (b) and (c), not with (a), the making of
epistemic contact. The agnosia patient makes visual epistemic contact with
the glove presented to him because the glove acts causally on his eyes. There
is, however, nothing in Aquinas's account of the concreated possession of the
intelligible forms in angels or the angels' ability to apply those forms that
explains the way in which, on Aquinas's view, angels, who lack senses, make
epistemic contact with particular things.

To summarize this brief exposition of Aquinas's account of angelic cognition, then, the claim that angels must cognize universally does not mean
that universals are the only objects of angelic cognition. Instead, Aquinas's
idea is that naturally inherent, universal intelligible forms are the media
through which angels render intelligible particular objects with which they
come into epistemic contact. And at least some of the perplexing features of
his account of angelic cognition can be cleared up by recognizing that
Aquinas is primarily concerned to explain the nature of angelic representations, rather than the way angels make epistemic contact with the particular
objects of their cognition.

God's cognition of creatures

These clarifications of Aquinas's theory of angelic cognition help us understand his account of God's knowledge. Among the things perplexing about
that account are Aquinas's claims that God cognizes things other than
himself in himself, "insofar as his essence contains a likeness of things other
than himself",[57] and that God cognizes by means of just one, perfectly
universal intelligible form. Both these claims can now be seen as logical
extensions of Aquinas's claims about angelic cognition.

Because Aquinas thinks of God as being itself, God's nature is for
Aquinas the most universal form through which all beings can be cognized.
The grandest unified *metaphysical* Theory of Everything would explain all
creatures not in terms of their fundamental particles and forces but in terms
of their participation in subsistent being. So for God to cognize created

things in himself, through his own nature, the intelligible form of his being, is to cognize them as deeply and understand them as fully as possible.[58] Nothing in this view of Aquinas's entails that *what* God knows is only universal, or that he knows only common natures and not particulars, any more than the physicist's deeper understanding of matter entails that he cannot know ordinary material individual things such as *this* cup. Similarly, the claim that the only intelligible form for God is his own nature does not entail that God cannot cognize individuals, because that unique intelligible form is simply *the medium through which* God cognizes individuals. So Aquinas says: "God cognizes his effects through his essence in the same way as a thing itself is cognized through a likeness of the thing."[59] As the human intellect cognizes a corporeal individual such as this cup through an intelligible form *cup*, so God's essence serves as the intelligible form through which he cognizes each and every created individual.

(There is, however, this relevant difference between the human intellect and the divine mind. Except in cases of introspection, for a human intellect an intelligible form is *only* the medium through which the intellect cognizes and not *also* what it cognizes. But God not only cognizes eternally through his essence; he also eternally cognizes his essence itself, since he knows himself primarily, and other things as well. And that's why Aquinas says that "God cognizes himself and other things in one cognition."[60])

So in the case of divine cognition, as in the case of angelic cognition, some of what is perplexing in Aquinas's account is cleared up if we take it as a theory of the nature of the similitude or intelligible form through which God knows and the way in which that divine similitude or form renders intelligible everything with which God is in epistemic contact, rather than as a theory about the way in which God is in epistemic contact with creatures or the way in which the one divine similitude is applied to the objects of God's cognition.

Intellective cognition of material particulars

There is, of course, still a problem about how Aquinas thinks an immaterial cognizer, such as God or an angel, can cognize *material* particulars. In the case of the human intellect, Aquinas insists that intellective cognition of material particulars requires the intellect's working together with the senses, because only the senses are in contact with material particulars. How, then, do God and the angels cognize material particulars, since they have no senses?

It is helpful in this connection to be clear about the nature of the problem for Aquinas. On his views, what is the difficulty in an immaterial intellect's cognizing a material object? And why does he think that direct human cognition of material particulars can be had only by means of the senses? Philosophers who raise objections to dualism standardly see a problem in an immaterial knower's knowing a material object because they suppose that knowledge requires the thing known to act causally on the knower, and they cannot imagine how an immaterial knower could be affected by the causal action of a material thing. But Aquinas would not see the problem in these terms; from his point of view, the main problem lies elsewhere.

Aquinas *would* agree that the intellective cognition of a material particular cannot be explained in terms of the immaterial mind's being directly affected by the causal action of a material object.[61] In this sense, he would be on the side of the contemporary objectors to dualism: for Aquinas, *nothing* material can act causally on the immaterial, not even on the immaterial human intellect. On his understanding of the process of human cognition, a material object of cognition exercises efficient causation in the cognitive process, but only to the point in the process at which Aquinas locates the phantasms, the processed deliverances of the senses.[62] At that point, the direction of efficient causation is reversed. In order for the intellect to cognize anything, the intellect must act causally on the phantasm.[63]

So where the human intellect becomes active in the cognitive process, at the threshold of intellective cognition, the chain of efficient causality exercised ultimately by the extramental material object comes to an end, and the human intellect initiates a causal chain in which the order of causation runs from the intellect to the phantasms, not the other way around.[64] The only causal relationship running *from* the direction of the material object all the way to the intellect is the *formal* causation through which the form of the extramental material object persists in the abstraction produced when the intellect strips away the individuating characteristics retained in the phantasm.

Consequently, for Aquinas the process of arriving at intellective cognition is never a matter of a material object's acting with efficient causality on an immaterial intellect. The claim that the material cannot act causally on the immaterial therefore does not pose problems for his account of the cognition of God and the angels, any more than it does for his account of the cognition had by the human intellect. He does not suppose that even human cognition occurs in virtue of such causation. So the problem for Aquinas of God's cognition of material particulars needs to be formulated differently.

In the first place, the problem as Aquinas sees it does not have to do with matter in a twentieth-century sense, every instance of which he would characterize as a composite of matter and form, but rather with matter apart from any forms. And, second, the problem arises in consequence of Aquinas's theory about how any cognition works. Cognition requires that a form or likeness of what is cognized be in the cognizer; cognition on the part of the immaterial human intellect requires that the forms of the extramental material things it cognizes be abstracted from those things. But a form or likeness of any material object is distinct from that object's matter. So, in acquiring an intelligible form of a material object abstracted from the object itself, the human intellect is coming into epistemic contact only with something non-material. It is not directly connected with the matter of the cognized object. But, on Aquinas's metaphysics, for material objects, matter is what individuates, not form. If an immaterial intellect is making contact only with the immaterial form of a material object, then it is not in contact with that which renders the object an individual thing.[65]

The real problem here for Aquinas is therefore not that an immaterial intellect cannot be affected by the causal action of a material thing, since on his view intellective cognition does not require such causation, but rather that in the nature of the case the immaterial intellect can come into direct contact only with the immaterial aspects of material particulars. Aquinas says:

> every form as such is universal, and so the addition of a form to a form cannot be the cause of individuation [for material particulars], because however many forms are gathered together at once, ... they do not constitute a particular ... Rather, the individuation of a form depends on the matter through which the form is limited to this or that determinate [thing].[66]

In the case of human intellective cognition, the intelligible forms through which human beings have cognition of extramental material objects are acquired from the cognized material objects, which begin the process of cognition by acting causally on the human senses. But utterly formless matter is entirely inert; because it is pure potentiality, it cannot act on anything. Consequently, matter considered just as such, formless matter, cannot act causally on a human cognizer in any way. Aquinas says:

> Because of the weakness of its being, since it is being only in potentiality, matter [by itself, apart from form] cannot be a source of action. And therefore a thing that acts on our soul acts only through form. And so the likeness of a thing imprinted on a sense and purified through several stages until it gets to the intellect is a likeness of a form only.[67]

Therefore, the human intellect cannot directly cognize the individuating material component in material objects. Consequently, the human intellect cannot know material particulars directly.

The problem of cognizing material particulars is solved as regards human beings because their senses are corporeal and receive corporeal impressions from the material particulars being sensed:

> A sense is a power of a corporeal organ. Now anything whatever is received in something in keeping with the recipient's mode [of

being] ... And, therefore, a sense has to receive corporeally and materially a likeness of the thing it senses.[68]

Moreover, Aquinas says:

> the object of any sensory power is a form insofar as it is in corporeal matter. Because matter of this sort is the source of individuation, every power of the sensory part [of the soul] cognizes particulars only.[69]

In other words, the senses, unlike the intellect, can be in contact with the matter of what is cognized, at least in this respect, that the senses are corporeally affected by the material things being sensed. The cognized material object acts causally on the matter of a sense organ and brings about a material change in it. By this means, a sense organ is in contact with the matter of a material object. By reflecting on, or "processing", the input that has its source in such corporeal impressions made by material objects on the corporeal senses, the immaterial intellect itself can cognize matter indirectly in turning to the phantasms. And so, Aquinas says, "the intellect cognizes both [universals and particulars], although not in the same way".[70]

But, of course, this way of resolving the problem as regards human intellective cognition is not available for divine or angelic cognition. God and angels do not acquire intelligible forms from the extramental things they cognize. Angels have their forms of things built into them at their creation by God, and God cognizes all the things he makes through the universal intelligible form that is his own nature. And neither God nor the angels receive corporeal impressions of material objects through senses. How, then, are they supposed to cognize corporeal individuals, including human beings, for instance? Or, to put the question more precisely, how do they cognize the individuating matter in the corporeal individuals they know, if they cannot do so by turning to the products of the senses as human intellects do?

For Aquinas, the answer to the question has to do with the fact that one of the things God creates is matter itself. That is, God not only makes composites of matter and form, as any craftsman or inventor does, but he also creates the formless matter that underlies the forms of any material object. It is this aspect of his creative activity that earns it the designation *ex nihilo*. As the "inventor" of matter, God cognizes it under the perfectly universal intelligible form that is his nature, and so of course he does not acquire his cognition from matter. Instead, he creates matter to instantiate the cognition of it he already has. And by means of this "inventor's" cognition of matter, God cognizes matter *itself* as human knowers cannot do. Aquinas says:

> The being of things, which is common to [their] form and matter, flows from the forms of things in the divine mind, and so these forms are related immediately to both form and matter [in created things] ... And in this way our mind has immaterial cognition of material things, but the divine mind and an angelic mind cognize material things more immaterially and yet [also] more perfectly.[71]

So for God and the angels, it poses no problem that formless matter cannot act on anything, because there is no need for them to acquire the form of matter from matter. The form of matter is antecedently in the mind of God, before he creates matter; and he builds this form into the minds of the angels, together with all other forms, at their creation. The form of matter is therefore available for both God and the angels to apply to material objects in cognition, together with the other forms instantiated in those objects. By this means, the very matter of an extramental material object is intelligible to God and to the angels, in virtue of the form of matter that they possess.

Aquinas thereby has solved the problem of the cognition of material objects by an immaterial cognizer as that problem arises for him, in the context of his metaphysics and his understanding of the nature of cognition. His solution allows him to explain in his terms how it is that an extramental material object is intelligible to an immaterial cognizer who cannot cognize material things through the senses.

Nonetheless, this solution leaves one perplexity unexplained. In the case of the cognition of material objects by a human cognizer, the operation of the senses explains *two* of the parts of the process of cognition. It explains not only how a material object causes a cognizer to acquire some forms of it that are necessary for the object's features and particularity to be intelligible to the cognizer, but it also explains how that cognizer comes into epistemic contact with that very object, rather than some other. In the case of the cognition of material objects by God and the angels, however, Aquinas's account in terms of a form of matter pre-existing in the intellect explains only how the cognized material object in its materiality is intelligible to God or to an angel. It does nothing to explain how God or an angel is in epistemic contact with *this* rather than *that* particular object. Given that the form of matter in the divine or angelic mind is just one form, how is it that by means of it the immaterial mind in question cognizes *this particular* material object and not some other? (I will reserve comment on this problem till the end of this chapter.)

The causative character of God's knowledge

Finally, we are now also in a position to consider Aquinas's claim that God's knowledge is causative. As I explained in the introduction to this chapter, this claim is often interpreted to mean that

(1) God knows everything that he knows in virtue of his knowledge's being the efficient cause of what he knows;

or the weaker version of this, namely,

(2) God knows everything that he knows which is in time in the actual world in virtue of his knowledge's being the efficient cause of this part of what he knows.

On even the weaker claim, our knowing, for example, that Brutus is one of Caesar's assassins depends on Brutus's action; God's knowing that Brutus is one of Caesar's assassins causes Brutus's action. For the reasons given above (as well as for the reasons that follow here), I think this interpretation of Aquinas's claim is mistaken.

It may be helpful here to underline what I am and what I am not denying. I am *not* denying that Aquinas holds any of these claims: (3) God's knowledge is causative (in some sense of 'causative'); (4) God is (in some sense of 'primary cause'[72]) the primary efficient cause of the existence of all created substances in the world; and (5) there are some actions, events, or states of affairs which are efficiently caused by God.[73] What seems to me mistaken as attributed to Aquinas is just claims (1) and (2) above, and the falsity of (1) and (2) is compatible with the truth of (3)–(5).

In my view, the attribution of two assumptions to Aquinas lies behind the mistaken interpretation of Aquinas's account of God's knowledge:

(Assumption A) the causation which God's knowledge has is efficient causation;

and

(Assumption B) what is effected by the causation of the divine cognition includes all actions, events, and states of affairs in the world.

I think both assumptions are false as attributed to Aquinas. (And, of course, if Aquinas does not hold the second assumption, then he also does not hold that, for everything God knows, God's knowledge "is itself [efficiently] causative of what is known".[74])

It is helpful to begin by asking carefully about the nature of the causation Aquinas attributes to God's knowledge. Although contemporary philosophy almost invariably has efficient causation in mind when it talks about causation, it is, of course, the case that Aquinas, following Aristotle, recognizes four different sorts of causes: material, final, and formal, as well as efficient.

Now Aquinas identifies God's own nature as the intelligible form through which God cognizes everything:

God cognizes his own nature perfectly, and so he cognizes it in every way in which it can be cognized. But it can be cognized not only as it is in itself, but [also] insofar as it can be participated in by creatures in some mode of likeness.[75]

So when God's nature is considered as the intelligible form through which God knows other things, the divine nature serves this function because of the ways in which created things can participate in it. In the mind of God, these ways are the divine ideas,[76] forms or likenesses[77] of possible imitations of God's nature. Aquinas says that they play a part in all of God's cognition of entities other than himself.[78]

The divine ideas, Aquinas likes to say, are analogous to the ideas a craftsman has. They are like the pattern the craftsman has in mind before he begins to make anything.[79] His favorite analogy to illustrate what he means by a divine idea is the pattern a builder has in mind as he begins to build a house.[80] It is in this same respect that the divine ideas constitute causes of the things created in accordance with them. In arguing that God's knowledge is the cause of what he knows, Aquinas says:

the knowledge of God is related to all created things as the knowledge of an artisan is related to artifacts. Now the knowledge of an artisan is the cause of artifacts; for insofar as the artisan operates through his intellect, the form in his intellect is the principle of his operation.[81]

The divine ideas are thus exemplars: any thing God creates has the form it has in imitation of the form that is the divine idea representative of that thing. But then the divine ideas are *formal* causes, not efficient causes:

A form is, in a certain respect, a cause of that which is formed in accordance with it, whether the forming takes place by way of the form's inhering, as in the case of intrinsic forms, or by way of imitation [of it], as in the case of exemplar forms.[82]

The pattern a builder has in mind as he begins to build a house is the formal cause of the house, not an efficient cause. And so Aquinas says:

in order for an individual thing to be cognized, the cognitive power must contain a likeness of it in its particularity ... Now the likeness of a cognized thing is in a cognizer in two ways. In one way, [it is in the cognizer] as caused by the thing, as in the case of those things that are cognized through a form abstracted from the things. In the other way, [it is the cognizer] as a cause of the thing [cognized], as is evident in the case of an artisan who cognizes an artifact through the form through which he makes it.[83]

It is because he understands the causation of God's knowledge as formal causation that Aquinas says about God's knowledge:

> Natural things are intermediates between the knowledge of God and our knowledge, for we receive knowledge from natural things, of which God is the cause by means of his knowledge. And so, as natural knowable [things] are prior to our knowledge and the measure of it, so the knowledge of God is prior to natural things and the measure of them. In just the same way a house is an intermediate between the knowledge of the artisan who makes it and the knowledge of the person who takes cognition of it from the house when it is already made.[84]

Consequently, when Aquinas says that God's knowledge is causative, he does not mean that God's act of cognition efficiently causes what God knows. He means rather that the divine ideas are formal causes of the things God creates or can create. That is why Aquinas can say in one and the same breath, as he does in the following passage, both that God's knowledge causes what God knows and that God knows things that do not exist because they are not caused to exist by God:

> The cognition of the divine intellect is related to other things as the cognition of an artisan to artifacts since he is the cause of things by his knowledge. But an artisan also cognizes those things which are not yet crafted (*artificiata*) by means of the cognition of his art ... And so nothing keeps there from being in the knowledge of an artisan those forms which are not yet externally produced. Therefore, in the same way, nothing keeps God from having knowledge of those things that do not exist.[85]

If God's knowledge is the formal cause of things, the causation in question is compatible with the non-existence of things, as efficient causation is not. What an efficient cause causes comes into existence; but a formal cause is simply the form of a thing, which may or may not come into existence, depending on whether or not it is brought into existence by the operation of an efficient cause.

These considerations make clear the mistake of attributing to Aquinas either Assumption A or Assumption B above. As I have shown, for Aquinas the causation of God's knowledge is formal causation, not efficient causation, and so he does not hold Assumption A. But for these same reasons, we can see that Aquinas does not hold Assumption B either. Medievals, including Aquinas, love the matter–form distinction and tend to apply it indiscriminately to virtually anything at all; but they are speaking figuratively when they do so, not literally or strictly.

Strictly or properly speaking, the formal cause of a thing is the form of an entity when it is either a form or a composite of matter and form. Anything that is a form or a composite of matter and form, however, is a substance or an artifact, or a part of a substance or artifact. Acts, events, and states of affairs are not substances, artifacts, or the parts of either, however. There are no artisans of states of affairs; builders build artifacts, not events or acts. The form of the house in the mind of the builder is thus the cause of the existence of the house; it is not the cause of all the states of affairs of the house, such as its being decrepit, or of the events that happen to the house, such as its burning down. And so formal causes are causes of things such as substances and artifacts; they are not causes of acts, events, or states of affairs.

It is therefore also a mistake to attribute Assumption B to Aquinas. The formal causation of God's knowledge is the formal cause of things with forms. Of course, if one knows completely the form of a thing, one thereby knows the features of the thing conferred on it by the form. The builder who knows completely the form of the house knows how many people the house will safely hold, for example. But it remains true that the form of the house in the mind of the builder is not the cause of the collapse of the house when too many people come into it.

Aquinas therefore holds neither Assumption A nor Assumption B. For this reason, interpretations of his account of God's knowledge that ascribe to Aquinas even the weaker claim (2) are mistaken. This conclusion is compatible with supposing that God is an efficient cause as well and that his efficient causality extends even to some acts, events, and states of affairs. The conclusion I have argued for here denies only that God's knowledge alone is an efficient cause and that it is a cause of everything, or everything in time in the world, that God knows. Denying this is not a disadvantage for Aquinas, however; it is rather a necessity, on pain of inconsistency, as I pointed out at the outset of this chapter. Finally, understanding the causation of God's knowledge on Aquinas's account as formal knowledge also rebuts the objection that Aquinas's account entails causal epistemic determinism. Formal causation of a thing is compatible with the absence of causal determination of that thing.

Epistemic contact

Although the preceding considerations resolve some of the problems with which this chapter began, insofar as they make it clear that Aquinas's account of God's knowledge does not constitute a species of Averroism and that it does not entail divine epistemic determinism of everything God knows, nonetheless an important problem remains. This chapter began with a question about how an omniscient immaterial God knows, a question to which Aquinas's account of God's knowledge seems to offer a detailed, defensible answer. But at least part of what the original question seeks is something that so far has not been addressed. Using the analysis of the process of cognition illustrated by the neurobiological study of agnosia, we can say that part of what is wanted as an answer to the question is an explanation of the way in which an omniscient immaterial God makes epistemic contact with things in the created world.

It is worth noticing here that although this analysis is well illustrated by contemporary neurobiology, the analysis itself is presupposed by Aquinas. So, for example, Aquinas presupposes the distinction between being in epistemic contact with something and rendering intelligible what one is in epistemic contact with. God renders temporal things intelligible in cognizing them through the intelligible form that is his essence, but he is in epistemic contact with temporal things because they are atemporally present to him. So, for example, in explaining God's knowledge of time, Aquinas tends to say things of this sort: "the whole course of time and the things that happen throughout all time are within his view as present and as suited to it".[86]

The third element in the analysis of the cognitive process, namely, applying a concept or intelligible form to what one is in epistemic contact with, is also presupposed in Aquinas's discussions of knowledge. For example, Aquinas says:

> every cognition is in accordance with some form, which is the source of cognition in the cognizer. But this sort of form can be considered in two ways. In one way, in keeping with the being that it has in the cognizer; in another way, in keeping with the relation it bears to the thing whose likeness it is. Considered in the first relationship, it makes the cognizer actually cognizant. Considered in the second relationship, however, it determines the cognition to some determinate cognizable thing.[87]

The intelligible form through which God cognizes his own nature makes him actually cognizant of everything he is in epistemic contact with. But, as Aquinas indicates, there also has to be a certain relationship between the intelligible form and what is cognized, a relationship that "determine[s] the cognition to some determinate cognizable thing".

Aquinas explicitly employs this analysis of cognition even with respect to God's knowledge. As we've seen, Aquinas argues that when an angel has a new cognition of something, it does not acquire a new representation or intelligible form; instead, it merely makes a new application of an intelligible form it has always had. Aquinas explains this feature of angelic cognition by reference to the divine cognition:

> this applying should be understood in accordance with the way God applies the [divine] ideas to cognize things. [God does] not [apply a divine idea] to something else as a medium [of cognition] that is [itself] cognizable; rather, [he applies it] to the thing cognized as the mode of cognizing [it].[88]

So Aquinas recognizes that the cognitive process involves more than possessing a concept or intelligible form, and here he identifies what else is needed as applying the intelligible form to the cognized thing.

On Aquinas's account of God's knowledge, then, for God, too, direct and immediate cognition of things outside his mind involves at least three elements: (a*) God's being in epistemic contact with everything he cognizes, (b*) God's possessing a concept or intelligible form of what he cognizes,[89] and (c*) God's applying that concept or form to what he is in epistemic contact with.

Most of Aquinas's explicit discussion of God's knowledge is an explanation of (b*), an attempt to say how God has the form requisite for cognition of things other than himself. Aquinas's understanding of the other two elements of God's cognition, however, is evident in what Aquinas says about them in his account of divine knowledge, his speculation about angelic cognition, and his general discussions of intellectual cognition.

Given the pre-eminence of the doctrine of God's absolute simplicity in Aquinas's philosophical theology and the difficulty of accounting for ideas of things in a simple God, the focus of Aquinas's attention is perhaps understandable. But it leaves us with problems, and one of them is the nature of God's epistemic contact with creatures.

Aquinas has a clear view of how epistemic contact is established when a human being cognizes an external object: the thing being cognized has an effect on the cognizer's senses, and that causal connection constitutes the epistemic contact. But, of course, this kind of explanation cannot be what accounts for God's epistemic contact with creatures. So how, on Aquinas's view, does God make epistemic contact with the created things he cognizes?

It sometimes looks as if Aquinas's answer to this question is not very different from the blank response, "He just does!"[90] In replying to questions about God's cognition of particular material things, Aquinas has a tendency to say such things as this:

> God does cognize individuals. For all the perfections found in creatures pre-exist in God in a higher way ... But cognizing individuals is a feature of our perfection, and so it is necessary that God cognize individuals. For even the Philosopher considered it absurd to

suppose that there is something that is cognized by us but not by God.[91]

Blank as this standard reply is, however, it does express the leading idea in his approach to an account of God's nature via an extrapolation from human nature: anything we can do (that involves no human imperfection), God can do better.

But a more forthcoming response can also be found in his writings. Aquinas divides all knowledge into two sorts:

> one sort is called the knowledge of vision, through which things that are, or will be, or were, are cognized. The other is the knowledge of simple awareness, through which one cognizes things that neither are, nor will be, nor were, but can be.[92]

And in passages making plain that Aquinas himself finds it acceptable to attribute "a perceptual paradigm of knowledge",[93] analogously understood, to God, Aquinas holds that God must have both these sorts of knowledge. Possibilities that are never actualized are cognized by God

> in accordance with the awareness of simple intellection [i.e., the knowledge of simple awareness]. On the other hand, God cognizes things that are present, past, or future with respect to us insofar as they are in his power, in their own causes, and in themselves. And [his] cognition of them is called awareness [i.e., knowledge] of vision.[94]

There are many other places where Aquinas talks about God's intellective observation,[95] God's view,[96] God's vision,[97] and God's gaze.[98] So the things with which God is in epistemic contact he renders intelligible through the intelligible form that is his essence and that is reflected and particularized in the divine ideas that are the formal causes of created things. But it looks very much as if Aquinas takes God to be in epistemic contact with creatures in virtue of metaphorically or analogously "seeing" them.

The claim that God's epistemic contact with creatures is a kind of "seeing" also helps explain why Aquinas insists on explaining God's knowledge of future contingents as he does. Aquinas takes the doctrine of divine eternity to be required to account for God's knowledge of future contingents; and the point of the doctrine is to support the claim that all the temporal things — whether they are past, present, or future with respect to us — are in fact present with respect to God. But it is hard to understand why God's mode of cognition would require its objects' presence, unless we recognize that Aquinas's attempt to parse divine epistemic contact with created things in terms of God's as it were "seeing" them. Seeing a thing does require it to be present to sight in some sense.

Aquinas's theory of God's epistemic contact with created things might then be construed as a matter of God's seeing, in some extended sense of 'seeing'. But there are problems with doing so.

The most obvious has to do with God's impassibility. If God's epistemic contact with creatures consists in "seeing" them atemporally, then his cognizing them and their doings does not compromise divine immutability; without time, change is, of course, impossible. But it seems nonetheless that any process which could count as seeing of contingents must also involve reception.[99] And since receiving is a kind of undergoing, it seems that God's "seeing" of creatures must be incompatible with his impassibility.

Now among the kinds of receiving or undergoing Aquinas recognizes, some involve deterioration or improvement; there is, for instance, getting sick and getting better. This is the kind of receiving or undergoing most obviously ruled out by divine impassibility. Then there is the reception or undergoing that is simply a component of completion, the actualization of a subject's natural potentialities.[100] A cognitive faculty's reception of forms is that kind of reception. Aquinas describes this sort of reception or undergoing in this way: "'undergoing' is [sometimes] used generally for any change, even if it pertains to the perfecting of a nature – as when understanding or sensing is said to be a kind of undergoing".[101]

And, of course, the perfect intellect of an impassible God could not *get perfected*. As Aquinas says, "the divine intellect is not in potentiality but is pure actuality".[102] Furthermore, as I pointed out just above, God cognizes even temporal things not successively but all at once, timelessly; and real potentiality is time-bound. As Aquinas understands the undergoing of cognition, however, it takes time: "Intellect … is said to undergo insofar as it is somehow in potentiality to intelligible things … *before* it understands."[103]

So God cannot have either of the sorts of receiving or undergoing at issue for Aquinas, deterioration or being completed or perfected by receiving information.

Nonetheless, it also seems as if God's intellect would not *be perfect* if it weren't somehow timelessly in receipt of what its "seeing" discloses, aware of things without first having been without that awareness. Furthermore, even in the case of the human intellect, the intellect understands by itself acting on data, not by being acted upon. So it seems that it is possible to hold consistently with Aquinas's other views that God's intellect as it were sees things but without undergoing and without being acted upon. In that case, God would "see" things but without there being any violation of his impassibility when he did so.

Even if there were no problem about divine impassibility, however, we might find Aquinas's talk of God's "seeing" mysterious; and the question analogous to that with which this chapter began might also be raised about it: how does God accomplish this "seeing"? As far as I can see, Aquinas provides no further help in analyzing God's epistemic contact than to hold that God applies his ideas to what he cognizes and that God atemporally "sees" things other than himself. In this respect, then, Aquinas's account is just incomplete.

It is worth noticing, however, that currently standard accounts of human cognition are also incomplete in analogous respects, contrary to what one might suppose. Although it is clear that concepts or mental representations have to be applied to what the cognizer is in epistemic contact with, no one has more than a rudimentary idea of what such application consists in or of what has gone wrong in agnosia patients who are no longer capable of it. Furthermore, although it is true that what is cognized acts causally on the cognizer's senses, for that causal connection to count as *epistemic* contact at all, the sensory data produced in that way must undergo some processing by the central nervous system. Causal contact between some object and say, an eye in a vat would not constitute epistemic contact. But sensory input by itself underdetermines the result of the central nervous system's processing.[104] How is the result of that processing related to the thing cognized, then? Or, to put it another way, how is it that the result of the processing constitutes epistemic contact with the extramental things that generated the sensory input? At the moment, at any rate, nobody knows.[105] The incompleteness of Aquinas's account of God's knowledge looks less surprising when we recognize that contemporary accounts of human knowledge are incomplete in the same way.

Conclusion

I have presented an interpretation of Aquinas's account of God's knowledge as an answer to the question, How does God know what he knows? I've shown one of the misinterpretations to which his account is liable, and I've argued that when his account is properly understood, it commits Aquinas to neither determinism nor Averroism. Insofar as the question about God's knowledge with which I started this chapter tacitly includes a question about God's epistemic contact with what he knows, Aquinas's account will not give us a complete answer. But, as I have suggested, this is a question that has not yet been answered regarding human cognition. It should not therefore be surprising that Aquinas provides no answer for it with regard to divine cognition. Furthermore, as Aquinas's rich, complicated account of divine cognition indicates, he fully realizes that there is more to cognition, divine or human, than epistemic contact. For the aspects of cognition beyond epistemic contact, Aquinas's account of God's knowledge is not only consistent with and illuminating of the rest of his monumental philosophical and theological system but also insightful as regards human cognition.

Part II

THE NATURE OF HUMAN BEINGS

6

FORMS AND BODIES
The soul

Introduction

Many philosophers suppose that the major monotheisms, and Christianity in particular, are committed to substance dualism of a Cartesian sort. Descartes explained his dualism in this way:

> my essence consists solely in the fact that I am a thinking thing. It is true that I may have (or, to anticipate, that I certainly have) a body that is very closely joined to me. But nevertheless, on the one hand I have a clear and distinct idea of myself, in so far as I am simply a thinking, non-extended thing; and on the other hand I have a distinct idea of body, in so far as this is simply an extended, non-thinking thing. And accordingly, it is certain that I am really distinct from my body, and can exist without it.[1]

On this Cartesian view, a person may have a body but is neither identical with it nor composed of it, and an intellectual process such as thinking occurs only in the non-material thing that is the person, not in the body. There are "close" connections between a person and his body. The cognitive processes of the person have effects on the body which that person has, and bodily processes, such as sensations, have effects on the person; so a person and his body interact causally. But intellectual cognitive functions are not exercised in or by the body; they take place in the thinking essence that is distinct from the body.

So understood, Cartesian dualism is widely regarded as false. If it is also the case that the major monotheisms have traditionally been committed to dualism of a Cartesian sort, then in the view of many philosophers the apparent or putative falsity of Cartesian dualism becomes an embarrassment for those religions. As a matter of historical fact, however, it is not true that a Cartesian sort of dualism has been the view traditionally espoused by all the major monotheisms. Aquinas, whose views surely represent one major strand of one major monotheism, is familiar with an account very like that of Cartesian dualism, which he associates with Plato; and he rejects it emphatically.

In this chapter, I will explore Aquinas's position. I will look at his rejection of a Cartesian sort of dualism in his attitude towards Platonism with regard to the soul and at the position he adopts in place of it. I will also consider the broader metaphysical issues within which Aquinas's account of the soul is situated, and I will examine the explanation Aquinas's account gives of the theological doctrine of the afterlife. Then I will turn to the vexed business of taxonomy. How should Aquinas's position be identified? For example, where – if anywhere – on the contemporary spectrum of opinions about the relations of mind and matter should Aquinas's account be located? Finally, I will briefly discuss the way Aquinas's account sheds light on contemporary attempts to find some intermediate between Cartesian dualism and eliminative materialism.

Aquinas's rejection of Cartesian dualism

In building his alternative to a Cartesian sort of dualism, Aquinas is guided by two complex, culturally conditioned intuitions, each of which can be conveniently summed up by a biblical passage. The first is God's speech to fallen Adam, which Aquinas takes to apply to all subsequent human beings: "dust thou art, and unto dust shalt thou return" (Gen. 3:19). The second is the line of Ecclesiastes about human beings at the moment of death: "Then shall the dust return to the earth as it was, and the spirit shall return to God who gave it" (Eccles. 12:7). On the first intuition, a human being is a material object, made out of the same sort of constituents as the earth is, and subject to dissolution by having those constituents resolved back into earth. On the second intuition, a human person survives death, whatever may happen to the body, because the spirit or soul continues to exist after the dissolution of the body. Aquinas thinks he can accommodate both these intuitions with his account of the human soul.

Sometimes the main difficulty in interpreting Aquinas lies in ferreting out just what his position on some subject is; interpreting his view of the nature of knowledge, for example, presents this sort of difficulty. But sometimes it is quite clear what Aquinas is claiming, and the difficulty in interpreting him lies in figuring out what his claims mean and why he supposed them to be true. Coming to grips with Aquinas's account of the soul presents the latter sort of difficulty. As is well known, Aquinas takes the soul to be the form of the body. What is much harder to grasp is what Aquinas means by this claim. A second and equally difficult question is whether his conception of the human soul will in fact allow him to reconcile both his apparently conflicting intuitions about the nature of a human being, namely, that a human being is made of matter, on the one hand, and that a human spirit survives death, on the other. It will help with both questions to begin by seeing the depth of Aquinas's commitment to the view that human beings are material objects and the vehemence with which he rejects what we tend to call 'Cartesian dualism'.

The position we commonly refer to as 'Cartesian dualism' Aquinas associates with Plato and thinks of as Platonism's account of the soul. As Aquinas understands Plato:

> Plato said ... that a human being is not something composed of soul and body; rather, a human being is a soul using a body, so that the soul is understood to be in the body somewhat as a sailor is in a ship.[2]

Aquinas typically rejects this position in no uncertain terms. So, for example, he says:

> Plato claimed that a human being is not a composite of soul and body but that a human being is the soul itself using a body, just as Peter is not a composite of a human being and clothes, but rather a human being using clothes. But this position is shown to be impossible. For an animal and a human being are natural, sense-perceptible things. But this would not be the case if a body and its parts did not belong to the essence of a human being and of an animal. Instead, on Plato's view, the whole essence of both a human being and an animal would be the soul, although the soul is not anything sense-perceptible or material. And for this reason it is impossible that [something that is] a human being and an animal be a soul using a body.[3]

In another place, he says:

> The difficulty of this question [whether a soul separated from the body can intellectually cognize something] stems from the fact that while the soul is conjoined to a body, it cannot intellectually cognize something without turning itself to phantasms ... But if this is not because of the nature of the soul but rather happens to it by accident because it is tied to a body, as the Platonists thought, then this question is easily resolved. For then when the impediment of the body is removed, the soul would return to its own nature, so that it could intellectually cognize intelligible things simply, as other separate substances [i.e., angels] do, and not by turning itself to phantasms. But on this view the soul would not be united to the body for the good of the soul, because on this view a soul united to a body would understand less well than when it is separated from the body ... and this [position] is irrational.[4]

193

Furthermore, Aquinas also raises an objection commonly leveled against Cartesian dualism. According to Aquinas, Platonists will have trouble explaining the way in which soul and body are joined. Platonists, Aquinas says, are committed to supposing that the soul is united to the body through some intermediary, because diverse, distinct substances cannot be bound together unless something unites them. And so certain Platonists postulate one or another spirit or humor as the medium between soul and body. But none of these devices is necessary, Aquinas says, if the soul is understood as the form of the body.[5]

As these and many other passages make clear, then, Aquinas recognizes a position he associates with Platonism which is very similar to, if not identical with, what we commonly take to be Cartesian dualism; and Aquinas rejects it unconditionally. Aquinas's emphatic repudiation of such Cartesian (or, as he would say, Platonic) dualism should be kept in mind as we consider Aquinas's own position.

Form as configuring: material forms

Because Aquinas takes the soul to be the form of the body and because of the focus on form in his account, it will also be helpful to say something briefly about Aquinas's general account of form.[6] Aquinas discusses forms in connection with God, angels, human beings, and non-human material objects. For our purposes in this chapter, it is perhaps best to begin with Aquinas's view of the nature of the forms of non-human material objects, which he sometimes calls 'material forms'.[7] Although Aquinas thinks that not all forms are forms of material objects, nevertheless on his view all material things are composites of matter and form. That is, earthworms, daisies, rocking chairs, amethyst clumps, and bread dough, share with all other material things, including human beings, the characteristic of having both matter and form as their metaphysical constituents.

A substantial form is the form in virtue of which a material composite is a member of the species to which it belongs, and it configures prime matter. The complete form (the substantial and accidental forms taken together) of a non-human material object is the arrangement or organization of the matter of that object in such a way that it constitutes that object rather than some other one and gives that object its causal powers. In general, form for Aquinas is not static but dynamic. That is why Aquinas thinks that when we use the names of the living body and its parts for the dead body and its parts, we use those words equivocally. The soul is the substantial form of the human body, and death separates it from the matter it previously organized. Once a human being dies and the soul is gone, Aquinas says, we use such words as 'flesh' or 'eye' equivocally if we apply them to parts of the corpse.[8] At death, the soul is replaced with a different, non-animating substantial form. The matter of the body is then configured in a substantially different way and so has a form different from the one it had before death.[9] That is why the body can be called 'a human body' only equivocally even immediately after death.

Unlike some of his contemporaries, Aquinas thought that any given substance has only one substantial form.[10] That is, a material substance such as a cat does not have one substantial form in virtue of which it is a cat, another in virtue of which it is an animal, a third in virtue of which it is a living thing, a fourth in virtue of which it is a material thing, and so on. On Aquinas's view, there is just one substantial form for any substance which makes it what it is; the one substantial form of a cat makes the cat a material object, a living thing, an animal, and a cat. When Aquinas says that the soul is the form of the body, he means that it is the single, substantial form of the body.

On Aquinas's view, as we increase complexity in systems, even systems of inanimate things, properties emerge which are properties of the whole system but not properties of the material parts of the system. For example, he says:

> the nobler a form is, the more it dominates corporeal matter and the less it is submerged in it and the more it exceeds it in its operation or power. And so we see that the form of a mixed body has a certain operation which is not caused from the qualities of the elements [of which that body is composed].[11]

And elsewhere he says:

> to the extent to which a form is more perfect, to that extent it surpasses [its] corporeal matter ... For the form of an element does not have any operation except that which arises by means of the active and passive qualities which are the dispositions of the corporeal matter [it informs]. But the form of a mineral body has an operation that exceeds the active and passive qualities ... as, for example, that a magnet attracts iron ... A vegetative soul has an operation which is aided by the organic active and passive qualities [of the matter it informs] but nonetheless it can surpass a quality of such a sort ... A sensitive soul has an operation to which the active and passive qualities [of the matter it informs] can in no way extend, except to the extent to which they are required for the composition of an organ by means of which this operation is exercised.[12]

On Aquinas's account of form, then, the fact that material objects are composites of matter and form means that even inanimate material objects can have emergent properties, and these emergent properties may bring with them further emergent properties, such as causal potentialities which belong to the whole but not to its parts.

It is not hard to illustrate Aquinas's idea with examples from contemporary biology. So, for example, the normal prion protein differs from the pathological prion protein that causes mad cow disease and its human variant in virtually no respect except the three-dimensional arrangement of the molecule. But normal prion protein is an innocuous part of ordinary neurons, while the differently structured disease-causing prion protein can afflict brains with spongiform degeneration.[13] Now the shape of a molecule results from the configuration of the components of the molecule, from their chemical and physical properties and the biochemical processes by which they causally interact with each other. The shape of the molecule is thus not just a sum of the shapes of the parts of that molecule; rather, the shape is an emergent property of the molecule as a whole.[14]

There are, of course, different understandings of the notion of emergent property.[15] As I am using 'emergent' here, a property is emergent in case it is a feature or property of a whole or system, is not a property of the parts of that system, and can be explained in terms of the properties of the parts of the system and the causal interactions among the parts.[16] On Aquinas's account, a thing may also, however, exemplify what John Searle calls "a much more adventurous conception" of emergence, in which a feature of the whole cannot be explained just in terms of the properties of the individual parts of the whole and the causal interactions among those parts.[17] In virtue of its shape (which is a feature of the whole system), the disease-causing prion protein has the causal power to destroy brain tissue (a causal power that is itself another feature of the whole system). But, for some large proteins, the shape of the biologically active molecule does not result just from the properties and causal interactions among the atoms that constitute the molecule;[18] and knowing the molecule's constituent atoms and the way those atoms can interact with one another is not enough to explain or predict the shape of the biologically active molecule. That is because the shape is produced by the interaction of the atoms of the molecule with enzymes or other molecules that catalyze folding.[19] But a molecule catalyzing folding is not itself a part of the prion protein being folded or its parts, and so the causal properties of the pathological prion protein cannot be explained just in terms of the parts of that protein itself. In this sort of case, then, the feature of being able to destroy brain tissue is emergent in Searle's "more adventurous" sense of 'emergent'.[20]

Furthermore, although accounts of emergentism are typically couched in terms of emergent *properties*, on Aquinas's way of thinking about material objects what can emerge when form is imposed on matter is not just properties but substances. When material components are combined into something higher level with a particular configuration, a substance will come into being.[21] So, for example, expounding a view of Aristotle's, Aquinas says:

> sometimes a composite has its species from something one, which is either a form ... or a composition ... or an organization ... In such cases, it must be the case that a composite is not those things out of which it is composed, as a syllable is not [its] letters. Just as this syllable 'BA' is not identical to these two letters 'B' and 'A', so neither is flesh identical to fire and earth [the elements of which it is composed]. And [Aristotle] proves this in the following way. If those things out of which the composition is formed are dissociated or separated from one another, ... the whole does not remain after the dissolution, just as flesh does not remain once [its] elements are separated [from each other], and the syllable does not remain once its letters are separated [from each other]. But ... the letters remain after the dissolution of the syllable, and fire and earth remain after the dissolution of the flesh. Therefore, a syllable is something more than [its] letters ... and in this way, similarly, flesh also is not only fire and earth (or heat and cold, by virtue of which the elements are commingled) but rather there is something else by means of which flesh is flesh.[22]

Aquinas's account is thus anti-reductionistic.[23] It is not true on his account that a material whole is nothing but its material parts or is identical to its material components.[24] The configuration of the whole will sometimes confer features, such as causal powers, on the whole which are not shared by the components of the whole.

In general, then, a substantial material form is the configurational state of a material object that makes that object a member of the kind or species to which it belongs and gives it the causal powers characteristic of things of that kind.

Forms as configured substances: angels

There is, however, another kind of form that plays an important role in Aquinas's thought. This is the sort of form that does not configure matter.

In arguing that God is not composed of matter and form, for example, Aquinas says:

> every agent acts by means of its form. And for this reason, a thing is related to its being an agent in the same way as it is related to its form. Therefore, it must be that something which is first and of itself an agent is primarily and of itself a form. But God is the first

197

agent, since he is the first efficient cause ... Therefore, through his essence God is form.[25]

Unlike material forms, the form that is God does not configure matter. More importantly, but equally obviously, the form that is God is not dependent on matter for its existence. Rather, it exists of itself, an immaterial and independently subsistent form. Aquinas explains the difference between a material form and a form entirely independent of matter in this way. He says:

> Those things which are composed of matter and form are not immediately an entity and one; rather, matter is a potential entity (*ens in potentia*) and becomes an actual entity through the advent of a form, which is for matter a cause of being. But a form does not have being through another form. And so if there is a subsistent form, it is immediately an entity and one.[26]

Clearly, there is a great difference between form of the sort that God is and the material forms informing non-human material objects. The doctrine of simplicity so complicates the discussion of God's nature, however, that focus on God as form is almost certainly more trouble than help in understanding Aquinas's notion of subsistent form. But we can readily enough leave considerations of God to one side because there is a useful and less complicated discussion of subsistent form in Aquinas's account of the angels. Aquinas himself makes a comparison of God and angels on this score; in the course of examining essence and accidents in angels, he says:

> a simple form which is pure act cannot be the subject of any accidents, because a subject is related to accidents as potentiality to actuality. And only God is of this sort [i.e., a simple form which is pure act] ... But a simple form which is not its own being but is related to it as potentiality to actuality can be the subject of accidents ... and such a simple form is an angel.[27]

So, like God, an angel is form existing on its own.

Aquinas does consider the question whether an angel is a composite of matter and form, and he discusses the answer that an angel is made out of form and a special sort of matter, a spiritual matter; but he rejects this answer decisively. An angel is not a sort of ghost, composed of ghostly stuff. Instead, speaking of angels, Aquinas says, "every intellectual substance is altogether immaterial."[28] So, for Aquinas, an angel is a subsistent immaterial form.[29]

We are naturally inclined to wonder how anything entirely immaterial could exist on its own, but for Aquinas the intuitions go the other way around. For example, in explaining that angels are incorruptible, he says:

nothing is corrupted except in virtue of the fact that its form is separated from matter. For this reason, since an angel is a subsistent form itself ... , it is impossible that its substance be corruptible. For what belongs to something of itself (*secundum se*) can never be separated from it ... But *being* belongs to a form of itself, for anything is a being in actuality insofar as it has a form, whereas matter is a being in actuality through a form. Therefore, a composite of matter and form ceases to be in actuality in virtue of the fact that the form is separated from the matter. But if the form subsists in its own being, as it does in the case of the angels, ... it cannot lose being. And so the immateriality of an angel is the reason why the angel is incorruptible of its own nature.[30]

Elsewhere, in the course of arguing that the human soul is not a composite of matter and form, Aquinas says:

although the soul is subsistent of itself (*per se*) it does not follow that it is composed of matter and form, because a form apart from matter can also subsist of itself. For although matter has being through a form and not conversely, nothing keeps a form from subsisting without matter, even though matter cannot exist without form.[31]

In addition, the immaterial form that an angel is can act and can engage in the activities characteristic of persons, namely, thought and volition. On Aquinas's view, angels have both intellect and will.[32] In comparing the cognitive and conative capacities of human beings and angels, Aquinas says:

in our soul there are certain powers whose operations are exercised by means of corporeal organs, and powers of this sort are acts of certain parts of the body, as vision in the eye and hearing in the ear ... But angels do not have bodies naturally united to them ... and so the only powers of the soul that can belong to them are intellect and will.[33]

But this is an advantage for the angels, not a defect in them. As Aquinas goes on to say: "it is appropriate for the order of the universe that the highest intellectual creature [i.e., an angel] be entirely intellective and not only partly [intellective], as our soul is."[34]

So an angel is a form; and in the case of angels, the form in question is an immaterial substance that exists on its own, with a certain set of capacities and powers superior to that of human beings, who are embodied. Clearly, a form of this sort is not a configurational state. Rather, it is a substance or thing that is itself configured in a certain way but that (like the form that is God) does not configure anything else, as material forms configure matter.

How are we to understand the conception of form that allows Aquinas to take both immaterial angels and the configuration of prime matter in material substances as forms? One way to think about his view is that, for Aquinas, to be is to be configured or to have a form; and everything, material or immaterial, is what it is in virtue of a form. We are inclined to suppose that there is something about matter itself which allows it to be configured. (Or perhaps we are so familiar and comfortable with the notion of configurations of matter that we don't suppose matter's ability to be configured requires any explanation.) But for Aquinas the ability of matter to be configured is just a consequence of the fact that matter has being of some sort. It was Augustine's position that being is a matter of having order, species, and mode, and Aquinas can be understood as adopting and developing this Augustinian sort of idea. An angel, for Aquinas, is immaterial but configured since it has order and species, that is, since it is a kind of thing with one rather than another set of characteristics; and anything that has being – whether that thing is material or immaterial – will be like this. Just in virtue of being, it will have configuration or form. Understanding this point helps to explain why although Aquinas is perfectly content to deny matter of God, he refuses to deny form of God: being, even divine being, is being configured.

The soul as subsisting form configuring matter

If a material form is a configurational state configuring matter and an angel is a configured immaterial subsistent form, what is the human soul? The end of a long story is that, in Aquinas's universe of spirit and matter, the human soul has a share in both the spiritual and material worlds. For Aquinas, the metaphysical world is ordered in such a way that at the top of the metaphysical hierarchy there are forms – the angels (or maybe God and the angels, depending on how one takes the implications of divine simplicity) – which exist independently and are not configurational constituents of anything else. Near the bottom of the hierarchy are forms that configure matter but do not exist independently of matter as configured things in their own right. The form of an amethyst is like this. And in the middle are human souls, the amphibians of this metaphysical world, occupying a niche in both the material and the spiritual realm. Like an angel, the human soul is itself a configured subsistent form; but like the forms of other material things, the human soul has the ability to configure matter.

The human soul, then, is a configured configurer. On the one hand, like an angel, it is able to exist and function on its own, apart from matter.[35] On the other hand, the human soul is not, as Plato thought, a spiritual substance moving a body which is also a substance in its own right; rather, the human soul is the substantial form constituting the material substance that a human being is, and it configures matter, as material forms do.[36] So, for Aquinas, the human soul is the noblest and highest of the forms that configure matter,[37] but it is the lowest in the rank of intellectual subsistent forms, because it is mixed with matter, as the intellectual subsistent forms that are angels are not.[38]

Aquinas sums up his position this way:

> the [human] soul has subsistent being, insofar as its being does not depend on the body but is rather elevated above corporeal matter. Nevertheless, the body receives a share in its being, in such a way that there is one being of soul and body, and this is the being of a human.[39]

In fact, he goes on to say,

> no part has the perfection of its nature when it is separated from [its] whole. And so since the soul is a part of human nature, it does not have the perfection of its nature except in union with the body ... And so, although the soul can exist and intellectively cognize when it is separated from the body, nonetheless it does not have the perfection of its nature when it is separated from the body.[40]

Now this view of the soul is the conclusion of a complicated discussion. To understand it, it may be helpful to begin with Aquinas's general concept of soul. The Latin translated 'soul' is Aquinas's generic term for the substantial form of a material object that is living. On his use of the term, then, plants have souls, too, not in the sense that they enjoy being talked to or in the sense that they may be reincarnated as something higher up the ladder of being in the next life, but only in the sense that plants are living things. On his view, a plant has a soul in virtue of the fact that it has a configuration of matter which allows for nutrition, growth, reproduction, and the other sorts of activities common to living things. Non-human animals have souls, since they, too, are living things; but the configuration of their matter allows them an operation not possible for plants, namely, perception. Unlike human souls, the souls of plants and non-human animals are nonetheless material forms, and even a material form that is a soul goes out of existence when the material composite it configures goes out of existence.[41]

The substantial form that configures a human being allows for still further sets of operations, namely, intellective and volitional processes. Because the human soul has this distinctive set of capacities, Aquinas tends to call it 'the intellective soul', or 'the rational soul' to distinguish it from the nutritive soul of plants and the sensitive (i.e., capable of perception) soul of animals generally. The intellective soul is thus that configuration of matter on the basis of which something exists as this living human body. There is not a configuration of matter that makes the body a human body and then another configuration that is the intellective soul.[42] As Aquinas says: "There is no other substantial form in human beings apart from the intellective soul."[43]

In virtue of this one form, a human being exists as an actual being, as a material object, as a living thing, as an animal, and as a human being with cognitive capacities.[44] For this reason, Aquinas tends also to call the soul the act of the body; the soul configures matter in such a way that the matter is actually a living human body.[45]

Since he takes the soul to be a kind of form, Aquinas holds that the soul is immaterial; the immateriality of the soul is for him a direct consequence of his view of the soul as a form.[46] Similarly, he takes the soul to be simple in virtue of its being an essence or nature. A soul is not simple in the way a point is,[47] Aquinas says; rather it is simple just in the sense that it is not the sort of thing that has a certain quantity.[48] On the other hand, considered with respect to what it effects rather than with respect to what it is – that is, considered in its powers or operations – the soul is manifold rather than simple, and the various parts of the body are configured by it in differing ways.[49]

Furthermore, because Aquinas sees the soul as the configuring form of the body, he says:

> although the soul is incorruptible, it is nonetheless in no genus other than [the genus] *body*, because since it is part of human nature, it does not belong to the soul itself to be in a genus or a species.[50]

In addition, as configuring matter, the soul has a spatial location; while the body is alive and the soul configures it, the soul is located where the body is.[51] Aquinas's views on this point are somewhat complicated. We can take the form of the body to be a whole in various ways, he says. Considered with regard to the wholeness of essence, for instance, the whole soul is entirely in each part of the body, just as whiteness is entirely in each part of a completely white thing. We can also, however, consider a thing whole with respect to its operations. Considered just with regard to wholeness of operation, the whole soul is not in each part of the body, since the operations of the soul are localized in various parts of the body, as, for example, sight is (on his view) localized in the eyes.

Some operations, such as intellect and will, are not localized in any particular organ of the body, Aquinas thinks,[52] although he does take it on medical authority that a lower-level cognitive faculty (which he calls 'particular reason') is located in the brain.[53] Nonetheless, he does not hold, as Descartes apparently did, that higher cognitive functions occur only in the soul and not in the body. On the contrary, Aquinas thinks that there is something misleading about attributing cognitive functions just to the soul itself. Rather, even such higher cognitive functions as understanding are to be attributed to the whole material composite that is the human being. So, for example, he says: "We *can* say that the soul understands in the same way that we can say that the eye sees; but it would be more appropriate to say that *a human being* understands *by means* of the soul."[54] And he specifically identifies the intellect itself with the form of the body: "the intellect, which is the source of intellective function, is the form of the human body".[55]

Finally, as his rejection of a Cartesian sort of dualism has made clear, Aquinas does not identify a human being with his soul.[56] Instead, it is his view that "a human being is not a soul only but rather a composite of soul and body."[57] (There is something redundant about this description of the composite since Aquinas thinks that there is a living human body only when matter is configured by the form that is the soul.[58] Given his view that the soul is the single substantial form of a living human body, we would expect him to say instead that a human being is a composite of matter and soul, not body and soul. Nonetheless, 'body and soul' is a common Thomistic description of the material composite that a human being is. It may be that the problem here is an artifact of translation; in some contexts, the Latin word translated 'body' ('*corpus*') refers just to matter.[59] Alternatively, Aquinas thinks that a human being is generated when the human soul replaces the merely animal soul of the fetus in the womb and that a human being is corrupted or decomposed when the human soul leaves the body and is replaced by whatever other substantial form is in the dead corpse.[60] And so he may use the Latin translated 'body' to refer to what is configured in these different ways in the transitions from fetus to living thing to corpse.)

It is therefore clear that, for Aquinas, the human soul resembles material forms in configuring matter and constituting a material object the kind of thing it is with the causal powers characteristic of things of that kind.

Aquinas on form: form as configured

At this point, it is not so difficult to see how Aquinas's account fits the first culturally conditioned intuition that shapes it, as I said at the outset of this chapter, namely, the intuition that human beings are dust and will return to dust. On his account, a human being is a material composite, with matter configured in a certain way by the form that is the soul. When the original configuration is lost and the composite begins to decompose, as happens at the death of a human being with the loss of the form that is the soul, that human being ceases to exist. But it is not so easy to see how Aquinas's account can accommodate the second culturally conditioned intuition informing it, namely, that at death the human soul does not cease to exist but rather persists when the composite of soul and body disintegrates.

203

That is, it is not immediately apparent how the view of the soul as configuring matter is compatible with the view of the soul as a configured subsistent form. We are naturally inclined to see little or no problem in the notion of an intellective configuration of matter (indeed, certain materialists suppose that matter configured in the way that the matter of the brain is configured just *is* the mind); but we tend to find problematic (or worse) the notion of a subsistent intellect existing and functioning apart from matter. In fact, at this point, we may think that Aquinas's general metaphysical account of the forms of material objects cannot accommodate the claim that the form which is a human soul persists and engages in mental acts after the death of the body. If the soul is the configuration of the matter of a human body, we might think, it must cease to exist when the body ceases to exist. How could a configuration of matter exist without the matter it configures?

Aquinas is aware of the tension between his two intuitions, and our sort of objection would not have surprised him. He himself imagines an objector making similar points. If the human soul is the form of the body, a putative objector asks, then it must be the case that it depends on the body for existence. But what depends on something else for existence, the objector protests, is not a thing and cannot exist on its own; consequently, neither can the soul, if it is the form of the body.[61] Elsewhere Aquinas also considers this objection: "forms dependent on matter as regards being do not have being themselves, strictly speaking; rather, the composites have being through the forms."[62] Therefore, the objection implies, the soul, which is the form of the body, has its being only in the being of the body and cannot exist or act apart from it.

But I point to this discussion in Aquinas's thought only to leave it to one side, partly because his reply to objections of this sort relies on a premise which is less believable to contemporary philosophers than the conclusion it is meant to support[63] and partly because, for Aquinas himself, the problem of the tension between his two intuitions presents itself the other way around. For him, the great difficulty lies in supposing that a subsistent form capable of existing and operating independently of matter is also the sort of thing that configures matter. Furthermore, even contemporary philosophers must grant that an immaterial mind is possible. An argument for the impossibility of an immaterial mind would be in effect an argument against the existence of God, and so far no one has produced such an argument that has garnered any substantial support. If an immaterial mind is possible, however, then perhaps the main obstacle to seeing Aquinas's views of the soul as consistent is the problem he himself addresses, namely, whether an immaterial mind can also be the form of the body, whether, that is, a configured subsistent form capable of existing apart from matter can also be a configurer of matter.

In discussing the problem as it presents itself to him, Aquinas canvasses the views of those thinkers known to him who, because of this sort of worry, concluded that the intellective soul could not be a matter-configuring form; the Cartesian sort of dualism Aquinas attributes to Plato is one of the views he discusses in this connection. Aquinas argues vehemently against each such view before going on to face what seems to him the hard question. He says, "And for these reasons it is evident that the soul is the form and quiddity of such a body ... But *how* this can be must be investigated."[64]

His investigation is not likely to be persuasive to contemporary readers. It consists in arguing that the human soul is the *highest* in the rank ordering of all the forms configuring material objects, because, unlike material forms, it has an operation (namely, intellective cognition) which surpasses the capacities of matter altogether, and the *lowest* in the rank ordering of subsistent forms able to exist independently of matter. Consequently, in the ranking of forms, the human soul is located right at the boundary between the material and the spiritual. For this reason, the soul partakes of some of the features of the spiritual world, but it is also able to be in contact with matter, so that the body informed by the soul is the highest in the order of material objects. Citing what he takes to be a Dionysian principle, Aquinas says:

> the highest of the lower order is always in contact with the lowest of the higher order ... And therefore the human soul, which is the lowest in the order of spiritual substances can communicate its being to the human body, which is most noble, so that one [thing] arises from the soul and the body, as from form and matter.[65]

Although Aquinas's argument here rests on premises more likely to be persuasive in his time than ours, his general idea may seem more plausible to us if we see that, in an analogous sort of way, we are also accustomed to the notion of an independently existing thing, configured in a certain way, that is nonetheless able to configure matter. So, for example, an enzyme catalyzing protein folding is an independently existing molecule with a complex configuration of its own. But it is also a configurer. When it is bound in the right way to a protein, it helps to fold the protein molecule, thereby reconfiguring that molecule in such a way as to make it biologically active. So as a configured thing, it can exist apart from the thing it configures; but it can also configure the matter of the protein it folds into a different form with different causal capacities from those the protein had before being so configured. A protein-folding enzyme is therefore a kind of configured configurer.

Something analogous can be said about the human soul on Aquinas's view. Of course, there are also significant disanalogies between the case of the enzyme and the case of the soul. Here are just some of them. (1) What is a configured configurer in the case of the enzyme is a matter-form composite; in the case of the soul, it is only a form. (2) The enzyme configures something which is a matter-form composite itself; the soul configures only unformed matter. (3) When the enzyme configures a protein, the result of the configuration is not one substance – the enzyme and the protein bound together in the process of folding the protein do not constitute one super-molecule; but the soul and the matter it configures do form one substance, an individual human being.[66] The example of the protein-folding enzyme thus cannot be taken as explanatory of everything perplexing in Aquinas's account of the soul; but it does perhaps serve as a heuristic example, helpful for making more plausible the notion of a config-ured configurer.

The special case of the soul

Understanding the soul in this way, as a configured configurer, a thing able to exist independently of matter but also able to configure matter, helps to explain some of the puzzling things Aquinas says about it.

For example, Aquinas takes the forms of material objects generally to come into existence with the existence of their composites; and although God is the ultimate or remote cause of the existence of such forms, the prox-imate cause is just the cause that brings about the existence of the composite. After canvassing various opinions that he takes to be mistaken about the forms of non-human material objects, Aquinas summarizes the flaws of those opinions in this way:

> All these [mistaken] opinions seem to have developed from a common root, because they were all seeking a cause for forms as if the forms themselves came into being in their own right. But, as Aristotle shows ... , what comes into being, properly speaking, is the composite. Now the forms of things that are corruptible some-times exist and sometimes do not exist, without its being the case that they themselves are generated or corrupted; rather the compos-ites are generated or corrupted ... So since like comes to be from like, we should not seek some immaterial form as the cause of corporeal forms, but rather some composite ... In this way, then, corporeal forms are caused not as infused from some immaterial form but as matter is brought from potentiality to actuality by some composite agent.[67]

But in this regard the human soul is different from all other forms that configure matter. It is created directly by God and infused into matter.[68] This is what we might expect Aquinas to hold once we recognize that for him the soul is a configured subsistent form, as the angels are; the angels, too, are created directly by God. No immaterial subsistent forms can be generated by the sort of natural generation that material objects are capable

206

of, according to Aquinas; immaterial subsistent forms can come into existence only by being created directly by God.[69] On the other hand, however, Aquinas rejects vehemently the notion that the soul can be created before the body and then infused into an already existent body. He says:

> if the soul is united to the body as its form and is naturally part of human nature, then it is completely impossible [for the soul to be created before the body] ... Since the soul is a part of human nature, it does not have its natural perfection unless it is united to the body. And so it would not have been fitting to create the soul without the body.[70]

That is why, he says, the soul is created in the body, and souls are produced simultaneously with human bodies,[71] at the culmination of human generation.[72] Aquinas is willing to maintain this position even in the face of what seem to him to be religiously worrisome objections. He considers an imaginary objector asking about children produced by adultery. If the divinely created human soul comes into existence only simultaneously with the body of which it is the form, the putative objector protests, and if children are sometimes the product of adulterous liaisons, will God not be concurring in the sin of adultery insofar as he creates a human soul to infuse into the product of the adultery? Rather than step back from his view of the strong connection between the soul and the matter it configures, Aquinas concedes part of the complaint of the objector. God does concur in the action of the adulterer in such a case, Aquinas says, though only insofar as that action is natural and therefore good; God fails to concur just with what is evil in the action of adultery.[73]

So because the form that is the human soul is a configured configurer, a subsistent form able to exist apart from matter but also able to configure matter, the soul has a double aspect. On the one hand, unlike the forms of other material objects, every soul is directly created by God, as an individual thing in its own right, with its own configuration. On the other hand, like the form of any material object, it exists in the composite it configures, and it comes into existence only with that composite, not before it.

On this way of understanding the form that is the human soul, it is also easier to see why Aquinas thinks that the soul makes matter be not just human but also this human being. The soul itself is an individual configured form, and each soul is as it were handcrafted by God to inform *this* matter.[74] Aquinas says:

> everything has its being and its individuation from the same source ... Therefore, as the being of the soul is from God as from an active principle ... so also the individuation of the soul, even if it has a

certain relationship to the body, does not perish when the body perishes.[75]

Given the double aspect of the soul, then, it is not surprising that Aquinas supposes that the individuality of a human person persists after death in the separated soul. Not only is there continuity of cognitive and conative faculties between the material object that is the human being and the separated soul, but the separated soul, as a configured form with a relation to *this* matter, is what makes a human being this particular individual.

Finally, this view of the human soul helps to alleviate some of the problems thought to be raised by the notion of the resurrection of the body. On Aquinas's view of the soul, there is, of course, mental continuity between a human person before death and after death. But the soul can also account for the sameness of the resurrected body. Since the soul was what made unformed prime matter this human being by configuring it in such a way that the matter is this living animal capable of intellective cognition, presumably in the resurrection of the body the soul can again make the unformed matter it informs this human being. Preservation of identity will not have to be guaranteed by recomposing the human being of the same bits of matter-form composites, such as atoms, as before; and puzzles about what happens when the same atoms have been part of more than one human being are avoided.

Aquinas's idea here is thus roughly analogous to one of Sydney Shoemaker's views about human persons. Shoemaker thinks that it is possible for there to be a brain-state transfer device which transfers a person's brain states from one body to another and thereby preserves an individual person in being through a succession of bodies. Shoemaker's brain states are presumably configurational states; and there is an interval, however small, in which the states are in the process of being transferred and so are no longer in the first body and not yet in the second.[76] On Aquinas's view, the interval in the transfer of the configuring soul from the old body to the new resurrected body may be very long, and in this interval the configuring soul can continue to operate, since it is itself something configured. Nonetheless, on both Aquinas's account and Shoemaker's, the imposition of the configurational state on new matter preserves the identity of the person.[77]

Cartesian dualism redivivus?

At this point it may seem that this interpretation of Aquinas's account has rescued it from some pressing problems only to enmesh it in all the equally difficult problems of Cartesian dualism, and that Aquinas has after all succumbed to the Platonic dualism from which he was so concerned to dissociate his own views. As I have explained Aquinas's account of the soul, does it not collapse into Cartesian or Platonic dualism? Is not Aquinas's view just another version of the ghost in the machine?

Here, I think, the answer is clearly 'no', and for reasons that are in a sense two sides of the same coin. On Cartesian dualism, (1) both the soul and the body are substances in their own right. Each can engage in acts independently of the other, and each can causally effect the other. Soul and body are somehow joined together in a human being; but (2) the soul is separate from the body in its functions, and that is why thinking goes on in the soul but cannot be in the body at the same time. On Aquinas's account, both (1) and (2) are false.

In the first place, although for Aquinas the separated soul exists on its own after death, it nonetheless is not a substance in its own right. Aquinas distinguishes two kinds of subsistent things that can exist on their own, those that are complete substances and those that just subsist, that is, that are able to exist on their own but are not complete substances. A severed hand[78] is a subsistent thing in this latter sense,[79] and so is the soul. Aquinas says:

> Not every particular substance is a hypostasis or a person but [only] that which has the complete nature of the species. So a hand or a foot cannot be called a hypostasis or a person, and similarly, neither can the soul, since it is [only] a part [of a complete human being].[80]

Similarly, in another place he says:

> if by 'a *this*' (*hoc aliquid*) [in the case of the soul] we understand a hypostasis or a person, or an individual located in a genus or a species, then [the human soul] cannot be said to be a *this*. But if a *this* is said to be anything capable of subsisting of itself, then in this way the soul is a *this*.[81]

And so Aquinas makes both these claims: "intellectual natures are subsistent forms, and although they exist in matter, their being does not depend on matter";[82] and "body and soul are not two actually existing substances, but instead one actually existing substance arises from these two".[83]

Therefore, although the soul is only a metaphysical part of the one substance that is a human being, it is nonetheless a subsistent thing.[84] Aquinas rejects the view that the soul is only a configurational state on the grounds that if the soul were only something such as a harmony, it could not exist on its own, and so "it would be only a form similar to other material forms".[85]

The soul, however, is not an *integral* part of a human being. If we think of integral parts as components that add to the quantity of the material whole they compose,[86] in the way that a roof is part of a house and a head is part of a body, then no forms are integral parts of the material objects to which they belong. When Aquinas lists the integral parts of a house, for example, he tends to list such things as foundation, walls, and roof; he would not add the form of the house as one more item on the list.[87] On the other hand, when we think of the metaphysical composition of a material object such as a biologically active protein, then an important part of what we consider is the configuration in which the molecule's component atoms are organized. There can thus be metaphysical, as well as integral, parts, in some extended sense of 'part';[88] and a form is a part of a whole only as a metaphysical part.

As a metaphysical part of this sort, a form could not interact causally with the matter it informs. It makes no sense to think, for example, of the configuration of a protein interacting causally with the matter of that protein. Rather, the form has causal influence in the sense that the composite has the causal influence it does because of its form.[89] Even intellective function, then, is implemented in the body, on Aquinas's account.

So Aquinas rejects both (1) and (2), which are characteristic of Cartesian dualism, and he does so because he takes the soul to be a configured configurer. The soul is a configured subsistent thing, but it is also a configurer of matter. And because it is a configurer of matter, it is not a complete substance in its own right; it is not even an integral part of a complete substance. For that reason, an embodied human being exercises efficient causality in virtue of the soul, but the soul does not exercise efficient causality on the matter of the body it informs. As far as that goes, the prime matter it informs could not exercise efficient causality on the soul either; the matter of a human being can engage in causal interactions only in virtue of being configured as it is into a living body, a configuration it has in virtue of the soul.

We can sum up the differences between Cartesian dualism and Aquinas's account by saying that on Cartesian dualism but not on Aquinas's account, the soul is only a configured subsistent form and not also a configurer; a Cartesian soul does not configure matter to constitute a body. In consequence of this difference, Aquinas's account is not vulnerable to the two main problems thought to afflict Cartesian dualism, namely, that it cannot explain the nature of the causal interaction between soul and body and that it divides cognitive functions into those that can be implemented only in the soul and those that can be implemented only in the body. On Aquinas's account, there is no efficient causal interaction between the soul and the matter it informs, and all human cognitive functions can be implemented in the body.

Dust and spirit

Does Aquinas then succeed in reconciling the two intuitions I said earlier guided his account of the soul, namely, that human beings are composed of dust and return to it, and that at death the spirit returns to God who gave it? The answer, I think, is 'yes'.

Since Aquinas thinks of a human being as a composite of matter and soul and since he recognizes that dead human bodies decay, he does in fact believe that a human being falls apart at death. The disembodied soul which persists is not the complete human being who was the composite but only a part of that human being.[90] In response to the question whether the saints in heaven can pray for us, an objector says: "the soul of Peter is not Peter. So if the souls of the saints pray for us when they are separated from the body, we ought not to call on St. Peter to pray for us but rather on the soul of St Peter." Aquinas's reply is to grant the point that the soul is not the complete human being but to argue for the appropriateness of calling the part (the soul) by the name of the whole (the composite of matter and form that Peter was and will be).[91] Since the disembodied soul still has its intellect and will, as well as other divinely aided cognitive faculties, it is in fact appropriate to address the soul of Peter as 'Peter'.

The disembodied soul after death is consequently something like the mirror image of a human being who is in a persistent vegetative state. A human being in an irreversible vegetative state is an incomplete human being. So, in a very different sense, is a disembodied soul, on Aquinas's view. When the soul of a person is separated from the body, Aquinas thinks, the cognitive powers that person had are curtailed and restricted; and, for certain cognitive functions, Aquinas feels constrained to give complicated considerations to show how the disembodied soul could engage in them at all.[92] As for knowledge of material things in the world that would ordinarily be cognized with sense perception, Aquinas attributes the disembodied soul's ability to cognize such things to divine intervention.[93]

On Aquinas's view, then, disembodied existence is not natural to the soul. If it weren't for the miserableness of the fallen human condition, which includes the necessity of dying – that is, the separation of soul and body – the soul would never exist in a disembodied state.[94] Furthermore, the soul's existence in a disembodied state is an impermanent as well as an unnatural condition. It is contrary to the nature of the soul to be without the body, Aquinas says, and nothing contrary to nature can be perpetual. Consequently, the soul's separation from the body cannot last.[95] In the general resurrection of the dead, at the Last Judgment, souls will be reimbodied. Consequently, except for the interim period when souls are separated from matter, human persons in the afterlife will be like human persons in this life, in the sense that they will be material composites of matter and form. After the period of disembodied existence, the soul will again exist as a constituent of a body, as it did before death.[96] Nevertheless, although existence apart from the body is an unnatural and impermanent condition for the soul, on Aquinas's view it is possible for the soul to exist and function in that condition.

For these reasons Aquinas can accept the claim that at death the spirit returns to God who made it. Given the way he understands this claim, however, it turns out after all not to be incompatible with the claim that human beings are dust.

To sum up, then, the soul is a configured subsistent form, able to exist on its own apart from matter but also able to configure matter into the living body of a human being. While it is possible for the soul to exist and (with divine help) exercise various cognitive functions apart from the body, that state is unnatural to it. In the natural condition, the soul configures matter; and when it is in its natural condition, human cognitive functions are to be attributed to the whole composite and not to the soul alone, although the whole composite exercises cognitive functions by means of the soul. If we can understand the intellective part of the human soul as roughly equivalent to the mind, then for Aquinas the mind is immaterial but implemented (in its natural condition) in matter. Mental properties are emergent, on this view, insofar as they are features which are dependent on the configuration and composition of the whole. A human being, who is a composite of matter and form, can engage in cognitive functions in virtue of his form, the soul; but in the natural condition, it is the whole composite and not the soul alone that understands and cognizes and the rest.[97]

Taxonomy: materialism without reductionism

How are we to understand Aquinas's account of the soul? It is clear that Aquinas rejects the Cartesian or Platonic sort of dualism. On the other hand, Aquinas seems clearly in the dualist camp somewhere since he thinks that there is an immaterial and subsistent constituent of the subject of cognitive function.

What sort of dualist is he? Since on his view the forms of material objects in general do not exist on their own and the soul is not a complete substance, we might think he should be classified just as some sort of property dualist. He does, however, hold that the soul can exist without the body, and his position is thus stronger than ordinary property dualisms. Maybe we should invent a new genus *subsistence dualism*, under which substance dualism will be one species and Aquinas's account of the soul another. But perhaps we need not be so fussy. It is clear that Aquinas's account of the soul is more nearly allied with substance dualism than with property dualism; and if we do not take 'substance' in 'substance dualism' too strictly (if it can include subsistent things that are not complete substances), then we can count Aquinas among the substance dualists.[98] In that case, we ought to categorize Aquinas as a non-Cartesian substance dualist and put him in the camp of those opposed to physicalism.

Matters are somewhat complicated here, however. Daniel Dennett takes it to be characteristic of dualism to hold that the mind is not composed of matter and that scientific investigation of the brain cannot teach us anything about the mind.[99] Shoemaker thinks that what characterizes dualism is the view that a person is something distinct from his body and so has any physical states only derivatively.[100] But if Dennett and Shoemaker are right about what dualism is, then Aquinas should not be counted among the dualists. Aquinas takes human beings to be matter-form composites, and he attributes cognition to the whole human being. Since he takes the subject that engages in cognition to be a material substance, it will be possible to investigate that subject by the methods for investigating matter. Furthermore, Patricia Churchland supposes it to be one of the main characteristics of physicalism to hold that "mental states are implemented in neural stuff".[101] But if this characterization of physicalism[102] is right, Aquinas should apparently be grouped with the physicalists. Although Aquinas mistakenly supposes that the intellect is tied to no particular bodily organ, he nonetheless holds that the intellectual soul is the form constituting the human body as a whole. On his view, therefore, mental states will be implemented in the matter of the body. His account of the soul is consequently compatible with supposing that mental states are implemented in neural stuff.

At this point it might occur to someone to suppose that it can hardly be surprising that Aquinas's account of the soul is not readily assimilable to either dualism or physicalism; the difficulty in categorizing Aquinas, such a person might think, stems from trying to insert a peculiarly medieval theory into the contemporary discussion, where it simply will not fit. But I think this is a mistaken attitude.

Consider, for example, Richard Boyd's defense of a functionalist version of materialism. Boyd argues that, although materialism is sometimes taken to include the claim that mental states are identical to physical states, materialism is in fact committed just to the claim that the mind is composed of matter. Boyd says: "Materialism, properly understood, does not entail the sort of mind-body identity statements against which the essentialist [i.e., anti-materialist] criticisms are directed."[103]

To argue for his claim, Boyd distinguishes compositional plasticity from configurational plasticity, in this way:

> Compositional plasticity is displayed by a type of state, event, or process to the extent that there are possible realizations of that state, event, or process that differ in the sorts of substances or causal factors that constitute them. Configurational plasticity, in contrast, is displayed by a type of state, event, or process to the extent that its possible token realizations differ in the structural configuration or arrangement of their constituent parts, events, substances, or causal factors.[104]

According to Boyd: "mental events, states, and processes are like computational states in being entirely configurational, that is, in possessing maximal compositional plasticity."[105]

In fact, on his account, mental events, states, and processes have no compositional properties essentially. The occurrence of some mental or psychological states in more than one animal species shows that mental states should not be identified with physical states, since it is highly unlikely that other animals share exactly our neurophysiological states; and it is even more unlikely that all logically possible animals that have some of the same mental states as human beings would have the same physiological states we do. For that reason as well as others, Boyd says, "materialism (in its most plausible version) entails that mental states are purely configurational"[106] and are not identical with physical states.[107]

Furthermore, on Boyd's view it is possible for mental events, states, and processes to exist without being realized in any matter at all.[108] He says, "any particular actual world mental event, state, or process could be – in some other possible world – nonphysically realized."[109]

Consequently, Boyd says: "A materialist account of mental phenomena is quite compatible with the view that there are possible worlds in which mental phenomena exist but are nonphysical."[110]

In fact, he maintains:

> it is ... fully compatible with a plausible materialist psychology that there should be a possible world in which there is no matter at all, but in which there are events, states, and processes that have all the nonrelational properties essential to the mental events, states, and processes manifested in the actual world.[111]

Mental processes and states must be the processes and states of something, however, and so on Boyd's view it must also be logically possible that there be a mind which is not realized in matter.[112]

Boyd thinks of himself as supporting materialism, and he takes his position to be a version of materialism without reductionism. It seems to me, however, that his position has some similarities to (though, of course, it is not identical with) that of Aquinas, who is not only a dualist but even a substance dualist (in a liberal sense of that phrase). Boyd's mental phenomena, like Aquinas's soul, are configurational;[113] like the soul in Aquinas's account, mental phenomena on Boyd's view have no essential compositional properties. Furthermore, both Boyd and Aquinas agree in supposing that it is possible for what is purely configurational to exist on its own apart from any material composition and to function in that condition. For both of them, then, it is possible that there be functioning, disembodied mental states.

It is tempting here to suppose that this comparison undercuts the materialism of Boyd's account[114] or to worry that it implies some sort of non-reductionistic materialism in Aquinas's.[115] For Aquinas, material objects are composites of matter and form, and a composite of matter and form can itself serve as matter for some other, more complex composite of matter and form. As complexity increases and new forms are produced in the increasingly complex composites, new substances as well as new properties will emerge. To reduce the composite to its constituent matter or to reduce the properties of the composite to just the properties of the composite's material components is to think that the form of the whole is nothing. But on Aquinas's view, the form of the whole, the configuration that makes the matter into the whole it composes, is an important ontological feature of things. And that is why, on his account, a material object cannot be reduced to its constituent matter.

But, in my view, the real lesson of the comparison and of this detailed examination of Aquinas's account of the soul is to show how misleading the dichotomy between materialism and dualism is. What Aquinas's account of the soul shows us is that a certain kind of (restricted rather than global) materialism — one that takes mental states to be implemented in bodily states — is compatible with a certain sort of dualism — one that is non-Cartesian in character. To this extent, examination of Aquinas's account supports Searle's claim that it is a mistake to suppose that one must choose between materialism and dualism.[116]

Although Boyd accepts the dichotomy between materialism and dualism and means to choose materialism, something he says in support of his position helps explain why the dichotomy is misleading or mistaken. He says:

> The issue [between materialism and dualism] ... has come to be described as the issue of whether the corresponding mental and physical states are identical [as many materialists have argued] or (as the dualist suggests) merely correlated ... This way of putting the question is fundamentally misleading. The issue is not identity versus correlation, but composition versus correlation.[117]

Boyd supposes that correlation is unsuccessful as an account of mind, and he (like Aquinas) builds his position around composition. As both Boyd and Aquinas recognize (in different ways), however, composition has a two-fold nature. On Aquinas's view, composition for material objects requires both matter and form; on Boyd's view, we can distinguish the configuration of a composite from the stuff in which that configuration is realized. If we focus on the material stuff and think that composites are identical with the matter that constitutes them, then we are likely to think the mental is identical with the physical. If we focus on configuration as the essential feature of the mental, our view will look dualistic. But in fact because a human mind is a complex configuration of a material object, a correct account of it will share features of both materialism and dualism. Furthermore, the hybrid nature of composition also helps to explain the strength of the debate over the nature of the mind. Because a human mind is implemented in a composite and

215

composition is a hybrid of matter and configuration, both materialist and anti-materialist intuitions can find strong support from a consideration of the characteristics of the mind.

Aquinas's account, then, helps us see that the battle lines between dualism and materialism are misdrawn.[118] It is possible to have a coherent account of the mind that satisfies intuitions of both dualists and materialists. It is unlikely, of course, that everyone will think Aquinas's account of the soul, including the soul's persistence after death, is coherent. But it is worth noting here that religious belief is not necessary for supposing that the soul can exist and function apart from the body. Boyd, too, thinks it is clear that there can be mental states, events, and processes even in a world in which there is no matter at all.[119] Furthermore, even if we cut out all of Aquinas's account that has to do with the afterlife, that is, if we assume that the soul in his account is just one more immaterial form of a material object, like the form of a protein, which exists only in the composite it helps constitute, Aquinas's account of the mind would nonetheless have the hybrid nature highlighted here. It would still take the mind to be something essentially immaterial or configurational but nonetheless – in human beings – realized in material components. And so it would still combine features of both dualism and materialism.

Aquinas's account of the soul, therefore, suggests that to make progress on a philosophical understanding of the nature of the mind (as distinct from a biological understanding of the mechanisms by which the mind operates), it would be good to break down the dichotomy between materialism and dualism that takes them to be incompatible positions. It also strongly suggests that Cartesian dualism is not essential to all the major traditions of the major monotheisms. For Aquinas, at any rate, the rejection of Cartesian dualism is entirely compatible with his view of the nature of the soul.

7

THE FOUNDATIONS OF
KNOWLEDGE

Introduction

Aquinas is sometimes taken to hold a foundationalist theory of knowledge.
So, for example, Nicholas Wolterstorff says:

> Foundationalism has been the reigning theory of theories in the
> West since the high Middle Ages. It can be traced back as far as
> Aristotle, and since the Middle Ages vast amounts of philosophical
> thought have been devoted to elaborating and defending it ...
> Aquinas offers one classic version of foundationalism.[1]

And Alvin Plantinga says:

> [W]e can get a better understanding of Aquinas ... if we see [him]
> as accepting some version of classical foundationalism. This is a
> picture or total way of looking at faith, knowledge, justified belief,
> rationality, and allied topics. This picture has been enormously
> popular in Western thought; and despite a substantial opposing
> groundswell, I think it remains the dominant way of thinking
> about these topics.[2]

Foundationalism is most frequently associated with Descartes, and the sort
of foundationalism ascribed to Aquinas is sometimes distinguished from
that attributed to Descartes. Plantinga, for example, distinguishes what he
calls 'ancient and medieval foundationalism' from the modern foundationalism commonly supposed to be in Descartes, Locke, and Leibniz, among
others; but Plantinga thinks Aquinas's brand of foundationalism has enough
in common with the foundationalism of Descartes and other early modern
philosophers that they can all be conflated under the heading 'classical foundationalism'.

But what exactly is being attributed to Aquinas here? Here is Plantinga's
description of classical foundationalism:

Foundationalism is best construed ... as a thesis about rational noetic structures ... According to the foundationalist a rational noetic structure will have a foundation – a set of beliefs not accepted on the basis of others; in a rational noetic structure some beliefs will be basic. Non-basic beliefs, of course, will be accepted on the basis of other beliefs, which may be accepted on the basis of still other beliefs, and so on until the foundations are reached. In a rational noetic structure, therefore, every non-basic belief is ultimately accepted on the basis of basic beliefs.[3]

A further and fundamental feature of classic varieties of foundationalism [is that] they all lay down certain conditions of proper basicality ... [A] belief to be properly basic (that is, basic in a rational noetic structure) must meet certain conditions ... Thomas Aquinas ... holds that a proposition is properly basic for a person only if it is self-evident to him or "evident to the senses" ... [T]he outstanding characteristic of a self-evident proposition is that one simply sees it to be true upon grasping or understanding it ... Aquinas and Locke ... held that a person, or at any rate a normal, well-formed human being, finds it impossible to withhold assent when considering a self-evident proposition ... [P]ropositions "evident to the senses" are also properly basic. By this latter term ... [Aquinas] means to refer to perceptual propositions – propositions whose truth or falsehood we can determine by looking or employing some other sense.[4]

This particular sort of foundationalism is currently thought to be in trouble; various philosophers, including Plantinga himself, have raised serious objections to it.

In the first place, this brand of foundationalism gives the counter-intuitive result that much of what we think we know is not to be counted as knowledge. The propositions which on classical foundationalism we can take to be properly basic do not entail (or even render probable) many of the apparently non-basic propositions we ordinarily suppose we know. Plantinga's examples include "all those propositions that entail ... that there are persons distinct from myself, or that the world has existed for more than five minutes".

In the second place, there are reasons for doubting whether classical foundationalism is right in confining the set of properly basic beliefs to those which are self-evident and evident to the senses. For example, memory beliefs, Plantinga argues, are neither self-evident nor evident to the senses, but they certainly seem to be properly basic. The belief that I walked to school this morning, rather than driving or cycling, is a belief I hold without basing it on other beliefs; and since it seems perfectly rational for me to take this belief as basic, this memory belief and others like it also seem to be properly basic beliefs.

Finally, Plantinga has argued that the central claims of this sort of foundationalism cannot themselves meet foundationalist criteria, because these central claims cannot be held as properly basic beliefs – they are not self-evident or evident to the senses – and it is difficult to see how they could be traced back to properly basic beliefs.

Plantinga's own favored theory of knowledge has certain features in common with reliabilism.[5] On Plantinga's account, when a person has enough warrant for a true belief, the belief counts as knowledge; and his complicated explanation of warrant includes this central claim: in order to have warrant, a person's belief must be true and acquired by a reliable process, when that person's cognitive faculties are functioning as they were designed to function in an environment in which they were designed to function. Given this understanding of the notion of warrant, on Plantinga's account beliefs with sufficient warrant constitute knowledge. This account is avowedly externalistic. One cannot tell just by looking within oneself and reflecting on the results of the introspection whether one's faculties are functioning as they were designed to function or whether the environment in which they are functioning is the appropriate one.

Plantinga concludes his case against the theory of knowledge he ascribes to Aquinas and others in the history of philosophy with the announcement that "classical foundationalism is bankrupt",[6] and he is not the only philosopher to make such a claim. In a recent book designed to acquaint students with current thinking about theories of knowledge, for example, Keith Lehrer ends his examination of foundationalism by claiming that as a theory of knowledge it "is a failure".[7]

So if the theory of knowledge held by Aquinas is classical foundationalism of this kind, then there are some good arguments for rejecting his views.

Of course, neither Wolterstorff nor Plantinga is a historian of medieval philosophy, and I began with their views for just that reason: to show that contemporary philosophers engaged in epistemology accept as commonplace this view of Aquinas's theory of knowledge. One historian of philosophy, however, who has expressly addressed the issue of foundationalism in the history of Western philosophy is T. H. Irwin. In his book *Aristotle's First Principles*,[8] Irwin argues that at least in the *Posterior Analytics*, Aristotle himself is a foundationalist. Irwin says:

> Aristotle therefore recognizes first principles with no further justification; but he denies that his view makes knowledge impossible, because he denies that demonstration requires demonstrable first principles. In denying this, he implies that in some cases complete justification is non-inferential, since it does not require derivation from other propositions. Non-inferentially justified first principles allow us to claim knowledge without facing an infinite regress or a

circle. Aristotle's conclusion implies a foundationalist doctrine, requiring true and non-inferentially justified beliefs as the basis of knowledge and justification.[9]

And Irwin takes the *Posterior Analytics* as an epistemological treatise in which Aristotle develops his foundationalism: "Aristotle's account of scientific knowledge develops from his metaphysical realism and his epistemological foundationalism";[10] and "[in the *Analytics* Aristotle] treated foundationalism as the only alternative to skepticism".[11]

Irwin himself takes a rather negative attitude towards this side of Aristotle's philosophy. According to Irwin:

> we must say that Aristotle's foundationalism in the *Analytics* results from a one-sided view of science and objectivity, and that this view needs considerable modification in the light of Aristotle's views on first philosophy.[12]

Irwin's views, of course, are not the only available interpretation of the *Posterior Analytics*.[13] Nonetheless, if his account of Aristotle is correct, it provides some confirmation for the common view of Aquinas as a foundationalist, since it would not be unreasonable to suppose that Aquinas simply accepted and developed the foundationalist theory of knowledge he found in Aristotle.

In this chapter I want to re-examine this picture of Aquinas's epistemology as an example of classical foundationalism.

Foundationalism

It will be helpful in this enterprise to have a little more clarity about the nature of the theory of knowledge that Aquinas is being taken to hold. On Plantinga's description of the type of foundationalist theory of knowledge he attributes to Aquinas, it includes the following claims:

(1) Some propositions are properly basic in the sense that it is rational to accept them without basing them on other propositions.
(2) Properly basic propositions include only propositions which are self-evident or evident to the senses, that is, propositions which can be known to be true either just by understanding their terms or by employing one or more of the senses.
(3) All non-basic propositions must be accepted, directly or indirectly, on the basis of properly basic propositions.

It is common to add one more set of conditions to this list. Wolterstorff stipulates that for classical foundationalists:

(4) the properly basic propositions are known with certitude;

and that consequently

(5) the propositions known on the basis of properly basic propositions can also be known with certitude.[14]

Lehrer emphasizes the search for a guarantee of truth, or for certainty, as the hallmark of foundationalism. He says:

> [A] central thesis of the traditional foundation theory was that basic beliefs are immune from error and refutation;[15]

> [S]ome beliefs *guarantee* their own truth. If my accepting something guarantees the truth of what I accept, then I am completely justified in accepting it for the purpose of obtaining truth and avoiding error. We are guaranteed success in our quest for truth and cannot fail.[16]

Finally, although it need not be so understood, classical foundationalism has been taken as a species of internalism, the view that only what is readily cognitively accessible to a person (for example, by reflection) is relevant to the justification of his beliefs. And although it is possible to combine features of both foundationalism and reliabilism, foundationalism has been distinguished from reliabilism, put forward as the view that knowledge stems from reliable states or processes not internally accessible to the knower.

Although both Plantinga and Wolterstorff freely speak of Aquinas as a foundationalist, or classical foundationalist, I want to avoid the sort of controversy which is sometimes raised by taxonomy. So I want to prescind from the precise terminology used by Plantinga, Wolterstorff, and other contemporary epistemologists who have made claims about Aquinas's theory of knowledge and focus just on internalism and the claims in (1)–(5) above. The idea of a theory of knowledge characterized by (1)–(5) is that there is a small set of propositions which we can know with certainty to be true without inferring them from anything else that we know, and that our non-basic beliefs will also be known with certainty if we base them on that small set of certainly true propositions. In Aquinas's case, the set of propositions which properly serves as the foundation for the non-basic beliefs is supposed to include just two groups of propositions: those whose truth is seen as soon as they are understood, and those whose truth is evident to the senses. As we examine Aquinas's views, I will be concerned to ask only whether he holds an epistemological theory which is internalist and which can be characterized by (1)–(5).

It will, of course, be helpful to have a noun by which to refer to this position rather than referring to it always by some clumsy circumlocution. So for ease of exposition I will refer to this theory as 'Foundationalism', capitalizing the term to remind the reader that it does not refer to foundationalism as a whole or to some commonly discussed species of foundationalism, but picks out instead only an epistemological position which is internalist and which is characterized by (1)–(5).

Evidence for Foundationalism in Aquinas

Why would anyone suppose Aquinas is a Foundationalist? One of the main reasons is that the Latin term for the subject of Aquinas's commentary on Aristotle's *Posterior Analytics* – namely, '*scientia*' – has often enough been translated as 'knowledge' and his commentary on that work of Aristotle's has consequently been taken to consist in an exposition of his theory of knowledge. Understood in this way, Aquinas's commentary can indeed give an appearance of Foundationalism.

There is a process of reasoning, Aquinas says, which yields its results necessarily, and in this process the certitude of *scientia* is acquired. (I will leave '*scientia*' untranslated, so as not to make any assumptions at the outset about the appropriate English equivalent for it; and I will render '*scire*' as 'have *scientia* of', or some other suitable circumlocution with '*scire*' in parenthesis after it, in order to signal to the reader that *scientia* is at issue.) Aquinas says, "*scientia* is cognition acquired through demonstration".[17]

The process of reasoning at issue here consists in demonstrative syllogisms.[18] Each demonstrative syllogism has two premises; and, according to Aquinas, these premises must be better known and prior to the conclusion.[19]

But demonstration does not give rise to an infinite regress. There are first principles of demonstration, and these are themselves indemonstrable.[20] Aquinas says: "It is not possible to acquire *scientia* of (*scire*) anything by demonstration unless there is prior cognition of the first, immediate principles."[21]

And so, according to Aquinas:

> *scientia* ... which is acquired by demonstration, proceeds from propositions which are true, first, and immediate, that is, which are not demonstrated by any intermediate but are evident by means of themselves (*per seipsas*). They are called "immediate" because they lack an intermediate demonstrating them, and "first" in relation to other propositions which are proved by means of them.[22]

There is no cognition that has more certitude than the cognition of such first principles, according to Aquinas, and first principles are the cause of certitude in one's cognition of other propositions.[23] They are not only necessary but known *per se*,[24] and any *scientia* takes its certitude from them.[25] On his views, there are different sorts of *scientia*, but mathematics is one of the paradigms.[26]

Clearly, all these claims give the appearance that Aquinas is committed to Foundationalism.

That appearance is only enhanced by what Aquinas has to say about the sorts of propositions which are first principles. On the one hand, Aquinas says that the first of all the principles are the law of non-contradiction and the law of excluded middle. But definitions, too, are principles of demonstration.[27] In fact, every proposition in which the predicate is in the definition of the subject is known *per se*.[28] On the other hand, Aquinas also says that propositions accepted by the senses, such as that the sun is now eclipsed, are the most known (*notissima*).[29]

Furthermore, on Aquinas's views, it seems that propositions which we know in virtue of understanding their terms – that is, self-evident propositions – and propositions evident to the senses are properly accepted as basic. All other propositions which form part of our knowledge must be accepted on the basis of these properly basic propositions. So we begin with properly basic propositions and proceed by means of demonstrative syllogisms to non-basic propositions. In this way, we begin with what can be known with certainty – the first, immediate, indemonstrable principles of demonstration – and move to non-basic propositions, which are deduced from the properly basic ones and so also count as knowledge known with certainty. Furthermore, introspective reflection seems to be enough to tell a person whether he has begun with the appropriate base and whether the rest of what he takes himself to know is derived in the appropriate way from that base.

These considerations can certainly make it seem as if Aquinas is committed to Foundationalism.

The problem

But just a little further exploration of Aquinas's views shows that this picture of Aquinas's theory of knowledge is irremediably flawed.

In the first place, there is ample evidence that Aquinas's notion of *scientia* is not equivalent to our notion of knowledge.

For Aquinas, *scientia* is not of contingent or corruptible things.[30] In fact, there is no *scientia* of individual things; demonstration always has to do with universals. Aquinas says, "Demonstration must always be on the basis of universals";[31] and "universals are the objects of our inquiry, just as they are the things of which we have *scientia*".[32]

Elsewhere, he says,

'Universal' is taken here as a certain suitability or adequation of a predicate to a subject, as when the predicate is not found apart from the subject or the subject without the predicate ... Demonstration is properly speaking of a universal of this sort.[33]

And, in another place he maintains:

[Aristotle] asserts that two things pertain to *scientia*. One of them is that it is universal, for there is no *scientia* of individual things susceptible to sense ... Besides things which are true and necessary and which cannot be otherwise, there are things which are true but not necessary, which can be otherwise; but it is evident ... that there is no *scientia* of such things.[34]

If '*scientia*' were Aquinas's term for knowledge, then we would have to attribute to him the view that we can have no knowledge of contingent, corruptible, or singular things; and that would be a very odd view of knowledge. It is also contrary to his explicitly argued claim that the human intellect can cognize (*cognoscere*) individual things and contingent things (although the intellect does so indirectly by working together with the senses).[35] Furthermore, it is at odds with Aquinas's claim that there is an act of intellect by which a human intellect cognizes itself.[36] Finally, it is hard to square with Aquinas's own claim, presented above, that propositions accepted on the basis of the senses, such as that the sun is now eclipsed, are most known (*notissima*).[37]

But there is further evidence which suggests not only that *scientia* is not Aquinas's equivalent of 'knowledge' but in fact that *scientia* should be understood as a special species of the broader genus *cognitio*, which looks like a much better candidate for an equivalent in Aquinas's thought to our notion of knowledge than *scientia* is.[38] (Actually, if Aquinas has a word which expresses what the English term 'knowledge' does, it is perhaps '*notitia*', although that Latin term does not have quite the range the English term does, and where we would expect to use the verb 'know', Aquinas uses not the verb cognate with '*notitia*' but rather '*cognosco*', 'cognize'.) When Aquinas explains '*scire*', the verb cognate with '*scientia*', he describes it in this way: "To have *scientia* (*scire*) of something is to cognize it perfectly (*perfecte*)."[39] In fact, Aquinas defines '*scire*' as Aristotle does: "To have *scientia* [of a thing] (*scire*) is to cognize the cause of the thing";[40] and he also says that "a cause is the intermediate in a demonstration which brings it about that we have *scientia* (*facit scire*)".[41]

In medieval logic, if we start with the highest genus in one of Aristotle's ten categories and progressively divide it into its subaltern genera and species by means of pairs of differentiae, we get a device known as a Porphyrian tree, which illustrates a set of structured relationships.[42] For example, the Porphyrian tree of substance begins with *substance*, which is divided into *corporeal substance* and *incorporeal substance* by the differentiae *corporeal* and *incorporeal*. Each of these subaltern genera of substance is divided in its turn until the single highest genus *substance* has been divided into all its subaltern genera and species. Medieval philosophers were fond of this device and extended its use as a means of showing structured relationships in many other areas besides the Aristotelian categories. Aquinas's explanations of *scientia* and *scire* given above, together with other things he says elsewhere, suggest that Aquinas has in mind a Porphyrian tree of cognition, with *scientia* as well as other species of cognition constituting the branches of the tree.[43]

So, for example, Aquinas says that *scientia* is one of several habits (*habitus*) of cognition which are related to what is true. There are five such habits, on his view, and all of them are species of cognition. Following Aristotle, Aquinas lists the five as art, wisdom, prudence, understanding, and *scientia*.[44] In another place, he says that a person is said to have understanding or *scientia* insofar as his intellect is perfect in cognizing truth.[45] Prudence and art have to do with the practical part of the soul, which reasons about things that can be done by us; prudence is right reason about things to be done, and art is right reason about things to be made. But wisdom, understanding, and *scientia* have to do with the speculative part of the soul. Understanding is a habit regarding first principles of demonstration. Wisdom has to do with causes which are ultimately first (that is, the highest or divine causes of things), and *scientia* has to do with lower causes.[46]

So here it looks as if the top of the Porphyrian tree in question is *cognitive habits with regard to what is true*, with a first division dividing these cognitive habits into those of the speculative intellect and those of the practical intellect.[47] Those of the practical intellect – prudence and art – are divided from one another insofar as one is a cognitive habit of the practical intellect regarding the truth with respect to things to be done and the other with regard to things to be made. Understanding is a cognitive habit of the speculative intellect regarding the truth with respect to first principles, unlike *scientia* and wisdom which have to do with the causes of things. And *scientia* is distinguished from wisdom because wisdom is a cognitive habit of the speculative intellect regarding truth with respect to the very highest causes of things,[48] and *scientia* is such a habit but with respect to causes other than those that are highest.

Furthermore, Aquinas tends to divide *scientia* itself into kinds, dependent on its subject matter, in much the same way as we distinguish sciences (or sciences and humanistic disciplines) from one another. So, for example, at the start of *ST* he considers carefully the question whether theology is a *scientia*.

So for all these reasons it seems clearly a mistake to render '*scientia*' simply as 'knowledge' and therefore even more of a mistake to interpret Aquinas's theory of *scientia* as a theory of knowledge. What he has to say about *scientia* cannot consequently be taken to express his views about the nature or structure of knowledge.

Evidence against ascribing Foundationalism to Aquinas

But what about the appearance of Foundationalism presented just above? What about Aquinas's apparent adherence to the view that there are properly basic beliefs, which ground all other propositions believed and which are known with certainty?

Properly basic beliefs for Aquinas are supposed to consist in propositions evident to the senses and self-evident propositions or propositions known with certainty to be true as soon as their terms are understood. It will be helpful to consider these two groups in turn.

It is true that Aquinas thinks the senses cannot be deceived as regards their proper objects;[49] but the proper objects of the senses are something below the propositional level.[50] Any belief about the world of physical objects based on the senses, such as the belief that there is a coffee cup in front of me or that there is a tree outside the window, is for Aquinas a deliverance of the intellect as well as the senses and constitutes a belief with regard to which we may be mistaken. Aquinas quotes with approval Augustine's dictum that we can make mistakes with respect to any of our senses, and he gives an affirmative answer to the question whether there can be falsity in sensory cognition. For example, he says:

> We are not deceived in the judgment by which we judge that we sense some thing. But from the fact that a sense is sometimes affected otherwise than as things are, it follows that that sense sometimes reports things to us otherwise than they are. And therefore by means of sense we make a mistake with regard to things, though not with regard to sensing itself.[51]

These claims on Aquinas's part, of course, do not show that it is wrong to attribute to him the view that propositions evident to the senses are properly basic beliefs. He surely does think that propositions evident to the senses are accepted without being based on other beliefs, and he also clearly thinks that, most of the time at any rate, we are rational in accepting such beliefs as basic. What Aquinas's claims about the fallibility of the senses do show, however, is that propositions based on sensory cognition may be false and that therefore they don't constitute a privileged class of propositions known with certainty. Consequently, a noetic structure in which the non-basic beliefs of a person are based on propositions based on sensory cognition may or may not constitute a set of beliefs known with certainty. On Aquinas's view, therefore, if the foundation includes propositions evident to the senses, there is no guarantee that the resulting structure comprises knowledge; it might consist in error instead.

Should we then understand Aquinas as a Foundationalist who restricts the certain foundations of knowledge to self-evident propositions? The evidence here too is against Foundationalist interpretations of Aquinas.

The candidates for self-evident propositions in Aquinas are the first principles of a *scientia*. Now these principles come in two sorts; what Aquinas (following Aristotle) calls 'the common principles', such as the law of non-contradiction, and what he labels 'the proper principles', such as *every man is an animal*.[52]

Common principles, unlike proper principles, are common to every *scientia*. They are not only true, indemonstrable, and known *per se*; but, in fact, Aquinas says, a common principle cannot be confirmed by an argument. It is known by the light of natural reason, and no one can form an opinion which is the contrary of a common principle.

Common principles, then, clearly look like candidates for the properly basic foundation of certain knowledge. It is, of course, obvious that common principles are basic; not only are they not derived from other propositions, but they cannot be, on Aquinas's view. And, equally clearly, there is no possibility here of falsity, as there was in the case of propositions based on sensory cognition; common principles are not only true but known by the light of natural reason itself. So common principles seem manifestly properly basic.

There are problems here, too, however. They arise from our cognition of common principles. On Aquinas's views, to say that common principles are known *per se* is not the same as saying that they are known *per se by us*.[53] We can think something is not a common principle when in fact it is. We can deny common principles out of bad intellectual habits or obstinacy, for example.[54] That is, on Aquinas's views, we cannot really deny common principles, in the sense that what we in fact believe really is the opposite of a common principle; but, Aquinas says, we can deny common principles orally ('*ore*')[55] and verbally ('*secundum vocem*'), in accordance with a false opinion or imagination.[56] As Aquinas puts it: "Nothing is so true that it cannot be denied verbally. For some people have denied orally even this most known principle: 'The same thing cannot both be and not be.'"[57]

For Aquinas, a common principle is known *per se* in the sense that if a person truly understands the terms of the principle, he will see that it must be true; but he might not truly understand the terms of the principle even though he can use those terms adequately in ordinary discourse. To take a particularly striking example, on Aquinas's view, the proposition that God exists is known *per se*. That is, if a person really understands the term 'God', he will also understand that God is simple and that therefore God's essence includes his existence, so that God not only exists but exists necessarily. But, of course, the proposition that God exists is not known *per se* by us.[58] On Aquinas's own views, it is perfectly possible for a person to be able to use the term 'God' adequately in ordinary discourse and not understand the term in such a way as to see that the proposition 'God exists' is necessarily true.

In the case in which a person denies a common principle, Aquinas will want to say both that the person who denies it does not really understand the principle and that in any case what that person takes to be the case does not constitute the opposite of the principle he is denying. But the interesting point for our purposes is that even though common principles are known by the light of natural reason, it is perfectly possible that what is in fact a common principle be rejected by someone as false (or at any rate possible that he should reject the common principle as he understands it). It is therefore also possible for a person to take what is in fact false as true and use it as a common principle. In such a case, he will be acting on a false imagination, or his verbal utterances will not correspond to any coherent concept; but he will be mistaken nonetheless.

Consequently, there is no guarantee that when a person begins with propositions which function as common principles for him, the resulting noetic structure will comprise knowledge. Just as in the case of propositions evident to the senses, the result might be error instead. Of course, whatever is suitably based on propositions that really are common principles will unquestionably be true and known. But the problem is that a cognizer might be confused, and in the place of genuine common principles he might have false propositions instead. If he is confused in this way, he is not really understanding the common principles at issue. The salient point, however, is that for all he knows he might be in the state of not really understanding the relevant common principles. Therefore, if he begins with propositions which function for him as common principles, the cognizer has no guarantee that what he builds on that foundation will even be true, let alone constitute something known with certainty.

What about proper principles, then? It seems even less likely that Aquinas's proper principles can serve as the foundations of knowledge on a Foundationalist theory of knowledge. To see why, we have to understand better what Aquinas means by the notion of a proper principle.

According to Aquinas, no *scientia* can reach its conclusions on the basis of common principles alone; proper principles are always required also.[59] Furthermore, there are very many proper principles. In fact, Aquinas says, following Aristotle, the number of principles is not much less than the number of conclusions.[60] These principles are universal propositions, and they describe a cause (or sometimes an effect) of something[61] (that is, a material, formal, efficient, or final cause or effect).[62]

Finally, the proper principles are always established by means of induction. According to Aquinas:

Demonstration proceeds from universals, but induction proceeds from particulars. Therefore, if universals, from which demonstration proceeds, could be cognized apart from induction, it would follow that a person could acquire *scientia* of things of which he did not have any sensory cognition (*sensus*). But it is impossible that universals be comprehended without induction.[63]

And so he says, "Universals, from which demonstration proceeds, do not become known (*nota*) to us except by induction;"[64] and, "it is necessary to cognize the first, universal principles by means of induction".[65]

For this reason, because first principles are acquired in this way, Aquinas says that, in a way, there are two roads to *scientia*; one is demonstration and the other is induction.[66] And elsewhere he says: "It is natural to human beings that they acquire *scientia* by means of the senses."[67]

Proper first principles, then, which are necessary to any *scientia*, are not basic at all, let alone properly basic. On the contrary, they are derived from other propositions by a process of reasoning, and the reasoning in question is induction. They are first in the process of demonstration, and so they are indemonstrable; but, as is evident here, that a principle is indemonstrable does not mean that it cannot be argued for or reasoned to in any way.

But, of course, induction is a notoriously uncertain mode of inference, as Aquinas himself recognizes: "a person who makes an induction by means of singulars to a universal does not demonstrate or syllogize with necessity."[68]

And Aquinas draws an analogy between induction and the method of analysis he calls 'division':

the method of division is analogous to the method of induction ... When something is proved syllogistically ... it is necessary that the conclusion be true if the premises are true. But this is not the case in the method of division.[69]

So not only is there no guarantee that what a cognizer uses as a proper first principle of *scientia* will be something known with certainty, there is not even a guarantee that what the cognizer starts with as a first principle will be true, since it is the result of induction.

Of course, since a genuine first principle is defined as true, if a cognizer begins with first principles, he will begin with something true. But since what we use as a first principle has to be the result of induction, what we use as first principles might very well not be genuine first principles at all, and there is no simple formal procedure for telling the genuine from the counterfeit.

Even when a cognizer does begin with a genuine first principle, however, he will not be starting with a properly basic proposition, since the genuine first principle he begins with will be derived by induction.

For these reasons, proper principles are no more candidates for properly basic beliefs in a Foundationalist theory of knowledge than common principles or propositions based on sensory cognition.

Finally, a word should be said about Aquinas's term '*certitudo*', which is generally translated just as 'certainty'. Aquinas is perfectly willing to talk about the possibility of error arising in demonstration. For example, following Aristotle, he says, "in order not to fall into mistakes in demonstration, one must be aware of the fact that often a universal seems to be demonstrated but in fact is not".[70]

Nonetheless, according to Aquinas, the process of demonstration produces "the *certitudo* of *scientia*".[71] And so what Aquinas says about the *certitudo* of *scientia* can give the appearance of supporting a Foundationalist interpretation of his epistemology.

But this appearance should not be taken at face value. Very little of Aquinas's commentary on the *Posterior Analytics* is devoted to an explanation of *certitudo*, but in the small space he gives to an exposition of the notion, he says things of this sort about it:

> *Scientia* is also certain cognition of a thing, but a person cannot cognize with *certitudo* anything which can be otherwise. And so it must also be the case that what we have *scientia* of cannot be otherwise than it is.[72]

Furthermore, Aquinas compares one *scientia* to another in order to determine which has more *certitudo* (or is *certior*) than the other. A *scientia* which knows *that* something is the case but does not know *why* it is the case has less *certitudo* than a *scientia* that knows both things.[73] Also, a *scientia* which is not about a subject that includes matter has more *certitudo* than a *scientia* that is about something material. For this reason, arithmetic has more *certitudo* than music.[74] In addition, on Aquinas's view, geometry has less *certitudo* than arithmetic;[75] a cause is *certior* than its effect; and a form is *certior* than matter.[76]

What exactly Aquinas has in mind with '*certitudo*' or '*certior*' is not clear. But clearly it would be a mistake to translate '*certitudo*' in such contexts as 'certainty'. Certainty, as we understand it, is a kind of relation between a knower and what is known, but it is difficult to see why anyone would suppose that such a relation could not obtain between a knower and a contingent state of affairs. And in the comparison of one *scientia* to another, of a cause to its effect, or of a form to matter, questions of the relation between knower and what is known do not seem to come into the discussion at all. For these reasons, we should be cautious about how we render Aquinas's term '*certitudo*'. It is not obvious what the concept of *certitudo* is in Aquinas's thought, but it is undoubtedly a mistake to take it simply as equivalent to our notion of certainty.

To summarize, then, on the view which interprets Aquinas as a Foundationalist, the foundation for knowledge on his theory of knowledge is constituted by propositions evident to the senses and the first principles of *scientia* known *per se*. These will be the properly basic propositions which are known with certainty and from which all other non-basic propositions known with certainty are derived. But, in fact, the evidence that Aquinas is a Foundationalist depends on interpreting '*scientia*' as equivalent to 'knowledge', and we have seen good reasons for supposing that such an interpretation is decidedly mistaken. Furthermore, as I have shown, on Aquinas's views, in one way or another, a person can be in error as regards all the propositions which are supposed to ground knowledge for him on the interpretation that Aquinas is a Foundationalist. The propositions which are supposed to be known with certainty according to that interpretation are not in fact guaranteed to be true on Aquinas's account and therefore obviously are not guaranteed to be known with certainty or to provide a certain foundation for other, non-basic propositions derived from them. Finally, as I have shown, among the first principles of any *scientia*, on Aquinas's account, are proper principles; and these are propositions which are not even basic, let alone properly basic, since they are derived by induction from other propositions.

These considerations by themselves seem to me enough to undermine the claim that Aquinas should be taken to be a Foundationalist. In what follows I want to consider what theory of knowledge Aquinas does hold. The evidence adduced in the following section seems to me to constitute further reason, if any more is needed, for rejecting the view of Aquinas as a Foundationalist.

Reliabilism in Aquinas's theory of knowledge

If Aquinas is not a Foundationalist, what theory of knowledge does he hold?

Like Aristotle, Aquinas is a metaphysical realist. That is, he assumes that there is an external world around us and that it has certain features independently of the operation of any created intellect, so that it is up to our minds to discover truths about the world, rather than simply inventing or creating them. On Aquinas's account, the human intellect was created by God for the purpose of discovering such truths about the world. He says:

> All natural things are the product of divine art ... And so God gives to everything the best disposition, not best simpliciter but best as ordered to its proper end ... The proximate end of the human body is the rational soul and its activities ... Therefore, I say that God constituted the human body in the best disposition appropriate to such a form [i.e., the soul] and its activities.[77]

Elsewhere, he says:

> A soul is united to a body in order to understand, which is [its]
> proper and principal activity. And consequently it is necessary that
> the body united to a rational soul be best suited to serve the soul in
> those things which are needed for understanding;[78]

and, he maintains, "a person is said to have understanding or *scientia* insofar
as his intellect is perfected to cognize what is true, which is the good of the
intellect".[79]

Not only did God make human beings in such a way as to be optimally
suited for the rational soul's cognition of what is true, on Aquinas's views,
but the fact that human beings are made in the image of God consists just
in their being cognizers of this sort. As Aquinas puts it, "only creatures that
have intellects are, strictly speaking, in the image of God".[80]

On his view,

> since human beings are said to be in the image of God in virtue of
> their having a nature that includes an intellect, such a nature is
> most in the image of God in virtue of being most able to imitate
> God;[81]

and he goes on to say:

> being in the image of God pertains to the mind alone ... Only in
> rational creatures is there found a likeness of God which counts as
> an image ... As far as a likeness of the divine nature is concerned,
> rational creatures seem somehow to attain a representation of [that]
> type in virtue of imitating God not only in this, that he is and lives,
> but especially in this, that he understands.[82]

So, on Aquinas's views, God has made human beings in his own image, and
they are made in his image in virtue of the fact that, like him, they are
cognizers; they can understand and know themselves, the world, and the
world's creator. Human beings can accomplish this feat just because God has
designed them to be cognizers and attainers of truth. Strictly speaking,
Aquinas's views about the way in which God has done so are outside the
scope of this chapter,[83] but a very brief word on this subject will be helpful
here nonetheless.

Human cognizing, on Aquinas's view, is a process which depends
primarily on two cognitive capacities (or sets of capacities): sense and intellect. (He does recognize other faculties as well, such as phantasia and
memory, but I am leaving them to one side here, for the sake of brevity.[84])
Aquinas's account of sensory cognition includes this claim: "With regard to

its proper object a sense is not deceived ... (unless perhaps by accident as a result of some impediment which happens as regards the [physical sense] organ)";[85] and in another place, speaking about proper sensibles, the non-propositional objects apprehended by one or another sense faculty, Aquinas says:

> With regard to its proper sensibles, a sense does not have false cognition, except by accident, and in only relatively few cases, because it does not receive the sensible form properly on account of some indisposition of the [physical sense] organ.[86]

This astonishing optimism as regards sensory cognition[87] is echoed by his view of the intellect: "The proper object of the intellect is the quiddity of a thing. And so as regards the quiddity of a thing, considered just as such, the intellect is not mistaken";[88] and he goes on to say, "in a simple consideration of the quiddity of a thing and of things cognized by means of it, the intellect is never deceived".[89]

Aquinas sees these claims about the senses and the intellect as connected. For example, he says:

> As a sense gets its form directly by a likeness of [its] proper sensibles, so the intellect gets its form by a likeness of the quiddity of a thing. And so, regarding the quiddity [of a thing], the intellect is not deceived, just as a sense is not deceived regarding [its] proper sensibles.[90]

For my purposes here, what is important about these implausible sounding claims is just the attitude Aquinas takes towards human cognitive capacities. On Aquinas's view, human cognitive capacities are designed by God for the express purpose of enabling human beings to be cognizers of the truth, as God himself is. In particular, when a human person uses the senses and the intellect as God designed them to be used in the environment suited to them, that is, in the world for which God designed human beings, then those faculties are absolutely reliable. In fact, not only are they reliable but as regards their proper objects it is even the case that, when they are functioning normally, neither the senses nor the intellect can be deceived or mistaken.

The nature of Aquinas's account of our cognitive capacities can be seen most graphically by considering what Aquinas has to say about Adam, the first human being created by God, in the period before Adam's fall, when Adam was still sinless. Sinless Adam, according to Aquinas, also was not deceived or in error with regard to any of his beliefs. Aquinas says:

> It could not be the case that, while innocence remained, a human intellect accepted anything false as true ... The rectitude of the

original condition is not compatible with any deception on the part of the intellect.[91]

And in another place, he says: "Every error is either guilt or punishment, and neither of these could be in the state of innocence; therefore, neither could error."[92] And he goes on to explain:

As the true is the good of the intellect, so the false is its evil ... If an opinion is false, it is a certain evil act on the part of the intellect. And so since in the state of innocence there was no corruption or evil, there could not be in the state of nature any false opinion ... And in this way in the intellect [of human beings in the original state of innocence] there could be no falsity.[93]

In a way, then, what has to be explained on Aquinas's views is not so much what accounts for the human ability to know as what accounts for the fact that human beings are sometimes in error. And, in fact, as the preceding quotations show, on Aquinas's views, because God has designed our cognitive capacities in such a way as to make us cognizers of the truth, it is only in our post-fall condition that error, deception, or false opinion is a possibility at all. As Aquinas sees it, error, deception, and false opinion have to be explained as either guilt or punishment.

It is not part of my purpose in this chapter to explain these views of Aquinas's about the design and function of human senses and intellect.[94] Here I want to call attention to these claims of Aquinas's about the senses and the intellect just to aid interpretation of his theory of knowledge. In light of Aquinas's views about human cognitive faculties, it seems reasonable to take his theory of knowledge as a species of externalism, with reliabilist elements. On Aquinas's account, when they function as they were designed to function in the environment in which they were designed to function, our cognitive faculties, and in particular our senses and intellect, work in a reliable way to yield knowledge of ourselves and everything else as well.

That this is Aquinas's understanding of the nature of knowledge helps explain the sort of discussion we find, for example, in his argument that the incarnate Christ has *scientia* acquired through experience. Aquinas does not argue for this conclusion by trying to make any claims about the kinds of beliefs that were basic for Christ or the way in which other beliefs of Christ's were derived from such foundations of Christ's noetic structure. Instead, he argues in this way that there was such *scientia* in Christ:

[W]e must say that in the soul of Christ there was not only a possible intellect but also an agent intellect. Now if in other things God and nature made nothing in vain ... ,it is all the more the case that nothing in the soul of Christ was in vain. But anything that did not have its proper function would be in vain ... Now the proper function of the agent intellect is to produce intelligible species in actuality by abstracting them from phantasms ... In this way, therefore, we must say that there were some intelligible species in Christ received in his possible intellect as a result of the action of [his] agent intellect. And this is what it is for there to be acquired *scientia* in him.[95]

For Aquinas, then, a human being's knowledge (in all its kinds, including *scientia*) is a function of that person's using the cognitive capacities God created in human beings as God designed them to be used in the world God created them to be used in.

As I will try to show in the next section, it is not at all surprising to find a theory of knowledge of this sort in a theist, which may help to explain why Aquinas's approach to knowledge bears a strong resemblance to the theory of knowledge Plantinga himself develops after rejecting the views he mistakenly attributes to Aquinas.

Aquinas's approach to epistemology

It might occur to someone to object at this point that if my interpretation of Aquinas's theory of knowledge is correct, we should expect to find some explicit statement of it somewhere in his works. In fact, what we have is largely a discussion (as, for example, in the commentary on Aristotle's *De anima*) of the way in which the mind makes epistemic contact with things and uses that contact to acquire information and an exposition (as, for example, in the commentary on the *Posterior Analytics*) of *scientia*, which on my interpretation turns out to be not knowledge simpliciter but only a certain species of cognition. If Aquinas holds a theory of knowledge of the sort I have sketched, not Foundationalism but an externalism with reliabilist elements, why is there not in his works some straightforward presentation and analysis of it? On the view that takes Aquinas to be a classical foundationalist, Aquinas's commentary on the *Posterior Analytics* is his epistemological treatise. On my interpretation, very little in Aquinas's writings constitutes an examination of theories of knowledge, and the commentary on the *Posterior Analytics* is not a presentation of Aquinas's epistemology. If my interpretation is correct, what would account for this paucity of interest in the nature of knowledge itself? (In a subsequent section, I will also say something about how we are to understand the commentary on the *Posterior Analytics*.)

To see the answer to this question, it helps to consider theories of knowledge in terms of an analogy. Suppose we are reflecting not on our cognitive capacities and theories of knowledge, but rather on race cars and theories of excellence in race car driving. Any good, complete manual presenting a theory of excellence in race car driving ought to include at least three parts. There might or might not be an introduction in which the manual explains what no one really needs to be told, namely, that excellence in race car driving is a matter of winning as many of the important races as possible. Then there needs to be (1) a section on race tracks, which says something about the environment in which the standard race car is designed to be driven. Next, there should be (2) a section on race cars themselves, and it should be divided into two parts. (2a) The first part should comprise information about the general mechanics of race cars; it should explain in general how such cars are built and how they are designed to work. (2b) The other part should evaluate the different firms which build such cars and should explain the extent to which various companies can be trusted to turn out excellent machinery. Finally, there ought to be (3) a section on race car drivers and what they need to do to drive well. This section should also have two parts. (3a) One part should present general advice on how to avoid crashes; (3b) the other should give information on what drivers can do to make their race cars go as fast and as far as possible.

As is evident, these parts of a theory of excellence in race car driving correspond roughly to elements in a complete theory of knowledge. Philosophical considerations about the environment in which our cognitive faculties operate, about what there is for our cognitive faculties to know, constitute part (1). Information about the way in which human cognitive faculties function (the sort of information currently given by neurobiology and cognitive psychology) and philosophical discussions of the reliability or non-reliability of human cognitive faculties respectively comprise the two parts of part (2). Epistemological theories about knowledge, about warrant, justification, and other central epistemological notions, fall under part (3); they give information on how to avoid falsehood and acquire truth. In modern epistemological theories, the emphasis has often seemed to be on the epistemological analogue to (3a), the avoidance of error and deception. But which of all these parts one emphasizes in one's epistemology or highlights for special concern is a function of one's whole worldview.

Given Aquinas's robust faith in a provident creator of the world who made human beings in his image in order that they might be, like himself, cognizers of the truth, it is not surprising that some elements of the theory do not get much explicit development or analysis in Aquinas's work. Aquinas takes for granted what might be in the epistemological analogue to the introduction, namely, that the goal aimed at in the use of human cognitive faculties is cognitive excellence or intellectual virtue. This view flows from his theological commitments and therefore does not receive lengthy argumentation. The epistemological analogue to the introduction, therefore, does not need or get a prominent place in Aquinas's discussions of human knowledge.

For roughly the same reason, it would be a mistake to look to Aquinas's work for detailed consideration of knowledge as a function of the reliable operation of human cognitive capacities. Given Aquinas's beliefs about God, it is not likely that the part of an epistemological theory corresponding to (2b), the section on the excellence of the equipment produced by various car makers, will be well developed in Aquinas's discussion of human knowledge. On Aquinas's views, the maker of human cognitive equipment is God, and his purpose in making that equipment is to enable human intellects to imitate him in his activity as a knower. This view is so fundamental to Aquinas's beliefs that he does not spend much argument on it. And it is entirely understandable that worries about the very possibility of knowledge, based on considerations of the unreliability of one or another human cognitive faculty, such as the worry raised, for example, by skepticism, should loom much larger in a theory of knowledge which is not firmly embedded in a theistic worldview.[96]

What is of far more interest to Aquinas than these issues is the analogue to (2a), the section on the mechanics of race cars. The epistemological equivalent of this section can be found in Aquinas's commentary on *De anima* and his other discussions of the way in which the human mind works, and he does give this subject considerable examination. (There is, of course, no reason why this part of Aquinas's thought cannot also be understood as part of his philosophy of mind. But insofar as his theory of knowledge takes knowledge to be a function of human cognitive capacities' operating as they were designed to operate, an explanation of the operations of human cognitive faculties will also be part of his theory of knowledge.)

As for the analogue to section (3), the driver's manual, the epistemological equivalent to (3) is a consideration of (3a′) how to avoid falsehood and (3b′) how to acquire truth, especially truths of a deep, significant, or far-ranging character. But here, too, which of these two parts one emphasizes is a function of one's general worldview. Aquinas does discuss, for example, the nature and detection of fallacies in reasoning or the way in which the mind can be deceived. But a driver who thought her car was built by God and she herself was under the direct providential care of God, who supposed that God himself wanted her to win races, might be less worried about the possibility of crashing and more concerned with doing her part to make the car go as far and as fast as possible. Similarly, Aquinas supposes that God is both the maker of human cognitive equipment and the one who designed that equipment for the purpose of acquiring truth. Consequently, it is not surprising to find that Aquinas devotes much less attention to questions about the avoidance of error or other undesirable cognitive states and much more attention to questions about the use of human cognitive capacities which yields the deepest or most important truths about the world and its creator.[97]

At any rate, expounding a method for acquiring significant and far-ranging truth is, in my view, the object of Aquinas's work on *scientia*, especially in his commentary on the *Posterior Analytics*, as I will show in the next section.

Aquinas's commentary on the *Posterior Analytics*

As we have seen, *scientia*, on Aquinas's view, is the cognition of the causes of things, where the causes in question are not divine causes but belong to a lower, created order of causes. As Aquinas puts it:

> it is obvious that a cause is the middle in a demonstration, which produces *scientia*, because to have *scientia* is to cognize the cause of a thing. But a cause is what is sought in all the aforesaid questions [in which demonstration plays a part].[98]

In retrospect, it seems clear that this description by itself should have given us pause about accepting an interpretation of Aquinas as a Foundationalist whose theory of *scientia* is a theory of knowledge. A Foundationalist theory of knowledge is a theory which explains what counts as knowledge and what does not and which explains the trustworthiness of what counts as knowledge. But, as Aquinas presents it, the theory of *scientia* is a different enterprise; for him, *scientia* is a matter of cognizing causes of things, of finding causal explanations for things, so that what is sought in a demonstration producing *scientia* is not the conclusion of a demonstrative syllogism but rather its premises.

That is why Aquinas says, for example:

> There are certain things which we would not ask about with [any] doubt if we were to see them, not because *scientia* consists in seeing but because the universal, with which *scientia* is concerned, would be obtained by means of experience, on the basis of the things seen. For instance, if we were to see glass as porous and see how the light is transmitted through the openings of the glass, we would have *scientia* (*sciremus*) of why the glass is transparent.[99]

Similarly, he says:

> Suppose ... that someone were on the moon itself and by sense perceived the interposition of the earth by its shadow. He would perceive by sense that the moon was then eclipsed by the shadow of the earth, but he would not for that reason have full *scientia* of the cause of the eclipse. For what causes an eclipse in general (*universaliter*) is the proper (*per se*) cause of the eclipse.[100]

And he explains the general point of that example in this way:

Scientia is superior to sense. For it is clear that cognition which is through a cause is nobler, but a proper (*per se*) cause is a universal cause ... and therefore cognition through a universal cause, which is the character of *scientia*, is more honorable. And because it is impossible to apprehend a universal cause by means of sense, it follows that *scientia*, which shows the universal cause, is not only more honorable than all sensory cognition but also than all other intellective cognition when it is of things which have a cause.[101]

Descriptions of these causes serve as the premises, rather than the conclusions, of demonstrative arguments. As Aquinas says in various places, "the middle of a demonstration is a cause";[102] and, he goes on to say, "by the middle of a demonstration all the causes [i.e., the formal, material, efficient, and final causes] are manifested, because any of these [four] causes can be taken as the middle of a demonstration".[103]

So, on Aquinas's views, demonstration is not a matter of starting with epistemically certain and properly basic beliefs and deducing conclusions which are consequently known with equal certainty, in order to have knowledge of a particularly rigorous sort. Rather, on his account, in order to find a demonstration we need to look for causes of what is described in the claim that is to be the conclusion of the demonstration. Once we have found the premises of a demonstration, we have *scientia* of the claim in the conclusion in virtue of having a causal explanation of the state of affairs described in the demonstration's conclusion. And what demonstration confers is not so much epistemic certainty as it is depth of understanding. Because Aquinas is often misunderstood on this score, Paul Durbin, in commenting on Aquinas's understanding of demonstration, says:

> After Descartes it has become necessary to distinguish Aristotelean "syllogismus" and "demonstratio" from a Cartesian, rationalist "deduction". Aristotle and St Thomas do not begin with self-evident principles and derive conclusions therefrom in a rationalist-deductive mode (even though *Posterior Analytics* is often interpreted this way); rather, they begin with a statement to be justified (it will become the "conclusion" only in a formal restatement of the argument) and "reduce" it back to its ultimate explanatory principles.[104]

When Aquinas himself describes what he is doing in his commentary on the *Posterior Analytics*, he describes his project in this way. On his view, there are two different processes human reason engages in; one is discovery, and the other is judgment. He says:

following the path of inquiry or discovery, human reasoning proceeds *from* certain things understood simply, and these are first principles. And, again, following the path of judgment, human reasoning returns by analysis *to* first principles and ponders these discovered principles.[105] (emphasis added)

So, according to Aquinas, when we are engaged in what he calls 'discovery', we reason *from* first principles to conclusions based on them. On the other hand, when we are concerned with what Aquinas calls 'judgment', we reason from other things back *to* first principles by means of analysis.

On the common account of Aquinas as a Foundationalist, his commentary on the *Posterior Analytics* (and his other putative discussions of epistemology) would thus count as a description of discovery, since in those discussions Aquinas is supposed to be explaining how we proceed from first principles to the conclusions of demonstrative syllogisms that are known with certainty in virtue of having been derived in the demonstrative way from those first principles.

But in his introduction to his commentary on the *Posterior Analytics*, Aquinas takes just the opposite view. In that introduction, Aquinas explains that there are three different reasoning processes examined in Aristotle's logical works. Only one of these processes, the first one, yields *scientia*. Aquinas describes that reasoning process in this way:

the part of logic which is principally devoted to the first process is called the judicative part, because judgment goes with the certitude of *scientia*. And because we cannot have certain judgment about effects except by analysis into first principles, this part is called "Analytics".[106]

And he goes on to say:

the certitude of judgment which is had by analysis is either from the form of a syllogism alone (and the *Prior Analytics*, which is about the syllogism considered unconditionally, is devoted to this), or it is also from the matter [of a syllogism] together with [the form], because [its] propositions are *per se* and necessary (and the *Posterior Analytics*, which is about the demonstrative syllogism, is devoted to this).[107]

On the other hand, Aquinas explicitly dissociates discovery, the reasoning *from* principles *to* conclusions, from *scientia*. He contrasts the analysis of demonstration, which on his view does lead to the certitude and *scientia*. with a second reasoning process which does not yield *scientia*; and this second process, he says, "is called 'discovery' ... The *Topics* or dialectic is devoted to this."[108] So is rhetoric, though in a somewhat different way, as Aquinas goes on to explain in this same passage. So on Aquinas's account discovery is a part of dialectic or rhetoric, rather than of demonstration; and what is covered in his commentary on the *Posterior Analytics* is not discovery but judgment.

But, on Aquinas's views, judgment is a matter of returning to first principles, rather than beginning from them and deducing other propositions from them. This process of reasoning, examined at length in the *Posterior Analytics,* is a matter of finding the premises or "middles" of a demonstrative syllogism; and these middles are, in general, the causes of what is described in the conclusion of a demonstrative syllogism. The process of finding middles and using them to make demonstrative syllogisms continues until the causes being used as middles are traced back to the first principles proper to the *scientia* in question.

So the subject matter Aquinas takes to be covered both in Aristotle's *Posterior Analytics* and in his own commentary on it has as its main emphasis finding ultimate causal explanations for what is described in the conclusions of demonstrative syllogisms. The point of this process is evidently to yield a deeper understanding of the nature of the state of affairs being described in the syllogistic conclusions.

This interpretation of Aquinas's views helps to clarify some of his examples presented above. For instance, on this interpretation, it is easier to understand Aquinas's example involving the lunar eclipse. Both the person who is on the moon watching the interposition that produces an eclipse of the moon on earth and the physicist who understands eclipses know that the moon is sometimes eclipsed (or is now eclipsed). But only the physicist has *scientia* of that fact because only the physicist understands the causes of eclipses in general. On this interpretation, then, a person has full *scientia* of something in virtue of knowing the general or the ultimate causal explanation of it.

Conclusion

On this interpretation of Aquinas's concept of *scientia* and theory of knowledge, then, how shall we translate *scientia*? 'Discipline', 'expertise', 'body of knowledge' are all possibilities, except that they leave us no easy analogue for the verb '*scire*'. 'Understanding' might do the job, except that it has unfortunately become the conventional translation for Aquinas's '*intellectus*'. Perhaps the best option is just to translate '*scientia*' by its cognate, 'science', with a reminder to the reader that science so understood ranges from, for example, mathematics to metaphysics. Understanding *scientia* as science in this broad sense will help us to digest some of Aquinas's examples of demonstration, which would be surprising and perplexing on a Foundationalist interpretation of his theory of knowledge.

For instance, in illustrating the different kinds of causes that can serve as the middle of a demonstration, Aquinas gives this example as a case of a demonstration in which the middle is an efficient cause:

> [Aristotle] presents an example of [a demonstration based on] an efficient cause using a certain story about the Greeks. Allied with certain other Greeks, the Athenians once invaded the Sardians, who were subject to the king of the Medes, and therefore the Medes invaded the Athenians. [Aristotle] says, therefore, that one can ask the reason why the war of the Medes with the Athenians occurred, and this reason why is a cause of the Athenians' being attacked by the Medes ... The middle ... in this case has to do with the Athenians who first began the war. And so it is clear that here a cause which is efficient (*primo movit*) is taken as a middle.[109]

It is not at all evident how this example could be construed on a Foundationalist interpretation of Aquinas. What combination of self-evident propositions and propositions evident to the senses of a person living in Aquinas's time could yield the conclusion that the Medes made war on the Athenians?[110] But on the account I have been developing here, it is possible to accommodate this example if we take 'science' broadly enough to include the social sciences as well.[111]

The fact that in this passage Aquinas is obviously discussing an example of Aristotle's should also serve to remind us that the question of the relation of Aquinas's theory of knowledge to that of Aristotle still remains. On Irwin's view of Aristotle's *Posterior Analytics*, Aristotle is a foundationalist, at least at the time of writing that work. I have been at pains to show that Aquinas's commentary on the *Posterior Analytics* cannot be interpreted as presenting his theory of knowledge as a whole, that '*scientia*' for Aquinas is not equivalent to 'knowledge', and that Aquinas's epistemological position is not correctly characterized as Foundationalism.

I am not certain what species of foundationalism Irwin is attributing to Aristotle; but if it is an internalist theory of knowledge or if it bears a family resemblance to Foundationalism, then, on my interpretation of Aquinas, there are two ways of thinking about Aquinas's relation to Aristotle. One is that Aquinas completely misunderstood the nature of Aristotle's treatise and that although he thought he was simply explaining and developing Aristotle's thought, in fact he was radically altering the nature of Aristotelian epistemology. The other is that Aquinas was an astute reader of Aristotle and that the evidence gathered here to reject the view of Aquinas as a Foundationalist is some reason to rethink at least one current account of Aristotle. Either of these possibilities is compatible with the interpretation of Aquinas I have defended here, but deciding which one to accept belongs to the province of historians of ancient philosophy and is outside the scope of this chapter.

On that score, then, this chapter will come to no judgment. When the issue is adjudicated, however, it should be resolved with a clear recognition of Aquinas as holding not Foundationalism but rather a sophisticated theological externalism with reliabilist elements, and his commentary on the *Posterior Analytics* should be understood not as a treatise presenting Aquinas's theory of knowledge but rather as an exposition of Aquinas's philosophy of science, where 'science' is very broadly understood to include all bodies of knowledge.

8

THE MECHANISMS OF
COGNITION

Introduction

Hannah and Tom are in the kitchen, talking; Hannah, momentarily distracted, stares intently out the kitchen window, which is outside the range of Tom's vision. "What are you looking at?" he says. "A cat," Hannah answers. "A big black and white one with a smudge on its nose. It's Max, the neighbors' cat. He's stalking birds. If I raised the bird feeders another three feet, Max couldn't get the birds so easily; but then the feeders would be a lot harder for me to fill, too. I should really talk to the neighbors about putting a bell on that cat." In this unremarkable exchange, Hannah does several very remarkable things, ranging from describing what she sees to reasoning discursively. There is currently an intense research effort to build machines that can do even the simplest part of what Hannah does so effortlessly here, but these attempts have not so far been remarkable for their success. How does Hannah do it?

This is a question about the mechanisms of cognition. In raising it, I am asking not about what constitutes one or another sort of cognition, but rather about the means and the processes by which cognition of all sorts is accomplished. Whatever we think about the nature of the mind, we all agree that Hannah's body is involved in her engaging in the cognitive processes manifested in the example. But how does Hannah achieve cognition? The light reflecting from the cat strikes the glass of the kitchen window as well as Hannah's eyes, and yet Hannah sees Max but the kitchen window does not. What is it about Hannah that enables her to use the light as she does?

Contemporary thinkers are interested in questions like these, and they attempt to solve them by research into neurobiology, computer science, and psychology, among other disciplines. Aquinas was interested in them, too. To explore them, he used astute and subtle observations, many of them not his own but derived from a long, largely Aristotelian tradition of thinking about human cognitive processes, together with theoretical inferences about faculties postulated to explain these observations.[1] In this chapter, I will be less concerned with his observations and inferences, or the traditions behind them, than with the theory that is the end result of them. The end result, in my view, is surprisingly insightful, with much to teach us even today.

I say '*surprisingly* insightful' not just because it is surprising that Aquinas produced so sophisticated a theory of cognition without any of the benefits of modern science and technology, but also because it is so hard for us to extract his theory and comprehend it. What he has to say about human cognitive processes is couched in an array of unfamiliar medieval technical terminology, and his remarks about it are often embedded in forbiddingly esoteric discussions, such as his arguments against the Averroists' theory of the unity of the agent intellect or his theorizing about the way in which the second person of the Trinity is related to the first. Worse yet, when he does use some terminology that is apparently familiar to us, such as 'form' or 'spiritual' or 'sensory cognition', we are likely to be misled all the more, because it turns out that the meanings he associates with such terms are different from those we are likely to attach to them. This state of affairs helps to explain the diversity of theories scholars have claimed to find in Aquinas's account of cognition. More patience and caution are needed here than in many other parts of his philosophical system.

Direct and unmediated cognition

It may also be helpful to clarify two points at the outset, which might otherwise cause confusion later on.

The first has to do with the notion of direct and unmediated cognition. Is Aquinas's account of cognition one that attributes to human beings direct and unmediated cognition of extramental reality, as historians of philosophy often say it is? The answer to this question depends not only on our reading of Aquinas, but also on what we mean by 'direct' and 'unmediated'. A full consideration of the relevant issues would take us too far afield, but for present purposes we can approach the question roughly in this way.

If by 'direct cognition' we mean that the cognizer apprehends the object of cognition in one indivisible act of cognition, without anything that counts as a means of cognition or a mechanism causing cognition, then on Aquinas's account perhaps only God knows anything directly. Similarly, if what we mean by 'unmediated' is that there is no intermediary process of any sort, including such processes as representation, between the cognizer and what she cognizes, then here, too, for Aquinas God alone will count as having unmediated cognition. But this is a fairly stringent interpretation of the notion of direct and unmediated cognition, and it has the implausible consequence that, on contemporary neurobiological accounts of the way in which human beings perceive things, no human being knows any extramental object with direct and unmediated cognition.

And so we might also consider a more plausible account of direct and unmediated cognition. On this less stringent account, by 'direct' cognition we mean just that a person cognizes something but does not cognize it solely in virtue of cognizing something else, as the viewer at home knows what is happening in the football game solely in virtue of knowing what is happening on the television screen. There is a correspondingly more moderate interpretation of 'unmediated cognition', too. In this sense, put roughly, a cognition is unmediated if there is no significant mechanism external to a cognizer through which he cognizes the object of his cognition.[2] In this sense, what is seen through a satellite's imaging system is mediated cognition, but what is seen unaided by such external devices is unmediated cognition, even if the cognition in question is mediated by the brain's processing.

On this more moderate interpretation of the notion of direct and unmediated cognition, Aquinas's account of cognition does ascribe direct and unmediated cognition to human beings.[3] Aquinas says:

> we say that corporeal creatures are seen *immediately* only when whatever in them can be conjoined to sight is conjoined to it. But they cannot be conjoined [to sight] by their essence because of [their] materiality, and so they are seen *immediately* just when their similitude[4] is conjoined to the intellect.[5] (my emphasis)

Blindsight and agnosia

The second preliminary point I want to make here has to do with perception. What Aquinas has to say about sensation is often taken as his account of perception, but whether this standard interpretation is right depends at least in part on what we take perception to be. In normal adult human beings, perception is a process that encompasses a great deal, ranging from the incoming visual data to the ultimate recognition of, say, a cat. Whether perception can still occur when some parts of the usual process are absent, and how many parts can be absent before we feel queasy about calling what remains 'perception', has been the subject of some dispute.

Neurobiology has made us particularly aware of some of the problems in this connection. There is, for example, the much-discussed phenomenon of blindsight. (This neurobiological debility and the one mentioned in the next paragraph will be helpful to us later in this chapter as well.) A patient with blindsight has no defects in his eyes and no neurological defects in the lower-level processing of visual data; but he will still be unable to have conscious access to the processed visual data. He will therefore claim, sincerely, to be blind. On the other hand, when asked just to guess whether a yardstick in his field of vision is vertical or horizontal, he has a very high percentage of correct 'guesses'. Shall we say that the blindsight patient perceives the yardstick? Here, although much of the patient's visual system is functioning properly, most of us would be inclined to answer 'no'.

246

Or, to take one more example, what shall we say about agnosia patients? These are patients who process visual data and have conscious access to that data but who cannot recognize what they perceive by means of the sense afflicted with agnosia. Although such patients can describe the objects they see (or touch, etc.) and although they are familiar with such objects, they have a profound inability to categorize those objects relying just on data from the afflicted sense.[6] Consequently, because of their disorder, visual agnosia patients function in some respects as if they were non-seeing. Shall we say that the agnosia patient perceives what is presented to the sense associated with the agnosia? Neurobiologists are accustomed to answer in the negative.[7]

Some philosophers who in effect agree with such neurological assessments argue that perception must consist in the whole process culminating in the recognition of objects. On their view, to see an extramental object – say, a cat – is to see it *as a cat*. On this way of thinking about perception, all seeing is seeing *as*. If perception is to be thought of in this way, then, as we shall see, sensory cognition on Aquinas's account should not be equated with perception. Rather, as I will argue, it consists just in the part of the process of perception which is still intact in agnosia patients; in the case of vision, this will be seeing, but without any seeing *as*.

With these preliminary cautions, we can now turn to Aquinas's account of the sensory powers.

The sensory powers

Aquinas thinks that there are five external senses – sight, hearing, touch, taste, and smell – and that each is a "power (*virtus*) in a corporeal organ".[8]

Each of the senses has both a proper "sensible" and a common "sensible". Aquinas tends to use the Latin translated 'sensible' as a noun to mean just that which the sense takes in, as distinct from what is cognized by the sense. So, for example, although the sense *object* I see in front of me is my coffee cup, the *sensible* taken in by sight is color, according to Aquinas (or light of different wave lengths, according to contemporary accounts). On Aquinas's view, the proper sensible of each sense is what that sense takes in primarily and what cannot be taken in by another sense. There are many proper sensibles for touch, for example, including hot and cold, wet and dry, heavy and light. The *common* sensibles are those that more than one sense can take in: movement, rest, number, shape, and size. Some of these – number, movement, and rest – can be discerned, at least sometimes in some conditions, by all five external senses; and some senses – sight and touch – are able to discern all the common sensibles in certain circumstances.[9]

Although what the senses take in are the proper and common sensibles, what is sensed by this means are extramental objects: "the senses when they are active are of singular things which are outside the soul."[10]

Besides the external senses, Aquinas recognizes a number of internal senses: the common sense, phantasia and imagination, the estimative power, and the memorative power. Like the external senses, these powers use corporeal organs, in particular, the brain. Phantasia and imagination are connected, and I will take them up at more length below. The memorative power is the storehouse for sensory impressions and is distinct from intellective memory; I will briefly discuss both sorts of memory after examining Aquinas's account of phantasia. The estimative power is similar to those animal instincts by which non-human animals sense what to seek out and what to flee, what is useful to them and what is hurtful.[11] In human beings, the estimative power compares "individual intentions", as intellect compares universal intentions;[12] it apprehends individual things insofar as they are "the terminus or the source of some action or passion".[13] Finally, the common sense is the power that integrates information from the various external senses. All the senses feed into the common sense, and impressions in any of the external senses are followed by impressions in the common sense. The common sense is therefore the power that enables us to discern the white from the sweet, which no individual external sense could do.[14] Aquinas is clearly right to hold that some integration among the senses is needed and that such integration requires a power other than the powers of the individual senses themselves.[15]

Except for a brief discussion of the memorative power, in what follows I will consider only phantasia and imagination among the internal senses. I will also leave to one side those parts of Aquinas's account that are not directly relevant to understanding his view of the cognitive faculties (as distinct, for example, from understanding his views of the way in which a cognitive faculty interacts with the will). So, for example, Aquinas has interesting things to say about recall and the way in which recall is to some limited extent under voluntary control;[16] he also makes remarks in various places about attention and the way in which the will can direct attention.[17] But I will leave these parts of his account to one side as well in the interest of focusing investigation on the heart of his account of cognition.

The nature of sensible *species*

Our senses contribute to cognition by putting us in epistemic contact with extramental material objects.[18] Aquinas says:

> Our cognition takes its beginning from things and proceeds in this way: it begins, first, in sense and is finished, second, in intellect, so that sense is found to be a kind of intermediary between things and the intellect.[19]

The senses participate in such cognition by receiving a "sensible *species*" from the extramental thing presented to them. What exactly a sensible *species*[20] is, however, is not so easy to determine. It has been taken to be everything from a pictorial image of a material object to the sense impressions which some philosophers suppose to be the primary objects of sensory awareness.[21] Consequently, it is wiser here to leave the term '*species*' in Latin and look at Aquinas's own description of the nature and function of a sensible *species*.

For Aquinas, a sensible *species* is the form of a matter-form composite. He says, "A sensory power is receptive of *species* without matter"[22]; and, in explaining the way in which a sensory power is acted on by what affects it, he remarks, "a sensory power receives form without matter".[23]

By thinking of a sensible *species* as an immaterial form, Aquinas is not taking it to be a sort of ghost or, on the other hand, as nothing more than a shape separated from the matter that it shapes. Rather, as I argued in an earlier chapter,[24] where material objects are concerned, by 'form' Aquinas generally means something like a configurational state. The form of a material object is the configurational state in which the matter of that object is arranged. The sensible *species* is thus the form or the configurational state of what is sensed, which the sensory power receives.

It is important to emphasize that a sensible *species* is not itself what is sensed. Instead it is the means by which the senses sense extramental things. There is room for confusion here, because Aquinas does talk about the sensory power apprehending the sensible *species*, and locutions of this sort can give the mistaken impression that what the senses sense, on Aquinas's view, is in fact the sensible *species*, contrary to what I just claimed. So, for example, Aquinas says:

> With regard to the apprehension of the senses, it is important to know that there is a certain apprehensive power which apprehends the sensible *species* when the sensible thing itself is present, and this is the sense itself. And there is another apprehensive power which apprehends the sensible *species* when the sensible thing is absent, and this is the imagination. And so the sense always apprehends a thing as it is, unless there is some impediment in the [sensory] organ.[25]

Especially because Aquinas talks about the sense's apprehending both an extramental thing and a sensible *species*, it is possible to suppose that 'apprehending' is for him a term of cognition, so that in this passage he is claiming that what the senses cognize is both the sensible *species* and extramental things.

But such an interpretation is contradicted by many passages in which he claims explicitly that the sensible *species* are *not* what the senses cognize. Rather they are just the means by which the senses participate in cognition:

"The sensible *species* is not what is sensed, but rather that by which a sense senses."[26]

Furthermore, in other places, Aquinas sometimes talks not so much of the senses' apprehending sensible *species* as of their *receiving* the *species*. So, for example, he says, "an animal by means of its sensitive soul not only receives the *species* of sensible things ... but also retains and preserves them".[27]

It is clear that just receiving is not necessarily a cognitive act for the senses; we don't suppose that our eyes perceive light just in virtue of taking in light. So it seems as if in some contexts 'apprehending' is a synonym of the non-cognitive 'receiving' for Aquinas.

In the light of these passages, it seems reasonable to take apprehending as a genus which can be divided into cognitive and non-cognitive acts (just as there can be, for example, cognitive and non-cognitive acts of grasping). When the senses apprehend some extramental thing, they have a cognitive grasp of it; but when they apprehend a sensible *species*, they simply receive it, without its being the case that the *species* they are receiving is itself the object of sensory cognition. This interpretation of apprehending is natural enough; and if we do not provide some such interpretation, we will have to ascribe to Aquinas an obvious contradiction, namely, that the senses both do and do not have sensible *species* as the objects of cognition.[28]

For these reasons, we should understand Aquinas's view of sensible *species* in this way: the sensible *species* is an immaterial form which is received by the senses although not cognized by them.

The reception of sensible *species*

Here, however, another apparent problem arises for Aquinas. On his view, the sensory powers are powers of bodily organs, and the sensible *species* or form is received by those bodily organs. So the *species* or form is imposed on the matter of the sense organ. But the imposition of form on matter is the way in which change and generation occur on Aquinas's account.[29] Since the *species* is the form of whatever it is that is being sensed, say, a stone, when that *species* is imposed on the eye, for example, it seems as if it ought to organize the matter of the eye as it organized the matter of the stone. In that case, imposing a form of the stone on the eye would not bring it about that the eye senses the stone; rather the eye would take on the characteristics of the stone.[30]

The solution to this problem lies in a distinction important for Aquinas's account of cognition. There are two ways a form can be received and a change occur. One way he calls "natural" or "material". The natural reception of a form in matter does make the newly resultant composite be whatever the form organizes it into. The form of a stone naturally or materially received in matter produces in that matter the characteristics of a stone.[31] Similarly, when the form of a quality such as sweet or red is received naturally, it makes the matter that receives it sweet or red. Aquinas says:

I call a change 'natural' insofar as a quality is received in its recipient according to the [kind of] being associated with the nature [of things] (*secundum esse naturae*), as when something is made cold or hot or moved with respect to place.[32]

There is another way a form can be received, however. Aquinas often says that a form is received in the recipient according to the mode of the recipient, that is, in the way the recipient is able to receive it.[33] In natural reception or change, the recipient of a form has the same disposition or potentiality as that from which the form comes, and that is why the form can be received in the same mode of being in the recipient as it had in that from which it gets the form. But sometimes,

> the material disposition for receiving [a form] on the part of the recipient is not similar to the material disposition on the part of the agent. And so [in such a case] the form is received in the recipient without matter, insofar as the recipient is assimilated to the agent as regards form, but not as regards matter. And, in this mode [of reception], a sense receives the form without the matter, because the form has a different mode of being in the sense from that which it has in the thing being sensed. For in the thing being sensed it has natural being, but in the sense it has intentional and spiritual being.[34]

Elsewhere he says:

> There are two kinds of change (*immutatio*): natural and spiritual. A change is natural insofar as the form of the agent is received in the recipient according to natural being, as when heat [is received] in what is made hot. But a change is spiritual insofar as the form of the agent is received in the recipient according to spiritual being, as when the form of a color is [received] in the pupil of the eye, which does not become colored as a result. For the operation of the senses, spiritual change is required, by means of which the intention[35] of the sensible form comes to be in the [bodily] organ of the sense. Otherwise, if natural change were sufficient for sensing, all natural bodies would sense, when they were altered.[36]

This distinction of Aquinas's between two different ways of receiving a form is couched in language unfamiliar to us. What does he mean by these claims about natural and spiritual reception of forms? The notion of a natural reception of a form is perhaps not so hard to understand. He thinks of a material object as a composite of matter and form, and the object's form is its configuration. When matter is configured in a certain way, say, with the configuration of a stone, the matter so configured is a stone. What is harder to understand is the "spiritual", "intentional", or "immaterial" reception of a form. Here the configurational state of something such as a stone is preserved and transferred to something else – the eye, for example. But it is transferred in such a way that it does not confer on the eye the substantial or accidental characteristics of a stone. A purple stone visually cognized does not make the eye purple even though the form of the stone's color is transferred to the eye.

So although the configurational state is somehow really conveyed to and present in the eye, it does not reconfigure the matter of the eye in the way it configures the matter of the stone. And yet how is this possible? If the eye really does accept the configurational state that gives some matter the features of a stone, why would not that configurational state also give the eye those same features? On the other hand, if the eye does not take on any and every features of a stone in virtue of receiving the forms that give those features to the stone, in what sense does the eye receive the configurational state of a stone?

It helps to see here that although Aquinas's terminology is unfamiliar to us, the phenomenon he wants to call attention to is not. Consider, for example, a street map. The map is effective in the use for which it was designed precisely because it is an instance of the spiritual reception of the form of material objects. The configurational state of the city's streets is transferred to the paper of the map, but it is transferred in such a way that the paper which receives that configurational state is not configured by it in the way that the matter of the streets is. Because the configurational state of the streets is successfully transferred to the paper of the map, the map enables its user to find her way around the city's streets. But because the configurational state is received "spiritually" in the paper, the map can be carried in the car. If the whole configurational form of the city streets were received in matter of the map's paper with natural reception (supposing such reception to be even possible), it would make that matter itself city streets. In that case, we would have a reproduction of the city's streets, but we would not have a map.

A map thus seems like a good example of the spiritual or immaterial reception of a form, and so does anything else in which a configurational state is preserved in an encoded fashion. Blueprints of a building and wiring charts are further examples.

Furthermore, we could have the spiritual reception of a form even in cases in which there is not the sort of one-to-one correspondence found in street maps or blueprints for buildings. Consider, for example, the way the configurational state of a protein is preserved in the code of DNA. There each amino acid constituting the protein is represented by a particular triplet of nucleic acids in DNA. Those who know the code of DNA can learn the constitution of a protein just by reading the ordered triplets of nucleic acids in a certain stretch of DNA. The configuration of the DNA contains the configuration of the amino acids of the protein, but it contains the protein's form in a spiritual way, as Aquinas would put it, because although the form of the protein is in the DNA, it is not in the DNA in such a way as to configure the DNA into the protein. What Aquinas refers to as the spiritual reception of an immaterial form, then, is what we are more likely to call encoded information.

Material change and reception of sensible *species*

Two more points about the reception of forms in the process of sensing are worth making here.

First, although the senses receive sensible *species* with spiritual reception, some senses *also* receive some of them with natural reception. The skin, for example, becomes hot when it senses something hot. Even in the case of sound, the local motion in the ear that conveys sound produces local motion in the inner ear. Sight is the major exception to this rule: "in the change (*immutatio*) in the power of sight, there is only spiritual change"[37], because in receiving color, the proper sensible for sight, the eye does not itself take on the color of the object it is sensing.

Second, the claim that a sense receives the sensible *species* with spiritual or intentional or immaterial reception does not by itself make clear whether or not that reception consists of a change in the matter of the sense. The intellect receives *species* with spiritual reception, but that spiritual reception is not itself a change in something material, because intellect does not operate in a bodily organ, according to Aquinas. On the other hand, as my examples above make clear, it is perfectly possible to have the spiritual reception of an immaterial form that consists in certain changes in matter, such as the lines printed on the street map.

Scholars have disputed the point,[38] but I think that the texts are decisively in favor of the conclusion that, for the senses, the spiritual reception of sensible *species* is a change in the matter of the bodily organ of the sense. Although it seems odd or even paradoxical to describe some changes in matter as the spiritual or immaterial reception of a form, it is a mistake, I think, to suppose that there must be anything ghostly about the spiritual reception of forms. For example, Aquinas says:

> A sense is a power in a corporeal organ ... Everything is received in something in the mode of [the recipient] ... And so it must be that a sense receives corporeally and materially the similitude of the thing which is sensed.[39]

In another place, he says: "Sense and imagination are powers attached to corporeal organs, and so similitudes of things are received in them materially, that is, with material conditions, although apart from matter."[40]

In yet another passage, he seems to be trying to ward off just the mistaken interpretation at issue here. He says:

> Because Aristotle said that a sense is receptive of *species* without matter ... someone could believe that a sense is not a power in a body (as the intellect is not). And, therefore, to rule this out, Aristotle assigns an organ to [each] sense. And he says that ... the primary organ of a sense is something in which there is such a power – i.e., a power receptive of *species* without matter.[41]

If the senses did undergo the spiritual reception of an immaterial form without a material change in a bodily organ, Aquinas is saying here, the senses would have been assimilated to the intellect, which differs from the senses, in his view, in virtue of not making use of a bodily organ.

Finally, Aquinas himself supposes that the medium between the object sensed and the sensory power – such as air, in the case of vision – also receives the sensible *species* with spiritual reception;[42] and since the medium is entirely material and has no soul of any sort, the only way it can receive anything is by a change affecting its matter. It is therefore clearly possible on his view for the spiritual reception of an immaterial form to consist in the alteration of matter.

For all these reasons, I am inclined to interpret Aquinas as thinking that a sensible *species* is an immaterial form received with immaterial or spiritual reception, but that this reception consists in a change in the matter of an organ of the body. The reception is "spiritual" or "immaterial" in the sense that, for example, the way in which the matter of DNA contains the forms of hemoglobin does not turn the matter of the DNA into hemoglobin. Or, as Aquinas would put it, the DNA is assimilated to the protein as regards the form but not as regards the matter. Aquinas's "spiritual" reception of forms is thus like the coding of maps or blueprints. This is, of course, also the way we ourselves think sensation occurs, encoded information being received in virtue of a change in the matter of a corporeal sense organ.

Medium and similitude

Since this process – the spiritual reception of an immaterial sensible *species* by means of a change in matter – is common to both sense organs and the medium between the sense organs and the thing sensed, it clearly is not itself sufficient for any cognitive process to occur. Before going on to consider what else is necessary for cognition, it will be helpful to consider briefly two more parts of Aquinas's account of sensible *species*: first, the nature of the media through which the *species* are propagated, and second, the way in which the *species* is a similitude of the thing sensed.

On Aquinas's account, sensing always takes place through a medium. Part of his reason for thinking so is that he accepts the principle which has been a staple of modern physics until very recently, namely, that there is no action at a distance: "Bodies do not change one another unless they touch one another."[43]

Since there is distance (however small) between an object sensed and the sense organ it affects, the sensible *species* must pass from the object into a medium, which propagates it to the sense organ. Air and water are external media for the senses.[44] For touch there is also an internal medium, namely, flesh, which conveys the sensible *species* to bodily organs of touch within the flesh.[45] For some of the senses, the sensible *species* is received in the medium with natural reception as well as a spiritual reception (just as in the case of some of the senses themselves). Sight is the main exception here, too. With regard to its medium, there is no natural reception of the *species*, and one cannot perceive the change by which the medium is affected. But the sensible *species* of all the senses affect the medium with spiritual reception.[46]

Finally, Aquinas often characterizes sensible *species* (as well as intelligible *species* and phantasms) as similitudes. The Latin '*similitudo*' is commonly translated 'likeness', and this translation has given some readers the impression that a similitude pictorially resembles the thing of which it is a similitude. But this is at best a very misleading impression. Some similitudes may be pictorial in character, but not all are. '*Similitudo*' is cognate with '*similis*' (the Latin for 'similar'); and things are similar insofar as they share qualities — or, as Aquinas would say, forms. And so, on his view, "similitude is grounded in an agreement in or sharing of forms. Consequently, there are many kinds of similitude, corresponding to the many ways of sharing forms."[47]

Aquinas makes many distinctions among similitudes or ways of sharing forms, but the one most relevant to our purposes is this:

> the similitude of two things to one another can be grounded in two [different] ways. In one way, insofar as there is sharing of a nature (*convenientia in natura*), and such a similitude is not needed between a cognizer and what is cognized. In another way, according to representation, and this [sort of] similitude is needed on the part of a cognizer with respect to what is cognized.[48]

He makes a related point in a different place:

> A similitude of one thing to another is found [to occur] in two [different] ways. In one way, according to the [kind of] being associated with the nature [of things], as the similitude of the heat of fire

is in the thing heated by the fire. In another way, as regards cognition, as the similitude of fire is in sight or touch.[49]

So similitude encompasses different kinds of agreement in form. Pictures or pictorial resemblances will count as similitudes, but so will the configuration of DNA, insofar as it shares forms with the proteins it codes for. For that matter, heat in the thing heated also is a similitude, since it is a form shared by both the heating agent and the thing heated. This last example is one in which the similitude is grounded in an agreement of nature, when the form of one thing is received in another with natural reception. But in cognition the similitude is based on the spiritual reception in the cognizer of the form of the thing cognized. A cognizer and the object of his cognition share a form, but the similitude in this case is a representation – and representations need not be pictorial in nature. It is therefore a mistake to take '*similitudo*' as indicating just a pictorial resemblance.

The notion of representation in this context may mislead some readers, and so it may be helpful to recall the point made at the outset of this chapter about direct and immediate cognition. Nothing in Aquinas's theory of similitudes as representations keeps him from holding that human beings cognize things in extramental reality directly and immediately, because such similitudes are only the means by which cognition occurs and are not themselves the objects of cognition. On Aquinas's view: "To cognize things by means of their similitudes existing in the cognizer is to cognize those things as they are in themselves, or in their own natures." [50]

Phantasms

After the activity of the senses, the next stage in the process of cognition involves the processing of phantasms. But Aquinas's views about phantasms are a perplexing part of his account of cognition since, at first glance, phantasms seem entirely superfluous as regards the cognition of extramental reality. Aquinas holds that there is no cognition of individual material objects without phantasms. And yet, at the outset, it is not clear why sensible and intelligible *species* (the intellect's analogue to sensible *species*) are not together sufficient to produce the cognition of some object presented to a sense. As far as that goes, it is not immediately clear why sensible *species* by themselves are not enough to bring about such cognition.

We can divide Aquinas's central thesis about phantasms in human cognition into two major parts. The first part is the claim that, for human beings, all cognition is dependent on phantasms. He says, for example:

> If the active intellect were related to the possible intellect as an active object is related to a power … , it would follow that we would immediately understand all things … But, as it is, the active intellect is

related not as an [active] object, but rather as what actualizes [cognitive] objects. What is required for this – besides the presence of the active intellect – is the presence of phantasms, the good disposition of the sensory powers, and practice at this sort of operation.[51]

In another place, he says: "In the course of [this] present life, in which our intellect is joined to a body that is not impassible, it is impossible for our intellect actually to understand anything except by turning to the phantasms."[52]

The second part of Aquinas's central thesis about phantasms is the claim that, for human beings, it is not possible to have any cognition of a material particular without a phantasm.

The role of phantasms in sensory cognition

I will leave this second claim for the subsequent section on the cognition of particulars; in this section I will confine the discussion to Aquinas's views on the nature and function of phantasms in order to examine the first claim, that cognition in general is dependent on phantasms.

Like sensible *species*, phantasms are similitudes of particular things;[53] and like sensible *species* they exist in corporeal organs.[54] In fact, they seem to be just similitudes of the same extramental things as the sensible *species* are. Furthermore, the form which is the sensible *species* is preserved in the phantasm, and the agent intellect abstracts that form from the phantasm in order to make possible intellectual functioning. Aquinas says, for example:

> The *species* of a thing, insofar as it is in the phantasms, is not actually intelligible, because the *species* is one with the intellect in actuality not in this way [that is, not in the way the *species* is in the phantasms], but rather insofar as the *species* is abstracted from the phantasms.[55]

Finally, the cognitive power that is phantasia is dependent on sensory powers. Although Aquinas reports approvingly Aristotle's position that "phantasia is not sense",[56] he says:

> There is a close relationship between phantasia and sense, because phantasia cannot arise without sense, and it occurs only in those [creatures] that have sense – that is, in animals. Furthermore, there is phantasia only of those things of which there is sense, that is, of those things which are the objects of sense (*sentiuntur*).[57]

And elsewhere he says: "Phantasia is nothing but motion produced by the senses in act".[58]

So, initially at least, it seems as if the phantasms are virtually identical to the sensible *species*. But what, then, is the difference between the sensible *species* of sensory powers and the phantasms of phantasia? And what is the role of phantasms in cognition?

An important clue is given by what Aquinas takes to be the etymology of 'phantasia'. According to Aquinas, "the name 'phantasia' is taken from vision or from appearing".[59] And a little later he explains: "The Greek '*phos*' is equivalent to 'light', and from there they get '*phanos*', which is appearance or illumination, and phantasia."[60]

Furthermore, he associates phantasia with something's appearing to us. For example, he says: "As [a creature] engaged in sensing is moved by sensible [*species*], so in the process of phantasia [a creature] is moved by certain appearances, which are called 'phantasms'."[61]

And elsewhere he cites Aristotle approvingly to the same effect: "Aristotle holds that animals that have phantasia are those to whom something appears in accordance with phantasia, even when they are not actually sensing."[62]

When a cognizer has such appearances without being engaged in the process of sensing, Aquinas sometimes speaks of the cognitive power in question as imagination, rather than phantasia, although he seems to regard imagination as a part of the same power that is phantasia; and another important clue to his view of phantasia comes from what he says about the process of imagining. He says: "The experience (*passio*) of phantasia is in us whenever we wish, because it is in our power to form something, as it were, 'appearing' before our eyes, such as gold mountains, or whatever we wish."[63]

Here, then, Aquinas describes a person who is having images of gold mountains in her mind as having an experience produced by the power of phantasia. Phantasia is also the cognitive power responsible for producing the images of dreams, in his view. You can see that phantasia is distinct from sense, he says, because a sleeper phantasizes, but she does not do so because she's actually sensing something.[64]

On his view, the process of imagination, which is operative also in sleep and which we can produce at will while awake, is a case of being moved by phantasms when we are not concurrently sensing something. Phantasia proper, as distinct from imagination, produces the analogous sort of experience when our senses are simultaneously receiving the *species* of things that are outside the mind and presented to the senses. And so Aquinas relates phantasia and imagination in this way:

> Every motion of phantasia which arises from the motion of the proper sensibles [of the sensory powers] is for the most part true [that is, is received in the cognitive power in the way in which it is in the thing sensed]. I say this with regard to cases in which the sensible is present, when the motion of phantasia is simultaneous with the

motion of the senses. But when the motion of phantasia occurs in the absence of [the motion of] the senses, then it is possible to be deceived even as regards proper sensibles. For sometimes absent things are imagined as white, although they are black.[65]

Finally, Aquinas sometimes talks about our "seeing" things in the phantasms. He says, for example: "When someone wants to understand something, he forms for himself phantasms, by way of examples, in which he, as it were, looks at (*inspiciat*) what he is concerned to understand."[66]

Similarly, in the course of discussing the difference between phantasia and opinion, Aquinas says, "when something appears to us in accordance with phantasia, we are as if we were regarding something in a picture".[67]

With these "as if" and "as it were" locutions, Aquinas, I think, is trying to capture a feature of perception that is hard for us to characterize, too, namely, its conscious character. He certainly does not mean to imply that we literally look at phantasms. The sense of sight, of course, could not literally see an immaterial phantasm, and Aquinas explicitly repudiates the view that phantasms are the objects of intellect's cognition. In arguing against Averroes's claim that there is only one intellect for the whole human *species*, for example, Aquinas remarks, "it cannot be said that my act of understanding differs from your act of understanding in virtue of the fact that our phantasms are different, because a phantasm is not something that is itself actually intellectively cognized".[68]

So it seems that for Aquinas, phantasia is the cognitive power that makes things appear to us or that gives us access to the sensory data taken in by the senses;[69] or, as we would put it, phantasia is the power that produces the conscious experience which is a component of ordinary sensing.[70]

Phantasia and consciousness

Understanding phantasia in this way helps explain the difference between phantasms and sensible *species*. On Aquinas's view, sensible *species* are not the objects of our cognition. What he says about phantasia strongly suggests that sensible *species* are not available for consciousness either and that this fact is one of the main differences between sensible *species* and phantasms. We can employ the power of phantasia at will, Aquinas thinks, to imagine things; in imagination, our mental experience includes the conscious appearances of things that are not present to our senses. Furthermore, the difference between phantasia proper and imagination is a matter of whether or not the sensory powers are operating simultaneously and in conjunction with the inner sense, and imagination obviously does involve conscious experience. So it seems reasonable to assume that for Aquina,s phantasia proper also produces in us conscious experiences, only conscious experience of the extramental reality being concurrently sensed.

On this way of understanding phantasia, the extramental things currently making a causal impact on the senses are consciously experienced by us because phantasia has further processed the sensible *species* of those things into phantasms. Without the phantasms, the sensible *species* alone would not produce conscious experience of what is sensed.

On this interpretation of phantasia, a person who had only sensible *species* but no phantasia would be like a blindsight patient. A blindsight patient receives visual input through his senses, and it is input which is to some extent and in some mode available to him in forming judgments about the external world – that the yardstick is horizontal, for example. But the blindsight patient reports sincerely of himself that he is blind, because the visual input is not accessible to his consciousness. It is hard to know how to describe his situation exactly, partly because we are still at a loss for a good way to describe consciousness, and so it is easier to think about what the blindsight patient cannot do, rather than describe what normal human beings usually do. Out of the incoming visual data from his normally functioning senses, the blindsight patient cannot get conscious visual experience of extramental reality. Using Aquinas's terminology, we can say that the visual sense of the blindsight patient is functioning normally, but that phantasia is not operating in him in connection with the visual sense. He has the sensible *species* of objects presented to his eyes, but no phantasms of them.

This explanation of phantasia helps explain why Aquinas supposes that there are two sorts of memorative powers, one associated with phantasia and one with intellect. Phantasia and the senses both belong to what Aquinas calls 'the sensitive soul', the part of the soul having to do with sensing. As part of the sensitive soul, the memorative power associated with phantasia functions to preserve and recall phantasms.[71] Presumably, memory at this level would consist of something like replaying the internal movie of previous sensory experience, though with some phenomenological indication that the sensory experience being reviewed is a past experience. It thus differs from the remembering associated with intellect, which need not have any associated imagery. That we in fact do have a memory faculty of the sort Aquinas associates with phantasia is made dramatically evident in clinical cases in which the sensory memory of an experience – the internal movie – has been suppressed but is subsequently released, sometimes being played over and over again to the torment of the rememberer.[72]

Sensory cognition and perception

When we combine the actions of the senses and the phantasia, have we then got Aquinas's account of what we would call perception? Or, to put the same question a slightly different way, is Aquinas's notion of sensory cognition equivalent to our notion of perception? The answer to questions of this sort depends, as I said at the outset, on what we take perception to be. If we accept the understanding of perception underlying the neurobiological description of agnosia as "the inability to perceive objects through otherwise normally functioning sensory channels",[73] then we would have to deny that on Aquinas's account the functioning of the sensory powers together with the phantasia gives us perception. It is true that, on the interpretation argued for here, sense and phantasia give us conscious experience of extramental objects and conscious access to sensory data about such objects. But a person who had only so much and no more of the cognitive processes Aquinas describes would be in the position of an agnosia patient who is agnosic for all senses. Even though a person with only senses and phantasia might be able to describe some of the properties of what he is sensing, the only answer he could give to any question of the form "*What* are you sensing?" would have to be "I don't know." If the agnosia patient cannot properly be said to perceive, although he has "normally functioning sensory channels" as well as conscious access to the data from those channels, then a person whose cognitive processes included only what is contained below the level of the intellect in Aquinas's account could not be said to perceive either.

That is because recognizing *what* one is perceiving depends on an act of intellect. In the example with which I began, Hannah's answer to the question "What are you looking at?" is "A cat". For Hannah to see what is presented to her vision *as a cat* requires what Aquinas calls the first operation of the intellect, namely, determining the quiddity or *whatness* of a thing.[74] Neither the senses alone nor the senses combined with phantasia can determine *what* it is that is being perceived. Doing so is the function of the intellect. A *fortiori*, the senses and phantasia together are not sufficient for perceptual judgments, such as "That's a cat", since a judgment of that sort requires what Aquinas calls compounding and dividing,[75] and that activity is the second operation of the intellect.

Aquinas's account of cognition, then, contains a distinction that is the equivalent of the distinction between seeing and seeing as. If it is possible for there to be seeing without any seeing as, then a person who was only seeing would be a person in whom sensory powers and phantasia were working, but whose intellect was not functioning in conjunction with that seeing.

Nothing in what I have said entails that, on Aquinas's account, there ever actually is seeing without seeing as, for normal adult human beings. Certainly, in the normal condition, on Aquinas's view, the senses and the phantasia function together with the intellect. But on his view, human cognitive processes are analyzable into different subsystems. The actions of some of those subsystems, namely, sensory powers and phantasia, are sufficient for seeing without being sufficient for seeing as.

By the same token, I do not mean to imply that for Aquinas cognition consists in a *temporal* sequence in which we first see and then see as. If there indeed is a temporal sequence of some sort, in most normal cases it is of such short duration as to be imperceptible; from a subjective point of view, an object is perceived – seen as a cup, for example – as soon as it is presented to the senses, if the perceiver's cognitive faculties are working properly.

Aquinas's central thesis about phantasms

Given this way of thinking about the functioning of phantasia, it is not so hard to understand the first part of Aquinas's central thesis about phantasms, namely, that cognition in general is dependent on phantasms. Aquinas does not mean that it is impossible for a human being in a condition of temporary sensory deprivation to think about, say, the Pythagorean theorem.[76] Rather he means that perception is the starting point for human cognition in general. A human being who came into existence deprived of every sensory power would be completely dysfunctional intellectually, too. On this way of interpreting his account, phantasms are essential for intellectual functioning because they are necessary for perception. So, for example, Aquinas says: "We cognize incorporeal things, for which there are no phantasms, by comparison with sensible bodies, for which there are phantasms."[77]

It is not the case, then, that every act of intellect is accompanied by an act of phantasia; rather, as part of perception phantasms are necessary for acts of cognition that use or depend on perception. Even many apparently purely intellectual acts will rely on perception and phantasms indirectly, since they will rely on inspection of examples drawn from things perceived or imagined.

We have done enough, I think, to understand the first part of Aquinas's central thesis about phantasms, namely, that cognition is dependent on them. But the second part of that thesis still remains, namely, that it is not possible to have any cognition of a material particular without a phantasm. For Aquinas, there is one sort of cognition which is always accompanied by the functioning of phantasia. On his view, without a concurrent act of phantasia it is not possible for the intellect to cognize a material particular. We will, however, be in a better position to understand this second part of his central claim about phantasms when we have looked in some detail at what he says about the functioning of the intellect, to which we can now turn.

Intelligible *species*

For the intellect, the analogue to the sensible *species* of the senses is what Aquinas calls 'the intelligible *species*'. Intelligible *species* share many of the characteristics of the sensible *species* and the phantasms. Like sensible *species* and phantasms, the intelligible *species* are immaterial forms that are means of cognition and similitudes of things outside the mind:

The similitude of a thing that is understood[78] – which is an intelligible *species* – is a form in accordance with which the intellect understands"[79];

[The] similitude of a visible thing is that in accordance with which the sense of vision sees; and the similitude of a thing that is understood – which is an intelligible *species* – is a form in accordance with which the intellect understands".[80]

As in the case of the sensory powers, what the intellect knows primarily is extramental reality, not the intelligible *species*: "the intelligible *species* is related to the intellect in this way: it is that by means of which (*id quo*) the intellect understands".[81]

The intellect, however, is self-reflective in a way the sensory powers are not; and so it also knows itself, its acts and processes. Consequently, the intelligible *species*, unlike the sensible *species*, is *also* an object of knowledge, but only when the intellect reflects on itself:

in one and the same act of reflection, the intellect understands both its own understanding and the *species* by means of which it understands; and so the understood *species* is, secondarily, what is understood, although what is understood primarily is the thing of which the intelligible *species* is the similitude.[82]

Like the sensible *species*, the intelligible *species* is received into the intellect in accordance with the mode of the knower, not in accordance with the mode in which the form inheres in the extramental object.[83] Consequently, the intelligible *species*, like the sensible *species*, is received with spiritual or immaterial or intentional reception, rather than with the natural reception it has in the extramental material object it informs. Unlike the sensible *species*, however, the spiritual reception of the immaterial form does not take place in a bodily organ and does not depend on material changes in such an organ, because on Aquinas's view the intellect is entirely immaterial.

The order of causation in intellective cognition

One of the biggest differences between the external senses and the intellect is that the intellect is active as well as passive. In the cognitive processes of the sensitive part of the soul, there is a causal chain that begins with an extramental object or set of objects. The extramental object causally affects the medium between that object and the sense it affects; the medium in turn makes an impression on the senses; and the senses affect the phantasia in such a way as to cause the production of the phantasms. But after the phantasms have been produced, the order of causation in the cognitive process is reversed. Phantasms do not act with efficient causation on the intellect. On the contrary, the intellect acts with efficient causation on the phantasms in the process Aquinas calls 'abstraction'.[84] In fact, according to Aquinas, the phantasms, lodged in a corporeal organ, could not act on the immaterial intellect, because, as he says frequently, "nothing corporeal can make an impression (*imprimere*) on an incorporeal thing".[85]

So for Aquinas, cognition is not just a matter of the impact extramental reality makes on the mind; it also depends on the intellect's action on the encoded information delivered and processed by the senses. Although he turns out to have been wrong in his view that the intellect uses no bodily organ, he has been amply vindicated in his view that cognition requires the intellect's active processing,[86] and not just its passive reception of sensory information.[87]

Aquinas thinks of the intellect as divided into an active part and a passive part. The active part, generally called 'the agent intellect', abstracts the intelligible *species* from the phantasms and deposits them in the passive part of the intellect, which is generally called 'the potential intellect' or 'the possible intellect'. Aquinas is concerned to defend the commonsensical view that each human being has an intellect of her own, as distinct from the view which he associates with Averroes and some of Aquinas's own colleagues (the so-called 'Latin Averroists') who were sympathetic to Averroes's position, namely, that there is only one intellect for the entire human *species*.[88] He also has to contend with an Augustinian tradition that takes divine illumination to be necessary for any act of cognition.[89] He of course credits God with being the source of human cognitive powers, but he denies that every human cognitive act requires a special divine act of illumination.[90]

The proper object of the intellect

Just as the external senses have proper objects, so the intellect also has its proper object, namely, the quiddity of a material thing, which it abstracts from the phantasms.[91] The process of abstraction is a matter of removing or ignoring the many material accidents of a thing as preserved in the phantasm and focusing instead just on the thing's quiddity. By 'quiddity' here Aquinas means that form of a thing that put it into one rather than another *species* or genus, its nature or essence. Natures do not exist in the world on their own; in the world they exist only as incorporated into the things that have natures.[92] Nonetheless, the agent intellect separates the quidditative form from a material thing, and that form is the intelligible *species* abstracted from the phantasms. So, Aquinas says: "to cognize what is in individual matter but not *as* it is in such matter is to abstract a form from individual matter, which the phantasms represent".[93]

And he goes on to say:

nothing keeps us from intellectively cognizing (*intelligi*) the color [of an apple] without intellectively cognizing the apple. Similarly, I hold that those things that are part of the nature (*ratio*) of any *species* of a material thing – such as a stone or human being or horse – can be considered apart from the individual principles, which are not part of the nature (*ratio*) of the *species*. And this is abstracting the universal from the particular, or the intelligible *species* from phantasms – that is, considering the nature (*natura*) of a *species* without considering the individual principles represented by the phantasms.[94]

In abstracting the intelligible *species* from the phantasm, then, the agent intellect strips the phantasm of the particular material characteristics of the thing whose similitude the phantasm is. But the abstraction does not strip from the phantasm every connection with matter. Aquinas says:

the intellect abstracts the *species* of a natural thing from individual sensible matter, but not from common sensible matter. For example, it abstracts the *species* of a human being from *this* flesh and *these* bones, which do not belong to the nature (*ratio*) of the *species* but rather are the parts of an individual ... But the *species* of a human being cannot be abstracted by the intellect from flesh and bones [generally considered].[95]

The operations of the intellect

When the agent intellect has accomplished the abstraction, it delivers the intelligible *species* to the potential intellect, which receives and preserves the form. Because the potential intellect can receive an infinite number of such forms, Aquinas often speaks of it as a blank slate, which can be written on over and over again. This metaphor is sometimes interpreted as if Aquinas were claiming that there is nothing innate in human intellect. But this is a misinterpretation of his metaphor. What he wants to call attention to is just the fact that the intellect, like a slate, can receive one form after another. But the metaphor should not be taken to mean that on Aquinas's view there is nothing hardwired into our intellects.

Aquinas does, in fact, think that there are no innate intelligible *species*; we must acquire all our intelligible *species* from the phantasms, and that is one of the reasons why cognition in general is dependent on phantasms. But he certainly assumes that a great deal of human cognition is built into us. He supposes not only that the world is the way it is and that things have the natures they have independent of human cognition, but also that human cognitive apparatus is natively so constructed that it will automatically cleave reality at these joints and cognize the natures of the things there are. That is, unlike metaphysical conventionalists, Aquinas supposes that the cookie dough of reality comes pre-cut into particular kinds of things; and, unlike Kantians, Aquinas assumes that we all naturally recognize those very kinds of things with the natures they really have. None of us has to be taught to divide the world into the so-called natural kinds, for example – as distinct from dividing it into such conventionally ordered units as one consisting of the property of redness, the Republic of China, and Robert Dole's left foot. When Tom asks Hannah what she's looking at, he expects her to name something in the Aristotelian category of substance, or – failing that – something in some other one of the ten categories. Even if Hannah's answer were artistic or unconventional – "I'm looking at the reflection of the pattern of the clouds in the water of the puddle left by the rain" – he would still understand her remark in terms of substances, qualities, and relations among them. But if her answer were a conventionalist's melange, he would be blankly perplexed. In this regard, then, Aquinas's account of human cognitive apparatus is very plausible.

Aquinas calls the simple acts of cognition by which we recognize and categorize things in the world around us 'the cognition of non-complexes', that is, cognitive acts which are not propositional but whose objects are the quiddities of individual things. Such non-propositional apprehension he calls 'the first operation of the intellect', as distinct from the second operation of the intellect, which is what he calls 'compounding and dividing'.

Composition or division occurs when the intellect combines its first apprehensions or divides them to form affirmative or negative "complexes" or propositional judgments.[96] It also occurs when the intellect combines its first apprehensions even in a non-propositional way. When Hannah says, referring to the cat, "a big black one with a smudge on its nose", she is compounding even though she is not forming a proposition.

Aquinas also thinks that we have built into us even the cognition of certain complexes: "the first principles, whose cognition is innate in us, are similitudes of uncreated truth".[97] On his view, all human beings are hard-wired for a small set of first principles, such as the law of non-contradiction, for example. And he thinks that this fact about human beings requires supposing that human cognitive faculties are created by God. So, for example, in rejecting the Averroistic line that there must be only one agent intellect for all human beings, he says it must nonetheless be the case that all our intellects derive from the one separate intellect that is God, because all human beings share a common set of first principles. "In this way," he says, "the sharing by [all] human beings of the first intelligible [principles] proves the unity of the separate intellect [that is God]."[98]

Intellected intention and perception

When the intelligible *species* has been received by the potential intellect, we are at a point in the intellective cognitive process analogous to the point in the process of sensory cognition when the sensible *species* has been received in a corporeal organ of the senses.[99] Like the sensible *species*, the intelligible *species* is not what is cognized; it is only the means of cognition. The intelligible *species* is also like the sensible *species* in being a form received spiritually or intentionally rather than naturally, so that it forms the intellect without turning the intellect into the thing that the form produces when it is received into matter naturally. And, finally, like the sensible *species*, the intelligible *species* is not part of conscious awareness. (Although the intellect can cognize the intelligible *species* by reflecting on its own acts, that sort of cognition is different from internal conscious awareness of the *species* themselves.) With regard to sensory cognition, conscious awareness of sensory data comes in at the level of the phantasms. The analogue in intellectual cognition to the phantasms is not the intelligible *species*, but something Aquinas calls the 'intellected intention'[100], 'concept' or 'internal word'.[101]

Although the abstracting of an intelligible *species* is the beginning or source of an act of intellection, that act of intellection is not complete until the intellect has used the intelligible *species* to form an intention. Thus Aquinas says:

> the intellect, informed by the *species* of a thing, forms in itself by an act of intellect a certain intention of the thing intellected; this intention is the nature (*ratio*) of the thing, which the definition signifies ... Since this intellected intention is as it were the terminus of an operation of the intellect, it is different from the intelligible *species* that actualizes the intellect; the intelligible *species* should be considered as the source (*principium*) of an operation of the intellect.[102]

The intellected intention is what finally allows the intellect to cognize an extramental thing:

> Because the intelligible *species*, which is a form of the intellect and the source for intellection, is a similitude of an external thing, it follows that the intellect forms an intention similar to that [extramental] thing ... And from the fact that the intellected intention is similar to an [extramental] thing, it follows that the intellect by forming an intention of this sort intellectively cognizes that thing.[103]

Aquinas explains in some detail what he means by 'intellected intention' in the course of his discussion of the generation of the second person of the Trinity. He says:

> It belongs to the nature (*ratio*) of an internal word, which is an intellected intention, that it proceeds from the person engaged in

intellection in accordance with his intellection, since it is as it were a terminus of intellectual operation; for in the process of intellection the intellect conceives and forms an intellected intention or concept, which is the internal word.[104]

And elsewhere in the same chapter he says:

> By 'intellected intention' I mean that which the intellect conceives in itself with regard to the thing understood. In us ... this is a certain similitude conceived in the intellect with regard to the thing understood. It is what is signified by external words. Hence, this intention is also called an 'internal word' ... And that this intention is not in us the thing understood is manifest from the fact that intellectively cognizing a thing is different from intellectively cognizing the intellected intention, which the intellect does when it reflects on its own work.[105]

The intellected intention is thus a mental concept corresponding to a spoken word and enabling us to cognize intellectively an extramental thing.

The cognitive process leading to the first operation of the intellect

So to get to what Aquinas calls 'the first operation of intellect', namely, the intellect's apprehension of the quiddity or the properties of some extramental thing, we need not only an intelligible *species* informing the potential intellect, but also the intellect's forming an intention of this sort. The intention is the mental concept formed in cognizing an extramental thing, and its formation is the end of the complicated process of impression on the senses and phantasms and intellective abstraction.

When Tom says to Hannah, "What are you looking at?" and Hannah answers, "A cat", Hannah's answer is dependent on her having a first operation of intellect of this sort. As Aquinas sees it, the process Hannah undergoes to recognize the cat works like this. First, the form of the cat is received into the air as encoded information; or, as Aquinas puts it, the sensible *species* is received spiritually by the medium. This encoded information, the spiritually received sensible *species*, is then transmitted through the air to Hannah's eyes, which undergo some material change in consequence. Then the senses impress the sensible *species* on an internal bodily organ in the brain which has the power of phantasia and produces phantasms, conscious awareness of sensory data without categorization – seeing without seeing as. The intellect then processes the encoded information in the phantasms, extracting just the intelligible *species* from them, abstracting from individuating material conditions and leaving only information about universal properties, beginning with the quiddity of the cat. The resulting intelligible *species* are received spiritually by the potential intellect. Actualized in this way by the intelligible *species*, the intellect engages in a further act, transforming the intelligible *species* into a mental concept, for example, the mental concept corresponding to the spoken word 'cat'. At that point, Hannah cognizes the cat as a cat.

Insofar as we think perceiving *as* to be requisite for perception, our notion of perception is equivalent to Aquinas's sensory cognition plus the first operation of the intellect. The senses and the phantasia together enable Hannah to get sensory data about the cat. But she does not get the concept *cat* from that data until the first operation of the intellect is completed. So Aquinas divides the process of recognizing a cat into four different stages, with four different subsystems operating at the different stages: the reception of sensible *species*; their processing into phantasms; the abstraction of intelligibile *species*; and their processing into intellected intentions.

That Aquinas is right to do so is confirmed by the fact that our recognition of a cat can be interrupted at roughly the junctures he picks out in the processing. The blindsight patient has sensible *species* but no phantasms. The visually agnosic patient has sensible *species*, phantasms, and intelligible *species*; he can use those intelligible *species* to recognize the cat by sound or by touch. But because he is visually agnosic, he cannot move from the intelligible *species* garnered from the visual sensible *species* to the intellected intention *cat*. So although he can describe the cat according to the way she visually appears to him, if we ask him what he is describing, he will say, "I don't know"; and if we ask him whether he sees a cat, he will answer, "no". Finally, in the case of certain neurological deficits, such as severe dementia, there may be fully functional sensory powers and even what Aquinas calls 'phantasia', without the patient's having any detectable intellectual functioning. Such a patient, for example, may track things of which she has conscious visual experience (as a blindsight patient cannot), without any indication that she comprehends the things happening around her or any sign of an ongoing inner mental life. In such a case, we seem to have the reception of sensible *species* and phantasms, but not intelligible *species* and their corresponding intentions.[106] Although Aquinas's account is complicated, then, its complication seems to reflect accurately the complexity of our cognitive processes as we currently understand them.[107]

Furthermore, Aquinas's way of thinking about the subsystems of our cognitive processing is not only tolerably accurate but also philosophically helpful. It is useful, for example, to think about the disability of an agnosia patient as an inability to extract the universal that is the quiddity from the mass of individuating characteristics presented to the senses. It gives us a helpful way to think about what at least many sorts of agnosia have in common and provides an insight into the nature of the deficit many agnosia patients have suffered. Consequently, this part of Aquinas's account is useful for thinking about the subsystems of the mind. Aquinas's position also contains a reasonable and irenic response to contemporary controversies over whether all perception is always a matter of "seeing" as.[108] Ordinary perception on the part of normal adults, on Aquinas's view, will consist in two components, one simply of "seeing" and the other — the first operation of intellect — of "seeing" as. Since these are distinct processes, it is possible to have one without the other in cognitively defective human beings. Whether we want to continue to use the name 'perception' for the process when it is missing one or the other of these components then looks more like a terminological dispute than a real philosophical issue.

Universality and the cognition of particulars

The proper object of the intellect, as we have seen, is a quiddity or nature or essence, and this quiddity is a universal. Thus, Aquinas says, "the intellect sees the universal existing in a particular".[109] Apprehending universals in this way, as I said, is the first operation of the intellect. The second operation is the forming of propositions, which Aquinas calls the process of compounding and dividing:

> [the intellect] first apprehends something about a thing, namely, the quiddity of that thing, which is the first and proper object of the intellect. Then it understands properties and accidents and relationships accompanying the essence of the thing, in accordance with which (secundum hoc) it must compound and divide one apprehended object from another. Then it must proceed from one composition and division to another, and this is reasoning.[110]

(Reasoning, the weaving together of complexes, is the last kind of operation of the intellect. When Hannah thinks about the best way to keep the cat out of her bird feeders, she is engaged in what Aquinas sometimes calls the third operation of the intellect, discursive reasoning.[111])

Besides the quiddity of an extramental thing, then, the intellect also cognizes the other properties of that thing, including its relationships. But all these properties are universals, and so what the intellect apprehends is universals.

This claim may appear peculiar, but its rightness can be seen by returning to the homely example with which I began. Suppose that Tom not only cannot see what Hannah is looking at outside the window; suppose that Tom has in fact been temporarily deprived of the use of all his senses but that Hannah, by some magic or futuristic neurobiological technology, can communicate her thoughts to him — her thoughts, but not her sensings or any of her sensory experiences. Suppose that Tom does not know Max the cat by acquaintance, and that Hannah is trying to describe Max for Tom. In answer to the question, "What are you looking at?", Hannah replies, "A cat." Here Hannah is reporting the first operation of the intellect, which has apprehended the quiddity in a material particular.[112] Then she reports on various accidents and relationships of the cat; she indicates the cat's size, coloration, and relationships to birds: a big black and white cat, stalking birds. All these features of the cat are universals, too.[113]

In fact, no matter how detailed or meticulous Hannah's observations are, anything she reports to Tom will still consist just in universals of this sort. The only way to cognize this very cat, this particular, is to begin by using the senses and pointing, metaphorically or literally, to the individual picked out by the senses, as Hannah does when she says, "That's Max!". And unless Tom, too, can make epistemic contact through his senses with Max, Tom will be restricted to cognizing the universals exemplified by Max, without being able to cognize the individual cat, Max.[114]

For reasons of this sort, Aquinas says:

> Our intellect is not able to cognize directly and primarily the individual among material things. The reason for this is that the principle of individuality in material things is the individual matter. But our intellect ... understands by abstracting the intelligible *species* from matter of this sort. Now what is abstracted from individual matter is a universal. And so our intellect is directly cognizant only of universals. It can cognize singulars indirectly and by means of a certain reflection.[115]

For a human person to cognize a particular, the intellect has to turn to the phantasms and so is dependent on the senses. Aquinas makes the point with an example about the cognition of flesh. There are two different ways in which the cognition of flesh occurs, he says:

> [It happens] in one way, [when] either the flesh itself and the quiddity of flesh are cognized by powers entirely different from one another. So, for example, the quiddity of flesh is cognized by the intellective power, and the flesh is cognized by the sensitive power. And this happens when the soul cognizes a singular by itself and the nature of a *species* by itself. [But] it happens in another way that the flesh is cognized, and the quiddity of the flesh – not that there are different powers; rather the same power cognizes both flesh and the quiddity of flesh, but in different ways. And this must be the case since the soul relates a universal to a particular ... And so the intellect cognizes both, but in different ways. For it cognizes the nature of a *species*, or a quiddity, by directly extending itself; it cognizes a singular, however, by a certain reflection, insofar as it

returns to (*redit super*) the phantasms, from which it abstracted the intelligible *species*.[116]

In returning to the phantasms and connecting a concept with a phantasm, the intellect anchors the concept, as it were, to a particular extramental thing. This is what Hannah does when she has sensory cognition of the cat – a process just involving sensory powers and phantasia – and also sees it as a cat – a process that involves intellect's apprehending the quiddity. The intellect's abstractive processing allows Hannah to see *as*, rather than just seeing. But the phantasms anchor that seeing *as* to this particular thing seen. So Aquinas says, "the potential intellect receives forms as actually intelligible because of the power of the agent intellect. But it receives them as similitudes of determinate things because of the cognition of phantasms."[117]

Hence, Aquinas says:

> Every [act of] cognition is in accordance with some form, which is the source of cognition in the one cognizing. But a form of this sort can be considered in two ways: in one way, in accordance with the being it has in the cognizer; in another way, in accordance with the relationship (*respectum*) it has to the [extramental] thing of which it is the similitude. In the first way, it causes the cognizer actually to cognize. In the second way, it determines the cognition to some determinate cognizable thing.[118]

In fact, according to Aquinas,

> a similitude existing in a cognitive power is not a source of the cognition of an [extramental] thing in accordance with the being which the similitude has in the cognitive power, but in accordance with the relationship which the similitude has to the cognized thing. And for this reason an [extramental] thing is cognized not by means of the mode in which the similitude has being in the one cognizing, but rather by means of the mode in which the similitude existing in the intellect is representative of that thing.[119]

Cognition of particulars and direct cognition

At this point, we might suppose that even if Aquinas's position is understandable, it is nonetheless worrisome. It is, we might think, bad enough epistemic news that human cognition is mediated first by sensible *species* and phantasms, and then by intelligible *species*, which are produced not by a causal chain extending from an extramental object to the intellect but rather by the action of the agent intellect on the phantasms. Now we are told that the entire, highly mediated process results only in indirect cognition of singular material objects. Furthermore, my interpretation of Aquinas here apparently belies the claim with which I began, namely, that for Aquinas human beings have direct cognition of extramental reality.

The appropriate response to this worry, as to many other worries with regard to various parts of Aquinas's thought, depends on remembering that Aquinas is no friend of reductionism of any kind. In this case, it requires recognizing the mistake in reducing a whole to its parts, the human knower to the subsystems that make up the mind.[120] Anyone (medieval or contemporary) interested in the mechanism of cognition will tend to analyze the mind into its components, the faculties or "modules" comprising it, and the processes of those components. There is a consequent temptation to associate cognition with the activity of just one of the components. The perplexity and unease generated by Aquinas's claim that the intellect knows individuals only indirectly stem from unreflectively equating Aquinas's account about what the intellect cognizes with his view of what a human person cognizes. But this is a mistake. An intellect is not identical with a human person, and the knower is the human person, not the intellect alone.

In other words, for Aquinas, cognition is a systems feature; it is to be ascribed to the whole human being, and not to one of her components, not even to the fanciest component, the intellect.

We are not likely to make a mistake of this sort when it comes to the senses. From the claim that hearing perceives what is white only accidentally, insofar as the thing that it hears is a white thing, we are not likely to suppose Aquinas thinks that human beings perceive white things only accidentally. But it is easier to fall into this mistake when it comes to claims about the intellect. When Aquinas says that the intellect perceives particulars only indirectly, we can become confused and form the mistaken notion that on his account human beings have only indirect cognition of material reality. But from the fact that one component of the cognitive apparatus perceives something indirectly, it does not follow that the cognizer herself perceives only indirectly in such cases. And so, as a general principle regarding the entire complex process of cognition, Aquinas holds that "to cognize things by means of their similitudes existing in the cognizer is to cognize them in themselves or in their own natures".[121]

Cognition as assimilation

We are now in a position to understand Aquinas's frequently repeated, frequently cited notion that "all cognition arises from the assimilation of the cognizer to the thing cognized",[122] that "the intellect in act *is* the thing understood in act",[123] so that "the soul is all things".[124]

This notion is often put forward in startling formulations. Speaking of the equivalent idea in Aristotle, Joseph Owens, for example, says, you *are* the things perceived or known. Knower and thing known ... become one and the same in the actuality of cognition. From the strictly epistemological standpoint, this thoroughgoing identity of knower and thing known is the most important and most funda-mental tenet in the Aristotelian conception of knowledge. Yet it is the tenet that evokes the hardest sales resistance in students, and is the last Aristotelian dictum to which they come to assent ... They do not like the idea of being a brown cow or a big bad wolf just because they are seeing those animals or thinking about them.[125]

When the idea is put in this way, it is hard not to sympathize with the sales-resistant students.

Putting the idea in this way gives rise to a host of perplexing questions, in addition to the counter-intuitiveness of the very idea troubling the student who is resistant to the claim that she is a wolf because she is thinking of a wolf. If it is the unity of the intellect and the thing known which produces cognition, why does the thing known not also become the intellect in the process of cognition? That is, why does the wolf not become a human intellect in the unity of the intellect and the thing known? Or to raise the epistemological correlate of this metaphysical question, if cognition is produced by unity between the wolf and the intellect, why is it the case that the intellect knows the wolf, but the wolf does not know the intellect? Why is cognition asymmetrical when it is produced by being one with, which is symmetrical? As far as that goes, why should unity be thought to be productive of cognition at all? When one thing is produced from two inanimate things, as, for example, when hydrogen and oxygen are combined into one substance, water, no cognition results. And even when at least one of the things involved in the union is endowed with intellect, it is not the case that just any union involving such a thing will produce cognition. If the wicked witch had turned Hansel into one of the decorations on her candy house, Hansel would have been united with the house (or at least with the house decoration), but we would not expect the witch's action to be enabling Hansel to cognize the house (or, for that matter, to be enabling the house to cognize Hansel).

Most but not all of these difficulties are artifacts of the startling formula-tion Owens gives the Aristotelian idea. The idea itself, at least in Aquinas's understanding of it, is significantly tamer and more sensible than such a formulation suggests. Aquinas thinks cognition is a kind of assimilation because he thinks that there is a similitude of the thing cognized in the cognizer. As we have seen, a similitude is a matter of sharing forms, and forms can be shared in a variety of ways. The cognizer is the thing cognized only in the sense that they share a form in one of these ways.

Furthermore, the sort of sharing at issue does not yield the symmetrical relationship that talk of unity between cognizer and cognized suggests;

rather, it is, sensibly enough, an asymmetrical relationship in which the form of the thing cognized is in the cognizer, but it is not the case that the form of the cognizer is in the thing cognized. In addition, the way in which the form of the thing cognized is in the cognizer is very far from making the cognizer *be* the thing cognized in any literal sense at all. In the mode in which the form is in the thing cognized, the form makes that thing what it is – a wolf, say. But in the mode in which the form is in the thing cognized, spiritually or intentionally, as encoded information, it does not make the cognizer be a wolf. Although when it is in the cognizer, it is the same form as the form in the wolf, the difference of mode makes it the case that the cognizer does not literally turn into a wolf when cognizing one.

So when Aquinas says that the intellect is all things, he is speaking in the same frame of mind we are in when we say, for example, "It won't be long before all our reference books will be on CD-readers." One can imagine some future historian laboring to explain this remark to students, who are wondering how a previous age could possibly have supposed that all those bulky books could be shoved through the little slot in the CD-reader. The intellect is all things in the sense that it can receive the forms of all things in a suitably encoded mode. Precisely because the intellect receives forms in an intentional or encoded fashion, the reception of those forms produces cognition in the intellect, though the same form received with natural reception in the thing cognized does not produce cognition in it.

What is required for cognition is thus some sort of representation. The original "presentation" of the form of the wolf in matter produces the wolf; the *re*-presentation of that form in the intellect produces cognition of the wolf.

Conclusion

We may still wonder why the intellect's representation of the forms of things outside the mind should produce cognition of those things. This is a question which can be taken in two ways. In asking it, we might want an explanation of this complex process's producing *cognition*, rather than simply producing non-cognitive causal effects in our cognitive apparatus. Alternatively, we might be looking for an explanation of this process's producing apprehensions and judgments in us that correspond reliably with the way the world really is.

We ourselves might be inclined to answer the second question by claiming that the reliability of our cognitive processes is a result of the way in which evolution has shaped our brains.[126] As I explain further in the chapter on the foundations of knowledge, Aquinas thinks that our cognitive processes are reliable because they are the products of our cognitive faculties, which were designed by a good God, who intended us to resemble him in being cognizers. So the answer to this question will be a function of the general worldview of the person who answers it, and there are different sorts of respectably reasonable answers corresponding to these different world-views.

But when it comes to the first question, why the form of the thing cognized received in the cognizer with spiritual reception should produce cognition, that is, why this particular set of processes should enable *cognition* to occur at all, I do not think that Aquinas's account has any good answer. This admission, however, should not be surprising. From Aquinas's point of view, the question is asking not whether God can be trusted to make our cognitive apparatus reliable, but rather how exactly the faculty produced by God manages to do the job of cognizing extramental things. The secular analogue to this query is the great question of contemporary neurobiology: what are the mechanisms that allow human beings to be conscious of the world around them? At present, we are not even agreed on the right methods for pursuing data that would count as evidence pertinent to this question.[127] As far as I know, no scientist or philosopher yet has been successful in finding an answer to it, in either its scientific or its philosophical form. So it is hardly surprising that Aquinas's account does not contain a good answer to it either.

Finally, although I have looked at Aquinas's theory of human cognition in some detail, I have by no means given an exhaustive account of it. A very important part of what is missing has to do with Aquinas's views of the relation between intellect and will in intellectual virtue and vice. I will return to consider this part of his theory in a later chapter.[128]

9

FREEDOM

Action, intellect and will

Introduction

For more than one reason, it is not easy to develop a comprehensive and satisfactory account of Aquinas's views of the nature of human freedom.

To begin with, most contemporary discussions of free will tend to belong to what is in fact a non-Thomistic tradition of thought about the topic.[1] In this tradition, human freedom ultimately is or depends on a property of just one component of human mental faculties, the will; and freedom most fundamentally consists in the will's ability to act autonomously in general and independently of the intellect in particular. This tradition has such a grip on the contemporary discussion, both for libertarians[2] and for their opponents, that Aquinas's account tends to be interpreted by its lights. As a result, the lineaments of the theory Aquinas holds are obscured. For Aquinas, as we will see, freedom with regard to willing is a property primarily of a human being, not of some particular component of a human being. Furthermore, the will is not independent of the intellect. On the contrary, the dynamic interactions of intellect and will yield freedom as an emergent property or a systems-level feature.[3]

Second, Aquinas gives a complicated analysis of the several acts of will associated with any free action of a person. Scholars sometimes pick out a subset of these acts or even just one of them as if for Aquinas freedom were lodged in that sort of act of will alone. So, for example, it is sometimes said that Aquinas has a particularly full treatment of free will in *De malo* 6 because in that text he discusses at length *liberum arbitrium*.[4] But, as we shall see, *liberum arbitrium* is not equivalent to free will in our sense,[5] and volitions characterized by *liberum arbitrium* are associated for Aquinas with only one sort of free act of will, namely, the sort he calls *electio*. *De malo* 6 is therefore not about freedom of the will as a whole but only about one of the acts of will, namely, *electio*, in which such freedom is exemplified. (In order to avoid confusion, I will leave both '*liberum arbitrium*' and '*electio*' untranslated here and let their meanings emerge from a consideration of Aquinas's use of them.)

For these reasons, as well as others, in order to understand Aquinas's views of human freedom, I will focus first on his account of the nature of intellect and will, the interactions between them, and the emergence of freedom from their interaction. Then I will discuss the kind of acts of will Aquinas associates with a free action of a person, such as voluntarily raising one's arm. With that background, I will look in detail at Aquinas's theory of freedom, in particular at his views of human ability to do otherwise and the relation of that ability to freedom. Finally, I will consider what answer can be given to a taxonomic question: Is Aquinas's theory a compatibilitist account, as is sometimes claimed, or is it a species of libertarianism?

Classifying Aquinas's theory of freedom is complicated because of his views of divine grace and the effect of grace on the will, and it is true in a sense that we cannot be entirely clear about Aquinas's theory of freedom without also understanding his account of grace.[6] But Aquinas's account of grace is a large subject, which cannot be treated in passing in this chapter. (In a subsequent chapter on grace and free will, I will say something about the way in which grace can work on the will without undermining its freedom, on Aquinas's views.)

Intellect and will

Contemporary philosophers tend to operate with a conception of the will as the mind's steering wheel, neutral in its own right but able to direct other parts of the person. Aquinas's conception of the will is different. He takes the will to be not a neutral faculty, but a bent or inclination. The will, he says, is a hunger, an appetite, for goodness.[7] By 'goodness' in this connection Aquinas means goodness in general, not this or that specific good thing; that is, the will is an inclination for what is good, where the phrase 'what is good' is used attributively and not referentially.[8]

By itself the will makes no determinations of goodness; apprehending or judging things as good is the business of the intellect. The intellect presents to the will as good certain things or actions under certain descriptions in particular circumstances, and the will wills them because it is an appetite for the good and they are presented to it as good. For this reason the intellect is said to move the will not as an efficient cause but as a final cause, because its presenting something as good moves the will as an end moves an appetite.[9] This is one reason for calling the will a 'moved mover' (as Aquinas notes that Aristotle does), because, in moving what is under its control, the will is moved by an object intellectively apprehended as good, or an "intellectively cognized appetible",[10] as Aquinas puts it.

Understood in this way, the will can be seen as part of a larger scheme. Because all things are created by a good God who wills what is good for his creatures, all things are created with an inclination of their own to the good, but of very different sorts. Some, like plants or even inanimate things, have a built-in inclination to the good apart from any cognition of the good. Aquinas sometimes calls this inclination 'a natural appetite'. The sort of thing Aquinas has in mind here is exemplified by, for example, plants naturally turning towards sunlight. Higher up the ladder of being are animals of certain sorts which are naturally inclined to the good but with some (sensory) cognition.[11] They can cognize particular goods, although they lack the ability to reflect on them or to think of them as good. Inclination dependent on limited cognition of this sort Aquinas calls 'sensory appetite'. Higher still on the ladder of being are human beings whose inclination to the good is dependent on intellect, which allows them not only to cognize particular goods but to think about them reflectively as good. Aquinas calls this inclination 'rational appetite', and it is what Aquinas takes the will to be.[12] So close is the association between intellect and will for Aquinas that he often speaks of the will as being in the intellect,[13] and he thinks that anything which has intellect must also have will.[14]

Understood as rational appetite, the will is the primary mover of all the powers of the soul (including itself) except the nutritive powers,[15] and it is also the efficient cause of motion in the body.[16] Most important for our purposes, the will exercises some degree of efficient causality over the intellect. In some circumstances, it can command the intellect directly to adopt or to reject a particular belief.[17] It can also move the intellect by directing it to attend to some things and to neglect others,[18] or even to stop thinking about something altogether. So, for example, while you are reading a magazine, you come across some organization's advertisement asking for money for children, with an emotionally powerful picture of a starving child. Your intellect recognizes that if you look at the advertisement for very long, you are likely to succumb to its emotional force. Intellect sees the goodness of contributing to the organization, but it also recognizes that if you give money to this organization, you will not have it for the new computer you have been coveting. Your desire for the new computer is strong and influences intellect to rank saving money for the computer as the best for you now in the circumstances in which you are. In consequence of the findings on the part of the intellect, and with this influence from the passions, the will directs the intellect to stop thinking about the advertisement and the organization, and (after a further interaction of intellect and will) you turn the page of your magazine.[19]

As this example shows, in addition to the will's control over the intellect, the passions – sorrow, fury, fear, etc. – can also influence the intellect, because in the grip of such a passion, something will seem good to a person which might not seem good to her otherwise.[20] The intellect, however, typically is not compelled by the passions in any way;[21] it can resist them, for example, by being aware of the passion and correcting for its effects on judgment, as one does when one leaves a letter written in anger until the next morning rather than mailing it right away. Furthermore, the passions are themselves theoretically subject to the will. In other animals, Aquinas says, motion follows directly from the sensitive appetite's positive or negative reaction. In human beings, however, the sensitive appetite awaits the command of the will, which is the superior appetite. The lower, sensitive appetite, Aquinas thinks, is not by itself sufficient to cause movement in other powers unless the higher appetite, the will, commands that movement.[22] That is why, for example, human beings can go on hunger strikes and stay on them to the point of starvation.

I raise the subject of the relation of the passions to intellect and will, however, only to put it to one side. Although Aquinas has many interesting things to say about the moral psychology of the passions, his complicated account of the intellect and the will and the freedom that emerges from their interaction is more than enough for the focus of this chapter. I will therefore introduce the passions into the discussion only when it is necessary to do so in order to understand what Aquinas has to say about the intellect and the will.

Just as the will can affect the intellect in various ways, so the intellect can move the will in more than one way. The will can be moved to will as distinct from not willing – this is the "exercise" of its act. Or it can be moved to will this rather than that particular thing – this is the "specification" of its act.[23]

There is nothing in this life that invariably and ineluctably moves the will to the exercise of its act, because it is always in a person's power to refuse to think about whatever is at issue and consequently to refrain from willing it.[24] Since the will wills something only in case the intellect presents it as some sort of good, the fact that the will can command the intellect to stop thinking about something means that the will can, indirectly, turn itself off, at least with regard to a particular action or issue. This is only a limited ability on the part of the will, however, since the apprehensions of the intellect can occur without any preceding act of will and so in some cases may force the issue back on the agent's attention. That is why, for example, the prisoner who wants not to think about what is happening in the next cell where other prisoners are being tortured will find that their screams make him recur to what he wants to stop thinking about.[25]

As far as the specification of the will's act is concerned, there is no object, other than happiness in this life and God in the next, which by its nature necessarily moves the will to want *that*.[26] Because God has created the will as a hunger for the good, the will by nature desires the good. And whatever is good to such a degree and in such a way that a person cannot help but see it as good, the will of that person wills by natural necessity. One's own happiness is of this sort,[27] and so a person necessarily wills happiness.[28] But even things which have a necessary connection to happiness are not willed necessarily unless the willer is cognizant of their necessary connection to happiness.[29] Except for happiness and those things so obviously connected with happiness that their connection is overwhelming and indubitable for a person, the will is not in general determined to one thing because of its relation to the intellect.

On Aquinas's account, the will wills only what the intellect presents at that time as good under some description. Acts of will, then, are for something apprehended or cognized as good at a particular time in particular circumstances, as distinct from something which is good considered unconditionally or abstractly. Besides happiness and the vision of God, all other things are such that they can in principle be considered good under some descriptions and not good under others, so that there is nothing about them which must constrain the will of any agent always to want them. So, for example, the further acquisition of money can be considered good under some descriptions in some circumstances – e.g., the means of sending the children to school – and not good under others – e.g., wages from an immoral and disgusting job.

Finally, the will can move itself in more than one way. It can move itself indirectly by commanding intellect to stop thinking about something, as in the example above. It can also move itself indirectly because in virtue of willing a certain end it moves itself to will the means to that end. That is, the will wills a certain means because it wills a particular end and because intellect presents that means as necessary, or the best in the circumstances, for attaining that end.

But a more direct control over itself is possible for the will, too. All the higher powers of the soul, Aquinas holds, are able to act on themselves.[30] So, for example, the intellect is able to cognize itself.[31] By the same token, the will can will to will. In fact, Aquinas confronts a problem that has troubled some contemporary hierarchical accounts of the will, namely, that there may be an infinite regress of higher-order willings. I can will that I will something, and I can also will that I will that I will something, and so on, apparently *ad infinitum*. Aquinas thinks, however, that in such an apparently infinite series, the will is not actually taking ever-higher orders of volition as its object. At some point, Aquinas thinks,[32] the apparently higher-order volitions collapse, and the object of the will is just whatever action was at issue at the beginning of the series of volitions.[33]

If the intellect does present something to the will as good, then, because the will is an appetite for the good, the will wills it – unless the will directs intellect to reconsider, to direct its attention to something else, or to stop considering the matter at hand. The will's doing this is, of course, a result of the intellect's presenting such actions on the part of the will as good, and such an act on the part of the intellect may itself be a result of previous acts on the part of the will directing the attention of the intellect.

One worry which arises here is that Aquinas's account commits him to an infinite regress of interactions between the intellect and the will, so that there is never a beginning for any action. How troublesome this worry appears depends in part on whether we start with some action an agent is doing and work backwards to ask why he did it, or whether we try to begin with something that in fact initiates an action.

So, for example, suppose you get up to answer the telephone when it rings, and we want to know why you did so. Then you might give some account of yourself, explaining why it seemed reasonable for you, rather than for your teenaged daughter, to get the phone. You might say, for example, that on this occasion your daughter had finally begun her piano practicing and you did not think she should be distracted. But now we might want to know why these considerations were effective with you. We might ask why you have this attitude towards your daughter's piano practicing, and you will find yourself giving some further explanation for this attitude on your part. And so on, in a process that looks as if it will never stop.

But suppose that instead of starting with the action of answering the telephone and working backwards in this way, we instead start with what in fact initiates the action. You are busily engaged trying to get the dirt and mildew out of the old camping equipment when the phone rings and you wish someone would answer it. A second's reflection, only half-consciously made, persuades you that, however inconvenient it is to drop the camping gear, you ought to get the phone yourself; and, with one degree of reluctance or another, you assent to doing so and move for the phone. Here there is no question of infinite regress. The action was started by your hearing and recognizing the ringing of the phone.

Thinking of your action in this way helps explain Aquinas's own reason for rejecting the worry about an infinite regress of this sort. Every act of willing, he thinks, is preceded by some apprehension on the part of the intellect, but not every apprehension on the part of the intellect need be preceded by an act of will,[34] so there is no danger of an infinite regress. Nonetheless, that the specter of an infinite regress is raised by beginning with an action and working backwards through successive sets of interactive cognitive and conative attitudes is an indication of the dynamic nature of the interaction between intellect and will. Any particular act on the part of intellect or will may be influenced by a whole array of preceding acts of intellect and will. That's why our past actions mold our character, and our character in turn shapes our actions.

It is apparent, then, that on Aquinas's account of intellect and will, the will is part of a dynamic feedback system composed primarily of the will and the intellect, but also including the passions. The interaction between will and intellect is so close and the acts of the two powers are so intertwined that Aquinas often finds it difficult to draw the line between them. So, for example, he says:

it happens sometimes that there is an act of the will in which something of the [preceding] act of reason remains ... and, vice versa, there is [sometimes] an act of reason in which something of the [preceding] act of will remains.[35]

That is why, for Aquinas, it sometimes *looks* as if (even if it is not in fact the case that) the will engages in acts of apprehension and the intellect engages in acts of willing.

If we remember this part of Aquinas's account and also take seriously his identification of the will as a hunger or appetite, we will be less likely to make a mistake and identify the will on his account as nothing more than a toggle switch with three positions: accept, reject, and off. Aquinas's account of the will is more complicated than such an identification implies. Because it is an appetite, the will can have dispositions, so that it can be more or less readily inclined to want something. It can will something with more or less strength.[36] It can give specific commands to body parts. Finally, under the pull of the passions, it can influence what intellect presents to it as good by selectively directing the attention of the intellect.

For this reason, too, although Aquinas's account of the will assigns a large role to intellect, he is not committed to seeing immoral actions simply as instances of mistakes in deliberation, since the intellect's deliberations are in many cases dependent on the will's influence. In cases of incontinence, where the intellect seems to be representing something as good which the will is not willing, Aquinas would say that the intellect, influenced by the will, is in fact being moved by opposed desires to represent the thing in question as both good (under one description) and not good (under a different description), so that the intellect is double-minded.[37] In the last analysis, what the intellect of the incontinent person represents as the best alternative in these circumstances at this time is not that which the agent takes to be good considered unconditionally or in the abstract.

Cases of incontinence illustrate the further complicating fact that the intellect need not present one simple, unified result to the will. Sometimes an agent is, as we say, entirely of one mind about something, and what the intellect presents to the will is one unified message that something is good now under this description in these circumstances. But what is no doubt also often the case is that an agent's intellect is not entirely unified. The doctor has recommended x-raying the agent's head to check for a sinus infection. On the one hand, the agent's intellect may recognize that the doctor is an expert in her field, so that her advice should be followed for that reason. On the other hand, however, the agent's intellect may be aware that even low-level x-rays are carcinogenic, and the intellect may raise a question about whether the doctor's ordering the x-ray reflects her concern to avoid malpractice law suits rather than her own view about what is necessary for the health of her patient. Furthermore, the influence of the passions may also complicate the case. It might be, for example, that a patient's intellect supposes some medical tests are in fact medically required, but his passions might recoil strongly from the tests, for one reason or another. In that case, his aversion to the tests may influence the intellect to give a divided verdict: on the one hand, it would be good to undergo the tests, because they are important for health; on the other hand, it would be bad to undergo the tests because they are fearful, painful, or otherwise repulsive. In such cases, there may be considerable interaction among intellect, will, and passions, until, in consequence of such iterated interaction, one side or another of the divided intellect becomes strong enough to override the other. This is a process familiar enough to anyone who has had to talk himself into doing something he originally feared or disliked. (I will say more about such iterated interactions involving the will in later sections of this chapter.)

The relation of freedom to intellect and will

One of the perplexing things about the preceding analysis of the relation of intellect to will is that it is not immediately apparent in what sense the will is free.

It is helpful in this connection to notice that Aquinas recognizes a distinction between freedom of action and freedom of willing.[38] He acknowledges, for example, that we can lose our freedom of action while retaining our freedom with regard to willing. Even when the will itself is not compelled or coerced in any way, he says, the members of the body can be impeded by some external cause so that they do not follow the command of the will.[39] While an agent might still be free with regard to his willing in such a case, he would not be free with regard to his actions, which in the case envisaged are at least in part under some control other than his own. In order for an agent to have freedom of action, then, it is not sufficient that his will be free in its willing of that action. It must at least also be the case that there is no external impediment to the action of the relevant body parts and that those parts are themselves functioning normally.

Consequently, freedom of action is not a property of just one component of a human being. Rather, it is a property of a whole system, the system comprised at least of the will and the members of the body. It emerges when the will is freely commanding a certain sort of movement and when the relevant bodily parts are functioning normally and are not kept by any cause external to the agent from being under the will's control. It is even more helpful to see that for Aquinas, freedom with regard to willing is also a feature of a whole system.

In explaining what constitutes a distinctly human action, Aquinas frames his explanation this way. What differentiates human beings from non-rational animals is that a human being is master of his acts, in virtue of having intellect and will. Consequently, no freedom with regard to willing remains for a person who, through madness, for example, has lost the use of his intellectual faculties.[40] Aquinas makes the same point another way by saying that the root of freedom is in the will as subject but in the reason as the cause.[41] That is, the property of freedom inheres in the will, which is the subject for the property, but it does so because of the intellect; the will's relations to and interactions with the intellect are the source of the freedom in the will. Freedom with regard to willing, then, is not a characteristic either of the will or of the intellect alone. Like freedom of action, freedom with regard to willing emerges from the functioning of a system, in this case the system comprised of the intellect and the will.

Furthermore, Aquinas also says that an agent is master of his acts or has his acts in his own power insofar as they are voluntary, and that it is a person's voluntary acts which make him subject to praise or blame.[42] But, in his view, whatever is voluntary requires an act of the intellect as well as an act of the will.[43] Seconding a view of Damascene's, Aquinas calls a voluntary act 'an act that is a rational operation'.[44] In fact, Aquinas holds that because the will has the relation it has to the intellect, all the acts of the will are voluntary, whether they are simple acts of will or are commands to some other power which the will controls.[45] Finally, in Aquinas's view, anything that takes away an agent's use of her intellectual faculties also takes away the voluntariness of her action.[46]

For Aquinas, a voluntary act is a special case of being moved by an intrinsic principle.[47] Whatever is moved by an intrinsic principle in such a way that it acts for an end which it cognizes as an end has within itself the principle of its action. Some creatures act with a limited cognition of the end for which they are acting, so that their acts are voluntary but in a limited sort of way. The acts of young children and some animals are voluntary in this way. Normal adult human beings, on the other hand, can have a full cognition of their ends, and so they can have complete voluntariness with regard to their acts.[48]

By the same token, and perhaps as a consequence of the same thought about the voluntary, Aquinas thinks that anything external to the agent which acted coercively on the agent's will would thereby destroy voluntariness. That the voluntary movement of the will be from an extrinsic principle, Aquinas says, is impossible.[49] This is not an empirical claim but a conceptual one. For something to be an act of will, it has to stem from an intrinsic source, in particular the will as informed by the intellect. So, Aquinas says, "an act of the will is nothing other than an inclination which proceeds from an interior cognizing principle ... but what is compelled or violent is from an extrinsic principle".[50]

If something extrinsic to the agent were to act on the will with efficient causation, then the tie of the will to the intellect, from which acts of will get their voluntary character, would be broken, and so the act of the will would not be voluntary – or to put it more nearly as Aquinas seems to think of it, in such a case it would not be a real act of the will at all.

We might wonder here why Aquinas would not grant that an act of will could be voluntary even if it were caused by an extrinsic principle, provided that the extrinsic principle produced its effects by operating directly on the agent's intellect and only thereby, indirectly, on the agent's will. Aquinas considers something like this question himself when he asks whether Satan could bring it about that a human being sin.[51] Aquinas subscribes to the demon-possession theory of mental illness, so he supposes that Satan can causally affect a human intellect by possessing it. But, in his view, this is to destroy it as a human intellect; an insane person has lost his reason. At any rate, if some external agent S has taken over entirely the intellect of some human being H, then the intellect that is operative in that human person is S's and not H's. In that case, what the will operative in H wills might be voluntary, but it would count as S's will, not H's, since the intellect that informs the willing is S's. In this case, there can be an extrinsic principle S which operates on the intellect of some other agent H, but the operation of the extrinsic principle will not give us an act of will that can count as H's. On the other hand, if we were to imagine Satan (or his twentieth-century counterpart, the evil neurosurgeon) invading H's intellect only partially, for example, by producing a thought or a train of thoughts, H's intellect will then examine that thought or set of thoughts and evaluate it, retaining or rejecting it according as it seems right to H to do so. In that case, however, any resulting voluntary acts of will stem from the reflections of H's intellect, not S's. Here again, then, we will not have a case in which a voluntary act of will on H's part is produced by an extrinsic principle S, operating through H's intellect.

So, worries about grace aside, it is clear that Aquinas is not a compatibilist. The causal chain resulting in any voluntary act on an agent's part has to originate in the agent's own intellect and will. If it originates in some cause external to the agent, the resulting act either will not be an act of the agent's will – as in the case of demon possession – or will not be an act of will at all. So while extrinsic principles may influence human volition, as, for example, we sometimes do when we persuade one another by arguments, causes external to an agent H cannot efficiently cause a voluntary act of will on H's part, either directly or indirectly.

If Aquinas is not a compatibilist, what sort of incompatibilist is he? Is he a libertarian? Although the outlines of Aquinas's theory of human freedom are now somewhat clearer, it still is not obvious in what sense the will – or the system of will and intellect – is supposed to be free. No doubt, part of what gives rise to this perplexity is the presupposition, common enough in contemporary discussions of free will, that libertarian free will includes or even just consists in the ability to do otherwise.[52] But in what sense is it possible for the will, or the will-and-intellect, to do otherwise on Aquinas's view?

To answer this question and to sort out the associated puzzle about libertarian free will, it is helpful to explicate Aquinas's account of *liberum arbitrium*, because it is often taken to constitute his theory of free will. That account, however, is inextricably linked to Aquinas's theory of action. Consequently, we will best approach our question regarding Aquinas's account of the will's ability to do otherwise not by attacking it head on but by proceeding obliquely, beginning with Aquinas's account of the nature of a full-blown human action[53] – one over which the agent is master, over which the agent has control, and for which the agent is subject to praise or blame.

Human action

Contemporary accounts, however they present the details, are likely to explain an action, such as raising one's hand, in terms of an agent's beliefs and desires, which combine to yield this action. By contrast, Aquinas's account of such an action explains it in terms of a much more structured and dynamic process.[54] Because it is complicated, I will first simply present it, reserving reflection on it till after the whole account has been sketched out.

The process which eventuates in the bodily motion of a human action begins, on Aquinas's view, with the intellect's cognition of the circumstances in which the agent finds herself and its judgment about what would be good, under some description, in these particular circumstances at this particular time. This judgment moves the will to a first act, a simple volition of an end. This judgment and its accompanying volition is the first of five sets of paired acts on the part of intellect and will. The next three sets all have to do with the means to the end considered and desired in this first judgment and volition.

Although the initial volition of the end is prior in explanatory order to the other acts of will in the sequence, it need not be separated by much or even any time from them:

> sometimes [the volition of the end] is temporally prior, as when someone first wants health and then afterwards, deliberating about how he can be restored to health, wills to send for a doctor in order to be made healthy.[55]

Because the intellect might in one act cognize both end and means, however, the willing of the end and of the means might also occur at once, as they would if the patient in Aquinas's example were simultaneously to wish to be healthy and to will on that account to send for the doctor.[56]

The second act of the will in the paired acts of intellect and will leading to voluntary bodily movement is the first of three acts of will associated with the means to the end wanted. This act of will is intention. Unlike the simple volition of the end, intention is an act of will which is related to the end but only as it can be achieved by certain means the agent believes are available to her. So Aquinas says, there is simple volition "by which we wish absolutely to have health", and then there is intention: "for when we are said to intend to have health, it is not just because we wish for it but because we want to achieve it by certain means".[57] Intention is therefore also dependent on a preceding act of intellect, namely, one which supposes that the end wanted can be achieved by the very person wishing for it, that achieving the end is now within the agent's power.

Aquinas distinguishes intention from another act of will related to means, third in the series of paired acts, namely, consent. Consent is the will's accepting the means the intellect proposes as suitable and efficacious for bringing about the end wanted. Intention is the act of will that follows the intellect's judgment that the agent is able to bring about the end at issue. Consent is the act of will that follows the intellect's judgment of the ways in which the agent can bring this about.[58]

Consent is thus also preceded by an act of intellect, which Aquinas calls 'counsel', in which the intellect determines means suitable for achieving the end wished for. If the intellect takes there to be several suitable means for reaching the end, the will may consent to all of them. So, for example, the intellect of a patient with a chronic back condition who wishes for health and intends to achieve it by some means involving medicine may determine a number of suitable alternatives, such as seeing an orthopedist, visiting a chiropractic clinic, or consulting a physical therapist for a regimen of exercise. The patient's will might consent to each of these alternatives as acceptable. On the other hand, the intellect may present to will a divided judgment of the sort discussed above. If the agent is strongly averse to surgery, for example, his intellect may give conflicting judgments about seeing an orthopedist, presenting it as a medically acceptable alternative but also presenting it as painful, expensive, and disruptive of life. In such a case, there will be further interactions among the intellect, the will, and the passions, till one side of the divided intellect dominates over the other. In such a case, although the intellect might originally present seeing the orthopedist as one of the medically suitable alternatives, in the end the will may not consent to that alternative. (I will say something more about such iterated interactions of intellect and will below.)

If there is more than one means that the will consents to, then the intellect ranks the alternatives and calculates which of these means would be best now in these circumstances. The end of this process on the intellect's part is the conclusion of a practical syllogism: this is what should be done now. The will then wills *this*, in an act of *electio*.

'*Electio*' is often translated 'choice', but this is a misleading translation. It suggests that the will is engaged in what is really the intellect's act of ranking alternative possibilities. In the act of *electio*, what the will does is accept the course of action that intellect proposes as the best. Furthermore, 'choice' ranges over cases which include acts of will that Aquinas would classify as simple volition of the end or intention.[59] For the sake of clarity, then, it seems better just to leave the term in Latin.

Electio and consent are not always different acts. So Aquinas says: "If only one means is found acceptable, then consent and *electio* do not differ really but only conceptually (*ratione*)."[60] If, for example, the intellect of the patient were convinced that chiropractors are quacks and that surgery is too risky a procedure for relieving back pain, then a review of his alternatives would suggest to his intellect that physical therapy is the only acceptable alternative. For his will, then, on that occasion, the acts of consent and *electio* would be the same.

Electio is generally followed by an act of intellect which Aquinas calls 'command' – intellect's issuing the imperative conclusion of its practical syllogism: "Do this!" – and an act of will called 'use', which is the will's causing one of the powers under its control to act. This is the last of the five sets of paired acts of intellect and will, and this is the point at which a bodily motion will take place, if what the will is directing is the motion of a part of the body.[61] Since the will has control over components of the person other than just body parts, however, this process can also conclude with the will's control over itself, as, for example in attempts at reform, when in consequence of a global volition (for example, to give up foods high in cholesterol) the will wills particular volitions (for example, willing to select North African chickpea stew from the menu, instead of steak).

So command and use are followed by the movement of something which the will has some control over, generally a movement of a part of the body, but on some occasions also some other faculty, such as the will itself. On the other hand, in consequence of some representation by the intellect, the will might also at this point exert control over the intellect – by, for example, causing intellect to reconsider the means, or to direct attention towards some things and away from others.

In general, then, Aquinas sees the hierarchically ordered interaction between will and intellect involved in producing a voluntary human action in this way:

I1   The intellect's determination that a particular end, under a certain description, is good now in these circumstances.

W1   A simple volition for that end.

I2   The intellect's determination that that end can be achieved by the willer, that the achievement of the end through some means is now and in these circumstances in the power of the willer.

W2   *Intention*: an act of will to try to achieve the end through some means.

I3   *Counsel*: the intellect's determination of the means suitable to achieve the end wanted. [If there is only one such means, then W3 collapses into W4, and I4 is omitted.]

W3   *Consent*: an act of will accepting the means the intellect proposes.

I4   The intellect's determination that *this* means is the best at this time in these circumstances.

W4   *Electio*: an act of will selecting the means the intellect proposes as best.

I5   *Command*: the intellect's imperative, "Do this!"

W5   *Use*: an act of will to exercise control over one of the things subject to the will, for example, a part of the body, the intellect, or the will itself.

This is a complicated picture of what goes into an action such as raising one's hand. But even so complicated a picture is a simplistic rendering of Aquinas's account.

To begin with, as I explained above, since the will exercises efficient causality on the intellect, it can at any time direct the intellect to reconsider a calculation or direct the intellect simply to stop considering some particular topic. (Of course, the will's doing so is a result of the intellect's maintaining that doing so is a good thing under some description in these circumstances.)

Furthermore, in some cases of complicated actions, at least some of the acts of intellect in the list I1–I5 (and thus also their consequent acts of will) can be accomplished only after a process of investigation involving a number of actions that themselves require an interaction of will and intellect. So, for example, Albert Speer reports that when his close friend Karl Hanke explained to him, with evident deep distress, that there were horrors occurring at Auschwitz, Speer realized that if he were to investigate, he might very well find that he himself must and could do something to affect what was happening there, but he saw at the same time that acting might cost him something. And so although he could not help believing his friend Hanke at least to some extent and sharing at least a little of Hanke's distress over whatever might be happening at Auschwitz, he willed not to investigate. Describing himself then, Speer wrote:

> I did not query him [Hanke]. I did not query Himmler, I did not query Hitler, I did not speak with personal friends. I did not investigate – for I did not want to know what was happening there ... from fear of discovering something which might have made me turn from my course, I had closed my eyes.[62]

Although Speer might well have wished that conditions were not as Hanke indicated they were in Auschwitz, he made sure to avoid information readily available to him in order to prevent the formation of the act of will Aquinas calls intention.

As this example indicates, in order to form an intention to try to bring about some end an agent may need a lengthy process of investigation, involving many subsidiary actions, so that a considerable time elapses between the original volition of the end and the intention to bring it about. There could be similar processes intervening elsewhere in the sequence of acts of intellect and will as well.

On the other hand, there may be little or no subjectively discernible temporal separation among these acts of intellect and will. Although there is a conceptual ordering among them, they need not have a corresponding temporal ordering. An agent might see an end and the sole acceptable means to that end simultaneously, for example, and act on it instantly. Similarly, although any act of will is dependent on and subsequent to an act of intellect, whatever temporal space there is between the two might be so small as to be practically indiscernible. From the agent's point of view, then, the entire sequence of I1–W5 may occur in the twinkling of an eye.

Finally, none of I1–W5 needs to be in the forefront of consciousness, done with transparent awareness. Any of these acts might be tacit, acts of which we could be made aware only by careful questioning and introspection after the fact. There is obviously a continuum of accessibility to consciousness, from acts done with self-conscious awareness to acts which can be brought up into consciousness only with probing by professional therapists. Any of I1–W5 might fall anywhere on that continuum.

In general, where the action is simple and the character of the agent is harmonious and well-integrated, I1–W5 are likely to occur seamlessly and tacitly. Their distinctness is easier to see in cases where the action is complicated or difficult and/or when the agent has serious internal conflicts. Consider, for example, the distinction between intention and consent, which might ordinarily be subjectively indiscernible in the antecedents of some simple action. Speer reports that at one point during the Nuremberg trials he felt suicidal and gave a great deal of thought to how he might kill himself. When his biographer, Gita Sereny, asked him whether he really had meant to kill himself then, he said, "Well, ... one fantasizes about such things, almost an intellectual exercise if you like – yes, I figured out how it could be done, but not with the intention of actually doing it."[63]

How are we to understand Speer here? One way to do so is to suppose that Speer, depressed and suicidal during his trial, began with a view that in his circumstances suicide was good, a volition for that end, a recognition that that end was in his power, an intention to accomplish it, and considerable deliberation about the various means by which it might be accomplished. But his will would not consent to any of those means, and so the original intention and volition unravelled as well. That is why although

291

he was by his own report suicidal and contemplating ways of killing himself, in the end he did not do so.

Suppose, however, that we put internally complicated characters and actions to one side and apply the analysis exemplified in I1–W5 to an actual case of raising one's hand. Consider this example Gita Sereny relates from her own teenage years. Walking through her native city in Austria, which had by then been occupied by the Germans, she unexpectedly came across a band of Nazi soldiers who had corralled a group of middle-aged Jews and were forcing them to scrub the sidewalks on their hands and knees with toothbrushes.[64] To the increase of Sereny's horror, she also recognized her old family doctor among the Jews. Although she was young, she was thoroughly aware of the dangers of intervening. Nonetheless, she waded into the crowd of onlookers, attracted the attention of the soldiers, and expressed passionate moral indignation. The crowd, in some confusion, began to disperse, and the Jews made their escape. Let us suppose she attracted the attention of the soldiers, at least in part, by raising her hand and waving her arm. Let us also suppose what most people would take for granted, that her raising her hand in these circumstances is a free action. How are we to explain the occurrence of this action?

On Aquinas's account, the process begins with (S-I1) a judgment on the part of Sereny's intellect that what is happening is horrible and that it would be good if it stopped. Then (S-W1) her will forms the simple volition that it stop. (S-I2) Her intellect considers whether it might not be in her power to do something to stop it and concludes that it is in her power. In consequence, (S-W2) her will resolves to do something, and as a result of that act of will, (S-I3) her intellect calculates what it might be possible for her to do, together with a determination of the costs to her of each means and a judgment about which of these costs renders the corresponding act unacceptable.

Her intellect need not determine these alternatives discursively or even linguistically. Sometimes when we consider alternative courses of action, we do so by picturing to ourselves the proposed action and then going on to imagine, in a computer-modeling sort of way, what would happen next if we did the proposed action, as well as how we would react to such subsequent events, and so on. So, for example, Sereny might in the flash of a psychological moment see herself in her mind's eye flying at the soldiers, or trying to create a diversion by feigning illness in front of them, or any of a number of alternatives. She might simultaneously realize that some of these alternatives would be ineffectual to gain her end and that others would work but would cost her too much.

If, by one mechanism or another, her intellect comes up with a number of effective and acceptable alternatives, (S-W3) her will will also assent to them; as her intellect presents one or another alternative, her will also will give a nod of assent to each. If there are several to which she finds herself consenting, then (S-I4) her intellect will rank them and present the one which, in the circumstances, under some description looks best now. Then (S-W4) her will will select that one in an act of *electio*. So, for example, we might suppose that after quickly sizing up the situation and seeing what she could do to interfere, Sereny rapidly comes to the view that she should intervene by first directing the soldiers' attention to herself with some gestures and then heaping moral indignation on them, and her will then consents to that means. At this point, we have the last act of intellect (S-I5) and will (S-W5) directing body parts to move; in consequence, she raises her hand, waves her arm, and starts to yell.

Furthermore, we may suppose, compatibly with this analysis, that from Sereny's subjective point of view, this entire process takes virtually no time and is largely tacit, so that she just finds herself, somewhat to her surprise, gesticulating and yelling at the soldiers. As I said, nothing in the postulation of this hierarchy of interactive intellections and volitions requires that any of it be done with full awareness and self-consciousness; the acts of intellect and will in question might be much nearer the bottom than the top of the continuum of accessibility to consciousness. But if we asked Sereny, after the fact, about why she acted as she did, on Aquinas's view the story she would tell (perhaps only with the probing of a skilled interlocuter) would give us the pieces of Aquinas's analysis of her action.

Furthermore, although the process may occur swiftly and tacitly, so that Sereny is not at the time aware of its components, at virtually any stage it is possible to imagine the story in such a way that the willings occur differently.

So, for example, after the first paired set of acts of intellect and will, Sereny's intellect, under the sway of the passions, might emphasize the dangers to her of intervention over the horror of the Nazi actions, so that what the intellect presents to the will is not one unified determination of what it would be good for her to do in these circumstances. In consequence of the intellect's double-minded emphasis of the danger, Sereny's will might command her intellect to stop thinking about this unpleasant scene or to begin attending to something else. This sort of aborting of the process leading to action, at the point between the first and the second paired set of acts of intellect and will, was characteristic of Speer in the years before 1943, and it helps to account for his learning a great deal about Nazi evils and yet never having a sense then that he could or should do anything about them.

Similarly, as we saw with the example of the suicidal Speer, at (S-I3) and (S-I4) there might be epicycles of interaction of the will and the intellect, in consequence of which the intellect might after all conclude that none of the alternatives available to achieve the end wanted are acceptable. If such epicycles occurred in her case, Sereny would give up or undo the original intention (S-W2).

Furthermore, because of the intellect's presentation of considerations against intervention, such as the danger to herself, Sereny's will might have misdirected the attention of her intellect in such a way that what she selected as a means to her goal were not in fact effective to achieve that goal but which were also not very costly for her. Such a misdirection of the intellect by the will characterized Speer when he was finally made unavoidably aware of Nazi horrors at the slave labor camp making rockets. He was appalled when he saw the conditions of the laborers, who lived in freezing caves without adequate ventilation or sanitation and who worked eighteen-hour shifts on starvation rations. On this occasion, he also could not hide from himself that it was within his power to do something about their conditions, since at that time he was the chief minister in charge of armament production. As was made plain during the Nuremberg trials, it was in fact open to Speer to refuse to employ slave laborers in armament production. But any sympathy for the plight of slave laborers would have brought him into open conflict with high-ranking Nazis, and this he wanted to avoid.[65] Consequently, in the circumstances, what Speer's intellect, influenced by the passions and misdirected by will, determined that it was best for him to do, the one thing he chose at the W4 level, was to order the construction of concentration camp barracks for the workers. The suffering occasioned by lack of proper food, clothing, ventilation, and sanitation was not alleviated by that means; nor was the problem of overwork under horrific conditions. And, of course, the monumental injustice of the slave labor itself was not addressed by the construction of barracks. Nonetheless, because his will selectively directed the attention of his intellect, Speer managed to persuade himself at the time that he had taken the best means available to him to stop the suffering of the workers.

So Aquinas's intricate analysis of action, which may look byzantine when we consider a simple action such as raising one's hand, looks considerably more understandable when we apply it to even simple actions in complicated circumstances, such as Sereny's. And it yields powerful and plausible explanations of the actions, and inactions, of a person such as Speer, who was seriously riven by internal conflicts.

Liberum arbitrium and the ability to do otherwise

When we say that Sereny's act of raising her hand is a free act, we mean that it is an act done with freedom of will, and Aquinas would agree. His explanation of freedom in such actions is often couched in terms of *liberum arbitrium*, and it is because of what Aquinas says about *liberum arbitrium* that he is generally supposed to see human freedom as a function of the will's ability to do otherwise.

It is true that Aquinas makes a strong connection between *liberum arbitrium* and the ability to do otherwise. In fact, although '*liberum arbitrium*' means 'free judgment', Aquinas sometimes sounds as if *liberum arbitrium* is just the power of the will to do otherwise than it does. So, for example, he says, "whoever has *liberum arbitrium* has it in his power to will or not to will, to do or not to do".[66]

Nonetheless, it is a mistake to suppose that '*liberum arbitrium*' is Aquinas's term for the freedom of the will in general. In fact, he explicitly associates *liberum arbitrium* with only one of the acts of will needed to produce a human action, namely, the act of will which is *electio*. So, for example, he says, "*liberum arbitrium* is that in accordance with which we have *electio*".[67] And in another place he says:

> with regard to intellective appetite, the will and *liberum arbitrium* – which is nothing but the power of *electio* – are related just as the intellect and reason are related with regard to intellective cognition[68] ... Now the act of *electio* is to desire something for the sake of obtaining something else, so that, strictly speaking, it has to do with means to an end ... Therefore, it is clear that the will is related to the power of *electio* – that is, to *liberum arbitrium* – just as intellect is related to reason.[69]

In discussing the will of angels, he worries about whether angels have *liberum arbitrium*, and he raises the worry in this way:

> It seems that there is no *liberum arbitrium* in angels, for the act of *liberum arbitrium* is *electio*, but there cannot be *electio* in angels since *electio* is an appetite associated with counsel, and counsel is a kind of investigation ... But angels do not cognize by investigation, because this pertains to the discursiveness of reason [which angels do not have].[70]

And elsewhere he associates the act of *liberum arbitrium* just with the selection of a means to an end,[71] which is *electio*.

So although, on Aquinas's account, *liberum arbitrium* involves being able to do otherwise, *liberum arbitrium* is not identical to freedom of the will in general, but instead picks out just the power of the will manifested in the act Aquinas calls *electio*, the will's assenting to the means apprehended as best for the end wanted.

Furthermore, not every free action has an act of *electio* in the series of acts of will and intellect producing that action. As we saw earlier, when the intellect finds only one acceptable means to an end, then the act of *electio* collapses into the act of consent, precisely because there are not alternatives available for the intellect and the will to act on.[72]

In addition, even understood narrowly as confined to the power of the will producing *electio*, *liberum arbitrium* is not a property of the will alone. It can be understood as a property of the will only insofar as the will itself is understood to be the rational appetite and to have a close tie to the intellect.

So, in some places Aquinas speaks of *liberum arbitrium* as if it were in fact a power of both the will and the intellect. When he is asking whether God has *liberum arbitrium*, one of the objections he raises begins with the uncontested remark that "*liberum arbitrium* is a faculty of reason and of will".[73] Elsewhere, speaking more precisely, he says:

> the nature of *liberum arbitrium* should be considered on the basis of *electio*. But both the cognitive power and the appetitive power contribute something to *electio*. From the cognitive power we need counsel, by which we determine what is to be preferred to what, and from the appetitive power we need the desire to accept what counsel has determined.[74]

That is why, he goes on to say, Aristotle supposed we ought to assign *electio* either to the "appetitive intellect" or to the "intellective appetite", phrases meant to indicate the intertwining of intellect and will in *liberum arbitrium*. (Of this pair, Aquinas opts for 'intellective appetite' – that is, the will understood as preceded by certain acts of intellect – as the more appropriate candidate for the faculty to which *liberum arbitrium* is to be assigned.) Furthermore, although he thinks that if we take *liberum arbitrium* to be a faculty rather than one of the powers of a faculty, then it is just the will itself, he nonetheless emphasizes that *liberum arbitrium* is the will understood as interwoven with and dependent on intellect.[75]

Finally, although Aquinas does associate *liberum arbitrium*, understood as *electio*, with the ability to do otherwise, the ability to do otherwise is not found only at the level of *electio*, as our consideration of the series I1–W5 has already shown us. It is possible for it to be manifested at any of the other stages as well.

This is not because at any stage the will may simply choose not to follow intellect,[76] or may act in some other way as a homunculus independent of intellect. It has instead to do with the relations between intellect and will. Insofar as the will has control over itself, this is an indirect control mediated by the intellect. It is a limited control as well, since there are intellective apprehensions which are not preceded by or dependent upon acts of will. The will may not always succeed, for example, in getting the intellect to stop thinking about something, because something in the environment causes the thought to recur repeatedly to the intellect, as in the case above regarding the screams of the tortured. But, within a limited range, the will can be effective at controlling the intellect, for example, by being able in some circumstances to redirect the attention of the intellect, and in that way the will can also have indirect control over itself. It is easy to imagine Sereny willing otherwise at one point or another throughout the series of I1–W5 in virtue of her having thought differently about the relevant issues, the risks associated with intervening, for example, or the means of intervening open to her and their likely effectiveness. She might even have aborted the entire series by directing her intellect to concentrate, for example, on some important task which needed her urgent attention then, and which was incompatible with her stopping to help the Jews.

Of course, the will's directing the intellect in any of these ways will itself depend on the intellect's presenting the will's doing so as good under some description in these circumstances. That is why a human agent's control over her own actions is a function of both the intellect and the will and is an emergent power or property, resulting from the dynamic interaction between the intellect and the will, rather than a static power localized in the structure of one particular faculty. On Aquinas's account of freedom, we have to attribute freedom to a human being with regard to willing or acting; for him, freedom is not just a property of one particular component of a human being, whether the will or the intellect.

Freedom and the ability to do otherwise

As we have seen, Aquinas supposes that human beings have control over their own actions and that this control is manifest, perhaps even specially evinced, in *electio*, which is an act of will involving the ability to do otherwise. But it is also important to recognize that, for Aquinas, the faculties that give a human being control over her actions — namely, the intellect and the will — are not themselves a function of or dependent on an ability to do otherwise. As long as these faculties are functioning normally (and, as we have seen, normal functioning precludes the will's being determined by anything outside the willer), then, on Aquinas's view, an agent has control over her actions and freedom with respect to her willing and acting, even if she cannot do otherwise.

We have already seen some sign of this attitude on Aquinas's part in his pointing out that in some cases *electio* collapses into consent, when the intellect presents to the will only one alternative as the means to achieve some end willed by the agent.[77] Such cases still count as acts over which an agent has control.

Another sign of the same attitude can be found in what Aquinas says about the limits of *liberum arbitrium*. Something can be outside the power of *liberum arbitrium* in two ways, he says. First, it can exceed the efficacy of the motive powers. For example, flying by flapping one's arms is not within the power of human *liberum arbitrium*, because flying exceeds the capacities of human powers of movement. Second, and this is the important point for our purposes, acts which we do under the sudden impetus of some passion, such as wrath or concupiscence, are outside the power of *liberum arbitrium* because such acts occur quickly, before reason can deliberate about them. An agent may be able to avoid letting passion have such effects in himself by paying careful attention; but an agent cannot always be paying careful attention.[78]

In unguarded moments, such passions can arise in an agent without the process of reason, even tacit reason, which is necessary to choice; and the agent in acting on such a passion is consequently unable to do otherwise on that occasion. If Aquinas supposed that *liberum arbitrium* were identical to free will or if he thought that the ability to do otherwise were in general essential to free will, he should go on to say here that acts done under the influence of passion are not free acts, since the agent in question is unable to do otherwise, and that therefore these acts are not sinful or blameworthy. What he in fact says is that such acts *are* sinful, but that they constitute only venial sins since their suddenness and their taking us by surprise provide us with some excuse.[79]

In *QDM* Aquinas argues at length that it is heretical to suppose that the will is moved of necessity to will whatever it wills, because such a supposition undermines all attributions of praise and blame, removes the impetus to deliberation, exhortation and precept, and so on. But in that very question where he is so concerned to establish the will's ability to will otherwise than it does, he also grants that the will does in fact sometimes will what it wills of necessity. This happens when what is willed is so altogether good that the intellect cannot find any description under which to present it as not good – as in the case of happiness. But it also happens in other sorts of cases as well, as, for example, when the intellect establishes very clearly that one course of action is in every respect superior to any other available. So Aquinas ends his discussion of this point with the conclusion that although the will is sometimes moved of necessity, it is not always so moved.[80]

What Aquinas means us to understand here, we might suppose, is that although the will sometimes wills something of necessity, it is free only when it is not moved of necessity; that is why, we might think, he is so concerned to show that the will is not *always* moved of necessity. But such an interpretation would be a mistake. In arguing that the will does will some things of necessity, Aquinas explains that there are two sorts of necessity which might be taken to operate on the will. One is the necessity of coercion, which occurs when some cause outside the agent causally produces in the will a volition for some particular thing.[81] This sort of necessity, Aquinas says, is incompatible with freedom. (In fact, as we saw earlier, there can be no such coercion of will for Aquinas, because he thinks that it is conceptually impossible for any necessity of this sort to operate on the will; coerced by external necessity, the will ceases to count as an intrinsic principle, and so it ceases to count as a *will*.) But there is also the necessity of natural inclination, Aquinas says. This is the sort of necessity by which the will wills, for example, those things whose goodness is overwhelmingly apparent to the agent. Necessity of this sort, according to Aquinas, is not repugnant to the will and does not take away the will's freedom.[82] Siding with Augustine, he says: "Freedom ... is opposed to the necessity of coercion, but not to the necessity of natural inclination."[83]

That is why Aquinas thinks that there can be freedom of will on the part of the redeemed in heaven who no longer have the ability to will evil.[84] Their inability to will anything but the good stems not from any extrinsic coercion being exercised on their wills but rather from the clear view their intellects have of the nature of the good: "Where there is no defect in apprehending and comparing, there can be no volition for evil with regard to those things which are ordered to the end, as is clear in the case of the blessed."[85]

Their intellects can no longer find descriptions under which to present as good things that are really evil. Although the blessed cannot will evil, they nonetheless will freely whatever good they will.

Elsewhere Aquinas contrasts the necessity of coercion with the necessity of the end. When someone is compelled by an extrinsic cause in such a way that he cannot do otherwise than he does, this is necessity of coercion, and it is altogether repugnant to the will, Aquinas says. But necessity of the end is different. It arises, for example, when the end desired can be attained in only one way, as when crossing the sea requires using a ship. This sort of necessity is in no way repugnant to the will, on Aquinas's view. But, Aquinas concludes, the necessity of natural inclination is similar in relevant respects to necessity of the end, and so necessity of natural inclination is also not repugnant to the will. For this sort of reason as well as others, Aquinas maintains that "natural necessity does not take away the freedom of the will".[86]

Clearly, then, Aquinas does not suppose that human freedom even as regards willing consists in or depends on the ability to do otherwise. Aquinas would consequently reject what is called the Principle of Alternative Possibilities (PAP). PAP has many different formulations, but they all share this claim:

> (PAP) A person has free will with regard to (or is morally responsible for) an action A only if he could have done otherwise than A.[87]

Aquinas would reject this principle not only for bodily actions but even, as we have seen, for acts of will.

Many contemporary philosophers also suppose that PAP is false. A standard strategy for showing that PAP is false is what has come to be known as a Frankfurt-style counterexample.[88] In such an example, a person P does an action A in circumstances that incline most people to conclude that P is doing A freely, but (in the example) there is some mechanism that would have operated to bring it about that P would have done A if P had not done A by himself. In the actual sequence of events presented in the counterexample, however, the mechanism does not operate, and P does do A by himself. So the counterexample is designed to make us think that P does A freely in the actual sequence of events although it is not the case that P could have done otherwise than A.[89] Frankfurt-style counterexamples can be constructed either for bodily actions, such as leaving a room, or for mental actions, such as deciding to leave a room.[90]

Some contemporary libertarians defend PAP by arguing strenuously against Frankfurt-style counterexamples.[91] But Aquinas would presumably find such counterexamples to PAP acceptable. In the actual sequence of events, P's doing A is not brought about by any cause extrinsic to P, and nothing in the counterexample keeps us from supposing that it is only P's own intellect and will which are responsible for P's doing A.

These reasons for the rejection of PAP do not have the implication that libertarian free will is never accompanied by alternative possibilities. On the contrary, as we have seen, Aquinas emphasizes human ability to do otherwise, for example in his account of *liberum arbitrium*. It may in fact be true on his view that in most cases in which an agent acts with free will, the agent can do otherwise. The ability to do otherwise would then be what medieval logic calls 'an associated accident', a non-essential property that accompanies its subject most or even all of the time. Nonetheless, on Aquinas's account, human freedom even with regard to willing does not depend on her having alternative possibilities available to her; it is possible for an agent to act freely even when she cannot act otherwise than she does.

In what sense does Aquinas count as a libertarian if this is his account of human freedom? To answer this question, we need to be clearer about what is required for a theory of free will to count as libertarian.

Libertarianism and causal determination

Libertarian free will is sometimes characterized in this way:

> (L) an act of will, such as a decision, is free only if [1] "the decision [is] not ... causally determined, and ... [2] the agent could have avoided making it."[92]

As we have seen, Aquinas does not accept the second conjunct of (L), (L2). Because of the implications of Frankfurt-type counterexamples, many contemporary philosophers also suppose that (L2) is too strong. So perhaps (L2) is not a necessary condition for libertarian free will. But what about (L1), the claim that a decision is free only if the decision is not causally[93] determined?[94]

In connection with (L1), it is important to ask what theory of mind a libertarian account of free will is to be embedded in. Suppose we assume, as perhaps most theories of mind now do, that there is some sort of correlation between a mental state and a set of neural firings. This will be a one–many correlation: there will need to be many neural firings to produce one mental state. The mental state of recognizing a girl across a crowded room as your daughter, for example, requires the firing of neurons from the retina through the superior colliculus, the lateral geniculate nucleus of the thalamus, and various parts of the visual cortex, and into those parts of the brain specialized for memory and the recognition of faces. The entire causal sequence of many neural firings is required to produce one mental state, which is an effect of the sequence.

This characterization of the mental state as causally brought about by a series of neural firings does not presuppose any particular sort of correlation between the mental and the physical. It is compatible with either type-type or token-token identity theories, but it does not presuppose either of them. By saying that mental states are correlated with neural sequences, I mean to make only a vague association between mental states and neural sequences, compatible with various theories of relations between mind and brain. Those who think that the mental is identical to the physical can suppose that the mental states and the neural sequences are correlated because the mental states are the neural sequences. Non-reductive materialists can take the correlation as some version of emergence or supervenience. As far as that goes, even dualists such as Aquinas, who takes the soul to be the form of the body, can accept this characterization of the mental as correlated with the physical in virtue of the mind's being implemented in configurations of the physical.[95] Only the most extreme versions of Cartesian substance dualism will reject it. On an extreme version of Cartesian dualism – which Descartes himself may have held – some mental states, such as thinking and willing, go on only in the immaterial soul and are not mirrored by or correlated with brain processes.[96]

On any theory of the mind, including Aquinas's, that sees a stronger tie between mind and body than extreme Cartesian dualism, there will be some sort of correlation (up to and including identity) between mental processes and brain processes. On such non-Cartesian theories, however exactly we interpret the correlation between a physical state and a mental state, the mental state is a causal outcome of physical states.

If (L1) is right, however, only those mental acts which are not so much as correlated with patterns of neural firings can count as free. But then libertarianism could be held only by extreme Cartesian dualists. And, clearly, there are committed libertarians who reject any form of Cartesian dualism.[97] So (L1) is also too strong; to avoid making libertarianism a theory only extreme Cartesian dualists can hold, it needs to be revised. Because libertarians identify themselves at least in part by their opposition to compatibilism, libertarianism does need to rule out as non-free mental or bodily acts that are causally determined by something outside the agent. The claim that a free act is the outcome of a causal chain which originates in some cause external to the agent's own intellect and will is incompatible with libertarian free will. But the mere claim that a free act is the outcome of a causal chain is not.[98]

A more reasonable version of the relevant necessary condition for libertarianism is therefore this:

(L1') a decision is free only if it is not the outcome of a causal chain that originates in a cause outside the agent.

An objection

At this point someone may object. If we bring contemporary theories of the nature of the mind into the discussion of Aquinas's theory of free will, the objector will argue, then (unless we accept extreme Cartesian dualism) no volition can be free in the sense specified in (L1') . So, insofar as Aquinas's account centrally includes (L1') , it can be shown to be false. For ease of discussion we can put the objector's point in contemporary terms by taking the physical states with which the mental is correlated to be neural states. Then the objector's point can be formulated this way:

(O) (1) there are no uncaused neural events, and (2) the chain of causation eventuating in a human action will be traceable ultimately to something outside the agent.

So if mental states are causally determined by neural states, they will also be determined, more remotely, by causes outside the agent, contrary to the stipulation in (L1') .

If correct, this objection, which presupposes that the mental is embedded in a complete causal nexus governing the whole realm of the physical, is fatal to Aquinas's theory of free will since on Aquinas's theory nothing outside the agent exercises efficient causality on the will.[99] So the objection is worth considering in some detail.

The objector will perhaps meet little opposition regarding (O1), the claim that all neural events are caused. Is he also right in (O2), the claim that the chain of causation for neural events will lead outside the agent? Are all brain processes causally determined, ultimately, by something outside the agent? We might suppose that they would have to be. Otherwise, it would seem, brain events would be insulated from the physical interactions of the surrounding extra-bodily environment. Or, to put the point in terms more suitable to Aquinas's account, if nothing in nature exercises efficient causality on the will, then it looks as if the causal nexus of events is incomplete or even magically interrupted at the level of the will (or the intellect and the will).

But the objector's way of looking at things, which will perhaps seem obviously right to many people, rests on philosophical convictions that include both reductionism and determinism, as well as the assumption of causal completeness at the microlevel. Although reductionism comes in many forms, its different forms share a common attitude: all the sciences are reducible to physics, and all scientific explanation is ultimately formulable solely in terms of the microstructural. But this attitude discounts the importance of form, as Aquinas thinks of it (or levels of organization, as contemporary philosophers of biology tend to say). It also discounts the causal efficacy things have in virtue of their form or level of organization. (This feature of reductionism perhaps helps explain why it has come under special attack in philosophy of biology.[100] Biological function is frequently a feature of the way in which the microstructural components of something are organized, rather than of the intrinsic properties of the microcomponents themselves.)

In his attack on reductionism in *The Disorder of Things*, John Dupré takes the examples in his arguments against reductionism from ecology and population genetics.[101] On reductionist views, Dupré says:

> events at the macrolevel, except insofar as they are understood as aggregates of events at the microlevel – that is, as reducible to the microlevel at least in principle – are causally inert. This ... is the classical picture of Laplacean determinism, except that it does not depend on determinism, only the causal completeness ... of the microlevel.[102]

But, as Dupré's examples from biology make clear: "there are genuinely causal entities at many different levels of organization. And this is enough to show that causal completeness at one particular level [the microlevel] is wholly incredible."[103]

Dupré thinks that commitment to reductionism was strongly motivated by a belief in determinism and in causal completeness at the microlevel.[104] Consequently, Dupré thinks his arguments against reductionism are also part of an argument against these views as well. His arguments against reductionism provide, he claims, an "inversion of the reductionist modus ponens (causal completeness requires reductionism) into ... [an] antireductionist modus tollens (the failure of reductionism implies the failure of causal completeness)".[105]

If Dupré is correct in his views, which support Aquinas's metaphysical attitude towards the importance of form,[106] then, while it is uncontroversial that neural events are causally influenced by events outside the agent, it is not at all clear that they are causally determined by events outside the agent. If reductionism is false, then, as Dupré says:

> there is no reason why changes at one level may not be explained in terms of causal processes at a higher, that is, more complex, level. In the case of human action, the physical changes involved in and resulting from a particular action may perfectly well be explained in

terms of the capacity of the agent to perform an action of that kind.[107]

So if form counts for something in our ontology, as Aquinas supposes it should, then reductionism, and with it determinism and the assumption of causal completeness at the microlevel, should also be rejected. In that case, there can be causal efficacy at various levels of organization, including the level of human agents. A person's intellect and will can exercise real causal efficacy, from the top down, in the way Aquinas supposes they do. Dupré says:

> humans have all kinds of causal capacities that nothing else in our world has ... There is no good reason for projecting these uniquely human capacities in a reductionist style onto inanimate bits of matter. Nor is there anything ultimately mysterious about partic- ular causal capacities being exhibited uniquely by certain very complex entities.[108]

So, if Dupré's arguments are correct, if Aquinas's attitude towards the onto- logical importance of form is correct, then (O2) is false. Consequently, it cannot count as a reason for rejecting (L1´), and Aquinas's account of free will as dependent on an agent's ability to initiate a causal chain leading to action is not undermined by the objection.

Aquinas among the libertarians

Of course, (L1´) is not sufficient, on Aquinas's account or on the views of contemporary libertarians, for libertarian free will. What else is to be added, if it is not some version of PAP?

For Aquinas, human freedom is vested in human cognitive capacities and in the connection of the will to those capacities. As long as human acts orig- inate in those faculties, those acts count as free, even if the agent could not have done otherwise in the circumstances or the act of will is necessitated by natural inclinations of the intellect and the will. On Aquinas's account, the causal chain culminating in a free mental or bodily act cannot originate in a cause extrinsic to the agent[109] just because it must have its ultimate source in the proper functioning of the agent's own intellect and will.

What is sufficient for libertarian free will, then, on Aquinas's account, is that the ultimate source of an action be the agent's own will and cognitive faculties. Since this condition entails (L1´), we can reformulate the charac- terization of libertarianism in this way:

> (L´) an act is free if and only if the ultimate cause of that act is the agent's own will and intellect.

This understanding of human freedom also helps explain why acts generated randomly are no more free than acts brought about by causes extrinsic to the agent. Random acts do not have their ultimate source in the agent's own intellect and will, any more than acts brought about by causes extrinsic to the agent.

Some contemporary philosophers share Aquinas's basic intuition about the nature of freedom. For example, John Martin Fischer's account of moral responsibility is like Aquinas's account of free actions in this respect: Fischer thinks that moral responsibility is a function of an agent's reasons-responsive mechanism.[110] And one way of understanding the point of contention between compatibilists and libertarians of any sort is in terms of this question:

(Q) Is it possible for the mind (or the brain) to be a reasons-responsive mechanism if the only candidates for the origin of mental events (or neural events) are random accidents or causes outside the agent?

A compatibilist will answer (Q) in the affirmative; a libertarian such as Aquinas will answer it in the negative.

Part of what makes it hard to adjudicate between compatibilists and libertarians here is that we are so far from understanding how the brain (or the mind implemented in matter) can be a reasons-responsive mechanism at all, on anybody's theory of mind. Except for extreme Cartesian dualists, most contemporary philosophers suppose that the brain does constitute a reasons-responsive mechanism, but it is hard to see how a biological organ such as the brain can respond to reasons or process information. Neurobiologists are in no position to give anything other than promissory notes on this subject, and the best philosophical attempts are ultimately unpersuasive even if ingenious.[111] But unless we understand how a biological organ such as the brain can be an information-processor or a reasons-responsive mechanism, we will not be able to give a neurobiological account of our cognitive functioning which successfully adjudicates the different answers to (Q) given by compatibilists and libertarians, such as Aquinas.

What Dupré's arguments indicate and what Aquinas's position shows is that the question is not settled in favor of compatibilism by philosophical considerations either. Looked at from the point of view of philosophy, compatibilism appears to be a sort of codicil to reductionism and determinism. If all macrophenomena are reducible to microstructural phenomena and if there is a complete causal story to be told at the microlevel, then if we as macroscopic agents are free with respect to any of our actions, that freedom has to be not only compatible with but in fact just a function of the complete causal story at the microlevel. On the other hand, if the metaphysical attitudes of Aquinas or Dupré are right, compatibilism is an unnecessary concession, an attempt to preserve what we commonly believe about our control over our actions in the face of a philosophically mistaken and scientifically premature commitment to reductionism and determinism.

Part III

THE NATURE OF HUMAN EXCELLENCE

10

A REPRESENTATIVE MORAL VIRTUE
Justice

Introduction

In recent decades, at least in certain philosophical circles, justice has lost some of its lustre as a virtue for establishing and sustaining good relationships in a society. In the view of some feminist philosophers, for example, ethics based on justice need to be supplemented, or even supplanted, by an "ethics of care". As Annette Baier says:

> 'care' is the new buzz-word. It is not ... mercy that is to season justice, but a less authoritarian humanitarian supplement, a felt concern for the good of others and for community with them. The 'cold jealous virtue of justice' (Hume) is found to be too cold, and it is 'warmer' more communitarian virtues and social ideals that are being called in to supplement it.[1]

As Baier explains it, the ethics of care is meant to be a challenge

> to the individualism of the Western tradition, to the fairly entrenched belief in the possibility and desirability of each person pursuing his own good in his own way, constrained only by a minimal formal common good namely a working legal apparatus that enforces contracts and protects individuals from undue interference by others.[2]

One of the problems with the ethics of justice and with liberalism in general, on Baier's view, is that the rules of justice, understood in a liberal sense,

> do little to protect the young or the dying or the starving or any of the relatively powerless against neglect, or to ensure an education that will form persons to be *capable* of conforming to an ethics of care and responsibility.[3]

309

One might add here that they also do little to protect the powerful from the corruption of their own power. One of the things that contributes to the corruption absolute power is said to produce is the extreme reluctance of those in the entourage of an absolute ruler to do anything but flatter him. Delusion and megalomania, fed by flattery, are common among such rulers, and the results have been disastrous for the communities they govern. (Think of the pathetic end of the Taiping rebellion, for example, or of the tragedies of Maoist China.) And yet, on an ethics of justice interpreted according to the sort of liberal principles Baier calls attention to, where an individual's pursuit of his own projects is constrained only by a "minimal formal common good", there is no obligation to care for the well-being of the state in general, or to care for the state by caring for the moral and spiritual welfare of its rulers, either by explicit social dissent or by any form of civil disobedience.

It may strike some readers as odd to speak of social dissent or civil disobedience as care, but it would be a serious mistake to suppose that all care is gentle, nurturing, and soft. Not much care is evinced for a person or an institution if one is content to let that person or institution go to moral ruin, and preventing the moral ruin of institutions or persons may require aggressive public opposition to them. There was more care for Henry VIII in More's intransigence than in Woolsey's compliance.

Among those Baier excoriates for holding blindly to an ethics of justice are not only modern liberal philosophers but also Thomas Aquinas, whose ethics she characterizes as "a very legalistic moral theory"[4] – a phrase intended to show how far his ethics is from incorporating any of the concerns of an ethics of care, which is presumably much harder to encapsulate in laws than an ethics of justice is.

It is true that Aquinas frequently discusses natural law in his account of justice and elsewhere in his ethics. But I think it is a mistake to take Aquinas's theory of ethics as built around laws. First of all, although natural law is a codification of ethics, the laws do not ground ethics; they only express what is grounded in the natures of things or in conventional agreements among human beings. Aquinas says:

> Something becomes just in two ways. In one way, from the very nature of things, and this is called 'natural justice' (*ius naturale*). And, in another way, from a certain agreement among human beings, and this is called 'positive justice' ... Written law, of course, contains natural justice but it does not establish it, because natural justice does not have its force from law but from nature.[5]

Aquinas understands even divine law in the same sort of way, as divided between natural justice and the divine analogue to positive justice. So, he says, the divine law

310

has partly to do with those things which are naturally just but whose justice is hidden from human beings, and partly with those things which become just by divine institution. And so divine justice (*ius*) can be divided by these two [categories] in the same way as human justice. For in the divine law, there are certain things which are prescribed because they are good and prohibited because they are evil, and certain other things which are good because they are prescribed and evil because they are prohibited.[6]

Second, Aquinas's own structuring of his treatment of ethics is not based on laws or rules of any kind. On the contrary, the structuring principle for his account of ethics is the virtues. Furthermore, even in describing and analyzing the virtues, he devotes very little space to rules which codify those virtues or prescribe the way a virtuous person would act. He devotes much more attention to explicating the relation among ethical dispositions, including the ordered relations among certain virtues or certain vices and the ordered opposition of particular virtues and particular vices.[7]

But, most interesting of all, many of the provisions that proponents of an ethics of care are most concerned to bring into ethics, such as care for those at the bottom of the social hierarchy, are in fact in Aquinas's ethics, and in a place where philosophers advocating an ethics of care would not expect to find them: subsumed under justice. Baier supposes that an ethics of care is needed to supplement an ethics of justice. As I will show in what follows, Aquinas supposes that caring of certain sorts is integral to justice itself. The results of this way of interweaving care and justice can be surprising. For example, on Aquinas's account, it is morally obligatory to relieve the needs of the poor, and the poor have a right to the things necessary for life, such as food, clothing, and shelter.[8]

One of the problems faced by those who think an ethics of care should supplant, rather than supplement, an ethics of justice[9] is that it is not immediately apparent how to ward off certain sorts of exploitation on an ethics of care alone, without reference to justice. If the value of caring for others is the fundamental ethical value, then it is not easy to explain why it is morally acceptable to withhold care for others in the interests of pursuing one's own projects. And yet if there is no morally acceptable way of doing so, caring can become deeply destructive for the one caring. So, for example, Virginia Woolf describes the "angel in the house" who cared utterly unselfishly for others in this way:

> she never had a mind or a wish of her own, but preferred to sympathize always with the minds and wishes of others ... I did my best to kill her. My excuse, if I were to be had up in a court of law, would be that I acted in self-defence. Had I not killed her she would have killed me.[10]

The problem for ethical theorists regarding the apparently competing claims of an ethics of care and an ethics of justice has a certain resemblance to the problem for political theorists regarding the difficulty of "reconciling the standpoint of the collectivity with the standpoint of the individual", as Thomas Nagel puts it:[11]

> The impersonal standpoint in each of us produces ... a powerful demand for universal impartiality and equality, while the personal standpoint gives rise to individualistic motives and requirements which present obstacles to the pursuit and realization of such ideals ... When we try to discover reasonable moral standards for the conduct of individuals and then try to integrate them with fair standards for the assessment of social and political institutions, there seems no satisfactory way of fitting the two together ... [T]he problem of designing institutions that do justice to the equal importance of all persons, without making unacceptable demands on individuals, has not been solved.[12]

The impersonal standpoint, which is egalitarian and holds that "no one is more important than anyone else",[13] is one that Nagel associates with theories of social justice, such as that of Rawls.[14] And yet it shares a certain kind of problem with the ethics of care: it makes utopian demands on an individual in the interests of others, because if "*{e}veryone's* life matters as much as his does, [then] his matters no more than anyone else's."[15] But each person has personal projects and personal relationships which are specially important to her, and to which she wants to devote herself. The person who treats everyone equally, like Woolf's utterly unselfish woman, will have to subordinate or deny those things which are especially important *to her*. Just as some feminists maintain that the ethics of care has to be tempered with the ethics of justice, so Nagel maintains that the impersonal standpoint has to be interwoven with the personal standpoint. According to Nagel, the main question for political philosophy is how to combine the two; as he puts it, "What, if anything, can we all agree that we should do, given that our motives are not merely impersonal?".[16]

Nagel also thinks that this question is extremely difficult, maybe even practically impossible, to answer. This is so particularly with regard to the great division which now exists between the rich and the poor, not only within any given society, but especially between one country and another. "The distance in standard of living between the industrialized democracies and the underdeveloped countries is staggering ... No one could say that such a situation is acceptable at any level."[17]

The impersonal standpoint (like the ethics of care) requires that human suffering be relieved. And yet any way of relieving the massive suffering of those on the lower end of the social spectrum seems to require unacceptable sacrifices of those at the upper end. Nagel says, "there is no alternative available in the short run which it would be unreasonable for anyone to reject, on the basis of a plausible mixture of personal and impersonal motives".[18]

Nagel thinks that the problems of combining the impersonal and the personal standpoints (like the problem of combining the ethics of care with the ethics of justice) is a theoretical problem, not just a practical problem stemming from the moral failures of individuals and institutions:

> My belief is not just that all social and political arrangements so far devised are unsatisfactory. That might be due to the failure of all actual systems to realize an ideal that we should all recognize as correct. But there is a deeper problem – not merely practical but theoretical: We do not yet possess an acceptable political ideal.[19]

But there is in fact such an ideal proposed in the history of philosophy. Aquinas's work on justice not only subsumes an ethics of care but also combines Nagel's personal and impersonal standpoints. This is particularly the case with regard to economic institutions and social relations between privileged and disadvantaged in a society. No doubt there would be insuperable practical difficulties in getting from today's liberal democracies to the sort of society envisaged in Aquinas's account of justice. But his account does constitute a political ideal in which care and justice, the personal and the impersonal standpoints, are combined not only with regard to economic goods but also with regard to other goods a society can and should provide.

In what follows, I will present Aquinas's account of justice in some detail and then return, at the end of the chapter, to discuss its combination of care and justice, and of the personal and impersonal standpoints. Even though this lengthy chapter will be devoted to a presentation of Aquinas's account of justice, I will nonetheless just be scratching the surface. For example, I will not explain the way Aquinas situates justice in the broader context of the virtues, the opposed "capital vices", the "gifts of the Holy Spirit", the theological virtue of charity, the "beatitudes", or any of the other medieval lore in which Aquinas typically embeds his account of a virtue.[20] Furthermore, I will also leave to one side Aquinas's considerable theoretical discussion of justice as a general and special virtue,[21] as well as the "parts" of justice, the virtues annexed to justice, and the natural law. My excuse for leaving these and various other topics to one side is the usual one, that it is not possible to do everything in one chapter. My main concern in what follows will be the way general and special justice structure relations among people in a just society,[22] on Aquinas's account, and the light his account sheds on the tension between concern for ourselves and concern for others, of the sort Nagel and Baier discuss.

Justice and the nature of the state

What makes a state good, according to Aquinas, is that it is governed by justice and by law. In fact, on Aquinas's view, the phrase 'by justice and by law' is something of a pleonasm, since he holds that an unjust law is not a law.[23] As I explained above, for Aquinas, political justice comes in two sorts: natural and legal (or positive). Aquinas makes an analogy between natural justice and the foundations of the sciences. Just as in *scientia*, theoretical knowledge, there are some things which are naturally known, such as the indemonstrable first principles, so in practical knowledge there are some things which are naturally known, such as that one should not steal.[24] Natural justice is the justice which people are by nature inclined to accept as just in virtue of such knowledge.[25] It is the same everywhere because human nature is the same everywhere. Positive justice, on the other hand, has to do with things which become just or unjust in virtue of the fact that there are laws about them, such as driving on one side of the road rather than the other. Positive or legal justice is grounded in natural justice, not in the sense that it can be derived from natural justice but rather in the sense that it is a determination of natural justice. Natural justice determines that a thief be punished; positive or legal justice determines that he be punished with a fine of so and so much.[26]

Aquinas is often said to have a "profoundly anti-egalitarian" political theory (as one writer puts it) and to advocate monarchy as the best form of government.[27] But, formulated in this way, these claims are highly misleading, at best.

To begin with, for Aquinas, if a human society is to be a just one, it must be ordered to the common good, that is, the good for everyone in that society. According to Aquinas: "The further a government recedes from the common good, the more unjust that government is."[28]

Law (that is, just law, the only sort Aquinas recognizes as genuine law) also must be ordered to the common good. Laws which aim not at the common good but at the advantage of the lawgiver, or which impose burdens unequally on persons in the community, are acts of violence rather than laws.[29] Furthermore, in explaining why custom generally has the force of law, Aquinas says that, for a free people, the consent of the people represented in the custom counts more than the authority of the sovereign does, since the sovereign of a free people has the power to frame only such laws as represent the consent of the people.[30]

Moreover, although Aquinas does think that the best form of government has only one ruler, a monarch, he also thinks that a ruler counts as a monarch only in case the ruler serves the common good. The *worst* form of government, on his view, is one in which the one person governing rules for his own sake, and not for the common good.[31] Moreover, he says:

> An oligarchy, in which the good of a few is sought, recedes further from the common good than does a democracy, in which the good of many is sought; and a tyrannical government, in which the good of only one is sought, recedes further still. For *many* is nearer to *absolutely all* than *a few* is, and *a few* is nearer than *only one*.[32]

The way Aquinas distinguishes a monarch from a tyrant makes it clear that during the period of the rule of sovereigns in Europe, including the period in which Aquinas lived, it is unlikely that there ever was a ruler who counted as a monarch in Aquinas's sense. A monarch, Aquinas says:

> does not assign more of the good things [of his society] to himself than to others (unless perhaps according to an appropriate ratio based on distributive justice). And so it follows that the ruler works not for his own advantage but for the advantage of others.[33]

And he goes on to say,

> Since the ruler works for the multitude, the multitude should give him a reward, namely, honor and glory, which are the greatest goods that can be given by human beings. But if there are some rulers for whom honor and glory are insufficient rewards and who seek wealth [instead], these are unjust and tyrannical.[34]

Furthermore, the kind of monarchy Aquinas recommends is not hereditary. In the best form of government, on his view, the ruler is chosen by the people and from among the people.[35] A monarch should also share power not only with other highly placed persons in government but also with all the people. Aquinas says:

> the best form of government is found in that state or kingdom in which one person, who rules over everyone, is put in charge because of his virtue, and under him are certain others who participate in ruling because of their virtue. And yet the government is everyone's business (*ad omnes pertinet*), not only because [the rulers] can be chosen *from among* everyone but also because they are chosen *by* everyone. This is the best form of government, compounded of monarchy, insofar as one person rules, and aristocracy, insofar as many participate in ruling because of their virtue, and democracy, that is, the power of the people, insofar as the rulers can be chosen from among the people and the choosing of the ruler is the people's business.[36]

Aquinas also recognizes that it is very easy for a person who starts out as a monarch to become a tyrant. Not only does the ruler need to be a very virtuous person, but also, "his power should be restrained so that he cannot easily slide into tyranny".[37] If a monarch does degenerate into a tyrant, then Aquinas holds that it is legitimate for the people to remove him, even by tyrannicide if his rule is noxious enough to the common good.[38] And although Aquinas holds that sedition is a serious moral wrong, he thinks there cannot be a case of sedition against a ruler who rules for his own advantage as opposed to the advantage of all the people:

> A tyrannical government is not just, because it is ordered not to the common good but rather to the private good of the ruler ... For this reason, disturbing such a government does not fit the definition of *sedition* ... Instead, it is the tyrannical ruler who is seditious, because he encourages discord and sedition in the people subject to him in order to be master in greater security.[39]

Clearly, then, what Aquinas actually advocates as the best form of government is not the sort of government familiar to us from the period of monarchy in modern Europe, but something much nearer to representational government.

Commutative and distributive justice

The recurrent emphasis on the common good in Aquinas's account of just laws and the well-ordered state might seem to some people to have a worrisomely utilitarian ring to it. This is a concern to which I will return at the end of the chapter, when we can consider it in the light of all Aquinas has to say about justice. But it is worth noticing at this stage that Aquinas is concerned to ward off the sorts of cases that have seemed to many philosophers to plague utilitarianism, such as those in which the well-being of individuals is sacrificed to the well-being of the community. So, for example, Aquinas clearly supposes that the communal welfare of a state is enhanced to the degree to which its citizens are Christian. One might suppose, then, that on Aquinas's views, Jews should be compelled to convert and their children should be baptized into the faith against their parents' will for the sake of the common good. But, in fact, Aquinas opposes both the forcible conversion of Jews and compulsory baptism for Jewish infants.[40] Furthermore, he thinks that in general "the Church does not have the right (*ad ecclesiam autem non pertinet*) to punish unbelief in those who have never received the faith."[41]

Concerning the forcible baptism of Jewish children, he says, "it would be against natural justice if, before a child reaches the age of reason, it is taken from the care of its parents or anything is done to it against the wishes of the parents."[42]

To begin to see why he takes such attitudes towards individuals and why his emphasis on the common good does not, apparently, saddle him with the problems common to certain sorts of utilitarianism, it is helpful to consider the Aristotelian distinction between commutative and distributive justice which Aquinas adopts and reworks.

Aquinas makes many divisions of justice,[43] but the division of justice into its species yields the two Aristotelian kinds of justice: commutative and distributive justice. Commutative justice governs relations between individuals within a state; distributive justice governs relations between an individual and the state as a whole.[44] In both cases, what is just is what is equal, and what is unjust is what is unequal; but what is equal is determined in different ways in the different species of justice.

What is equal is a mean between more and less, Aristotle says. For commutative justice, that mean is arithmetical.[45] That is, it is an equality of quantity:[46] "the just is nothing other than having the same amount after a transaction as before."[47]

So if at the beginning of a transaction, Joe has $50 worth of firewood and Tom has $75 worth of mulch, then if Joe gives Tom half his firewood but gets nothing in return, they will not have the same amount after the transaction as before. To restore justice in this situation, Tom needs to give $25 worth of mulch, or just $25, to Joe, so that both again have property valued at the same amount as before their transaction.[48]

For distributive justice, on the other hand, the mean is geometric, a matter of proportionality. Any society has certain common goods to distribute – money and honor, for example – and certain burdens to impose – expenses and labor;[49] and these all need to be distributed fairly. The mean for such distribution, however, is a matter of proportionality. If laborers are paid equally for doing unequal amounts of work, the mean of distributive justice is not preserved.[50] If Joe has worked twice the time Tom has, the two workers are treated equally if Joe is given twice what Tom is given.[51]

Just distribution is thus proportional to desert, but what counts as desert varies from society to society. In aristocracies, it is virtue, Aquinas says; in oligarchies, wealth or nobility of birth. In democracy, it is being a free citizen, so that the goods of the society are equally distributed to all.[52]

Although the terms in which Aquinas's discussion is couched sometimes suggest that the transactions of distributive and commutative exchange are largely economic, the same general analysis holds, Aquinas thinks, even when what is being exchanged is not economic or even readily measurable. So, for example, he thinks that if one man hits another in such a way as to cause an injury, there is a commutative injustice.[53] Something has been taken from or inflicted on the one injured without compensation, and the one hitting has gained, at least in power, over his victim. And so, after the blow, the two stand in a different relation from that in which they were before. Consequently, they do not have the same after the "transaction" as they did before it.[54]

For these sorts of reasons, Aquinas thinks that it is an injustice to kill an innocent person, to steal, to think ill of another person without sufficient cause[55] − or to baptize Jewish infants against the will of their parents. The sorts of cases which have been thought to trouble certain varieties of utilitarianism tend to involve circumstances in which the rights of some individual are violated for the sake of the general welfare. Any such case will involve an injustice towards the individual in question, on Aquinas's view. And, he says: "no one ought to injure another unjustly in order to promote the common good."[56]

Commutative justice and equality

The way Aquinas understands commutative justice leads him into a decidedly uncapitalistic attitude towards economic exchange. This attitude can be readily surmised from his general characterization of injustice:

> we speak of injustice with regard to inequality between one person and another, as for example when a person wants to have more [than another person has] of goods such as riches and honors and less of evils such as labor and losses.[57]

And he often characterizes justice in such a way as to bring out its connection with equality as well: "it is characteristic of justice ... to direct a human being in his relations with others, for justice implies equality of a certain sort."[58]

But we do not really need to do any surmising, because Aquinas spells out his economic views in great detail. He has strenuous standards for what constitutes bare *justice* in regard to economic exchange. To begin with, on his view, the point of buying and selling is the common advantage of both parties. Insofar as one party is considerably more advantaged or more burdened than the other, the exchange is not just.

In addition, Aquinas thinks there is a just price for a thing, which is measured not by the demand for that thing but rather by the thing's own worth. It is not entirely clear how Aquinas supposes the worth of a thing is to be assessed, apart from demand for it, but he is quite explicit about the wrongness of disregarding such worth in financial transactions: "to sell a thing for more than it is worth or to buy it for less than it is worth is in itself unjust and unlawful".[59]

Even in case the buyer has a great need for what is being sold, the seller cannot justly raise the price unless he himself would suffer a corresponding loss by selling. Demand alone is not a just reason for raising prices. On the contrary, Aquinas thinks that the Golden Rule applies even to economic exchange: "No one wants something to be sold to him for more than it is worth. Consequently, no one ought to sell something to another for more than it is worth."[60]

Furthermore, Aquinas is opposed to what we might call 'economic luck'. Any sort of conscious deceit with regard to buying and selling constitutes fraud, in Aquinas's view. But in addition to fraud, an exchange is unjust if the seller or buyer is unwittingly disadvantaged. A seller who does not know the faults of something he sells is not guilty of fraud, but he still has to make compensation for the faults when they are revealed.[61] On the other hand, if a seller makes a mistake and sells gold thinking it to be copper, the buyer has to make restitution when the mistake comes to light.[62]

Aquinas supposes that the injustice of unequal economic exchange, of the sorts just sketched, has serious moral and theological consequences. For Aquinas, if an act of wrongdoing is of sufficient moral gravity, it breaks relations between the agent who does it and a good God, thereby imperiling the agent's salvation. It constitutes a mortal sin, a moral wrongdoing that is spiritually deadly to the wrongdoer. Unjust economic exchange is a moral wrong of this sort. Worse yet, until A restores to B what A has gained unjustly from B (for example by buying as copper from B what B did not know to be gold), the injustice of A's act remains. That is why Aquinas says, "it is necessary to salvation to restore to a person what was taken away from him unjustly".[63]

For my purposes here, what is important is not the theology in these lines, but the uncompromising moral attitude towards economic injustice which they reveal.

As is well known, like other medievals of his day, Aquinas is strongly opposed to usury, that is, to the practice of charging interest on money lent. One of his reasons for opposing usury is commonly cited, namely, that (in his view and the view of many medievals) the use of money is not the kind of thing which should be sold. But he also has another reason, which shows his attitude towards economic exchanges: "it is manifest that this leads to inequality, which is contrary to justice".[64]

Because the money gained by usury is gained unjustly, on Aquinas's view, he thinks that it too must be restored on pain of losing one's salvation. When the Duchess of Brabant asks Aquinas whether she could lawfully expropriate property from the Jews since they have gained it by usury, Aquinas concurs wholeheartedly, since it is unjust to keep what is unjustly acquired. Only, he explains to the Duchess, it would of course be equally unjust for *her* to keep what she takes from the Jews, on the same grounds, namely, that it is unjust to keep what was gotten by usury. On the other hand, if the Duchess's intention is to find the people from whom the property was taken by usury and restore that property to them, that would be acceptable.[65]

It should be evident at this point that the entire notion of profit in exchange is problematic for Aquinas. For example, when he asks whether it is lawful to sell something for a higher price than was paid for it, the first objection he considers against an affirmative answer is this:

> If a man ... sells a thing for more than he paid for it, then it must be the case either that he bought it for less than it is worth or that he sold it for more than it is worth.[66]

And, as we have just seen, either practice is unjust, on Aquinas's view. In reply, Aquinas concedes, with some reluctance,[67] that "profit, which is what trade aims at, ... does not by itself imply anything having to do with vice or contrary to virtue",[68] although he still thinks that trading for profit has something base about it since it serves the lust for money. Nonetheless, Aquinas explains, by trading, a man might seek only moderate profit for the upkeep of his household. In that case, he is not seeking profit itself, but only an appropriate reward for his labor in the business of trading.

In the same spirit, Aquinas asks whether it is lawful for lawyers to charge for their services. He answers that it is lawful, just as it is lawful for doctors to charge for their services, but in both cases only if the fee is moderate and takes into account the client's ability to pay. If doctors or lawyers take an immoderate fee, they act wickedly and against justice.[69]

Economics and Old Testament law

To understand Aquinas's view of economic justice, it is also helpful to look briefly at Aquinas's attitude towards the economic measures in Old Testament law. Aquinas accepts the traditional view that this law is no longer binding on Christians, who live under a new dispensation; but he thinks it would nonetheless be morally acceptable for a Christian ruler to govern his state by it.[70] Furthermore, Aquinas argues, in a long article headed by a dozen objections to the contrary, there is something fitting about what the Old Testament law enjoins.[71] He is particularly supportive of Old Testament laws regulating property.

Some contemporary philosophers maintain that property is held justly in case it is part of an initial just distribution of resources or it is acquired as a result of a just transfer from someone who himself holds it justly. So, for example, Robert Nozick's entitlement theory of property rests on three main principles:

1   a principle of transfer – whatever is justly acquired can be freely transferred;

2   a principle of just initial acquisition;

3   a principle of rectification of injustice – how to deal with holdings if they were unjustly acquired or transferred.[72]

Coupled with an account (such as Nozick's) of an absolute right to property, these principles give us a fairly unrestrained capitalism.

Like Nozick, Aquinas thinks that there needs to be a just initial acquisition, and he approves of the Old Testament system because its principle of initial acquisition consists in the granting of equal shares: "The [Old Testament] law provided a threefold remedy with regard to the regulation of possessions. The first [was] that possessions should be distributed equally, in accordance with the number of men."[73]

It is clear from his views of buying and selling, presented above, that Aquinas thinks there also needs to be a just system of transfer as well as a system for rectifying unjust transfers. In discussing Old Testament law, he supports a principle that has some resemblance to Nozick's first principle, namely, that "private persons have power over the things they possess, and so they can transfer them at will among themselves, for example, by buying, selling, or giving".[74]

So far, then, the account of ownership Aquinas finds in the Old Testament and approves of looks very much like Nozick's. But Aquinas also adduces a principle from Old Testament law which makes his own account decidedly uncapitalistic and different from Nozick's: "A second remedy is that possessions should not be alienated for ever, but after a certain time should revert to their [original] possessors."[75]

Old Testament law prescribes that every fiftieth year must be a Jubilee year. In that year, possessions revert to their original owners. It is clear that this rule does not apply to every thing that can be bought and sold, because the Old Testament itself mentions certain exceptions; but, among the things that do revert, the law specifically includes land and slaves. In the Jubilee year, slaves bought anytime in the half-century before go free, and land reverts to those who sold it within the preceding Jubilee period.[76] It is clear that this rule applied in an agrarian economy makes the accumulation of vast wealth much more difficult.

That, in fact, seems to be the intent of the rule. The long list of commands about things which have been bought and must be returned in the Jubilee year is punctuated by lines of this sort: "You shall not therefore oppress one another, but you shall fear your God" (Lev. 25:17).

Aquinas himself understands the Old Testament economic laws to have this purpose. The judicial precepts of the Old Testament, Aquinas says, have as their aim preserving equality among men.[77] He himself shares the view he attributes to those precepts. Riches are called 'riches of iniquity', he says, because wealth is not distributed equally among all people, but some are affluent while others are in need.[78]

The economic system endorsed by these principles of ownership, which Aquinas approves of in his review of Old Testament law, looks a little like a game of Monopoly with time limits. Players begin with equal shares. Then unbridled capitalism operates for a fixed period – half a century, according to Leviticus. At that point, more or less everything reverts to the original position. Whether such an economic system ever was feasible in any society is not clear. What is interesting for my purposes here is that Aquinas supposes that if such a system were feasible, it would be just because it would help to promote and preserve economic equality.

Theft and alms: morally acceptable ownership

In fact, however, Aquinas's position is even less favorable to capitalism than his approval of the Old Testament law suggests. Consider, for example, what he says about theft. Theft is so serious a moral wrong that, on Aquinas's view, it counts as a mortal sin. The question then arises for him whether it is similarly an act of mortal sin to steal because of need. Aquinas's answer is more than a little surprising; it is expressed succinctly in the *sed contra* of the reply:

> In cases of need, all things are common. And so it does not seem to
> be a sin [of any kind] if one person [in great need] takes a thing
> belonging to [the abundance of] another, for it has been made
> common as a result of [his] need.[79]

Although theft is always a mortal sin, taking in need what belongs to another's abundance does not count as mortal sin because it does not count as theft.[80]

As far as that goes, Aquinas thinks it *is* a mortal sin to acquire or keep more property than is necessary to sustain one in one's condition in life,[81] by which he means not only the sort of job and position in society an individual has[82] but also the number and nature of his dependents.[83] In fact, in considering an argument that failure to give to the poor constitutes theft on the part of the rich, he objects, but only on the grounds that theft, strictly speaking, requires secrecy. Nonetheless, he concedes the general point of the argument; keeping back what is due to another, he says, inflicts the same sort of injury as theft.[84] Similarly, he quotes with approval Augustine's claim that the person who refuses to give tithes keeps what belongs to another since the tithes are given to the ministers of the Church for the use of the poor.[85]

For reasons of this sort, he also thinks that almsgiving is morally obligatory.[86] Although he treats almsgiving in connection with his discussion of charity in *ST*, so that almsgiving is a free expression of love, he also thinks that the failure to give alms is a mortal sin.[87] He considers an objection based on a Nozick-like view of rights over property: since it is lawful for everyone to use and keep what is his own, almsgiving cannot be morally obligatory. Aquinas's response is interesting and important for my purposes here. Although our possessions belong to us as regards *ownership*, he says, as regards the *use* of these possessions they belong not only to us but also to all those who could be helped by what we have left over after attending to our own needs. And he quotes with approval Basil's claim: "It is the hungry man's bread that you withhold, the naked man's cloak that you have stored away, the shoe of the barefoot that you have left to rot, the money of the needy that you have buried underground."[88]

Contrast this with, for example, Locke's position on property:

> if [a person] would give us Nuts for a piece of Metal, pleased with its colour; or exchange his Sheep for Shells, or Wool for a sparkling Pebble, or a Diamond, and keep those by him all his Life, he invaded not the Right of others, he might heap up as much of these durable things as he pleased; the *exceeding of the bounds of his* just *Property* not lying in the largeness of his Possession, but the perishing of any thing uselessly in it.[89]

Waste, not wealth, is troubling to Locke. Unlike Aquinas, he supposes that there is a right to unlimited accumulation of property and that the inequality attendant on it is just.[90] Locke's political philosophy is consequently compatible with capitalism in a way Aquinas's is not.[91]

A puzzle: morally acceptable ownership and commutative justice

At this point, however, a puzzle arises, because Aquinas's views about the obligation to give alms seem in tension with what he says about commutative justice.

Suppose that an almsgiver A, who has property equivalent to $100, meets a beggar B, who has property equivalent to only $1. Suppose, then, that A gives B something worth $1. Exchanges of this sort are morally obligatory, on Aquinas's view. But at the end of the exchange A has property equivalent to $99, and B has property worth $2.

What, then, becomes of Aquinas's Aristotelian view of commutative justice? On that view, an exchange between two individuals will be just if what they exchange is of equal value, and their positions at the end of the exchange are the same as they were at the beginning. But if one is obligated to give away all one's possessions that are not needed to sustain one in one's condition in life, if one is obligated to give alms, then the poor have a right to an exchange in which the poor person gives nothing at all.[92] If almsgiver A required beggar B to give A back the equivalent of $1 (in money or in property) because A had given B $1, A would be violating his obligations towards the poor. Consequently, the obligatoriness of almsgiving appears to violate rather than preserve justice in commutative exchanges. If when B begs alms of A, what A and B exchange is equal in value, the commutativity of this exchange makes it unjust, not just, since in such a case A would be failing to give alms to B and so would be violating the almsgiving obligation. On the other hand, an exchange which does constitute almsgiving seems to be an exchange that violates the conditions for commutative justice.

So it looks as if either Aquinas's account of commutative exchanges gives us a formula for justice-preserving exchanges between individuals in a society, or Aquinas is right in holding that failure to give alms is an injustice, but not both.

One way to resolve this puzzle is to recognize that there is not for Aquinas the absolute right of ownership which Nozick supposes there is. Understanding the root of the difference between Aquinas's view of morally acceptable ownership and a view such as Nozick's helps to explain not only Aquinas's attitude towards almsgiving but also other economic views of his.

In two different questions, Aquinas asks whether it is natural and whether it is lawful for a human being to possess anything at all. His answers to both questions are in the affirmative, but highly nuanced.[93]

In reality, all things belong only to God, he says. It is human agreement, added to natural justice and supplementing it, which allows certain people to claim certain things as their own. Consequently, it is appropriate for human beings to *hold* certain things as their property, and to *acquire* and *dispose* of certain things as their own. On the other hand, God's purpose is that the earth should sustain his people, and human agreements cannot contravene God's purposes. Therefore, when it comes to the *use* of property, a person ought to hold his possessions not as his own but as (in principle) common, that is, ready to use them for the common good.[94] For this reason, Aquinas says that a rich man does not act unlawfully if he precludes others in taking possession of something that was common, but he acts wrongfully if he indiscriminately prevents others from its use.[95]

It is clear that ownership in this sense is something much less absolute than Nozick has in mind. It resembles in some but not all respects the sort of ownership with which the federal government owns public parks, where the ownership consists largely in a duty to preserve and maintain the land for the use of all people in the society. It is perhaps most nearly like the kind of ownership with which the wage earner in a family owns the money she makes. The money she earns is certainly *her* money; she can rightfully hold it or dispose of it at her discretion, as her own. On the other hand, it is also clear that she does wrong if she does not consider the needs of her whole family in the way in which she uses her money. If she buys imported designer furniture instead of food or medical care needed for her children, she is blameworthy, even if it is her own money that she spends on the furniture. Aquinas thinks it is similarly morally obligatory for people who have property in abundance to consider the needs of the poor in general in deciding how to use the property they own.

This attitude of Aquinas's towards ownership also explains his view that taking from someone else's abundance to relieve a great need is not theft, however much it may resemble what is prohibited as theft. In case of great need, the human agreement that certain things belong to certain people is void, and things become common. That is why what one person takes from the abundance of another person to alleviate his need becomes the property of the needy man by reason of his need.[96] Since all things really belong to God and God has ordained them for the sustenance of all his creatures, it is not theft if one person in great need takes from the abundance of another. Distribution of God's property in accordance with God's will and purposes cannot count as theft.[97]

Clearly, this attitude towards property also helps explain Aquinas's view that what the rich have in abundance is owed to the poor to relieve their need:

> Things which belong to human justice (*jus*) cannot derogate from natural or divine justice. Now according to the natural order established by divine providence, the purpose of earthly things is the succoring of human needs. For this reason, the division and appropriation of things stemming from human justice does not alter the fact that human needs must be met from things of this sort. And for that reason, the things which some people have in superabundance is owed, by natural justice, for the sustenance of the poor.[98]

These passages suggest a way to reconcile the tension between Aquinas's account of commutative justice and his attitude towards such things as almsgiving, theft, and the Old Testament law of the Jubilee year. As far as almsgiving and other religiously motivated economic exchanges are concerned, although the exchanges are between one individual and another within a society, nonetheless what is at issue is not a commutative exchange. If such exchanges fit anywhere within the species of justice, they would seem to fall more nearly under *distributive* rather than *commutative* justice. Insofar as everything *really* belongs to God, God plays a role analogous to the role of society in more usual explanations of distributive justice. Furthermore, in holding or disposing of property any human being is in effect acting as God's agent, helping to effect the distribution of property within a society.[99]

I do not mean to say that almsgiving should be interpreted literally as an instance of distributive justice. Aquinas does not include almsgiving within his treatise on justice in *ST*, and it is clear that on his view almsgiving falls under justice only if justice is considered as a general virtue, comprising all moral obligation. My point is only that while the formal features of alms-giving, an exchange of property between two individuals within a state, make almsgiving appear to fall within the range of exchanges governed by commutative justice, the appearance is misleading. In fact, what Aquinas has to say about the nature and limits of ownership shows that these exchanges, in spite of their appearance, share certain important features with those exchanges that are governed by distributive justice.

It is easiest to apply this interpretation to Aquinas's remarks about the Jubilee year. In the fiftieth year, A has to restore to B land A bought from B in the preceding half-century, even though B gives A nothing in return. If we think of the exchange as a commutative exchange between two individuals in a society, it looks as if Aquinas is committed to saying that it is both just and unjust – unjust by the rules of commutative justice,[100] but just insofar as it conforms to the precepts regarding the Jubilee year.[101] But if we take the exchange to be a case in which A is acting, as it were, unofficially or even unwittingly, as God's agent in the process of arranging a distribution of what belongs to God in accordance with God's purposes, then the puzzle disappears.[102] Certain sorts of economic exchange between individuals in a society, which seem to be cases of commutative exchanges,[103] are, on this interpretation, better understood as being more nearly like distributive exchanges.

For the same reason, there is no violation of commutative justice when A fulfills a moral obligation by giving alms to B and getting nothing in return. Contrary to appearances, this is not the sort of exchange to which commutative justice applies. It is rather a matter of distributing what ultimately belongs to God in accordance with God's purposes.

Two more things are worth noticing here as regards Aquinas's economic views. First of all, the distinction between the deserving and the unde-serving poor, which plays a large role in the Enlightenment and Victorian periods,[104] does not so much as rear its head in Aquinas's remarks on almsgiving. Aquinas argues that it is a mortal sin to keep more of one's property than is necessary to sustain one in one's condition in life, but he says nothing about the moral characteristics persons must have in order to qualify as recipients of alms. On the contrary, the only thing he mentions in connection with the recipient of alms is the recipient's poverty. In explaining the conditions for almsgiving, Aquinas says that two things are necessary, one on the part of the giver and one on the part of the recipient: on the part of the giver, that he have a surplus; on the part of the recip-ient, that he have a need.[105]

Similarly, in arguing that a person in extreme need can simply help himself to the property of the person who has abundant possessions, Aquinas makes no qualifications on the basis of the way in which such a person came to be in extreme need. In much the same spirit, Aquinas cautions the Duchess of Brabant about the limits of morally acceptable expropriation of the Jews. She can legitimately expropriate the property of the Jews if she wants to find those persons from whom the Jews made money by usury and restore to those persons what was taken from them by usury. Nonetheless, he says, her expropriation has to be limited by the needs of the Jews. Even the proceeds of usury, which from Aquinas's point of view are like the proceeds of theft, cannot be taken away from the Jews if they are among the necessary resources of life for them.[106]

Second, one of the ways of distinguishing types of societies from one another, on Aquinas's view, is the nature of the desert in accordance with which they make distribution. In an aristocratic society, those who receive a larger distribution of goods are the virtuous; in an oligarchic society, they are those who are nobly born or who already have wealth. In democratic societies, distribution is made equally to all.[107]

It is worth asking what sort of society Aquinas is in effect recommending in the type of distribution he advocates.

It certainly is not an oligarchy. Honor is one of the goods to be distributed in a society. But, on Aquinas's view, whoever honors a rich person because of his wealth does a serious wrong,[108] and the wrong in question is a violation of *distributive* justice.[109]

It does not seem to be aristocracy either, however. In considering what is owed to the poor, Aquinas looks only to the fact that the poor are in need, and not at all to the question of whether the poor have the right sort of virtuous moral character for distribution to be made to them.

It is true that in a just society as Aquinas envisages it, there will not be equal shares for all since, within certain bounds, he seems content to let individuals accumulate goods at will. On the other hand, the prohibition against retaining more of one's possessions than is needed is clearly designed to keep the inequalities among persons small.[110] So, if we consider the kinds of societies Aquinas recognizes, the type of distribution Aquinas recommends, which is designed to promote equality among all the people in the society, makes his just society look more like a democracy than like any other kind of society he recognizes.

Corporal and spiritual almsgiving

So far I have discussed almsgiving in terms of giving money or other property to the poor. But, in fact, Aquinas recognizes two sorts of alms: corporal and spiritual. Corporal almsdeeds are feeding the hungry, giving drink to the thirsty, clothing the naked, finding shelter for the homeless, visiting the sick, ransoming the captive, and burying the dead. Spiritual almsdeeds, on the other hand, are instructing the ignorant, counseling the doubtful, comforting the sorrowful, giving moral reproof to a wrongdoer, forgiving injuries, bearing with those who trouble us, and praying for all. All of these are a kind of alms, too, in Aquinas's view, and like corporal almsgiving, they are a matter of obligation. I want to focus just on giving moral reproof to a wrongdoer. Aquinas's designation for this activity is handier than the clumsy locution I have translated it into, and so from here on I will use his expression: "fraternal correction"; but the reader should remember that the sort of correction at issue here is moral.[111] Fraternal correction, as we shall see, raises a more troublesome version of the puzzle posed by Aquinas's views of alms owed to the poor.

The primary good aimed at by fraternal correction is the amendment of the wrongdoer. Its secondary aim is to remedy the wrongful act of the wrongdoer insofar as that act affects others. In either case, it is obligatory.[112]

There are some limited circumstances in which failing to reprove a wrongdoer is *not* a serious moral wrong.[113] The most important of these occurs when it seems very probable that the wrongdoer will get morally worse as a result of correction (although, as I explain below, this consideration may be overridden by the needs of the community).[114] Furthermore, there is no obligation to seek out wrongdoers in order to reprove them, or to spy on people in order to know what their wrong actions are. There is a still further set of constraints derived from the primary aim of fraternal correction: one must find the proper way and the proper time in which to engage in fraternal correction; not just any mode of fraternal correction is morally acceptable, let alone obligatory.[115] Finally, of course, the one accusing needs to have good evidence of the guilt of the accused.[116] Slander and gossip are serious moral wrongs, too.[117]

On the other hand, however, fraternal correction *is* a matter of moral obligation in those cases in which we know about someone else's serious wrongdoing, the opportunity arises to offer him correction in the proper way, and there is no very strong reason to suppose that reproving the wrongdoing will make him worse. In such circumstances, the omission of fraternal correction is a serious moral failing. In fact, Aquinas quotes with approval Augustine's line that the failure to correct a sinner makes one worse than the sinner himself.[118]

Furthermore, the obligation to reprove a wrongdoer holds even when the wrongdoer is superior in some official sense to the one doing the reproving. Sanctity of office or person provides no exception either; fraternal correction is obligatory even when the wrongdoer is a priest or church official.[119] In such cases, the one reproving should take special care to be respectful and to give the admonition in private if possible. But in cases of grave wrongdoing which endangers others in the society, even public denunciation of church officials is obligatory if private admonition is unavailing.[120]

In general, private admonition ought to precede public denunciation; but if the wrongdoing is public and the welfare of those affected by the wrongdoing is in jeopardy, then public denunciation is required. The one doing the reproving must try to protect the good name of the wrongdoer, but if only public denunciation will keep the wrongdoer from seriously harming others, then public denunciation as a first step is obligatory.[121]

Aquinas is not blind to the fact that sometimes fraternal correction, whether private or public, comes at quite a cost to the person engaging in it. But he takes a stern line in this regard. The moral wrong of failing to engage in fraternal correction is not lessened because the one in a position to reprove is afraid of the wrongdoer and what he can do. Failure to reprove is a serious moral wrong even if one fails to reprove the wrongdoer because one believes that doing so can result in death to oneself, or at least great harm.[122] Quoting Augustine with approval, Aquinas says, "when ... one fears what people may think, or that one may suffer grievous pain or death",[123] omitting fraternal correction is still a mortal sin.

Connected to this view of private and public dissent is Aquinas's attitude towards flattery. Flattery is discussed in the treatise on justice in *ST*, and what Aquinas says about it is, in a sense, the other side of the coin of his views about fraternal correction.[124]

There are certain circumstances in which flattery is not a serious moral wrong, as, for example, when it does not encourage the one flattered in wrongdoing, or when it arises from something as harmless as a general desire to please. But sometimes flattery praises something which is in fact morally wrong, so that it is an encouragement to the one flattered to act wrongly. In such a case, flattery is a mortal sin. Furthermore, it remains a mortal sin even if the flatterer does not intend to lead the flattered person into wrongdoing, but the flattery has such an effect anyway. So, for example, Mao Tse Tung's doctor, Li Zhisui, by his own admission, habitually flattered Mao not with the conscious intention of making Mao morally worse but just in order to stay in his good graces.[125] On Aquinas's view of flattery, however, insofar as the continual flattery to which Mao was subjected did make him morally worse, then even though the flatterers did not intend their flattery to have such an effect, the flattery was itself a serious moral wrong.[126]

As Aquinas's views about fraternal correction make clear, it is not enough simply to refrain from participating in another's wrongdoing by omitting to flatter him. One is also obligated to speak out. That is, one is obligated to rebuke, in some suitable way, those wrongdoers whom one is in a position to correct, either with private admonition or with publicly expressed social dissent. Doing so is not an act of heroism, an act of supererogatory goodness, or an act conforming to the counsels of perfection. Failure to engage in fraternal correction is a serious enough moral wrong that it imperils one's eternal salvation and counts as a mortal sin. For Aquinas, the spiritual almsdeed of fraternal correction, like the corporal almsdeed of succoring the poor, is a matter of justice — general justice in some cases, commutative or distributive justice in others.

A puzzle: fraternal correction and commutative justice

There is something puzzling as well as impressive in this stern attitude of Aquinas's. Consider, for example, what he says about detraction. Detraction comes in various forms, but one kind has to do with false accusation. We have a case of detraction of this sort when A publicly makes certain claims about wrongdoing on B's part in order to do a significant injury to B's reputation, although A does not have good evidence for the accusation and B is in fact not guilty of such wrongdoing.[127] Detraction is a violation of commutative justice.[128] Aquinas's idea here seems to be that in engaging in detraction against B, A is taking something of value from B, some part of his good name, and giving nothing of equal or greater value in return.[129] The resulting exchange is thus unjust.

But engaging in fraternal correction or social dissent at the cost of serious harm to oneself is also an exchange in which one gives something – one's social standing, economic well-being, or even one's life – and receives in return no benefit for oneself. Fraternal correction differs from detraction largely in the evidence and motive of the accuser, and the truth or falsity of the accusation.[130] If it violates justice for a victim of detraction to lose something of value to himself and gain nothing of value in return, as Aquinas holds with regard to detraction, then why is it morally obligatory in cases of fraternal correction for a person to give up something – perhaps something of much greater value than reputation – with no return?

Pointing out that fraternal correction does not count for Aquinas as an instance of commutative justice is not helpful. What one wants to know, in effect, is *why* it is not. Given the sort of principle underlying Aquinas's account of commutative justice, it seems as if it should not be morally obligatory on his view for someone to give up something of value to himself without any provision for his receiving something of equal worth.[131]

Of course, it is perhaps this very feature of fraternal correction that accounts for its being included as a species of almsgiving. And this way of putting the puzzle calls attention to the connection between this case, in the genus of spiritual alms, and the case of giving one's goods to the poor, in the genus of corporal alms. Succoring the poor is also obligatory, and in that case, too, the one giving alms gives up something of value to himself and does not receive anything in return.

In the case of corporal almsgiving, which also raised a puzzle in connection with commutative justice, the solution to the puzzle was to recognize that what looks like an exchange of the sort regulated by commutative justice is in fact more nearly like an exchange governed by distributive justice. Because of Aquinas's views of the nature of property, there is no absolute right of ownership; on Aquinas's account, an individual has a right neither to unlimited accumulation nor to total control over the disposal of what is, formally speaking, his own. Because all property really is God's, and because God's purposes encompass the well-being of all his creatures, those purposes take precedence over an individual's right to control what he otherwise can legitimately regard as belonging to him.

Can Aquinas's attitude towards corporal alms, as interpreted here, give some insight into his attitude towards the spiritual alms of fraternal correction? I am inclined to think so.

To see why, it is helpful to digress briefly and consider what Aquinas says about suicide. In *ST*, suicide is discussed in the question on murder, and Aquinas treats the topic of murder in connection with his account of the vices opposed to commutative justice.[132] It is not so hard to see why murder should count as a violation of commutative justice, but in what sense could suicide also count as such a violation? One cannot take away from oneself more than one gets in return. Aquinas considers an argument of this sort in the first objection in the article on suicide. Murder is contrary to justice, the objection goes, but no one can do an injustice to oneself; therefore, suicide cannot fall under the prohibition against murder.[133]

In the reply to the objection, Aquinas grants the objection's central premise that no one can do an injustice to himself. But, Aquinas says, suicide is an injustice against the community and against God.[134] This attitude is explained in the body of the article. In the second reason Aquinas gives for the prohibition against suicide, echoing Aristotle, he says, "every part, as a part, belongs to the whole. Now every man is part of a community; and so, as a part, he belongs to the community. Consequently, he injures the community by killing himself."[135]

This attitude towards the relations between an individual and his community occurs frequently in Aquinas's thought. Is it lawful, Aquinas asks, for a person A to cut off a part of B's body which poses no threat to B's life, even if B consents to A's doing so?[136] The answer Aquinas argues for is 'no' – unless A happens to be a person entrusted by the community with some official responsibility and there is some reason relating to the whole community for doing so. And the reason that Aquinas gives for his general negative answer is that, insofar as B is a part of the whole which is the community, the community is injured if B suffers a mutilation.[137] Elsewhere, in explaining why laws must aim at the common good, he says: "A human being is a part of a group (*multitudo*), and for that reason every human being, in what he is and what he has, belongs to the group."[138]

Furthermore, although each person belongs to his community, in an even more fundamental sense each person belongs to God. That is why committing suicide is also an injustice against God: "A person who takes his own life sins against God, just as a someone who kills the slave of another sins against the master of that slave."[139]

The idea underlying the prohibition on suicide is thus similar to Aquinas's basic idea about property. An individual can justly lay claim to certain possessions as his own, but only within certain limits, since in reality everything belongs to God and God intends property for the welfare of the whole human community. That is why no individual person has absolute control over his property. The purposes of God, who is the true owner of all property, trump the purposes of the human owners of that property; and human beings can deal justly with their property only if they do not violate God's purposes. In a similar sort of way, human beings have control over themselves, in virtue of having been created by God with intellect and will;[140] but they do not have absolute rights of disposal over themselves. In reality, *all things*, human beings too, belong to God, and his purposes include the welfare of the whole community. Human beings can conduct their lives justly, can dispose of themselves as they think best, only to the extent to which they do not thereby violate God's purposes.

So almsgiving looks like a commutative exchange; in some respects, it is very similar to exchanges which are truly commutative, such as buying and selling. But, in fact, almsgiving is not a commutative exchange, because it has to do with distribution of property in accordance with the good of the whole community on the basis of the purposes of God. Analogously, fraternal correction looks like a commutative exchange, and it has features in common with a sin that Aquinas takes to be a genuine (but unjust) commutative exchange, namely, detraction. But, in fact, fraternal correction is not a commutative exchange, because it has to do with the way in which an individual's life is used, for the good of the whole community, in accordance with the purposes of God.

Spiritual and corporal almsgiving: a question

This is, of course, only the beginning of a suggestion for reconciling Aquinas's views of fraternal correction with his account of justice. But it should be enough to remind us of the issues with which this chapter began.

In connection with Aquinas's approval of Old Testament law about the Jubilee year, I said that the economic system Aquinas is recommending looks a little like Monopoly with limits. In a sense, that analogy is also appropriate for Aquinas's views of almsgiving, spiritual and corporal. It is morally permissible to accumulate property in an unbridled sort of way, but only up to a point. At that point in the process of accumulation, the Monopoly game is over. One has to give away one's property as alms, and it is God's purposes, not those of the human owner, which ultimately determine the disposition of the property. Similarly, one can justly devote oneself to one's own projects and plans, but only up to a certain point. At that point, one's life belongs to the community, and it is lived justly only insofar as it furthers God's purposes, which include the well-being of the whole community.

But what is this certain point? And how do we know that it does not pose the same problems as the ethics of care or the impersonal standpoint, namely, swallowing up individuals and their personal projects for the sake of meeting the needs of others? Alternatively, how do we know that it does not permit so much to the individual that the communal welfare is jeopardized? Here, of course, we are returning to the issues raised by Baier and Nagel.

The first thing to see here is that the concerns prompted by Aquinas's account are more nearly like those raised by the ethics of care and the impersonal standpoint than like those raised by their opposed counterparts, the "ethics of justice" and the personal standpoint. According to Baier, Western tradition, and the "ethics of justice" which has dominated it, are characterized by a belief that an individual's pursuit of his own projects should be "constrained only by a minimal formal common good namely a working legal apparatus that enforces contracts and protects individuals from undue interference by others".[141] But, clearly, Aquinas, who is undoubtedly part of the Western tradition, holds no such belief. His account of justice makes strenuous demands on the individual for the sake of a common good which is not minimal or formal only.

It should also be clear that Aquinas's ethics of justice is very different from the ethics of justice Baier attributes to liberalism, which on her view does "little to protect the young or the dying or the starving or any of the relatively powerless against neglect".[142] On Aquinas's view, as we have seen, it is morally obligatory not only to relieve the material needs of the poor but also to care for the spiritual and moral well-being of others. I have focused on only one example of such an obligation, the obligation of fraternal correction, and I have argued that Aquinas's views have the result that, in certain circumstances, moral reproof and even social dissent is obligatory. But, as I said above, there are other species of spiritual almsgiving besides fraternal correction, including, for example, instructing the ignorant; and all of these other species are obligatory, too. Many of the features of an ethics of care, including its emphasis on protection of the powerless and on the importance of education, are thus subsumed by Aquinas under justice,[143] understood as a general or as a specific virtue.[144]

Insofar as the purposes of any individual with regard to his property or his life can be trumped by God's purposes, and God's purposes include the welfare of the whole community, it seems as if, on Aquinas's account, the impersonal standpoint takes precedence over any individual's personal projects and preferences. So the question with regard to Aquinas's account will be the first of the two questions I raised at the start of this section: does Aquinas's account not, like the ethics of care and the impersonal standpoint, run into the danger of swallowing up individuals and their own pursuits for the sake of the well-being of others? Will not Aquinas's just person be like Virginia Woolf's "angel", whether in the house or in the community, namely, a person who sacrifices herself to the point of self-destruction?

It is true that Aquinas stoutly maintains that it is never right to treat an individual unjustly for the sake of the common good.[145] But this line loses some of its power to reassure when we remember Aquinas's views of alms-giving. He also thinks that there is no injustice to individuals in their being morally obligated to sacrifice their well-being or even their lives for the sake of fraternal correction and the good it brings to the community.

Care, impartiality, and justice

At this point, it may seem as if Aquinas does not reconcile care and justice, the impersonal and the personal standpoint, contrary to my claim at the outset of this chapter. Rather, it may seem that he supports just one side – care, the impersonal standpoint – in the disputes between these positions. Consequently, the demands his account of justice makes on individuals can appear much too strenuous. But this is a mistaken appearance.

Consider, first of all, one important difference between the two cases of almsgiving at issue here – relieving the poor and fraternal correction at the cost of some sacrifice – and the instances of commutative exchange which these cases of almsgiving resemble in some respects – unfair mercantile exchanges and detraction. In an unfair mercantile exchange, one of the participants gets less than he gives. In cases of detraction, one of the partici-pants is deprived of something (the goods associated with a good name) without getting anything in return. In either sort of case, the person who suffers a commutative injustice typically does so involuntarily.[146] On the other hand, although a person engaged in spiritual or corporal almsgiving loses something of value to him and gets nothing in return, he does so voluntarily. It is true that he is guilty of a mortal sin, on Aquinas's view, if he does not do so, but it remains the case that it is up to the individual whether to commit mortal sin or not. The biblical line which covers alms-giving is "It is more blessed to give than to receive", not "It is more blessed to be taken from than to receive."

So, on Aquinas's account, although strenuous demands are made on indi-viduals, it is up to those individuals whether or not to act in accordance with those demands. If they were forced into doing so, they would resemble the victims in cases of unfair mercantile exchange or detraction. But then they would also be treated unjustly; and, as Aquinas says, it is not acceptable to treat individuals unjustly even for a communal good which outweighs the good of those individuals.

But what about the sort of case Virginia Woolf worries about, in which one person sacrifices herself, altogether voluntarily, for the sake of others in a way which strikes us as entirely unfair and destructive to her? Do we have to say that on Aquinas's account her sacrifice will count as almsgiving in virtue of being voluntary? And will it turn out on Aquinas's account that such sacrifice is morally obligatory for her?

Consider, for example, Shakespeare's Ophelia, who suppresses her own desires and docilely submits to the desires of those around her, who use her as a pawn in their own plans, until she loses her reason and then, finally, her life. Does Ophelia's submissiveness count as obligatory almsgiving?[147]

Here I think the answer is clearly 'no', and the reasons for that answer help us see the way in which Aquinas's account contains protection for individuals. Consider, for example, just the relations between Ophelia and her father Polonius. The point of almsgiving is to help a person in some great moral or material need. Material need, of course, is not at issue in the case of Polonius. What about moral need? Does his daughter's submissiveness promote his moral welfare? It seems clear that it does not. Ophelia's well-being is of less importance to Polonius than his ingratiating himself with Claudius, the king; that is why he is willing to use her, for example, just as bait for Hamlet in order to get information for the king. But when Polonius treats her in that way, Ophelia seems as much the victim of a commutative injustice on Polonius's part as she would have been if she had been the victim of detraction or a fraudulent sale. Insofar as Ophelia's docility makes it easy for Polonius to continue treating her unjustly, she makes him morally worse, rather than better. In fact, one might suppose that if almsgiving of the sort Aquinas defends comes into Ophelia's story, it should be the almsgiving of paternal correction. Resistance to her father, not submission, would have been useful for making him morally better and therefore would have counted as almsgiving on Aquinas's account of the conditions for morally obligatory almsgiving.[148]

So the sorts of cases which worried Woolf, in which one person voluntarily lets herself be used by others who have little or no concern for her welfare, are not sanctioned by Aquinas's account of justice either. Such a person is allowing herself to be treated with commutative injustice, and in so doing is making the person she serves morally worse, not better. Nothing in Aquinas's account of almsgiving requires her to do so. On the contrary, what he says about fraternal correction and its purpose suggests that she has a moral obligation to resist such treatment, not submit to it. For these reasons, too, although Aquinas's account includes many of the provisions that are thought to distinguish an ethics of care from an ethics of justice, including morally obligatory concern for the needy, his account is not vulnerable to some of the criticisms leveled against an ethics of care. The fact that he includes these provisions within an account of justice means that he has a principled way of adjudicating between care for others and appropriate concern with oneself.

Human flourishing: the moral obligation of fraternal correction and the impersonal standpoint

One might nonetheless suppose that, even with these worries put to one side, Aquinas demands from individuals an unreasonable concern for others or for the welfare of the community. Too much emphasis is put on the impersonal standpoint, one might think, and not enough room is left for a person's own projects and preferences. For some people, this objection might be prompted most by Aquinas's views about the moral obligation not to keep more of one's wealth than is necessary for one's condition in life. But I think the objection arises with most force in connection with Aquinas's attitude towards fraternal correction. If you live in a bad community, social dissent can be disastrous to your well-being; it can cost you your job, your standing in the community, your children, your life. How can there be a moral obligation to wreck one's life for the good of the community (or for the bare possibility of the good of the community, since it is clear that fraternal correction might be entirely unsuccessful)?

But I think that this question, whose force I feel, underestimates the power of evil in a bad community.[149] To see what I mean here, notice that the question has an implied presupposition, namely, that in a bad community a person who does not engage in fraternal correction or social dissent *can* avoid wrecking his life, *can* flourish, *can* promote his own well-being. Is this presupposition true?

Consider, for example, Nazi Germany. The slightest open dissent was generally met with sanctions, including fines, jail terms, loss of jobs or pensions, internment in camps, and even death. Is it true that those who did not dissent, who managed to survive in their positions, pursuing their own projects, succeeded in flourishing or maintaining their well-being?

Think, for example, of Albert Speer, who only gained in opportunities to flourish as an architect as a result of his willingness to placate Hitler. Or consider Gerhard Kittel, who was a much respected biblical scholar at Tübingen during the Nazi period. Kittel maintained his position there in part because he joined the Nazi Party and was willing to lend his expertise to Nazi causes when called on.[150] Because he did not make trouble for the Nazis, Kittel was able to produce his influential work *Theologisches Wörterbuch zum Neuen Testament* during the Nazi period.

And yet, given a choice, which of us would choose to live a life like Speer's or Kittel's? Kittel died shortly after the war, at the age of 59, in world-wide disgrace for his collaboration. The war that gave such scope to Speer's talents also destroyed what he had built, and what remains of his work is largely his disgraceful reputation as Hitler's architect. On the other hand, we now idealize men like Dietrich Bonhoeffer, who actively resisted and suffered dreadfully for it.

No doubt, in the event, most of us would in fact have made choices more like Kittel's than like Bonhoeffer's. But that is a different point, a sad point about how ideals and reality diverge. The question at issue here is about ideals: who among us would rather have had Kittel's life than Bonhoeffer's?

So perhaps the unfortunate truth is that in a bad community, the kind in which social dissent is visited with severe sanctions, avoiding dissent is just as destructive to one's flourishing as engaging in it, though in different ways.

Perhaps, in fact, the qualifying phrase 'in different ways' explains why Aquinas's insistence on the obligatory character of fraternal correction is less stern than it seems to be. Franz Stangl, an ordinary German without special gifts, rose through the Nazi ranks by cooperating, instead of dissenting, no matter how horrible the assignment given him, until he became commandant of Treblinka. By failing to dissent, he protected his position, his income, his family, his own security in the system, perhaps even his life. His *material* well-being was achieved by his failure to dissent. But the cost was tremendous. He became a person who could oversee the gassing of thousands of Jewish men, women, and children with a relatively quiet mind.

At the end of his life, Stangl said to his biographer, Gita Sereny: "My guilt is that I am still here ... I should have died. That is my guilt."[151] Stangl thought, perhaps self-protectively, that he would have paid for dissent with his life. But at the end, he judged, somewhat paradoxically, that he would have had a better life had he chosen death. I concur with that judgment. And if that judgment is right, then perhaps Aquinas's claim about the moral obligatoriness of fraternal correction even in the face of serious consequences to oneself is not stern but only realistic. In a truly bad society, the best or perhaps even the only hope for human flourishing may include terrible suffering or early death.

Thought of in this way, Aquinas's account of justice does not in fact favor the impersonal standpoint over an individual's pursuit of his own well-being. Rather, in some circumstances, in some societies, the best or only way to pursue one's own well-being is by pursuing the good for all.

Conclusion

To sum up, then, Aquinas's account of justice constitutes a political theory which is not "profoundly anti-egalitarian" and monarchical,[152] but, on the contrary, egalitarian, representative, and profoundly anti-capitalistic.

Unlike some political theories which fit that same description, however, Aquinas's political theory succeeds in accommodating the personal standpoint and making a place for it within the impersonal point of view. Although Aquinas places a heavy emphasis on communal welfare and on the obligations of individuals to promote that welfare, his position does not allow individuals and their projects to be swallowed up by communal concerns. His view of commutative justice rules out as wrong taking something of value from an innocent, unwilling individual solely for the sake of the common good, without giving him in return something he values at least as much.

Furthermore, even Aquinas's strenuous views of what individuals ought to be willing to give for the sake of the communal welfare are tempered with constraints. The moral requirement of alms for the poor requires that a person give away what he does not need for his condition in life. What is appropriate to an individual's condition in life, however, is clearly a somewhat flexible matter; nothing in the requirement regarding alms has the implication that every moral person must embrace Franciscan (or even Dominican) poverty. The requirement regarding fraternal correction can impose a very high cost on individuals in the interests of the common good, but only in societies so wretchedly bad, in part or in whole, that an individual's flourishing is, arguably, more likely to be attained by incurring this high cost than by avoiding it.

Aquinas's account of justice therefore gives us what Nagel thinks is extremely difficult or even impossible to attain, namely, a political ideal which weaves together in some reasonable manner the personal and the impersonal standpoints. I certainly do not mean to suggest that in my view Aquinas's account of justice gives us a practically useful political model of a just society. No doubt, this is a political ideal whose implementation is virtually inconceivable. As a practical model, it seems reasonable to think, Aquinas's account would be bound to fail. But the failure would stem from common human faults, and not from the account's inability to combine the personal and impersonal into an acceptable political ideal. The account itself is a political ideal that gives appropriate weight both to the proper concerns of individuals for their own projects and to the welfare of society as a whole.

Considered as part of his ethical theory, Aquinas's account of justice is very far from constituting a "legalistic moral theory" that recognizes only a minimal formal common good and neglects the interests of the less privileged in society. The defects of liberal theories of justice, which some philosophers suppose need to be remedied with an ethics of care, are absent in Aquinas's account of justice. The common good which constrains individuals on his account is robust, and it is a matter of justice that the needs of the poor and powerless be met. In this way, then, he subsumes many of the concerns of an ethics of care into his "ethics of justice". On the other hand, because these concerns are met in the context of justice, because justice, not care, is the fundamental ethical value governing relations with others, Aquinas's account can give a principled explanation, difficult to come by on the ethics of care, of the moral unacceptability of letting oneself be exploited by others. His account of justice thus interweaves the concerns of justice and care in such a way as to preserve the insights of an ethics of care but without incurring its costs.

If we understand justice as Aquinas does, then, it seems to me that it has lost none of its luster as a virtue for establishing and sustaining good, and caring, relations in a morally acceptable society.

11

A REPRESENTATIVE INTELLECTUAL VIRTUE
Wisdom

Introduction

Aquinas thinks that there are intellectual virtues as well as moral virtues, and he takes wisdom to be chief among them. His account of wisdom constitutes a rich contribution not only to ethics but also to philosophy of mind. His discussion, however, is set in a web of medieval lore, about the gifts of the Holy Spirit, the beatitudes, the cardinal vices, and so on; and it also presupposes his theory of the relations between intellect and will, some but not all of which has been touched on in a previous chapter. In order to capture what is plausible and explanatorily useful about Aquinas's account of wisdom, therefore, it is necessary to approach it with a wide-angle lens, including both an examination of his theory of the will's control over belief and a consideration of the larger philosophical and theological context in which his account is lodged.

For Aquinas, wisdom is a virtue in the sense that the will plays a role in acquiring and maintaining it.[1] The idea of an intellectual virtue in this sense is not so common now.[2] In contemporary culture, it is more customary to think in terms of excellences, rather than virtues, of the intellect; and the paradigm excellence of mind currently valued is intelligence or smartness. We say admiringly of some academic whose philosophical positions strike us as utterly wrong-headed that, although his views are widely agreed to be mistaken, he himself is so smart.

Of course, it is not entirely clear, even by our lights today, what smartness or intelligence is supposed to be. Intelligence is generally taken to be an innate, genetically determined characteristic. On the other hand, psychologists carefully control the distribution of intelligence tests, on the grounds that scores go up significantly with each retaking of the test – which, of course, suggests that the tests measure a quality that can be gotten or at least increased through experience. Furthermore, although it used to be common among psychologists and is still widely held by others, the belief that intelligence is a unitary quality of the mind is almost surely false; psychologists now acknowledge that intelligence is composed of "many discrete [intellectual functions] that work together ... smoothly when the brain is intact".[3]

One widely used intelligence test is the revised Wechsler Adult Intelligence Scale, or WAIS-R. It turns out, however, that the IQ scores obtained from the WAIS-R do not adequately indicate even serious neurological deficits and disorders;[4] it is possible to have significant neurological deficits and test normally on the WAIS-R. In addition, part of what we measure in IQ tests is just the speed with which a person can use the intellectual abilities he has; there are time limits for various WAIS-R subtests. Finally, as one well-known neurobiologist, Michael Gazzaniga concludes, in split-brain patients whose brain hemispheres are disconnected, "isolating essentially half the cortex from the dominant left hemisphere causes no major changes in intellectual function".[5] This result leads Gazzaniga to claim that "specialized circuits in the left brain are managing the complex task of human intelligence".[6] But another possibility, of course, is that what intelligence tests are measuring as smartness is simply a matter of the speedy use of solely left-brain skills.

By contrast, what Aquinas values in wisdom is not the speed of information processing or, as far as that goes, any other feature of the processing itself; what is important for him is, we might say, the product of that processing. Wisdom is *scientia* (or knowledge)[7] of the most fundamental causes of things; it is a matter of having a certain understanding of reality. Furthermore, Aquinas thinks that wisdom is acquired, not innate, and he thinks that the will has a role in its acquisition. We currently tend to hold that a person's intelligence is not under her control; being smart is a matter of genetic good fortune, not a matter of effort or choice. But wisdom, on Aquinas's account, is a function both of intellect and of will. His account of wisdom thus presupposes that the will has a significant role in the production and maintenance of belief.

Because this claim about the effect of the will on belief seems false to many contemporary philosophers, I will begin with a discussion of Aquinas's views about the role of will in belief formation, and I will examine some current reasons for supposing that Aquinas's views about the effects of will on belief are false. Next, I will lay out the web of medieval ethical lore within which Aquinas's discussion of wisdom is set, and I will attempt to explicate his view of wisdom by focusing on wisdom's opposed vice, namely, folly. I will then argue that Aquinas's account of wisdom and folly gives a good explanation of a common but puzzling ethical phenomenon. Finally, I will conclude by briefly relating Aquinas's account of wisdom to hierarchical theories of freedom of the will, and I will show how on Aquinas's account wisdom is crucially connected to an agent's inner peace and harmony.

Will and belief

I have dealt with Aquinas's account of the intellect and the will at length in an earlier chapter, but it will be helpful to have a brief summary here. On

Aquinas's views, the intellect presents to the will as good certain things under certain descriptions, and the will wills them because the will is an appetite for the good and they are apprehended as good. For this reason the intellect is said to move the will not as an efficient cause but as a final cause, because what is understood as good moves the will as an end.[8]

What the intellect determines with respect to goodness is somewhat complicated, however, because, on Aquinas's views, the intellect is itself moved by other things. In the first place, the will moves the intellect as an efficient cause, for example, by commanding it directly to adopt a belief[9] or by directing it to attend to some things and to neglect others.[10] The will does so only in case the intellect represents doing so at that time, under some description, as good. Every act of willing is thus preceded by some apprehension on the part of the intellect, although not every apprehension on the part of the intellect need be preceded by an act of will.[11] In the second place, the passions – sorrow, fury, fear, etc. – can influence the intellect, because in the grip of a passion, such as fury, something will seem good to a person which would not seem good to her if she were calm.[12] The intellect, however, typically is not compelled by the passions in any way; it can resist them,[13] for example, by being aware of the passion and correcting for its effects on judgment.

It should be apparent, then, that on Aquinas's account of intellect and will, the will is part of a dynamic feedback system composed of the will, the intellect, and the passions. Any willing is influenced in important ways, but not caused or compelled, by previous willings and is the result of an often complicated interaction of the intellect and the will.

Finally, Aquinas not only holds that the will can command the intellect, but he also makes some helpful remarks about the manner in which the will commands all the powers under its control. The will is ordered to the good in general while all the other powers of the soul are ordered to particular goods, but there is order among active powers so that the power which regards a universal end (goodness in general, in this case) moves the powers which regard particular ends. Consequently, the will moves the other powers of the soul (with the exception of the vegetative powers, which are not under its control) with efficient causation, just as the general who aims at the common good of the whole army moves by his command the captains of individual companies, each of whom aims at the good of his own company.[14] So, for example, the power of sight has a good towards which it is directed, namely, the apprehension of color; and the intellect has a good towards which it is directed, namely, the cognition of truth. Because the will is directed to the good in general, however, it governs these powers which are directed towards particular goods.[15]

In other words, Aquinas's idea is that the will works in accordance with the nature of the power of the soul it is commanding in order to help that power achieve the good it was created to achieve; as we might put it, the will works in accordance with the design plan[16] of the faculties it governs, not against them.[17] It is an implication of Aquinas's position here that we do not have voluntary control over belief in cases where our cognitive capacities, acting according to their nature, have been abundantly or sufficiently moved by their objects.[18]

An objection

The part of Aquinas's account about the interaction of the will and the intellect that is likely to strike contemporary philosophers as most objectionable is Aquinas's view that the will can exercise control over the intellect.

Of course, not all philosophers in recent times have supposed that the will has no role in the production and maintenance of belief. The deontological tradition in epistemology, for example, seems committed to the view that the will can significantly influence belief. For example, Clifford's famous dictum that it is always wrong for anyone to believe anything on insufficient evidence seems to presuppose that we have some voluntary control over our beliefs. There is no point in issuing proclamations to people about what it is wrong for them to do unless it is in some sense up to them whether or not they do the acts in question.[19] Roderick Chisholm also (at least at one time in the development of his views) built his epistemology on a strong commitment to the role of the will in belief. According to Chisholm,

> If self-control is what is essential to activity, some of our beliefs, our believings, would seem to be acts. When a man deliberates and comes finally to a conclusion, his decision is as much within his control as is any other deed we attribute to him.[20]

But this tradition in epistemology has come under attack in recent years, for example, by William Alston[21] and Alvin Plantinga, among others.[22] One of the objections against it has been the argument that the will does not have the sort of role in producing and sustaining belief that such deontological conceptions require. In fact, it has even been argued that the will cannot have such a role in belief. Because Aquinas's account of wisdom depends on the claim that the will can sometimes determine intellect, it is important to look at the contemporary arguments which seem to call this claim into question.[23]

Winters's argument against believing at will

Bernard Williams has argued that it is impossible to believe at will.[24] His arguments have been criticized effectively by Barbara Winters,[25] but she herself sides with Williams to the extent of arguing for a weaker version of his claim. According to Winters,

[this] general principle related to believing at will [is true]: [namely,] it is impossible to believe that one believes p and that one's belief of p originated and is sustained in a way that has no connection with p's truth.[26]

Now the principle Winters cites is in fact false, contrary to her claim; and it is not hard to find counterexamples to it. Consider someone who finds herself believing that she must wash her hands although she can see that they are clean and she knows that she has just washed them twelve times in the last hour. She will recognize, unless she is hopelessly psychotic, that her belief that she must wash her hands is a belief which has originated and is sustained in a way that has no connection with that belief's truth; but she might recognize that she is afflicted with the belief nonetheless. She might be double-minded or in some other way irrational; she might in some way also believe that it is not true that she must wash her hands. What makes her miserable is that in spite of everything she finds that she cannot get rid of the belief that she must wash her hands. Psychotherapy is a successful business just because Winters's principle is false. Many people make appointments with therapists as a result of believing of themselves that they hold some belief p but that that belief has arisen and is sustained without the appropriate connection to truth; and so they enlist the help of therapists to rid themselves of their belief p.[27]

Or consider someone undergoing a major change in worldview, someone (for example) in the process of jettisoning all the Baptist religious beliefs inculcated in him as a child. Such a person might well find himself, to his considerable annoyance, still believing that drinking is morally wrong, and he might give himself periodic stern lectures on the subject. What the lectures would consist in, presumably, is explaining to himself that his belief in the wrongness of drinking originated and is sustained in a way which has no connection with that belief's truth. But the fact that he has to give himself these lectures repeatedly shows that, even in his own view, the belief persists nonetheless. We might suppose that his lectures show he also does not believe that drinking is wrong. But unless he supposed that he perceived in himself the belief that drinking is wrong, his lectures to himself would be hard to explain. So he is also an example of someone who violates Winters's principle; he believes in full consciousness that he believes drinking is wrong and that his belief that drinking is wrong is not appropriately connected to truth considerations.

Suppose for the sake of argument, however, that Winters's principle were true. Contrary to what Winters argues, it nonetheless would not follow that we have no voluntary control over any of our beliefs. The philosophical controversy regarding voluntary control over belief, as Winters explains, "concerns whether the model of free basic action can be applied to belief acquisition",[28] as Winters glosses believing at will.[29] But we could have voluntary control over belief, the model of free basic action could be applied to believing, even if Winters's principle were true. That is because Winters's account of what is necessary for anything to count as a case of believing at will is much too strong.[30]

According to Winters, " [t]o constitute a genuine case of believing at will":

(1) "the belief [in question] must have been acquired directly and as a result of intending to hold it";

(2) "the belief [must] be acquired independently of any consideration about its truth";

and

(3) "the action of acquiring the belief at will [must] be performed with the agent fully aware that he or she is attempting to arrive at the belief in this way."[31]

But there can be cases of free basic belief acquisition that do not meet these conditions; if these conditions do in fact capture what it is to believe at will, then not being able to believe at will is compatible with a robust degree of voluntary control over belief and also with free basic belief acquisition.

To see that this is so, it is helpful to notice that there can be cases of free basic action involving bodily movement that do not meet the appropriate analogues of (1)–(3). That is, if we think of the appropriate analogues of (1)–(3) as capturing, analogously, what it is to move at will, then there can be free basic actions of moving a body part which are not instances of moving at will.[32]

Consider, for example, the free basic action of moving your hand and arm to scratch your head. This is an action which is performed directly, in normal human beings, but not necessarily always as a result of intending to perform it. The action might be absent-minded; you might not even notice that you are moving your hand and arm in this way. The action might be an example of parapraxis; you were intending to smooth your hair, but, distracted by what you were thinking about, you scratched your head instead. So, the appropriate analogue to condition (1) is not a general condition on free basic action.

The same is true of condition (3) and its appropriate analogue for free basic action of all sorts. For the same or similar reasons as before, it is not in general true that to count as free and basic an action must be performed with the agent fully aware that she is attempting to perform the action in this way. Many free basic actions are performed with less than full awareness. Besides absent-minded actions and instances of parapraxis, which involve the will's commanding muscles of the limbs, there are also cases involving the will's commanding muscles of the mouth and larynx; Freudian slips, instantly regretted and socially embarrassing interjections, and utterances one just finds oneself giving voice to are all cases of the will's commanding muscles with less than the agent's full awareness that she is attempting to perform the action in this way.[33]

So neither the analogue of condition (1) nor the analogue of condition (3) is a condition on free basic actions which involve muscle movement. But if the analogues of (1) and (3) do not hold for all these sorts of free basic actions, why suppose that (1) and (3) should hold in cases where what the will is governing is belief? To support such a supposition, we would need to find a difference between mental acts and bodily acts that made the conditions for free basic action much more stringent in the case of mental acts than in the case of bodily acts, and it is hard to imagine what such a difference might be.

I have so far left to one side consideration of condition (2) because the way in which it is too strong is harder to see but also more important.

In general (though perhaps with some exceptions), our cognitive faculties are aimed at truth, whatever other purposes there may be for them. Their design plan is such that when they are operating according to it, they function fairly reliably to arrive at truth; or, as Aquinas puts it, each power is directed to some suitable good proper to it, and the intellect is directed to the knowledge of the truth.[34] If the will commands the intellect to acquire belief "independently of any consideration about its truth", then the will is commanding the intellect to act against its design plan, rather than in accordance with it.[35]

It plainly is not a necessary condition on free basic action in general, however, that the will be able to act against the design plan of the system it is commanding. On the contrary, it is clear that in order to have a free basic action, the will must command in accordance with the design plan of the system it is commanding. So, for example, the will can be successful in commanding the head and neck to move only in case the volition is in accordance with the design plan of those parts. One might will that the head rotate a full circle around the neck, but (as long as the head and neck are formed in the normal way) one cannot will so successfully, and there can be no such basic action. Similarly, if the legs are not monstrously deformed, the will cannot successfully command the muscles of the lower leg to move in such a way that the leg folds over on itself with the toes touching the fronts of the thighs. The design plan of the leg will not permit that sort of motion, and there are no free basic actions of that sort.

Free basic actions, then, have to be in accordance with and not contrary to the design plan of the system or module or body part the will is commanding when the free basic action involves muscle movement. It does not seem unreasonable to suppose, as Aquinas clearly does, that this must also be the case when the free basic action involves a mental act. Aquinas thinks that, when the will moves the other powers of the soul, it is to help them achieve the particular goods to which they are directed.[36] Since our cognitive faculties are in general aimed at truth, however, an attempt to command the intellect to acquire a belief independently of any consideration of the truth of that belief would be for the will to attempt to govern the intellect against, rather than in accordance with, its design plan.[37] One might attempt to will in this way, but (as long as the cognitive faculties are not malfunctioning or defective) one could not will so successfully, and there can be no such free basic actions.

Condition (2) and its analogue for bodily movement are thus too strong as conditions on free basic action. Consequently, that there are no free basic actions involving belief which meet Condition (2) tells us very little about whether we have voluntary control over beliefs.

Showing that there are not or cannot be such things as believings at will, then, where the conditions for believing at will are (1)–(3) above, is not sufficient to determine whether "the model of free basic action" can be applied to belief.

Alston's counterexamples

The approach of Williams and Winters is not the only tactic for arguing that the model of free basic action cannot be applied to belief. William Alston is another philosopher who takes this view, and his tactic, as he explains it, is just to get us to ask ourselves whether it is in fact in our power successfully to will to believe. His first example, designed to show us that it is not, is this: "Can you, at this moment, start to believe that the United States is still a colony of Great Britain, just by deciding to do so?"[38] Since we in fact know that the United States is not still a colony, to ask whether we can adopt the opposite belief just by deciding to do so is to ask whether the will can successfully command the intellect to act contrary to its design plan. But this is the sort of thing, as we have seen, which the will cannot do in other cases, for example, when it is commanding body parts, and so it is not surprising to discover that the will cannot do so in the case of believing either.

Alston's other examples are like the first in this regard. It is not the case either, he says, that we have voluntary control as regards such obviously true beliefs as perceptual beliefs. If I had such control, Alston says, then I would

> have effective voluntary control over whether I do or do not believe that the tree has leaves on it when I see a tree with leaves on it just before me in broad daylight with my eyesight working perfectly. And it is perfectly clear that in this situation I have no power at all to refrain from that belief.[39]

But if the will were to command refraining from the belief that the tree has leaves on it in this situation, it would obviously be trying to govern the perceptual cognitive faculties (or the perceptual faculties together with other cognitive faculties of judgment) in a way contrary to their design plan. Perceptual faculties are designed to report with some reliability about whatever is presented to perceptual organs, and the will cannot successfully direct them to do otherwise, however much it may want to do so. When, near the end of Orwell's *1984*, Big Brother offers to end his torture of Winston if Winston will only believe that the four fingers he sees in front of him are five, the torture continues for some time, despite Winston's passionate efforts to make it stop by trying to alter his perceptual beliefs.[40]

But once we see what the problem is with examples such as Alston's, it is not difficult to generate different examples that do, in fact, support the intuition that we sometimes have voluntary control over beliefs.

This is the case even for perceptual beliefs. Consider, for example, a man separated unwillingly from the woman he loves. Missing her desperately, he finds himself seeing her everywhere, till he gets tired of (as we say) his eyes playing tricks on him.[41] The next time he thinks he sees her, he says to himself sternly, "Stop that! You know it can't be her!"; and with that command the woman he was looking at no longer looks to him like the woman he loves, and he no longer has the perceptual belief, "That's Anna!"

Furthermore, not only can the will successfully command the rejection of perceptual belief in this way, but it can also successfully command that a certain perceptual belief occur. You are reading a psychology book on perception which contains a picture that can be seen either as a young woman or as an old lady. You see the old lady and not the young woman, but the book tells you that normal, non-brain-damaged adults see the picture both ways. Consternated, you will to see the young woman; and the result is that you do now see her. You do not work out the lines delineating that figure, crossword puzzle fashion; you just suddenly see her. Because of the will's command, the image of the young woman emerges from the lines that had been the old lady; you simply see her, all at once, and you form the belief "There's the young woman!".[42] Here the perception and the perceptual belief are simultaneously acquired as a direct result of the will's command.[43]

In these two cases, the occurrent belief (or the rejection of an occurrent belief) that the will brings about is in accordance with the agent's dispositional beliefs. That is, in these cases the will is not bringing about a belief (or the rejection of a belief) "independently of any consideration of its truth". Nonetheless, that the agent has (or rejects) the occurrent belief she does is a direct result of the will's commands.

There are also reasons for supposing that we have voluntary control of this sort over memory and to that extent over memory beliefs.[44] More importantly for our purposes here, there are cases as regards the intellect as well. For example, consider Smith, who grew up in a racist part of Boston and became imbued with the racist views of the surrounding culture, but whose worldview changes in college and who becomes determined to eradicate racism in himself. When Smith catches himself with a racist belief, he says to himself, "Stop it! Don't think such a thing!". And as a result of this imperative on the part of his will, his intellect rejects the racist belief in question, at least at the moment. Or consider someone who finds himself believing, compulsively, that he must wash his hands yet again; or a person who notices that he is depressed and finds himself believing that he is worthless and would be better off dead; or a person who becomes furious with a colleague and finds himself believing that nothing he could do to her would be bad enough. In each case, the will may intervene, commanding the intellect to reject the belief in question. Here, as in the cases involving perceptual beliefs, the acquisition or rejection of an occurrent belief in consequence of the directives of the will is in accordance with the dispositional beliefs of the agent, and the change in occurrent beliefs is not made "independently of considerations of truth". But it remains the case that the agent's acquisition or rejection of a belief on the occasion in question is the direct result of the will's commands.

Someone might suppose that the control of the will over belief in these cases is only indirect, that the will governs belief by having the intellect review the relevant evidence, thus strengthening a belief (or weakening its competitors). Perhaps in some cases this view is correct, but surely not in all. When the person afflicted with the belief that he must wash his hands wills to reject that belief, he does not do so by reviewing the evidence available to him about whether or not his hands need washing. He recognizes the compulsive hand-washing belief as an old enemy and, without any intervening cognitive calculations, wills straightway to reject it. Cases of this sort can be part of fierce and ongoing internal battles. Sometimes the will is not successful, and a person seeks external help from friends or religious counselors or therapists. But sometimes the will is successful, and the willer wins her battles by herself because her will has been effective in getting her intellect to abandon the compulsive or depressive or vengeful beliefs she wills not to have.

There are also the opposite sorts of cases, where a person wants a belief, where one's will in fact commands one's intellect to adopt a specific belief. Smith finds himself walking the long way home at night to avoid the graveyard. As a result of his will's stern commands to his intellect, his intellect forms the belief that there is nothing to fear in the graveyard, and he takes the short-cut home. What accounts for Smith's disciplining the fear he still feels and walking nonetheless through the graveyard is not that he is being courageous about ghosts or even recklessly taking his chances with whatever stalks in the cemetery, but rather that his will's directives have resulted in his intellect's holding the occurrent belief that there is nothing to fear in the graveyard. (This belief could, of course, coexist in an irrational way with opposed occurrent or dispositional beliefs as well as with emotions inconsistent with the belief that there is nothing to fear.) As before, the will might govern belief indirectly, by bringing about a review of the evidence; what is more likely in this sort of case, however, is that both the fear and the internal struggle are old and familiar, and the will governs belief directly, without any intervening review of the evidence.

These examples, and many others like them, show that we do have considerable direct voluntary control over belief and that believing or refraining from believing can be a free basic action.[45] A simple way to find such examples is to look for cases where the will is working in accordance with the design plan of the cognitive faculties, or even cases such as those given above where the will is correcting the action of a cognitive faculty that is beginning to go wrong in some way.[46] Aquinas is right to hold that the will can move the intellect as an efficient cause in cases where the will is working with the powers of the soul, directing them in accordance with the aims they have by nature.

It is important, however, to add here that the will can also work with the design plan of what it commands in such a way as to damage it rather than aid its functioning. In the most extreme case, the will can work with the design plan of the muscles in such a way as to render those muscles, and all others, permanently dysfunctional; suicide is the most obvious example. But there are plenty of smaller-scale examples. Pitchers hurt their arms pitching; ballerinas injure their legs and feet dancing; keyboard operators develop carpal tunnel syndrome on the job; and so on. In all these cases, the will is working with the design plan of the relevant body parts but by that means making them less functional or bringing about damage to them.[47] Aquinas thinks that there can be such a deleterious effect of the will on cognitive capacities as well, and not just on body parts. By working with the design plan of the intellect, the will can misdirect the intellect, as well as aid its functioning. The misdirection works by immediate indirect control, rather than direct control, as we shall see when we look more closely at what Aquinas has to say about wisdom.[48]

Wisdom as one of the intellectual virtues

Aquinas's understanding of virtue is complicated, but for present purposes we can understand him as characterizing a virtue much as Aristotle does: a virtue is a habit or disposition which makes the power it is a disposition of apt to work well.[49] For intellectual virtues, the power in question is primarily the intellect or reason. Aquinas divides intellect or reason into speculative reason and practical reason, and he assigns three virtues to the former and two to the latter.[50] The two virtues of practical intellect are prudence and art.[51] The three virtues of the speculative intellect are wisdom, *scientia*, and understanding. Understanding is a matter of grasping first principles, the starting points for the various sorts of sciences. *Scientia* involves comprehension of the causes of things and recognition of the way in which things are related to their causes. Wisdom is a particular kind of comprehension of causes; it consists in understanding the highest (or as we would say, most fundamental) causes of everything and seeing everything else in the world in its relation to those highest (most fundamental) causes.[52]

What one thinks these highest causes are depends on the rest of one's worldview. Aquinas, who knew Aristotle did not hold a worldview identical with his own, supposes that for Aristotle the grasp of the most fundamental causes belongs to metaphysics (or metaphysics and some natural theology), so that, Aquinas thinks, for Aristotle wisdom is a matter of mastering metaphysics.[53] For Aquinas, the highest or most fundamental cause is, of course, God, so that on Aquinas's account wisdom is a matter of knowing God's nature, God's actions, and God's decrees.[54] Just as we today suppose that all the sciences will be understood best if the scientist begins with a solid foundation in physics and sees the other sciences in the light of that foundation, so Aquinas supposes that physics and all the sciences, including metaphysics, will be understood most deeply and most excellently by someone who has a good grasp of God's nature and actions.[55] We and Aquinas, then, share the conviction that there is a hierarchy of knowledge about the world and that a cognitive agent's knowledge is held with more depth and richness if she knows the foundations (or as Aquinas would say, the pinnacle) of that hierarchy. On his view, the foundation, or the pinnacle, consists in the attributes and actions of the creator of the world, and knowing these is an intellectual virtue.

Understood just in this way, an intellectual virtue need not be a product of the will as well as the intellect. Most of what Aquinas has to say about wisdom, however, has to do not with wisdom as an acquisition of human reason but with wisdom as a gift of the Holy Spirit; and, so understood, wisdom does involve the will as well as the intellect. In order to understand all Aquinas has to say about wisdom, then, we have to see it in its context among the gifts. When we see his account of wisdom in that context and in the web of the other connections in which he locates it, then it turns out that wisdom is not just one part of a rather boring taxonomy of cognitive excellences, but is instead the culmination of a complex interaction between the will and the intellect which is intimately connected to moral goodness.

Three, maybe even four, of the intellectual virtues have a twin among the gifts of the Holy Spirit.[56] The seven gifts of the Holy Spirit are courage, piety, fear, counsel (*consilium*), understanding, *scientia*, and wisdom. Besides understanding, *scientia*, and wisdom, prudence among the intellectual virtues also seems to have an analogue among the gifts, because the gifts include counsel, and counsel is regularly coupled with prudence. Alone among the intellectual virtues, art has no twin in the gifts of the Holy Spirit.

There are two main differences between the intellectual virtues and their twins among the gifts.[57] The first has to do with origin. To put it roughly, if, for example, *scientia* is something we have acquired ourselves through the use of reason, then it counts as an intellectual virtue. If, on the other hand, God gets the credit for our having it, then it counts as a gift. The second has to do with quality. *Scientia* as a gift is more excellent, more deep, rich, and far-ranging, than *scientia* as a virtue. So if a person manifests *scientia* in an especially excellent way, then, on Aquinas's view, that *scientia* should be judged as coming from God and counted as a gift from the Holy Spirit.[58]

Given this way of distinguishing between the intellectual virtues and the gifts of the Holy Spirit, it is not surprising that Aquinas pays relatively little attention to the intellectual virtues and substantial attention to their twins among the gifts. On the other hand, in his discussions of the intellectual virtues-as-gifts, Aquinas devotes virtually no space to discussion of the divine origins of the gifts or to the way in which God infuses these gifts into the mind or to the way in which grace and human free will cooperate during the process of divine infusion. In short, his discussion of wisdom, *scientia*, and understanding considered as gifts of the Holy Spirit looks in all relevant respects indistinguishable from what we might have expected to find in a discussion of the intellectual virtues. In working on wisdom, then, I will follow his lead and consider wisdom not as an intellectual virtue but as a gift of the Holy Spirit, but I will leave to one side (as he himself does) any specifically theological issues raised by his claim that wisdom is infused by God.

Wisdom in its context

Besides the five intellectual virtues and the seven gifts of the Holy Spirit, Aquinas also recognizes four other groups relevant to his discussion of wisdom.

First, there are the seven principal virtues. These consist in the three theological virtues, faith, hope, and charity, together with the four cardinal moral virtues, courage, justice, temperance, and prudence.[59] Second, there are the seven deadly sins or capital vices. Beginning with the worst and progressing to the least, these are pride, envy, wrath, sloth, avarice, gluttony, and lust. (There are many more mortal sins than these, but these seven are picked out as the sources from which the rest flow and to which the rest can in some sense be reduced.[60])

Third, there are the twelve fruits of the Holy Spirit: faith, charity, joy, peace, patience, long-suffering, goodness, benevolence, meekness, moderation, continence, and chastity.[61] The virtues, vices, and gifts are habits or dispositions. The fruits of the Holy Spirit, on the other hand, are to be understood either as acts — acts of self-discipline with regard to kicking the dog, for example — or else as mental states resulting from such actions.

Fourth and last, there are the seven beatitudes or blessings, a series of claims attributed to Christ in the Gospels. They begin "blessed are", followed by a human action or attribute to which blessing is attributed, and they finish by assigning a reward to go with that blessing. Seven (or eight, depending on how one counts) actions or attributes are picked out for blessing: Blessed are they that hunger and thirst after justice; blessed are the peacemakers, the meek, the poor in spirit, the mourners, the merciful, and the pure in heart.[62]

In examining wisdom, as well as the other virtues, Aquinas works by interweaving all the items from all of these lists. So, for example, for each of the seven principal virtues, he presents and discusses the associated gifts, fruits, and beatitudes, and the opposed vices, including both the secondary vices and the cardinal vices from which those secondary vices stem. For wisdom in particular, it helps in understanding his position to see his account of the virtue in the context of all these connections.

Wisdom and charity

The three gifts associated with the speculative intellect (*scientia*, understanding, and wisdom) are linked to the three theological virtues (faith, hope, and charity). None of the intellectual virtues or their twins among the gifts of the Holy Spirit are associated with hope. Faith, on the other hand, has two intellectual virtues-as-gifts associated with it, namely, understanding and *scientia*.[63] Wisdom is the gift associated with charity.

Acts of faith are the fruit connected to faith, and two beatitudes are given for it: blessed are those who are pure of heart and who mourn sin. The theological virtue of faith, in other words, is said to eventuate in acts of faith and to be produced in those whose hearts or wills are pure – that is, not internally divided – and who mourn or grieve over moral wrongdoing.

Each of the gifts associated with faith also has vices coupled with it. The vices opposed to the gift of understanding are dullness of sense and blindness of mind; and the vice opposed to *scientia* is culpable ignorance. All of these opposed vices are said to stem from the lesser or carnal vices on the list of the capital vices. The idea here seems to be that the carnal vices result in a certain culpable ignorance and mental dullness; and these in their turn get in the way of understanding and *scientia*.[64]

The tie that Aquinas sees between wrong ethical choices and consequent intellectual defect is brought out even more strongly in his discussion of wisdom. The theological virtue with which wisdom is linked is charity or love of God. Since on the doctrine of simplicity, God is identical with goodness, charity is also a love of goodness,[65] and, for my purposes here, I will understand it in this way. On Aquinas's view, charity or a love of goodness gives rise to wisdom, and wisdom and charity together eventuate in the fruits of peace and joy.[66] The beatitude associated with wisdom is "Blessed are the peacemakers ...".[67] The vice opposed to wisdom is, predictably enough, folly; and folly, on his view, has its source in the deadly sin of *luxuria*, taken either narrowly as lust or broadly as the absence of self-discipline with regard to worldly desires.[68] (The nature of all these connections and associations will emerge in the next sections of this chapter.)

As an intellectual virtue, wisdom is an excellence of the speculative intellect. It is a sort of super *scientia*, grasping the highest cause or causes of everything and enabling a person to make decisive judgments about the way in which other things, such as human actions, are related to that highest cause.[69] Since God is the highest cause and also perfect goodness, judging human acts in relation to the highest cause is a matter of discerning good or right actions from bad or wrong actions. For this reason, wisdom as a gift is a disposition informing both the speculative and the practical intellect.[70]

Understood in this way, wisdom is incompatible with any mortal sin, Aquinas says.[71] That is, a person who is guilty of pride, envy, wrath, sloth, avarice, gluttony, or lust — or of the other mortal sins which flow from these — will undermine or destroy wisdom in herself. (Why Aquinas should think so will emerge in the next sections of the chapter.)

Perhaps the first thing that should strike us here is how far we have come from wisdom in what Aquinas takes to be the Aristotelian sense of the mastery of metaphysics (or metaphysics and Aristotelian natural theology). The mastery of metaphysics, we naturally suppose, could be had by anyone in any moral or emotional state. It could be had by Hitler, for example, and on a day when he had neither peace nor joy, to say nothing of peacemaking and a passion for goodness. But on Aquinas's understanding of wisdom, an excellence of the intellect is linked together with certain actions and dispositions in the will and also with certain states of emotion.

Wisdom is not alone among the intellectual virtues or gifts in being treated in this way, as the preceding remarks on faith show. Understanding and *scientia* are dealt with in the same way. The carnal vices lead to the mental states opposite to understanding and *scientia*, so that presumably the absence of the carnal vices is a prerequisite to either understanding or *scientia*. Furthermore, the first beatitude associated with faith, "Blessed are the pure in heart ...", indicates that a moral state is a concomitant of the intellectual condition of understanding and *scientia*. The second associated beatitude, "Blessed are they who mourn ...", apparently refers to a state which includes certain emotions, so that the intellectual dispositions of understanding and *scientia* on Aquinas's account are also linked to the passions.

On Aquinas's account of wisdom, then, a person's moral wrongdoing will produce deficiencies in both her speculative and her practical intellect. In its effects on her speculative intellect, it will make her less capable of understanding God and goodness, theology and ethics. It will also undermine her practical intellect, leaving her prone not only to wrong moral judgments in general but also to wrong moral judgments about herself and particular actions of hers, and so it will lead to self-deception. She will think her moral standards are appropriate and her moral judgments are correct when they are not. In other words, on Aquinas's view, morally wrong choices on the part of the will misprogram both the speculative and practical intellect, resulting in a skewed view of God and goodness, wrong moral judgments, erring conscience, and self-deception.

If this process gets bad enough, it eventuates in the vice opposed to wisdom, namely, folly. We will understand Aquinas's notion of the role of the will in wisdom and the connection between wisdom and moral goodness better if we consider what he has to say about folly.

Folly: contemporary examples

By way of a general characterization of folly, Aquinas says that it implies a certain apathy of heart and dullness of mind.[72] What is more interesting, I think, are the various descriptions he gives of the fool. He presents three of them, all taken from Isidore of Seville: a fool is one who through dullness remains unmoved; a fool is one who is unconcerned when he is injured; and a fool is one whom shame does not incite to sorrow.[73] What do these claims about the fool mean, and what do they have to do with the way in which wisdom is supposed to be undermined by moral wrongdoing?

It is helpful here to consider a particular case, and there is a good case to be found in the movie *What's Love Got to Do with It?*, the story of Ike and Tina Turner. (For the sake of argument, I will assume that the movie is completely veridical. Partisans of Ike Turner may take what is said here as a fictional, rather than a historical, example.) According to the movie, Anna Mae (Tina's real name) was a good person and a talented musician. Ike, on the other hand, had a limited talent and was a rotten person besides. He was a drug addict and a drunk, a womanizer and a wife-beater.

After the movie was released, media people contacted Ike to ask whether the movie portrayal of him was accurate. In particular, the reporters wanted to know whether he had really beaten Anna Mae in that way. In general, Ike conceded the movie's accuracy but complained about the consequent negative assessment of himself. As for the particular complaint about wife-beating, he granted that he had frequently beaten Anna Mae, but (he explained) only when she made him really mad. Through his abuse, Ike Turner lost a talented, beautiful, internationally acclaimed woman who had at least at the outset loved him, and his shameful actions were subsequently portrayed in revolting detail for movie audiences throughout the country. But his reaction to the events of his life and the movie's revelations seemed to come to a mixture of perplexity and indifference. Without disputing the movie's portrayal of him, he nonetheless seemed at a loss to understand the consequent disparagement of himself. In fact, his agent said at the time that

Ike was contemplating a movie telling his side of the story. In his movie, no doubt, he would beat his wife bloody, but audiences would get to see that she was making him mad when he did it.

Ike's behavior towards Anna Mae was outrageous; but what is more interesting for my purposes here is Ike's reaction to the release of the movie, which he acknowledged to be basically accurate as regards his actions, if not his motivation. His reputation in the country fell precipitously; the movie did him incalculable damage in a host of respects ranging from financial and professional to personal and emotional. For present purposes, we can take shame as a person's recognition that others around him hold a morally low opinion of him, when that low opinion is correct.[74] A shamed person, in other words, is someone who ought to have low self-esteem and who recognizes that other people see him in this way. (This is a sense of 'shame' in which a person can be shamed without feeling shamed.) So we might say of Ike Turner that the release of the movie has both shamed and injured him. But what is frustrating about his response to the movie is that he does not seem to care. Ike thus fits Aquinas's (and Isidore's) definition of a fool. Shame is not inciting him to any sorrow over what he has done or become – it is not making him feel shamed. Ike Turner's condition here is not unrepresentative of what we find when we look at people habituated to major moral evil and then brought face to face with outrage in public reaction. Consider white South Africans supporting apartheid, or Eichmann at his trial in Jerusalem. Like Ike Turner, they seem to fit Aquinas's definition of a fool: the shame their actions elicit evokes no sorrow for those actions in them, and the injury done them by their public shaming does not produce in them any deep moral concern. The camp doctor at Auschwitz, Johann Paul Kremer, personally murdered many people in dreadful scientific experiments. In his diaries, published after the war, he details both his murders and his opinion of himself as an upstanding citizen, a devoted family man, a morally good person. He thinks of himself as a person of great moral sensitivity even as he notes the pain and suffering he causes the Jews in the camp.[75] Nothing about his public disgrace at his two trials and convictions after the war seems to have changed his mind.[76] In Aquinas's sense, he is a paradigm of a fool.

How does a person get to be in such a morally frightening condition? Nazis are made; they are not born. One of the most insightful studies of the making of a Nazi is Gita Sereny's biography of Franz Stangl, the commandant of Treblinka.[77] She shows the way in which each serious instance of moral wrongdoing on Stangl's part made it easier for him to take the next and further step into moral evil; the move into moral monstrosity is slow and gradual. When he was first assigned to head a euthanasia clinic, Stangl was morally repelled by what the Nazis were doing. But he was afraid that he would lose his job or even his position among the Nazis if he made any trouble, and so he talked himself into thinking first that euthanasia was a necessary evil and then that it was in fact a favor to those killed.[78] Having dulled himself in this way, he found it easier to take the next step into evil, where again he had to choose between, on the one hand, losing his promotion or his position or even his security in the system and, on the other, losing further moral ground. In each case, he protected his position and security at the cost of morality. Nothing in his trial or his consequent disgrace and prison term could shake his conviction that in all his actions he was a morally good person, even a humane and morally sensitive person, who did what he did just because he was following orders, in a morally appropriate spirit of civic and military obedience. Nothing about the revulsion in which he was held by the whole world after the war gave him any serious pause.

Folly: intellect and will

Aquinas's account of wisdom and folly gives theoretical background for these contemporary examples of folly, and his theory of the relation between intellect and will provides an explanation of how a person can become a moral monster such as Stangl was.[79]

Like Ike Turner, though clearly in a radically more serious way, Stangl is a fool, a person whom shame does not incite to sorrow and who is unconcerned when he is injured. He has a severely impaired speculative intellect, unable to apprehend correctly the highest causes of things, including the nature of moral goodness; and in consequence his practical intellect is also grossly deficient in its ability to make particular moral judgments. The result is that he is self-deceived and morally monstrous. What has brought him to this condition is a disinclination, made habitual from long practice, to discipline his desires for worldly well-being when they conflict with morality.[80]

The reason these morally wrong choices can have the effect of misprogramming the intellect in both its speculative and its practical parts is explained by the will's ability to exercise control over the intellect – in this case, indirect but immediate control.

Stangl wanted to accept his appointment at the euthanasia institute, or, at any rate, he preferred doing so to the other alternatives open to him; but he was also horrified by the nature of the assignment. In the beginning, he was double-minded, wavering between thinking he must accept the assignment and thinking that he would not be able to stick it out. "After the first two or three days," Stangl told Sereny, "... I didn't think I could stand it ... I ... couldn't eat – you know, one just couldn't".[81] In the end, however, he did – all things considered – want to accept and remain in his assignment. As Aquinas holds, though, a wrong action can be willed by the will only in case the intellect has succeeded in finding some description under which it seems good.[82] And so in a case in which the will wants what in fact is not good, as a result of the command of the will the intellect directs its attention to just the evidence which supports the goodness of what the will wants and turns away from any countervailing evidence.

This seems a fairly good description of what happened in Stangl's case. Sereny asked him whether he succeeded in convincing himself that what he was doing was right. Yes, he explained, he did so in virtue of reflecting on an encounter he had with a Catholic nun, who was in favor of euthanasia for disabled children. Speaking of a severely disabled sixteen-year-old child who was not taken for euthanasia, the nun said, "Just look at him ... No good to himself or anyone else. How could they refuse to deliver him from this miserable life?". Commenting on this speech by the nun, tacitly approved by an accompanying priest, Stangl said, "Here was a Catholic nun, a Mother Superior, and a priest. And they thought it was right. Who was I then, to doubt what was being done?".[83] Here Stangl's will has directed intellect to reflect on this one encounter and on the fact that the person who gave moral approval to euthanasia was a person whose office generally carries moral authority, namely, a nun. On the other hand, there was abundant evidence available to Stangl to indicate that many Protestant and Catholic clergy were strongly opposed to euthanasia.[84] He found euthanasia morally acceptable on the basis of one nun's approval of it only because his will was also directing the attention of his intellect away from the countervailing evidence.[85]

Because he succeeded in approving euthanasia as morally acceptable or even morally good, to this extent Stangl misprogrammed his intellect, and the next step was easier to take. The misprogrammed intellect allows the will to want as good what it might have rejected before the misprogramming of the intellect; and the warped will, in turn, misprograms the intellect further. So the will and the intellect are in a dynamic interaction which allows each of them to corrupt the other, one step at a time. Aquinas's theory, then, makes it easier to understand the well-documented fact that the descent into moral monstrosity tends to be gradual rather than precipitous, and it also shows, at least in part, how it is that conscience becomes dulled. Stangl went from the euthanasia institute at Hartheim to one at Bernburg, where those "eligible" for euthanasia included perfectly healthy political prisoners. From there he went to Lublin where he was gradually inducted into the secrets of the death camps until he accepted the assignment of supervising Sobibor. When Sereny asked him how he felt when he first came in contact with the gassing of Jews at Sobibor, he answered, "At Sobibor one could avoid seeing almost all of it."[86] In Treblinka, he could not help but see it, and he called what he saw "Dante['s Inferno] come to life"; but he accepted his posting as commandant to that death camp.[87] In response to Sereny's question how he could have stilled his conscience into accepting, he said, "the only way I could live was by compartmentalizing my thinking"[88]– by which he meant willing not to think about a great deal.

With every wrong action, then, there is a misprogramming of the intellect; and the misprogrammed intellect twists the will, which in turn misprograms the intellect further. These misprogrammings can progress till they reach the point where a man like Stangl, who at first almost could not bear the painless death of the severely disabled, subsequently was able to oversee with a quietened conscience tortures and killings that now sicken those who just read pale descriptions of them.[89]

Furthermore, breaking into the cycle of the spiraling corruption of intellect and will, on Aquinas's account of the interaction of these faculties, clearly will be difficult. The outrage of virtually the whole civilized world was not enough to turn Stangl from his conviction that he had never been responsible for any serious evil, that he had always done what he ought to have done in the circumstances. The shame of his internationally publicized trial and the deluge of shaming publications documenting his part in mass murder inspired him to no repentance or moral sorrow. Why this should be so is easier to see on Aquinas's theory of intellect and will. A severely misprogrammed intellect with a correspondingly twisted will will be hard to fix, because all of the previous misprogramming will have to be undone, one piece after another,[90] but this will be an undoing for which the agent has no will or desire, or which his will is even set against, and which his intellect does not find good. Consequently, the corrupting interaction of will and intellect will continue. In his self-deceived state, Stangl does not see his actions or himself as the rest of the world does, and he does not want to do so either. That is why shame produces no sorrow in him. His moral evil has made him a fool.

So wisdom is undermined by moral wrongdoing because morally wrong choices corrupt not only the will but also the intellect. Because of the way in which the will and the intellect interact, it is not possible, on Aquinas's account, for a person to have the intellectual virtue of wisdom without a corresponding moral excellence in the will.

Wisdom and peace

Although there is a great deal more to be said about Aquinas's account of wisdom, I want to conclude by considering briefly the beatitude Aquinas associates with wisdom. The wise person is a peacemaker, on Aquinas's view, and that in two respects. First, he is able to make peace for others by helping them sort out the rights and wrongs of their differences. Secondly, he is able to make peace within himself.[91]

It is not so hard to understand why Aquinas would think that wisdom, understood in his way, enables a wise person to be a peacemaker for others. But it is somewhat more difficult to see what it is about wisdom that produces peace in the person who has it. We can gain some insight into Aquinas's point here if we think of the will as a hierarchically ordered faculty. Harry Frankfurt's work on the will has made clear that persons can have not only first-order desires and volitions – desires or volitions to do something – but also second-order desires and volitions – desires or volitions to have a will of a certain sort.[92] This hierarchy in the will makes possible a variety of internal conflicts. There can be conflicting first-order desires, as when a person both desires to smoke and desires not to smoke. And there can be conflicts between first- and second-order desires, as when a person has a second-order desire for a will that wills not to smoke and a first-order desire to smoke. And, finally, there can be conflicts on the second-order level, as there would be in a person who was conflicted about whether or not to undertake a reform of his smoking habits. Frankfurt's idea is that for a person to be free, there needs to be harmony within the will. A free person's second-order desires and volitions cannot be in disagreement with his first-order volitions.

It is clear that Frankfurtian harmony in the will is needed for peace as well as freedom. An agent whose will is divided against itself is an agent who is at war with himself. Unless the agent's will is unified in its desires, whatever such an agent does or gets for himself, he will not have what he wants.

Now Frankfurt thinks that there can be harmony in the will whatever the will wills, as long as the will is unified in that wanting. That is, if Stangl wanted to have the will of a mass murderer and if his first-order volitions were in harmony with that second-order volition and he had no discordant willings, then to that extent on Frankfurt's, theory Stangl would be free and (we might add) at peace with himself. But Aquinas would not agree with Frankfurt on this score. On Aquinas's view, moral evil will always result in internal divisions in the self, in disharmony in the will and corresponding double-mindedness in the intellect; and so moral evil is incompatible with inner peace.[93] For single-mindedness and harmony in the will, on Aquinas's account, we need moral goodness and the wisdom that moral goodness accompanies.

For Aquinas, no one ever becomes so evil that there is nothing in his intellect or will which holds back from the evil he is immersed in, which disapproves of that evil or which desires something better. Aquinas's account is thus a much more optimistic view of human beings than Frankfurt's is. Frankfurt's view allows a person to be utterly unified in evil. For Aquinas, a morally evil person will always be divided within himself. Somewhere, however deeply buried in the psychic structure, there will be some part of the evildoer's intellect and will which dissents from the evil approved of by the rest of the intellect and desired by the rest of the will. And so, Aquinas thinks, in distinction from Frankfurt, that to the extent to which the will wills moral wrongdoing, to that extent the agent's peace is undermined. That is why Aquinas connects peace and wisdom. A moral monster such as Franz Stangl, on Aquinas's view, is not only a fool but also a restless person.

Conclusion

To comprehend Aquinas's theory of wisdom, we must understand it not only in the web of Aquinas's moral categories – the deadly sins and principal virtues, the beatitudes and the fruits of the Holy Spirit – but also in the context of Aquinas's views of intellect and will. We have to be clear about Aquinas's rich account of the nature of the will and of the way in which the will interacts with the intellect. I have tried to show that, contrary to much contemporary opinion, Aquinas is right in supposing the will can influence belief, both directly and also indirectly. Furthermore, on Aquinas's theory of the intellect and will, the relations between them are not simple but dynamic and full of interactive feedback; each can progressively shape and influence the other. As a result, it is possible for there to be a series of morally wrong acts which culminates in a bland and self-satisfied moral monstrosity, corrupting the intellect as well as the will.

Wisdom is the virtue opposed to this sort of vice, on Aquinas's account. Understood in this way, wisdom turns out to be a mixed moral and intellectual excellence; and it is noteworthy that on Aquinas's view all true excellence of intellect – wisdom, understanding, and *scientia* – is possible only in connection with moral excellence as well. Wisdom, in particular, is undermined by moral evil. A person devoid of wisdom is a fool: he is mistaken in the things he believes to be good and right and desires as such; his conscience is dulled; and he is hugely self-deceived about his own actions and character. No one is born a fool; a person becomes a fool gradually, as a result of a series of wrongdoing in which his will and intellect progressively misprogram one another, as Aquinas's account of intellect and will explains. Aquinas's conception of wisdom thus gives us some understanding of the perplexing phenomenon Hannah Arendt called "the banality of evil", signaled, for example, by the lack of anguish or remorse or even insight on the part of an Eichmann or a Stangl.[94] For Aquinas, the evil a person does can have the fearful consequence of making him morally stupid.

Wisdom, on the other hand, carries powerful benefits with it, among the chief of which is inner peace. Because Aquinas has an essentially optimistic attitude towards human beings and human nature, he supposes that moral evil will always fragment a person, that no person, however morally monstrous, can ever be wholly unified in willing and approving of what is objectively wrong. That is why there is no peace for the wicked; peace is the natural reward for the wise.

In explaining just this much of Aquinas's account of wisdom, I have left a great deal to one side. I have hardly discussed the connection between wisdom and charity, and I have said only a little about the fruits and beatitude Aquinas associates with wisdom. Space does not permit a full consideration of the whole of Aquinas's conception of wisdom, but this is, I think, enough to see that it constitutes an impressive and useful contribution to moral psychology.

12

A REPRESENTATIVE
THEOLOGICAL VIRTUE

Faith

Introduction

Faith is the first of the theological virtues, and Aquinas's account of it is both rich and puzzling. The puzzles center on justification, one might say, where justification is to be understood in two different ways. According to Aquinas, a person who acquires faith forms an assent to a group of propositions under the influence of a volition which has the effect of moving the intellect to an assent it otherwise would not have formed. Because the intellect arrives at the beliefs of faith through the influence of the will, there is some question about whether a person is justified in holding those beliefs and if so, why. On the other hand, on Aquinas's views, the volition in virtue of which the intellect is moved to assent to faith is produced in a person by divine grace, and God alone is responsible for it. Nonetheless, this volition and the faith it engenders justify a person in the theological sense of 'justification': a person's combined act of will and intellectual assent is the necessary and sufficient condition for her salvation and it renders her acceptable to God. If there seems to be too much influence of a person's volitional control for epistemological justification, on Aquinas's account, there seems to be too little of it for theological justification. In this chapter, I will look at Aquinas's account of faith in order to show its resources for dealing with both sets of puzzles.

Will and intellectual assent

On Aquinas's view of the relations between the intellect and the will, the will has a role to play in many, though not all, acts of the intellect.[1] That this is so can be seen just from Aquinas's claim that the will can command the intellect to attend or not to attend to something. But the will also enters into acts of the intellect in another way, because the will has a more direct role to play in certain sorts of intellectual assent (*assensus*), that is, in a person's acceptance of a proposition or set of propositions.[2]

According to Aquinas, intellectual assent can be brought about in different ways. Assent to a proposition can be brought about entirely by the object of the intellect. Aquinas gives as examples cases in which a person assents to first principles and to the conclusions of demonstrations.[3] In either of these sorts of cases, the object of the intellectual act (the first principle or conclusion of the demonstration) moves the intellect by itself and produces intellectual assent without the will's acting on the intellect. Aquinas describes such cases by saying that the object of the intellectual act is itself sufficient to move the intellect to assent. By this expression he seems to mean that, as a result of a particular person's cognitive relation to what is being cognized, the cognizer is at that time in an epistemic state in which it is natural and easy for him to assent to a certain proposition and difficult or even psychologically impossible for him not to assent. Aquinas's examples are abstruse, but there are plenty of homely examples. So, for instance, consider a mother who watches the facial expressions and body language of the judge evaluating her son's piano recital and who finds herself assenting, whether she wants to do so or not, to the proposition that the judge dislikes her son's performance.

In other cases, however, intellectual assent is obtained in a different way, on Aquinas's view, because the intellect is moved to assent not by its object but by the will; in such a case, the intellect assents to one proposition rather than another under the influence of the will and on the basis of considerations sufficient to move the will but not the intellect.[4] Considerations are sufficient to move the will when it is natural and easy for a particular willer to form a desire or volition for something and difficult or even impossible for him not to form it. Homely cases of this sort are also abundant.[5] For example, the mother watching the judge's reaction to her son's piano recital might believe irrationally and unfairly that it is the judge's bias against her son which makes him dislikes her son's performance, and her belief might result not from good evidence against the judge but from some evidence combined with what she wants to think of the judge for one powerful motive or another.

On Aquinas's view, when the object of an intellectual act *is* sufficient to move the intellect by itself, there is no room for the will to have a role in bringing about intellectual assent. If the mother's evidence that the judge is not prejudiced against her son were overwhelming, then it would not be possible for her to form the belief that the judge is prejudiced against her son's piano performance, no matter how much she may want to do so. Nothing in Aquinas's account of the relations between the intellect and the will contravenes the common view that we do not have direct voluntary control over our beliefs in such cases.[6] But in cases where the object of the intellect is *not* sufficient to move the intellect by itself, then Aquinas thinks that it is possible for the will to have an effect on intellectual assent to propositions. In this way, a person's will can influence his beliefs.[7]

The sorts of cases in which the will influences belief that are most likely to occur to us are those in which the will acts on the intellect for the worse, as in the example above in which the mother believes the judge is prejudiced. But it is also possible to think of examples in which the will's influence on the intellect is apparently for the better, epistemically speaking. In George Eliot's *Middlemarch*, Dorothea Casaubon finds her friend and admirer Will Ladislaw in a compromising embrace with the wife of one of his friends. Although it is possible (and in the novel is in fact the case) that there is an exonerating explanation of Ladislaw's conduct, the evidence available to Dorothea strongly suggests that Ladislaw's behavior is treacherous. But because of her commitment to him, Dorothea, in spite of the evidence, cleaves to her view that Ladislaw is a good man, not a scoundrel and a traitor.[8] As becomes clear to Dorothea and to the reader of the novel, Dorothea's belief based on her desires about her relationship to Ladislaw is veridical; without the influence of her will on her intellect, Dorothea would have formed a false belief about Ladislaw.

The will's role in faith

On Aquinas's view, in faith the will plays a role analogous to that played by Dorothea's desires regarding Ladislaw in *Middlemarch*. It influences the intellect in a way that leads the intellect to assent to a proposition that is veridical when the object of the intellect is sufficient by itself to move the will but not the intellect.

According to Aquinas, the object of faith is in fact God himself; but since in this life our minds cannot comprehend God directly or immediately, the object of faith is more properly considered as propositions about God.[9]

Assent to the propositions of faith, on Aquinas's view, lies in the middle between knowledge and opinion.[10] In faith, the intellect assents to these propositions, but that assent is generated by the will's acting on the intellect. Even together with whatever else is known or believed by a person, the propositions of faith are not sufficient to move the intellect of any human person in this life to assent; when it assents to the propositions of faith, a human person's intellect does so under the influence of the will, which *is* sufficiently moved by the object in question to act on the intellect to bring about its assent.[11] In this respect, faith is unlike knowledge but like opinion, in which the will also has a role in the generation of assent. On the other hand, faith holds to its object with certainty,[12] without any hesitation or hanging back; and in this respect faith is like knowledge and unlike opinion.[13]

To see why the object is sufficient to move the will, it helps to remember Aquinas's view of the will: the will is by nature an appetite for the good. The ultimate good, however, and the final end of the will, can be thought of in either of two ways. On the one hand, what the will wants as the greatest of goods is the happiness of the willer. On the other hand, that greatest good is in fact God; union with him is perfect happiness for every created person.

The propositions of faith present the ultimate good under both these descriptions, namely, as the happiness of eternal life in union with God; and they present it as available to the believer. For a person coming to faith, the will is drawn to the great good presented in the propositions of faith; and in consequence it influences the intellect to assent to them. A motion on the part of both the intellect and the will is thus required for faith. Furthermore, in consequence of this influence of the will on the intellect, the intellect cleaves to the propositions of faith with the sort of certainty normally found only in cases of knowledge.[14]

Formed faith

This description of Aquinas's conception of faith can be misleading, however, because it is not sufficient to distinguish between the faith of committed religious believers and the faith of devils.[15] On the medieval tradition Aquinas accepts, the devils also believe, but their faith is not salvific faith. The belief of the devils does not cause them to trust in God and be saved; it just causes them to tremble.[16]

The propositions of faith are not exactly the same set of propositions for human beings and for demons. There are some propositions that count as propositions of faith only for human beings, on traditional Christian doctrine, because with respect to those propositions the devils have knowledge rather than faith (the proposition that God exists is an example). But even the devils have to rely on belief rather than knowledge for some of the propositions taken as propositions of faith by human believers, such as that the man Jesus is the incarnate Son of God, or that Christ will come again to establish the kingdom of heaven on earth. At least until a certain point in history, nothing in the devils' experience of God or the supernatural realm puts them in a position to know that *this* particular human being has a dual nature or is God's chosen means of restoring the earth. With regard to such propositions, on Aquinas's account, the difference between devils and religious believers is not that believers have faith and devils do not, but rather that devils do not have what Aquinas calls 'formed faith', whereas believers do.[17]

The difference between formed and unformed faith is a function of the different ways in which the will can bring the intellect to assent. The will can move the intellect in different ways, two of which are relevant here, according to Aquinas.[18] In the case of those who have formed faith, the will moves the intellect to assent to the propositions of faith because the will is drawn by its hunger for what is in fact God's goodness. The resulting faith is called 'formed faith' because in it the intellectual assent to the propositions of faith takes its form from the charity or love of goodness that animates the will. In the case of the devils, however, the faith they have is not so much informed as deformed by malice,[19] a hatred of what is in fact true goodness,[20] and a love of the (relative) good of power instead.

The belief of the devils thus arises in a way different from the way in which formed faith arises. Like those with formed faith, the devils believe the propositions of faith without seeing their truth for themselves, because with regard to these propositions, for devils as well as for human beings, the object of the intellect is not sufficient by itself to move the intellect to assent. But, in the case of the devils, their wills command their intellects to assent to the teachings of the Church, according to Aquinas, because the devils see the power accompanying those who promulgate these teachings, and so they see manifest signs that the propositions of faith are from God.[21] The belief of the devils, Aquinas says, is thus the sort of belief a person would have if he heard a prophet first foretell the future and then raise a person from the dead. The miracle of resurrecting the dead is not any sort of direct evidence that the future event foretold will in fact occur, but seeing the power of the miracle would incline an observer moved by considerations of power to believe that the prophet was in touch with the deity and so also to believe that the prediction was veridical.

This example implies that what Aquinas means by the manifest signs inclining the devils to belief are signs primarily of the power behind those promulgating what is to be believed, and only indirectly of the truth of what is believed. If we now take into account Aquinas's claim that what distinguishes diabolical belief from salvific faith in God is the kind of contribution made by the will to intellectual assent, we will have a clearer understanding of Aquinas's distinction between unformed and formed faith. For both kinds of faith, the will brings about intellectual assent in virtue of certain strong desires; but in the case of formed faith, the desire in question is a desire directed towards real moral and metaphysical goodness, and in the case of the faith of the devils it is directed towards the good of power.

When it is formed faith, faith is a virtue, a habit that contributes to perfecting a power or capacity. Since both the will and the intellect are involved in faith, for faith to be a virtue it has to contribute to perfecting the will as well as the intellect. Now, for Aquinas, the intellect is perfected by the acquisition of truth; and since the propositions of faith are in his view true, the beliefs accepted in faith are perfective of the intellect. In this respect, there is no difference between faith that is a virtue and the faith of the devils. The difference comes with regard to the will. In formed faith, the will moves the intellect to assent to the propositions of faith because of the will's love of and desire for God's goodness. The wills of the devils, on the other hand, are drawn not by a love of goodness but rather by their reaction to power, a reaction in which malice is a powerful component. So faith in the devils is not perfective of their wills. Consequently, the faith of the devils, unformed by charity or love of God's goodness, does not count as a virtue, since the will is one of the two powers involved in faith.[22]

On Aquinas's account of faith, then, the propositions of faith entertained by a believer's intellect are not sufficient to move the intellect to assent; but the will of a person coming to faith is drawn by the good of eternal life in union with God which the propositions of faith taken together present. Because the will is drawn to this good, it moves the intellect to assent to the propositions of faith; and it moves the intellect in such a way that the consequent intellectual assent has the kind of conviction or certitude ordinarily found only in cases of knowledge. Because the propositions of faith are true, faith contributes to the perfection of the intellect; and because the will in faith desires what is in fact its ultimate good, faith contributes to the perfection of the will. For this reason, faith informed by love of goodness is a virtue, as the faith of the demons is not.

Objections

This summary of Aquinas's account of faith raises a host of questions and objections. Here I want to focus on just three of them.[23]

Objection (1)

The role Aquinas assigns to the will in faith makes it seem as if faith is without epistemic justification and, furthermore, seems to lay Aquinas open to the sort of charge Freudians often level against religious belief, namely, that faith is simply another case of wish-fulfillment belief.

If a believer's intellectual assent to the propositions of faith results primarily from her will's being drawn to the good represented in those propositions, there seems to be no reason for supposing that the propositions of faith are justified for her. In order for a belief to be justified, there are certain criteria the belief must satisfy. A believer must have acquired it by a reliable method, or it must cohere in the right sorts of ways with her other beliefs, or she must violate no epistemic obligations in holding it, or something else of the sort. In one or another of these ways, depending on the epistemological theory we adopt, we form judgments about whether a belief is justified and whether a believer is entitled to some reasonable confidence in supposing that what she believes is in fact true.[24] In general, Aquinas shares such views, and he espouses (his interpretation of) an Aristotelian epistemology.[25] But in the case of faith, epistemological considerations seem not to play a major evaluative role at all for Aquinas. What, then, keeps faith from being unjustified? On the other hand, if there is some way of warding off this sort of objection, then it seems as if precisely analogous sorts of reasoning ought to support as justified any belief a person wants to be true, such as Cromwell's false and unjustified but firmly held belief during his last illness that he would be completely restored to health and continue to lead the nation.

Objection (2)

Since faith is based at least largely on the action of the will because the object of faith is not sufficient by itself to move the intellect to assent, why should faith be thought to have any certainty? The certainty of a set of beliefs seems to be or be dependent on some epistemic property of those beliefs. But on Aquinas's account, the certainty of faith results from the *will's* being moved by the object of faith. Why would Aquinas suppose that an act of will can give rise to certainty of beliefs?

Objection (3)

Aquinas thinks that faith is a virtue which perfects the intellect as well as the will. But why should he think so? Should not human intellectual assent be obtained on the basis of considerations that by themselves are sufficient to move the intellect to assent, as in cases of knowledge? There seems to be something inappropriate about obtaining intellectual assent as a result of the will's being drawn to goodness rather than by the intellect's being moved by the evidence, the sort of inappropriateness there is, for example, in using a sewing machine to join two pieces of cloth by gluing the two pieces of cloth together and using the machine as a weight to hold them in place as the glue dries. Even in Aquinas's terms, on his theology, there is something apparently unsuitable about the process of coming to faith as Aquinas explains it. Since God is omniscient and omnipotent, as well as the designer and creator of human intellects, he could easily provide the sort of object for the intellect which would enable the intellect to come to belief in the propositions of faith on the basis of considerations relevant to truth alone. He could, for example, make the propositions of faith so evident that they move the intellect all the way to knowledge. Why does he not do so? And why should Aquinas think that faith generated by the will's influence on the intellect is a virtue perfective of the intellect?

The relation of faith to goodness: Objection (1)

Objection (1) has two parts. On the one hand, it argues that the propositions of faith are unjustified for a believer, because it is the will's inclining to the good presented in them, rather than the intellect's being sufficiently moved by its object, that is responsible for the intellect's assent to those propositions. On the other hand, the objection runs, if there is some way of justifying beliefs acquired and held in this way, it seems that this will also justify in general every wish-fulfillment belief.

Aquinas's metaphysics of goodness gives him a response to the first part of this objection. The easiest way to see that this is so is to focus on a particular proposition of faith, namely, the proposition that God exists. Although Aquinas thinks that this proposition can be known to be true by natural reason, he also holds that not all people are in a position to know it by natural reason and that those who are not are justified in holding it as a proposition of faith. (For different propositions of faith, such as that Christ rose from the dead, different but analogous if more complicated responses can be given.[26])

To see how to respond to the objection with regard to the proposition of faith that God exists, we need to consider the connection Aquinas makes between being and goodness. The central thesis of Aquinas's meta-ethics is that the terms 'being' and 'goodness' are the same in reference but different in sense.[27] The expressions 'being' and 'goodness' are thus analogous to the expressions 'the morning star' and 'the evening star': they refer to the same thing but with different senses.

Aquinas takes God to be essentially and uniquely being itself. Given his meta-ethical thesis, it is no surprise to discover that Aquinas also takes God to be essentially and uniquely goodness itself. Since 'goodness' and 'being' are the same in reference, where there is being there is also goodness, at least goodness in some respect and to some degree. For that reason, on Aquinas's account, even the worst of creatures, even Satan, is not wholly bad, but has some goodness in some respect. It is helpful here, however, to see that on Aquinas's views the relationship between being and goodness also holds the other way around. The presence of goodness also entails the presence of being.

Now Aquinas takes metaphysical being to be something broader and more complicated than mere existence in the actual world; so the claim that where there is goodness, there is being does not entail the simplistic conclusion that any good thing we can imagine actually exists. Aquinas's equation of being and goodness does not imply, for example, that any good fictional character has existence, even existence of some peculiar or attenuated sort. So in the case of any limited good, however exactly we explain the attribution of being to it, on Aquinas's account the being it has will also be limited and need not include actual existence.

In the case of perfect goodness, on the other hand, things are different. The sort of being correlated with perfect goodness is perfect being, and Aquinas maintains that perfect being includes not only existence but even necessary existence.[28] Given Aquinas's central meta-ethical claim about being and goodness, then, where there is perfect goodness, there is also necessarily existent perfect being.[29]

So if what the will hungers for is goodness that is perfect and unlimited, and if, largely because of that hunger on the part of the will, the intellect is moved to assent to the proposition that what is hungered for exists, the resulting belief will not be unjustified; an intellect that assents to the proposition that God exists on the basis of the will's hungering for God's perfect goodness *will* be reliably right, because of the connection between goodness and being. On Aquinas's views, the design plan of the intellect, which allows it to be moved by the will in such cases, and the nature of metaphysical reality are such that in these circumstances the intellect's assent to the proposition that God exists is justified. On the other hand, if the will hungers for a certain good thing whose goodness falls short of perfect goodness, and if the intellect is moved to assent to the proposition that that thing exists because of that hunger on the part of the will, the resulting belief will not be similarly justified. This is so because, although it follows from Aquinas's basic meta-ethical thesis that any particular good thing that is limited in goodness has being of some sort, it does not follow that it has perfect being and so actually exists.

It is helpful in this connection to make a distinction among levels of justification. We can distinguish between S's being justified in believing p, on the one hand, and S's being justified in believing that she is justified in believing p, on the other. As William Alston has been at pains to argue, a person S might be justified in believing p without being justified in believing that she is justified in believing p.[30]

The explanation of the justification for the propositions of faith provided by Aquinas's account of being and goodness gives reasons for thinking that a believer is justified in believing that God exists, but not for thinking that a believer is justified in believing that he is so justified. Aquinas's views explain what it is about reality and our relation to it that accounts for the justification of a belief in God's existence acquired in consequence of the will's being drawn to the goodness of God. In ordinary cases, as in the kinds of cases good experimental design is intended to prevent in science, beliefs stemming primarily from the will's moving the intellect to assent to something because of the will's hungering for some good would not have much (if any) justification. Because goodness and being are correlative on Aquinas's account of the metaphysics of goodness, limited goods have limited being, so that they may or may not actually exist. But if the will moves the intellect to assent to the existence of God on the basis of the will's hungering for what is perfect goodness, then in that case, on Aquinas's account, the resulting belief will have a great deal of justification. On Aquinas's account of the nature of God as the perfect being, the relation of perfect being and perfect goodness, and the design plan for the will and the intellect, a belief in the existence of God formed in this way is reliably true.

But to say this is not to say that on Aquinas's account we are justified in believing that we are justified in believing that God exists. We might not have a good argument for (or we might not even accept) some or all of the metaphysical theory in question here; or we might accept it but not believe that any goodness is perfect, so that the will's hungering for the good represented by the propositions of faith is just another instance of the will's hungering for a limited good. And Aquinas's account gives us no certain procedure for deciding whether a good that the will hungers for is a perfect or a limited good. For these reasons, although Aquinas's account of the metaphysics of being and goodness explains why a believer S is justified in believing the propositions held in faith, it does not give us an argument that a person is justified in believing that she is justified in believing that God exists on the basis of her will's desire of goodness.

Nothing in Aquinas's metaphysics of goodness, however, justifies wish-fulfillment beliefs in general. In wish-fulfillment beliefs, such as the belief of a lazy, untalented student that he has done well in an exam he did not study for, the will moves the intellect to assent to the truth of a proposition asserting the existence of some good because of the will's desire for that good. But since for Aquinas, limited goods may fail to exist, nothing in the will's hungering for limited goodness gives a person a reason for supposing that a proposition ascribing existence to a limited good is true; and so the belief that there is such a good which results from this process is unjustified. Although therefore a belief in God's existence formed in consequence of the will's desire for God's goodness is justified, nothing in Aquinas's account has the result that any wish-fulfillment belief is equally justified or likely to be true.

Finally, besides the worry about the epistemological status of wish-fulfillment beliefs, we are inclined to find such beliefs objectionable because we think allowing will to guide intellect as it does in the case of wish-fulfillment beliefs is bound to lead to frustration or disappointment. On Aquinas's account, while this may be true of wish-fulfillment beliefs in general, it is not true with regard to faith. According to Aquinas, happiness is the ultimate end for the will, and a person wills it necessarily.[31] But a person's true happiness consists in her uniting with God. Therefore, the hunger of the will is not stilled until the willer is either in union with God or inexorably on the road to union with God, with the other desires of the will in harmony with that final goal. As Augustine puts it, addressing God: "Our hearts are restless till they rest in you." But if the will's restless hunger prompts the willer to assent to the propositions of faith, her faith initiates a sequence which has her salvation as its conclusion. For these reasons, on Aquinas's account, letting the will's hunger for goodness govern beliefs and actions subsequent on those beliefs is not an obstacle to human flourishing in the long run. If the process of following the will's hunger is carried on to its full conclusion, if a person does not give up prematurely and settle for something ultimately unsatisfactory to her (as she may be inclined to do in consequence of preferring her own immediate pleasure or power to greater goods), then allowing her hunger for goodness to govern her beliefs will eventuate not in frustration but rather in her having what she wants. (The section on faith and justification below supports this same conclusion but with a different emphasis and explanation.)

Faith and certainty: Objection (2)

The reply to Objection (1) may serve only to exacerbate the worry in Objection (2), that nothing in Aquinas's theory can account for the certainty of faith. Aquinas's account of goodness and being explains what it is about the world which, on Aquinas's metaphysics, makes the belief that God exists justified when the intellect assents under the influence of the will; but on this basis alone, a person is not similarly justified in believing that that belief is in fact so justified. It seems, then, that Aquinas is not entitled to say that a believer has certainty with regard to the propositions of faith when the intellect assents to them under the influence of the will.

There is one sense in which Aquinas concedes the point of this objection. Drawing a distinction with at least some similarity to that between levels of justification, Aquinas says we can think of certainty in two different ways: either in terms of the cause of the certainty of the truth of the propositions believed or as a characteristic of the person believing those propositions.[32] According to Aquinas, the cause of the certainty of the propositions of faith is something altogether necessary, namely, God himself. Considered with regard to the cause of the certainty of the truth of the propositions of faith, then, faith is at least as certain as any other true beliefs entertained by human reason. On the other hand, if we consider the certainty of faith with regard to the person who believes, then the certainty of faith is considerably less than the certainty of many things about which human beings have knowledge, because some or all the propositions of faith are beyond reason for any human being.[33]

Aquinas's position here may strike us as disappointing. He begins with the apparently bold claim that the *propositions* of faith have the same sort of certainty as mathematical propositions known to be true; but, looked at more closely, this claim is apparently compatible with the claim that *believers* cannot be anything like as certain about the propositions of faith as mathematicians can be about mathematical truths. What exactly is this distinction of Aquinas's with regard to certainty? And does it undermine what is generally seen as a key characteristic of faith, namely, the deep confidence of believers in the truth of the propositions believed?

One way to understand Aquinas's distinction with regard to certainty is also in terms of levels of justification. Perhaps what he has in mind is that a person S who believes the propositions of faith is as justified in holding those beliefs as it is possible for him to be, because the "cause of the certainty" of the propositions of faith is God himself. But it does not follow that S is justified to the same degree in believing that he is justified in believing the propositions of faith, so that with respect to this level of justification the believer is more justified as regards, for instance, mathematical truths he knows than as regards the propositions of faith.

Though this approach might be a promising beginning for understanding Aquinas's distinction, it seems to offer no help with the main point of Objection (2), because, on the face of it, it seems as if it is the higher-order level of justification that must play a role in the assurance of religious believers. Does Aquinas's point about the certainty of faith leave him unable to account for the confidence believers have in the truth of the propositions believed in faith?

If Aquinas thought that believers' confidence consisted solely in an intellectual state or condition, then the answer to this question might be affirmative. But his view is more complicated because of the role of will in faith. Consequently, on Aquinas's account of faith, we can explain the confidence of believers in the propositions of faith in two different ways, based either on intellect or on will.

As regards intellect, a believer might not be in a position to know, or even to have a great deal of justification in the belief, that his belief in the propositions of faith is justified. Nonetheless, he is still in a position to know that if the propositions of faith are true, then his happiness can be achieved and the deepest desires of his heart can be fulfilled only by adherence to the propositions of faith. And in that case, on Aquinas's view, a religious believer will hold these propositions with the greatest possible commitment because of the desire of the will. On Aquinas's account of the relations between intellect and will, then, because the will can act on the intellect with efficient causation, the will's whole-hearted commitment to the good in question also has the result that the intellect's assent to the propositions of faith has maximal conviction. This way of interpreting Aquinas's position thus helps to explain his claim that, although in the case of faith, the object of the intellect is not sufficient to move the intellect by itself, it is sufficient to move the will, and the will then in turn moves the intellect to the sort of unwavering assent given in cases of knowledge.

The purpose of faith: Objection (3)

These replies to Objections (1) and (2) only sharpen the point of Objection (3). Why would Aquinas think that the will's moving the intellect to assent to the propositions of faith is the way such assent *ought* to be obtained? Some philosophers have supposed that if there is an omnipotent, omniscient, perfectly good God, he should have provided sufficient evidence of his existence. But Aquinas plainly takes it to be an important feature of faith that the object of intellect in the case of faith is not enough by itself to move the intellect and that the intellect has to be moved instead by the will, drawn to the good represented in the propositions of faith.

To understand why Aquinas takes this position, it is important to see what he thinks the point of faith is. Both intellect and will have a role in faith, but we tend to assume unreflectively that the first and most important effect the acquisition of faith produces in the believer is a change in intellectual states. Consequently, we might suppose, the immediate point of faith is some alteration of the intellect. If we think of the efficacy of faith in this way, it is certainly understandable that we should feel some perplexity. Why would an omniscient, omnipotent God, himself the creator of the intellect, arrange things in such a way that certain crucial states of intellect must be brought about by means that bypass the natural functioning of the intellect?

Aquinas, however, sees the role of faith differently. On Aquinas's view, the most important immediate point of faith is not its influence on the intellect, but its effects with regard to the will. Of course, given the kind of connection Aquinas postulates between intellect and will, the effects on the will also have effects on the intellect, in one way or another. But, on Aquinas's view, the purpose of the changes brought about in the acquisition of faith has to do primarily with changes in the will. These changes are the start of the process of justification by faith, the *sine qua non* of salvation (and the subject of more detailed discussion in subsequent sections).

But if the act of will in faith has the importance it does in the scheme of salvation, then since on Aquinas's theory the will is also moved by the intellect, the point of Objection (3) may seem only to be strengthened. In view of all that has just been said, a proponent of this objection might hold, is it not clear that a good God ought to make sure that everyone has this act of will by making the propositions of faith manifest to everyone in virtue of making the object of the intellect sufficient by itself to move the intellect? If unbelievers could be convinced of the truth of the propositions of faith, the objector might suppose, then they also would come to the desire of goodness that is the act of will in faith.

Suppose, however, that a person were to see manifestly and evidently the truth of the propositions of faith. Then what such a person would know is that there exists an entity of unlimited power, the ruler of the universe, who draws human beings into union with himself through the redemptive power of the incarnate Christ. If such a person were then to ally herself with God, it might be because of an attraction to God's goodness, or it might also be because of a desire to be on the side of power, as in the case of the unformed faith of the devils.

Since, on the doctrine of original sin, human beings are already marred by a tendency to prefer their own power to greater goods, there is consequently a serious danger in allowing the things asserted in the propositions of faith to be overwhelmingly obvious. It is like the danger of attracting overweight people to Weight Watchers meetings by promising to begin the meetings with a lavish banquet, although this is a limited danger, because one could plan more ascetic meetings for later. Eventually, one could decouple the excessive desire for food and the desire for the good of temperance represented by Weight Watchers meetings, so that the former desire would be diminished and the latter enhanced. But in the case of God, if it once becomes overwhelmingly obvious that an omniscient, omnipotent, perfectly good God exists and has a redemptive plan of the sort presented in the propositions of faith, then it also becomes overwhelmingly obvious that human beings can be on the side of power in allying themselves with goodness.[34] In that case, however, it ceases to be possible to decouple the desire for power and the desire for goodness, so that the former is diminished and the latter is enhanced.

What these considerations suggest is that the failure to provide sufficient evidence for all the propositions of faith and the requirement that intellectual assent be produced by the will's attraction to goodness not only are no embarrassment for Aquinas's account of faith, but in fact constitute an important means of furthering the purpose he takes faith to have, namely, the salvation of post-Fall human beings.

Epistemological justification

There is, then, another way of thinking about faith, which assigns a central role to the will in the production of faith and which sees the purpose of faith in its effect on the will, rather than in its influence on the intellect. Nothing in this position of Aquinas's, of course, denies reason a role in the life of faith. Aquinas is part of a tradition going back at least as far as Augustine, which takes faith to be the prerequisite for understanding and which accords reason an important part in the process of coming to understanding. Furthermore, although on Aquinas's view it would be a mistake to suppose that faith is *acquired* by an exercise of reason, reason may nonetheless clear away some intellectual obstacles that bar the believer's way to faith. On this way of thinking about faith, the intellect assents to the propositions of faith in virtue of the will's moving it to assent because of the will's desire for God's goodness when the object of the intellect is not sufficient by itself to move the intellect. Nonetheless, the resulting belief is not simply a case of wish-fulfillment beliefs. Aquinas's metaphysics of being and goodness gives an explanation for why belief in the propositions of faith is justified, in a way that other wish-fulfillment beliefs could not be. In addition, although the metaphysics of goodness and being explains the certitude of faith as regards the propositions believed, it is the will's cleaving to God's goodness that explains the certitude of faith as regards the believer.

Finally, Aquinas's account of faith has the advantage of explaining why an omniscient, omnipotent, perfectly good God would let the epistemic relation of human beings to himself rest on faith, rather than knowledge, and why a person's having faith should be thought to be meritorious in any way, because it holds volitionally produced faith to be the beginning of salvation for a person, in the process of justification by faith, to which I now turn.[35]

Theological justification: introduction

That we are justified by faith is one of the fundamental claims of Christian doctrine, variously understood but equally accepted by all traditional Christian theologians, including Aquinas. On the traditional understanding, all human beings are marred by original sin, which means, among other things, that a post-Fall person has a will which tends to will what he ought not to will, and that that inborn defect of will results sooner or later in sinful actions, with consequent moral deterioration. In such a state a person cannot be united with God in heaven but is rather destined to be left to himself in hell. God in his goodness, however, has provided salvation from this state, which is available for all, though not all avail themselves of it.

What is the nature of this salvation? Either of two answers to this question is equally appropriate, and Aquinas subscribes to both of them. On the one hand, there is the doctrine of justification by faith, which explains that we are rescued from the evil in ourselves not because of any successful moral struggles on our part but rather by faith. On the other hand, there is the doctrine of the atonement, which explains that salvation is won for us by Christ's passion and death. The connection between these two answers is not apparent at first glance.

Generally speaking, Aquinas understands justification by faith as necessary and sufficient for salvation. It involves acceptance by God apart from any moral virtue on the part of the person being justified, but it is also the beginning of the process by which a person is made righteous and acquires the virtues; that is, on Aquinas's understanding of the doctrine, justification by faith initiates the process by which real change for the better is effected in the character of the person being justified.

Understood in this way, there is something puzzling about the doctrine that faith justifies. If faith is understood in Aquinas's terms as the intellect's assenting to the propositions of faith, the problem is that a person's being committed to religious beliefs seems compatible with a persistent lack of the virtues, as witness some of the unsavory characters who have undoubtedly been sincere adherents to Christianity. And it hardly seems consonant with divine goodness to make God's acceptance of a person dependent on that person's holding certain beliefs, as distinct from a person's moral state.

The doctrine of the atonement, that we are saved from sin by Christ's passion and death, is problematic in part because it is a second answer to the question about the nature of salvation. If faith in God can justify a person, and if justification is sufficient for salvation, what is the role of the atonement in salvation? But there are other puzzles as well. If Christ's passion and death save post-Fall human beings, how do they do so?[36] What is the nature of the benefit which his passion and death produce? In particular, how is that benefit appropriated to the person redeemed by faith in order for that person to be saved? And how is this benefit related to the beneficial effects of justifying faith?

Faith and justification

For justification, Aquinas says, the following three things are required: (1) an infusion of grace; (2) an act of will on the part of the person being justified; and (3) the remission of sins. These elements can be understood as: (1) the motion of the mover (God's infusion of grace); (2) the motion of what is moved (the mind's act of will); and (3) the consummation of the motion or the attainment of the end (the process of remission or removal of sins).[37] So to understand Aquinas's account of justification by faith, we need to consider each of these three elements of justification.

It is easiest to begin with (3), the attainment of the end of justification. By 'justification', according to Aquinas, we mean movement towards justice, and justice in this case consists in rectitude or right order in a person's mind and will, so that his passions are subject to his rational faculties (including the rational appetite that is the will), and his rational faculties are subject to God. Justification is the process by which someone who was previously an unrepentant sinner changes direction and has his intellect and will directed to God. In this process his habits of sinning are gradually removed as a result of the changes wrought in his intellect and will by God's grace.

Aquinas recognizes that someone might suppose justification consists simply in God's not imputing sin to the person being justified, that is, that justification is only God's forgiveness of sins and not also change in the character of the person being justified. But Aquinas thinks, on the contrary, that in forgiving a person's sin, God works a change in the nature of the sinner.[38] Such a conclusion is consistent with Aquinas's general emphasis on God as active rather than passive. When *we* love someone, Aquinas says, we take account of some good, real or apparent, in that person; but when *God* loves someone, he is causing, not taking account of, good in that person. And, similarly, for God to refrain from imputing a sin is for God to effect a change for the better in the intrinsic properties of the person to whom the sin is not imputed.[39] So for Aquinas the process of justification is the process by which a person is gradually changed from being a sinner to being righteous, although the end of the process, the complete removal of all sin from the person justified, does not occur in this life.

To understand element (1) of justification, God's infusion of grace, we need to be clearer about one of Aquinas's several divisions of grace, namely, the division between operating and cooperating grace. Operating and cooperating grace are the same grace, Aquinas says, but distinguished on the basis of the effects produced in the mind of the believer.[40] Grace that is the source of meritorious acts a person performs is cooperating grace, but grace that justifies or heals a person's soul is operating grace. In other words, God is responsible for all that is good in us. Sometimes, however, what is good in us is also to be attributed to us, not because we could do any good without God but simply because our will cooperates with God, who moves us to a good work by his *cooperating* grace.[41] But the process of justification is different. In this case all the work is done by God alone, and so the grace of God which justifies a person is *operating* grace.

Echoing Augustine's famous line that God who made us without our consent will not justify us without it,[42] Aquinas says that God does not justify us "without ourselves": simultaneous with God's justifying us, he says, we consent to God's justice in an act of free will, which constitutes element (2) in the process of justification.[43] Operating grace comes to a person suddenly, Aquinas says. The preparation for operating grace may take a period of time (during which God may be working providentially in a person's life), but the actual infusion of operating grace is instantaneous.[44] And the act of free will which is part of justification is simultaneous with the infusion of operating grace.[45] The infusion of grace is prior in nature, or logically prior, to the act of free will, in the sense that the willing is dependent on the grace rather than the other way around; but temporally they occur together and at once.

It is true that Aquinas thinks God causes this act of free will in us, and, of course, the extent to which Aquinas is a theological determinist is a vexed issue.[46] But Aquinas makes many claims insisting on the freedom of the will. For example, he denies emphatically that God's action on the will compels the will to will what it wills. Grace acts on the soul not with efficient causality, he says, but rather with formal causality.[47] Furthermore, although God moves the will in infusing operating grace, God moves everything in accordance with its own nature; but it is part of human nature to have free will, and so God moves the will in such a way that the will remains free.[48] Finally, on Aquinas's view, a person is not forced towards virtue by divine grace. It is natural to human beings to act voluntarily and to control their own acts, but coercion is contrary to a human being's acting in this way. Since, however, God provides for all things in accordance with their nature, God's grace does not exclude from us the free act of our will.[49] So, however Aquinas thinks that divine grace operates on the will, however we are to settle the long-standing controversies over Aquinas's views on grace and free will, in this chapter I propose to take him at his word and assume that on his view grace does not coerce the will or keep the will from its own natural operation and voluntariness. (I have reserved detailed discussion of this issue for Chapter 13 on grace and free will.)

As for element (2) in justification, the act of will concomitant with operating grace, on Aquinas's account, always has two parts. The entire process of justification, which only begins with element (2), is a movement in which God brings a person from a state of sin to a state of justice, and so a person who is being justified must consider both ends of this motion and form an act of will regarding both. By an act of free will the person being justified must want to withdraw from his sins and draw near to God's goodness. Consequently, the act of will concomitant with operating grace must have two parts, one in which a person detests his sins and one in which he longs for divine goodness or righteousness.[50]

What Aquinas says about the role of free will in justification seems to blur the distinction between operating grace and cooperating grace, which depends on whether or not the will cooperates with God's grace. If both operating and cooperating grace are concomitant with an act of free will, how are we to distinguish one sort of grace from the other? In two ways, I think. In the first place, when God infuses cooperating grace, grace and the will cooperate to produce some third thing, a mental or physical action. But operating grace has as its end just a particular act of will itself. The effect of operating grace, Aquinas says, is an effect in which the mind is moved but does not move, and it has to do with that interior act of the will by which the will first begins to will God's goodness.[51] This volition constitutes, in effect, an act of assent to the workings of operating grace.[52] Second, when the will cooperates with cooperating grace, some work can be attributed to the will as well as to God's grace. That is why Aquinas says that God's infusing cooperating grace into a person's soul is a source of merit for that person. The act of will associated with operating grace, however, while it is a full-fledged action of the will on the part of the person being justified, is not an action in which some labor can be attributed to the person willing or in which he can be said to have acquired merit just as a result of the willing.

Aquinas's example of a person being justified by operating grace is Paul on the road to Damascus. He acknowledges that this case is an example of a rare method of justification, but it nonetheless elucidates the elements he thinks essential for the process. Paul was converted suddenly because of a vision he had while traveling to Damascus; but his assent to Christianity in consequence of his vision still constitutes the twofold act of will in faith which accompanies operating grace. We can contrast this twofold act of will with, for example, the decision Paul makes to continue his missionary activity after being stoned in Lystra. That Paul wills to continue preaching instead of becoming discouraged or frightened and so withdrawing from the work shows him to be virtuous; this act of will on Paul's part can be attributed to Paul as a good work and increases Paul's merit. Consequently, on Aquinas's account, it must have as its source God's cooperating grace, which had as its aim Paul's continuing to preach the gospel. On the other hand, the very act of will in which Paul adopts Christianity is not something Paul labors at in any way, so that it is not attributable to Paul as a good *work*. Rather, all the work in this case is on God's part, and attributable to his providence and grace; Paul's only contribution is not to refuse the grace God is infusing in him. For that reason it also does not increase Paul's merit;[53] not to refuse it seems the least Paul can do in the circumstances.[54]

So the immediate effect of God's infusing operating grace in this case is the act of will which constitutes Paul's assent to grace in his acceptance of Christianity, and cooperating and operating grace are distinguished on the basis of the will's role in being acted on by grace or acting with grace to produce some other mental or physical action.

In discussing justification, Aquinas emphasizes the twofold nature of the requisite act of will: it consists first in a longing for the goodness of God, and, second, in a detestation of one's sins. The first part of the act of will involved in justification is thus just the act of will involved in faith, and the second part is derived from the first. If a person has some notion of the goodness of God and loves it, he will also simultaneously hate those things about himself which are opposed to God's goodness and which by comparison with it look loathsome. So one reason justification involves faith is that the act of will which is a constituent of faith is just the act of will required for justification.

Justification by means of faith

On Aquinas's account of faith and grace, a human being Nathan is justified when God operates on Nathan in such a way as to bring Nathan to assent to the propositions of faith and to generate a corresponding twofold act of will. In consequence, Nathan desires God's goodness and hates his own sins, and (among the other propositions of faith he believes) he believes that God fulfills such desires as his because God justifies believers through Christ. But by 'believers' here is meant just those who have the faith which justifies, or more specifically, those who believe what Nathan believes and will as he does. If we spell out the implications of what Nathan believes, we will say that as regards belief Nathan is justified by believing (implicitly or explicitly) that God justifies those who believe that God justifies them. If we now also include Aquinas's understanding of justification as God's bringing a person to righteousness, then, on Aquinas's view, as regards the intellectual component of justification by faith, the process of making Nathan righteous is begun by Nathan's believing that God will make him righteous, and it continues so long as Nathan maintains this belief, until the culmination of the process when Nathan is made perfectly righteous.

The act of will which accompanies this belief in the process of justification is one in which the will draws near to goodness by longing for it and hating its sin.[55] In other words, the act of will accompanying Nathan's justifying belief that God will justify him is Nathan's desire for God's doing so, based on a yearning for the goodness of God and a disgust for his sins, for those things in himself which he sees as contrary to God's goodness.

In short, Nathan's part in the process of coming to righteousness is to believe that God will make him righteous and to want God to do so. And God's undertaking to justify those who have faith is a commitment to bring to righteousness those who believe he will do so and who want him to do so.

This account of justification by faith may seem to savor of the notion that wishes are horses and therefore beggars ride, but in this particular case there is something to be said for that notion. The act of will that is part of the process of justification constitutes a desire for God's bringing the believer to righteousness. But this act of will is equivalent, logically and perhaps also psychologically, to willing that God make the believer's will righteous. To desire God's goodness, in the sense intended here, is to want righteousness, and the righteousness of any person depends first of all on his will's willing what it ought to will. Similarly, to repudiate one's sins is to want not to engage in those sins any longer and so to have a will which wills what it should. So the act of will involved in justification is a will to will what one ought to will. Such a will is a second-order volition, a volition in which the will operates reflexively to command itself.[56]

If Nathan has a second-order volition of this sort,[57] then God can bring about changes in Nathan's first-order desires and volitions to bring them into accord with that second-order volition, thereby removing Nathan's sin and making him righteous, a process of moral improvement which culminates (after death) in a state of perfect righteousness. If God were simply to alter a first-order volition of Nathan's without Nathan's having such a second-order volition, it seems clear that God would be violating Nathan's free will, since, as Aquinas also thinks, if a person's volition is altered as a direct result of the exercise of efficient causality on the part of some external agent, that volition is not free.[58] But if God brings about a volition in Nathan (either directly, by operating on his will, or indirectly in some way) when Nathan has a second-order volition that God do so, then in altering some first-order volition in Nathan, God does not undermine Nathan's free will but instead enhances or evokes it.[59]

Nathan's own second-order volition brings it about that he has the first-order volition he does, not in the sense that it is the strength or even the agency of Nathan's second-order volition that produces the desired first-order volition in him, but rather in the sense that unless Nathan had had such a second-order volition God would not have acted on his first-order volitions. If Nathan's second-order volition had been different, his first-order volition would have been different also, because to produce in him a first-order volition discordant with his second-order desires would be to undermine his freedom of will; and that is something which God, who does not undermine the nature of his creatures, would not do.

Someone might object that if God can alter first-order volitions in the face of a believer's second-order volitions that he do so, and if Nathan has a second-order volition that God bring him to righteousness, then the entire process of Nathan's justification would be completed at the very instant at which Nathan frames his second-order volition, because in response to that second-order volition, God can make Nathan entirely righteous without violating his free will. But this objection rests on a confusion about the content of the second-order volition involved in justification. Nathan's second-order volition consists in a general willingness to have God alter his will to make him righteous. But unlike the second-order volition, say, to have the volition not to smoke, the content of this volition is vague. It consists in a general submission to God and an effective desire to let God remake one's character. But a willingness of this sort is psychologically compatible with stubbornly holding on to any number of sins. When George Eliot's Romola experiences a powerful desire to have God transform her, her newfound submission to God and desire for goodness at first co-exist with a virulent hatred of her husband. Making a sinner righteous, then, will be a process in which a believer's specific volitions are brought into harmony with the governing second-order volition assenting to God's bringing her to righteousness, with the consequent gradual alteration in first-order volitions.[60] Unlike the act of free will requisite for justification, which occurs at an instant, this part of the process takes time.

Someone might also object that this interpretation of Aquinas's account of the role of the believer's will in justification mistakenly makes him Pelagian, or at least semi-Pelagian. It is clear that theological determinism, on the one hand, and some form of Pelagianism, on the other, are the Scylla and Charybdis between which an orthodox account of justification by faith must steer. As I explain Aquinas's account here, it clearly avoids theological determinism, because it claims that God performs some act in response to something done just by a human will.

Whether or not this account avoids Pelagianism and semi-Pelagianism can be assessed more readily if we first remind ourselves briefly of the nature of those heresies. Pelagianism was condemned at the Council of Carthage in 418 because it denied the doctrine of original sin, maintained the view that a person can achieve perfect righteousness without the grace of God, and understood grace to be, for example, the sort of mental illumination which comes from reading the Bible. Aquinas's account as I have presented it here clearly avoids Pelagianism.

But what about semi-Pelagianism? Semi-Pelagianism held that God awards grace in response to the meritorious first act of human free will, which acts to request grace. On Aquinas's account of operating grace, although a believer's second-order volition is a necessary condition for God's acting on the believer's first-order volitions, the believer does not form any good act of will apart from grace, including the act of will in faith that initiates his justification. On Aquinas's view, God alone is responsible for bringing about the requisite second-order volition on the believer's part. How, exactly, Aquinas takes God's grace to bring this volition about is, of course, a vexed issue, and one which I address in Chapter 13 on grace and free will. For present purposes it is enough to note Aquinas's claim that the believer's second-order volition is a result of divine grace. Whether Aquinas can consistently hold that God's grace brings about the believer's volition in the process of justification and also that that volition is free is obviously controversial. But as long as Aquinas's account insists on this claim about the relation of operating grace to that volition, it is not guilty of semi-Pelagianism either.[61]

The theological import of justification

The combined act of intellect and will which constitutes the faith by which a person is justified on Aquinas's view thus works something like a drug which cures cancer but takes time to do so. Suppose that a person Aaron is dying of cancer but that a miracle drug is found in time. The drug is guaranteed to cure the cancer as long as Aaron takes it, but he has to take it for many years before it completes its work. When this drug is first brought to Aaron and he consents to take it, his friends will be inclined to say, with rejoicing, that the crisis is over because the doctor has cured his cancer with the new drug.

Now, of course, in one sense the claim of the friends is clearly false. Aaron's cancer will not *really* be cured till many years after the first administration of the drug; and in that long interval it will still be true to say that he has cancer. On the other hand, however, we do sometimes say that a state of affairs obtains once we have passed the turning point after which it is reasonable to assume that that state of affairs will surely follow. So, for example, we say that we paid the rent when what we actually did was put a check in the mail or that we made the coffee when what we did was to start the coffee machine. In such cases, and others like them, we act as if the end of the process has been accomplished although we know that the process is not finished, because what strikes us as the necessary condition most within our control or most likely to be omitted has in fact been met, and without further worry we can reasonably expect the end to follow. In this way there is something natural and understandable about saying of Aaron that the doctor has cured his cancer when what we mean is that the doctor has administered a drug which will cure Aaron's cancer if he continues to take it over a period of years.[62]

Analogously, once Nathan has formed the act of will which accompanies the intellectual component of faith, there is a sense in which it is true to say that God has fixed the defect in his will and healed him. The will of God is that all human beings be saved;[63] the weak link in the chain of events required for Nathan's salvation lies in Nathan himself. That is why if Nathan is not saved, the blame is to be imputed to him and not to God. And for this reason, once Nathan has the intellectual and volitional components of faith, we can correctly say that he is saved from his sin and made righteous. As long as Aaron takes the drug, his cure will surely follow; and as long as Nathan has faith, God will bring him to righteousness. On the other hand, of course, even while he takes the drug, Aaron's body still has cancer cells; and even when Nathan's second-order volition is that God make him righteous, Nathan may still be inclined to any number of evils. In this sense, Aquinas's theory of justification is compatible with the thought expressed in Luther's famous line *"simul justus et peccator"*[64] ("righteous and sinful at once");[65] and it gives a helpful insight into Paul's claim that God quickens the dead and calls those things that are not as though they were.[66]

Aquinas's theory of justification by faith also gives a consistent and interesting reading of various other well-known Pauline passages about justification by faith. On Aquinas's theory, for example, God is just and a justifier of those that believe.[67] He is a justifier of those that believe because he brings believers to righteousness, and he is just himself because in the process of justification he really does eradicate sin. Those he takes to himself are those who have been made righteous, in a process extending through this life and culminating in the next. Furthermore, it is clear why "the works of the law" can justify no one. On Aquinas's theory, justification is the process whereby a person who was not righteous is changed and brought to righteousness.[68] But to do the works of the law is to do what is righteous. Anyone who does the works of the law is not thereby being changed from unrighteousness to righteousness but is already at the end or at least in the middle of the transformation. Justification involves getting a will which was bent on evil to turn to what is good. It is not that the will of a person before justification is constrained in some way towards evil; the problem is rather that such a will does not want the good. Any person who did the works of the law, however, would have a will which already willed the good. Even a person who is only beginning a struggle to do the works of the law, a person, that is, who is trying, often unsuccessfully, to do those things that satisfy the law, is a person whose will is bent on good, at least to the extent of wanting to *try* to do the works of the law. Therefore, the works of the law, that is, righteous actions, cannot accomplish the transformation of an evil will into a good one. That is why even the initial assent to grace, which constitutes the volitional part of faith, must be a result of God's work on the believer. Since that initial willing is a hungering for goodness and to that extent a righteous willing, a will which forms that volition has already been turned to righteousness to some extent.

Finally, on this account of Aquinas's, it is clear in what sense believers are children of Abraham, as Paul claims.[69] Abraham was justified by believing in God's promise; believers are Abraham's seed, Paul says, and so heirs of his promise.[70] But the promise, according to Paul, is the promise of justification by faith: "the scripture, foreseeing that God would justify the heathen through faith, preached before the gospel unto Abraham, saying, 'In thee shall all nations be blessed'."[71] Therefore, according to these passages, a believer is justified by believing what Abraham believed, namely, that God will justify him through faith; and this is the very view of justification by faith Aquinas's theory provides.[72]

Faith: the resolution of some puzzles

On Aquinas's account of justification by faith, it is easy to see why a person's having faith has an impact on her moral character. Insofar as a desire for a good will is morally preferable to the absence of that desire, to the state in which a person does not recognize her moral shortcomings or is indifferent to them, a person who comes to faith undergoes a moral improvement simply in virtue of acquiring faith. Furthermore, once a believer has the second-order volition at issue in justification by faith, God can work on the believer's first-order desires and volitions to bring her to righteousness without violating her freedom of will. On the other hand, it is also easy to see why having faith is compatible with the perpetration of evil, even the perpetration of evils in the name of Christianity. As we saw before, the second-order volition involved in faith is a volition whose content is vague and compatible with volitions (whether first-order or second-order) to do what is evil. The movement towards righteousness which is begun with the believer's second-order volition in faith is carried out in a process which takes time, a process in which more and more of a believer's will and intellect are brought into harmony with the general second-order volition desiring goodness and detesting sin. Aquinas's theory also explains why a person who is justified finds acceptance with God, because the nature of the volitional component of faith is such that it enables God to unite a believer with himself, insofar as that volition allows God to make the believer morally good without violating his freedom of will.

In a complaint which is a variant on that we considered in connection with epistemological justification, someone might object here that, even so, the act of will in faith is not open to everyone, because some people are ignorant of the claims of Christianity on which the will of faith is based. Consequently it may still seem morally unacceptable for God to base his acceptance of a person on faith, even on Aquinas's understanding of faith. What Aquinas's account shows, however, is that God's requiring faith for justification is not an arbitrary constraint, because without the volitional component of faith, God's acting on the will to make it good would violate its freedom. What this objection amounts to, then, is the complaint that a good God should have done more to make the beliefs requisite for faith available to all people. The objection is thus in effect part of the problem of evil, which lies outside the scope of this chapter.

But perhaps something can be done to blunt the edge of this objection even in the context of this chapter. The objection apparently presupposes that only those people who have specifically and explicitly Christian beliefs can have the will of faith. This, however, is a presupposition which Aquinas denies. It is important to distinguish the essential characteristics of the object of faith from its accidents, Aquinas says; and it is possible to be rightly related to the object of faith without knowing some of the truths contained in Scripture.[73] On Aquinas's view, some of those who lived before the advent of Christ or who lived in places where Christianity was not known might nonetheless have been saved because they were rightly related to the object of faith even if they did not explicitly hold the articles of faith. Pagans before the time of Christ, for example, might have implicit faith, believing in the providence of God who frees men in his own way and in ways known to those to whom he has revealed the truth.[74] Implicit faith is salvific, too.

Atonement and the will

The way in which Aquinas's account solves these puzzles about faith may leave the puzzle about the atonement's role looking only more intractable. On Aquinas's account, faith justifies because it includes a second-order volition assenting to God's doing the work of justification in the believer. There seems no need, in fact no room, in this process for the atonement. If God can do the work of making a believer righteous in virtue of the believer's assent to God's work, then what is the role of the atonement in salvation? Why should God not have done the entire work of justification without the suffering and death of the incarnate Christ? On the other hand, if we can describe the atonement in such a way as to make it an integral part of salvation, what is its relation to the process of justification by faith? How does the atonement contribute to justification if justification consists in God's eliciting and responding to the believer's second-order volition assenting to God's justification of him?[75]

To see how the doctrine of the atonement and the doctrine of justification by faith fit together for Aquinas, it helps to reflect on the way the atonement is related to the act of will involved in faith. Consider, for example, Rosamond Lydgate in George Eliot's *Middlemarch*. Her prodigality, social climbing, and selfish manipulation of her husband bring him to ruin, forcing him to give up his aspirations to do medical research and causing him to lead a life he despises. Insofar as she gives religion any thought at all, Rosamond might fairly be said to be vaguely theistic, but no one would ever say of her that she has a will which desires God's goodness and detests her own sin. How is Rosamond to be brought to such a will?

We could, of course, suppose that God simply produces such a will in her, moving her directly from the evil state in which her will refuses grace to a state in which it assents to grace, because free will, like everything else, is in the control of an omnipotent God; that is, we might suppose that God could simply determine her will.[76] But this response seems to me to increase, not lessen, the puzzle over the atonement. If with a single act of will God could produce the volitions he wants in human beings, the volitions necessary for salvation, why would he instead save people by submitting Christ to the pain of crucifixion? And why would he not produce this volition in everybody, so that all people are saved? Because this approach is problematic and also seems to contradict various things Aquinas says about the freedom of the will of faith, in this chapter I am simply leaving to one side answers which maintain that the act of will requisite for justification is produced directly by God alone without there being in any way a divine response to something in the believer. In Chapter 13 on grace and free will, I argue at some length for an interpretation of Aquinas's views which eschews such divine determinism.

We might suppose, alternatively, that Rosamond can herself produce the act of will necessary to salvation. Absent worries about Pelagianism, it does appear that people reform themselves. The story of Rosamond's brother, Fred Vincy, gives us an excellent example of a scapegrace who puts the indolence and self-indulgence of his youth behind him to become a temperate and productive man.

But the reforms of Fred Vincy are piecemeal and, by comparison with the reform produced by conversion, small. When he considers the money he loses at billiards or the weeks and months of his life he fritters away, he can see for himself that he falls far short of his own ideal of human life; consequently, he may resolve to quit billiards and take up some useful profession. What is required for justification, however, is seeing that what needs reforming is not this or that practice but the whole desperately wicked human heart.

What Rosamond needs in order to be converted, then, is not that she should subject some practice of hers to criticism in light of her own standard of values but something much more radical. It is not that she must reform some leaning of her will in light of her will's overarching disposition, but that her whole will undergo a moral rebirth. That she herself cannot effect these changes requisite for conversion seems clear. In wanting such a change she would already be exercising a changed will.

But if we are not to account for the act of will necessary for justification by attributing it to Rosamond or to God's determining Rosamond's will without any contribution from her will, how are we to account for it? To answer that question, it is helpful to consider in some detail what changes there would have to be in Rosamond in order for her to form the act of will involved in faith.

First, she will have to recognize at least that some of what she has done is seriously wrong, and then she will have to care about that fact. She will have to come to understand further that the evil she has done is symptomatic of a much deeper disorder in her will, a disorder which has alienated her from God, and she will have to have some desire that that disorder be remedied. She will need to suppose that she is capable of moral rebirth, so that she does not despair of herself, but she will also need to recognize that she needs help in order to effect such a moral change. Finally, she must come to see that God can work the desired moral transformation in her even if she cannot do so herself. This belief will itself depend on other beliefs, perhaps most importantly on the belief that her past evil has not left her permanently separated from God and that God is willing to renew her. Finally, she must have some desire that God change her in this way; what she sees of God must inspire her with some desire to draw nearer.

No doubt many things in a person's life can contribute to readying her for and inviting her to this transformation. Rosamond's one stirring of genuine altruism is a result of the self-disregarding compassion shown her by Dorothea Casaubon. Such stirrings or softenings of the heart are the harbingers of a moral rebirth; and, except for cases such as that of Paul on the road to Damascus, perhaps all instances of moral renewal are preceded by such experiences. But in order for their promise to be fulfilled, the heart of a person such as Rosamond must not only stir or soften but crack and melt. The cold, proud self-will and self-love which have animated her must break and give way to a new understanding of goodness and a new desire to follow it.

When the providentially ordered circumstances and the choices of her life have left her ready, reflection on the passion and death of Christ will be the wedge that cracks her heart. Christ's willingness to die for the spiritually poor and lost sets a standard by which Rosamond can measure herself and see the petty egotism which has been the basis of her character and actions. The same events also show her God's great love for her. God, who sees Rosamond's failings clearly, responds to her evil not by abandoning her in anger and disgust but by coming to draw her to himself. If Dorothea's generous and compassionate move towards Rosamond can soften her heart, Christ's passion and death will crack it, if anything can do so at all.

The notion of a heart's cracking or melting is, of course, a metaphor. To speak of something's cracking or melting is to describe something's giving way to an external force after (or in spite of) some internal resistance or disinclination. To say that a heart cracks or melts, then, is to imply that a will which previously was resistant or disinclined towards something urged on it by someone (or something) else gives over its dissent and leaves off its resistance.[77]

We can consequently explain the connection between the atonement and justification by faith in this way. Before he is justified, a person has a resistance or disinclination towards the second-order volition in which sinners detest their sin and long for God's goodness, a volition towards which the providence of God urges him. When a person has been readied (or perhaps as in the case of Paul does not need to be readied) by past experience and grace, the passion and death of Christ are the means for subduing the sinner's final resistance to such a volition. The internal opposition to undergoing the wholesale changes and the humbling entailed by such a volition is broken by the suffering of Christ and the love it shows.

But, as I argue in detail in Chapter 13 on grace and free will, the quelling of dissent need not be equivalent to freely willed assent. If we can distinguish the breaking down of refusal from the positive good of assent – and Aquinas's philosophical psychology makes it plain that we can – then God can avail himself of the absence of refusal to infuse the previously refused grace, in order to move the will from quiescence all the way to assent. On this view, God's grace is what produces the second-order volition requisite for justification, as Aquinas's theory of justification claims; and yet because God does so only in the absence of the refusal of grace, he does not coerce the will or undermine its freedom, but is instead responsive to it. Nonetheless, all forms of Pelagianism are avoided since there is nothing good in a human person's will that is not produced in it by God's grace. Consequently, in addition to the many other benefits the atonement works for human beings, there is this very important one: the atonement cracks the will's resistance to grace so that God may reform it without violating it.[78]

In this way, Aquinas's theory of justification by faith, together with his view of the nature of the will, can be shown to have the resources for a solution to the puzzles which I raised earlier. Using Aquinas's theory of justification, then, we can show both why faith justifies and how the atonement is related to that faith.

Conclusion

Aquinas's account of faith, the first of the theological virtues, raises questions related to epistemology and philosophical theology, having to do with justification variously understood. These questions need to be considered within the context of Aquinas's metaphysics and philosophy of mind, as well as his understanding of the theology immediately relevant to his account of faith. When we consider them within this broader context, it is apparent that Aquinas's philosophy and theology have the resources to give defensible answers to the questions regarding epistemological justification as well as a defensible explanation of the doctrine of justification by faith.

13

GRACE AND FREE WILL

Introduction

On Aquinas's account of faith and grace, a human being is justified when God operates on him in such a way as to bring him to faith with its two-part act of will. In consequence of God's operating grace, that person desires God's goodness and hates his own sins; as I argued in Chapter 12 on faith, this is a second-order act of will for a will that wills what it ought to will. But how are we to understand the genesis of this second-order act of will? At this point, we are ready finally to turn to the vexed question of the relation of grace and free will. According to Aquinas, the second-order act of free will in justifying faith is produced in a person by the divine infusion of operating grace; the will does not cooperate with God in this act but is simply moved by him. Nonetheless, Aquinas holds, this act of will is still free.

The problem of the relation of grace to free will in Aquinas's thought is, of course, at the center of the longstanding conflict between Molina and Bañez and their intellectual descendants, and the conflict has seemed to many to be irresoluble. In a spirit of altogether appropriate diffidence, however, I want to suggest that it is not impossible to see a way in which to maintain compatibly both Aquinas's claim that divine grace produces the act of will necessary for justification and that that act of will is free in a non-compatibilist sense. Whether Aquinas himself actually held the position I am about to suggest or whether he would even have liked this position if he had not held it but could have seen it with all its implications and ramifications will no doubt always be controversial. What I want to show is just that his views allow for this interpretation, that the interpretation combines his views on grace and free will into one consistent whole, and that without falling into any form of Pelagianism this interpretation vests ultimate responsibility for the configuration of the justifying second-order act of will in the believer. I myself think that the interpretation I present here *is* Aquinas's own view, but I will not argue for that conclusion here. My purpose here is only to show that there is one way of rendering Aquinas's account of grace and free will consistent, without covertly eviscerating his claims about either grace or free will.

389

The will as an internal principle of action

The first thing to see in this connection is Aquinas's insistence that *nothing* operates on the will with efficient causation. For example, Aquinas canvasses the necessity involved in the operation of each of the four Aristotelian causes – material, formal, final and agent or efficient; and he argues that there can be no causation of the will of this last sort, because any such causation is, in his view, coercive. But, he maintains, "necessity of coercion is entirely repugnant to the will ... It is impossible for something to be coerced or violent *simpliciter* and [also] voluntary".[1]

Elsewhere he says:

> if the will is moved by any external principle, the motion will be violent. By being moved by an external principle, I mean a principle which moves in the manner of an agent and not in the manner of an end. But the violent is altogether repugnant to the voluntary. It is therefore impossible that the will be moved by an external principle as an agent cause. Rather, every motion of the will must proceed from an interior principle.[2]

In an article of *Quaestiones disputatae de veritate* (*QDV*) in which he hammers home the same point, he affirms what he takes to be Augustine's claim to the same effect: "the necessity of compulsion cannot in any way apply to the will".[3]

Aquinas does not waver from this conviction even when it comes to divinely infused grace. So, for example, he says:

> God moves everything in accordance with its own manner ... And so he also moves human beings to justice in accordance with the condition of human nature. But in accordance with his own nature a human being has free choice. And so in a human being who has the use of free choice, there is no motion from God to justice without a motion of free choice.[4]

In *Summa contra gentiles* (*SCG*) he says:

> Now it might seem to someone that a human being is compelled to some good action by the divine aid [of grace] ... But it is plainly shown that this is not true. For divine providence provides for all things in accordance with their own manner ... But it is characteristic of a human being (and every rational nature) that he acts voluntarily and is master of his own acts ... and compulsion is contrary to this. Therefore God does not compel a human being to good action by his aid [of grace].[5]

In another place in *QDV* he sums up his position by saying: "God can change the will with necessity, but he cannot compel it."[6]

The infusion of grace and formal causality

What does it mean, however, to say that God can change the will with necessity but cannot compel it? How is this possible? If an omnipotent God changes something with necessity, how could it possibly be true that God does not also compel it?

Aquinas himself answers this question in some detail, and it is worth quoting his answer at length. He says:

> to will something is to be inclined to it. But compulsion or violence is contrary to the inclination of the thing compelled. Therefore, when God moves the will, he brings it about that an inclination succeeds a previous inclination in such a way that the first is removed and the second remains. And so that to which he leads the will is not contrary to an inclination now existent but rather to an inclination previously inhering [in the will]. And so there is no violence or compulsion.
>
> Similarly, there is in a stone an inclination to a downward place, because of its heaviness; and while this inclination remains, if the stone is thrown upward there will be violence. If, however, God removed from the stone the inclination of heaviness and gave it an inclination of lightness, then its upward motion would not be violent for it. In this way, a change of motion can be without violence. [And] this is the way in which we should understand that God changes the will without its being the case that he compels the will ...
>
> God changes the will in two ways. In one way, by moving it only, as when he moves the will to will something, without impressing any form on the will, as when he brings it about, without the addition of any disposition, that a human being wills something that he previously did not will. In another way, [God changes the will] by impressing some form on the will itself. For just as from the very nature which God gave to the will the will is inclined to will something ... so too from something added on to it, as grace or virtue is, the soul is further inclined to will something to which it was not previously determined by a natural inclination.
>
> This added-on inclination is sometimes complete and sometimes incomplete. When it is complete, it brings about a necessary inclination for that which it determines in such a way that the will is inclined by nature to desire the end of necessity, as happens among the blessed ... But sometimes the added-on form is not complete in

> every way, as is the case with wayfarers. And then the will is
> inclined because of the added-on form, but not of necessity.[7]

Aquinas is here calling attention to what he takes to be an important difference in the way in which God can change the will. But just what is this
difference, and why does it matter to him?

The example he gives having to do with the motion of a stone is helpful
in this regard, I think. On his view, a stone is configured in such a way that
it is inclined to fall downward. If the stone is thrown upward while it still
has this configuration, then, on Aquinas's views, some violence or compulsion is exercised on the stone, because the stone is moved contrary to its own
inclination or configuration. But it is possible to change the configuration of
the stone. The configuration that makes the stone inclined to fall downward
could be removed by God, and the stone could instead be given a new inclination, an inclination to move upward. In that case, the stone would
presumably be like fire; it would be naturally inclined to move upward. If
God were to alter the configuration of the stone in this way, then he would
change the stone in such a way as to make the stone move upward. But now
the upward motion would not occur as a result of any compulsion or
violence on God's part.

In the same way, Aquinas emphasizes in one place after another that
God's giving of grace is not simply God's willing that a human will will
something or other. Rather, it is God's infusing of a form, the form of grace,
after a previous form in the human will has been removed. Because grace
justifies the person who receives it, Aquinas takes the previous form, which
is removed or expelled, to be the form of culpability or guilt; this is the
configuration of the will before it detests sin and loves the goodness of God.
So, elsewhere in *QDV*, Aquinas says:

> grace which is and inheres expels guilt – not that guilt which is
> but that guilt which previously was and [now] is not. For grace
> does not expel guilt in the manner of an efficient cause; for if it
> did, then it would have to be the case that grace acted on
> existing guilt to expel it ... Rather, grace expels guilt in the
> manner of a formal cause (*formaliter*). For from the very fact that
> grace inheres in its subject as a form, it follows that guilt is not
> in the subject.[8]

And in another place, he says: "God brings about graced spiritual being in
us without the intervention of any agent [cause], but still with the intervention of a created form – and this is grace."[9] And so, on his view, "grace
does not expel guilt in the manner of an efficient cause (*effective*) but in the
manner of a formal cause (*formaliter*)."[10]

Aquinas goes to great lengths to explain what the manner of a formal cause is in cases such as this. For example, in arguing that justification occurs in an instant, he says:

> when some mean must be recognized between the endpoints of a change, the transition from one endpoint to another must be successive, because that which is moved continuously must first be changed to the mean before it is changed to the final endpoint ... But when there cannot be a mean between the two endpoints of a change or motion ... , then the transition from one endpoint to the other does not occur in [a period of] time but rather in an instant. And this happens when the two endpoints of a motion or change are ... privation and form ... And so I say that the endpoints of justification are grace and the privation of grace. Between these there is no mean ... and therefore the transition from one to the other is in an instant, ... And so the whole justification of an impious person occurs in an instant.[11]

For Aquinas, then, the will of a person before she comes to justifying faith is characterized by a configuration which is culpable. God could simply will that such a person will to detest sin and love God's goodness. But if he did so while that culpable configuration remains in her will, he would compel the will and exercise violence on it. In his goodness, however, God deals with all things in accordance with their nature, and so, according to Aquinas, God does not deal violently with the will. Instead of compelling it to will something, God instead gives the will a new configuration after the old configuration has been removed. As Aquinas says, the endpoints of the change that constitute God's infusion of grace are *not* two opposite forms, but rather a privation of a form and a form. So in the process of justification, the culpable configuration of the will is removed, leaving the will with a privation – an absence of a configuration as regards sin and goodness. Then in turn this privation is taken away by the form of grace which God adds to the will.[12] And so divinely infused grace gives the will a configuration with regard to something not by restructuring some configuration present in the will but by adding a configuration to a will which lacks a configuration in this regard. It is for this reason that Aquinas says that divinely infused grace operates on the will in the manner of a formal cause and not in the manner of an efficient cause.

The privation of form and quiescence in the will

But why think that this somewhat complicated scholastic distinction is of any help here? Why think, for example, that there is any less force or compulsion exercised on the will because God alters its configuration with a formal cause rather than an efficient cause? A potter who reshapes a cup into a saucer might be thought to deal forcibly with the cup; but a potter who shapes a formless lump of clay into a saucer also seems to exercise compulsion on the clay. So why suppose that the will is free in its act because its configuration is infused by God in the manner of a formal cause? If God controls the configuration of a human will, it hardly seems to matter whether he does so with formal or with efficient causation. Why, then, does Aquinas place so much emphasis on the distinction?

The answer, in my view, has to do with Aquinas's insistence that grace is infused into a will which has a privation of the opposite form. Grace configures the will into a detestation of past sins and a love of God's goodness; grace, however, introduces this configuration into a will which was but is no longer configured with a love of sin and a repugnance to God's goodness. To understand why this point matters so much to Aquinas, we first have to consider further his notion of the privation of form in the will. How are we to understand the will in the state of privation of form in this regard? And, more importantly, what accounts for this privation?

It helps in this connection to call to mind Aquinas's view of the nature of the will. According to Aquinas, the will can assent to something or reject it, but it can also simply do nothing at all. It can just be turned off; it can be inactive or quiescent.[13] Sometimes the will is determined to want something by the nature of the will's object, Aquinas says, but the exercise of the will – whether the will is turned off or not – is always in the power of the will itself.[14] Furthermore, in principle, the will can move directly from any one of these positions to another. That is, in general, it can move from rejecting to quiescence, from quiescence to assenting, from assenting to rejecting, and so on. The will's motion is thus analogous to bodily motion, on Aquinas's views. I can walk east or walk west, but I can also simply cease walking east; and my ceasing to walk east is not by itself an instance of my walking west. Furthermore, I can move from walking east to ceasing to walk east without having to walk west in order to do so. Finally, my ceasing to walk east is not a special kind of walking; it is simply the absence of walking, an inactivity or quiescence in those particular bodily parts that function to produce walking.

If this view of the will is right, then on Aquinas's metaphysics there are at least three possibilities for the will as regards the configuration of grace: the will can detest its past sins and love God's goodness (call this 'an acceptance of grace'); it can love its past sins and reject God's goodness (call this 'a refusal of grace'); or it can simply be quiescent or turned off. When it is quiescent, the will does not refuse grace, but it does not accept it either. As Aquinas understands justification by faith, a post-Fall adult person has a will which refuses grace until at some moment the refusal of grace gives way to a privation of form, an absence of a configuration in the will, or a state of quiescence. Only when the will is in this state does God infuse grace into the will.

Aquinas does not discuss the subjective phenomenology of a person in a state of quiescence in the will with regard to something or other. But here is one way to understand his idea. Consider a person suffering a bad allergic reaction to a bee sting who nonetheless vigorously refuses his doctor's injection of the desperately needed antidote to the allergen because he has a phobic fear of needles. Such a person might not be able to bring himself to will that the doctor give him the injection. That is, if the doctor asks him whether he will accept the injection, he might not be able to bring himself to say 'yes'. But he might nonetheless be able to stop actively refusing the injection, knowing that if he ceases to refuse it, the doctor will press it on him. If he does this, then his will is quiescent with regard to the injection, neither accepting it nor refusing it, but simply turned off in relation to the injection.

It seems to me that cases of this sort in which the will fails either to reject or to assent are more common than we might originally suppose and not so hard to grasp intuitively. To take another example, consider a man who is trying with the help of a friend to conquer his hysterical fear of touching snakes because there is some overwhelming need for him to come into contact with snakes. The terrified person might be brought to the point of ceasing to exclaim vehemently "I can't! I can't!" when his friend holds out a live snake to him, but he might still not be able to bring himself to do anything that constitutes assenting to touching the snake. What characterizes a case of this sort, I think, is that a person who has a powerful resistance to something, perhaps something which someone else is urging on him, finally gives up his resistance without, however, being able actually to give full-fledged assent to what the other is urging. If we inquire of the friend who put the snake into the hands of the phobic person whether the phobic assented to the contact, she may grin and say, "Hardly!". But if we then ask her in some dismay whether she forced the snake on the unwilling phobic, she will stoutly, and quite correctly, deny the charge.

Aquinas's post-Fall person whose will is quiescent with respect to grace is in an analogous case. Consequently, on Aquinas's view, when God gives the grace of justifying faith to such a person, he is infusing that grace into a human will which has ceased to reject it but which has not accepted it either. The will is in a state of privation in this respect; it is inactive.

Quiescence in the will

It may be helpful here to reflect in more detail on the nature of quiescence in the will.[15] Aquinas makes a close connection between the intellect and the will, which I have discussed in detail in the chapter on freedom. Consequently, depending on the condition of an agent's intellect, there are several ways in which the will can come to be quiescent, on Aquinas's views.

First, consider a particular act A which a person S might do but with regard to which the will of S is quiescent. And let the act in question be S's divorcing his wife. S's will might be quiescent with regard to A because S's intellect has never thought about the possibility of doing or not doing A. Although S is unhappy living with his wife, he is used to his unhappiness; and it has never occurred to him that he might end his marriage. So S's intellect forms no judgments about A, simply because considerations of divorce have not come into his mind. In this case, S's will does not reject A or assent to A; it is simply quiescent. This sort of quiescence is a consequence of *simple inattention* on the part of S's intellect.

Second, it is also possible that S's will is quiescent with respect to A because S is overwhelmed by attention to something else. For example, S might be struggling to come to terms with painful and risky medical procedures for a recently diagnosed illness that is hard to cure. In the circumstances, his unhappiness with his marriage is pushed to the back of his mind. In this condition, S's intellect does not form any judgments about A because S's intellect is occupied with other things. Consequently, S's will is quiescent with regard to A, and the quiescence is a matter of inattention on the part of S's intellect; but in this case the inattention is a *distracted inattention*, which pushes considerations of divorce out of S's mind, rather than the simple inattention of the preceding case.

Third, it might also be the case that S's will is quiescent because S does not want to think about his marriage at this stage in his life. For example, suppose that S is a mathematician who feels sure he is on the verge of a major mathematical breakthrough which will make his career, and he is worried that if he lets anything distract him from his work, he will find that the muse has deserted him when he returns to that work. So when he finds himself reflecting on ending his unhappy marriage, he sternly commands himself to stop thinking about his marriage now. In this case, S's will is quiescent with regard to A, but it is quiescent because S's intellect has reached a conclusion, namely, that in the circumstances the best thing to do now is not to think about his marriage. In consequence of that judgment on the part of S's intellect, S's will commands S's intellect not to think about S's marriage, S's intellect obeys the will's command, and *in the end* S's will is quiescent with regard to A. In this case, the final quiescence of S's will is still a function of inattention on the part of S's intellect, but it is what we might call '*willed inattention*'.[16]

Fourth, on the other hand, S's intellect might have reflected on the condition of his marriage, but it might not have been able to reach any integrated judgment. S might see powerful reasons for dissolving his marriage and also see powerful reasons for keeping it going; and even with all the wrestling with the issue he can muster, S might not be able to reach any single conclusion one way or another. When his reflections come to an end, when he has considered everything he sees as relevant to the decision, S is still deeply double-minded. In this condition, on Aquinas's understanding to the relation of the intellect and the will, S's will is also quiescent, but that is because S's intellect is unable to reach a judgment about what it would be best to do now in these circumstances. In this case, the quiescence of S's will is not a matter of any sort of inattention. It is more nearly a case of a real, internal *abstention*. The will refrains from willing anything because S's intellect cannot reach a single judgment.

It is worth noting here that none of these kinds of quiescence can be exactly the kind Aquinas has in mind in his account of justifying faith. That is because in all of these cases – simple inattention, distracted inattention, willed inattention, and abstention – the quiescence of the will is not one in which the will's quiescence is a privation of a previously inhering form. In all of these four cases, the will is quiescent in the sense that it has no configuration with regard to A; but the absence of configuration with regard to A does not follow a previous configuration with regard to A.

To have a case of the sort Aquinas describes in his account of justifying faith, we would have to imagine that the agent previously had a particular configuration of will with regard to some action – in fact, that he rejected doing that action – and that that configuration gives place to quiescence of the will with regard to the action in question. So consider Henry VIII of England at the time when Henry was besotted with infatuation for Anne Boleyn and determined to divorce Catherine of Aragon in order to marry Anne, and let the act in question be sending Anne away in order to be faithful to Catherine. At that time, with regard to this action, Henry's will was in the configuration of rejection; he wanted to divorce Catherine, and he passionately rejected dismissing Anne. On Aquinas's views of the relation of the intellect to the will, Henry's will can be in this condition only in case Henry's intellect yields single-mindedly the judgment that, in the circumstances, the best thing to do now is not to send Anne away but rather to divorce Catherine. ('Best' in this judgment need not be morally best. On Aquinas's account, the will wills only what the intellect judges best to do in the circumstances now, but Aquinas takes the good to range over the moral, the pleasant, and the useful; and what the intellect judges to be best might be a species of the pleasant or the useful, rather than the moral.)

It is, of course, possible that Henry might then have changed his mind. His counselors might have convinced him, for example, that the disruption to his realm likely to follow a divorce would be too high a price to pay even for the sake of marriage to Anne. In that case, his intellect would have abandoned its former judgment and adopted the judgment that sending Anne away for the sake of remaining in his marriage to Catherine was the best, that is, the most useful, thing to do in the circumstances now. Or the counselors might have prevailed on Henry's notoriously fearful conscience to convince him that God would damn him to hell if he divorced his wife. In that case, too, though for different reasons, Henry's intellect would have formed the judgment that sending Anne away was the best thing to do in the circumstances.

But if Henry changed his mind in this way, if Henry's intellect formed a judgment of this sort, then his will would have changed from rejecting the action in question to assenting to it, on Aquinas's account of the relations between the intellect and the will. But this is not the sort of change in the will that is at issue in justification by faith, where rejection is followed by quiescence. What would have to happen in the intellect to account for the sort of change Aquinas describes in his account of justifying faith, where the configuration of rejection in the will is followed by a privation of configuration in the will?

We could, of course, suppose that Henry's intellect just moves into one of the states of inattention described above. He could simply lose interest in the whole matter of divorce, say, perhaps because Anne Boleyn died; or he might stop considering the matter because he was distracted by civil unrest and the need to protect his throne. Then we would have a case in which simple inattention or distracted inattention caused quiescence in the will; and in such a case we would in fact have quiescence which succeeded rejection with regard to the action in question. But cases of this sort would still fall short of meeting Aquinas's description of the quiescence in justification, I think, because there is at least a suggestion in the texts at issue that quiescence of the will is at least part of the means by which the preceding rejection in the will is driven out or expelled, as Aquinas says. In the cases involving Henry I have just sketched, quiescence succeeds rejection but does not seem in any sense instrumental in removing it.

Finally, considerations of the homely examples I gave above to illustrate the subjective phenomenology of Aquinas's notion of quiescence in the will suggest still another possibility, however. In the grip of a terror of needles, the intellect of the phobic person in the bee sting case is vehemently opposed to the idea of letting the doctor give the needed injection, and so the phobic's will rejects yielding to the doctor. But there is a side of his intellect which also understands the importance of the injection. It is a side that has been ineffective in the face of the phobic's passionate fear of needles. But the doctor's importunities and exhortations may strengthen it significantly, by calling to the forefront of the phobic's mind something he had suppressed, by actualizing beliefs the phobic was antecedently disposed to believe but did not attend to, and/or by trying to build some passion on the other side of the issue. By these means on the part of the doctor, the phobic's intellect may come to find much more significant and weighty the considerations for letting the doctor give him the shot.

If these considerations come to outweigh decisively the thoughts that were originally responsible for the phobic's rejecting the shot, then the phobic's intellect will yield the result that accepting the injection is the best thing to do now in these circumstances; and the phobic's will will move from its original rejection of the shot to accepting it. But in the homely example I gave, the doctor's persuasion is not enough to move the phobic to assent to the doctor's giving him the injection; the phobic's will moves from rejecting the doctor's administering the shot only to quiescence. It must be, then, that in the circumstances the considerations on the side of accepting the injection become, in one way or another, just weighty enough for the phobic that the phobic's intellect becomes divided against itself. The original considerations which yielded the judgment that the shot was to be rejected remain, but they are countered by new considerations pushing in the direction of the judgment that the shot is to be accepted. The result is that, as in the case of abstention I described above, the intellect becomes locked in indecision, unable to resolve the conflict within itself into one single, integrated judgment. In the face of this blockage in the intellect, the phobic's will becomes quiescent. But now the quiescence can appropriately be said to drive out the rejection.

In this final case, it is not simply that the will is inactive because the intellect has lapsed into inattention of some sort. Rather, the will becomes inactive because the intellect has come to be divided against itself. The shift in the intellect's considerations is responsible for the alteration of the configuration in the will. And so it seems appropriate to describe the change in the will to quiescence as the expelling or driving out of the preceding rejection. (Of course, other things also play a role in this process. The circumstances which help to produce the division in the intellect – and Aquinas would take these to be providentially ordered – also make a contribution. In the case of the phobic in the bee sting case, the doctor's persuasive speeches about the importance of the injection have some influence on the process by which the phobic becomes divided in intellect; in this non-determinative sense, the doctor's speeches also contribute to driving out the will's rejection of the necessary shot.)

Someone might wonder what difference it would make to this case if the phobic knew that the doctor would give him the injection as soon as his will ceased rejecting it.[17] If the phobic knew that quiescence in his will would have the same effect as his assenting to the injection, why would not quiescence in his will be equivalent to assent? The first thing to say in response to this question is that the phenomenology is different in the two cases. In order for the will to assent, the intellect has to reach the conclusion that assenting to the injection is the best thing to do in these circumstances, and the will has to will accordingly. A mind in such a condition is reasonably well integrated. But when the will is quiescent in the way it is in the case of the phobic, the intellect is strongly divided against itself; the will is quiescent because the intellect can reach no single conclusion. A mind in this condition is torn and in tension with itself. So, the condition of the intellect is significantly different in the two cases, and there is consequently also a considerable difference in the condition of the will. If the intellect gives a single judgment that in the circumstances, the best thing to do now is to accept the injection, the person in question will form the corresponding act of will. But the will of the person whose intellect is stymied in irresoluble internal division forms no act of will at all.

Furthermore, it is important to see that even if the phobic knew that the doctor would take quiescence in his will as sufficient for giving him the shot, and even with all the considerations influencing him in the direction of accepting the injection, the phobic might not be able to get himself all the way to assent to the shot because his fear of needles might be too great for him to conquer. Quiescence in the circumstances may be the best he can do. It might nonetheless be the case that the phobic is not neutral in this struggle within himself. Even if his will is quiescent with regard to the action of letting the doctor give him the injection, he might *want* one side or another of his internally divided mind to prevail. That is, we can imagine that although the phobic's intellect is divided and his will is consequently quiescent as regards permitting the doctor to give him the injection, the phobic's intellect judges that it would be good if he could conquer his phobia of needles, so that the phobic has a second-order desire[18] for a will that wills to accept the injection. To desire a will that accepts the injection is not, of course, the same as a will that accepts the injection, nor is a second-order desire for a certain first-order act of will a sufficient condition for forming such an act of will, as anyone can attest who has ever begun a difficult reform of himself.

So it is possible that a person S with a quiescent will is in this sort of condition. After originally having a will in a configuration of rejection as regards some act A, A's intellect moves into a double-minded state with regard to A, so that A's will moves from rejection to quiescence. But S's intellect simultaneously forms the judgment that it would be good if one side of the internal division were to win the struggle; and S consequently forms the higher-order desire for a will that wills to assent – without, however, actually forming the will to assent. Although the psychology as I have described it is complicated, it does seem to describe appropriately people in the process of serious psychological change. To pick just one famous case, as Augustine recounts his struggle with himself to accept a life of celibacy, he seems for a short time to have been in a condition of this sort. After reading the texts which moved him strongly in the direction of accepting celibacy, he ran impetuously to a solitary place and wept bitterly. In the course of his weeping, he heard the child's voice which prompted him to read a portion of Scripture; and after his reading of that text, he finally assented to adopting the celibate lifestyle. While he was still in the fit of weeping, then, he had not yet formed that assent, but it is also true that he was not any longer in the simple condition of wholeheartedly rejecting celibacy which marked him previously either. The weeping seems to have been an expression of the conflict in his mind and of the accompanying stymied quiescence of his will, which was not able either to reject celibacy or to assent to it either.

And yet it is perfectly clear from Augustine's description of himself in his *Confessions* that he himself was not a neutral party to the warring parts of himself. He had a higher-order desire[19] for a will that willed celibacy even while he was unable to form an act of will accepting celibacy. He had this higher-order desire because his intellect, which could not reach a single, integrated conclusion that accepting celibacy was the best thing in the circumstances now (a conclusion about what act to do now), nonetheless did form the judgment that Augustine's being in the state of willing celibacy would be the morally best state of will for Augustine (a judgment about moral rank-orderings of states of will). It is important to be clear that the higher-order desire in question here is not itself an act of will. If it were an act of will, it would be effective in its command to the will to be in a certain condition. As it is, it is a self-reflexive and ineffective desire for a condition of will other than the one in which the will actually is. There is thus no act of will at the higher-order level in such a person, any more than there is an act of will in a person who has some desire to grade her term papers but not enough desire to will to do so.

And so we can even suppose that the person whose will is quiescent both knows and also desires that his quiescence of will will be followed by an infusion of grace. We need not make such a supposition; but it is a coherent possibility, exemplified in cases of complicated internal division such as that represented by Augustine's experience in the garden, and nothing in Aquinas's account of justification or of the nature of the will rules it out.

Quiescence, alternative possibilities and Pelagianism

Because Aquinas thinks that it is always in the will's own power to be quiescent or not, it is open to us to suppose that for Aquinas the will is moved from the rejection of grace to quiescence by the human willer herself. There is nothing Pelagian or even semi-Pelagian about this view, however. What characterizes all forms of Pelagianism is the claim that a human being is capable of some good act without grace. But a will which is quiescent in the way at issue here is not a good will. The configuration that grace introduces into such a will is the will to detest sin and want goodness, and this is the configuration that the quiescent will lacks. But, clearly, a will which does not so much as will to will goodness is not a good will. (And the point remains the same even if the person whose will is quiescent has some ineffective higher-order desire for a will that is not quiescent. To do no more than wish ineffectively that one wanted a will that willed the good is still to be in a morally lamentable condition.) It is true that a will in this condition is better than a will which wants sin and does not will to will goodness. But comparatives do not suppose positives. One thing can be better than another and yet not be good.

Someone might object here that, even so, the *movement* towards quiescence is a movement in the direction of the good and that therefore the person who moves to quiescence of will has done something good. But here it is important to remember that on Aquinas's account the will's lapsing into quiescence is not itself another act of will, any more than ceasing to walk east is another act of walking. But since the lapsing into quiescence is not an act of will at all, it can hardly be considered a *good* act. So in this respect, too, Pelagianism is warded off.

Consequently, without risk of falling into Pelagianism, we can suppose that it is up to a human willer, and to her alone, whether her will refuses grace or is quiescent with regard to grace. As I have been at pains to show, this is not to say that the human willer at issue looks at the options of refusing grace or being quiescent with regard to grace and forms a decision about which of the options should characterize her will. Rather, it is to claim just that control over whether her will acts or fails to act is vested ultimately only in her.

Consequently, insofar as it is open to a human person to be simply quiescent in will in this way, then with regard to the will of faith, before the infusion of grace, there are two alternative possibilities for a human willer – rejection and quiescence – neither of which is a good act of will. On Aquinas's view, God infuses grace only into a will which is in the quiescent condition; the change brought about by the infusion of grace, as Aquinas explains in detail, is the change from a privation of a form to the possession of the form. And so it is possible to suppose that for Aquinas, although the will of faith is brought about entirely by God with operating grace, nonetheless a human person is herself still ultimately in control of the state of her own will. That is because it is up to her either to refuse grace or to fail to refuse grace. Although her options are just to refuse grace or to be quiescent with regard to grace, it is still only her own intellect and will that determine which of these positions her will is in, and God's giving of grace depends on the position of her will.

Nonetheless, since what God is responsive to in a human will does not count as a good act of will, it is possible to hold compatibly with this position the anti-Pelagian thesis that any good act on the part of a human will is brought about by grace. Consequently, without danger of any form of Pelagianism, it is possible to hold that a post-Fall human being who cannot form a good act of will apart from grace can nonetheless control whether or not his will refuses grace. In ceasing to refuse grace, he brings himself into a quiescent condition to which God responds by giving him the grace that produces in him the good will of justifying faith.

Conclusion

On the position I have just outlined, then, we can explain Aquinas's account of justification by faith in this way. A normal adult human being[20] in a post-Fall condition who is not converted or in the process of being converted refuses grace continually, even if she is not aware of doing so. Before she is justified, she has a resistance or disinclination towards the second-order volition in which sinners detest their sin and long for God's goodness, the act of will towards which the providence of God urges her. At some point, however, in the way I discussed in the chapter on faith, her refusal of grace may be quelled. But the quelling of refusal is not equivalent to assent. A person can cease to refuse grace without assenting to it, on Aquinas's views. Instead, she can just be quiescent in will. If she is, then God, who offers grace to every human being, immediately infuses in her the previously refused grace; God avails himself of the absence of refusal on her part to produce in her the good will of justifying faith.

Consequently, it is possible to hold consistently both that the will of faith, like any good will whatsoever in a human being, is brought about only by God's grace, but that a human being is still ultimately in control of the state of her will, insofar as it is up to her either to refuse grace or to fail to refuse grace, and God's giving of grace depends on the state of her will.[21] Nonetheless, all forms of Pelagianism are avoided since nothing in these claims requires Aquinas to give up the view that there is nothing good in a human person's will which is not produced in it by God's grace.

Because ultimate control over the state of her will is vested in the person being justified, Aquinas's account (on this interpretation of it) can give an answer to the question Augustine wrestled with, namely, why God does not cause the justifying act of will in everyone. Whether or not God causes that act of will in a person is dependent on whether or not that person's will has ceased to reject grace, and that is something for which she herself is ultimately responsible. Furthermore, since a human being not only is ultimately responsible for her state of will but also has alternative possibilities with regard to willing, it does seem right to hold, as (on this interpretation) Aquinas does, that the justifying act of will is a free act, and even free in a libertarian sense.

But is the interpretation I have sketched here really right? That is, does the textual evidence support the conclusion that this is the position Aquinas in fact held? There are certainly some texts of Aquinas's which could be used to argue for an affirmative answer. So, for example, in a section of SCG in which Aquinas argues that grace is necessary for faith, he also has a chapter in which he explains why, in his view, a person who does not come to faith is nonetheless responsible for his unregenerate condition. Aquinas says:[22]

> one must consider that although a person cannot merit or produce
> grace by a motion of free will, he can nonetheless impede himself

from receiving grace ... And so this is in the power of free will: to impede the reception of the divine grace or not to impede it. For this reason the person who provides an obstacle to the reception of divine grace merits the blame imputed to him. For insofar as it lies in him himself, God is prepared to give grace to everyone ... But the only people deprived of grace are the ones who provide in themselves an obstacle to grace.[23]

As I said above, however, interpretations of Aquinas's account of grace and free will have been so controversial in the past that arguments for one interpretation over another are more likely to prompt contention than to produce convergence of view. And so my aim here is the more modest one of simply showing one way in which Aquinas's account of human psychology, and especially his view of the nature of the will, makes it possible to combine consistently the claims Aquinas holds as regards grace and the free will of justifying faith. I myself am strongly inclined to think that this is in fact the position Aquinas himself held, but all I am arguing for here is that this position is available to Aquinas whether or not he availed himself of it.

Part IV

GOD'S RELATIONSHIP TO HUMAN BEINGS

14

THE METAPHYSICS OF THE INCARNATION

Introduction

Aquinas's interpretation of the metaphysics of the incarnation is an attempt to make sense out of a theological doctrine bequeathed to him as a traditional and central part of Christian belief. In this chapter, I want to explicate his interpretation of the doctrine and go some way towards defending it. It is *not* my intent to argue that the formulation of the doctrine he accepts as traditional is the only orthodox one, or that his interpretation of that formulation is the only appropriate interpretation of the doctrine, or that his interpretation is the best way to understand biblical statements about the nature of Christ. It is also *not* part of my purpose to show that Aquinas's interpretation is completely intelligible and coherent or philosophically defensible in every respect. Rather, my aim in this chapter is a limited one: to explicate Aquinas's interpretation of the doctrine of the incarnation in terms of his metaphysics in such a way as to clarify and support both his understanding of the doctrine and his metaphysics.

The formulation of the doctrine of the Incarnation which Aquinas accepts and takes as binding on Christians is the one put forward at Chalcedon in 451 AD: Christ is one hypostasis, one person, with two natures, one fully human and the other fully divine. Stating the Chalcedonian formulation is one thing; explaining what it means is another. Aquinas relies heavily on his general metaphysical theory to provide one interpretation of the Chalcedonian formulation.[1] On the other hand, the doctrine of the incarnation stretches that metaphysics almost to the breaking point. Consequently, in the course of considering the incarnation, Aquinas is compelled to explain his metaphysics with some care, in order to argue that, contrary to appearances, the doctrine of the incarnation does not serve as a counterexample to any of his general metaphysical claims. Some of his most helpful explanations of various parts of his metaphysics can thus be found in his discussions of the incarnation. In this chapter, I will be concerned primarily with the way in which Aquinas understands the Chalcedonian formula, the resources his interpretation of the formula has for handling familiar objections to the doctrine of the incarnation, and the view of the mind of Christ to which his interpretation is committed.

Incarnation: the doctrinal claims on Aquinas's interpretation

The Chalcedonian formula says that Christ is one person with two natures. On Aquinas's understanding of the doctrine, the one person of Christ[2] is the second person of the triune God.[3] Consequently, all that is true of deity is true of the person of Christ. He is outside time; his knowledge, power, and goodness are not limited, and so on. In short, because the person of Christ is the second person of the Trinity, divine nature is the nature of that person.[4] If we ignore for the present the complications raised by the doctrine of simplicity, we can skip these clumsy circumlocutions and say that the person of Christ has a divine nature in virtue of being a divine person.[5]

At a certain moment in time, the second person of the Trinity assumed a human nature. That is to say, the second person added to himself another nature, in addition to the divine nature already his own.[6] According to Aquinas, the moment of the assumption is the moment of the conception of Jesus. Ordinarily, Aquinas thinks, a fetus does not become human at conception; rather, at a certain moment in its development, the fetus loses whatever substantial form it has and gains the substantial form of a human being. In the case of Jesus, however, for reasons which are not directly relevant to my concerns here, the substantial form of a human being is infused at conception, and the conceptus is human from the first instant of its existence, which is thus also the first moment of time of the assumption of human nature.[7]

There is a complication here, however, that arises from the doctrine of divine eternity. Although the assumption of a human nature occurred at a moment of time t, the second person of the Trinity is not himself in time; rather, he is eternal. There is no succession in eternity, no *before* and *after*. So it is not the case in eternity that after this moment t but not before it God has assumed human nature. On the contrary, each moment in time is simultaneous with the whole of God's atemporal life. The whole of God's life is thus simultaneous with the assumption of human nature at t.[8] So the assumption of human nature which takes place at t in time is not something new that occurs in the life of an atemporal God in eternity. Rather, there never was a part of God's life when the second person of the Trinity had not assumed human nature. The incarnation is thus not a change in God.[9]

For Aquinas, the nature of a material substance is conferred by a substantial form which is an individual; and a substantial form is an individual in virtue of its configuring matter under indeterminate dimensions.[10] So when the second person of the Trinity assumes human nature, he assumes a particular substantial form and the matter it configures.[11]

Like every other human substantial form, the substantial form assumed by Christ configures matter into a human body and confers those properties essential to human beings, including rationality. In virtue of having two natures, Christ therefore has two "operations", as Aquinas puts it.[12] On the one hand, in his divine nature, he has the operations proper to the deity. On the other hand, in his human nature, Christ has a complete and fully human mind, and he also has a rational appetite, that is to say, a complete and fully human will. Since intellect and will also characterize the divine nature, in virtue of having two natures, Christ also has two intellects[13] and two wills,[14] one human and one divine.[15]

Furthermore, different things can be true of these intellects and these wills. The human intellect can fail to know something that the divine intellect knows.[16] As for the will, it is impossible that Christ sin, through either his divine or his human will.[17] But it is possible for Christ's human will to be (sinlessly) out of accord with the divine will, at least as regards desire. Consequently, the human will of Christ can (and did) desire what the divine will rules out.[18] When the human will of Christ desires not to die, for example, there is a non-sinful discord of this sort between the divine and the human wills.[19]

For these reasons, the multiplicity of the natures is preserved. However the unity of Christ is to be explained, it is not a unity of nature.[20]

Now for a subsisting thing to have a complete human nature is just for it to have a human soul and body. But for a subsisting thing to have a human soul and body is, apparently, just for it to be an individual substance that is a human being, on Aquinas's metaphysics. Furthermore, to be an individual human substance is to be a human person, for Aquinas. Consequently, it seems as if, on Aquinas's views, there must be a human person as well as a divine person in Christ. Aquinas's response to this sort of worry is to grant that *in general* a human soul configuring a human body composes a human person but that *in the special case of Christ*, although there is a human soul and body, they do not comprise a human person.

Aquinas's metaphysical claims about substance include the denial that any substance includes a substance within it. Instead, anything that is or would be a substance existing on its own ceases to be a substance in its own right when it is included within a larger whole. So because, in the case of Christ, the substantial form of a human being and the matter it configures are part of a larger composite, which includes the second person of the Trinity and the divine nature, in this one case the substantial form of a human being and the matter it configures do not constitute a human person. If they existed on their own, outside of the composite which is the incarnate Christ, the human soul and body of Christ would certainly constitute a human person. But conjoined in Christ, they do not, in virtue of being subsumed into the whole composite.[21]

There is therefore just one person in Christ, and that person is divine. Because this one person has two natures, however, that one divine person subsists in both natures[22] and can operate through either one (or both).[23]

The two natures of Christ are united into one thing in this one person, so that the unity of the incarnate Christ is a unity in person. (Since the person is a supposit or a hypostasis,[24] this unity is sometimes also referred to as 'a hypostatic union'.) But the principle of unification of the natures in the person is unique to Christ.[25] On the one hand, the divine person does not configure the human body and soul as a substantial form. The divine person is not a form configuring matter; the divine person is a complete thing in its own right, as the substantial form of a material composite is not.[26] On the other hand, the human soul and body do not come to the divine person as an accident comes to an already existing thing, because the human nature is a component of the substance of Christ.[27] The unity of the person and the natures in Christ is also not a union in nature, since there are two distinct natures in Christ that cannot be conflated into one. So the human nature of Christ is not united to the person of Christ in any of the ways in which the constituents of a substance are usually united, either by having the form of the whole configure the constituent in question, or by coming together to form a nature, or by coming to the composite as an accident of the whole. Rather, the union of the constituents of the incarnate Christ is effected in a completely unique way. (Later in this chapter I will say something about the difficulty made by these claims of Aquinas's.)

Three questions

There are perhaps three main questions to ask of this, as of any other, interpretation of the Chalcedonian formula of the doctrine of the incarnation.

First, does the interpretation succeed in preserving the Chalcedonian formula, or does it instead alter the doctrine, overtly or by implication, in the process of interpreting it? An interpretation of the doctrine which covertly multiplied the persons or conflated the natures of Christ into one, for example, would be an interpretation which was not successful in preserving the Chalcedonian formula.

Second, does the interpretation give us a logically coherent position? An interpretation which in effect predicates contradictory attributes of one and the same thing would not be a logically coherent position. Does the interpretation have the resources to show that in predicating the attributes of divinity and humanity of one and the same thing, it is not simply making inconsistent claims?

Finally, we ordinarily think of a person as an entity with a mind and a will. Even in the bizarre disorder of multiple personalities in one organism, one personality at a time is present in a body, so that there is one will and one mind operative at a time. There are rare cases of dicephalic twins where one physically indissoluble biological organism is governed by two minds and two wills, but just for that reason most of us suppose that such an organism somehow constitutes (or at least is governed by) *two* persons, not one. Apart from worries about the logical coherence of the doctrine of the incarnation, is there any way to explain one person with two minds and two wills that makes psychological sense? What would it be for one person to be split in this way and yet constitute one person? If one mind knows the date of the last judgment and the other mind does not, what are we to say about the mental or cognitive state of the one person? Or, to put the same point another way, how could two minds constitute one person without thereby collapsing into one mind?

If Aquinas's interpretation does not have the resources to answer this third question, it will in effect have multiplied the persons in Christ. If, as things are in this world, two minds cannot comprise one person even if both minds are in one organism, then however much Aquinas may insist on the Chalcedonian orthodoxy of his interpretation, his interpretation will deviate from the Chalcedonian formula just in virtue of holding that there are two minds in the incarnate Christ. It will be an implication of his position that there are two persons in Christ.

On the other hand, unless there is some way of making sense of the claim that one thing can have apparently contradictory human and divine attributes, Aquinas's interpretation will not be successful in modeling the Chalcedonian separation of the natures of Christ. If his segregation of the apparently incompatible attributes into distinct natures is nothing but a complicated way of predicating incompatible properties of the same thing, then on his interpretation there will in effect be just one (logically incoherent) nature of Christ, a conjunctive nature having incompatible divine and human properties.[28] In effect, then, Aquinas's interpretation will have conflated the two natures mandated by the Chalcedonian formula into just one.[29]

For these reasons, the first question, whether Aquinas's interpretation of the doctrine is faithful to the Chalcedonian formulation, is best answered by considering whether or not Aquinas's interpretation has the resources to deal successfully with the second and third questions.

The second question: logical incoherence

There is certainly a *prima facie* case to be made for the objection that the doctrine of the incarnation attributes contradictory properties to one and the same thing. On the doctrine of the incarnation, Christ is said to be limited in power and not limited in power, for example. Being limited in power and not being limited in power are contradictory properties, and both properties are attributed to one and the same thing, namely, Christ. So, on the face of it, it seems as if the objection is right.

One traditional way, employed also by Aquinas, of defending the Chalcedonian formula against this objection is by means of reduplicative propositions (where a simple reduplicative proposition generally has this form: X *qua* Y *is* F).[30] According to the reduplicative strategy for rebutting the objection, the fact that both limited and unlimited power are attributed to Christ does not show the Chalcedonian formula of the incarnation incoherent because omnipotence is predicated of Christ in his divine nature and lack of omnipotence is predicated of him in his human nature.[31] Consequently, on the reduplicative strategy, the attributes that are incompatible with each other are also segregated from each other in the incarnate Christ in virtue of inhering in different natures of his.

The reduplicative strategy is not much in favor in contemporary philosophical theology. One apparently plausible criticism of it runs along these lines. For any reduplicative proposition of the form '*x* as A is N and *x* as B is not N', if "the reduplication predicates being A of *x* and predicates being B of *x*" and if "being N is entailed by being A, and not being N is entailed by being B",[32] then the reduplicative proposition is nothing more than a complicated way of predicating contradictory attributes of its subject *x*.[33]

Aquinas's metaphysics, and especially his attitude towards constitution, give a response to this sort of objection to the reduplication strategy, however.[34] On Aquinas's views, there is a distinction between a property a whole has in its own right and a property it has in virtue of having a constituent that has that property in its own right; it is possible for a whole to "borrow" a property from one of its constituents.[35]

This distinction between ways in which a whole can have a property gives us one helpful manner in which to analyze reduplicative locutions of the form *x qua* A *is* N. In such a locution, the property of being N is predicated of *x*, but it is predicated of *x* just in virtue of the fact that *x* has a constituent C which has the property of being N in its own right.

So, for example, consider the molecule CAT/Enhancer-Binding Protein (C/EBP).[36] C/EBP is a two-part molecule or dimer, each of whose subunits is a protein with an alpha helix coil.[37] The molecule has the property of being coiled in the alpha helix manner, but it has that property in virtue of the fact that it has subunits which are coiled in that way. The whole molecule "borrows"[38] these properties from its constituent subunits. 'C/EBP *qua* dimer with coiled subunits has the property of being coiled in the alpha helix manner' thus predicates a property of the whole molecule which the molecule borrows from a part. *Being coiled in the alpha helix manner* is predicated of C/EBP in virtue of the fact that the molecule's subunit is coiled in that way.

On the other hand, C/EBP is a conglomerate of two such subunits which bend away from each other in a limp Y-shape at one end of the molecule. So this is also true: 'C/EBP *qua* Y-shaped is not coiled in the alpha helix manner'. Here again a borrowed property is being attributed to the whole.

C/EBP has a constituent C – in this case, the Y-shaped end of the molecule – which has in its own right the property *not being coiled in the alpha helix manner*.

At this point, someone might suppose that when in a *qua* locution we attribute to the molecule C/EBP the property *being coiled*, we are in effect just attributing to it the property *having a coiled part*, and when we attribute to it the property *not being coiled*, we are just attributing to it the property *having a part that is not coiled*. Clearly, there is no incoherence here, but that is because these are not incompatible properties. But the problem with this approach is that, on this way of analyzing *qua* locutions, the properties which really are incompatible – *being coiled* and *not being coiled* – are not being attributed to the molecule; they are being attributed only to its parts.

But this line cannot be right. A thing which has a coiled part really is itself coiled in some respect or to some degree. Similarly, in virtue of having an end that is Y-shaped, the whole itself is really not coiled in that respect or to that degree. If a student, seeing a diagram of the molecule C/EBP for the first time, were to try to describe it to someone unfamiliar with its shape, she might well say, "Well, it's a sort of complicated coiled, Y-shaped molecule." So the incompatible properties *being coiled* and *not being coiled* are attributes of the whole molecule; they are not just attributes of different parts of the molecule. It is better therefore to understand the reduplicative locution in question as attributing the apparently incompatible properties to the molecule itself.

But because these are borrowed properties, because on this analysis of the reduplicative locution the molecule does not have these properties in its own right, there is no incoherence in the claim that the molecule is both coiled and not coiled. As long as reduplicative locutions are understood in this way, it is clear that both *qua* locutions – '*x* as A is N' and '*x* as B is not N' – can be true without any violation of the laws of logic. The two reduplicative claims taken together do not have the result that we are giving a logically incoherent account of *x*, because, although contradictory attributes are being predicated of the same subject, they are not being predicated in the same respect. C/EBP is coiled in virtue of having a constituent which is coiled in the alpha helix manner, and it is not coiled in virtue of having a constituent which is Y-shaped.[39]

Analogously, some of the properties attributed to Christ are properties borrowed from his constituent natures. So, for example, Christ is limited in power and not limited in power, but he borrows the first attribute from his human nature and the second from his divine nature.[40] So he has the property of being limited in power just in virtue of having a constituent, namely, human nature, which has the property of being limited in power in its own right; he has the property of not being limited in power just in virtue of having a different constituent, divine nature, which has the property in its own right. Because the incompatible properties are borrowed properties,

Christ does not have them in the same respect. And so it is no more incoherent to attribute both properties to Christ than it is to attribute being coiled and not being coiled to C/EBP.

Someone who rejects the reduplicative strategy might repudiate this attempt to resuscitate it in connection with the Chalcedonian formula, on the grounds that the case of the C/EBP molecule and the case of the incarnate Christ are not suitably analogous. The molecule has integral or physical parts – the coiled subunit, the Y-shaped end of the molecule – which have certain properties, and we attribute those properties to the whole molecule only because the molecule has these integral parts. But in the case of Christ, the natures are not integral parts; insofar as they are any sort of part at all, they are metaphysical parts. Metaphysical parts are not physically segregated bits of the whole, and so it seems that a whole cannot borrow properties from them. Metaphysical parts are not really segregated from each other, as physical parts are segregated from one another in space. Consequently, it appears that the original objection to the reduplicative strategy still stands. The reduplicative strategy can be defended against that objection by the notion of borrowed properties only in case the properties are borrowed from physical constituents of the whole.

This conclusion, however, and the line of thought that supports it seem to me mistaken. It is true that the case of Christ differs from the case of the molecule insofar as the parts in question in the case of Christ are not integral or physical parts. But it is false that a whole borrows properties from its parts only in case the parts are physical parts.

Consider, for example, Mark Twain's *Letters to the Earth*. Whatever exactly a work of fiction is, it is not a physical object, and its constituents are not physical either. Twain's *Letters to the Earth* is a passionate indictment of Christianity based largely on a dark and hard-hitting review of the suffering in the world and what Twain takes to be the stupid and insipid nature of Christian attempts to explain it away. As such, *Letters to the Earth* is a serious complaint against Christianity, and Twain meant it to be. On the other hand, the attack is carried out by means of Twain's characteristic biting humor. As such, *Letters to the Earth* is comic. So the work *qua* attack on Christianity is serious (and therefore not funny); *qua* work of satire, on the other hand, it is very funny.

In fact, one might argue that a satire is a work which uses various forms of humor as a means to a sober end. Jokes and sarcasm are parts which are woven together by the configuring serious purpose of the whole. The comic bits and the overriding purpose are therefore *some* sort of constituents of the whole, but certainly not integral or physical constituents. Nonetheless, it is clear that the whole can borrow properties from these non-physical, non-integral constituents, just as the molecule C/EBP can borrow properties from its integral parts. That is why Twain's work taken as a whole is correctly characterized both as a hilarious piece of satire and as a deathly earnest attack on religion. Because the properties of the whole are borrowed from the constituents in this way, there is no more incoherence in saying of the work that it is funny and not funny than there is in saying that C/EBP is coiled and not coiled. The work is funny in one respect and not funny in another, just as C/EBP is coiled in one part and not coiled in another.

So a whole can borrow properties from its constituents even if those constituents are not integral or physical parts of the whole. Consequently, there is no reason for denying that Christ can have properties borrowed from either his human nature or his divine nature, even if the natures are not integral or physical parts of Christ. Furthermore, because each of the incompatible properties is had in its own right by a different constituent of the whole and because they attach to the whole only derivatively, in consequence of the fact that the whole has these constituents, there is no incoherence in attributing both otherwise incompatible properties to the one whole.

Therefore, the objection to the reduplicative strategy fails. The objection would succeed if the attributes in question were attributes of the whole not borrowed from the parts. In that case, incompatible properties would be predicated of the same thing in the same respect, and that would be incoherent. But the point of the reduplicative strategy is to segregate the incompatible properties into different constituents of the whole and to attribute them to the whole derivatively, and Aquinas's metaphysics of composite things supports this use of the reduplicative strategy. Aquinas's metaphysics therefore provides a way to support his interpretation of the Chalcedonian formula against the charge of incoherence.

The third question: the logical problem

Even if the reduplicative strategy supported by Aquinas's metaphysics successfully defends Aquinas's interpretation of the doctrine of the incarnation against the general charge of logical incoherence, a serious question remains having to do with the cognitive and conative states of Christ. What sense does it make to attribute these to Christ derivatively? As I will show, it seems that the attempt to answer this question raises again, in a special way, the issue of the logical incoherence of the doctrine of the incarnation. This issue and the question that gives rise to it pose two serious problems for Aquinas's interpretation of the Chalcedonian formula, which we can call, respectively, 'the logical problem' and 'the psychological problem'. Since I have already said something about the nature of the psychological problem, I will begin here by presenting the logical problem and then turn to what can be said by way of a solution to both problems.

Ordinarily, one would suppose that desires, volitions, beliefs, doubts, and so on are had by the whole person and had non-derivatively. Consequently, one would think, properties such as the property of knowing something or other and the property of desiring something or other are properties that a person has in her own right. Aquinas himself takes this view as regards perception and cognition.[41] On Aquinas's interpretation of the doctrine of the incarnation, however, even properties involving intellect and will have to be attributed to the whole person derivatively. Christ *qua* God knows the whole essence of God; Christ *qua* human being does not.[42] In his divine nature Christ is omniscient; in his human nature he is not. Similarly, Christ *qua* human being desires that he not die; Christ *qua* God lacks this desire. Because Christ has two intellects and two wills which are radically different from each other, even properties involving intellect and will are predicated of the whole person Christ in virtue of being predicated of some constituent of the person.

But how are we to understand this part of Aquinas's interpretation of the doctrine of the incarnation? In general, we think that we have to take the reliability of our cognitive faculties on faith, because the very cognitive capacities whose reliability is at issue would have to be used in order to check on that reliability. But one cannot take off one's mind like a hat to examine it, we think; the mind whose reliability one may like to investigate is the only mind one has. On Aquinas's interpretation, it is as if Christ were an exception to these general claims. Christ, and Christ alone, has an alternative set of cognitive (and conative) capacities.

But what sense can be made of this view? How are these disparate minds and wills constituents of one person? Or, to put the same question the other way around, why should not we suppose that where there are two minds and wills there are also two persons? Furthermore, if even with two minds and wills Christ is somehow just one person, how are we to understand the psychological state of this one person?

Consider, for example, questions of knowledge. Do both intellects operate at once? Does Christ simultaneously know and not know the mind of God? Aquinas calls attention to the fact that Christ is said to wonder at something, and Aquinas points out that a person cannot feel wonder if he knows everything.[43] How are we to account for wonder in a person who has an omniscient mind as one constituent? Does Christ have the ability to alternate between intellects? And if he alternates between them, which will decides which intellect he will use? The human will? The divine will? And which will decides which will makes the decision which intellect to use?

The first thing to see here is that the answers to some of these questions are implicit in Aquinas's interpretation of the Chalcedonian formula. The person of Christ is the second person of the Trinity. That person is divine and has all the standard divine attributes, and these attributes are essential to the person, not accidental. Consequently, it is not possible for the person of Christ to be without the divine attributes. The human nature of Christ is added to the divine person, who assumes human nature. So it is possible that the person Christ sometimes operates with and through his human nature

416

and sometimes does not. But it is not possible that the person Christ operates without the divine nature. Christ can therefore alternate between operating with just his divine mind and operating with both his human and divine mind. He cannot alternate between operating with his divine mind and operating with his human mind alone. A similar point applies to the will. The human will of Christ may be switched on or off, as it were, but the divine will is always on.

Now an omnipotent being may bind himself in such a way that at a given time he is unable to do something. His omnipotence is not thereby undermined, provided that he is able at any given moment to release himself from the self-imposed bond.[44] Omnipotence is a matter of being able to do everything (with the usual complicated qualifications, which I omit here for the sake of simplicity), and a being who is unable to do something because of a bond he is able to undo retains the *power* to do everything. Consequently, even when he is bound, he is still *able*, in some sense of the term, to do everything. So Christ can operate in his human nature with limited power while still being omnipotent, provided that it is up to him whether he operates with divine or human power. But I mention this feature of omnipotence just in order to highlight the fact that omniscience is not like this. It is not a matter of being *able* to know everything. Rather, it is a matter of *actually* knowing everything there is to know (with the usual complicated qualifications, which I also omit here). So if the person of Christ is essentially omniscient, it is not possible for him not to know something. Consequently, if the divine mind of Christ is always operative, the person Christ is always omniscient; and, as omniscient, he actually knows everything. But, then, in what sense is it also true that he sometimes fails to know something, as he does when he engages in wonder?

The success of the reduplicative strategy depends on being able to segregate the incompatible attributes of Christ into the two natures of Christ, so that Christ has a human attribute in one respect and a divine attribute in another respect. The strategy might work even for properties that a person ordinarily has non-derivatively, such as the property of knowing something, as long as Aquinas's interpretation can keep even these attributes segregated. If Christ were able to alternate between human and divine minds, for example, then the reduplicative strategy would work even for such properties as the property of knowing something. Christ could know something when he was operating with his divine mind and not know it when he was operating with his human mind, and so he would know in one respect and not know in another respect. But, on Aquinas's interpretation, the divine mind is always operative, and so the person Christ always knows everything. In that case, it is difficult to see how the incompatible divine and human properties regarding knowledge can be kept segregated from each other. If a person always knows everything, then how could it be true that he sometimes also fails to know something?

Analogous questions can be raised as regards desires and volitions. God is not divided within himself as regards his desires. He desires wholeheartedly whatever he desires. But since the divine mind is always operative in Christ, then, it seems, Christ always desires wholeheartedly whatever he desires. On the other hand, insofar as the human desires of Christ sometimes are in opposition to divine desires, as they are when Christ desires not to die, then it will also be true that the person Christ does not desire wholeheartedly whatever he desires. His divine will has some desires that are opposed to the desires of his human will, and so there will be division within the structure of the desires of Christ. But how can it be true of the same person that his desires are always integrated and wholehearted and that they are sometimes divided against themselves?

For these reasons, even if the reduplicative strategy works in general, it seems not to work for at least some properties involving intellect and will. And so, in addition to the psychological problem, the problem of how to model the mental state of one person with two minds, the logical problem, the worry about logical incoherence of the doctrine, arises here too. The difficulty is that the two natures are hard to keep segregated when it comes to intellect and will. If there is one person with two minds, and if he does not simply alternate between the two minds, then it seems as if the two minds are united into one supermind in the one person. In that case, the two natures are also conflated, at least in respect of intellect and will, and this supernature seems to have incompatible states of intellect and will.

The psychological problem

It helps considerably in connection with the psychological problem to reflect on cases in which more ordinary agents operate with discrepant cognitive capacities.

To begin with a simple case, suppose that an actor Art has 20/20 vision but that he is preparing to play the role of a person Victor with severely impaired vision. Suppose that Art wants to know what it feels like to experience the world as Vicktor does; on the other hand, he does not want to take any chances of falling and hurting himself, so that he is unavailable for the role. Consequently, he has his ophthalmologist make him *one* contact lens that will impair his vision *in one eye* (say, the left eye) to the same degree to which Victor's vision is impaired. When he wears his one contact lens in his left eye and puts a patch over his right eye, he sees the world as Vicktor does (leaving questions of depth perception to one side). On the other hand, when he puts the patch over the eye with the contact lens in it, he sees the world with 20/20 vision. By this system, Art will see the world both as an excellent visual perceiver sees it and as the visually impaired Victor sees it. He will see the thing in front of him as a hamburger with lettuce, tomato, and onions, and he will see it as an indistinct blob, whose nature he cannot identify; and he will know what it is like to see it both ways.

This example gives us some insight into the notion of a person's choosing to operate through a cognitive capacity: Art can choose to see through his left eye or through his right eye. The example also gives us some help in understanding what it would be like for one person to have discrepant perceptual capacities, one of which gives much less information about the world than the other. Of course, in this case, Art alternates between these cognitive capacities. The organization of the visual system in the human brain is such that alternating between the two visual cognitive capacities is the only possibility. If Art opened both his eyes while he was wearing his one contact lens, he would not see simultaneously what he sees alternately when he uses first one and then the other eye.

But if the human nervous system were constructed in such a way that Art could do so, then there would be one person simultaneously using two differing visual capacities that gave two very different sorts of epistemic access to the same part of the extramental world. Consequently, even though Art really is just one person, it is at least conceptually possible that Art could visually perceive and also not visually perceive the same thing at the same time. There is no incoherence in these claims because the disparate visual experiences are conveyed through different visual capacities to a mind which has both capacities operative at once. In this conceptually possible case, Art would perceive and not perceive the hamburger simultaneously; but he would perceive it through his right eye and fail to perceive it through his left eye.

Actual cases that come closer to this imagined state of Art's can be found in the neurobiological literature on agnosia.[45] A person with a visual agnosia is a person who is unable to perceive what a thing is, even though her visual system is functioning normally otherwise. So, for example, if a visual agnosic – call her 'Anna' – is shown a pen and asked, "What is it?", she will say, "I don't know"; and that will also be her answer if she is asked whether there is a pen in the room. On the other hand, asked to describe the object in front of her and presented to her visual system, she will accurately characterize the features of the pen: it is long, black, cylindrical, and so on. The problem for Anna is that, although she is getting visual information about the pen, she cannot use that information to identify the pen as a pen. This inability, however, affects *only* the visual system. If we put the pen in Anna's hand, she will say, "Oh, it's a pen!". This recognition of the pen by touch does not put an end to the visual agnosia, however. Even after having identified the pen as a pen by touching it, Anna does not *see* it as a pen when she looks at it.[46]

Now consider Anna's perceptual state as she looks at the pen when it is in her hand. She does not recognize this thing in front of her as a pen when she looks at it; she does recognize it as a pen when she touches it. When she looks at it while touching it, she is in fact doing what it was just conceptually possible that Art do in the thought experiment in which he has discrepant visual capacities simultaneously operative: Anna is using two differing perceptual capacities that give her at one and the same time two very different sorts of epistemic access to the same part of the extramental world. She is just one person, and yet it is true that at the same time she recognizes and fails to recognize this thing as a pen. She recognizes it through one perceptual capacity and simultaneously fails to recognize it through another. The disparate perceptual experiences are conveyed to the same person through different perceptual capacities.

Of course, when Anna sees the pen, Anna knows that what is in her hand is a pen; but she knows this fact because she recognizes the pen in her hand through touch. It remains true that she does not recognize it through vision. When she looks at the pen in her hand, her visual system does not tell her what it is which she sees. In a simpler version of the same kind, the severely visually impaired Victor might recognize the actor Art by the sound of his voice; and by this means he would then know that the person he was seeing was Art. But it would remain the case that when he looked at Art, he failed to recognize Art through vision.

It is important to see that in these cases, there is no conflation of cognitive capacities into one. Even though Anna is undoubtedly one person, Anna can have simultaneous discrepant perceptual experiences through touch and through vision; and nothing about the fact that touch gives her recognition of the pen implies that she also gets recognition of the pen through vision. Although both perceptual capacities convey information to one and the same person, the capacities themselves remain separate, and the perceptual experiences of the one pen also remain different.

So far, my examples have had to do with perception, but the difficult case for Aquinas's account has to do with knowledge. And it does seem that whatever Anna's discrepant perceptual experiences might be, there is just one resultant state of knowledge for her: she knows that what is in front of her is a pen. Is there any way to extend cases such as that involving the discrepant perceptual experiences of a person with visual agnosia to cases in which one person has at one and the same time different states of knowledge about the same part of extramental reality? I think that we can find cases roughly of this sort in science fiction stories such as Robert Heinlein's *The Puppetmasters*.

In science fiction stories of this sort, an alien invader of some super-intelligent race enters the mind of a human person in such a way as to be able to operate simultaneously through the human being's mind and through his own. So, for example, operating through his own mind the alien knows that an alien invasion of earth is in process, in virtue of remembering having landed on earth with the ships from his home planet and knowing what he himself is currently doing. There is no similar memory or awareness in the human mind through which the alien is simultaneously operating, however; and so when the human mind sees the alien spaceship for the first time, that mind will be surprised and wonder at what is happening.

Because the alien is operating with both minds simultaneously, he can fail to be surprised through his own alien mind and feel surprise through the human mind he is also using. That is, just as Art can look through a contact lens and thereby see what Victor sees when Victor looks at the same scene, so the alien can operate through all the faculties of the mind of the human person the alien has taken over. To that extent, the alien can not only see what the human mind sees when he looks out at a certain scene through the perceptual system of the human body he has invaded, but the alien can also be in the cognitive state that that human mind has in consequence of looking at that scene. So operating through his own mind, the alien does not feel surprise at the presence of the spaceship, and he knows what it is doing there; but operating through the human mind of his victim, the alien lacks the relevant knowledge and feels the surprise of the human mind.

In these circumstances, the alien will be in a cognitive situation which is a complicated analogue to Anna's when she recognizes the pen through one perceptual capacity and fails to recognize it through another. Just as in Anna's case, the fact that the alien knows something through one cognitive capacity does not imply that he knows the same thing through the other. He knows the spaceship has landed through the cognitive operation of his alien mind; he feels surprise and wonder at the sight of the spaceship through the cognitive operation of the human mind.

The alien is thus simultaneously using two different minds that give two very different kinds of epistemic access to reality. His epistemic state is thus roughly analogous to the perceptual state of Art with the obscuring contact lens in place. Art can look at the world with visual capacities equivalent to Victor's in power as well as with Art's own visual capacities; and when Art does looks at the world through Victor's sort of vision, he sees much more obscurely than he would if he saw that same part of the world through the visual capacity he himself ordinarily has. In an analogous way, the alien can cognize the world through his own mind or through the human mind he has taken over, and the different minds will give him different epistemic access to the world around him. He will cognize more obscurely, as it were, when his mind cognizes through the human mind than he would if he cognized that same part of the world through the cognitive capacities he has without the addition of the human mind.

So the alien can know something (that an alien invasion is in progress, for example) through his alien mind that he does not know through the human mind he has taken over; and even though he does know this in his own alien mind, he continues not to know it when he is cognizing through his added-on human mind. It is as if each mind were something like Art's eyes with and without the contact lens. The alien can, as it were, look out at the world through his own superior cognitive capacities while at the same time looking out through the more clouded, less sensitive cognitive capacities of his human victim's mind; and he can simultaneously "see" the world through both sets of capacities, analogous to the way in which Art could perceive the world if he could simultaneously see through each eye, with and without the contact lens.

Consequently, although the alien is just one person, at the same time he knows that an alien invasion is in progress and does not know it. But there is no logical incoherence here, because he knows it through his alien mind and fails to know it through the human mind he has taken over. The disparate cognitive states are conveyed to the same person through different minds.

It is clear that we can tell a similar story as regards desires. The alien can feel desire through his alien mind, or he can feel it through the human mind he has taken over.

The case of volitions or acts of will is only somewhat trickier, because a volition or an act of will is a desire that moves an organism all the way to action if nothing external to the will impedes it. One might suppose that one person could not operate with two wills because if the wills were really different, then in principle they could be discordant. But on the definition of volition just given, any act of will has to move to action unless externally impeded. How then could the same entity have discordant wills? If nothing external impeded, then each will would have to move to action. If through his alien mind, the alien willed that the human body he has invaded sit down, and through his human mind he willed that the body stand up, it seems that the body would have to do the impossible: stand up and sit down simultaneously. This sort of difficulty is easily handled, however, just by recognizing that the human will counts as something external to the alien will, and vice versa. If the alien's desire that the human body sit down is not effective because of the contrary human will, it can nonetheless count as a volition which is impeded by something outside itself.

So, if we take all these cases together, the cases of Art, Anna, and the alien, we can perhaps get some intuitive grip on the notion that one and the same person can operate through more than one intellect and will. The divine intellect and will are always operative, but the person of Christ can simultaneously operate with and through a human intellect and will.

The logical problem

With this much said about the psychological problem, the logical problem can be dealt with expeditiously.

On Aquinas's interpretation of the doctrine of the incarnation, the divine assumption of a human nature is like the alien's adding to himself the mind of a human being, but with a fairly important difference. The alien invades an entity who is a person in his own right and who was accustomed to having his body and his mind to himself until the alien invaded it.

Consequently, when the alien invades his human victim, there are two persons in one organism, the alien and the human. In Christ's case, the human nature is added to Christ from conception; the human nature in question is always Christ's. Any human experiences had by means of this human nature are had by the person Christ, who always has the human body to himself.[47] So when Christ assumes a human nature, the only person in the human body is the person of Christ.[48]

With this very significant difference, the science fiction story gives us some idea of how the reduplicative strategy can be applied also to properties involving intellect and will, so that Aquinas's interpretation can be saved from imputations of incoherence even in cases of such mental properties as knowing and not knowing something. Christ can operate simultaneously through a human and a divine mind. And so, *qua* divine, he comprehends the whole essence of God; *qua* human, he does not. The natures are thus not conflated into one supernature to which we have to attribute incompatible properties. The reduplicative strategy can be successfully employed even for cognitive and conative states in Christ.

Conclusion: the three questions posed at the outset

At the outset of this chapter, I posed three questions for Aquinas's interpretation of the Chalcedonian formulation of the doctrine of the incarnation. Does it succeed in remaining faithful to the Chalcedonian formula? Does it give us a logically coherent account of the incarnation? And is there any way to understand the notion of one person with two minds and two wills that makes psychological sense?

The preceding considerations make clear, I think, what the answer to the first question is: Aquinas's interpretation of the doctrine of the incarnation is faithful to the Chalcedonian formula it wants to explain. Aquinas's metaphysics includes an understanding of constitution which supports the reduplicative strategy. It thus also has the resources to ward off the charge that the doctrine of the incarnation is logically incoherent. It does so just in virtue of keeping the natures of Christ separate, so that the properties of the two natures are segregated from each other and not joined together into one super-nature. In addition, Aquinas's version of the reduplicative strategy can be shown to work even for properties involving intellect and will, such as the properties of knowing and not knowing something. So Aquinas's interpretation gives a logically consistent explanation of the claim Christ is *one* person with *two* natures, even as regards the claims about Christ's minds and wills. Finally, insight into the manner in which the reduplicative strategy can be made to work even for the minds and wills of Christ clarifies Aquinas's interpretation of one person operating in and through two different natures. It is possible to make psychological sense out of this interpretation by thinking about it in connection with cases from neurobiology and science fiction.

We may still wonder, however, whether Aquinas's metaphysics can support the claim that the person and the natures are united together in a union of person. The one person and the two natures have somehow to combine into one thing on Aquinas's interpretation. Since the person of Christ is divine, and since the deity is simple, on Aquinas's views, the person of Christ and the divine nature are as united, are as much one, as it is conceptually possible for anything to be. So, on this score, the real question for Aquinas's interpretation has to do with the assumption of human nature. How is human nature added to the simple divine person in order to make the resulting composite one thing? What mode of union unites the human nature to the person of Christ?

Aquinas himself struggled with this question.[49] The problem for him is that his metaphysics provides for a limited number of ways in which components can come together to compose one thing. There is union in nature, in which differing components are united in the one nature conferred by one substantial form. There is the union of an accident with the supposit in which it inheres. And then there is the union by which a substantial form comes together with the matter it configures to form one supposit.[50]

But none of these modes of union can be the mode of union that unites the human nature to the person of Christ. It cannot be union in nature, both because the two natures of Christ are not combined into one and because the relata for the union include a person as well as a nature.[51] It cannot be the union by which an accident is united with a supposit, because natures are not accidents, and the human nature of Christ is not an accident of his, as his hair color and weight are.[52] Finally, it cannot be the union of a substantial form and matter.[53] Aquinas, like most medievals, is willing to use the conceptual division into form and matter very broadly, and so he might be willing to think of the human nature of Christ as a sort of matter. But the second person of the Trinity is not the sort of thing that configures matter. It is more perfect for something to be simple in its nature, Aquinas says, than for it to be united to something as a substantial form is united to matter;[54] and so it is not possible for the second person of the Trinity to be the form of a body.[55] So none of the modes of union for combining components into one thing is the mode of union in person for Christ.

Or, to put the same problem in another way, Christ is a person; a person is an individual substance of a rational nature; and a substance is a thing configured by a substantial form. But the only substantial form in Christ is the human soul, and it configures only one constituent in Christ, the human body; it does not configure the whole composite. The divine person cannot configure the composite either. So what does configure the components of the whole into one thing?

Aquinas himself concedes that he has no answer to this question.[56] If the mode of union for Christ *were* any of the modes of union his metaphysics recognizes, then, he says, it would be the mode of union between a substantial form and the matter it configures.[57] But since this mode of union is also ruled out as a mode of uniting the human nature of Christ to the person of Christ, the best that can be said is that whatever exactly the mode of union is for Christ, it is analogous to the mode of union of substantial form and matter into one supposit. Strictly speaking, Aquinas is compelled to conclude, the mode of union for Christ is unique.[58] It is not the same as any other union found among created things, and therefore it cannot be analyzed in terms used to understand any other sort of union. In fact, Aquinas thinks, we have to grant that this mode of union is in a certain respect incomprehensible.[59] He says, "to explain this union perfectly is not possible for human beings".[60]

In this sense, then, Aquinas's interpretation is incomplete. It succeeds in faithfully interpreting the Chalcedonian formula, as far as it goes. It succeeds in defending the Chalcedonian formula against important objections to it, and it succeeds in giving us some limited intuitive grasp of what the mental life of a being such as the incarnate Christ would be like. But it is not successful in giving a complete analysis of the doctrine of the incarnation. On Aquinas's interpretation, the doctrine in its entirety is finally incomprehensible to us.

But, of course, it is not clear that this feature of Aquinas's interpretation is a defect in it. Given the doctrine of the incarnation, it would be astonishing if anything else in the world were characterized by the same mode of union as that ascribed to Christ. And if the mode of union for Christ is unique to him, it becomes at least easier to understand why it should be incomprehensible to us. We tend to understand things by finding patterns among apparently disparate things or by mapping the obscure onto the familiar. Both these moves are ruled out for something which is like nothing else on earth. In this sense, then, in its very incompleteness, Aquinas's interpretation of the doctrine gives the result which reason should lead us to expect. It is not reasonable to expect that everything can be explained in its entirety by reason; and if the doctrine of the incarnation is correct, then the incarnation itself is a prime example of the sort of thing human reason could be expected to fail to comprehend completely. Furthermore, the doctrine of the incarnation is traditionally reckoned among the theological mysteries, as Aquinas also knows and accepts.[61] But if Aquinas's interpretation claimed to make the doctrine fully comprehensible, it would not be an interpretation of a *mystery*.

So in failing to give a complete explanation of the doctrine, in leaving something which is beyond human comprehension, Aquinas is also being faithful to the Chalcedonian council, which took the doctrine of the incarnation to be a mystery.[62]

It is important to see, however, that this failure of Aquinas's interpretation to explain the doctrine completely is not equivalent to a failure to show that the doctrine is defensible. If there were an argument that the mode of union needed to unite the human nature to the person of Christ is impossible, then the inability of Aquinas's interpretation to explain and defend the mode of union would leave the doctrine undefended. But I know of no such argument, and it is hard to see what such an argument would be. It could hardly be based on a failure to find such a mode of union in anything familiar to us since the mode of union for Christ is explicitly claimed to be unique to him. And since, in its claim that the mode of union is a mystery, Aquinas's interpretation fails to specify the nature of the mode of union, so an argument that this particular mode of union is incoherent is also not possible. If the mode of union is left completely unspecified, one can hardly claim that it has incompatible properties.

I conclude therefore that Aquinas's interpretation of the doctrine of the Incarnation, as it is explained and supported by his metaphysics, is a philosophically sophisticated, rich, and powerful account which is faithful to the Chalcedonian formula and successful in defending it against some of the formidable objections commonly leveled against it.

15

ATONEMENT

Introduction

The doctrine of the atonement, the doctrine that God has resolved the problem of human evil by means of the suffering and death of Christ, is the central doctrine of Christianity; and yet not much attention has been paid to it by contemporary philosophers of religion. Perhaps one of the reasons for this comparative neglect is that many philosophers know this doctrine only in the version which tends to be promulgated by unreflective believers who are more to be admired for devotion than for philosophical expertise. This popular account of the atonement is often assumed to be just the theory of the atonement held by such Christian thinkers as Aquinas (or some other notable philosophical theologian), but careful consideration shows that Aquinas's theory (and no doubt also that of other thoughtful and sophisticated theologians in the history of the Christian tradition) differs significantly from the popular account with which many philosophers are familiar.

The popular account in question tends to consist in the following set of claims (or something approximately like it):

> A *popular version of the doctrine:* Human beings by their evil actions have offended God. This sin or offense against God generates a kind of debt, a debt so enormous that human beings by themselves can never repay it. God has the power, of course, to cancel this debt, but God is perfectly just, and it would be a violation of perfect justice to cancel a debt without extracting the payment owed. Therefore, God cannot simply forgive a person's sin; as a just judge he must sentence all people to everlasting torment as the just punishment for their sin. God is also infinitely merciful, however; and so he brings it about that he himself pays their debt in full, by assuming human nature as the incarnate Christ and in that nature enduring the penalty which would otherwise have been imposed on human beings. In consequence, the sins of ordinary human beings are

forgiven; and, by God's mercy exercised through Christ's passion, human beings are saved from sin and hell and brought to heaven.

There are many problems with this version of the doctrine of the atonement. To begin with, contrary to what it intends, this version of the doctrine does not, in fact, present God as forgiving human sin. To forgive a debtor is to fail to exact all that is in justice due. But, according to (P), God does exact every bit of the debt owed him by human beings; he allows none of it to go unpaid. As (P) tells the story, God himself fully pays the debt owed him. This part of the story is perplexing; but what it shows is only that God himself has arranged for the debt to be paid in full, not that he has agreed to overlook any part of the debt.

The proponent of (P) might claim that God's forgiveness consists precisely in his not requiring that *we* pay the debt for sin but rather his paying it himself for us in the person of Christ. But it is hard to see what constitutes forgiveness on this claim. Suppose that Daniel owes Sarah $1000 and cannot pay it, but Sarah's daughter Marion, who is Daniel's good friend, does pay Sarah the whole $1000 on Daniel's behalf. Is there any sense in which Sarah can be said to forgive the debt? On the contrary, Sarah has been repaid in full and has foregone none of what was owed her.

The proponent of (P) will say that God's justice precludes his overlooking the debt and that therefore, in himself paying the debt owed him, he has shown mercy and forgiveness in the only way he can. And, the proponent of (P) will say, surely our intuitions about Sarah's forgiveness would be different if it turned out that although her justice did not allow her to cancel Daniel's debt, Sarah had instructed her daughter to pay the debt. The case for (P) is also strengthened by remembering that, on the doctrine of the Trinity, Christ is one in being with God the Father, so that the one paying the debt is the same as the one to whom the debt is paid.

Apart from the other perplexities raised by this rejoinder, however, it seems not to emphasize God's justice but to rest on a denial of it. For all the talk of debt is really a metaphor. What (P) is in fact telling us is that any human being's sins are so great that it is a violation of justice not to punish that person with damnation. What God does in response, however, is to punish not the sinner but a perfectly innocent person instead (a person who, even on the doctrine of the Trinity, is not the same person as God the Father, who does the punishing). But how is this just? Suppose that a mother with two sons, one innocent and one disobedient, inflicted all her disobedient son's justly deserved punishment on her innocent son, on the grounds that the disobedient one was too little to bear his punishment and her justice required her to punish someone. We would not praise her justice, but rather condemn her as barbaric, even if the innocent son had assented to this procedure. If the mother could after all forego punishing the disobedient son, why did she not just do so without inflicting suffering on the other child? And how is justice served by punishing a completely innocent person?

428

Furthermore, the account given in (P) is inconsistent both with itself and with another fundamental Christian doctrine. In the first place, (P) claims that in his suffering and death on the cross Christ paid the full penalty for all human sin so that human beings would not have to pay it; and yet it also claims that the penalty for sin is everlasting damnation. But no matter what sort of agony Christ experienced in his crucifixion, it certainly was not (and was not equivalent to) everlasting punishment, if for no other reason than that Christ's suffering came to an end. Second, (P) maintains that Christ pays the penalty for all sin in full so that human beings do not have to do so. But it is a fundamental Christian doctrine that God justly condemns some people to everlasting punishment in hell. If Christ has paid the penalty for sin completely, how is God just in demanding that some people pay the penalty again?

The proponent of (P) may try to answer both these objections by altering his account to say that the penalty Christ pays for human beings is his death and suffering. But this answer is no real help. On Christian doctrine, the punishment for sin is not just death but hell, so that this alteration of (P) has the infelicitous result that what Christ undergoes in his substitutionary suffering is not the traditionally assigned penalty for sin. But even if it were, Christ's suffering would not remove the penalty from human beings since they all suffer death anyway.

Finally, it is not clear what the atonement accomplishes, on the account given in (P). According to Christian doctrine, the main problem with human evil is that it leaves human beings alienated from God. Human beings tend to will what they ought not to will, and so their wills are not in conformity with God's will. Consequently, they do not live in peace with God now, and in that state they cannot be united to God in heaven. Now, according to (P), the atonement consists in Christ's paying the penalty for sin. But nothing in (P) suggests in any way that the atonement alters human nature and proclivities which are responsible for sin. In (P)'s version of the doctrine, the atonement is efficacious to remove not sinful nature or proclivities for moral evil, but only the penalty for sin. In that case, however, the atonement is not really an atonement; for, as (P) tells it, the atonement leaves human beings with just the same tendencies to will what is contrary to God's will, so that their wills are no more conformable to God's will, they are no more tending towards unity with God, than they were before the atonement.

It seems to me, then, that the version of the doctrine of the atonement in (P) is subject to serious philosophical and theological objections. But often enough when we find a piece of Christian doctrine which looks highly problematic in popular theology, it turns out to be a somewhat distorted version of an idea which was once presented with philosophical and theological sophistication in the work of philosophical theologians in the history of Christian thought. In this chapter I want to look carefully at Aquinas's interpretation of the doctrine of the atonement, which is one of the best treatments of the doctrine I know. Although it is indebted to other interpretations of the doctrine in the preceding history of medieval thought, some of which (such as that of Anselm) it resembles in one way or another, it is nonetheless one of the most philosophically sophisticated and theologically insightful of the medieval accounts.

The problems solved by the atonement

Aquinas assigns a number of roles to Christ's passion and death;[1] but, roughly speaking, they can all be subsumed under two general functions, namely, (as he puts it) making satisfaction and meriting grace. These functions correspond to two different problems posed by moral evil.

To see these problems and the difference between them, consider two friends, Susan and David. Suppose that these two have been best friends for years, but that very recently (unbeknownst to Susan) David has become an alcoholic, and that he is given to driving while drunk, although he is generally successful in concealing his condition when he drives. Suppose that on one occasion, when he has Susan's small daughter in his car and is nonetheless driving drunk, he has a bad car accident; the child is killed, and David's alcoholism becomes a matter of public knowledge. If Susan and David are not to be permanently alienated despite this dreadful event, there will be two obstacles to their continued friendship: first, the problem of dealing with the moral wrong David has done (I will call this 'the problem of past sin') and, second, the problem of dealing with the moral wrong David is likely to do, given that he is still an alcoholic (I will call this 'the problem of future sin').

Aquinas believes that the atonement is God's solution to both these problems.[2] Christ's passion and death, insofar as they serve to make satisfaction, are the solution to the problem of past sin; and, insofar as Christ merits grace by his passion and death, they are the solution to the problem of future sin. So, Aquinas says, Christ's suffering and dying have two principal effects: satisfaction for our past sins and salvation from our sinful nature.[3]

I will begin with Aquinas's understanding of the atonement as making satisfaction for sin.

The popular account and Aquinas's account

At first glance, the Thomistic account of the atonement as making satisfaction sounds perilously like (P). Here is an example of the sort of thing Aquinas tends to say about making satisfaction:

The Thomistic account (*T*): "[Christ] willed to suffer that he might make satisfaction for our sins. And he suffered for us those things which we deserved to suffer because of the sin of our first parent. The chief of these is death, to which all other human sufferings are ordered as to their end ... Accordingly, Christ also willed to suffer death for our sins so that, without any fault of His own by himself bearing the penalty we owed, he might free us from the sentence of death, in the way that anyone would be freed from a penalty he owed if another person undertook the penalty for him."[4]

To understand Aquinas's account of this function of the atonement, however, and to see why it is in fact different from the views in (P), we need to see what Aquinas means by satisfaction and the importance he attaches to it.

Satisfaction, Aquinas says, removes the debt of punishment for sin.[5] But, according to Aquinas, if God had willed to free human beings from sin without any satisfaction, he would not have acted against justice; for if God forgives sin without satisfaction — without removal, that is, of the debt of punishment — he wrongs no one, just as anyone who overlooks a trespass against himself acts mercifully and not unjustly.[6] In fact, Aquinas says:

a judge who has to punish a fault committed against another ... cannot remit the fault or penalty without injustice. But God has no one superior to him; rather he himself is the highest and universal good of the whole world. And for this reason, if [God] remits sin, which is defined as a fault from its being committed against [God] himself, he does no one an injury, just as any human being who, without [requiring] satisfaction, remits an offense committed against himself does not act unjustly but is merciful.[7]

And so, on Aquinas's view, it is not necessary that satisfaction be made for human sins.

Nonetheless, Aquinas holds, there was no more suitable way of healing our nature than by making satisfaction.[8] According to Aquinas:

Something is said to be necessary for an end in two ways. In one way, [as] that without which something cannot be ... ; in another way, [as] that by means of which one arrives at the end in a better and more suitable manner, as, for example, a horse is necessary for a journey. In the first way, it was not necessary for God to become incarnate in order to restore human nature, for by his omnipotent power God was able to restore human nature in many other ways. But in the second way it was necessary for God to become incarnate in order to restore human nature.[9]

And so Aquinas concludes: "by his passion Christ made satisfaction for the sin of the human race, and in this way a human being is made free [from sin] by the justice of Christ."[10]

These remarks strongly suggest that for Aquinas the problem of past sin is understood differently from the way it is understood in (P). On (P), the problem with the sins a person such as David has committed is that they have resulted in God's alienation from David and in God's consequent inability to refrain from punishing him, without satisfactions having been made. But, on Aquinas's account, David is alienated from God, who is free to require satisfaction or to forego it; and the problem is a problem in human nature. This is a large and important difference. How one interprets the doctrine of the atonement depends most fundamentally on how one understands the nature of the problem the atonement was meant to solve. For (P), the main obstacle to human salvation lies, in effect, in God himself, whose justice constrains him to damn human beings unless atonement is made. For Aquinas, the main obstacle lies in sinful human nature, which damns human beings unless it is repaired or restored by the atonement.

Aquinas's notion of satisfaction: support and illustration

Support for this reading of Aquinas's account can be found in Aquinas's general theory of satisfaction as one of the three integral parts of penance (the other two being contrition and confession).[11] Aquinas's emphasis in his discussion of all the parts of penance is on the sinner, not on the person sinned against. So, for example, Aquinas sees penance in general as a kind of medicine for sin.[12] It consists in detesting one's sin and purposing to change one's life for the better,[13] and it aims primarily at the restoration of friendship between the wrongdoer and the one wronged.[14] In discussing the remission of sins, which is on his view the goal of penance, Aquinas maintains that sins are remitted when the soul of the *offender* is at peace with the one offended.[15] As he goes on to explain:

> this peace consists in the love with which God loves us. Now on the part of the act of God, the love of God is eternal and immutable. But with regard to the effect which it impresses on us, it is sometimes interrupted, insofar as we sometimes fall away from it and sometimes recover again. Now the effect of divine love on us, which is lost through sin, is grace, by which a human being is made worthy of eternal life.[16]

So the function of satisfaction for Aquinas is not to placate a wrathful God or in some other way remove the constraints which compel God to damn sinners. Instead, the function of satisfaction is to restore a sinner to a state of harmony with God by repairing or restoring in the sinner what sin has damaged.

We can understand the gist of Aquinas's idea about the way in which the making of satisfaction for a wrong done achieves this end by considering a homely example of minor evil. Suppose Anna is the mother of a feisty boy, Nathan, who loves soccer. Anna, on the other hand, loves flowers and has asked her son repeatedly not to play soccer on the side of the house where her flower beds are. But Nathan does play with his soccer ball near the flower beds, and the inevitable occurs: some of the flowers are trampled. Nathan, however, is so interested in his ball playing that he stops just long enough to run into the house and say, "Sorry, Mom, I trampled your flowers" before he returns to his game. What he has done then presents his mother with two problems, one regarding the flowers and one regarding her son. She has lost some of her flowers, and it will take her some time, energy and money to replace them. But her real problem is with her son, as she must see. In the first place, he does not love what she loves; if he had had any care for the flowers, he would have played with his soccer ball in a different place. And second, he does not love her as she would like him to do, because although he knows *she* loves her flowers, he does not have a care for the flowers for her sake. So what Nathan has done has created some distance between himself and his mother. His will and hers are not in harmony, and he does not love her as he might.

In the example, in recognition of his misdeed, Nathan has offered only a hasty and casual apology and nothing more. If, however, he had any real care for his mother or her flowers, if he were really sorry for what he has done, he would also have done what he could to fix the damage. And his mother would have been very glad of his efforts, even if they were clumsy and ultimately unsuccessful, because they would have manifested a change of heart: after the fact, at any rate, Nathan would have had a care for his mother and for her flowers. And so by his efforts at undoing the damage caused by his action, he would have restored a harmony of will and love between himself and his mother which his wrong action had disrupted. In Aquinas's terms, Nathan would then have made satisfaction for his sin. The chief value of this satisfaction is not so much that it restores Anna's flowers. If Nathan's efforts are clumsy enough, the flowers may even be worse off than if he had not tried to improve their condition. Rather, the value of the satisfaction is that it restores the harmonious and loving relationship between Anna and her son.

A view of this sort, I think, underlies Aquinas's claim that, in the case of either punishment or satisfaction for sin, the important considerations have to do with the state of the sinner or the one satisfying, rather than with the state of the one sinned against.[17] So, for example, in *SCG*, in the reply to the twentieth objection where the context is a discussion of the acceptability of vicarious satisfaction, Aquinas says:

> Although when it comes to punishment of sins, the person who sinned is the one who must be punished ... , nonetheless when it comes to satisfaction one person can bear the penalty of another.

> [This is] because when a penalty for a sin is inflicted, the iniquity of the person who is punished is weighed; but, in the case of satisfaction, when someone voluntarily assumes a penalty in order to please someone who was wronged, the charity and benevolence of the person making satisfaction is considered.[18]

Just as suitable punishment is based on the state of the sinner, so also acceptable satisfaction for sin is based not on demands or needs of the person wronged but on the state of soul of the person making the satisfaction.

In fact, on Aquinas's view, the whole goal of penance, of which satisfaction is a part, is the remission of past sin. He says: "The detestation of [one's] past sins belongs to penance, together with the purpose of changing [one's] life for the better, which is, as it were, the goal of penance."[19]

But, according to Aquinas, the will moves away from past sin by moving in a direction opposed to those movements which previously inclined it to sin. Doing so requires being sorry for past sin in such a way that the past sin comes to be against one's present will. Aquinas says:

> A human being who is rising again after [falling into] sin must both be penitent with regard to the past sin and also intend to avoid future sins. For if he did not intend to desist from sin, the sin in itself would not be contrary to [his] will. And if he willed to desist from sin but were not to sorrow for the past sin, that very sin that he did would not be contrary to [his] will.[20]

Elsewhere he says:

> although the act of sin, by which a human being distanced himself from the light of reason and the divine law, ceases, the person himself does not immediately return to the [state] in which he was [before he sinned]. Rather, there is necessary some motion of the will contrary to the previous motion [of the will in sinning].[21]

In my homely example illustrating Aquinas's notion of satisfaction, when Nathan attempts to rectify the damage he has done, he shows that he is truly sorry for his action, that if he had it to do over again, he would be more careful — in short, that he now wills the opposite of what he willed when he hurt his mother's flowers and feelings.

Vicarious satisfaction

Vicarious satisfaction is much easier to understand on this way of thinking about satisfaction. Suppose that Nathan is too little to make any satisfaction himself. Perhaps to rectify the damage he would need to buy and plant new flowers, but he has no money and is too small either to go to the store or to use a shovel. If he is truly sorry for trampling the flowers, what can he do? Suppose that he has an older brother Aaron, who can do what Nathan cannot. And suppose that Nathan explains his predicament to his brother and asks his brother to buy flowers and plant them for him. If Aaron loves his brother enough, he may then use his own time and money to undo his brother's mischief. If Nathan's will really is set on some restitution for his misdeed, he will have returned to harmony with his mother even if all the actual work of restitution was done solely by Aaron. In this context, just in virtue of allying himself with Aaron's restitution, Nathan shows he cares for his mother and for the things she values; and so he restores the close relationship with his mother although Aaron is the one who restores the garden.

In this way, then, it is possible for one person to make satisfaction for another's sins. Because, on Aquinas's view, the point of making satisfaction is to return the wrongdoer's will to conformity with the will of the person wronged, rather than to inflict retributive punishment on the wrongdoer or to placate the person wronged, it is possible for the satisfaction to be made by a substitute, provided that the wrongdoer allies himself with the substitute in willing to undo as far as possible the damage he has done. So Aquinas thinks that one person can make satisfaction for another only to the extent to which they are united,[22] or that one person can atone for another insofar as they are one in charity.[23] He says, for example:

> the penalty of satisfaction is in a certain sense voluntary. It can happen that those who differ with respect to guilt [worthy of] penalty are one with respect to the will in a union of love. For this reason, sometimes someone who has not sinned voluntarily bears the penalty for another person.[24]

Now the story in which Aaron makes vicarious satisfaction for Nathan's wrong action has obvious analogies to the doctrine of Christ's atonement; but, of course, it is also disanalogous in many ways. We can, however, alter the story till many of the disanalogies vanish, and the vicarious satisfaction is much closer to that of the atonement. Suppose, for example, that instead of Nathan's asking Aaron for help, he just continues playing soccer but that *Aaron* comes to *him* and asks if he would like to have Aaron fix the damage for him. That the initiation of restitution lies with Aaron is no hindrance to the subsequent reconciliation between Nathan and his mother. Provided that Nathan does now have a care for his mother and her concerns, it does not matter to their reconciliation whether the credit for his change of heart is due to Nathan himself or to his brother. The salient fact is that Nathan's will is now in harmony with his mother's.

Or, finally, suppose that Nathan shows no signs of any interest in restitution or reconciliation with his mother. If Anna were, like the mother of

Aeneas, endowed with the power of transforming herself, and if she really loved her son, she might appear to him in disguise and in that disguise try to talk him into letting *her* make his restitution for him. If we think of the problem between Nathan and Anna as consisting in her loss of flowers or her distress over the damage to the flowers, then, of course, this story is just farcical, for in this story Anna is in effect giving flowers to herself. But if we understand, as Aquinas does, that the real problem lies in Nathan's will, which is turned away from his mother's, and if we suppose not that Anna is wrathful and vengeful towards her son but rather deeply loving, then the story makes good sense. For by this complicated and somewhat demeaning method, Anna may succeed in turning her son's will and love back to her, so that the harmony of their relationship is restored. As long as Nathan wills heartily to undo the wrong he did, it does not matter whether he himself or someone else, including even Anna, actually does the work of making restitution. And this version of the story of Anna and Nathan is analogous in relevant respects to the vicarious satisfaction of the atonement, on Aquinas's understanding of the notion of making satisfaction.

Satisfaction and the debt of punishment for sin

So although both (P) and Aquinas's account (T) are couched in terms of a debt of punishment for past sin committed, they reflect two different ways of understanding the notion of incurring a debt of punishment. That in (P) rests on a conception of God which makes him seem something like an accountant keeping double-column books on the universe. When a person commits a sin, a debt of guilt is registered in one column which must be balanced on the same line in the other column by the payment of a punishment which compensates for the guilt. This view raises a problem about how the books could ever balance if the debt is to be paid by someone other than the sinner, because the debt stems from guilt, and guilt is not a transferable commodity.

Aquinas, on the other hand, has a different understanding of the notion of incurring a debt of punishment, which in turn rests on a different conception of God. This is a conception of God more nearly analogous to a parent than to an accountant. For a good parent, a misbehaved child incurs a debt of punishment for his misbehavior, not because the parent is trying to keep the spiritual books of the household balanced, but rather because the parent loves the child, and everything from old wives' tales to psychological theory suggests that negative reinforcement contributes to extinguishing the negatively reinforced behavior if the child cannot be otherwise persuaded to give it up. The parent's concern is with the child, that the child develop into the best person she can be and that there be a loving relationship between the child and her parent. Any punishing, then, is strictly a means to the end of making the child a good person in harmony with the parent. If punishment is the only hope for achieving that end, then a good parent will not omit punishment – but for the parent, unlike the celestial accountant, the occurrence of the punishment in itself does not produce the end desired.

So when a person sins, both on (P) and on (T), he incurs a debt of punishment. On (P), the sin results in a debt of guilt in that person's accounts, which must be paid back somehow. If the sinner could pay back the debt, as on (P) he cannot, then God would be satisfied (in more than one sense of the term). But on (T), God is not concerned to balance the accounts. He is concerned with the sinner. What he wants is for that person to love what God loves and to be in harmony with God. His aim, then, is to turn that person around; and what will satisfy him is not repayment, but the goodness and love of his creature. Punishment is one means to that end; but it is a desperate means, because while punishment is known for its efficacy in extinguishing punished behavior, it is not famous for its effectiveness at winning hearts.

So while Anna in my story may well hold some punishment in reserve for her son, if she is a wise as well as a loving mother, she will try some other means first. If she forces Nathan to fix the flower bed as punishment for his sin, he may repent, or alternatively he may hate flowers all his life. On the other hand, if she provides vicarious satisfaction for her son, in the way Aquinas understands vicarious satisfaction, she eases his return to her. She invites rather than forces his compliance. She counts as sufficient for reconciliation his willingness to undo his mischief and does not require his actually restoring the garden. And finally, in the person of the substitute making vicarious satisfaction, she sets before him a living model of what he should be if he were up for it, so that he does not need to initiate the desired state of mind in himself, but needs just to watch and copy someone else's. So if Anna in a spirit of love sends Aaron to offer to fix the damage on his brother's behalf, she stands a better chance of getting what she wants: not compensation, but the heart and mind of her disobedient son.

For Aquinas, then, the aim of any satisfaction (including vicarious satisfaction) is not to make debts and payments balance but to restore a sinner to harmony with God. On this view, a person making vicarious satisfaction is not providing compensatory payment so much as acting the part of a template representing the desired character or action, in accordance with which the sinner can align his own will and inclinations to achieve a state of mind which it is at least unlikely he would have achieved on his own. That is why, speaking of Christ's passion, Aquinas remarks, "by this human beings know how much God loves them, and by this they are stimulated to love God [in return]; and the perfection of human salvation consists in this";[25] and in listing the ways in which human beings are saved by Christ's passion, Aquinas says, "he gave us an example of obedience, humility, constancy, justice, and other virtues shown in the passion of Christ, and these are necessary to human salvation".[26]

The atonement is thus the means to salvation for human beings not in virtue of altering something about or for God, but rather in virtue of helping human beings to a new and better state of will towards their past sins and towards God and his goodness.

A question

Focusing on this aim of satisfaction helps to answer a question that may occur to someone at this point.[27] If the aim of making satisfaction is just a sinner's repentance, why bother with restoration? In the example of the trampled flowers, why not just forget about the garden and the whole notion of satisfaction and aim solely at producing repentance? Aquinas says that it *was* open to God to deal with sin in just that way, that nothing required God to deal with sin by means of satisfaction (vicarious or otherwise).[28] Nonetheless, it is not hard to see the usefulness of requiring the restoration accomplished in satisfaction. In the first place, if a person is truly sorry for a sin, he will *want* the evil he has done to be undone in whatever way and to whatever extent possible; and there is something right about this desire of his being fulfilled. In the second place, true repentance, being sorry for a sin and resolving not to repeat it, is difficult. People are apt to deceive themselves into thinking that they have achieved it when they have, in fact, just had some short-lived remorse; people who find their way easily into remorse can also easily find their way out of it and back into their sin. Participation in making compensation for the wrong done – even the indirect involvement of making satisfaction vicariously – helps turn remorse into repentance; the willing of restoration, voluntarily undertaken in contrition, helps strengthen the will in its resolution of repentance.

These considerations show that there is some value in the restoration involved in making satisfaction for a wrong done, and they also clarify the usefulness of vicarious satisfaction, even when the one making satisfaction is the same as the one wronged. But it is not yet clear *how* Christ is supposed to make satisfaction, on Aquinas's account. It is not clear, that is, what the theological equivalent of restoring the flowers is.

The restoration effected by Christ's making satisfaction

According to Aquinas, Christ makes satisfaction for all the sins of the human race in his passion and death, that is, in the suffering which leads up to and includes his dying in physical and psychological pain.[29] Something in what Christ endured in dying, in other words, rectifies what was disordered or destroyed by the past sins of human beings.

But what is it that the past sin of human beings has ruined? In general, a person sins by preferring his own immediate power or pleasure over greater good. Human sin has pride and selfishness at its root, then, and it constitutes disobedience to God, whose will it contravenes. So what is most directly ruined by the sins human beings have committed is human intellect and will; a proud, selfish, disobedient mind and heart are the theological analogue of the trampled garden. In Aquinas's terms, the immediate effect of sin is to leave something like a stain on the soul;[30] and the cumulative stains of sin lessen or destroy the soul's comeliness,[31] so that by sinning a person directly mars part of God's creation, namely, himself.

The restoration involved in making satisfaction for human sinning, then, is a matter of presenting God with an instance of human nature which is marked by perfect obedience, humility, and charity and which is at least as precious in God's eyes as the marring of humanity by sin is offensive. But this is just what the second person of the Trinity does by taking on human nature and voluntarily suffering a painful and shameful death. By being willing to move from the exaltation of deity to the humiliation of crucifixion, Christ shows boundless humility; and by consenting to suffer the agony of his passion and death because God willed it when something in his own nature shrank powerfully from it, Christ manifests absolute obedience.[32] Finally, because he undertakes all his suffering and humiliation out of love for sinful human beings, Christ exhibits the most intense charity. So in his passion and death, Christ restores what sin has marred in human nature, because he gives God a particularly precious instance of human nature with the greatest possible humility, obedience, and charity. So one answer to the question why Christ had to suffer is that humility, obedience, and charity are present in suffering that is voluntarily and obediently endured for someone else's sake in a way in which they could not be, for example, in Christ's preaching or healing the sick.[33]

In this way, then, because of his divine nature and because of the extent of his humility, obedience, and charity,[34] Christ made satisfaction for all the sins of the human race.[35]

Availing oneself of Christ's having made satisfaction

It is clear on Aquinas's account of the nature and purpose of making satisfaction – as it is not clear on (P) – why Christ's having made satisfaction for all human sins does not entail that there be no human beings in hell. For Aquinas, satisfaction for sin made by a substitute for the sinner effects reconciliation between the sinner and the one sinned against only in case the sinner allies himself with the substitute by willing the restitution the substitute makes. The benefit of Christ's making satisfaction is unavailing unless a person applies it to himself by accepting Christ's suffering and death as making satisfaction for his own sins and by being united to Christ in love.

To ally oneself with Christ's making satisfaction involves, first of all, having faith in his passion. As Aquinas says, "the passion of Christ is applied to us by faith".[36] That is, availing oneself of Christ's vicarious satisfaction involves believing that the incarnate Christ suffered for the sake of human beings and in their stead. But this belief by itself is not enough, as we can see by remembering the example of satisfaction in my example. Nathan might believe that Aaron was restoring the flowers for his sake and in his stead and yet, in a fit of perversity, hate what Aaron is doing. In that case, on Aquinas's understanding of making satisfaction [but not on that which (P) employs], Aaron's action would not be successful in producing reconciliation between Nathan and his mother.

Consequently, according to Aquinas, for Christ's passion to be applied to a person, that person must have both faith and charity. He must not only believe that Christ has made satisfaction for his past sin; he must also have the love of God and of goodness which makes him glad of the fact. So, Aquinas says:

> The faith by which we are cleansed from sin is not lifeless faith, which can exist even with sin, but rather it is faith informed by charity ... And by this means sins are remitted by the power of the passion of Christ.[37]

In such a case, then, the mind and heart of the sinner cleave to Christ, and the benefit of Christ's making satisfaction in his passion and death is extended to that sinner for the remission of his sin[38] and for reconciling himself with God.

In this way, too, we can see that although Aquinas's account superficially resembles (P), it is in fact very different from it. Aquinas sees the problem of the alienation between God and human beings as consisting not in God's wrathfulness towards human beings or in his inability to avoid damning them but rather in human withdrawal from God. And he understands Christ's passion as atoning, as producing reconciliation between God and human beings, not because God in his justice must inflict the punishment for sin on someone and the innocent Christ substitutes for guilty human beings, but rather because by allying their hearts and minds with Christ in his passion as he makes satisfaction for their past sins, human beings are converted to a state of mind in harmony with God's will with regard to what they have done.

There is real mercy and forgiveness on Aquinas's account, because, according to Aquinas, God does not require the penalties for sins either from human beings or from Christ. God does not inflict Christ's suffering on Christ as a punishment for human sins; rather God receives it as an act of making satisfaction whose goal is the alteration of human intellects and wills. The homely example drives this point home. In accepting Aaron's restoration of her flowers, Anna does not inflict restoration of the flowers on Aaron as punishment even if she is the instigator of his action. The purpose of Aaron's action (and Anna's participation in it) is not to make sure that there is punishment to balance the misdeed done by Nathan but rather to change Nathan's will with regard to his past deed in such a way that he is again in harmony with his mother.

And so it is clear on Aquinas's account, as it is not on (P), why not all people experience the benefit of the atonement, namely, because on Aquinas's account it is not possible for Christ's atoning action to be efficacious for anyone unless that person allies himself with Christ's act of making satisfaction.

Finally, Aquinas's account, unlike (P), provides some comprehensible connection between Christ's atoning action and the remission of past sin, because, according to Aquinas's account, when a person allies himself with Christ's making satisfaction, he wills the contrary of the pride, selfishness, and disobedience he willed when he sinned, and in *this* willing he moves away from the past sin he committed.[39]

The second problem

If we return now to the example of Susan and her alcoholic friend David with which I began, we can see that Aquinas's account of the atonement as making satisfaction is only part of the solution to the problem of human evil. According to the story in that example, David drove while drunk and in consequence killed Susan's child. One way of restoring Susan and David to friendship with each other again afterwards, on Aquinas's view, is for David (or someone else acting for David) to make satisfaction for the evil David did by offering Susan something which she would not have had otherwise and which she values as much as (or almost as much as) what she lost, thereby evincing the real care for Susan and for what she loves which David lacked in the actions that resulted in the death of Susan's daughter. Suppose, for example, that Susan has a second child who is dying from kidney disease and for whom a donor has not been found; and suppose (*mirabile dictu*) that David's tissues are compatible with those of the sick child. If in a spirit of contrition, David donates one of his kidneys and thereby saves Susan's sick child from death, he goes a long way towards restoring his friendship with Susan.

But even in such rare felicitous circumstances, their friendship will not be restored to its previous state as long as David remains an alcoholic, and Susan knows this about him. In his current condition David does not share many of Susan's most important concerns and desires; and, as he and Susan both know, he may at any time again do something as terrible as killing a child.

Analogously, although Aquinas's account of the atonement as making satisfaction explains how Christ's passion remits past sin, this account by itself is not enough to show that Christ's passion solves the problem of human evil, because simply making satisfaction for past sin still leaves a person with the same proclivities to do evil in the future. Taken just in its function of making satisfaction, Christ's passion does not alter human proneness to evil, the disordered relationship among human reason, will, and passions which, on Aquinas's view, is responsible for the tendency of human beings to sin.[40] This disordered condition of human nature constitutes the problem of future sin.

Aquinas, however, thinks that Christ's passion also helps with this problem. He says, "by his passion Christ not only freed man from sin but also merited for man justifying grace and the glory of beatitude".[41] On Aquinas's view, Christ's passion is like a medicine for sin[42] available to cure sin in all ages of human history.[43] And so he says:

> by his passion Christ freed us from [our] sins causally, that is, [by] constituting (*instituens*) the cause of our being freed. And from this all sins at any time can be remitted, whether they are past or present or future, as if a doctor were to prepare a medicine by means of which all sicknesses could be cured, even in the future.[44]

For Aquinas, Christ's passion and death are, as he puts it, both a remedy of satisfaction and a sacrament of salvation.[45] Christ's suffering thus has *two* principal beneficial effects: satisfaction for one's past sins and salvation from one's sinful nature.[46]

When Aquinas's account of Christ's passion as making satisfaction is supplemented by an explanation of the passion as Christ's meriting grace and thereby healing the sinfulness of the human mind and will, Aquinas's interpretation of the doctrine of the atonement also explains how the passion and death of Christ provide a solution to the problem of future sin.

Christ's meriting grace

This second part of Aquinas's interpretation of the doctrine of the atonement is more complicated and difficult than his explanation of the atonement as making satisfaction. It is couched in the technical terminology of medieval theology; it is set in the context of Aquinas's elaborate treatment of the nature and varieties of God's grace; and on first hearing it is likely to strike a contemporary audience as obscure and implausible at best. In what follows I will give a brief summary of the salient points of Aquinas's account, presenting just as much of his work on grace as I need to do in order to make this part of his interpretation of the doctrine of the atonement intelligible and without pausing to comment on the many questions Aquinas's views raise. After this uncritical presentation I will try to illustrate Aquinas's interpretation with a concrete case in order to give some insight into the general idea that animates his views. With the help of this concrete case, we will be in a position to consider whether Aquinas is successful in arguing that the atonement, taken in the way he understands it, is a solution to the problem of future sin.

According to Aquinas, Christ is the head of the Church;[47] and since all human beings are potentially members of the Church, Christ is (at least potentially) the head of the whole human race.[48] By saying that Christ is the head, Aquinas means that he is first among human beings in order, perfection, and power;[49] but, more importantly, he also means that together Christ and human beings form one mystical body, analogous to the physical body formed by the head and other members of a human body.[50] All human beings are potentially, and believers are actually, part of this mystical body. In his passion Christ merits grace sufficient to cure all human sin;[51] and as head of the body of the Church, he infuses the grace he has merited into those persons actually united with him in this mystical body.[52]

For someone to merit something is for him to bring it about that some good thing should in justice be given him, and the source of Christ's merit that provides grace for human beings is his will.[53] In the last analysis, good things for human beings are those which contribute to obtaining eternal life, and so the grace that Christ merits is grace bringing salvation to human beings. Now an action meriting eternal life must be an action done out of charity.[54] In fact, charity is the root of all merit[55] because it is the love of God,[56] who is goodness personified,[57] and the love of other persons and things for the sake of goodness. Without charity, then, no true virtue is possible,[58] and charity is, as it were, the form of all virtuous acts.[59] But Christ in his passion suffered out of the deepest charity, for he voluntarily accepted great suffering and death out of love for all human beings.[60] His suffering was intense, both physically and psychically, partly because during his passion he grieved for all the sins of the human race at once,[61] and partly because there is more charity involved when a greater person submits to suffering for the sake of others.[62] So because of the intensity of his love for human beings, Christ merits grace leading to eternal life; and as the head of all human beings (at least potentially), he merits this grace for all people.

Grace and salvation

To understand this part of Aquinas's interpretation of the doctrine of the atonement, we have to be clear about at least a part of his complicated account of grace. (Although Aquinas recognizes several species of grace, in what follows I will not generally distinguish among these kinds of grace, because the distinctions are not necessary for my purposes here.[63]) In general, Aquinas thinks of the grace necessary for salvation in this way:

> a human being is said to have the grace of God not only in virtue of the fact that he is loved by God in eternal life, but in virtue of the fact

that there is given to him some gift by means of which he is worthy
of eternal life ... For otherwise a person existing in mortal sin could
be said to be in grace if 'grace' meant divine acceptance alone, since it
is possible for some sinner to be predestined to eternal life.[64]

Explaining the work of grace, Aquinas says, "by grace the will of a human
being is changed, for grace is what prepares the human will to will the
good".[65] For Aquinas, grace is a habit or disposition bestowed in virtue of
Christ's passion by the Holy Spirit on a person, inclining that person towards
freely complying with God's precepts and prohibitions.[66] This disposition is
bestowed when a person's mind is illuminated to know things which exceed
reason and when his affections in consequence cleave to God in love, being
inclined to do all the things such love requires.[67] The end or purpose of this
grace is the union of a human person with God.[68] Grace accomplishes this
end by inclining the natural powers of the mind to the love of God and by
making that love come easily and pleasantly.[69]

Nonetheless, this inclining of a person's mind and will to charity is
always accomplished by the Holy Spirit by means of a free act[70] of that
person's will.[71] While grace is being infused into a person, that person
assents to the process in an act of free will,[72] so that the infusion of grace is
simultaneous with the movement of the will.[73] According to Aquinas:

> the motion of the free will, which occurs in the justification of an
> impious person, is the ultimate disposition to grace. For this reason,
> in one and the same instant there is the infusion of grace together
> with this motion of the free will ... The act of penitence is comprised
> in this motion ... And so, insofar as the motion of free will in peni-
> tence is more or less intense, to this degree the penitent receives
> greater or lesser grace.[74]

And so, on Aquinas's views, no one comes to God by grace without freely
willing to do so.[75] He says, "in adults, who can know and love God, there is
required some use of free will by means of which they may know and love
God; and this is conversion to God".[76]

It is God who moves a person towards charity, from which the virtues
flow. But God moves everything in accordance with the nature of the thing
moved; and since it is part of human nature to have free will, God's movement of a person in the process of infusing grace does not take place without
a movement of free will.[77]

Furthermore, what grace confers is a habitual disposition. But one can
always act against a disposition or habit, and so a person in grace is always
capable of sinning.[78] And, finally, grace is available to all human beings; the
only human beings who are deprived of grace are those who offer an obstacle
to grace within themselves.[79]

Grace itself is not a virtue;[80] but it helps ready the will for virtue by giving it a disposition, by preparing the will to love God and to act rightly.[81] So grace gives rise to all the virtues,[82] and especially the theological virtues, faith, hope, and charity.[83] The process of the infusion of grace and the consequent effects of grace on the mind of the person receiving it is the process of sanctification, in which a person's sinful nature is slowly converted into a righteous character. Thus, Aquinas says, there are five effects of grace in human beings: (1) healing of the soul; (2) desire of the good; (3) carrying out the good desired; (4) perseverance in good; and (5) attainment of eternal life.[84]

Grace and Christ's passion

Even if this account of grace were entirely clear and wholly plausible as a solution to the problem of future sin, however, it would not yet suffice as part of an interpretation of the doctrine of the atonement, because so far we have no connection between the bestowal of grace, on the one hand, and Christ's passion and death, on the other. That connection is provided by Aquinas's theory of the means by which God has chosen to bestow grace, particularly in the sacraments. According to Aquinas:

> One must hold that the sacraments of the new law are, in a certain way, the cause of grace ... Neither the sacraments nor any created thing can give grace in the manner of a cause acting *per se* ... but the sacraments function as an instrument of grace ... [T]he humanity of Christ is an instrumental cause of [our] justification, and this cause is applied to us spiritually by faith and corporeally by the sacraments ... [T]he passion of Christ is said to work in the sacraments of the new law, and in this way the sacraments of the new law are the cause of grace, working as it were as an instrument of grace.[85]

There is no way that salvation from sin can occur without grace, Aquinas says,[86] and he holds that the sacraments, particularly the Eucharist, confer this grace. Partaking of the Eucharist is not necessary to salvation,[87] but, according to Aquinas:

> the grace of the sacraments is especially ordained to two [ends], namely, to taking away the defects of past sins, insofar as they have passed away in act and remain in guilt, and furthermore to perfecting the soul in those things that pertain to the worship of God according to the religion of the Christian life. Now it is manifest ... that Christ has freed us from our sins especially by his passion ... And so it is manifest that the sacraments of the Church

have their virtue particularly from the passion of Christ, and the power (*virtus*) of this is joined to us by the reception of the sacraments. As a sign of this, from Christ's side, while he was hanging on the cross, there flowed water and blood, one of which pertains to baptism, and the other to the Eucharist, which are the most powerful sacraments.[88]

And so Aquinas says, "the Eucharist is the sacrament of the passion of Christ insofar as a human being is perfected [by means of it] in union to Christ in his passion (*Christus passus*)".[89]

Grace is thus involved in all the sacraments, but the one most important for Aquinas's interpretation of the doctrine of the atonement is the Eucharist: "The most perfect sacrament is that in which the body of Christ is really contained, namely, the Eucharist, and it is the consummation of all the others."[90]

On his view, Christ's passion works its effect of saving human beings from their proclivity to (future) sin through all the sacraments,[91] but particularly through the Eucharist. The sacraments are for the spiritual life what certain physical things are for bodily life, according to Aquinas;[92] the Eucharist is nourishment for the psyche, and it provides growth in virtue[93] precisely by conferring grace.[94] In fact, Aquinas says, "this sacrament has in itself the power of conferring grace ... And so it is due to the efficacy of its power that even from a desire of it a person attains grace, by which he is revived spiritually."[95]

Obviously, the sacrament of the Eucharist is intimately related to Christ's passion. On Aquinas's theology of the sacraments, in accordance with Christ's institution at the last supper, Christ's body and blood are actually, literally, present in the sacrament. Christ's body, however, is not in the sacrament as a physical body is in a place, that is, contained by the place and filling it. Rather it is in the sacrament only substantially, as being the substance of what was bread. Thus Christ's body is in the (apparent) bread in such a way that the whole body of Christ is comprised in every part of the bread.[96] (Something roughly similar applies also to the wine, but I omit the details here.) Furthermore, the nature of the Eucharist is such that when a believer partakes of it, he does not turn the sacrament into his substance, as happens when he eats other food, but instead he becomes part of the body of Christ and is incorporated into the body of Christ. Aquinas says, "there is this difference between corporeal and spiritual food: corporeal food is converted into the substance of the human being who is nourished [by it] ... but spiritual food converts a human being into itself".[97] This process, however, occurs only in those who partake of the Eucharist appropriately. Although the grace Christ merited by his passion is sufficient for undoing bad habits acquired in the past and preventing further sin in the future, it is efficacious to cure the sinful tendencies only of those united to him. The uniting is effected by faith and love.[98] Aquinas says:

> the power of Christ is joined to us by means of faith. Now the power of remitting sins in a certain special way belongs to Christ's passion. And therefore by means of faith in his passion human beings are specially freed from sins ... And therefore the power of the sacraments, which are ordained to taking away sins, is principally from faith in the passion of Christ.[99]

The faith in question here is living faith, what Aquinas tends to call 'faith informed by charity'. And although charity or love of God can be stimulated by other examples of God's love for his creatures, it is stirred especially by reflection on Christ's passion.[100] So, for example, in one of the many passages in which he makes the point, Aquinas claims that we are freed from our sinful nature by the passion of Christ in three ways, the first of which is "by means of stimulating us to charity, because, as the Apostle says in Romans 5, 'God commends his charity to us since when we were enemies, Christ died for us." ' [101]

Union with Christ in love is thus needed to receive this sacrament appropriately; but union (or perhaps increased union through increased love) is also the effect of this sacrament, since in the sacrament a believer receives Christ within himself in such a way as to become incorporated into the body of Christ.[102] So the effect of the sacrament for those who receive it with charity, that is, with the right sort of will, is that they are united with Christ to such an extent that they become part of the body of Christ.[103] But if a person is part of the body of Christ, then the grace Christ merited on the cross by his passion flows into that person. By this means, the grace won by Christ's passion is bestowed through the Eucharist on those who partake of the sacrament appropriately.[104] The result of the believer's becoming part of the body of Christ and receiving grace from Christ is that his mind and will are strengthened against future sin, because by the grace bestowed through the sacrament a believer's love of God and love of goodness is stimulated and strengthened.[105] In the sacrament of the Eucharist, Aquinas says (in one of the few lyrical passages in his scholastic prose), a believer's soul is inebriated by the sweetness of the divine goodness.[106]

This is so because, when a person cleaves to Christ in faith and love in this way, an act of free will is elicited in him simultaneous with the infusing of Christ's grace. The act of free will is directed both towards past sins and towards future acts; in this act of will, a person hates his past sin and loves God's goodness. In consequence, the believer withdraws from sin and draws nearer to righteousness.[107] Simultaneously with this free act of willing on the believer's part, God infuses grace into the believer's soul. God adds to the believer's mind and will a disposition inclining the believer towards the good and away from sin. The repetition of this cooperative action of free willing and the simultaneous infusion of grace is the process of gradually conforming the believer's mind and character to Christ's, a process whose culmination is eternal life with Christ in the afterlife.[108]

So the atonement solves the problem of future sin because by means of the sacrament of the Eucharist, a union of love is effected between a believer and Christ such that the grace merited by Christ in his passion is transferred to the believer in one cooperative divine and human action in which the believer freely loves God's goodness and hates his own sin, and God adds to the believer a strengthened disposition for the good, with the result that in the course of time, the believer comes to be more righteous and more like Christ.

Illustration and explanation

Because Aquinas's account of grace is complex and problematic, this part of his theory of the atonement may leave us cold and uncomprehending. It is, for example, not clear how God could infuse the grace of a disposition for willing the good into a believer simultaneously with a free act of will for the good on the believer's part. And why should it take a religious ceremony like the Eucharist for God to bestow this grace? Furthermore, the connection Aquinas makes between Christ's passion and the bestowal of grace through the Eucharist is not immediately obvious. The talk of the mystical body of Christ is more perplexing than helpful, and it is difficult to see why it was necessary for Christ to suffer in order to effect this mystical body. The transfer of grace, which was merited by Christ in his passion, to believers united to Christ in charity raises moral and metaphysical problems. The nature of grace is or at least includes a disposition to goodness, and it is hard to understand how this disposition of Christ's could be directly transferred from him to another person, no matter how they are joined together. And finally, it is not clear why a good God could not and would not simply bestow grace directly without the suffering of Christ's passion or the ritual of the Eucharist.

Part of the trouble we have in understanding Aquinas's account, I think, stems from the fact that he explains in medieval metaphysical terms what we would be more inclined to explain in psychological terms. But it is possible, I think, to see what Aquinas has in mind if we think through his claims in terms of a concrete case. Doing so will not explain the details of the metaphysics in which Aquinas's interpretation is couched; but I believe it will clarify Aquinas's general idea of the way in which the atonement solves the problem of future sin, and it will provide answers to some (but not all) of the questions I just raised about this part of Aquinas's account.

So consider again David, an alcoholic who kills a child while driving drunk. Suppose that David is a Christian (of a Thomistic sort) and that shortly after his dreadful accident, still in the grip of his alcoholism but nonetheless full of sorrow and remorse over his killing of the child, he returns to church; and in this state of sorrow and remorse he participates in the sacrament of the Eucharist. What will this experience be like for David?

Consider first what he believes (on the supposition that he is a Thomistic sort of Christian). He believes that he has done something morally reprehensible and that he did it because of his continuing enslavement to alcohol, and he will see himself in consequence as a hateful person. Since he is a Christian, however, he also believes that God does not hate him but rather *loves* him intensely. God himself is perfectly good, holy in righteousness, and he also sees completely all the evil in David's will and actions. And yet Christ's love for David, for the hateful, alcoholic David, was so great that he voluntarily undertook the shame and agony of crucifixion for him. And for what purpose? To heal David of his sin; to offer for David what David himself could not offer to God, so that he might be reconciled to God, no matter what awful evil he had done, and to transform David from something hateful into someone holy, into someone like Christ.

Furthermore, Christ's great love for David is not just part of some old historical narrative or abstruse theological argument. On the contrary, the divine person who loves David so intensely as to die for him in order to keep David from dying in his sin is right there then in the sacrament, present to David's spirit even if hidden from his eyes. In fact, not only is he present, but (David will believe) in the sacrament of the Eucharist the God who loves him comes closer to him and is more intimately united to him than it is possible for two created persons to be in this life. That is because, David himself believes (since he is a Thomistic Christian), in receiving the sacrament David receives the body and blood of Christ in such a way that he himself becomes a part of the body of Christ, bound together with Christ into one spiritual entity.

If David believes all this, what is the effect on him likely to be?[109] In the first place, his feelings of guilt will be assuaged; Christ has made satisfaction to God for David's sin and restored the relationship between David and God which David's past sin had disrupted. In consequence, David's hostility to himself will be alleviated; the judge most in a position to despise and condemn him instead loves him and means to rescue him from his evil. Then, too, David's hope for himself will be strengthened. God, who sees David as he is and who can do anything, is himself on David's side. It is God's intention that David be turned into a righteous person, at peace with God and with himself. And if God be for him, what can be against him? Furthermore, David will feel a great debt of gratitude to Christ, who suffered so to free him, and with that gratitude will come a determination that Christ's suffering should not be for nothing. Finally, David will feel a surge of love for Christ, who so loved him, and also a sense of joy, for the divine person who loves David is present to him *now* and united with him.

As long as David is in this frame of mind, what chance has his addiction got of retaining its mastery over him? To use Aquinas's terminology for a moment, what David has done in this state is to cleave to Christ in charity and thus to will freely to draw near to righteousness and withdraw from sin.

If at some other time out of love for David, God were simply to alter David's will, in such a way as to strengthen a determination in David not to drink, for example, he would be destroying David's free will, because he would be making David will contrary to what David himself wills absent the divine intervention. But if God acts on David's will while David is in the frame of mind outlined above, if in these circumstances God strengthens David's will in its resolution to stop drinking, he is not violating David's will, for in these circumstances David has in effect a second-order will for a will not to drink.[110] In other words, the beliefs and desires stimulated in David by the Eucharist and reflection on Christ's passion evoke in David a will to have a will that wills not to drink. In giving David grace when David has a second-order will of this sort, God infuses David with a disposition (of one degree of strength or another) to first-order willing against drinking; but that God does so in no way detracts from the freedom of David's will because it is David's own (second-order) will that he have a (first-order) will against drinking. In strengthening David's will in its resolution, then, God does not undermine the freedom of his will but rather cooperates with it to produce the state of will which David himself wills to have. This is, I think, the sort of thing Aquinas has in mind when he says that the grace bestowed to help human beings will the good *cooperates* with free will and is infused simultaneously with an action of free will.[111] (A different and much more complicated question has to do with the relation between Christ's passion and grace which is operating, rather than cooperating; but I have already discussed that question in Chapter 12 on faith, because it is intimately bound up with Aquinas's understanding of the nature of justifying faith, and so I omit it here.)

It is clear that if David's response to the sacrament is of the ordinary human variety, if it is not the unusually powerful and life-transforming conversion of the sort had by Paul on the road to Damascus, David's exalted state of mind will fade, and his second-order resolution will weaken. Even so, however, he will have made some progress, because God will have acted to alter David's will simultaneously with David's free (second-order) will to have a will that wills the good, to enable David to be successful in repudiating his past sin and drawing nearer to the goodness of God. But not even omnipotence can make David's will stronger in its willing of goodness than David wills it to be, on pain of violating David's will. Without the sudden wholesale conversion of will of the sort experienced by Paul, David will also have a strong disposition towards first-order willings to drink, which will undermine his second-order willing to have a will not to drink and which will thus resist God's grace.[112] So David's road away from his sin and towards the goodness he wants in himself will take time, during which some second-order willing and some grace will occur together, in consequence of which there will be more divine strengthening of David's will in willing the good, and this strengthening in turn will stimulate further cooperative willing and grace.[113]

On the basis of this sort of concrete case illustrating Aquinas's interpretation of the doctrine of the atonement as providing a solution to the problem of future sin, we can sketch some answers to the questions with which I began this section.

We can understand the bestowal of grace in the process of the sanctification of a believer as God's simultaneous cooperation with the believer's willing to have a will for the good. Such grace is tied to the Eucharist because (for believers of the sort Aquinas has in mind) it is the Eucharist which breaks down a believer's resistance to grace and thus contributes to producing that second-order willing. Both the bestowal of grace and the second-order willing associated with the Eucharist are connected to Christ's passion, because it is Christ's love as manifested in his passion which elicits the believer's love and consequent willingness to repudiate his sin and will the good. It is also clear why God could not bestow grace directly without Christ's passion. The commemoration of Christ's passion in the Eucharist serves to undermine a person's refusal of grace, so that God's bestowal of grace does not violate the will of that person. On this way of understanding Aquinas, then, whatever else the mystical body of Christ may be, it is or at least essentially includes a union of minds and wills, when the believer values and wants what Christ does, in the love engendered by the intimacy and poignancy of the Eucharist.

In this sort of way, it is also possible to see what Aquinas has in mind with his claim that Christ's grace is transferred to a believer through the Eucharist. When David acquires grace on partaking of the Eucharist, it is not because some moral disposition of Christ is magically plucked from Christ and transplanted into David. Instead in loving Christ because he believes Christ loves him and wants David's love in return, with all that that love of Christ's implies in the context, David allies himself with Christ and takes on a frame of mind like that which he believes characterized Christ in his passion, namely, charity accompanied by a hatred of sin (in David's case, his own sin) and a love of goodness. In this frame of mind David forms a second-order willing to have first-order willings of the sort he believes he ought to have, so that God can simultaneously infuse in David (to the degree suitable to the condition of David's second-order will) a disposition to will not to drink without thereby violating the freedom of David's will.

In this way, then, Christ's grace is transferred from Christ to David, not in the way that tulip bulbs are transferred from one plot to another but rather in the way that understanding is sometimes transferred from one mind to another, by the two minds being joined together in certain aims and beliefs and one mind's being kindled and illuminated by the other.

Conclusion and caveat

If we combine the two main parts of Aquinas's interpretation of the doctrine of the atonement, Christ's passion as making satisfaction and Christ's passion as meriting grace, we can see that Aquinas has an interpretation of the doctrine which can handle the problems of both past and future sin.

If we return to the story of Susan and David, we can see that this story is in many (but certainly not all) respects analogous to the Christian view of the relationship between God and a post-Fall human being. To reconcile Susan and David requires David's doing what he can to make satisfaction for the evil he has already done and then his abandoning his addiction. On Aquinas's interpretation of the doctrine of the atonement, a post-Fall human person is alienated from God because of the sins he has already committed and because of his on-going tendency to will the contrary of what God wills, generally his own pleasure or power in preference to greater goods. Christ out of love for humans initiates the process of making satisfaction by offering in his passion what human beings cannot offer to God, namely, an instance of human nature with perfect humility, obedience, and love of God. In addition, for a human being and God to be at one again, a person needs to convert from his post-Fall disordered nature with its inclination to evil to a new Christ-like character inclined to goodness. On Aquinas's interpretation of the doctrine of the atonement, Christ also provides the means for effecting this conversion by his passion and by its commemoration in the Eucharist. The love manifested by Christ's passion and the loving union experienced by the believer in the Eucharist call forth the believer's love of Christ, together with a second-order will to will goodness and withdraw from sin. Simultaneous with this free second-order will on the believer's part, God gives the believer's will supernatural aid by infusing in it a disposition for the good, thereby assisting and strengthening the will to will the good, without violating the believer's free will.

Finally, although I have canvassed many elements of Aquinas's interpretation of the atonement, there are still others that I have left to one side. For example, readers familiar with other theories of the atonement, such as Calvin's, may wonder at the fact that there is here hardly any mention of the work of the Holy Spirit, which features significantly in Calvin's account, as in the theories of some other theologians. In fact, however, Aquinas's interpretation does assign a prominent place to the Holy Spirit, because on Aquinas's view the grace bestowed through the sacraments is given by the Holy Spirit,[114] so that the infusion of grace is the Holy Spirit working in the heart. But covering all the complexities and elaborations of Aquinas's account of the atonement is more than can be managed in one chapter, and so I have left to one side any issues which could be omitted without distorting the heart of Aquinas's interpretation. The work of the Holy Spirit is one such matter; the role of Christ's resurrection in the process of atonement is another.

There is, however, one idea important in theories of the atonement found, for example, in the Reformation which is not mentioned in this chapter because, as far as I can see, it is not in Aquinas. Luther, for example, in his explanation of the atonement, emphasizes the idea that Christ somehow actually bears all human sin; that is, in some way all the sins ever committed in human history are transferred to Christ's soul in his suffering on the cross. There is no similar or analogous claim in Aquinas's account. There is consequently some problem for Aquinas in squaring his account with the New Testament story of the passion. At any rate, the cry of dereliction from the cross is certainly easier to explain on Luther's view than on Aquinas's interpretation; and so is Christ's agony in the garden of Gethsemane. For Aquinas, it is difficult to explain why the incarnate deity should have been in such torment over his death when so many of the merely human martyrs went gladly, even cheerfully, to death by tortures worse than crucifixion.

We might be tempted to suppose that Aquinas's interpretation does not include an idea such as Luther's because Luther's idea makes no sense and so did not occur to Aquinas; sins, we might think, cannot be transferred like money in bank accounts. But, in fact, Luther's idea is less counter-intuitive than it seems at first, and Aquinas has the philosophical concepts and distinctions necessary for supporting something at least resembling it.

For example, Aquinas distinguishes between the very act of sinning itself and what he calls 'the stain on the soul' left by that sinful action.[115] By 'the stain on the soul' Aquinas understands the effects wrought on the intellect and will by the past act of sin which remain after the act is over, even when the past sin has been repented. Whatever exactly Aquinas meant these effects to be, it seems to me that among the effects left by past sin are the distressing knowledge of what it feels like to be a person who has committed a particular sin and the tormenting awareness of what it is like to want to do such an evil action. It is, arguably, possible to have a stain on the soul, so understood, without having the very act of sin which usually precedes it. To take just one example, a powerful scene in a movie portraying a brutal sexual assault may succeed in evoking in some receptive members of the audience a mild version of the stain on the soul ordinarily produced only by the evil action itself.

Something like Luther's idea could thus be explained in Aquinas's own terms by claiming that in his passion Christ acquires all the stains on the soul produced by all the sins of all human beings, or at least of the human beings with whom Christ is united.[116] The (foreseen) horror and pain of such a burden would certainly explain the agony in Gethsemane and the cry of dereliction on the cross. And that Christ suffer in such a way could perhaps be explained as a necessary concomitant of Aquinas's idea that a believer is united to Christ in the mystical body of Christ through the Eucharist. If David is united with Christ in this way, then Christ is also united with David. In my example, David experiences that uniting as allying himself with an overwhelmingly holy, loving person. By parity of reasoning, then, one might argue that Christ experiences the uniting as allying himself with a selfish, alcoholic killer of a child, with the mind and heart of that killer somehow one with his own.

So it is possible for Aquinas's account of the atonement to accommodate something like Luther's idea. That Aquinas has no equivalent idea stems, I think, from his tendency to emphasize the divine nature of Christ at the expense of his human nature, rather than from any philosophical absurdity (in Aquinas's terms or ours) in the version of Luther's idea at issue here. But Aquinas's theory of the atonement would have been theologically more powerful, in my view, and also perhaps more humanly compelling, if it had included something equivalent to this idea.

Finally, it is, of course, clear that Aquinas's account is not the only theory of the atonement that is an alternative to the unreflective (P) with which this chapter began. Anselm, Abelard, Luther, Calvin, and John of the Cross, to name just a few, also worked out sophisticated theories of the atonement. What my examination of Aquinas's account shows is not the preferability of his version to any of these others but rather just the nature of one defensible theory of the atonement and the general constraints on any acceptable account. Aquinas's theory of the atonement is a reflective analogue of (P). As Aquinas explains it, Christ in virtue of his passion really does solve the problem of human evil and really does make people at one with God. Whatever the details of other theories of the atonement, they must explain how the atonement solves the problem both of past and of future sin; and they must do so, like Aquinas's account, in a way which does not undermine God's justice and mercy or human nature.

16

PROVIDENCE AND SUFFERING

Introduction

In this chapter, I am going to examine Aquinas's views of providence and human suffering by considering his interpretation of the story of Job. Because, however, Aquinas's biblical commentaries are less well known than his other philosophical or theological works, it may be helpful to begin this discussion with a very brief word about Aquinas's biblical commentaries in general and his commentary on Job in particular. Aquinas wrote commentaries on five books of the Old Testament (Psalms, Job, Isaiah, Jeremiah, and Lamentations), two Gospels (Matthew and John), and the Pauline epistles. Though these biblical commentaries have not received the same sort of attention as some of his other works, such as *Summa theologiae* or *Summa contra gentiles*, they are nonetheless a treasure trove of his philosophical and theological thought.[1] The commentary on Job in particular is one of Aquinas's more mature and polished commentaries. Unlike many of his commentaries, which are preserved in the form of a *reportatio*, a transcription of Aquinas's lecturers by someone who attended them, the commentary on Job is an *expositio*, material reworked and revised by Aquinas himself.[2] The commentary sheds light on Aquinas's understanding of God's providence and especially of the relation between God's providence and human suffering. Aquinas does discuss providence in other works as well, most notably in Book III of *Summa contra gentiles*, which is roughly contemporary with the commentary on Job; and he considers problems involving suffering in many of the biblical commentaries, especially those on the Pauline epistles.[3] But the book of Job is the paradigmatic presentation of the problem of evil for anyone trying to reconcile the existence of God with the presence of evil in the world, and it is therefore particularly interesting to see how Aquinas interprets this book. So, although when it is appropriate, I turn to other works of Aquinas's, including *Summa contra gentiles* and the commentaries on the Pauline epistles, my focus here is on Aquinas's commentary on Job. I will begin with some general remarks about Aquinas's views of providence and then turn to Aquinas's interpretation of the role of providence in the book of Job.

God's providence

The notion of God's providence is derived from the concept of his goodness. Because on the doctrine of simplicity the divine nature is identical with goodness, the goodness of creatures is measured by their relationship to God.[4] For human persons in particular, the ultimate good and the final fulfillment of their natures consists in union with God. And because God is good, he does what is good for his creatures. In his dealings with human beings, then, God's ultimate aim, which takes precedence over all others, is to return human beings to himself, to unite them to himself in heaven. The plan by which he directs the lives of human beings, influences their characters, and orders the events of their lives in order to achieve his aim is his providence; the actual working out of his plan is the divine governance.[5] For the sake of brevity in what follows, I will refer to both the plan and its execution as 'God's providence'.

Consonant with traditional Christian doctrine, it is Aquinas's claim that everything in the world is subject to divine providence. Comprised in this claim are two beliefs:

(1) God in his providence directs all things in the world to their ultimate good, that is, to himself;[6]

and

(2) God's will is always fulfilled.[7]

In other words, Aquinas believes that everything that happens happens under God's control and is chosen or allowed by him because it contributes to the ultimate good of creatures by drawing them back to him.

There are obvious objections to this claim about providence, and Aquinas considers some of them from different approaches at several places in his writings. These objections fall into two groups. Those of the first group argue against the claim itself; those of the second group argue that the particular mechanism by which divine providence is said to operate is not open to God as a means of governance.[8] I will leave the objections of the second group to one side and concentrate on those of the first group.[9]

To begin with, it seems evident that God's will is not always fulfilled; in fact, there is apparently even a biblical warrant for the claim that it is not. 1 Timothy 2:4 says that "God would have all men to be saved"; but it is Christian doctrine that not all human beings are saved, and therefore it seems that the will of God is not always fulfilled. Besides, the point of God's giving human beings free will is evidently to enable them to govern themselves and make their own choices; but in that case it is possible for human persons to will something discordant with God's will. Furthermore, traditional Christianity holds that some of God's creatures, most notably Satan but also some human beings, rebel against God; to rebel, however, is just to pit one's will against God's and deliberately act contrary to God's will. Finally, it seems that considerations of God's justice require us to say that God's will is not always fulfilled, because unless some creatures acted contrary to God's will, it seems that God would not be just in punishing them, as he is said to do.[10]

In reply Aquinas says that God always wills what is good, but sometimes what is good absolutely considered is not good in the circumstances. In such cases God may be said to have an inclination (*velleitas*) for the good absolutely considered, but what he actually wills is what is good in the circumstances.[11]

To see what Aquinas means, consider, for example, a mother who dotes on her son. If she could, she would no doubt be glad always to live in happy harmony with her child; but when he engages in deliberate mischief, she wills to scold him. What is good absolutely considered, namely, that she be pleasant to her child, is not good in the circumstances in which he misbehaves; what is good in those circumstances is that she scold him. Therefore, as a good mother who wills what is good for her son, when she is confronted with her son's misbehavior, she wills to scold him.

Is some part of her will frustrated when she scolds him? Not if by 'will' here we mean an occurrent act of will, as distinct from a wish, desire, longing, or inclination. The mother would like to live at peace with her son, and she herself may be quite frustrated when his misbehavior keeps her from the happy relations with him which she desires; but these facts tell us only something about her emotions and aims, not about her will. In the face of her son's mischief her *will* is to scold him; and her will is fulfilled even if she has a longing which is unsatisfied when she and her son are at variance. Again, someone might suppose that the mother's will is contravened nonetheless just by the fact that her son does not will to do what he ought to do. But this objection also confuses an aim or longing with an act of will. The mother can yearn for her son to do what is right, but unless his doing what he ought to do is something she can bring about herself (as it is not so long as he has free will), *she* cannot form an act of will the content of which is what *he* does.

Similarly, Aquinas says, when God considers human persons just as human, what is good for them is that they be saved, and hence a perfectly good God has an inclination (or wish or desire) to save them all. But since some persons refuse grace and persist in sin, what God actually wills is not to save some of them.[12] The technical but familiar way to describe this situation, employed by Aquinas,[13] is to say that God antecedently wills what is good absolutely, but he consequently wills the good in the circumstances. God antecedently wills all persons to be saved; but he consequently wills that some not be saved.

The distinction between antecedent and consequent will Aquinas uses is convenient, as long as it does not mislead us into thinking that God wills first one thing and then another,[14] or that his antecedent will is what he really wills while his consequent will is what he settles for.[15] Rather what God has ordained for his creatures insofar as it lies just in God himself to determine is what God is said to will in his antecedent will. But when a created person, because of some defect he introduces into himself, hinders himself from coming to the end God ordained for him, then God's willing nonetheless to bring that person to as much goodness as he is capable of (given the state of his will) is God's consequent will.[16]

As Aquinas describes it, then, God's antecedent will is what God would will as good in the abstract, apart from the actual circumstances which obtain, as the mother in the example wills in the abstract that she might live harmoniously with her son; but what God in fact actually wills, given the circumstances that obtain, is said to be God's consequent will. For this reason Aquinas says that God's antecedent will is not strictly speaking his will at all but rather something like an inclination on God's part. What God actually wills, all the acts of will which God forms, are acts of consequent will; and understood as part of God's consequent will, all God's acts of will are fulfilled.[17]

The objections to Aquinas's account of providence presented above can all be handled with the distinction between God's antecedent and consequent will. The biblical text that says God wills all men to be saved is referring to God's antecedent will; given that some people do not repent, it is God's consequent will that not all be saved. Furthermore, when human beings sin or rebel and so apparently will something against God's will, it is God's antecedent, not his consequent, will they contravene; his consequent will is always fulfilled.[18]

In other words, when in the biblical story Jonah disobeys God's injunction and runs away, what are we to suppose about God's acts of will as regards Jonah's action? If God then had the *volition* that Jonah should not disobey him, he could have brought about what he willed by, for example, simply undermining Jonah's free will and causing Jonah to will to obey. Jonah's disobeying is compatible with the existence of an omniscient and omnipotent deity only on the assumption that God's will does not dissent from Jonah's disobedience. In the circumstances, namely, Jonah's rebelliousness, the best thing for God to will (the story leads us to believe) is that Jonah be allowed to disobey, and God consequently so wills.[19]

Jonah's disobedience is thus consonant with God's consequent will, which is not frustrated by what Jonah does. The initial command God gives Jonah in the story shows that Jonah's subsequent choice is not in accord with the way God would like things to be, but to say this is not to say that there is an act of God's will which is frustrated when Jonah disobeys God's command, as long as we can distinguish inclinations, desires, wishes, or longings (or their divine equivalents) from acts of will. The notion of an agent's antecedent volition is thus the notion of a desire of some sort which is nonetheless not made at the agent's volition;[20] the agent's volitions are comprised in the notion of his consequent will. Therefore, we can say that Jonah's rebellion contravenes God's antecedent but not his consequent will, and that even in a case of disobedience such as Jonah's there is no unfulfilled act of God's will.

Finally, God's justice in punishing a person for willing what is in accord only with God's consequent and not his antecedent will is also explainable on Aquinas's view. That a certain act is in accord with God's consequent will does not mean that the act is a good one, only that allowing the agent to perform that act is in the circumstances a good thing. Analogously, a mother might decide to allow her child to make his own mistakes and so have it as her consequent will that he be allowed to forego studying for the sake of socializing, but she might nonetheless be just in punishing him for the resulting bad grade.

This solution to the preceding objections, however, leads directly to another set of objections, because we might suppose that if evil acts are in accord with God's consequent will, then in some sense or other God himself wills moral evil and is responsible for it. In reply, Aquinas says that it is not part of God's will to exclude from his creatures entirely the power of falling away from the good or the exercise of that power.[21] It is one of Aquinas's favorite principles that God does not destroy the nature of anything he has made.[22] But it would destroy the nature of human beings if God kept them from ever doing anything evil, since the nature he has given them enables them to make significant choices for themselves. Consequently, God neither wills that moral evils occur nor wills that they do not occur. Rather he sometimes wills to permit such evils to occur when human persons have chosen to do evil, because if he always failed to give such permission, he would be acting contrary to (and to that extent destroying) the nature of human beings.[23] Therefore, in his consequent will God sometimes gives his consent to moral evil because to do otherwise would require undermining the nature he created, and the loss of being and hence of goodness entailed by doing so is a greater loss of being than whatever loss may be incurred by the evil God permits.[24]

Finally, we might suppose that the doctrine of providence Aquinas espouses has the philosophically and theologically absurd consequence that there is no contingency in the world.[25] If God's will is always fulfilled, then things must go as God wills; so, apparently, nothing occurs by chance, and (even worse) whatever happens, happens of necessity. This conclusion, as Aquinas says, obviously goes against common opinion.[26] But, in fact, on Aquinas's view, that God's will does not impose necessity on all things willed by God is a consequence of the efficacy of God's will, which extends both to the production of the effect willed and to the manner in which that effect occurs. Not only do those things happen that God wills to happen, but they happen necessarily or contingently according to his will.[27] The modality of the effects of God's will is not a result of direct divine fiat, though. Rather, some things happen contingently because God has prepared contingent causes from which contingent effects eventuate. For example, by creating human beings with free will, God has prepared contingent causes from which contingent effects result, namely, all those effects dependent on human choice.[28] Consequently, although everything that happens happens as part of God's providential plan, it does not follow that God's governance imposes necessity on all the things governed.[29]

Aquinas's approach to Job

With this much consideration of Aquinas's general account of providence, we are now in a position to turn to Aquinas's exposition of the book of Job. Contemporary readers tend to think of the subject of the book as the problem of evil. Since the book itself says that Job was innocent and since the book is equally clear about the fact that Job's suffering is (indirectly) caused by God, who grants Satan permission to afflict him, it seems to contemporary readers that the story of Job's suffering is hard to reconcile with the claim that there is an omnipotent, omniscient, perfectly good God. How could such a being allow an innocent person to suffer the loss of his property, the death of his children, a painful and disfiguring disease, and the other sufferings Job endured? And so the story of innocent Job, horribly afflicted with undeserved suffering, seems to many people representative of the kind of evil with which any theodicy must come to grips. But Aquinas sees the problems in the book of Job differently. He seems not to recognize that suffering in the world, of the quantity and quality of Job's, calls into question God's goodness, let alone God's existence. Instead Aquinas understands the book as an attempt to come to grips with the nature and operations of divine providence. How does God direct his creatures? Does the suffering of innocent persons require us to say that divine providence is not extended to human affairs? Of course, this question is clearly connected to the one we today generally find in the book of Job. But the difference between the contemporary approach to Job and the one Aquinas adopts is instructive for understanding Aquinas's view of the relation between God and evil.

On Aquinas's account, the problem with Job's friends is that they have a wrong view of the way providence operates. They suppose that providence assigns adversities in this life as a punishment for sins and earthly prosperity as a reward for virtue. Job, however, has a more correct view of providence, according to Aquinas, because he recognizes that a good and loving God will nonetheless allow the worst sorts of adversities to befall a virtuous person also. The disputation constituted by the speeches of Job and his friends is a disputation concerning the correct understanding of this aspect of the operations of providence. What is of more interest to us here than the details of this disputation, as Aquinas understands it, is his analysis of the reasons the friends take such a wrong view of providence. In connection with one of Eliphaz's speeches, Aquinas says:

> If in this life human beings are rewarded by God for good deeds and punished for bad, as Eliphaz was endeavoring to establish, it apparently follows that the ultimate goal for human beings is in this life. But Job intends to rebut this opinion, and he wants to show that the present life of human beings does not contain [that] ultimate goal, but is related to it as motion is related to rest and the road to its end.[30]

Constraints on theodicy

Aquinas's idea, then, is that the things that happen to a person in this life can be justified only by reference to her or his state in the afterlife. That a medieval Christian thinker should have an other-worldly view comes as no surprise, but it is at first glance perplexing to see that Aquinas thinks taking the other world into account will settle questions about how providence operates. For we might suppose that even if all that happens in a person's life is simply a prolegomenon to her state in the afterlife, nothing in this claim allays the concerns raised by seeing that in this world bad things happen to good people. Job's comforters take the line they do, that suffering is punishment for sins, just because they see no other way to maintain God's goodness and justice. It is hard to see how indicating the existence of an afterlife would change their minds. Because Aquinas has always in mind the thought that the days of our lives here are short while the afterlife is unending,[31] he naturally supposes that things having to do with the afterlife are more important than the things having to do with this life. But nothing in this attitude of his is incompatible with supposing that if God is good, things in this life ought to go well, at least for the just, if not for everybody.

We might suppose that Aquinas is here presupposing a view familiar to us from contemporary discussions of the problem of evil: God's reasons for allowing suffering are mysterious, and we do not know what sort of justification, if any, there is for God's allowing evil; but the immeasurable good of union with God in heaven recompenses all the finite evils we suffer here.[32] The benefits of the afterlife do not justify God's allowing evil, but they do make up for the suffering of people who experience evil, in the sense that in union with God such people find their sufferings more than compensated. But Aquinas adopts a line different from this. His line makes constructing an adequate theodicy more difficult but also (to my mind) more satisfying if successful. He supposes that we *can* know, at least in general, the good that justifies God's allowing evil. And he accepts basically the same constraints as those some contemporary philosophers insist on: if a good God allows evil, it can only be because the evil in question produces a benefit for the sufferer and one that God could not provide without the suffering.[33]

In his commentary on Romans, Aquinas distinguishes between the way providence works with respect to persons, on the one hand, and the rest of creation, on the other hand. As part of his defense of the line that all things work together for good for those who love God, Aquinas says this:

> Whatever happens on earth, even if it is evil, turns out for the good of the whole world. Because as Augustine says in the *Enchiridion*, God is so good that he would never permit any evil if he were not also so powerful that from any evil he could draw out a good. But the evil does not always turn out for the good of the thing in connection with which the evil occurs, because although the corruption of one animal turns out for the good of the whole world – insofar as one animal is generated from the corruption of another – nonetheless it does not turn out for the good of the animal which is corrupted. The reason for this is that the good of the whole world is willed by God for its own sake, and all the parts of the world are ordered to this [end]. The same reasoning appears to apply with regard to the order of the noblest parts [of the world] with respect to the other parts, because the evil of the other parts is ordered to the good of the noblest parts. But whatever happens with regard to the noblest parts is ordered only to the good of those parts themselves, because care is taken of them for their own sake, and for their sake care is taken of other things ... But among the best of all the parts of the world are God's saints ... He takes care of them in such a way that he does not allow any evil for them which he does not turn into their good.[34]

In discussing providence in *Summa contra gentiles*, Aquinas takes the same line. In a chapter appropriately headed "Rational creatures are governed for their own sake but others are governed in subordination to them", Aquinas repeatedly argues for the conclusion that "by divine providence, for creatures with intellects provision is made for their own sake, but for other creatures provision is made for the sake of those with intellects".[35]

In fact, Aquinas not only accepts the biblical line that (by divine providence) all things work together for good for those (rational creatures) who love God, but he has a particularly strong interpretation of it. How are we to understand the expression "all things" in this line? he asks in his commentary on Romans. The general claim that for created persons God permits only those evils he can turn into goods for them is, Aquinas says:

> plainly true when it comes to the painful evils that [created persons] suffer. That is why it says in the gloss that the humility [of

those who love God] is stimulated by their weakness, their patience by affliction, their wisdom by opposition, and their benevolence by animosity.[36]

But what about the evils that are sins? Are they also among the things which work together for good for those who love God? Aquinas makes the point perfectly clear:

> Some people say that sins are not included under 'all things' [in the biblical passage] … But against this is the passage in the gloss: … if some among the saints go astray and turn aside, even this God makes efficacious for good for them … [S]uch people rise again [from their fall] with greater charity, since the good of human beings is charity … They return more humble and better instructed.[37]

So Aquinas adopts a line different from the one some contemporary philosophers argue for. He apparently believes that we can and in some cases do know the goods which justify suffering. On the other hand, like some contemporary philosophers, Aquinas feels that (at least for creatures with minds) suffering is justified only in case it is a means to good for the sufferer herself. And Aquinas's examples of such good all have at least a natural, if not a necessary, connection with the evil in question: patience brought about by affliction, humility brought about by the experience of sin and repentance.

What shall we say then about Aquinas's approach to Job? Given his understanding of the constraints governing theodicy, how shall we explain Aquinas's view that the perplexities of the story and the inadequacies of the comforters can all be satisfactorily accounted for by the recognition that there is an afterlife and that rewards and punishments are distributed there rather than in this life? The first part of the explanation comes from Aquinas's attitude towards happiness; the second part stems from his account of suffering.

Aquinas's attitude towards human happiness

That human beings naturally desire their own happiness is a commonplace of Western philosophy. And we also suppose that any good person, but especially a perfectly good divine person, will desire the happiness of other persons. What raises the problem of evil for us is watching cases in which, it seems to us, God is not doing enough to promote the happiness of his creatures, or is permitting their unhappiness, or even, as in Job's case, is actively conniving at the unhappiness of one of his creatures. But then in order to investigate the problem of evil we need first to be reflective about the nature of human happiness. It is noteworthy that in his long treatment of providence in *Summa contra gentiles*, Aquinas has virtually no discussion of what we would consider the problem of evil but fifteen chapters on the nature of human happiness.

What exactly happens to Job that makes us wonder about God's goodness? (We might also ask about what happens to Job's animals, Job's children, or Job's wife, because questions about God's goodness obviously arise in connection with them, too; but I will focus here on Job alone.) Job loses his animals, the basis of wealth in his society. Afflicted with a miserable skin disease, he loses his health. And he loses his children, all of whom are killed in one day. We might term these losses Job's first-order afflictions. These first-order afflictions are the cause of further, second-order afflictions for him, the most notable of which is his disgrace in his own society. In consequence of the way in which his society interprets his troubles, he becomes a pariah among those who once honored him. And, finally, because Job's friends react very negatively to his insistence that he is innocent, their response to the way in which Job sees his first- and second-order afflictions provides yet more suffering for him, a third-order suffering. Because his reactions to his first- and second-order suffering differ radically from theirs, he finds himself deeply at odds with the very people who might have been a source of comfort to him – first, his wife and then the men closest to him. (His conflict with God, to which Aquinas is oblivious, seems to me the most important part of this third-order affliction, but I will leave it to one side here, and not only because Aquinas is insensitive to it. Since this part of Job's misery stems from his inability to understand how the God he trusted could let such things happen to him, the enterprise of theodicy is itself an attempt to explain this part of Job's suffering.)

We naturally take Job's losses to constitute the destruction of his happiness. But if we look at the chapters on happiness in *Summa contra gentiles*, we find Aquinas arguing the following claims: happiness does not consist in wealth,[38] happiness does not consist in the goods of the body such as health,[39] and happiness does not consist in honors.[40] Happiness is the greatest of goods, on Aquinas's account; and any good which is not by nature completely shareable, that is, which is such that in giving it to others one has less of it, is only a small good. Most, if not all, the gifts of fortune will therefore count just as small goods, on Aquinas's view. There is enough of medieval Christianity left in twentieth-century Western culture that many of us can read such claims and vaguely affirm them without paying much attention to what they mean. But on this view of Aquinas's, if happiness does not consist in health, honor, or riches, then it does not follow that a person who does not have these things is without happiness. It is therefore not immediately clear, contrary to what we unreflectively assume, that Job's happiness is destroyed in consequence of not having these things.

Two things are worth noticing here. First, even with all his otherworldly focus, Aquinas is not a Stoic. Among the many chapters in *Summa contra gentiles* saying what happiness does not consist in, there is no chapter saying that happiness does not consist in loving relations with other persons. Unlike some ancient philosophers, Aquinas does not understand happiness as a matter of self-sufficiency. So Aquinas's arguments about what happiness does not consist in are not relevant to one of Job's losses, the loss of his children, or to the third-order afflictions of discord with his wife and friends. It is true that the dreadful suffering Job experiences at the death of his good and virtuous children becomes transformed on Aquinas's views from the unbearable awfulness of total loss to the bitter but temporary pain of separation. In being united to God in love, a person is also united with others; for Aquinas, the ultimate good of union with God, like any great good, is by nature shareable. Nonetheless, Aquinas recognizes that there is pain in the absence of a person whom one loves (as the last section of this chapter, on consolation, makes clear). So, on Aquinas's views, even if Job is only temporarily separated from his children, their absence causes suffering for him.

Second, even if health, honor, riches, and the other things on Aquinas's list do not constitute happiness, it might nonetheless be the case that the loss of them or the presence of their opposites – sickness, disgrace, impoverishment – produces so much pain as to make happiness impossible. On Aquinas's view, human happiness consists in the contemplation of God. Apart from worries over whether human cognitive faculties are capable of contemplating God in this life, one might wonder whether pain and suffering do not interfere with such contemplation. And, in fact, as part of the evidence for the conclusion that true happiness cannot be achieved in this life, Aquinas himself says that weaknesses and misfortunes can impede the functions which must be exercised for happiness.[41]

Consequently, even if, as Aquinas thinks, happiness consists in contemplation of God rather than in the gifts of fortune, so that the loss of health, honor or riches does not by itself entail the loss of happiness, Aquinas apparently recognizes that it is possible for misfortune in any of its varieties to be an obstacle to happiness. So although it is helpful to understand Aquinas's views of happiness, we also need to consider his account of suffering in order to understand his approach to the book of Job.

Aquinas's attitude towards pain and suffering

When from the standpoint of religion we reflect on the many evils of the world – murder, rape, torture, the oppression of apartheid, the evils of nuclear armament, the horrors of Auschwitz and Treblinka – we can hardly avoid wondering how a good God could let such things occur. But another thing to wonder about is the nature of human beings, who in all cultures and all ages can be so vicious to one another. On Aquinas's view, all human beings have a terminal cancer of soul, a proneness to evil which invariably eventuates in sin and which in the right circumstances blows up into monstrosity. On his view, even "our senses and our thoughts are prone to evil".[42] The pure and innocent among human beings are no exception to this claim. When the biblical text says that Job was righteous, Aquinas takes the text to mean that Job was pure by human standards. By the objective, uncurved standards of God, even Job was infected with the radical human tendencies towards evil.[43] No human being who remains uncured of this disease can see God. On Aquinas's view, then, the primary obstacle to contemplation of God, in which human happiness consists, is the sinful character of human beings.

Aquinas thinks that pain and suffering of all sorts are God's medicine for this spiritual cancer; and he emphasizes this view repeatedly. In his commentary on the Apostles' Creed, he says:

> If all the pain a human being suffers is from God, then he ought to bear it patiently, both because it is from God and because it is ordered toward good; for pains purge sins, bring evildoers to humility, and stimulate good people to love of God.[44]

In his commentary on Thessalonians he says:

> As water extinguishes a burning fire, so tribulations extinguish the force of concupiscent desires, so that human beings do not follow them at will ... Therefore, [the Church] is not destroyed [by tribulations] but lifted up by them, and in the first place by the lifting up of the mind to God, as Gregory says: the evils which bear us down here drive us to go to God.[45]

He comments in great detail on the line in Hebrews: "whom the Lord loves he chastens".[46] He says:

> All the saints who have pleased God have gone through many tribulations by which they were made the sons of God.[47]

> Since pains are a sort of medicine, we should apparently judge correction and medicine the same way. Now medicine in the taking of it is bitter and loathsome, but its end is desirable and intensely sweet. So discipline is also. It is hard to bear, but it blossoms into the best outcome.[48]

The same general point appears recurrently in the commentary on Job. Arguing that temporal goods such as those Job lost are given and taken away according to God's will, Aquinas says:

someone's suffering adversity would not be pleasing to God except for the sake of some good coming from the adversity. And so although adversity is in itself bitter and gives rise to sadness, it should nonetheless be agreeable [to us] when we consider its usefulness, on account of which it is pleasing to God ... For in his reason a person rejoices over the taking of bitter medicine because of the hope of health, even though in his senses he is troubled.[49]

In commenting on a line in Job containing the complaint that God sometimes does not hear a needy person's prayers, Aquinas says:

Now it sometimes happens that God hearkens not to a person's pleas but rather to his advantage. A doctor does not hearken to the pleas of the sick person who requests that the bitter medicine be taken away (supposing that the doctor does not take it away because he knows that it contributes to health); instead he hearkens to [the patient's] advantage, because by doing so he produces health, which the sick person wants most of all. In the same way, God does not remove tribulations from the person stuck in them, even though he prays earnestly for God to do so, because God knows these tribulations help him forward to final salvation. And so although God truly does hearken, the person stuck in afflictions believes that God has not hearkened to him.[50]

In fact, on Aquinas's view, the better the person, the more likely it is that he will experience suffering. In explicating two metaphors of Job's,[51] comparing human beings in this life to soldiers on a military campaign and to employees, Aquinas makes the point in this way:

It is plain that the general of an army does not spare [his] more active soldiers dangers or exertions, but as the plan of battle requires, he sometimes lays them open to greater dangers and greater exertions. But after the attainment of victory, he bestows greater honor on the more active soldiers. So also the head of a household assigns greater exertions to his better servants, but when it is time to reward them, he lavishes greater gifts on them. And so neither is it characteristic of divine providence that it should exempt good people more from the adversities and exertions of the present life, but rather that it reward them more at the end.[52]

In his commentary on Thessalonians, Aquinas makes the same point in a slightly different way: "Many who are alive [in the eschaton] will be tried in the persecution of Antichrist, and they will surpass in greatness the many who had previously died."[53]

And in his commentary on Philippians, he makes the point more generally: "from sufferings borne here a person attains to glory".[54]

With this background, then, we should not be surprised to find Aquinas affirming Paul's line in Romans that we should be glad of suffering:

> It is a sign of the ardent hope which we have on account of Christ that we glory not only because of [our] hope of the glory to come, but we glory even regarding the evils which we suffer for it. And so [Paul] says that we not only glory (that is, in our hope of glory), but we glory even in tribulations, by which we attain to glory.[55]

The oddness of Aquinas's views

In Plato's *Gorgias*, Callicles accuses Socrates of turning the world upside down; if Socrates's views are correct, Callicles says, "Everything we do is the exact opposite of what we ought to do."[56] Aquinas's views here also seem upside down. If he is right, everything we typically think about what counts as evil in the world is the exact opposite of what we ought to think. The topsy-turvy nature of this view of evil in the world is made vivid by a passage in a much earlier commentary on Job by Gregory the Great, whose views on this score are similar to Aquinas's. The ways of Providence are often hard to understand, Gregory says, but they are

> still more mysterious when things go well with good people here, and ill with bad people ... When things go well with good people here, and ill with bad people, a great uncertainty arises whether good people receive good so that they might be stimulated to grow into something [even] better or whether by a just and secret judgment they see the rewards of their deeds here so that they may be void of the rewards of the life to come ... Therefore since the human mind is hemmed in by the thick fog of its uncertainty among the divine judgments, when holy people see the prosperity of this world coming to them, they are troubled with a frightening suspicion. For they are afraid that they might receive the fruits of their labors here; they are afraid that divine justice detects a secret wound in them and, heaping external rewards on them, drives them away from internal ones ... Consequently, holy people are more fearful of prosperity in this world than of adversity.[57]

In other words, since in Gregory's view it is so difficult to understand how a just and benevolent providence could allow *good* things to happen to good people, when good people see that there is no adversity in their lives, they cannot help but wonder whether they are not after all to be counted among the wicked. For that reason, prosperity is more frightening to them than adversity.

Such an upside-down view of evil is the foreseeable conclusion of Aquinas's twin accounts of happiness and suffering. True happiness consists in the contemplation of God, shared and enjoyed together by all the redeemed in heaven. But the spiritual cancer which infects all human beings, even those who count as pure and innocent by human standards, makes it impossible for people to be united with God (or with each other) in heaven. Suffering is a kind of medicine for that disease.[58] Furthermore, at least for those who assent to the process and are eventually saved from their sinfulness, there is a direct connection between the amount of suffering in this life and the degree of glory in the life to come. Given such views, the sort of topsy-turvy thought represented by the passage from Gregory the Great is less surprising. If suffering is the chemotherapy for spiritual cancer, the patients whose regimen does not include any are the only ones for whom the prognosis is really bad.

This attitude on Aquinas's part also helps to explain his reaction to the book of Job. Like Aquinas, we take the attitude we do towards Job because of the values, the metaphysics, the general worldview we bring to the book. Because *we* assume, unreflectively, that temporal well-being is a necessary constituent of happiness (or even the whole of it), we also suppose that Job's losses undermine or destroy his happiness. Consequently, we wonder how God could count as good if he allowed these things to happen to a good person such as a Job, or we take stories of undeserved suffering to constitute evidence for thinking there is no God. Aquinas, on the other hand, begins with the conviction that neither God's goodness nor his existence are in doubt, either for the characters in the story of Job or for the readers of that story. Therefore, on his view, those who go astray in considering sufferings such as Job's do so because, like Job's comforters, they mistakenly suppose that happiness and unhappiness are functions just of things in this life. And so Aquinas takes the book of Job to be trying to instill in us the conviction that there is another life after this one, that our happiness lies there rather than here, and that we attain to that happiness only through suffering.[59] On Aquinas's view, Job has more suffering than ordinary people not because he is morally worse than ordinary, as the comforters assume, but just because he is better. Because he is a better soldier in the war against his own evil and a better servant of God's, God can give him more to bear here; and when this period of earthly life is over, his glory will also be surpassing.

Concerns about Aquinas's view

For many people, the reaction to this view of Aquinas's will be indignation. If we take it not as piously platitudinous but as a serious expression of otherworldliness, we are likely to find it so alien to our own sensitivities that we reject it as outrageous. I think that there are two primary forms such a reaction will take.

Our more articulate reaction is likely to center on the thought that this view constitutes a reprehensible callousness towards human affliction and misfortune and a disgusting willingness to accept evil.[60] Concern for others is a good part of what prompts this reaction; the asceticism and otherworldliness of Aquinas's sort of attitude seem to rule out all attempts to alleviate the suffering of other people. And, of course, an emphasis on otherworldliness *has* in the past been used in abominable ways as a basis for exploiting and oppressing the poor and defenseless. When the labor movement in the USA was trying to protect workers through unionization, part of its strategy was to cast opprobrium on hope in an afterlife. Instead of offering decent conditions and fair wages, union organizers said, the exploitative bosses held out to their workers the hope of "pie in the sky when we die". In fact, if what we take away from Aquinas's text is just the general conclusion that on his view pain and adversity are good things, then his view will yield results worthy not only of vituperation but of ridicule as well. We might suppose, for example, that his views entail the claim that anesthetics are to be eschewed[61] or, more generally, that any attempt to palliate or end anyone's pain is a bad thing.

What should we say about such an objection? One thing worth noticing at the outset is that it is perhaps not quite so obvious as one might at first suppose where callousness lies in this discussion. If, contrary to what Aquinas supposes, human happiness requires the gifts of fortune, then people in contemporary wealthy and developed countries, or just the middle and upper classes in them, will have a vastly greater share of happiness, and the bulk of the world's population will be ruled out of that state. Aquinas's alien otherworldliness at least has the implication that the highest human good of happiness is not another monopoly of the industrialized nations.

But the more detailed and appropriate response to our emotive reaction in both its altruistic and its more general forms consists in seeing that on Aquinas's view suffering is good not *simpliciter* but only *secundum quid*. That is, suffering is not good in itself but only conditionally, insofar as it is a means to an end. On Aquinas's view: "The evils which are in this world are not to be desired for their own sake but insofar as they are ordered to some good."[62]

In itself suffering is a bad thing; it acquires positive value only when it contributes to spiritual well-being. We have no trouble seeing this sort of point when it comes to chemotherapy. In chemotherapy toxic drugs are administered to the patient, and the patient's friends and family are grateful for the treatments; but no one gets confused and supposes that it is then all right to allow the patient to ingest any sort of poisonous substance or that the medical personnel who administer the drugs are as a result in favor of administering poison generally.

It is sometimes easy to confuse conditional goods with non-conditional ones. The development of muscles is a conditional good, to be valued insofar as it contributes to health and strength and their accompanying attractiveness, but steroid users can mistakenly value it as a good in its own right. No doubt, even those steroid users who are not ignorant of the dangers of steroids would claim that they took the drugs to enhance their bodies. But their behavior belies their explanation and suggests that they have lost sight of the purported purpose; bulking up of muscles appears to have become a good in itself in their eyes, even if it is harmful to health in the long run. Similarly, not eating is good only *secundum quid*, insofar as it leads to a healthier and more attractive body, but anorexics misprogram themselves to value it even when it leads to an ugly destruction of health. An anorexic might believe of herself that she was continuing to diet because dieting is a good means to a more attractive body; but in the face of her distressing skeletal appearance, it would be hard not to suppose that she had lost sight of the goal she professed to want in her obsessed valuing of the means. It is clear from the stories of ascetic excesses in the patristic and medieval periods that it is possible to become confused in the same sort of way about the conditional good of suffering. According to the stories, Simeon Stylites spent thirty-seven years living on top of pillars, the last of which was sixty feet high and only six feet wide. He is reputed to have come close to death on one occasion as a result of wearing next to his skin an abrasive material which grew into the skin and infected it.[63] It seems not unreasonable to take him as a spiritual anorexic, mistaking a conditional good for a non-conditional one. Perhaps he believed of himself that his purpose for self-denial was spiritual progress, but like the anorexic he appears to have become obsessed with the means at the expense of the goal. No doubt, part of what the Renaissance found so repulsive about the Middle Ages was a certain tendency on the part of medievals to engage in prolonged and apparently pointless bouts of self-destructive asceticism.

But how do we know that Simeon Stylites, or one of the other over-rigorous ascetics of the patristic period, is the medieval analogue to a neurotic and unstoppable dieter? It is not so hard to know the difference between healthy dieting and anorexia, but how would we know with regard to suffering when it was serving the function of spiritual health and so was good rather than destructive? The answer, I think, is that we cannot always know. Sometimes in dealing with conditional goods we have to rely on experts. The steroids which some misguided athletes take to their misfortune are also important therapeutic drugs for certain sorts of cancers; but we learn this fact from medical experts, and we have to rely on them to administer the drugs in such a way that they contribute to health rather than destruction. In the case of suffering and its role in redemption, it seems clear that very often we do not know whether the suffering of a particular person on a particular occasion is a help towards spiritual health or a spiritual analogue to anorexic fasting. Here, too, we have to rely on experts – only the expertise in this case, which requires omniscient insight into the history and psychology of the sufferer, is an expertise that God alone possesses.[64]

But is it possible for us to avail ourselves of that expertise? Barring direct divine revelation, can we know in any given case whether God intends some suffering as a cure for evil or whether a particular degree of suffering will not produce spiritual toxicosis instead? Aquinas's views support an affirmative answer to this question.

In the first place, when we see someone suffer as a result of human injustice, then on Aquinas's view (other things being equal) we have a clear obligation to do what is in our power to stop the suffering, *ceteris paribus*.[65] Injustice is a mortal sin which separates a person from God; in intervening we help to rescue not only the victim of the injustice but also the perpetrator, whose condition on Aquinas's view is otherwise apparently terminal. Furthermore, there is nothing in Aquinas's attitude towards suffering which is incompatible with a robust program of social justice. Job, in arguing for his innocence, points not just to the fact that he has not exploited any of those dependent on him but that he has even been particularly attentive to the needs of the poor and downtrodden;[66] and Aquinas comments on these passages with evident approval, as he has to do, given his view that corporal and spiritual almsgiving is obligatory.[67]

More generally, one way (though not the only way) to tell if any particular suffering on the part of a given individual is ordained by God to spiritual health is if we try to alleviate that suffering and it turns out not to be possible to do so. Part of what makes Simeon Stylites repulsive to us is that he not only does not try to avoid suffering but even deliberately seeks it out for its own sake.[68] Gregory the Great's line, on the other hand, implies that redemptive suffering cannot be instigated by us but has to be received from God's hand. Otherwise, the good men who tremble at their prosperity could stop trembling and just flagellate themselves to put a stop to their worrisome lack of adversity.

For these reasons the concern that Aquinas's account prompts indifference to suffering is mistaken; and if our indignation at his views is based on this concern, it is misplaced. But perhaps our negative reaction to Aquinas's account of evil stems from attitudes more complicated and less amenable to crisp articulation. Renaissance attitudes towards the Middle Ages were something like Callicles's reaction to Socrates. The Renaissance thought the Middle Ages had turned human values upside down, and it found medieval worldviews repellent because it saw them as inhuman. As intellectual descendants of the Renaissance (more nearly than of the Middle Ages), we might feel somewhat the same way about Aquinas's view of the world: any life really lived in accordance with this worldview would be wretched, inhumanly repudiating all the loveliness and goodness of this world, unnaturally withdrawing from all that makes life worthwhile.

Aquinas is not oblivious to this problem. For that matter, neither is the apostle Paul. "If in this life only we have hope in Christ," he says, "we are of all people most miserable."[69] In commenting on this passage, Aquinas says:

> If there is no resurrection of the dead, it follows that there is no good for human beings other than in this life. And if this is the case, then those people are more miserable who suffer many evils and tribulations in this life. Therefore, since the apostles and Christians [generally] suffer more tribulations, it follows that they, who enjoy less of the goods of this world, would be more miserable than other people.

The very fact that Aquinas feels he needs to explicate this point in some detail highlights the difference between our worldview and his; no one has to explain to us that those who suffer more evils in this world are more miserable than others. But what Aquinas goes on to say spells out explicitly the difference between the worldview of his culture and our own. And so he continues:

> If there were no resurrection of the dead, people would not think it was a power and a glory to abandon all that can give pleasure and to bear the pains of death and dishonor; instead they would think it was stupid.

He assumes that Christians are people who do glory in tribulations, and so he ends his commentary on this passage in Corinthians by saying, "And so it is clear that [if there were no resurrection of the dead, Christians] would be more miserable than other people."[70]

So Aquinas's account of evil has inherent in it a response to objections of the Renaissance variety. If you suppose that fast-food-munching couch potatoes are just as healthy or healthier than nutrition-conscious physical-fitness advocates, you will of course find all the emphasis of the exercisers on diet and physical training perplexing or neurotic or worse. Denying oneself appealing foods and forcing oneself to sweat and strain in exercise are conditional goods only. Unless you share the view that these things do lead to desirable ends, you will not find them good in any sense. Similarly, if we do not share the worldview that holds that there is an afterlife, that true happiness consists in union with God in the afterlife, and that suffering helps us to attain that happiness, we will naturally find Aquinas's valuing suffering even as a conditional good appalling or crazy.

Consolation

Even those who share with Aquinas the conviction that there is an afterlife and that the truest or deepest happiness is to be found in it might nonetheless feel queasy about or alienated from his account of evil. For many people, the supposition that suffering has the therapeutic value Aquinas claims for it will not be enough; they will still feel that there is something frighteningly inhuman in a worldview that tells us not only that the whole of our life on earth will be one prolonged spiritual analogue to chemotherapy but also that we ought to rejoice in that state of affairs. And so they are likely to side with the Renaissance humanist repudiation of such a worldview. I, too, think the Renaissance humanists were right to reject this worldview, but I think it would be a mistake to take it as the correct description of Aquinas's account. There is a more humane side to the medieval view of suffering which the Renaissance humanists missed. As Aquinas explains it, this part of his account applies primarily to the suffering of fully functional adults who are Christians. (I think it is possible to see in Aquinas's thought a way in which to transpose his line so that it applies also to the suffering of children and non-Christian adults.[71] For the sake of brevity, however, I will consider it here only in the form he gives it, in which it applies to Christian adults with normally functioning faculties.)

The missing element has to do with the work of the Holy Spirit. On Aquinas's view, the Holy Spirit works in the hearts of those who believe in God and also produces spiritual consolation. The Holy Spirit, Aquinas says, "purges us from sin", "illumines the intellect", "brings us to keep the commandments", "confirms our hope in eternal life", "counsels us in our perplexities about the will of God", and "brings us to love God".[72] The Holy Spirit guides towards truth those whom it fills and helps them to conquer their weaknesses[73] so that they can become the sort of people they are glad to be. Most importantly, the Holy Spirit fills a person with a sense of the love of God and his nearness, so that one of the principal effects of the Holy Spirit is joy.[74]

The Holy Spirit perfects us, both inwardly and outwardly, Aquinas holds; and so, he says:

> the ultimate perfection, by which a person is made perfect inwardly, is joy, which stems from the presence of what is loved. Whoever has the love of God, however, already has what he loves, as is said in 1 John 4:16: "whoever abides in the love of God abides in God, and God abides in him." And joy wells up from this.[75]

> When [Paul] says "the Lord is near," he points out the cause of joy, because a person rejoices at the nearness of his friend.[76]

Perhaps there is no greater joy than the presence of the person you love when that person loves you to the fulfillment of your heart's desire.[77] Joy of that sort, Aquinas says, is not destroyed by either pain or tribulation. In order to keep joy whole, even in the adversities of this life, the Holy Spirit protects people against the evils they encounter:

> and first against the evil which disturbs peace, since peace is disturbed by adversities. But with regard to adversities the Holy Spirit perfects [us] through patience, which enables [us] to bear adversities patiently ... Second, against the evil which arrests joy, namely, the wait for what is loved. To this evil, the Spirit opposes long-suffering, which is not broken by the waiting.[78]

In this way and others, on Aquinas's view, the Holy Spirit makes human joy whole, even in the midst of pain.

But what about Job, we might think at this point. Was he not someone who faced his troubles without consolation from God? Aquinas thinks, after all, that God sometimes heeds a suffering person's advantage rather than his prayer, and it is in connection with Job that Aquinas develops that line. If the sufferer cannot see that advantage, then, as even Aquinas recognizes, the sufferer may not be consoled but rather be afflicted in spirit also.[79] But I think Aquinas would be inclined to deny the characterization of Job as someone who suffers without divine consolation. One of the longest speeches attributed to God in the Bible is the speech he makes to Job; and when God's speech is finished, Job says, "I had heard of you before with the hearing of the ear, but now my eye sees you."[80] Whatever else we need to say about the complicated relations between God and Job, and that is no doubt a great deal, it is clear that with his views of happiness Aquinas would certainly attribute deep, sweet consolation to anyone who could truly claim to be seeing God. Furthermore, part of the benefit of Christianity, on Aquinas's account, is bringing home to believers that there is a point to suffering, so as to ward off the kind of theological perplexity and anguish many people see in Job. In his passion, Christ not only makes atonement for sinners but also sets them an example, so that they will understand that the path to redemption goes through suffering.[81] The lesson learned for us by Job and the example presented by Christ make it easier for others afterwards, Aquinas thinks, to endure suffering without losing spiritual consolation during the period of pain.[82]

In fact, Aquinas thinks that for Christians, the inner sweetness of God's consolation increases directly with the troubles of this life. At the start of his commentary on 1 Thessalonians, he quotes with approval the line in 2 Corinthians which says that "as the sufferings of Christ abound in us, so our consolation also abounds by Christ" (2 Cor.1:5). And in explaining that line, in his commentary on 2 Corinthians, he describes spiritual consolation in this way:

> People need to be supported in the evils that happen to them. And this is what consolation is, strictly speaking. Because if a person did not have something in which his heart could rest when he is overcome with evils, he could not bear up [under them]. And so one person consoles another when he offers him some relief, in which he can rest in the midst of evils. And although in some evils one human being can take consolation and rest and support in another, nonetheless it is only God who consoles us in all [our] evils.[83]

Even in our sins, which from Aquinas's point of view are more frightening than adversity, because unlike adversity they separate us from God, Aquinas holds, we are consoled by God; that is why, Aquinas says, Paul calls him the God of *all* consolation.[84]

Conclusion

The Renaissance saw the Middle Ages as inhuman in part because it no longer shared the medieval worldview and in part because it had missed this side of the medieval story. On Aquinas's account, Christianity does not call people to a life of self-denying wretchedness but to a life of joy, even in the midst of pain and trouble. Without joy, Aquinas says, no progress is possible in the Christian life.[85]

Aquinas's attitude towards evil is clearly as different from the attitude common today as Socrates's attitude towards the good life is different from Callicles's. Aquinas's analysis of the reaction of Job's comforters would also, I think, be his analysis of the reaction to evil common in our contemporary culture:

> Human beings are made up of a spiritual nature and of earthly flesh. Consequently, evil for human beings consists in their abandoning spiritual goods, to which they are directed in virtue of [having] rational minds, and their cleaving to earthly goods, which suit them in virtue of [having] earthly flesh.[86]

Job's loquacious friends did not understand the spiritual consolation of Job, and so he adds:

> "You, [God,] have put their heart far from learning" – that is, from the spiritual learning [which comes from] you, by which you teach [human beings] to disdain temporal goods and to hope for spiritual ones. And because they put their hope only in things low and

476

temporal, they could not reach a spiritual plane to be placed next to God.[87]

It certainly does seem true, at any rate, that there is a correlation between the degree to which we associate human good with things in this world and the extent to which we see the problem of evil in its contemporary form. The story of the metamorphosis from the medieval worldview to our own is, of course, in large part a matter of a shift from a religious to a secular outlook. But even among Christians we can chart the change from the otherworldly approach of the medievals to the more common contemporary attitudes. We can see this change in its beginnings in, for example, the pious Christian adherents of the *devotio moderna*, a religious movement important in the Netherlands, particularly in the fifteenth century. There was a distinctly non-medieval attitude in the *devotio moderna* in its tendency to conflate temporal and spiritual goods and in its emphasis on the religious importance of temporal concerns. Commenting on the death of a recently appointed principal of a school for religious instruction, an anonymous adherent of this movement raises the problem of evil in a way which is devout but altogether different from Aquinas's approach. He says:

> Permit me to take a moment here to allude to the wondrous and secret judgments of our Lord God, not as if scrutinizing them in a reproachful way but rather as humbly venerating the inscrutable. It is quite amazing that our fathers and brothers had set out with a single will and labored at their own expense, to the honor of God and for the salvation of souls, to erect a school here in Emmerich to do exercises with boys and clerics ... And now after much care and trouble, everything had been brought to a good state: we had a learned and suitable man for rector, the venerable Master Arnold of Hildesheim ... Then, behold, ... our Lord God, as if totally unconcerned with all that we had in hand, which had just begun to flower, suddenly and unexpectedly threw it all into confusion and decline, nearly reducing it to nothing. For just as the sheep are dispersed when the shepherd is struck down, so when our beloved brother [Master Arnold] died the whole school was thrown into confusion. The youths left in swarms ... not, it is to be feared, without some danger to their souls ... Nonetheless, to [him] be the honor and the glory now and through the ages, to him whose judgments, though hidden, are yet never unjust.[88]

Between the attitude of this author, who finds adversity for God's people fundamentally inexplicable, and the attitude of Aquinas, there is a world of difference.

In this chapter I have only expounded Aquinas's views of evil; I have not sought to argue for them, although they seem to me impressive and admirable in many ways. No doubt, a thorough philosophical defense or refutation of his views would require book-length treatment. But what Aquinas's interpretation of Job and his general account of evil show us, whether we are inclined to accept or reject them, is that our approach to the problem of evil is a consequence of our attitude towards much larger issues, such as the nature of human happiness and the goal of human life. To make progress on the problem of evil, in my view, we need to face up to these larger issues in a reflective way. One of the benefits of the history of philosophy, especially the history of philosophy from periods such as the Middle Ages whose cultures are so different from our own, is that it helps us to see the otherwise unnoticed and unexamined assumptions we bring to philosophical issues such as the problem of evil. Aquinas's worldview, characterized by a renunciation of the things of this world and a rush toward sheaven, is a particularly good one to juxtapose to the worldview of our culture, steeped in comforts and seeking pleasure. "Theodocies", says Terrence Tilley in his passionate denunciation of them, "construct consoling dreams to distract our gaze from real evils."[89] What reflection on Aquinas's account helps us to see is that in evaluating this claim and others like it, hostile to theodicy, everything depends on what one takes to be dream and what one takes to be reality.[90]

NOTES

Introduction: life and overview of Aquinas's thought

1 *SCG* I.2.11.
2 *SCG* IV.1.
3 *Expositio super Job* 7.1–4.
4 *Expositio super Job* 9.16.
5 *In Sent* II.14.1.2.
6 *In DDN* prologue; *QDM* 16.1 ad 3.
7 René Antoine Gauthier (ed.) Sancti Thomae de Aquino: Opera Omnia iussu Leonis XIII P.M. edita, Tomus XLV, 1: *Sentencia libri de anima*, (Rome: Commissio Leonina, 1984), pp. 275–282.
8 Martha C. Nussbuam, "The Text of Aristotle's *De anima*", in M.C. Nussbaum and A.O. Rorty (eds), *Essays on Aristotle's De anima* (Oxford: Clarendon Press, 1992), pp. 3–4.
9 T. H. Irwin (1992) "Who Discovered the Will?", in J.E. Tomberlin (ed.), *Philosophical Perspectives 6: Ethics* (Atascadero, CA: Ridgeview, 1992), p. 467.
10 *In DC* I.22.
11 *De perfectione spiritualis vitae* 26.
12 *DUI* prologue.
13 *DUI* prologue.
14 Simon Tugwell, O.P., *Albert and Thomas: Selected Writings*, *The Classics of Western Spirituality* (Mahwah, NJ: Paulist Press, 1998), p. 226.
15 I. Brady, "John Pecham and the Background of Aquinas' *De Aeternitate Mundi*", in A.A. Maurer (ed.), *St. Thomas Aquinas 1274–1974: Commemorative Studies* (Toronto: Pontifical Institute of Mediaeval Studies, 1974), vol. II, pp. 141–178.
16 See Claire le Brun-Gouanvic (ed.), *Ystoria sancti Thome de Aquino de Guillaume de Tocco (1323)* (Toronto: Pontifical Institute of Mediaeval Studies, 1996), c. 47.
17 See e.g., *SCG* III.25; *In BDT* 5.4; 6.1.
18 *QDV* I.1.
19 *QDV* I.1.
20 *ST* Ia.5.1.
21 See, e.g., *SCG* I.37; III.3.
22 *ST* Ia.5.1.
23 See, e.g., *ST* IaIIae.1.5; 94.2; *SCG* III.3; *QDV* 21.1–2.
24 *ST* Ia.15.1c.
25 *ST* Ia.15.1.
26 *ST* Ia.75.1.
27 *ST* Ia.75.2.

28 *QDA* I.
29 *In Meta* I.1.3–4.
30 *ST* Ia.85.2 ad 1.
31 *ST* Ia.12.4.
32 *ST* Ia.85.1 ad 5.
33 *ST* Ia.12.4.
34 *In PA* II.20.14.
35 *ST* Ia.85.5; *In DA* II.12.377.
36 *SCG* I.3.16.
37 *ST* Ia.85.5.
38 *In PA* I.7.5–8.
39 *In PA* I.10;33.
40 *In PA* I.5.7.
41 *In PA* I.2.9.
42 P.T. Durbin, *St Thomas Aquinas: Summa Theologiae*, Blackfriars edition and translation, vol. XII (New York: McGraw-Hill, 1968), p. 82.
43 *In PA* prologue.
44 *ST* Ia.80.1.
45 *ST* Ia.81.3.
46 *ST* Ia.81.3 ad 3.
47 *Politics* I. 2.
48 *ST* Ia.81.3 ad 2.
49 *QDV* 24.7 ad 6.
50 See, e.g., *ST* IaIIae.6.4.
51 See, e.g., *ST* IaIIae.9.6.
52 *ST* IaIIae.6–17.
53 *ST* IaIIae.1.1.
54 *ST* IaIIae.1.8; 3.8.
55 *ST* IaIIae.18.5.
56 *ST* IaIIae.50.5 ad 3.
57 *ST* IaIIae.50.5, ad 3.
58 *ST* IaIIae.90.4.
59 *ST* IaIIae.94.2.
60 *ST* IaIIae.91.3.
61 *ST* IaIIae.92.1, ad 4.
62 *ST* IaIIae.91.1.
63 *ST* Ia.1.2.
64 *SCG* I.1.2.
65 *SCG* I.1.3.
66 *SCG* II.4.874.
67 *SCG* I.1.5.
68 *SCG* II.4.875.
69 *SCG* I.1.6.
70 *SCG* I.9.57.
71 *ST* Ia.1.1. ad 2.
72 *ST* Ia.1.1.
73 *ST* Ia.2, intro.
74 *ST* Ia.1.7.
75 *ST* Ia.1.2.
76 *Expositio super librum Boethii De trinitate 2.2, ad.7.*
77 *ST* Ia.32.1.
78 *ST* Ia.32.1.

1 Metaphysics: a theory of things

1 Aquinas himself does not confine his discussion of metaphysics to just one section of his work, and so further discussion of his metaphysics can also be found in Chapters 6 and 14 on the soul and on the incarnation.

2 By 'thing' in this context I mean approximately – but perhaps only approximately – what Aquinas meant by the Latin expression '*hoc aliquid*', which might be rendered into English roughly as 'a *this*'. I put the point in the text in a hedged way, because there is some unclarity as regards Aquinas's concept of a *hoc aliquid*. In *In Meta* VII.3.1323, e.g., he says that only a substance is a *hoc aliquid*, but elsewhere he says that, e.g., parts of substances such as severed hands and the substantial soul also count as examples of a subsistent thing or a *hoc aliquid* (see, e.g., *ST* IaIIae.72.2). Finally, by 'thing' in this context, I do not mean what Aquinas meant by '*res*', although that Latin word is often translated into English as 'thing'. For Aquinas, strictly speaking, *res* is found throughout the ten categories, and so it ranges much more broadly than *thing* or *hoc aliquid*, as that notion is used in this chapter. It should perhaps be added that sometimes Aquinas uses '*res*' as broadly and loosely as 'thing' is used in English. We say, e.g.: "That situation is the kind of thing that occurs only in bad dreams." Things in such a loose sense are not at issue here either.

3 Not everything that is appropriately designated the matter of something counts as a thing; similarly, not every form constituting a whole is a thing, on Aquinas's view. In what follows, I will try to clarify what matter and which forms are things for him and his reasons for thinking so. In general, the forms configuring immaterial substances and the form configuring human beings are things in his view; the forms of other material substances and the forms of artifacts are metaphysical parts of a thing but are not themselves things.

4 To take just one example, contemporary philosophy takes an essential property to be one which a thing has in every possible world in which it exists. In general, however, Aquinas thinks it is possible that God might have acted otherwise than he did (see, e.g., *QDP* 1.5). e.g., Aquinas holds that God creates but that God might not have created. It apparently follows that in this world God has the property of creating, and that there is some possible world in which God does not have this property. On the contemporary understanding of essential and accidental properties, God's property of creating is thus an accidental property of his. But Aquinas holds that there is only essence in God and no accidental properties. What exactly Aquinas means by his modal terms is a subject of debate. For further discussion of this issue, see Chapter 3 on God's simplicity.

5 There is a very helpful discussion of Aristotle's concept of form in Marjorie Grene's "Aristotle and Modern Biology", *Journal of the History of Ideas* 33 (1972): 395–424. She argues that Aristotle's concept of form is very like the contemporary biological concepts of organization or information. (I am grateful to Shawn Floyd for calling Grene's article to my attention.) For a helpful attempt to explicate a notion at least closely related to the Aristotelian concept of form which is at issue in this part of Aquinas's metaphysics, see Kit Fine, "Things and Their Parts", in *Midwest Studies in Philosophy* 23 (1999): 61–74. Fine does an admirable job of discussing this notion in the context of contemporary mereology and showing what the Aristotelian notion can do that cannot be done equally well with mereological schemes. He says:

> I should like to suggest that we take the bold step of recognizing a new kind of whole. Given objects *a*, *b*, *c*, ... and given a relation *R* that may

> hold or fail to hold of those objects at any given time, we suppose that there is a new object – what one may call 'the objects $a, b, c, \ldots$ in the relation R.
>
> (p. 65)

He also makes a helpful distinction between what he calls 'temporary' and 'timeless' parts. This distinction has some resemblance to the distinction I make later between integral and metaphysical parts (though perhaps Fine himself might think the resemblance fairly attenuated).

6 See, e.g., *SCG* IV.36 (3740).

7 See, e.g., *DPN* 2 (346).

8 A helpful discussion of this molecule and its properties can be found in Steven Lanier McKnight, "Molecular Zippers in Gene Regulation", *Scientific American* 264 (1991): 54–64.

9 *DPN* 3 (354); see also *In Meta* V.4.795–798 and VII.2.1284. The role of prime matter in Aquinas's metaphysics is sometimes misunderstood because Aquinas's notion of the elements is not taken into account. So, e.g., Peter van Inwagen thinks that he differs from Aristotle (and consequently others, such as Aquinas, who accept the notion of prime matter) because, unlike the upholders of prime matter, he believes that "matter is ultimately particulate" (*Material Beings*, Ithaca, NY: Cornell University Press, 1990, p. 3 and p. 15). But van Inwagen is clearly concerned with the ultimate constituents into which actually existing material objects could be decomposed. Aquinas also thinks that the ultimate constituents into which a material object can be decomposed are particulate, in the sense that they are matter-form composites which cannot be divided into any smaller matter-form composites. Prime matter is never actual; its existence is only potential and conceptual. Consequently, prime matter could never be one of the actual constituents into which a material thing could be decomposed. The division of form from prime matter can occur only in thought.

10 *DPN* 2 (349); see also *In Meta* VII.2.1289–1292.

11 *DPN* 1 (340).

12 For Aquinas's view that the form of a thing confers certain causal powers on that thing, see, e.g., *SCG* IV.36 (3740) and *In Meta* VII.11.1519.

13 For some discussion of immaterial forms and immaterial substances such as angels, see Chapter 6 on the soul.

14 For the claims about what substantial and accidental forms configure, see, e.g., *DPN* 1 (339).

15 For the claims about what the forms bring into existence, see *DPN* 1 (339).

16 Lynne Rudder Baker makes an interesting case for the claim that sometimes the primary kind of a thing is given not simply by characteristics intrinsic to the thing, as Aquinas's Aristotelian analysis here suggests, but rather by external, relational or historical features of the thing. See Lynne Rudder Baker, *Persons and Bodies: A Constitution View* (Cambridge: Cambridge University Press, 2000), pp. 46–58.) So, e.g., a flag is a flag rather than just a piece of cloth because of the circumstances in which it exists, circumstances which include certain social and political conventions. I think that she is right on this score, but that her view completes Aquinas's position rather than undermining anything in it.

17 See, e.g., *SCG* IV.48 (3834–3835).

18 To avoid confusion, it might also be helpful here to emphasize that Aquinas's point is a point about substances. Statues are not substances but artifacts; for Aquinas there can be more than one substantial form in an artifact. See also the discussion in Chapter 6 on the soul.

19 Someone might wonder why one should not say that the new composite has the substantial form of a barnacle–starfish, so that the new composite would after all count as a substance. It helps in this connection to understand the notion of a form as a dynamic organization and a substantial form as the dynamic organization that confers on the organized thing those properties essential to its being a member of a particular species. On Aquinas's view, a substance cannot have more than one substantial form. So if the composite barnacle–starfish were a substance, it would have only one substantial form. In that case, the substantial form of the barnacle and the substantial form of the starfish would be replaced by one single new substantial form. But when the barnacle attaches to the starfish, it certainly seems as if the species-conferring dynamic organization of the barnacle remains the same, and so does the species-conferring dynamic organization of the starfish. The barnacle does not cease to be a barnacle in virtue of its attaching to the starfish, and the starfish does not cease to be a starfish in virtue of having a barnacle attached to it. Consequently, each of them retains its original substantial form after the barnacle's attaching itself to the starfish, and there are two substantial forms in the composite. For this reason, the resulting composite does not have its own substantial form and does not count as a substance.

20 See, e.g., *ST* IIIa.2.1.

21 *DPN* 1 (342).

22 Cf. *DPN* 3 (354), where Aquinas talks about water being divided into water until it is divided into the smallest bits that are still water, namely, the element *water*.

23 See, e.g., *CT* 211 (410), where Aquinas discusses the case in which the combination of elements constitutes a complete inanimate thing which is a suppositum, that is, an individual in the genus of substance.

24 *SCG* IV.35 (3732); cf. also *In Meta* VII.17.1680 and VII.16.1633.

25 See, e.g., *CT* 211 (409–410) where Aquinas discusses the way in which elements combine and uses the examples of flesh and a hand to make this point.

26 *In Meta* VII.16.1633.

27 *SCG* IV.49 (3846).

28 For an analogous attitude in service of a different metaphysical position, see Eric Olson, *The Human Animal* (Oxford: Oxford University Press, 1997), pp. 135–140.

29 See, e.g., *ST* IIIa.5.3, where Aquinas explains that such flesh which is not informed by the substantial form of a human being is called 'flesh' only equivocally, and *ST* IIIa.5.4 where he makes the more general claim that there is no true human flesh which is not completed by a human soul. (Cf. *In DA* II.1.226 and *In Meta*, VII.9.1519.) See also *In Meta* VII.11.1519 and *SCG* IV.36 (3740) where Aquinas explains that the substantial form of a thing confers on that thing operations proper to it.

30 *ST* IIIa.2.1.

31 It would seem that a mixture existing on its own is just another case of the sort of composite listed under (iii): a composite of prime matter and substantial form. It may be that Aquinas lists it as a category by itself because he thinks that in a mixture the elements that came together to form it are not entirely absorbed into the whole but are still "virtually present", that is, present in their powers although not present as substances. Cf. *SCG* II.56.

32 See also, e.g., *SCG* IV.35 (3730–3734), which has a slightly more detailed taxonomy of composites. Aquinas distinguishes there between the composition of one from many which is accomplished only by order, as in a city composed of

many houses, and composition accomplished by order and binding together, as in a house conjoined of various parts.

33 See, e.g., *CT* 211 (410–411), where Aquinas explains this general point in connection with the composition of the incarnate Christ.

34 For more discussion of Aquinas's views of emergent properties and substances, see Chapter 6 on the soul.

35 *ST* Ia.76.1.

36 See, e.g., *CT* 212 (418).

37 *In Meta* VII.16.1635–1636.

38 See, e.g., *In Meta* VII.13.1588 and VII.16.1633.

39 Cf. *In Meta* VII.16.1635–1636.

40 The point of saying that they go out of existence as things in their own right is to preclude the misunderstanding that these things cease to exist *simpliciter*. They continue to exist as components of the whole. Analogously, when an apple is eaten, it ceases to exist as an apple, but all its matter continues to exist and (at least for a time) constitutes some of the components within the eater.

41 See, e.g., *De unione verbi incarnati* 2 where Aquinas explains in some detail the difference between a substance and a part of a substance. See also *ST* IIIa.2.2 ad 3; *ST* Ia.75.2 ad 1; *QDA* un.1 corpus and ad 3; and *ST* IaIIae.72.2, where Aquinas says:

> things are found to differ in species in two ways, in one way from the fact that each [of the differing things] has a [different] complete species, as a horse and a cow differ in species, and in another way insofar as difference in species is found in accordance with difference in the degree of some generation or motion, as a building is a complete generation of a house, but the laying of the foundation and the raising of a wall constitute an incomplete species.

42 Cf., e.g., *In Sent* II.3.1.4.

43 For further discussion of the soul as part of the human being, see Chapter 6 on the soul.

44 Fine says of a hylomorphic whole, which he takes to be a composite of material components ordered by a certain relation:

> it is a composite of a very special sort. For the components and the relation do not come together as coequals, as in a regular mereological sum. Rather, the relation R preserves its predicative role and somehow serves to modify or qualify the components. However, the result of the modification is not a fact or a state. It is a whole, whose components are linked by the relation, rather than the fact or state of the components being so linked.
>
> (1999, p. 65)

45 See, e.g., *QQ* V.2.1, where Aquinas explains why a part of a substance is not itself a substance; see also *CT* 211 (409).

46 For technical reasons involving medieval logic, it is not possible for Aquinas to give a definition, in his sense of 'definition', for substance. That is because a definition for him consists in an analysis of the thing to be defined into genus and differentia. But because substance is a genus which does not itself belong to any higher genus, it is not possible to assign substance to a genus. Consequently, substance cannot be defined in the usual medieval way.

47 See, e.g., *QQ* 9.3.1 ad 2. In other places, he gives somewhat different characterizations. So, e.g., in *De unione verbi incarnati* 2, he describes substance as that to

which it belongs to subsist *per se* and *in se*, whereas it belongs to an accident to be in something else. In this passage, he stresses that substance exists not only *per se* but also *in se*, in order to distinguish a substance from a part of a substance. A part of a substance does not exist *in se*; it exists in the whole substance of which it is a part. See also *De unione verbi incarnati* 2 ad 3.

48 Sometimes Aquinas delineates a substance in terms of an Aristotelian condition for substances: a substance is what has an intrinsic principle of motion. This condition looks promising when one thinks of animate substances; but Aquinas also recognizes inanimate substances, and there the Aristotelian condition looks much less promising. Water is a substance, and so is a quantity of water. It has an intrinsic principle of motion insofar as it is naturally inclined to fall to the earth. But the same can be said of an axe. It is true that the axe is inclined to fall to the earth only insofar as it is material, and not insofar as it is an axe; but, then, the same thing seems to be true of a quantity of water.

49 Some philosophers make a distinction between individuals and particulars, but for purposes of this chapter I will use the terms 'individual' and 'particular' interchangeably.

50 See, e.g., *DEE* 3 (18), and cf. *In Meta* VII.11.1521.

51 *ST* Ia.50.1 and Ia.50.5.

52 *ST* Ia.50.2.

53 The qualification 'composite' has to be added, because the point here does not apply to something, such as God, which is simple. An immaterial substance such as an angel is composite insofar as there is a distinction between the angel and the properties it has. There is also a distinction between one essential property and another in the angel, and there is a distinction between the angel's essential properties and its accidental properties.

54 See, e.g., David Lewis, "The Problem of Temporary Intrinsics", in *On the Plurality of Worlds* (Oxford: Blackwell, 1986) and Dean Zimmerman, "Temporary Intrinsics and Presentism", in *Metaphysics: The Big Questions,* Peter van Inwagen and Dean Zimmerman (eds) (Malden, MA: Blackwell, 1998), pp. 206–219; Lewis's paper is reprinted in the same volume, pp. 204–206.

55 Whether or not an analogue of this problem occurs in connection with (LII) is a question that is outside the scope of this chapter, which is concerned with medieval metaphysics.

56 *In BDT* 2.4.2; cf. also *ST* Ia.119.1 and *QDP* 9.1.

57 See, e.g., *De unione verbi incarnati* 1 corpus; see also *De unione verbi incarnati* 2 ad 6 where Aquinas explains that the name of a species signifies a nature.

58 Perhaps the most detailed exposition of this view of his is in his *In BDT* 2.4.2.

59 *In BDT* 2.4.2. Aquinas does not always describe his position on this score in the same way, and the variation in terminology suggests to some scholars either a development in his thought or a series of changes of mind. The issue is complicated, and so I am leaving it to one side here. Cf. *In Meta* VII.2.1283 for a helpful discussion of matter and its dimensions. For the discussion of the scholarly controversy, see John Wippel, *The Metaphysical Thought of Thomas Aquinas: From Finite Being to Uncreated Being* (Washington, DC: Catholic University of America Press, 2000), pp. 357–373.

60 *In BDT* 2.4.2.

61 Although Aquinas does not focus on continuity in connection with matter under indeterminate dimensions, he does emphasize continuity as a basis for unity in certain circumstances. See, e.g., *In Meta* V.7.849–858.

62 Cf., e.g., *ST* IIIa.3.7 ad 1 where Aquinas says that a substantial form is multiplied in accordance with the division of matter.

63 This is so even for the properties medieval logicians call '*propria*'. A *proprium* is a property which all and only the members of a species have and which they have always. The capacity for laughter, or risibility, is a *proprium* of human beings. *Propria* are classified by medieval logicians as a kind of accident just in virtue of the fact that, although the members of a species never lack the *propria* characteristic of that species, if a member of that species were to lack a *proprium* of the species, it would not be the case that it therefore ceased to be a member of the species in which the *proprium* is found.

64 God has no accidents, but it is also not true to say that God *has* a substantial form, because in the case of a simple God it is not possible to make a distinction between him and his nature.

65 See, e.g., *ST* IIIa.4.4 sed contra and corpus. See also Chapter 7 on the foundations of knowledge.

66 See, e.g., *In Meta* VII.17.1672–1674. There Aquinas says that in cases in which the composite is one thing, the composite is not identical with its components; rather the composite is something over and above its components. For interesting contemporary arguments against the reduction of wholes to their parts, see Mark Johnston, "Constitution is Not Identity", *Mind* 101 (1992): 89–105, and Lynne Rudder Baker, "Why Constitution is Not Identity", *Journal of Philosophy* 94 (1997): 599–621. For an excellent discussion of the constitution relation, see Lynne Rudder Baker, "Unity Without Identity: A New Look at Material Constitution", *Midwest Studies in Philosophy* 23 (1999): 144–165. Cf. also Baker (2000).

67 These are not synonymous for him; although they pick out the same thing in reality (for this point, see, e.g., *SCG* IV.38 [3766]), they pick it out under slightly different designations, because 'suppositum' is a term of second intention and 'hypostasis' is a term of first intention. This complexity of medieval logic is one I will ignore here, for the sake of brevity. For the distinction, see, e.g., *De unione verbi incarnati* 2 corpus.

68 Aquinas gives a helpful explanation of his use of these terms in *De unione verbi incarnati* 2; see also *QQ* V.2.1.

69 *ST* IIIa.2.2.

70 See, e.g., *De unione verbi incarnati* 1 where Aquinas says that a suppositum will not be the same as a nature in anything in which there is either accident or individual matter, because in that case the suppositum is related to the nature by means of an addition. See also *SCG* IV.40 (3781) where Aquinas explains the distinction between a singular and its quiddity or nature and goes on to explain that a supposit such as Socrates is not identical to his substantial form because in his normal or natural condition he is also constituted of designated matter.

71 I am grateful to Brian Leftow for calling this passage to my attention.

72 *In I Cor* Chapter 15, 1.2.

73 For Aquinas, a person is an individual substance of a rational nature; a human being is an individual substance of a rational *animal* nature. Since these are not the same, some scholars have argued in conversation that my interpretation needs a separate argument to handle texts that appear to deny that a disembodied soul is not a human being. I am happy to consider this a separate objection, though I think it is worth pointing out that while there is a difference between a person and a human being for Aquinas, there is no difference between a human person and a human being.

74 See, e.g., *SCG* II.57, where Aquinas argues at length against Plato's attempt to show that a human being is identical to a soul.

75 See, e.g., *ST* Suppl.69.2.

76 *ST* Suppl.70.2–3.

77 *ST* Suppl.69.3.

78 *ST* Suppl.69.4–5.

79 See, e.g., Eric Olson, *The Human Animal* (Oxford: Oxford University Press, 1997).

80 Contemporary ways of harmonizing Leibniz's Law with change over time (see, e.g., Lewis [1986], and Zimmerman [1998]) might offer Aquinas a way out here if they were compatible with the rest of Aquinas's metaphysics, but it is not clear that they are.

81 It is perhaps worth pointing out in this connection that the counterexample involving Cicero and Tully which I gave to show that indiscernibility of properties at a time and coincident identity are not sufficient for identity on Aquinas's views is given its force by a temporal discontinuity in the existence of what is being referred to by 'Cicero' and 'Tully'.

82 Aquinas would therefore share Peter van Inwagen's intuition that two objects (or substances) cannot be composed of all and only the same proper parts at the same time (van Inwagen [1990, p. 5]).

83 Peter van Inwagen, "Composition as Identity", in James Tomberlin (ed.), *Philosophical Perspectives*, vol. 8 (Atascadero, CA: Ridgeview Publishing Co., 1994), pp. 207–219. Aquinas makes the point explicitly in *In Meta* VII.13.1588; see also *ST* IIIa.17.1 obj. 1, where Aquinas says that where there is one thing and another, there are two things, not one. (Although this line occurs in the objection, it is not disputed in the reply to the objection.)

84 Baker (1999, p. 151).

85 In fact, as I explained above, on Aquinas's view, it is possible to decompose a material whole into matter and form in such a way that the matter is itself a composite of matter and form. There are thus levels of organization in a complex material composite, and in consequence there will also be nested sets of constitution relations. Baker gives an interesting argument for the claim that even in such cases, constitution is not a transitive relation; see Baker (1999, p. 164, n. 30).

86 This is for technical reasons involving medieval logic as well as metaphysics. A thing's nature is what is signified by the name of the species of that thing. But a species is defined in terms of genus and differentia.

87 See, e.g., *SCG* IV.41 (3787–3789).

88 See, e.g., *SCG* IV.36 (3740) where Aquinas claims that there is an operation proper to the nature of anything which derives from the substantial form of that thing. See also *ST* IIIa.17.2 where Aquinas says that a supposit is that which exists and a nature is that whereby it exists.

89 *ST* III.2.3.

90 *SCG* IV.48 (3835).

91 For further discussion of this topic, see Chapter 14 on the incarnation.

92 Baker speaks in this connection of something's having a property independently, rather than in its own right, and she gives a helpful analysis of what it is for anything to have a property independently. See Baker (1999, pp. 151–160).

93 The metaphor of borrowing here is Baker's; see Baker (1999, pp. 151–160).

94 Baker (1999, pp. 159–160).

95 *ST* Ia.76.1.

96 *SCG* IV.48 (3835).

97 *ST* Ia.75.2 ad 2.

98 Unlike the case of human beings, in the case of these substances temporal continuity of the substantial form is not enough just because their forms cannot exist apart from the composite.

99 In Fine (1999), Fine tries to provide hylomorphic theories of wholes and parts with a distinction which explains and accounts for the fact that sometimes a

change of parts is compatible with the continued existence of the whole of which they are parts and sometimes it is not. As Fine puts it, a material composite has both a rigid embodiment (one which cannot be changed compatibly with the continued existence of the composite) and a variable embodiment (which can be changed without the composite's going out of existence). Fine's explanation and use of this distinction are helpful, but, as far as I can see, they do not provide all that is needed for a principled way of drawing the line between a change of matter which is just an alteration and one which constitutes generation of something new.

2 Goodness

1 *ST* IIaIIae.122 and IIaIIae.140, respectively.
2 For more discussion of this lore, and especially for some discussion of the relation between the intellectual virtues and their twins among the gifts of the Holy Spirit, see Chapter 11 on wisdom.
3 See, e.g., Robert B. Louden, "On Some Vices of Virtue Ethics", *American Philosophical Quarterly* 21 (1984): 227–236; Gregory E. Pence, "Recent Work on Virtues", *American Philosophical Quarterly* 21 (1984): 281–297.
4 *ST* Ia.5.1. Aquinas's treatment of this thesis about being and goodness is a particularly important development in a long and complicated tradition; cf. Scott MacDonald (ed.), *Being and Goodness* (Ithaca, NY: Cornell University Press, 1991).
5 The claim is set in the context of the medieval lore of the transcendentals, which are part of the metaphysical underpinnings of the claim. It is not possible to deal with the transcendentals here; but for a helpful treatment of the subject, see Jan Aertsen, *Medieval Philosophy and the Transcendentals: The Case of Thomas Aquinas* (Leiden: E. J. Brill, 1996). It would be particularly interesting to show the connection Aquinas sees between goodness and beauty, which is either a transcendental or a quasi-transcendental; see, e.g., Umberto Eco, *Problem Estetico in Tommaso d'Aquino* (Cambridge, MA: Harvard University Press, 1988). For a moving treatment of beauty in art, nature, and religion, see John Foley, *Creativity and the Roots of Liturgy* (Portland, OR: Pastoral Press, 1994).
6 *ST* Ia.5.1. See also *SCG* I.37; III.3. Cf. Aristotle, *Nicomachean Ethics* I 1, 1094a1–3.
7 For discussion of the relation between intellect and will in the process leading to moral wrongdoing, see Chapter 11 on wisdom.
8 *SCG* I.37.
9 *SCG* I.37.
10 *SCG* I.38.
11 *SCG* I.39.
12 *SCG* I.37.
13 *SCG* III.3, *passim*.
14 See, e.g., *ST* IaIIae.1.5.
15 When the thing described is a rational being, the object of its aim will include its conception of the fulfillment of its nature, which can be more or less mistaken. Objectively evil objects of desire are desired because they are perceived as good for the desirer to have.
16 *ST* IaIIae.1.6.
17 *ST* IaIIae.1.7.
18 *SCG* III.3.
19 *SCG* I.37; cf. also *ST* Ia.5.1.
20 *ST* Ia.5.5; cf. also *QDV* 21.6.

21 *ST* Ia.48.3.
22 *CT* 109; see also *ST* Ia.48.3.
23 *CT* 115.
24 See, e.g., Augustine, *Confessions*, Bk. VII.
25 See Chapter 1 on things.
26 *ST* IaIIae.85.4.
27 T. H. Irwin's "The Metaphysical and Psychological Basis of Aristotle's Ethics", in Amélie Rorty (ed.), *Essays on Aristotle's Ethics* (Berkeley, CA: University of California Press, 1984), pp. 35–53, is particularly useful here because of Aquinas's dependence on Aristotle. On the relevant role of substantial form in particular, see esp. pp. 37–39 of Irwin's article.
28 See, e.g., *DEE* 2.
29 *DEE* 3.
30 A contemporary counterpart of this view of forms might be seen in Sydney Shoemaker's "Causality and Properties", in Peter van Inwagen (ed.), *Time and Cause* (Dordrecht: Reidel, 1980), pp. 109–135; reprinted in Shoemaker, *Identity, Cause, and Mind* (Cambridge: Cambridge University Press, 1984), pp. 206–233.
31 *SCG* III.7.
32 *ST* IaIIae.55.2.
33 See, e.g., *SCG* I.42 (n. 343):

> The differentia that specifies a genus does not complete the nature (*rationem*), of the genus; instead, it is through the differentia that the genus acquires its being in actuality. For there is a complete nature of *animal* before the addition of *rational*, but an animal cannot be in actuality unless it is rational or irrational.

34 *ST* Ia.48.5.
35 *ST* Ia.48.6.
36 *ST* IaIIae.3.2.
37 *ST* IaIIae.49.4, esp. ad 1.
38 See, e.g., *SCG* III.16.3.
39 See, e.g., *ST* IaIIae.18.1.
40 *ST* Ia.5.1, s.c. Cf. Augustine, *De doctrina christiana* I 32.
41 See, e.g., *SCG* III.7, *passim*.
42 *SCG* III.15, *passim*.
43 See, e.g., *ST* Ia.5.3ad 2:

> No being can be called bad or evil insofar as it is a being, but insofar as it lacks some sort of being – as a human being is called evil insofar as it lacks the being of virtue and an eye is called bad insofar as it lacks clarity of sight.

44 See, e.g., *SCG* III.20, III.22.
45 *ST* IaIIae.94.3.
46 *ST* IaIIae.18.5.
47 *ST* IaIIae.18.5 ad 2.
48 *ST* IaIIae.55.1; cf. also *ST* IaIIae.55.2.
49 *ST* IaIIae.63.1.
50 *ST* IaIIae.58.3.
51 *ST* IaIIae.18.5 ad 1.
52 *SCG* III.7: "Therefore, since badness or evil is a privation of that which is natural, it cannot be natural to anything."

53 See, e.g., *ST* IaIIae.71.2.

54 *ST* Ia.59.1.

55 *ST* Ia.59.1; cf. *SCG* II.47 and *QDV* 23.1. See also Chapter 3 on simplicity.

56 See, e.g., *SCG* III.9 and *ST* IaIIae.18.5. For a discussion of the relation of the intellect and will in actions that are freely willed and for which an agent is morally responsible, see Chapter 9 on freedom.

57 For a helpful survey, examples, and much else of relevance, see Jaegwon Kim, "Concepts of Supervenience", *Philosophy and Phenomenological Research* 45 (1984): 153–177; reprinted in his *Supervenience and Mind* (Cambridge: Cambridge University Press, 1993).

58 John Campbell and Robert Pargetter, "Goodness and Fragility", *American Philosophical Quarterly* 23 (1986): 155–165.

> The relationship between fragility, fragility phenomena and the basis of the fragility is given by two identities. (1) being fragile = having some property which is responsible for being such that (X is dropped, X breaks), etc. and (2) The property which is responsible for object O's being such that (O is dropped, O breaks), etc. = having chemical bonding B. This explicates the 'because' relation for fragility, i.e., it tells us what is meant when we say that O is fragile because it has bonding B. And when we say that object N is fragile because it has bonding A, clause (1) remains unchanged and clause (2) is changed in the obvious way.
>
> (p. 161)

59 I say 'apparently' here because sometimes Aquinas distinguishes between reason as a discursive faculty, which characterizes human beings but not angels, and intellection, which is not discursive and which angels employ. This additional complication has to be left to one side here.

60 *ST* Ia.5.1 obj. 1.

61 Someone might object here that Hitler's conduct of the war and his governing of Germany during his time in power were very smart, so that, on Aquinas's connection between reason and morality, Aquinas is stuck with calling Hitler good. But this objection relies on a confused conflation of a certain kind of cleverness with rationality. For some discussion of the distinction, see the beginning of Chapter 11 on wisdom.

62 *ST* Ia.5.1 obj. 3.

63 The capacity for reproduction is a potentiality human beings share with all living things.

64 The *ceteris paribus* clause in this claim is important. Even though species A outranks species B in the way described, it is theoretically possible that a particular individual of species B might outrank an individual of species A. Suppose that there are angels, that angels constitute a species as human beings do, that the species *angel* outranks the species *human being*, and that Satan is a fallen angel. It is theoretically possible that Mother Teresa outranks Satan in the relevant sense even though the amount of being available to an angel is greater than that available to any human being. For if Mother Teresa has actualized virtually all of her specifying potentiality and Satan very little of his, it will be possible to ascribe more being and hence more goodness to Mother Theresa than to Satan.

65 See, e.g., *ST* IaIIae.60, *passim*. For a good discussion of the Aristotelian background, see, e.g., L. A. Kosman, "Being Properly Affected: Virtues and Feelings in Aristotle's Ethics", in Amélie Rorty (ed.), *Essays on Aristotle's Ethics* (Berkeley, CA: University of California Press, 1984), pp. 103–116.

66 *ST* IaIIae.61.2.

67 See, e.g., *ST* IaIIae.57.5; IaIIae.58.4; IIaIIae.47–56.
68 *ST* IaIIae.57.5.
69 See, e.g., *ST* IaIIae.60.4.
70 See, e.g., *ST* IaIIae.61.2; IIaIIae.57–71.
71 *ST* IaIIae.58.1 ad 2.
72 For a clear, succinct presentation of some of this material in more detail, see, e.g., Alan Donagan, "Aquinas on Human Action", in N. Kretzmann, A. Kenny and J. Pinborg (eds), *The Cambridge History of Later Medieval Philosophy* (Cambridge: Cambridge University Press, 1982), pp. 642–654.
73 Aquinas's "Treatise on Action" is contained in *ST* IaIIae.6–17; IaIIae.18–21 are concerned with the evaluation of actions.
74 For this distinction, see *ST* IaIIae.1.1.
75 On the object of an action, see, e.g., *ST* IaIIae.10.2; IaIIae.18.2.
76 *ST* IaIIae.18.5.
77 *ST* IaIIae.18.5 ad 3.
78 On the end of an action, see, e.g., *ST* IaIIae.1.1–3; IaIIae.18.4–6.
79 *ST* IaIIae.1.3 ad 3.
80 For some of the complications, see, e.g., *ST* IaIIae.18.7.
81 On specifying an action, see, e.g., *ST* IaIIae.1.3; IaIIae.18. 2, 5, 7.
82 On the circumstances of an action, see esp. *ST* IaIIae.7, *passim*.
83 On the role of circumstances in the evaluation of actions, see, e.g., *ST* IaIIae.18.3, 10, 11.
84 *ST* IaIIae.18.8.
85 See, e.g., *ST* IaIIae.7.2 ad 2.
86 On Aquinas's treatment of issues of this sort regarding decrees or laws see Norman Kretzmann, "*Lex iniusta non est lex:* Laws on Trial in Aquinas's Court of Conscience," *American Journal of Jurisprudence* 33 (1988): 99–122.
87 See, e.g., *ST* IIaIIae.123, *passim*.
88 *ST* IIaIIae.64.6.
89 *ST* IIaIIae.64.6 obj. 2 and ad 2.
90 *ST* IaIIae.1.3.
91 *ST* IaIIae.1.3 ad 1.
92 For a well-known form of the problem in the hospital case, see Philippa Foot, "The Problem of Abortion and the Doctrine of Double Effect", in her *Virtues and Vices* (Berkeley, CA: University of California Press, 1978), pp. 19–32.
93 *ST* IIaIIae.64.6.
94 *ST* IIaIIae.64.2.
95 In addition to the moral repugnance many readers will feel towards this position on Aquinas's part, there are philosophical problems as well. e.g., it is hard to know why, on Aquinas's own views, capital punishment would not be ruled out as immoral by the central meta-ethical thesis if the society could be adequately protected from the wrongdoer by some means (such as imprisonment, e.g.) other than killing him. For a moving argument that any killing of human beings is always immoral, see John Kavanaugh, *Who Count As Persons?: Human Identity and the Ethics of Killing* (Washington, DC: Georgetown University Press, 2001).
96 For a detailed discussion of Aquinas's views of distributive and commutative justice, see Chapter 10 on justice.
97 *ST* IIaIIae.61.1.
98 Cf., e.g., *ST* IIaIIae.57.1 and IIaIIae.61.2.
99 See, e.g., *ST* IIaIIae.77, *passim*.
100 See *ST* IIaIIae.73, *passim*; for comparisons of slander (or "backbiting") with theft or murder, see esp. IIaIIae.73.3.

101 To see the way in which Aquinas reconciles this attitude towards murder with his acceptance of capital punishment, it is important to take seriously Aquinas's view that a society has a being of its own and that the harm which a criminal can do to a society may be great enough to warrant the loss of being and goodness attendant on killing him. In that case, killing the criminal, on Aquinas's view, is not a violation of commutative justice. For discussion of the complexities of Aquinas's views of commutative justice, see Chapter 10 on justice.

102 On murder as a vice in opposition to commutative justice and the vice "by which a man does the greatest harm to his neighbor", see *ST* IIaIIae.64, *passim*.

103 *ST* IaIIae.18.4.

104 *ST* IaIIae.18.4 ad 3.

105 Someone might nonetheless wonder whether Esther's actions are not subject to Aquinas's moral censure of suicide. For a discussion of Aquinas's views of suicide, see Chapter 10 on justice.

106 Samuel Scheffler, "Agent-Centred Restrictions, Rationality, and the Virtues", *Mind* 94 (1985): 409–419. In this article Scheffler is commenting on Philippa Foot's "Utilitarianism and the Virtues", *Proceedings and Addresses of the American Philosophical Association* 57 (1983): 273–283; also (a revised version) *Mind* 94 (1985): 196–209. For Scheffler's own resolution of the puzzle of agent-centered restrictions, see his book *The Rejection of Consequentialism* (Oxford: Clarendon Press, 1982).

107 For one recent and sophisticated treatment of the topic, see Mark Murphy, *Natural Law and Practical Rationality*, Cambridge Studies in Philosophy and Law (Cambridge: Cambridge University Press, 2001).

108 Ralph McInerny, *Aquinas on Human Action: A Theory of Practice* (Washington, DC: Catholic University of America Press, 1992), p. 110.

109 Ralph McInerny, *Ethica Thomistica: The Moral Philosophy of Thomas Aquinas* (Washington, DC: Catholic University of America Press, revised edition 1997), pp. 46 and 47.

110 John Finnis, *Aquinas: Moral, Political, and Legal Theory* (Oxford: Oxford University Press, 1998), p. 135.

111 *ST* IaIIae.91.2.

112 *ST* IaIIae.91.1.

113 *ST* IaIIae.91.2.

114 *ST* IaIIae.93.6.

115 *ST* IaIIae.19.4 ad 3.

116 *ST* IaIIae.19.10 ad 1; cf. also *ST* IaIIae.21.1.

117 *ST* IaIIae.90.4 ad 1.

118 *ST* IaIIae.94.2.

119 *ST* IaIIae.94.6.

120 *ST* IaIIae.94.3.

121 *ST* IaIIae.94.3.

122 *ST* IaIIae.93.6.

123 *QDV* 16.

124 For further discussion of Aquinas's theory of angelic knowledge, see Chapter 5 on God's knowledge.

125 *QDV* 17.

126 *QDV* 16.2–3.

127 *QDV* 17.2.

128 *QDV* 17.4.

129 See, e.g., *ST* Ia.2.3; Ia.3.4, 7; Ia.6.3. Bonaventure, Aquinas's contemporary and colleague at the University of Paris, forthrightly identifies God as the single

referent of 'being' and 'goodness' in his own version of the central thesis, interpreting the Old Testament as emphasizing being, the New Testament as emphasizing goodness (see, e.g., *Itinerarium mentis in deum*, V 2).

130 *ST* Ia.6.3.

131 *ST* Ia.3.3.

3 God's simplicity

1 This doctrine has also been the subject of a voluminous literature. The most sustained and sophisticated attack on Aquinas's position can be found in Christopher Hughes, *A Complex Theory of a Simple God* (Ithaca, NY: Cornell University Press, 1989). Hughes's attack, however, seems to me based on misunderstandings of crucial elements of Aquinas's metaphysics, as reviewers have pointed out (see, e.g., David B. Burrell's review in *The Journal of Religion* 72 (1992): 120–121), and so I will not consider it here, in the interests of keeping this chapter from expanding past all reasonable bounds.

2 The derivation of divine simplicity from such considerations is apparent in Aquinas's *QDP* 7.1, as Mark D. Jordan has recently pointed out in his article "The Names of God and the Being of Names", in Alfred J. Freddoso (ed.), *The Existence and Nature of God* (Notre Dame, IN: University of Notre Dame Press, 1983), pp. 161–190; see esp. pp. 176–179.

3 On the combination of biblical data and rational theology in Christianity see Thomas V. Morris, "The God of Abraham, Isaac, and Anselm", *Faith and Philosophy* 1 (1984): 177–187.

4 See, e.g., Augustine, *De trinitate* VI, 7–8; Anselm, *Monologion* XVII; Aquinas (besides the source cited in n.2 above), *SCG* I.18, I.21–23, I.31; *ST* Ia.3. For the development, criticism, and defense of the doctrine in recent philosophical literature, see, e.g., Jordan (1983); Daniel Bennett, "The Divine Simplicity", *Journal of Philosophy* 66 (1969): 628–637; Richard LaCroix, "Augustine on the Simplicity of God", *New Scholasticism* 51 (1977): 453–469; James F. Ross, *Philosophical Theology* (Indianapolis and New York: Bobbs-Merrill, 1969), esp. pp. 51–63; Alvin Plantinga, *Does God Have a Nature?* (Milwaukee: Marquette University Press, 1980), esp. pp. 26–61; Nicholas Wolterstorff, "Divine Simplicity", in James E. Tomberlin (ed.), *Philosophical Perspectives, 5: Philosophy of Religion* (Atascadero, CA: Ridgeview Publishing Company, 1991), and "Divine Simplicity" in Kelly James Clark (ed.), *Our Knowledge of God: Essays in Natural and Philosophical Theology* (Dordrecht: Kluwer Academic Publishers, 1992), pp. 133–150; and in particular the inter-related articles by William E. Mann, including "The Divine Attributes", *American Philosophical Quarterly* 12 (1975): 151–159; "Divine Simplicity", *Religious Studies* (1982): 451–471; and "Simplicity and Immutability in God", *International Philosophical Quarterly* 23 (1983): 267–276.

5 See, e.g., Simo Knuuttila, *Modalities in Medieval Philosophy* (London: Routledge, 1993).

6 *ST* Ia.3.3 ad 3.

7 *ST* Ia.13.2.

8 *ST* Ia.13.2 obj. 1.

9 *ST* Ia.13.2 ad 1.

10 See, in this connection, particularly *SCG* I.14.

11 Peter of Spain, *Tractatus*, ed. L. M. De Rijk (Amsterdam: Van Gorcum & Co., 1972), p. 21.

12 *ST* Ia.3.1–2.

13 *ST* Ia.10.1.

14 *ST* Ia.9.1.

15 *ST* Ia.3.6.

16 In Chapter 4 of his *De trinitate* Boethius draws a distinction between what might be called intrinsic and extrinsic predicates, attempting to found it on a distinction between the first three and the remaining seven Aristotelian categories. Cf. Eleonore Stump, "Hamartia in Christian Belief: Boethius on the Trinity", in Donald Stump *et al.* (eds), *Hamartia: The Concept of Error in the Western Tradition* (New York: The Edwin Mellen Press, 1983), pp. 131–148.

17 *ST* Ia.3.3.

18 *ST* Ia.3.5.

19 The most familiar problems of this sort are associated with the claim that there can be no real distinction between what God is and its being the case that he is; for God, as for no non-simple entity, essence and existence must be identical. Robert M. Adams has worked at rebutting the familiar philosophical objections to the essence–existence connection and to the concept of necessary existence; see his "Has It Been Proved that All Real Existence is Contingent?", *American Philosophical Quarterly* 8 (1971): 284–291 and "Divine Necessity", *Journal of Philosophy* 80 (1983): 741–752.

20 There are, of course, also problems arising from claim (1), but those involving the denial of temporality are taken up in Chapter 4 on God's eternity.

21 Entities existing only at an instant could satisfy that description, and they are sometimes discussed, notably by Duns Scotus. But there is some reason for wondering whether strictly instantaneous temporal existence is really possible.

22 For a discussion of God's eternality and God's relations with time on Aquinas's account, see Chapter 4 on God's eternity.

23 *SCG* I.76.

24 For a discussion of the essential connection between divine goodness and the manifestation of it in things other than God, see Norman Kretzmann, "Goodness, Knowledge, and Indeterminacy in the Philosophy of Thomas Aquinas", *Journal of Philosophy* 80 (1983): 631–649.

25 See *SCG* I.77.

26 *ST* Ia.13.4.

27 In a discussion of a much earlier version of the arguments in this chapter, Bowman Clarke raised a criticism that has occurred to others as well. He claimed that it is "plainly false" that perfect power is identical with perfect knowledge "unless perfect power bears no resemblance to power, and perfect knowledge to knowledge". While there is indeed an essential resemblance between creaturely attributes such as power and their perfect counterparts among the conceptually distinguishable divine attributes, the resemblance must be confined to the formal, abstract aspect of the attribute. God in his perfect power can raise 100 pounds a foot off the floor, and a man can raise 100 pounds a foot off the floor; but it is inconceivable that the means by which a temporal, material creature achieves that result with some effort be like an omnipotent God's doing it in any respect other than, perhaps, the fact that an act of will initiates it. In this same vein, Clarke also objected to the summit-slope analogy, pointing out that a summit is not a perfect slope. At least part of the trouble here is with the apparent contrast between 'perfection' in the sense of 'ideal 'and 'perfection' in the etymologically fundamental sense of 'culmination', 'completion'. In that latter, more directly relevant sense, the single summit is indeed the perfection of all the slopes. The slope-summit analogy was intended to suggest that the idea that perfect A and perfect B might be identical despite the plain difference between A and B cannot simply be dismissed as incoherent. Here is one more analogy offered with that same intention. Consider two sets of geometrical

elements: A (three two-inch line segments lying parallel to one another) and B (three 6-degree angles with one-inch legs lying with their vertices toward a single point). In this analogy the analogue for the perfection/completion of A and of B is the construction of closed figures involving all three elements of each; and, of course, the resultant figures are identical two-inch equilateral triangles, despite the essential differences between A and B. (I am grateful to Sydney Shoemaker for help with this analogy.)

28 See Chapter 4 on God's eternity.

29 The question whether God could do what he does not do, or refrain from doing what he does, is a well-recognized problem in the tradition of rational theology. Aquinas, for instance, discusses it several times, e.g., *In Sent* I.43.1.1–2; *SCG* II23, 26–27; *QDP* 1.5; *ST* Ia.25.5. I discuss this question further later in this chapter.

30 This apparent diversity is clearly expressed by Aquinas in such passages as these: "God necessarily wills his own being and his own goodness, and he *cannot* will the contrary" (*SCG* I.80); "in respect of himself God has only volition, but in respect of other things he has selection (*electio*). Selection, however, is always accomplished by means of free choice. Therefore, free choice is suited to God" (*SCG* I.88): "free choice is spoken of in respect of things one wills *not* necessarily but of one's own accord" (ibid.). Notice that even though God's existence and attributes are conceived of here as being *willed* by God, they are expressly excluded from among the objects of God's free choice. This diversity is discussed further later in this chapter.

31 For developments of this last sort, see, e.g., Nelson Pike, "Omnipotence and God's Ability to Sin", *American Philosophical Quarterly* 6 (1969): 208–216; Thomas V. Morris, "The Necessity of God's Goodness", in *Anselmian Explorations: Essays in Philosophical Theology* (Notre Dame, IN: University of Notre Dame Press, 1987), pp. 42–69; William Rowe, "The Problem of Divine Perfection and Freedom", in Eleonore Stump (ed.), *Reasoned Faith* (Ithaca, NY: Cornell University Press, 1993), pp. 223–247.

32 The notion of *liberum arbitrium* is not equivalent to our notion of free will but is rather a narrower concept falling under the broader concept of freedom in the will. For more explanation of Aquinas's understanding of *liberum arbitrium*, see Chapter 9 on freedom.

33 See, e.g., *SCG* II.23.

34 *ST* Ia.19.10.

35 See, e.g., Peter Geach, *Providence and Evil* (Cambridge: Cambridge University Press, 1977), esp. Chapters I and II; Joshua Hoffman, "Can God Do Evil?", *Southern Journal of Philosophy* 17 (1979): 213–220; Jerome Gellman, "Omnipotence and Impeccability", *The New Scholasticism* 51 (1977): 21–37.

36 For good surveys of the difficulties and significant contributions to the discussion, see Thomas P. Flint and Alfred J. Freddoso, "Maximal Power", in *The Existence and Nature of God* (n. 2 above), pp. 81–113; Edward Wierenga, "Omnipotence Defined", *Philosophy and Phenomenological Research* 43 (1983): 363–376 (including a useful bibliography of literature on the subject).

37 The conception of God's goodness as exercising final causation, a conception at the heart of Aquinas's account of creation and its relationship to God, seems particularly likely to emphasize the esthetic aspect of perfect goodness at the expense of the moral. See Kretzmann (1983, esp. p. 637).

38 This principle, of course, has more than a family resemblance to the much discussed Principle of Alternative Possibilities (PAP). In Chapter 9 on freedom, I argue at length for the claim that Aquinas rejects PAP.

39 For a more detailed discussion of Aquinas's views of free will, see Chapter 9 on freedom.
40 It is not easy to provide a satisfactory translation of *'appetitus'*, especially in a single word: 'desire', 'tendency', 'inclination', 'attraction' are all more or less unsatisfactory possibilities. The basic sense of the verb *'appeto'* involves the notion of striving after, which also seems to play a part in Aquinas's account of the will. Perhaps the least unsatisfactory one-word counterpart of *'appetitus'* is 'wanting', as long as 'wanting' is not understood as implying the absence of the object of *appetitus*. On this basis we could say that for Aquinas the will is a self-directed intellectual wanting of the good, or a self-directed wanting of what is good, essentially connected with some understanding of goodness in general.
41 *ST* Ia.59.1; cf. *SCG* II.47 and *QDV* 23.1.
42 See, e.g., *ST* Ia.83.1; IaIIae.13.16; *QDV* 22.6; *QDM* 6.
43 *ST* Ia.82.1.
44 *ST* Ia.82.1.
45 *ST* Ia.82.1.
46 See, e.g., *ST* Ia.82.1: "in practical matters the end plays the role played by the principle in speculative matters, as is said in *Physics* II [9]".
47 *ST* Ia.82.1.
48 *ST* Ia.82.4.
49 *ST* Ia.82.4.
50 For a more detailed defense of this claim, see Chapter 9 on freedom.
51 *SCG* I.80.
52 *QDV* 23.4.
53 *SCG* I.74.
54 *SCG* I.88.
55 Cf. *SCG* I.86.
56 In this connection, see also Chapter 1 on Aquinas's theory of things.
57 *ST* Ia.3.6: "in Deo accidens esse non potest". See also *QDP* 7.4: "absque omni dubitatione, tenendum est quod in Deo nullum sit accidens".
58 *ST* Ia.25.5.
59 *QDP* 1.5 ad 9.
60 *QDV* 24.3 ad 3.
61 Cf., e.g., *QDP* 3.15.
62 Reginald Garrigou-Lagrange, *The One God* (St Louis and London: Herder, 1943), pp. 190–191.
63 Garrigou-Lagrange (1943, pp. 511–512).
64 Peter of Spain (1972, p. 23).
65 See Knuuttila (1993, esp. pp. 99–137). Knuuttila argues that what he calls a 'dynamic' model of modality, that ties modality to time (as distinguished from a 'synchronic' model that understands modality in terms of synchronic possible worlds), was common in the thirteenth century.
66 See, e.g., *QDP* 7.4 s.c. The Latin I have rendered 'cannot change over time' is *'sit immutabilis'*; and someone might suppose that my rendering is unwarrantedly tendentious. But the preceding line in the text has to do with the corruption of the subject, which is certainly a change or alteration over time, as distinct from a difference across possible worlds.
67 For more detailed discussion of Aquinas's account of accidents, see Chapter 1 on Aquinas's theory of things.
68 *DEE* 6.34–35.
69 *QDP* 7.4 s.c.
70 *ST* Ia.19.3 obj. 4.
71 *ST* Ia.19.3 ad 4.

72 That angels change across possible worlds is a consequence of Aquinas's claim that in this world angels know creatures and his claim that God's creating is not necessary but a result of divine free choice.

73 *QDP* 7.4.

74 *ST* IIaIIae.83.16 s.c.

75 David Ray Griffin, *God, Power, and Evil: A Process Theodicy* (Philadelphia, PA: Westminster Press, 1976), p. 74; I am grateful to Theodore Vitali for this reference. Griffin builds an attack against the consistency of Aquinas's theology on the basis of this interpretation of Aquinas's understanding of simplicity; some Thomists seem to share Griffin's interpretation, but they apparently see this interpretation as a strength of Aquinas's position. See, e.g., Reginald Garrigou-Lagrange, *God: His Existence and Nature*, 5th edn, trans. Dom Bede Rose (St Louis, MO: Herder, 1955), p. 546. I discuss Garrigou-Lagrange's position further a little later in the chapter.

76 Griffin (1976, p. 77).

77 Griffin (1976, p. 77).

78 For further discussion of these claims, see Chapter 4 on God's eternity.

79 I am here operating with a simplistic and clumsy notion of responsiveness. To see something of the complications that would be needed to refine this account of divine responsiveness, see the roughly analogous discussion of reasons-responsiveness in John Martin Fischer and Mark Ravizza, *Responsibility and Control: A Theory of Moral Responsibility* (Cambridge: Cambridge University Press, 1998). Nothing in the additional complication is excluded by simplicity, in my view.

80 I am grateful to Theodore Vitali for calling my attention to the need to address these other worries.

81 See in this connection the discussion of God's immutability in *ST* Ia.9.1.

82 For more discussion of this and related claims, see Chapter 4 on God's eternity.

83 *SCG* I.85:

> Vult enim Deus omnia quae requiruntur ad rem quam vult, ut dictum est (cap. 83). Sed aliquibus rebus secundum modum suae naturae competit quod sint contingentes, non necessariae. Igitur vult aliquas res esse contingentes. Efficacia autem divinae voluntatis exigit ut non solum sit quod Deus vult esse, sed etiam ut hoc modo sit sicut Deus vult illud esse: ... Igitur efficacia divinae voluntatis contingentiam non tollit.

84 *SCG* I.85:

> Necessitas ex suppositione in causa non potest concludere necessitatem absolutam in effectu. Deus autem vult aliquid in creatura non necessitate absoluta, sed solum necessitate quae est ex suppositione, ut supra (capp. 81 sqq.) ostensum est. Ex voluntate igitur divina non potest concludi in rebus creatis necessitas absoluta. Haec autem sola excludit contingentiam.

85 *SCG* I.85.

86 For an account of Boethius's explanation of all contingency in terms of free will, see Norman Kretzmann, "*Nos Ipsi Principia Sumus*: Boethius and the Basis of Contingency", in Tamar Rudavsky (ed.), *Divine Omniscience and Omnipotence in Medieval Philosophy* (Dordrecht: D. Reidel, 1984), pp. 23–50.

87 I am grateful to Theodore Vitali for calling my attention to the need to address this argument explicitly.

88 Reginald Garrigou-Lagrange, *God: His Existence and Nature* (St Louis, MO,: Herder, 1955), pp. 546–547.
89 Garrigou-Lagrange (1936, pp. 538–539).
90 See Chapter 8 on the mechanisms of cognition for further discussion.
91 For further discussion of this issue, see Chapter 5 on God's knowledge.
92 For discussion of the notion of simultaneity at issue here, see Chapter 4 on God's eternity.
93 *ST* Ia.25.1; cf. also *QDP* 1.1.
94 *ST* Ia.25.1 ad 1.
95 In addition, if the director wills freely what he wills, then, on Aquinas's view of the nature of free will, nothing is acting on the will with causal efficacy; if the will were efficiently caused to will what it wills, it would not be free. For Aquinas's view of the nature of freedom in the will, see Chapter 9 on freedom. And for more discussion of God's responsiveness in connection with this issue, see Chapter 4 on God's eternity.
96 I Samuel I: 19–20.
97 *In Phil* 4.1. The translation in the text is mine, but a helpful translation of the whole work can be found in *Commentary on Saint Paul's First Letter to the Thessalonians and the Letter to the Philippians*, trans. F. R. Larcher and M. Duffy (Albany, NY: Magi Books, 1969); the passage I cited is found on p. 113 of the translation.
98 Someone might suppose that Paul and Aquinas are here both talking just about the incarnate Christ, and so Aquinas's lines have to do just with a human person. But, on Aquinas's view, the incarnate Christ is just one person and that person is divine. (See Chapter 14 on the incarnation for discussion of this claim.) Consequently, even if 'Lord' in this connection refers to Christ, the person to whom it refers is a divine person. Therefore, the point being made in the text stands, even on this interpretation of 'Lord'.
99 Cf. *ST* Ia.19.3.
100 There are elements of Aquinas's theology not directly relevant to those under consideration here that suggest he is not entitled to this claim; see Kretzmann (1983, esp. pp. 632–638).
101 It is clear that this account rests on a particular understanding of potentiality, one that distinguishes sharply between potentiality and real possibility. An exposition of Aquinas's theory of potentiality is outside the scope of this chapter, but such an exposition is more than is needed for present purposes in any case. Aquinas's solution to the problem of freedom and conditional necessity, which rests on his notion of potentiality, is a solution to a problem raised by his claim that God is essentially without unactualized potentialities. Consideration of whether his use of '*potentia*' matches the prevailing use of the word 'potentiality' is, then, in an important respect irrelevant to an evaluation of his position; the problem and his solution to it could always be reformulated in different terminology. So in this context the only important consideration regarding Aquinas's conception of potentiality is whether or not it is consistent, and there is no reason to think that it is not.
102 Christopher Hughes raised an objection of this sort to an earlier version of this position.
103 Most of this treatment of the issue of religious morality is adapted from Norman Kretzmann, "Abraham, Isaac, and Euthyphro: God and the Basis of Morality", in D.Stump *et al.* (1983, pp. 27–50).
104 For an interesting, sophisticated treatment of divine-command theories of morality, see, e.g., Philip Quinn, *Divine Commands and Moral Requirements* (Oxford: Clarendon Press, 1978) and Robert Merrihew Adams, "A Modified

Divine Command Theory of Ethical Wrongness", in Gene Outka and John P. Reeder, Jr. (eds), *Religion and Morality* (Garden City, NY: Doubleday Anchor, 1973), pp. 318–347; R. M. Adams, "Divine Command Metaethics Modified Again", *Journal of Religious Ethics* 7 (1979): 66–79; and R. M. Adams, "Divine Commands and the Social Nature of Obligation", *Faith and Philosophy* 4:3 (July 1987): 262–275. For Adams's most recent work on ethics and religion, see *Finite and Infinite Goods: A Framework for Ethics* (New York: Oxford University Press, 1999).

105 See Chapter 2 on goodness for more discussion of these issues.

106 See also Scott MacDonald (ed.), *Being and Goodness* (Ithaca, NY: Cornell University Press, 1991).

107 See, e.g., "On the Radical Origination of Things", trans. Leroy E. Loemker in *Gottfried Wilhelm Leibniz: Philosophical Papers and Letters*, 2nd edn (Dordrecht: D. Reidel, 1969), pp. 486–491.

108 In his book *The Existence of God* (Oxford: Clarendon Press, 1979), p. 132.

109 Swinburne (1979, p. 130).

110 William Rowe, "Rationalistic Theology and Some Principles of Explanation", *Faith and Philosophy* 1 (1984): 357–369.

4 God's eternity

1 At least one contemporary philosopher of religion has rejected the concept of divine eternality on the grounds that it is incompatible with biblical theology and, in particular, with the doctrine of divine redemption. "God the Redeemer cannot be a God eternal. This is so because God the Redeemer is a God who changes" (Nicholas Wolterstorff, "God Everlasting", in Clifton J. Orlebeke and Lewis B. Smedes (eds), *God and the Good* [Grand Rapids, MI: Eerdmans, 1975], pp. 181–203, on p. 182). It will become clear in the course of this chapter that, pace Wolterstorff, Aquinas's interpretation of God as eternal can be shown to be compatible with the other doctrines of orthodox Christianity, including the doctrine of redemption, even in their biblical formulations. Passages that have been or might be offered in evidence of a biblical conception of divine eternality include Malachi 3:6; John 8:58; James 1:17.

2 For other defenses of Aquinas's position, see Brian Leftow, *Time and Eternity* (Ithaca, NY: Cornell University Press, 1991), whose interpretation of the doctrine of eternity is somewhat different from that defended in this chapter.

3 Ed. E. K. Rand, in H. F. Stewart, E. K. Rand, and S. J. Tester, *Boethius: The Theological Tractates and The Consolation of Philosophy* (London and Cambridge, MA: Harvard University Press, 1973). The extract source is *CP*, 422.5–424.31.

4 There are at least two misleading features of this passage. In the first place, Boethius says that God's eternality *always* has to do with present *time*. In the second place, Boethius's etymology of 'sempiternity' is mistaken. '*Sempiternitas*' is an abstract noun constructed directly on '*semper*', somewhat as we might construct 'alwaysness'. His etymology is not only false but misleading, associating 'sempiternity' with 'eternity' in a context in which he has been distinguishing between sempiternity and eternity. Extract source is *DT*, 20.64–22.77.

5 Cf. Romano Ameno, "Probabile fonte della nozione boeziana di eternità", *Filosofia* I (1950); 365–373. See also note 6 below.

6 "*Aeternitas igitur est interminabilis vitae tota simul et perfecta possessio*", *CP*, p. 422.9–11. This definition closely parallels the definition developed by Plotinus in *Enneads* iii 7: "The life, then, which belongs to that which exists and is in being, all together and full, completely without-extension-or-interval, is what

we are looking for, eternity" (A. H. Armstrong (ed.), *Plotinus* (London and Cambridge, MA: Harvard University Press, 1967), vol. 3, p. 304.37–39). The way in which Boethius introduces eternity suggests that he considers himself to be presenting a familiar philosophical concept associated with a recognized definition. The parallel between the Plotinian and Boethian definitions is closest in their middle elements: 'z   *homou pasa kai plerës*' / '*vitae tota simul et perfecta*'. Plotinus describes the possessor of this life, and Boethius does not; but, in view of the fact that Boethius is talking about God, he, too, would surely describe the possessor of eternity as 'that which exists and is in being'. The most interesting difference between the two definitions is that the Plotinian has 'completely without-extension-or-interval' and the Boethian has 'illimitable', which suggests that Boethius takes eternity to include duration but Plotinus does not. In the rest of *Enneads* iii 7, however, Plotinus goes on to derive duration from his definition and to stress its importance in the concept. For an excellent presentation and discussion of Plotinus on eternity and time, see Werner Beierwaltes, *Plotin über Ewigkeit und Zeit* (*Enneade* iii 7) (Frankfurt am Main: Klostermann, 1967).

7   The many medieval discussions of the possibility that the world is 'eternal' really concern the possibility that it is sempiternal, and most often their concern is only with the possibility that the world had no beginning in time. Thomas Aquinas provides an important summary and critique of such discussions in *SCG* II.32–8.

8   See, e.g.,*CP,* p. 424.51–56.

9   The weight of tradition both before and after Boethius strongly favors interpreting illimitable life as involving infinite duration, beginningless as well as endless. Boethius throughout the *Consolation*, and especially in passage *CP*, is plainly working in the Platonic tradition, and both Plato and Plotinus understand eternal existence in that sense. See, e.g., Plato, *Timaeus* 37d–38c; Plotinus, *Enneads* iii 7 (and cf. note 6 above). Augustine, who is an earlier and in general an even more important source for medieval philosophy and theology than Boethius and who is even more clearly in the Platonist tradition, understands and uses this classic concept of eternity (see, e.g., *Confessions*, Bk. xi, ch. 11; *The City of God*, Bk. xi, ch. 21); but his influence on the medieval discussion of eternity seems not to have been so direct or important as Boethius's. As for the period after Boethius, Aquinas, e.g., also interprets the element of illimitable life in the notion of eternity as involving duration, as I show below.

10   Notice that these characteristics of a temporal entity's possession of its life apply not just to finite temporal lives but even to a temporal life of beginningless, endless duration – a sempiternal life.

11   *QDV* 12.6: "it belongs to God to cognize future things as present, with certainty, as Boethius says, because his gaze is measured by eternity, which is all at once (*totum simul*)".

12   See, e.g., *QDV* 2.12.

13   *ST* Ia.10.1 obj.2.

14   Cf. also *ST* Ia.39.8 obj.1 and corpus; *ST* Ia.46.1 obj.8 and ad 8.

15   In "Time(s), Eternity, and Duration" (*International Journal for Philosophy of Religion* 22 [1987]: 3–19) Herbert Nelson claims that it is a mistake to include Aquinas among those who take duration to be part of the concept of eternity, even though Nelson himself concedes that Aquinas uses the Latin term translated 'duration' to characterize the existence of a timeless God (ibid., p. 11). Nelson cites *In Sent.* VIII.2.1 ad 6 in support of this view (ibid., p. 11, n. 10). Aquinas does distinguish eternity from duration in that text as well as in other passages in that same article. But Nelson has apparently overlooked the parallel

between this discussion in Aquinas's early *Sentences* commentary and that in *ST* Ia.10.1, which contains his more mature views on the same issues. Both texts present six precisely parallel objections to the claim that the Boethian definition of eternity is correct. But for each passage in the *Sentences* commentary that separates eternity and duration, the corresponding passage in *ST* unequivocally unites them. e.g., although Obj. 2 in each text argues that *existence* ought to replace *life* in the definition, the argument in *ST* (though not in the relevant passage in the *Sentences* commentary) is based on a premiss that eternity signifies "a sort of duration", a premiss that Aquinas leaves unchallenged in his rejoinder to the objection. Again, in both texts Obj. 4 argues that the phase 'all at once' should not be included in the definition. The objection's argument in the *Sentences* commentary depends on the claim that the definition of duration includes having non-simultaneous parts, a definition that obviously cannot be applied to successionless eternity. But that part of the argument is omitted from the parallel objection in *ST*. Finally, Obj. 6 in both texts argues against the inclusion of *possession* in the definition, and the objection's argument is based on the claim that eternity has the essential character (*ratio*) of duration. But that claim is disputed in the rejoinder to Obj. 6 in the *Sentences* commentary, whereas in the parallel passage in *ST* it is accepted and the reply instead stresses the absence of change and loss in this mode of existence. So it seems reasonable to infer that any worries Aquinas may have had at an early stage of his career about attributing duration to eternity he had abandoned some fourteen years later, when he wrote *ST* Ia.

16 So, e.g., Anthony Kenny says: "The whole concept of a timeless eternity, the whole of which is simultaneous with every part of time, seems to be radically incoherent." ("Divine Foreknowledge and Human Freedom", in Anthony Kenny (ed.), *Aquinas: A Collection of Critical Essays* (Garden City, NY: Anchor Books, 1969), p. 264). Elsewhere, in discussing Aquinas's concept of God as eternal, Kenny says, "the doctrine of a timeless person is an incoherent one" (*The God of the Philosophers*, Oxford: Clarendon Press, 1979, p. 40).

17 To talk of events constituting the life of God is to speak only roughly and analogously; for some explanation of the problems with this locution, cf. Chapter 3 on God's simplicity.

18 *ST* Ia.10.11.

19 *QDV* 12.6.

20 *QDV* 12.6 corpus.

21 *ST* Ia.14.13; see also *SCG* I.66.

22 In the interest of simplicity and brevity, the subsequent discussion will focus largely on coexistence, taking it as covering co-occurrence too.

23 The medieval concept of the *aevum* or of *aeviternitas* is complicated but it does not seem to be the concept of a third mode of existence, on a par with time and eternity. See, e.g., *ST* Ia.10.5–6.

24 *ST* Ia.10.4 obj.1.

25 *ST* Ia.10.4 ad 1.

26 For careful discussion of the connections between relativity theory and the doctrine of eternity, see William Lane Craig, *Time and Eternity: Exploring God's Relationship to Time* (Wheaton, IL: Crossway, 2001) and *God, Time and Eternity* (Dordrecht: Kluwer Academic Publishers, 2001). Craig's conclusions are opposed to those of this chapter, but it is not possible to look at his arguments in detail here.

27 The adaptation of this example is a simplified version of Wesley C. Salmon's presentation of it in his *Space, Time, and Motion* (Minneapolis, MN: University of Minnesota Press, 1980), pp. 73–81. For my purposes here, it is sufficient simply

to cite the example. An understanding of its significance for relativity theory requires a consideration of a presentation as full (and clear) as Salmon's.

28 Salmon (1980, pp. 73–76).

29 It is important to understand that by 'observer' in this context I mean only that thing, animate or inanimate, with respect to which the reference frame is picked out and with respect to which the simultaneity of events within the reference frame is determined. In the train example there are two human observers, but the example could have been set up just as well if the observers had been nothing more than devices, primitive or sophisticated, for recording flashes of light.

30 I am here making use of a revision of the original definition of ET-simultaneity which Norman Kretzmann and I devised in our "Eternity", *Journal of Philosophy* 78 (1981): 429–458. We presented and defended the revised definition in our "Eternity, Awareness, and Action", *Faith and Philosophy* 9 (1992): 463–482. Cf. also our "Prophecy, Past Truth, and Eternity", in James Tomberlin (ed.), *Philosophical Perspectives*, 5 (1991): 395–424.

31 And, of course, there may not be more than one; cf. Chapter 3 on God's simplicity.

32 Since no eternal entity or event can itself be an element in a temporal series, no temporal entity or event can be earlier or later than the whole life or than any part of the life of an eternal entity. It is not clear that it makes sense to think in terms of parts of atemporal duration (cf. *ST* Ia.10.1 ad 3); but even if it does, it cannot make sense to think of any such part as earlier or later than anything temporal. If the Battle of Waterloo were earlier than some part of atemporal duration, it would be uniquely simultaneous with one other part of atemporal duration, in which case one part of atemporal duration would be earlier than another, which is impossible.

33 In the development of the classic concept of eternity, geometric models were sometimes introduced in an attempt to clarify the relationship I am here calling ET-simultaneity. There are passages in Boethius's work, for instance (*Consolation*, Bk. iv, prose 6; *De trinitate*, pp. 364.78–366.82), which suggests that Boethius took the relationship between time and eternity to be analogous to that between the circumference and the center of a circle. Aquinas developed this sort of analogy in connection with an account of an eternal entity's apprehension of temporal events:

> Furthermore, God's understanding, just like his being, does not have succession; it is, therefore, always enduring all at once, which belongs to the nature of eternity. The duration of time, on the other hand, is extended in the succession of before and after. Thus the relationship of eternity to the whole duration of time is like the relationship of an indivisible to a continuum – not indeed of an indivisible that is a limit of the continuum, which is not present to each part of the continuum (an instant of time bears a likeness to that), but of the indivisible that is outside the continuum and nevertheless coexists with each part of the continuum or with a designated point in the continuum. For, since time does not extend beyond change, eternity, which is entirely beyond change, is nothing belonging to time; on the other hand, since the being of what is eternal is never lacking, eternity in its presentness is present to each time or instant of time. A sort of example of this can be seen in a circle. For a designated point on the circumference, although it is an indivisible, does not coexist together with another point as regards position since it is the order of position that produces the continuity of the circumference. But the centre, which is

outside the circumference, is directly opposite any designated point on the circumference. In this way, whatever is in any part of time coexists with what is eternal as being present to it even though past or future with respect to another part of time. But nothing can coexist with what is eternal in its presentness except as a whole, for it does not have the duration of succession. And so in its eternity the divine understanding perceives as present whatever takes place during the whole course of time. It is not the case, however, that what takes place in a certain part of time has been existent always. It remains, therefore, that God has knowledge of those things that, as regards the course of time, are not yet.

(*SCG* I.66)

34 In *The Consolation of Philosophy* Boethius introduces and develops the concept of eternity primarily in order to argue that divine omniscience is compatible with human freedom, and he does so by demonstrating that omniscience on the part of an eternal entity need not, cannot, involve foreknowledge.

35 This way of looking at eternity and time need not conflict with the idea that there is an absolute temporal present, that temporal passage is real rather than mind-dependent. One frame of reference in respect of which to determine presentness might be all of time itself.

36 The claim that Antichrist's birth is really future rests on the assumption around which we all organize our lives, the view that the temporal present is absolute, that the expressions 'the present', 'the past', and 'the future' are uniquely (and differently) referring expressions on each occasion of their use, that 'now' is an essential indexical. On the notion of an essential indexical see John Perry, "The Problem of the Essential Indexical", *Nous* 13 (1979): 3–21.

37 Most clearly in fr. 8. For excellent examples of both sides of the controversy over the presence of the concept of eternity in Parmenides, see G. E. L. Owen, "Plato and Parmenides on the Timeless Present", *Monist* L (1966): 317–340; and Malcolm Schofield, "Did Parmenides Discover Eternity?", *Archiv für Geschichte der Philosophie* 52 (1970): 113–135.

38 See notes 6 and 9 above.

39 For some discussion of this analysis of time in Aristotle and Augustine, see Fred Miller, "Aristotle on the Reality of Time", *Archiv für Geschichte der Philosophie* 61 (1974): 132–155; and Norman Kretzmann, "Time Exists – But Hardly, or Obscurely (*Physics* iv, 10; 217b29–218a33)", *Aristotelian Society Supplementary Volume* I (1976), pp. 91–114.

40 See, e.g., Herbert Nelson, "Time(s), Eternity, and Duration", *International Journal for Philosophy of Religion* 22 (1987): 3–19; cf. also Paul Fitzgerald, "Stump and Kretzmann on Time and Eternity", *The Journal of Philosophy* 82 (1985): 260–269.

41 For a good, brief introduction, see James F. Ross, "Analogy as a Rule of Meaning for Religious Language", *International Philosophical Quarterly* 1 (1961): 468–502 (reprinted in A. Kenny (ed.), *Aquinas: A Collection of Critical Essays* (Garden City, NY: Doubleday & Co., 1969); for a more extended treatment, see James Ross's *Portraying Analogy* (Cambridge: Cambridge University Press, 1981).

42 For further discussion of Aquinas's views on this issue, see Chapter 3 on God's simplicity.

43 *ST* Ia.13.5.

44 *ST* Ia.13.5.

45 *QQ* 12.2.un.

46 William Kneale has taken this notion to be genuinely incoherent and among the most important reasons for rejecting the classic concept of eternity. See his

"Time and Eternity in Theology", *Proceedings of the Aristotelian Society* 61 (1960): 87–108; also his article "Eternity" in Paul Edwards (ed.), *The Encyclopedia of Philosophy* (New York: Macmillan, 1967), vol. 3, pp. 63–66. Cf. Martha Kneale, "Eternity and Sempiternity", *Proceedings of the Aristotelian Society,* 69 (1968–9): 223–238.

47 *ST* Ia.18.3.
48 *SCG* I.98.
49 *SCG* I.99.
50 *SCG* I.89.
51 *SCG* I.90.
52 Cf., e.g., *SCG* I.90–91.
53 *SCG* I.91.
54 Anthony Kenny, "Divine Foreknowledge and Human Freedom", in A. Kenny (ed.), *Aquinas: A Collection of Critical Essays* (Garden City, NY: Anchor Books, 1969), pp. 255–70, 264.
55 *ST* Ia.22.2.
56 For arguments to this same conclusion based on divine simplicity, see Chapter 3 on God's simplicity.
57 Nelson Pike, *God and Timelessness* (London: Routledge and Kegan Paul, 1970), pp. 104–105.
58 Cf., e.g., *SCG* II.15–17.
59 Cf., e.g., *ST* IIaIIae.83.
60 For Aquinas's account of these and related issues, see Chapter 14 on the incarnation.
61 *SCG* II.19.
62 These ambiguities, like the two interpretations provided for consideration I above, are of the sort extensively investigated by medieval logicians under their distinction between the compounded and divided senses of propositions. Thus (9a) and (10a) present the compounded senses of propositions (9) and (10), whereas (9b) and (10b) present their divided senses.

63   One can be immediately aware only of what is *present* for one to be aware of; what else, after all, can 'immediate' mean? If God is timeless, he can be immediately aware of (supposedly) temporal facts only if these facts *really are* timeless after all. If, on the other hand, the world really is temporal, only a temporal God can be immediately aware of it – and then only of its *present*, not of its past or future

                                     (William Hasker, *God, Time, and Knowledge*, Ithaca, NY, and London: Cornell University Press, 1989, p. 169)

64 *In Gal* 5.6. There is an English translation of this work: *Commentary on Saint Paul's Epistle to the Galatians by St. Thomas Aquinas*, trans. F. R. Larcher and Richard Murphy (Albany, NY: Magi Books, 1966); for this passage, see pp. 179–180.
65 *ST* Ia.43.3.
66 Consider relationships of direct awareness in which the subject and object are of different orders of dimensionality. A three-dimensional observer can be and very frequently is effortlessly aware of a two-dimensional object as such; an imagined two-dimensional observer could not be aware of a three-dimensional object as three-dimensional.
67 For more discussion of what is needed in general for God to be responsive to human beings, see Chapter 3 on God's simplicity.
68 I Samuel 1: 9–20.

69 For a discussion of other philosophical problems associated with petitionary prayer see Eleonore Stump, "Petitionary Prayer", *American Philosophical Quarterly*, 16 (1979): 81–91.

70 But see Chapter 14 on the incarnation.

71 *ST* IIIa.16.8.

72 In connection with statements such as (14), Aquinas introduces a nuance which is interesting but not relevant to my purposes here. On his view, the *qua* qualification can be omitted any time no one could be in any doubt that it is needed, as in the case of the statement that Christ died, since (in Aquinas's view) no one could suppose that death can be attributed to God. He says:

> we do not say that an Ethiopian is white, but that he is white with regard to his teeth, but we do say without a determination that he is curly, because [curliness] could be fittingly attributed to him only with regard to his hair.
> (*ST* IIIa.16.8)

73 Cf., e.g., *ST* IIIa.16.1 and IIIa.16.4, where Aquinas says that since Christ is one hypostasis, even though he has two natures, the same names can be applied to that one hypostasis.

74 Although Boethius treats of the incarnation and the dual nature of Christ in his theological tractates, especially in his *Contra Eutychen et Nestorium*, he does not apply his concept of eternity in those discussions as Aquinas applies it. (For Aquinas's views on the incarnation of Christ and especially on the dual nature of Christ, see Chapter 14 on the incarnation.)

75 Including, e.g., God's knowledge of what time it is now, the compatibility of omniscience and immutability, and the openness of the future, among many others. For some consideration of such additional issues, cf. Eleonore Stump and Norman Kretzmann, "Eternity", *Journal of Philosophy* 78 (1981): 429–458; "Eternity, Awareness, and Action", *Faith and Philosophy* 9 (1992): 463–482; and "Prophecy, Past Truth, and Eternity", in James Tomberlin (ed.), *Philosophical Perspectives*, 5 (1991): 395–424.

76 Aristotle, *Nicomachean Ethics*, vi, 2.

77 Although the concept of *the* past, dependent on the concept of the absolute temporal present, has no application for an eternal entity, for an omniscient eternal entity there is the awareness of your past, your present, your future as of 1 January 1970, and of your past, your present, your future as of 1 January 1980, and so on for every temporal entity of any date in its duration.

78 These observations regarding God's relationship to the past might suggest further issues regarding petitionary prayer. It is obviously absurd to pray in 1980 that Napoleon win at Waterloo when one knows what God does not bring about at Waterloo, but it might not seem absurd – at least not in the same way – to pray in 1980 that Napoleon lose at Waterloo. After all, your prayer and the battle are alike present to God; why should your prayer not be efficacious in bringing about Napoleon's defeat? But, as a petition addressed to the will of God, a prayer is also an expression of the will of the one who prays it, and any temporal entity who prays in 1980, 'Let Napoleon lose at Waterloo', is to that extent pretending to have atemporal knowledge and an atemporal will. The only appropriate version of that prayer is 'Let Napoleon have lost at Waterloo', and for one who knows the outcome of the battle more than a hundred and fifty years ago, that prayer is pointless and in that sense absurd. But a prayer prayed in ignorance of the outcome of a past event is not pointless in that way. (I am thus disagreeing with Peter Geach, when he claims that "A prayer for something to have happened is simply an absurdity, regardless of the utterer's

knowledge or ignorance of how things went" (*God and the Soul* (London: Routledge and Kegan Paul, 1969), p. 90.) On the hypothesis that there is an eternal, omniscient, omnipotent God, the praying of such a prayer would indeed qualify as "the only instance of behaviour, on the part of ordinary people whose mental processes we can understand, designed to affect the past and coming quite naturally to us" (Michael Dummett, "Bringing About the Past", *Philosophical Review* 73 (1964): 341). Dummett does not draw on the concept of divine eternality, but, if it is acceptable in its own right, its introduction would lead to a modification and strengthening of some of the claims he makes – e.g., "I am not asking God that, even if my son has drowned, He should *now* make him not to have drowned; I am asking that, at the time of the disaster, He should then have made my son not to drown at that time" (ibid., p. 342).

79 What I present here is essentially Boethius's line against the suggestion that divine omniscience and human freedom are incompatible, a line in which he was followed by many medievals, especially Aquinas. On Aquinas's use of the Boethian solution, see Kenny (1969).

80 *QDV* 2.12.

81 Various thinkers have raised sophisticated and complicated objections to the position Aquinas adopts in this connection; space does not permit a more detailed evaluation of those objections here. For some consideration of these issues, see Stump and Kretzmann (1991).

82 *QDV* 2.12 ad 1.

83 *QDV* 2.12 ad 2.

5 God's knowledge

1 What exactly the doctrine of impassibility is on Aquinas's understanding of it is a matter worth investigation. For some discussion, see Chapter 3 on God's simplicity.

2 Leo Elders, *The Philosophical Theology of St. Thomas Aquinas*, Studien und Texte zur Geistesgeschichte des Mittelalters (New York: E. J. Brill, 1990).

3 Elders (1990, p. 234).

4 Elders (1990, p. 230).

5 Elders (1990, p. 234).

6 Elders (1990, p. 238).

7 Brian Shanley, "Eternal Knowledge of the Temporal in Aquinas", *American Catholic Philosophical Quarterly* 71 (1997): 205. (For a reply to this paper of Shanley's, see Eleonore Stump and Norman Kretzmann, "Eternity and God's Knowledge: A Reply to Shanley", *The American Catholic Philosophical Quarterly* 72 (1998): 439–445.)

8 See, e.g., *SCG* I.66.

9 *QDV* 2.8.

10 See, e.g., *ST* IaIIae.79.1. Cf.also Norman Kretzmann, "God Among the Causes of Moral Evil: Hardening of Hearts and Spiritual Blinding", *Philosophical Topics* 16 (1988): 189–214.

11 In "Divine Causation and Human Freedom in Aquinas", *American Catholic Philosophical Quarterly* 72 (1998): 99–122, Brian Shanley seems to think it is possible to reconcile freedom and divine causality by showing that for Aquinas even the free human will is not independent of God. Certainly, for Aquinas, nothing creaturely is independent of God. But the problem is this. For Aquinas, human beings have *liberum arbitrium*, and *liberum arbitrium* is the ability to do otherwise than one does: "we are said to have *liberum arbitrium* because we can take up one thing, having rejected another, which is what it is to choose." (*ST*

Ia.83.3). On Shanley's interpretation of Aquinas as holding that God's knowledge is causal, however, God causes everything (or everything temporal) that he knows. Since God knows human acts, on Shanley's view God's knowledge causes those human acts. But if God causes human acts, then in what sense is it possible for any human being to act otherwise than she does? Clearly, it is not possible that God cause a person to do some act A and yet she does not-A. Is 'ability to do otherwise' here supposed to have just the compatibilist sense of 'ability to do otherwise if one chose to do otherwise'? On compatibilism, there is no genuinely open future for human beings; on the theological analogue to compatibilism, there is no genuinely open future for human beings because God determines the future in every respect. Surely, that is not the view Shanley means us to attribute to Aquinas. And yet in what sense is there an open future for human beings if God knows the future and God's knowledge causes everything he knows? Furthermore, Shanley seems not to recognize what his view of God's knowledge as causal commits him to. He says, "God moves the will efficiently by inclining it interiorly. How this can be so without violating human freedom is the key question" (Shanley, 1998, p. 112; footnote omitted). But if God's knowledge is causal, as Shanley argues, God does not just incline the will interiorly. He causes it to be in whatever state it is in. If God did not cause the states of the will, he would not know them, on Shanley's view. Shanley argues that God's action on the will "is not coercive" (ibid., p. 113). But, on Shanley's view, if a human will is in state A, God knows that it is, and his knowing it causes the will to be in state A. And it is very hard to see how God's *causing* the will to be in state A does not constitute coercing the will to be in state A. Is it possible that God could cause the will to be in state A and yet the will could be in some other state?

12 *QDV* 2.15 ad 1.
13 Notice that this determinism is *causal* and therefore not to be confused with the much-discussed alleged incompatibility of divine foreknowledge and human freedom.
14 See, e.g., *ST* Ia.14.3 and *SCG* I.66.
15 *QDV* 2.12.
16 Elders (1990, p. 237).
17 Ibid., p.239.
18 Ibid., p.238.
19 See, e.g., *ST* Ia.14.13.
20 *ST* Ia.14.8.
21 *SCG* I.65.530.
22 *SCG* I.49.412.
23 See, e.g., *SCG* I.63.521, and *QDV* 10.4 obj. 5.
24 For some discussion of Aquinas's views of the means by which cognition arises, see Chapter 8 on the mechanisms of cognition.
25 *ST* Ia.55.2 obj. 1; *ST* Ia.14.1. 'Understand' is a standard translation of Aquinas's '*intelligere*', but it can be misleading. As Aquinas uses '*intelligere*', even a case of your recognizing that something you see is a tree counts as intellect's understanding. (For further discussion of Aquinas's views of the intellect and its operations, see Chapter 8 on the mechanisms of cognition.)
26 *ST* Ia.14.5.
27 *SCG* I.46.389.
28 *SCG* I.31.281. See also, e.g., *QDV* 8.10 and *ST* Ia.55.3.
29 For a brief but representative instance of this complaint, see Daniel Dennett, *Consciousness Explained* (Boston: Little, Brown, 1991), pp. 33–37.
30 See, e.g., *ST* Ia.85.1 and Ia.86.1, and *In DA* III.12–13.

31 *ST* Ia.14.6. See also, e.g., *SCG* I.65; *QDV* 2.5; *QDP* 6.1; and *In Sent* I.36.1.1.
32 *ST* Ia.14.11.
33 See, e.g., *SCG* III.76.
34 *ST* Ia.55.2. See also *ST* Ia.54.4 ad 1; and *QDV* 8.9.
35 *QQ* 7.1.3 ad 1.
36 *ST* Ia.89; see also *ST* Ia.55.3.
37 *QDV* 10.5 ad 6.
38 See, e.g., *QDV* 10.4.
39 *ST* Ia.57.2 s.c.
40 Another helpful analogue to God's knowledge is the knowledge the separated human soul is supposed to have after death but before the resurrection of the body. The separated soul also knows embodied individuals although it lacks corporeal senses; and Aquinas holds that after death it can cognize, as angels do, through forms that are not acquired from the cognized things. (See, e.g., *ST* Ia.89.1.3 and 4; and *QQ* 3.9.1.) The discussion we are about to develop could, therefore, have been based on the separated soul's cognition rather than on angelic cognition. But special problems in Aquinas's discussion of the knowledge separated souls are supposed to have make it more appropriate in this connection to focus on his account of angelic cognition.
41 *ST* Ia.55.3 ad 2.
42 See, e.g., *ST* Ia.57.1; Ia.85.1 and 5; and *In DA* III.8. See also Norman Kretzmann, "Infallibility, Error, and Ignorance", in Richard Bosley and Martin Tweedale (eds), *Aristotle and His Medieval Interpreters* (*Canadian Journal of Philosophy*, supplementary volume 17 [1991]), pp. 159–194.
43 See, e.g., *In DA* 111.8.705, 706, 712, and 713.
44 *In DA* III.8.712–713.
45 *In DA* III.8.712–713. See also, e.g., *ST* Ia.86.1 and Ia.85.1.
46 *In DA* III.8.718. See also *ST* Ia.85.2.
47 Oliver Sacks, *The Man Who Mistook His Wife for a Hat* (New York: Summit Books, 1985), p. 13. For an excellent recent neurobiological study of agnosias, see Martha J. Farah, *Visual Agnosia* (Cambridge, MA: MIT Press, 1990). In *Principles of Neural Science* by Eric Kandel, James Schwartz, and Thomas Jessell (New York: Elsevier, 1991), agnosia is defined as "the inability to perceive objects through otherwise normally functioning sensory channels" (p. 831). Not all agnosias are visual. e.g., astereognosia, which is caused by damage to the parietal cortex, is "an inability to recognize the form of objects by touch even though there is no pronounced loss of somatosensory sensitivity" (ibid.).
48 For the sake of brevity, I am glossing over many complications here, but two of them should be at least noted. In the first place, agnosia is a puzzling phenomenon. I introduce it here as a helpful illustration; but if the example were pressed, it would raise more questions than it answers. For instance, one odd feature of agnosia is that the patient plainly *can* identify *some* genus to which the thing he sees belongs. To cognize a glove as a continuous surface is to cognize that particular universally, but the universal serving as the medium of cognition in that case is very abstract, nothing like the thing's proximate genus, let alone its species. Second, although I present the discussion here in terms of the *quod quid est* of whatever is being cognized, what is at issue in cognizing a particular universally cannot be only the genera and species to which the cognized thing belongs. For the medievals, universals consist not only in genera and species but also in the rest of the predicables, including differentiae, propria, and accidents. Therefore, in recognizing that the thing he sees has five outpouchings, the agnosia patient is also cognizing a particular through the medium of a universal. And so any conscious awareness of any shareable charac-

teristic of any thing presented to the senses counts as cognizing that particular universally.

49 *ST* Ia.55.3.

50 Epistemic contact should be understood as a component in perception or in divine analogues to perception. Though I certainly do not have a set of necessary and sufficient conditions for the notion of epistemic contact, we can take a rough characterization of it from contemporary neurobiology. According to contemporary neurobiological theories of perception, after incoming sensory data have been processed at low levels, they are processed further by various other "modules" or "systems", including one that connects sensory data to conscious awareness and one that matches sensory data to information stored in associative memory. (For a clear, simple discussion of the connections between, e.g., visual sensory data and associative memory, see Stephen Kosslyn and Oliver Koenig, *Wet Mind: The New Cognitive Neuroscience* (New York: Macmillan, 1992), pp. 52–58.) By 'epistemic contact' I mean the result of the central nervous system's processing of sensory data that does *not* include the matching of the data to information stored in associative memory. I take this description of epistemic contact to be roughly equivalent to the following description in Aquinas's terms: the apprehension of the accidents of some extramental thing without any apprehension of that thing's *quod quid est*.

51 Since the prerequisite sensory experience in the case discussed here would typically be the experience of cups, it may seem that our representations have to be acquired from the particular extramental things cognized in order for there to be cognition of things outside the mind. But, of course, we can be and sometimes are equipped ahead of time with an intelligible form we need in order to recognize something the first time we encounter it. The acquisition of intelligible forms can be carried out conceptually, e.g., by imagination.

52 *QQ* 7.1.3.

53 *ST* Ia.85.2, s.c. See also *In DA* III.8.

54 In many passages, Aquinas is concerned to rule out the possibility that the intelligible form is itself the object of cognition in ordinary cases of cognition, in which people cognize external particulars. In his recent book *Cognition: An Epistemological Inquiry* (Houston, TX: Center for Thomistic Studies, 1992), Joseph Owens is similarly concerned to show that the direct object of the intellect is not an intelligible form but some extramental object. He is so concerned to rule out the possibility of skepticism, however, that he goes to the other extreme and maintains that for Aquinas there is unmediated awareness of things in the world. Aquinas's position seems to stand somewhere between the position Owens ascribes to him and the position Aquinas himself is ruling out. Owens is right to hold that the object of ordinary intellective cognition is part of extramental reality and not some internal state of the intellect's. But, on the other hand, it takes a process on the part of the intellect to reach the state in which it has cognition of some extramental object, and that process is mediated by intelligible forms. *Pace* Owens, then, an intelligible form is, therefore, the medium between the cognizer and the thing cognized. The nature of Aquinas's position can be seen clearly, e.g., in *QQ* 7.1.1:

> One should know that in intellective vision there can be three sorts of intermediary ... [The second sort of] intermediary is that by which it sees, and this is the intelligible species, which determines the possible intellect and is related to the possible intellect as the species of a rock is related to the eye [which sees the rock] ... Consequently, the first and the second

[sort of] intermediary do not produce mediated vision, for a person is said to see a rock immediately, although he sees it by means of a species of the rock received in the eye and by means of light.

55 For the difference between an intelligible form and a concept, on Aquinas's views, and the relation between them, see Chapter 8 on the mechanisms of cognition.

56 *QQ* 7.1.3, obj. 3.: "quamvis nihil recipiat, tamen formam quam apud se habebat prius, applicat ad particulare quod de novo fit"; ad 3: "applicatio illa est intelligenda per modum illum quo Deus ideas ad res cognoscendas applicat, non sicut medium cognoscibile ad aliud, sed sicut modus cognoscendi ad rem cognitam."

57 *ST* Ia.14.5.

58 In putting the point this way, I am simplifying for the sake of brevity. Aquinas's account has an additional complexity we cannot examine here. For some idea of the complexity, see *QDV* 2.3 and 4; also *QQ* 7.1.1.

59 *QDV* 2.3.

60 *QDV* 2.3.

61 There is, of course, a parallel problem regarding the way an immaterial entity can causally act on a material entity. But this is unlikely to have seemed problematic to a traditional theist such as Aquinas, who believes that an immaterial God causally affects his material creatures.

62 *ST* Ia.84.6.

63 For further discussion of this topic, see Chapter 8 on the mechanisms of cognition.

64 For some comparative discussion of these claims of Aquinas's about the workings of the intellect, see my "Ockham on Sensory Cognition", in Paul Spade (ed.), *The Cambridge Companion to Ockham* (Cambridge: Cambridge University Press, 1999), pp. 168–203.

65 For further discussion of these metaphysical views of Aquinas's, see Chapter 1 on Aquinas's theory of things.

66 *QQ* 7.1.3.

67 *QDV* 2.5. See also *QDV* 10.4.

68 *In DA* II.12.377.

69 *ST* Ia.85.1.

70 *In DA* III.8.712–13. See also, e.g., *ST* Ia.86.1 and Ia.85.1.

71 *QDV* 10.4. See also *QDV* 10.5 and 2.5–6.

72 For a clear and helpful statement of the nature of God's primary causality in its relation to a secondary cause, see *SCG* I.68, where Aquinas says:

> The control (*dominium*) which the will has over its own acts, by means of which there is in the will the power to will or not to will, excludes the determination of the power to one thing and [also] the violence of a cause which acts [on the will] from outside [the willer]. But it does not exclude the influence of a superior cause, from which the will has its being and its function. And so with respect to the motion of the will there remains the causality of the primary cause, which is God.

73 See Chapter 13 on grace and free will. I have also discussed God's causing acts of will in "Sanctification, Hardening of the Heart, and Frankfurt's Concept of Free Will", *Journal of Philosophy* 85 (1988): 395–420. Reprinted in John Martin Fischer and Mark Ravizza (eds), *Perspectives on Moral Responsibility* (Ithaca, NY: Cornell University Press, 1993), pp. 211–234; and "Augustine on Free Will", in

Eleonore Stump and Norman Kretzmann (eds), *The Cambridge Companion to Augustine* (Cambridge: Cambridge University Press, 2001), pp. 124–147.

74 Shanley (1997, p. 205).

75 *ST* Ia.15.2.

76 *ST* Ia.15.1 ad 2. See also *QDV* 3.2.

77 See, e.g., *QDV* 3.1: "ideas latine possumus dicere species vel formas." See also *QDV* 3.3: "idea est ratio rei, vel similitudo."

78 *QDV* 3.3. See also *ST* Ia.15.3 s.c.

79 *ST* Ia.15.1.

80 See, e.g., *ST* Ia.15.2.

81 *ST* Ia.14.8.

82 *QDV* 3.3. See also *QDV* 3.1.

83 *QQ* 7.1.3.

84 *ST* Ia.14.8 ad 3.

85 *SCG* I.66.

86 *QDP* 16.7 In our article "Eternity, Awareness, and Action" (*Faith and Philosophy* 9 [1992]: 463–482), Norman Kretzmann and I discuss some of the problems associated with epistemic and causal relationships between an eternal being and temporal beings.

87 *QDV* 10.4. See also *QDV* 3.1.

88 *QQ* 7.1.3 ad 3.

89 For Aquinas's theological understanding of the divine concept or inner word as the second person of the Trinity, see my "Word and Incarnation", in Marco Olivetti (ed.), *Incarnation* (Padua: Edam, 1999), pp. 543–554.

90 In correspondence Alvin Plantinga has suggested that it is a mistake to look for a mechanism by means of which God knows. He points out that we do not look for a mechanism by means of which God exercises his omnipotence. In the case of divine power we are content just to note that omnipotence enables God to do whatever is at issue, without investigating the means by which an omnipotent being could do what he does. This line has its attractions. It might also explain some of the peculiar slant of Aquinas's discussion of God's knowledge. Aquinas, too, might think there is nothing to discuss regarding the mechanism by means of which God knows, but that what must be discussed is how a simple God could know anything if knowledge requires representations or intelligible forms. If that is Aquinas's view, we should expect to find virtually nothing in his texts on how God applies his representations or makes epistemic contact with things but quite a lot on how a simple God can have intelligible forms in his intellect. So Plantinga's suggestion has some plausibility as the basis for an interpretation of Aquinas's approach. On the other hand, it also looks like a better line with which to end an investigation of God's knowledge than one with which to begin it.

91 *ST* Ia.14.11. See also *ST* Ia.57.1 and Ia.84.1.

92 *QQ* 3.2.3.

93 Shanley (1997, p. 205).

94 *SCG* I.66.550–51.

95 See, e.g., *SCG* 1.67.557. See also *CT* 1.133; *ST* Ia.14.13.

96 *QDP* 16.7.

97 See, e.g., *ST* Ia.14.9 and Ia.14.12; also *QDV* 2.12.

98 See, e.g., *ST* Ia.14.13: "Unde manifestum est quod contingentia et infallibiliter a Deo cognoscuntur, inquantum subduntur divino conspectui secundum suam pracentialitatem."

99 For this *a priori* truth, he also has Aristotelian authority: *De anima* II.11.423b26–424a10 and III.4.429a13–18.

100 See, e.g., *ST* IaIIae.22.1; Ia.79.2.
101 *ST* Ia.97.2.
102 *ST* Ia.79.2.
103 *In DA* III.9.722. See also *SCG* I.16.133: "quod est potentia, nondum est."
104 See note 66 above.
105 It is, of course, possible to suppose that evolution or God has constructed human beings in such a way that their cognitive processing yields reliable information about the world around them. For a critical discussion of such a claim about evolution, see Alvin Plantinga, *Warrant and Proper Function* (Oxford: Oxford University Press, 1993). But attempts to solve the puzzle by pointing to evolution or God's creative activity do not seem to get us very far if what we are interested in is the mechanism by which human cognitive processing is reliably related to what it cognizes.

6 Forms and bodies: the soul

1 Meditation VI, in *The Philosophical Writings of Descartes*, trans. John Cottingham, Robert Stoothoff and Dugald Murdoch (Cambridge: Cambridge University Press, 1984), vol. II, p. 54. In other places, Descartes seems to hold that a complete human being is a compound of body and soul; see, e.g., his reply to objections, in *The Philosophical Writings of Descartes*, vol. II, pp. 299–300. How this position is to be reconciled with the position in the quotation from Meditation VI is not entirely clear; but my interest in this paper is only in the dualism commonly associated with Descartes, regardless of whether or not Descartes himself actually held it. For discussion of the extent to which Descartes held Cartesian dualism, see, e.g., Margaret Wilson, *Descartes* (London: Routledge and Kegan Paul, 1978), pp. 177–185, and Tad Schmaltz, "Descartes and Malebranche on Mind and Mind–Body Union", *The Philosophical Review* 101 (1992): 281–325.
2 *QDSC* un.2.
3 *SCG* II.57.
4 *ST* Ia.89.1. For further discussion, see Chapter 7 on the foundations of knowledge.
5 *QDA* un.9.
6 For further discussion of the metaphysical issues raised here and in subsequent sections in connection with Aquinas's theory of forms, see Chapter 1 on Aquinas's theory of things.
7 See, e.g., *QDA* un.1.
8 *QDA* un.9.
9 *In DA* II.11.226.
10 Cf., e.g., *QDSC* un.3. For a good account of this medieval controversy over substantial forms, see, e.g., Anton Pegis, *St. Thomas and the Problem of the Soul in the Thirteenth Century* (Toronto: Pontifical Institute of Mediaeval Studies, reprinted 1983). See also the discussion in Chapter 1 on Aquinas's theory of things.
11 *ST* Ia.76.1.
12 *QDSC* un.2.
13 See, e.g., Ziwei Huang, Jean-Marc Gabriel, Michael Baldwin *et al.*, "Proposed Three-dimensional Structure for the Cellular Prion Protein", *Proceedings of the National Academy of Sciences*, 91 (1994): 7139–7143.
14 For a very helpful discussion of the history of the notion of emergent properties, see Brian McLaughlin, "The Rise and Fall of British Emergentism", in Ansgar Beckermann, Hans Flohr, and Jaegwon Kim (eds), *Emergence or Reduction? Essays*

on the Prospects of Nonreductive Physicalism (Berlin: Walter de Gruyter, 1992), pp. 49–93.

15 It is interesting to note that in Samuel Alexander's influential early account of emergent properties, they are identified with configurational patterns and explicitly associated with the historical distinction between matter and form. Alexander says: "To adopt the ancient distinction of form and matter, the kind of existent from which the new quality emerges is the 'matter' which assumes a certain complexity of configuration and to this pattern or universal corresponds the new emergent quality." (Quoted in Timothy O'Connor, "Emergent Properties", *American Philosophical Quarterly* 31 (1994): 91–104. O'Connor's article is a helpful discussion of emergent properties.) For a useful discussion of reasons for preferring one formulation of the notion of emergence over another, see Robert L. Klee, "Micro-determinism and Concepts of Emergence", *Philosophy of Science* 51 (1984): 44–63.

16 Cf., e.g., John Searle, *The Rediscovery of the Mind* (Cambridge, MA: MIT Press, 1992), p. 111.

17 Searle (1992, p. 112).

18 There is some room for ambiguity and confusion here. On some accounts of emergence, e.g., a property of a system is emergent if it could not have been predicted from knowledge of the properties of the parts of the system or if the microstructure of a system does not completely determine the property in question. But it is not entirely clear what is to count as the microstructure of the system or the properties of the parts. In particular, we can be thinking of the properties of the parts in two ways: (i) as the properties of the parts taken *singillatim*, that is, the properties had by the molecule's constituent elementary particles, taken individually, (ii) as the properties the parts in fact have when they are organized into the whole, that is, the properties the constituent elementary particles have in the configuration which the molecule has in its final, biologically active form. I am taking 'properties of the parts' in sense (i) here. In sense (i), it is true to say, as biochemists do, that the folded shape of a protein cannot always be derived from even perfect knowledge of the biochemical properties of the components of the protein, including their causal interactions (since it might be the case that the protein achieves that folded shape only with the help of enzymes, e.g.). It would not be true to say this in sense (ii). If we take 'properties of the parts' in sense (ii), then we smuggle the configuration, or the form of the whole, into the properties of the parts of the whole. In sense (ii), it would be very surprising if there were features of the whole system that were not explainable in terms of or determined by the causal interactions of the parts of the whole, since the features of the system are a function of the configuration of the whole and that configuration is in effect being counted among the properties of the parts.

19 See, e.g., Frederic M. Richards, "The Protein Folding Problem", *Scientific American* 264 (1991): 54–63. According to Richards, for relatively small proteins, folding is a function of the properties and causal potentialities among the constituents of the protein, but "some large proteins have recently been shown to need folding help from other proteins known as chaperonins" (ibid., p. 54). Richards thinks of proteins with 300 or fewer amino acids as small proteins.

20 Whether such an emergent property of a whole system should be counted as supervening on the properties of its components depends, in part, on two things. (The type of supervenience at issue here is what is sometimes called 'multiple domain supervenience'; see, e.g., Jaegwon Kim, "Supervenience for Multiple Domains", reprinted in *Supervenience and Mind* (Cambridge: Cambridge University Press, 1993), pp. 109–130. A helpful formulation of such a supervenience relation

with respect to wholes and parts is given in O'Connor 1994, p. 96). (1) Whether it is possible for the parts to have the properties they have without the whole system's having the emergent feature in question depends on what we think is to be included among the properties of the parts and whether the configuration of the whole is somehow included among them. If we think of the properties of the parts only in sense (i) of note 18 above, then the emergent property will not be supervenient on the properties of the parts, since it is possible for the parts to exist and have those properties without the whole's having the emergent property in question – as would be the case, e.g., if we synthesized a large protein but did not succeed in catalyzing its folding, so that it was not biologically active. (2) Whether it is possible to have the systems feature in question exemplified by different constituents with different properties is at least in part a function of how abstract the description of the systems feature at issue is. Being able to regulate genes is one thing; being able to regulate genes by fitting a leucine zipper of such-and-such a size into the major groove of a DNA helix is another. The intuitive idea behind supervenience is that the supervenient property is dependent upon and determined by the subvening properties. My point here is that whether or not we have such dependence and determination in the case of emergent properties depends, among other things, on whether or not the configuration of the whole is tacitly included among the properties of the parts and on the specificity with which we pick out the supervenient property.

21 Giving a principled distinction between configurations of material components that combine their components into one thing from those that bring the components together without combining them into one thing is difficult. (For a good account of the problems, see Peter van Inwagen, *Material Beings* (Ithaca, NY: Cornell University Press, 1990). It is not clear to me that Aquinas has the resources for giving an adequate distinction of this sort, but see, e.g., *In Meta* VII.17.1672–1674. There Aquinas says that in cases in which the composite is one thing, the composite is not identical with its components; rather the composite is something over and above its components.

22 *In Meta* VII.17.1673–1674.

23 For a helpful discussion of the general problem of reductionism relevant to the issues considered here, see Alan Garfinkel, "Reductionism", in Richard Boyd, Philip Gasper, and J.D. Trout (eds), *The Philosophy of Science* (Cambridge, MA: MIT Press, 1993), pp. 443–459. Garfinkel argues against reductionism by trying to show that reductive microexplanations are often not sufficient to explain the macrophenomena they are intended to explain and reduce. He says:

> A macrostate, a higher level state of the organization of a thing, or a state of the social relations between one thing and another can have a particular realization which, in some sense, "is" that state in this case. But the explanation of the higher order state will not proceed via the microexplanation of the microstate which it happens to "be". Instead, the explanation will seek its own level.
>
> (ibid., p. 449)

Aquinas would agree, and Aquinas's account of the relation of matter and form in material objects helps explain Garfinkel's point. In Aquinas's terminology, a biological system has a form as well as material constituents, so that the system is not identical to the material constituents alone; and some of the properties of the system are a consequence of the form of the system as a whole. Garfinkel himself recognizes the aptness of the historical distinction between matter and form for his argument against reductionism. He says, "the independence of levels of explanation … can be found in Aristotle's remark that in explanation it is the form and not the matter that counts" (1993, p. 149). See also Philip Kitcher, "1953 and All That: A Tale of Two Sciences", in *The Philosophy of Science*, op. cit., pp. 553–570. Kitcher, who rejects reductionism in biology, argues for the strongly anti-reductionist claim that sometimes descriptions of higher-level processes are needed to explain events at a lower level.

24 For an interesting contemporary argument against the reduction of wholes to their parts, see Peter van Inwagen, "Composition as Identity", in James Tomberlin (ed.), *Philosophical Perspectives*, vol. 8 (Atascadero, CA: Ridgeview Publishing Co., 1994), pp. 207–219.

25 *ST* Ia.3.2.

26 *QDSC* un.1 ad 5.

27 *ST* Ia.54.3 ad 2.

28 *ST* Ia.50.2.

29 In this connection, see also *SCG* II.51.

30 *ST* Ia.50.5.

31 *QDSC* un.1 ad 6.

32 See, e.g., the extensive discussion of angelic knowledge and willing in *ST* Ia.54–60.

33 *ST* Ia.54.5.

34 *ST* Ia.54.5.

35 Cf., e.g., *ST* Ia.75.6.

36 Cf., e.g., *ST* Ia.76.1.

37 See, e.g., *ST* Ia.76.1.

38 See, e.g., *ST* Ia.75.7 ad 3 and *QDA* un.8.

39 *QDSC* un.2 ad 3.

40 *QDSC* un.2 ad 5.

41 Cf., e.g., *ST* Ia.75.3.

42 See, e.g., *QDSC* un.4.

43 *ST* Ia.76.4.

44 *ST* Ia.76.6 ad 1.

45 *ST* Ia.75.1.

46 *ST* Ia.75.5.

47 For some arguments that the soul is simple in the way that a point is, see Philip Quinn, "Tiny Selves: Chisholm on the Simplicity of the Soul", in Louis E. Hahn (ed.), *Roderick M. Chisholm* (Chicago: Open Court Press, 1997).

48 *QDA* un.10 ad 18.

49 *QDA* un.9 ad 14.

50 *QDSC* un.2 ad 16.

51 Aquinas therefore would not agree with Hoffman and Rosencrantz, who define the soul as lacking a spatial location. See Joshua Hoffman and Gary Rosencrantz, "Are Souls Unintelligible?", in James Tomberlin (ed.), *Philosophical Perspectives*, vol. 5 (Atascadero, CA: Ridgeview Publishing Co., 1991), p. 183.

52 *ST* Ia.76.8. See also the discussion in *QDA* un.10 and *SCG* II.72.

53 *ST* Ia.78.4.

54 *ST* Ia.75.2 ad 2; emphasis added.

55 *ST* Ia.76.1.

56 Contrast Chisholm here, who uses 'soul' to mean the same thing as 'person'. See Roderick Chisholm, "On the Simplicity of the Soul", in James Tomberlin (ed.), *Philosophical Perspectives*, vol. 5, op. cit., p. 167.

57 *ST* Ia.75.4.

58 The possible identification of human agents that Chisholm quickly dismisses, namely, that a human person is his (living) body, is therefore close to the one Aquinas espouses; for Aquinas, the 'is' in that claim must be the 'is' of constitution (see Chapter 1 on Aquinas's theory of things for a discussion of Aquinas's views of constitution and identity). Chisholm's reasons for rejecting this include his mereological essentialism and his conviction that a person could lose a part of his body and still continue to exist. Aquinas shares Chisholm's conviction that a person can persist through the loss of a part of his substance, but he would not accept Chisholm's mereological essentialism for human beings. See Roderick Chisholm, "On the Simplicity of the Soul", in James Tomberlin (ed.), *Philosophical Perspectives*, vol. 5, op. cit., p. 168.

59 In some versions of the Porphyrian tree in logic texts, e.g., *'corpus'* is the name for the genus that encompasses all material things, both animate and inanimate.

60 Cf., e.g., *QDSC* un.3 ad 12 and ad 13. The production of a human body is not itself instantaneous; Aquinas does not think that at conception the fetus is a human being.

61 *QDA* un.1 obj.12.

62 *SCG* II.51.

63 Aquinas's general argument for the soul's ability to exist on its own apart from matter depends crucially on the premiss that the soul's operation of intellective cognition is an operation which could not be carried out by any material organ of a body, as vision *is* carried out, on his view, by the eye.

64 *QDSC* un.2.

65 *QDSC* un.2.

66 There are other disanalogies as well. e.g., the enzyme is a substance in its own right; the soul is not.

67 *ST* Ia.65.4.

68 See, e.g., *ST* Ia.90.2.

69 See, e.g., *ST* Ia.118.2.

70 *ST* Ia.90.4.

71 See, e.g., *ST* Ia.76.3 ad 3.

72 *ST* Ia.118.2–3.

73 *ST* Ia.118.2 ad 5.

74 But see also the other issues having to do with the individuation of the soul discussed in Chapter 1 on Aquinas's theory of things.

75 *QDA* un.1 ad 2.

76 Shoemaker gives no indication that he thinks the BST device is person-preserving only in case it transfers brain states instantaneously or that brain states are such that they can be transferred only if the process of transfer takes no time.

77 See Sydney Shoemaker and Richard Swinburne, *Personal Identity* (Oxford: Basil Blackwell, 1984), pp. 108–111.

78 *ST* Ia.75.2 ad 1. It is not entirely clear what Aquinas has in mind with the distinction between a complete and an incomplete substance, but the idea seems to be something like this: the definition of an incomplete substance will include reference to a primary substance, as the definition of a complete substance will not.

79 See *QDA* un.1 corpus and ad 3, and *ST* IaIIae.72.2, where Aquinas says:

> things are found to differ in species in two ways, in one way from the fact that each [of the differing things] has a [different] complete species, as a horse and a cat differ in species, and in another way insofar as difference in species is found in accordance with difference in the degree of some genera-

tion or motion, as a building is a complete generation of a house, but the laying of the foundation and the raising of a wall constitute an incomplete species.

See also *In DA* II.1.215.

80 *ST* Ia.75.4 ad 2.
81 *QDSC* un.2 ad 16.
82 *SCG* II.51.
83 *SCG* II.69.
84 Swinburne is therefore mistaken in claiming that on Aquinas's view a soul is itself a substance; see Sydney Shoemaker and Richard Swinburne, *Personal Identity* (Oxford: Basil Blackwell, 1984), p. 32.
85 *QDA* un.1.
86 These are what Aquinas calls 'integral' parts, as distinct from metaphysical parts. For further discussion on the distinction, see Chapter 1 on Aquinas's theory of things.
87 See also *In Meta* VII.17.1679–1680 where Aquinas explains that the form of a material composite is not an element of the composite in the way that its material components are; rather the form is what Aquinas calls a 'principle' of the constitution of the composite.
88 For further discussion of the distinction between metaphysical and integral parts, see Chapter 1 on Aquinas's theory of things.
89 And, of course, the separated soul after death can exert causal influence apart from any connection with or to the matter of its body.
90 Aquinas would therefore not accept the claim that anything which is embodied is necessarily embodied. For interesting arguments that the claim should in fact not be accepted, see Stephen Yablo, "The Real Distinction Between Mind and Body", *The Canadian Journal of Philosophy*, supplementary volume 16 (1990), p. 197.
91 *ST* IIaIIae.83.11.
92 Richard Swinburne asserts that on Aquinas's account there is no memory in the separated soul [*The Evolution of the Soul* (Oxford: Clarendon Press, 1986), p. 306]; but Swinburne is mistaken here. He supports his point by referring to *SCG* II.81.14, where Aquinas says that recollection is not in the separated soul. But in that passage Aquinas goes on to say that the denial of recollection in the separated soul is false if by 'recollection' we mean the understanding of things which the person cognized before (in the embodied state). Whatever exactly Aquinas means by 'recollection' here, then, it is not to be equated with memory in general.
93 *ST* Ia.89.1 and 89.8.
94 *ST* IaIIae.85.5 and 85.6.
95 *SCG* IV.79.
96 What are we to say about the human person here? The question is somewhat difficult to answer just because the contemporary notion of personhood does not map neatly on to medieval concepts; certainly the medieval term *'persona'* is not exactly equivalent to our 'person'. As far as I can see, Aquinas's notion of a human being is as close to our notion of person as anything else in his account of human nature. If this is right, then for Aquinas the person, as it were, falls apart at death. Nonetheless, although the soul is just a part of a person, it is the part that has intellect and will, so that there is a sense in which, on his account, the person survives death, since the person part that is the soul thinks and wills even if it is not a complete person in its own right. (This is no doubt at least part of

the reason why he thinks it is appropriate to call the soul of Peter 'Peter', as he claims we should do in his discussion of prayer to the saints in heaven.) In this sense, the soul is different from other forms of material objects. The form of a cathedral without the matter it configures might be considered a part of the cathedral, in some sense of part, but even if (*per impossibile*) the form somehow survived the dissolution of the form-matter composite that is the cathedral, we would not think the survival of this part of the cathedral counted as the survival of the cathedral. For further discussion of this issue, see Chapter 1 on Aquinas's theory of things.

97 Aquinas's account thus satisfies Chisholm's constraint, which Chisholm thinks is supported by our strong intuitions, that the mind must be a thing of some sort and cannot be identified with anything like a set of properties. (Chisholm, 1991, p. 169). On Chisholm's view, the mind must be a substance. For Aquinas, as I explain, when the mind exists in its disembodied state in the separated soul, it is a subsistent thing but still only a part of a substance, like a severed hand, and not a whole substance in its own right.

98 Stephen Yablo says that any "substance dualism worthy of the name maintains at least that (1) I am not identical to my body" ("The Real Distinction Between Mind and Body", in *The Canadian Journal of Philosophy*, supplementary volume 16 (1990), p. 150). Whether or not Aquinas meets this test for substance dualism depends on how (1) is understood. If we take (1) literally as it stands (and this is how Yablo himself interprets it), then Aquinas accepts it, since in some sense the corpse of a person also counts as that person's body. On the other hand, if we are to understand 'body' in (1) as referring to a living human body, then Aquinas would reject (1) since he thinks that a human being is the matter-form composite of a living human body.

99 Dennett (1991, pp. 33–37).

100 Sydney Shoemaker, *Identity, Cause, and Mind* (Cambridge: Cambridge University Press, 1984), p. 141.

101 Patricia Churchland, *Neurophilosophy. Toward a Unified Science of the Mind/Brain* (Cambridge, MA: MIT Press, 1990), p. 352.

102 This is admittedly a very restricted sense of 'physicalism'. For some attempt to clarify the different senses of 'physicalism' in current use, see Howard Robinson (ed.), *Objections to Physicalism* (Oxford: Clarendon Press, 1993).

103 Richard Boyd, "Materialism without Reductionism: What Physicalism Does Not Entail", in Ned Block (ed.), *Readings in Philosophy of Psychology*, vol. 1 (Cambridge, MA: Harvard University Press, 1980), p. 85.

104 Boyd (1980, p. 88).

105 Boyd (1980, p. 88).

106 Boyd (1980, p. 97).

107 Boyd in fact qualifies this thesis with a distinction between narrow and broad construals of the scope of states, events, and processes; but this distinction does not alter his general point and is not relevant to the issues at hand.

108 Boyd asserts this claim with very little argument; for considerable careful and interesting argument for the claim, see Stephen Yablo, "The Real Distinction Between Mind and Body", *The Canadian Journal of Philosophy*, supplementary volume 16 (1990): 149–201.

109 Boyd (1980, p. 101).

110 Boyd (1980, p .85).

111 Boyd (1980, p. 97).

112 Unless I have misunderstood Boyd and he thinks it is possible for there to be functioning mental phenomena existing on their own apart from both a body and a mind. Something similar to or even identical with such a peculiar theory

seems to be held by N. M. L. Nathan, who says, "A person could be a series of volitions connected causally or by their contents, or ... a single continuous activity in which all succession and variety belongs to the content of that activity" (see his "Weak Materialism", in Howard Robinson, 1993, p. 223).

113 Furthermore, Boyd like Aquinas takes configurational events, states, or processes as dynamic, since he supposes that such dynamic conditions as information-processing are configurational.

114 For someone who sees positions such as Boyd's as dualist, see Stephen Yablo (1990, p. 151) (where Yablo describes the claim that a human mind could have existed in the absence of all material objects a "genuinely challenging form of dualism") and "Mental Causation", *The Philosophical Review* 101 (1992): 246.

115 This is the sense of materialism Howard Robinson has in mind when he says, "One could, e.g., have a materialist or physicalist theory of man and hence of the human mind, whilst believing in the existence of non-human immaterial spirits" (Robinson, 1993, p. 2).

116 See John Searle (1992, p. 28).

117 Searle (1992, p. 102).

118 For detailed and elaborate consideration of arguments for this conclusion, see David Braine, *The Human Person. Animal and Spirit* (Notre Dame, IN: University of Notre Dame Press, 1992). For arguments that Aquinas's account of the soul occupies a halfway house between dualism and materialism, see Brian Davies, *The Thought of Thomas Aquinas* (Oxford: Clarendon Press, 1992). Davies's discussion is very helpful, but a better way to describe Aquinas's position, in my view, is as showing the mistakenness of the dichotomy between materialism and dualism.

119 And if it is logically possible for disembodied minds to exist and function, then on Aquinas's understanding of omnipotence, God can bring about such a state in this world.

7 The foundations of knowledge

1 *Reason Within the Bounds of Religion* (Grand Rapids, MI: Eerdmans 1984), 2nd edn, p. 30. Wolterstorff has since altered his view; see "The Migration of the Theistic Arguments: From Natural Theology to Evidentialist Apologetics", in Robert Audi and William Wainwright (eds), *Rationality and Religious Belief* (Ithaca, NY: Cornell University Press, 1986), pp. 38–81.

2 "Reason and Belief in God", in Alvin Plantinga and Nicholas Wolterstorff (eds), *Faith and Rationality: Reason and Belief in God* (Notre Dame, IN: University of Notre Dame Press 1983), p. 48. For Plantinga's later views, however, see *Warrant: The Current Debate* (Oxford: Oxford University Press, 1983), pp.183–184, and *Warranted Christian Belief* (Oxford: Oxford University Press, 2000), pp. 167–186.

3 Plantinga (1983, p. 52).

4 Plantinga (1983, pp. 55–57).

5 For Plantinga's theory of knowledge, see his trilogy on warrant: *Warrant: The Current Debate* (Oxford: Oxford University Press, 1993); *Warrant and Proper Function* (Oxford: Oxford University Press, 1993); and *Warranted Christian Belief* (Oxford: Oxford University Press, 2000).

6 Plantinga (1983, p. 62).

7 *Theory of Knowledge* (Boulder, CO: Westview Press, 1990), p. 62.

8 Oxford: Clarendon Press, 1988.

9 Irwin (1988, pp. 130–131).

10 Irwin (1988, p. 134).

11 Irwin (1988, p. 197); see also pp.139–141, 148–150, 315, 318, 326, 482–483.
12 Irwin (1988, p. 473).
13 For a different interpretation of the nature and purpose of Aristotle's *Posterior Analytics*, see, e.g., Jonathan Barnes, "Aristotle's Theory of Demonstration", in Jonathan Barnes, Malcolm Schofield, and Richard Sorabji (eds), *Articles on Aristotle* (London: Duckworth, 1975), pp. 65–87.
14 Wolterstorff (1984, pp. 24–25); cf. also p. 36.
15 Lehrer (1990, p. 42).
16 Lehrer (1990, p. 40).
17 *In PA* II.1 [408].
18 *In PA* proemium. (In places where it might be particularly helpful for scholarly readers, I have also included in square brackets the number in the Marietti edition of the paragraph in which a quotation can be found. Also, because of the nature of the controversy at issue in this chapter, I have frequently included in footnotes the Latin text for short quotations. It would, of course, have been good to give the Latin for all the quoted passages everywhere in this book, but considerations of space rule out doing so.)
19 *In PA* I.4.
20 *In PA* I.35.
21 *In PA* II.20.
22 *In PA* I.4:

> *scientia* … quae per demonstrationem acquiritur, procedat ex proposition-ibus veris, primis et immediatis, id est quae non per aliquod medium demonstrantur, sed per seipsas sunt manifestae (quae quidem immediatae dicuntur, in quantum carent medio demonstrante; primae autem in ordine ad alias propositiones, quae per eas probantur).

23 *In PA* II.20.
24 Cf., e.g., *In PA* proemium; I.9.
25 *In PA* I.42.
26 *In PA* I.1.
27 *In PA* I.20; see also II.2.
28 *In PA* I.5 and I.9.
29 *In PA* I.16.
30 *ST* Ia.79.9; *In PA* I.4, I.16: "neque demonstratio, neque *scientia* est corrupt-ibilium." Aquinas does think that we have *scientia* of the natural world, but we have it in virtue of the fact that we have *scientia* of the universal causes which operate in nature. See, e.g., *In PA* I.42.
31 *In PA* I.16.
32 *In PA* II.1: "ea quae quaeruntur sunt universalia, sicut et ea quae sciuntur."
33 *In PA* I.11.
34 *In PA* I.44 [396]: "ponit duo ad eam pertinere: quorum unum est quod sit universalis. Non enim *scientia* est de singularibus sub sensu cadentibus"; [397] "praeter vera necessaria, quae non contingunt aliter se habere, sunt quaedam vera non necessaria, quae contingit aliter se habere. Manifestum est autem ex praedictis, quod circa huiusmodi non est *scientia*."
35 Cf., e.g., *ST* Ia.86.1 and 86.3
36 *ST* Ia.87.1.
37 It is true that sometimes Aquinas uses '*scientia*' in a very broad sense. So, e.g., in *ST* IIIa.9.1, speaking about the knowledge of the incarnate Christ, Aquinas says, "here we are taking '*scientia*' broadly for any cognition of the human intellect." But it is clear that, in general, Aquinas uses the term in a

much more restricted sense, and that is why his claims about what a human person cognizes by intellect or sense are different from his claims about *scientia*.

38 In fact, there are some passages in which Aquinas uses *'cognitio'* in a way that would not allow *'cognitio'* to be translated 'knowledge': as, e.g., when he occasionally talks of a false cognition.

39 *In PA* I.4 [32]: "scire aliquid est perfecte cognoscere ipsum."

40 *In PA* I.13 [116]: "scire est causam rei cognoscere"; see also I.4 and I.42.

41 *In PA* II.1: "causa est medium in demonstratione, quae facit *scire*."

42 For a discussion of this part of medieval logic, see my *Dialectic and Its Place in the Development of Medieval Logic* (Ithaca, NY: Cornell University Press, 1989).

43 In this connection, see especially *QDVC* 7.

44 *In PA* I.44; cf. also *ST* IaIIae.57.1–4.

45 *QDVC* 7.

46 Cf. *In Meta* I.11.34; see also *In NE* VI.11–6.

47 Technically speaking, it requires *two* divisions to accomplish the distinction between the dispositions of the speculative intellect and those of the practical intellect, because differentiae in a Porphyrian tree always come in pairs of contrary opposites. The same technical point applies to the rest of the discussion of this putative Porphyrian tree.

48 "Highest cause" is the phrase Aquinas uses in his description of wisdom; 'most fundamental cause' is what we would be inclined to say. For some discussion of this issue, see Chapter 11 on wisdom.

49 *ST* Ia.17.2.

50 For a discussion of the processes of sensory cognition and the proper objects of sense cognition, see Chapter 8 on the mechanisms of cognition.

51 *ST* Ia.17.2 ad 1:

> non decipiamur in judicio quo judicamus nos sentire aliquid. Sed ex eo quod sensus aliter afficitur interdum quam res sit, sequitur quod nuntiet nobis rem aliter quam sit aliquando. Et ex hoc fallimur per sensum circa rem, non circa ipsum sentire.

52 For the distinction between common principles and proper principles, see, e.g., *In PA* I.17, I.18, I.43.

53 For this distinction, see, e.g., *In PA* I.4, I.5.

54 *In PA* I.27 [222 – 224].

55 *In PA* I.19.

56 *In PA* I.27 [223].

57 *In PA* I.19 [161]: "nihil est adeo verum, quin voce possit negari. Nam et hoc principium notissimum, quod non contingat idem esse et non esse, quidam ore negaverunt."

58 *SCG* I.11:

> simpliciter quidem Deum esse per se notum est: cum hoc ipsum quod Deus est, sit suum esse. Sed quia hoc ipsum quod Deus est mente concipere non possumus, remanet ignotum quoad nos. Sicut omne totum sua parte maius esse, per se notum est simpliciter: ei autem qui rationem totius mente non conciperet, oporteret esse ignotum.

59 *In PA* I.43:

non possunt esse aliqua principia communia, ex quibus solum omnia syllogizentur … quia genera entium sunt diversa, et diversa sunt principia quae sunt solum quantitatum principia, ab his quae solum sunt principia qualitatum: quae oportet coassumere principiis communibus ad concludendum in qualibet materia.

60 *In PA* I.43 [388]: "principia non sunt multum pauciora conclusionibus".

61 Cf., e.g., *In PA* I.4 [42]: "demonstrationis propositiones sint causae conclusionis, quia tunc scimus, cum causas cognoscimus"; [43] "Ex singularibus autem quae sunt in sensu, non sunt demonstrationes, sed ex universalibus tantum, quae sunt in intellectu."

62 Cf., e.g., *In PA* I.10; II.9.

63 *In PA* I.30:

demonstratio procedit ex universalibus; inductio autem procedit ex particularibus. Si ergo universalia, ex quibus procedit demonstratio, cognosci possent absque inductione, sequeretur quod homo posset accipere *scientia*m eorum, quorum non habet sensum. Sed impossibile est universalia speculari absque inductione.

Cf. also, e.g., *In Meta* I.11.

64 *In PA* I.30: "universalia, ex quibus demonstratio procedit, non fiunt nobis nota, nisi per inductionem."

65 *In PA* II.20: "necesse est prima universalia cognoscere per inductionem."

66 *In PA* I.30: "duplex est modus acquirendi *scientiam*. Unus quidem per demonstrationem, alius autem per inductionem."

67 *ST* Ia.101.1.

68 *In PA* II.4: "Ille enim qui inducit per singularia ad universale, non demonstrat neque syllogizat ex necessitate."

69 *In PA* II.4 [445], "ita se habet in via divisionis, sicut et in via inductionis …. Cum enim aliquid syllogistice probatur, necesse est quod conclusio sit vera, praemissis existentibus veris. Hoc autem non accidit in via divisionis."

70 *In PA* I.12: "quod non accidat in demonstratione peccatum, oportet non latere quod multoties videtur demonstrari universale, non autem demonstratur."

71 *In PA* proemium: "Est enim aliquis rationis processus necessitatem inducens, in quo non est possibile veritatis defectum; et per huiusmodi rationis processum scientiae certitudo acquiritur."

72 *In PA* I.4: "scientia est etiam certa cognitio rei; quod autem contingit aliter se habere, non potest aliquis per certitudinèm cognoscere; ideo ulterius oportet quod id quod scitur non possit aliter se habere."

73 *In PA* I.41 [357].

74 *In PA* I.41 [358].

75 *In PA* I.41 [359].

76 *In PA* I.41 [360].

77 *ST* Ia.91.3:

omnes res naturales productae sunt ab arte divina …. Sic igitur Deus unicuique rei naturali dedit optimam dispositionem, non quidem simpliciter, sed secundum ordinem ad proprium finem… Finis autem proximus humani corporis est anima rationalis et operationes ipsius… Dico ergo quod Deus instituit corpus humanum in optima dispositione secundum convenientiam ad talem formam et ad tales operationes.

Cf. also *ST* Ia.76.5.

78 *QDA* 8.15: "anima unitur corpori propter intelligere, quae est propria et princi-palis operatio. Et ideo requiritur quod corpus unitum animae rationali sit optime dispositum ad serviendum animae in his quae sunt necessaria ad intelli-gendum."

79 *QDVC* 7: "Dicitur enim aliquis intelligens vel sciens secundum quod eius intel-lectus perfectus est ad cognoscendum verum; quod quidem est bonum intellectus."

80 *ST* Ia.93.2: "solae intellectuales creaturae, proprie loquendo, sunt ad imaginem Dei."

81 *ST* Ia.93.4: "cum homo secundum intellectualem naturam ad imaginem Dei esse dicatur, secundum hoc est maxime ad imaginem Dei, secundum quod intel-lectualis natura Deum maxime imitari potest."

82 *ST* Ia.93.6:

> Esse ergo ad imaginem Dei pertinet solum ad mentem ... in sola creatura rationali invenitur similitudo Dei per modum imaginis .... Nam quantum ad similitudinem divinae naturae pertinet, creaturae rationales videntur quodammodo ad repraesentationem speciei pertingere, inquantum imitantur Deum non solum in hoc quod est et vivit, sed etiam in hoc quod intelligit.

83 See Chapter 8 on the mechanisms of cognition.

84 Further discussion of faculties other than the senses and the intellect can be found in Chapter 8 on the mechanisms of cognition.

85 *ST* Ia.85.6: "Sensus enim circa proprium objectum non decipitur ... nisi forte per accidens, ex impedimento circa organum contingente."

86 *ST* Ia.17.2: "circa propria sensibilia sensus non habet falsam cognitionem nisi per accidens et ut in paucioribus, ex eo scilicet quod propter indispositionem organi non convenienter recipit formam sensibilem"; cf. also *ST* Ia.17.2 ad 2: "falsitas dicitur non esse propria sensui, quia non decipitur circa proprium objectum."

87 It might occur to someone to wonder how this optimism is compatible with the position in a text cited earlier, in which Aquinas accepts the possibility of falsity in sensory cognition. The optimism about the senses has to do just with the reception by a sense of its proper object. Senses also have common objects and accidental objects, and with regard to these falsity is possible even in an other-wise properly functioning sense organ (cf., e.g., *ST* Ia.17.2). In addition, judgment based on the senses' reception of their object, which is propositional, involves intellect's operation on sensory information, and error in such percep-tual judgments is also possible.

88 *ST* Ia.85.6: "Obiectum autem proprium intellectus est quidditas rei. Unde circa quidditatem rei, per se loquendo, intellectus non fallitur."

89 *ST* Ia.85.6 ad 1: "in absoluta consideratione quidditatis rei, et eorum quae per eam cognoscuntur, intellectus nunquam decipitur."

90 *ST* Ia.17.3: "Sicut autem sensus informatur directe similitudine propriorum sensibilium, ita intellectus informatur similitudine quidditatis rei. Unde circa quod quid est intellectus non decipitur: sicut neque sensus circa sensibilia propria."

91 *ST* Ia.94.4: "non poterat esse quod, innocentia manente, intellectus hominis alicui falso acquiesceret quasi vero ... rectitudo primi status non compatiebatur aliquam deceptionem circa intellectum."

92 *QDV* 18.6 s.c.: "omnis error vel est culpa, vel poena: quorum neutrum in statu innocentiae esse poterat. Ergo nec error."

93 *QDV* 18.6:

> sicut verum est bonum intellectus, ita falsum malum ipsius ... si ipsa opinio falsa, sit quidam malus actus intellectus. Unde cum in statu innocentiae non fuerit aliqua corruptio vel aliquod malum, non potuit esse in statu innocentiae aliqua falsa opinio ... ita in intellectu eius nulla falsitas esse potuisset.

94 Both these topics are discussed in detail in Chapter 8 on the mechanisms of cognition.

95 *ST* IIIa.9.4; cf. also *QDV* 20.1 ad 2.

96 Although it has seemed to some contemporary thinkers that a theory of knowledge at least similar to Aquinas's can form part of a non-theistic worldview. For God as the guarantor of the reliability of human cognitive equipment, on the view of some thinkers it is possible to substitute evolution and to suppose that the theory of evolution provides roughly the same support for such a theory of knowledge that Aquinas's theism does. For further discussion cf., e.g., Alvin Plantinga, "An Evolutionary Argument Against Naturalism", *Logos* 12 (1992): 27–49; see also *Warrant and Proper Function* (Oxford: Oxford University Press, 1993), Chapters 11 and 12.

97 Of course, this story will be considerably complicated if we add to it Aquinas's views concerning the effects of sin on the will and his account of the relations between intellect and will, but these additional considerations will only complicate and not undermine the epistemological story I have argued for here.

98 *In PA* II.1 [414]: "Manifestum est enim quod causa est medium in demonstratione, quae facit scire; quia scire est causam rei cognoscere. Causa autem est quod quaeritur in omnibus praedictis quaestionibus."

99 *In PA* I.42:

> Quaedam enim sunt de quibus non quaereremus dubitando, si ea vidissemus; non quidem eo quod scientia consistat in videndo, sed in quantum ex rebus visis per viam experimenti accipitur universale, de quo est scientia. Puta si videremus vitrum perforatum, et quomodo lumen pertransit per foramina vitri, sciremus propter quid vitrum est transparens.

100 *In PA* I.42:

> Ponamus ergo quod aliquis esset in ipsa luna, et sensu perciperet interpositionem terrae per umbram ipsius: sensu quidem perciperet quod luna tunc deficeret ex umbra terrae, sed non propter hoc sciret totaliter causam eclipsis. Illud enim est per se causa eclipsis, quod causat universaliter eclipsim.

101 *In PA* I.42:

> scientia est potior quam sensus. Manifestum est enim quod cognitio quae est per causam, nobilior est: causa autem per se est universalis causa, ut jam dictum est; et ideo cognitio per universalem causam, qualis est scientia, est honorabilis. Et quia huiusmodi universalem causam impossibile est apprehendere per sensum, ideo consequens est quod scientia, quae ostendit

> causam universalem, non solum sit honorabilior omni sensitiva cognitione, sed etiam omni alia intellectiva cognitione, dummodo sit de rebus quae habent causam.

See also *In Meta* I.1.

102 *In PA* II.9 [491]: "medium demonstrationis sit causa."

103 *In PA* II.9 [491]: "per medium demonstrationis omnes hae causae manifestantur; quia quaelibet harum causarum potest accipi ut medium demonstrationis."

104 Paul T. Durbin, trans., *St. Thomas Aquinas. Summa theologiae*, vol. 12 (New York: Blackfriars and McGraw-Hill 1968), p. 82, note a to *ST* Ia.85.7.

105 *ST* Ia.79.8: "ratiocinatio humana, secundum viam inquisitionis vel inventionis, procedit a quibusdam simpliciter intellectis, quae sunt prima principia; et rursus, in via iudicii, resolvendo redit ad prima principia, ad quae inventa examinat."

106 *In PA* proemium [6]:

> Pars autem Logicae, quae primo deservit processui, pars Iudicativa dicitur, eo quod iudicium est cum certitudine scientiae. Et quia iudicium certum de effectibus haberi non potest nisi resolvendo in prima principia, ideo pars haec Analytica vocatur, idest resolutoria.

107 *In PA* proemium [6]:

> Certitudo autem iudicii, quae per resolutionem habetur, est, vel ex ipsa forma syllogismi tantum et ad hoc ordinatur liber *Priorum analyticorum*, qui est de syllogismo simpliciter; vel etiam cum hoc ex materia, quia sumuntur propositiones per se et necessariae, et ad hoc ordinatur liber *Posteriorum analyticorum*, qui est de syllogismo demonstrativo.

108 *In PA* proemium [6]:

> Secundo autem rationis processui deservit alia pars logicae, quae dicitur Inventiva .... Per hiusmodi enim processum, quandoque quidem, etsi non fiat scientia, fit tamen fides vel opinio propter probabilitatem propositionum, ex quibus proceditur ... et ad hoc ordinatur Topica sive Dialectica .... Quandoque vero, non fit complete fides vel opinio, sed suspicio quaedam .... Et ad hoc ordinatur Rhetorica.

109 *In PA* II.9 [497]:

> ponit exemplum de causa movente, tangens quamdam Graecorum historiam: videlicet quod Athenienses quondam, adiunctis sibi quibusdam aliis Graecis, invaserunt Sardenses, qui erant subiecti regi Medorum; et ideo Medi invaserunt Athenienses. Dicit ergo quod quaeri potest propter quid bellum Medorum factum est cum Atheniensibus; et hoc propter quid est causa quare Athenienses impugnati sunt a Medis ... Hoc autem... quod est medium, pertinet ad Athenienses, qui prius bellum inceperunt. Et sic patet quod hic accipitur quasi medium causa quae primo movit.

110 Someone might suppose that an eye-witness to the events could just *see* the Medes making war on the Athenians and so conclude that this example is meant to be a demonstrative syllogism just for such people, but this objection is confused. In the first place, Aquinas presents this example as a demonstrative

syllogism without any indication that it is restricted to people living contemporaneously with the events at issue. Second, much more is involved in the notion of making war than the things an eye-witness to the actions of the Medes could know through self-evident propositions and propositions evident to the senses, as Aquinas's example itself makes clear. The Medes constituted a political entity with a governing structure of some sort; following the conventions of the time, the Medes made an official decision to engage in a series of hostile activities against another political entity, Athens, for a reason deemed weighty enough to warrant the hostility by the officially sanctioned decision-making authority among the Medes. It is because the notion of making war involves conventions of all these sorts that Aquinas accepts as the efficient cause of what the Medes do to the Athenians an action of the Athenians against the Sardinians.

111 Although even so there remains the difficulty of explaining how the premises of this putative demonstration fit the description of demonstrative premises – that is, universal, necessary, and so on.

8 The mechanisms of cognition

1 Aquinas's views were themselves one pole around which subsequent storms of discussion swirled. For some discussion of these discussions, see, e.g., Steven P. Marrone, *Truth and Scientific Knowledge in the Thought of Henry of Ghent* (Cambridge, MA: The Medieval Academy of America, 1985), and Katharine Tachau, *Vision and Certitude in the Age of Ockham: Optics, Epistemology and the Foundations of Semantics 1250–1345* (Leiden: E. J. Brill, 1988). See also Katharine Tachau, "The Problem of the *species in medio* at Oxford in the Generation after Ockham", *Mediaeval Studies* 44 (1982): 394–443.

2 Making the rough distinctions given here precise would take considerably more work than is appropriate in this context. e.g., it does not seem sensible to say that wearers of contact lenses see what they see with mediated cognition; it does seem right to suppose that use of an electron microscope produces mediated cognition; and it is hard to be clear about the categorization of cognition resulting from the use of an ordinary light microscope. So 'significant' in this description is an indication of a vagueness that a more precise formulation might succeed in removing.

3 It is only with these provisos that I concur with Joseph Owens's claim that for Aquinas human beings have direct and unmediated cognition of the external world. See Joseph Owens, *Cognition: An Epistemological Inquiry* (Houston, TX: Center for Thomistic Studies, 1992). See also Joseph Owens, "Aristotle and Aquinas on Cognition", in Richard Bosley and Martin Tweedale (eds), *Aristotle and His Medieval Interpreters*, *Canadian Journal of Philosophy*, supplementary volume (Calgary: University of Calgary Press, 1992), pp. 103–123. Owens seems to me to underplay the degree to which Aquinas, like other philosophers, has to take the reliability of human cognitive faculties on trust. For a discussion of Aquinas on the reliability of human cognitive faculties, see the chapter on the foundations of knowledge. See also Norman Kretzmann, "Infallibility, Error, and Ignorance", in *Aristotle and His Medieval Interpreters* (1992b), for an excellent discussion of Aquinas's views on the reliability of human cognitive faculties.

4 The Latin which I have rendered 'similitude' is '*similitudo*' and is usually translated 'likeness'. That translation, however, often leads people into supposing that a *similitudo* is a pictorial representation or that it is supposed to resemble whatever it is a *similitudo* of. These are very misleading impressions. It is better,

in my view, to proceed cautiously here, too, and simply anglicize the Latin, presenting it as a technical term. I have taken the same approach to various other Latin technical terms in this chapter.

5 *In Sent* IV.49.2.1. ad 16:

> creaturae corporales non dicuntur immediate videri, nisi quando id quod in eis est conjungibile visui, ei conjungitur: non sunt autem conjungibiles per essentiam suam ratione materialitatis; et ideo tunc immediate videntur quando eorum similitudo intellectui conjungitur.

I am indebted to Robert Pasnau for this reference.

6 The title of Oliver Sacks's well-known book is taken from such an agnosia case: *The Man Who Mistook His Wife for a Hat*. The visual agnosia patient in that book did see his wife, in some sense, but without seeing her *as* his wife (or even as a human being). See Oliver Sacks, *The Man Who Mistook His Wife For a Hat* (New York: Summit Books, 1985). For a helpful recent study of agnosia, see Martha J. Farah, *Visual Agnosia* (Cambridge, MA: MIT Press, 1990).

7 See, e.g., Eric Kandell, James Schwartz, and Thomas Jessell, *Principles of Neural Science*, 3rd edn (New York: Elsevier, 1991), p. 831.

8 *In DA* II.12.377.

9 *In DA* II.13.384–386.

10 *In DA* II.13.375. See also *In DA* II.5.284, where Aquinas contrasts sense and intellect on this score, that sense is of particular things while intellect has to do with universals.

11 *ST* Ia.78.4.

12 *In DA* II.13.396.

13 *In DA* II.13.398.

14 *ST* Ia.78.4 ad 2.

15 Discovering how the brain achieves integration across processing systems is a pressing problem in contemporary neurobiology, too, and we know much less about it than we would like. Among the little we know so far is that the senses feed into the thalamus and that significant integration of the senses occurs there.

16 See, e.g., *In DA* III.4.633.

17 See, e.g., *SCG* I.55.458.

18 See the discussion of epistemic contact in the chapter on God's knowledge.

19 *QDV* 1.11.

20 In this context, '*species*' is the Latin for form or image rather than the species of a genus.

21 To take just a few examples of the way in which '*species*' has been understood, Martin Tweedale says: "the visual species can be viewed as a little colored image that is propagated through the air and comes to exist in the eye." ("Mental Representation in Later Medieval Scholasticism", in J.-C. Smith (ed.), *Historical Foundations of Cognitive Science* (Dordrecht: Kluwer Academic Publishers, 1990), pp. 35–52.) F. C. Copleston takes sensible *species* as sense-impressions; according to Aquinas, he says: "Our organs of sense are affected by external objects, and we receive sense-impressions." (*Aquinas*, Baltimore, MD: Penguin Books, 1955, reprinted 1970), p. 181. And Anthony Kenny tends to translate '*species*' in the intellect as 'ideas' or 'concepts'; see e.g., A. Kenny, *Aquinas on Mind*, (London: Routledge, 1993), pp. 91–92, 94, 96.

22 *In DA* II.24.555.

23 *In DA* II.24.553.

24 See Chapter 1 on Aquinas's theory of things.

25 *QDV* 1.11.

26 *ST* Ia.85.2 s.c.

27 *ST* Ia.78.4.

28 For interesting arguments to a conclusion opposed to my interpretation, see Robert Pasnau's *Theories of Cognition in the Later Middle Ages* (Cambridge: Cambridge University Press, 1997).

29 Cf. Chapter 1 on Aquinas's theory of things.

30 Some scholars explain Aquinas's theory of cognition in formulations that make it seem as if Aquinas would welcome the conclusion that the cognizer becomes the thing cognized. I discuss such formulations and the parts of Aquinas's theory of cognition that give rise to them in the last section of this chapter.

31 Someone might suppose that the form of a stone could be received naturally or materially in matter without producing a stone; e.g., a stone might be pressed into mud, thereby bringing it about that the mud receives the form of the stone, but it nonetheless would not be the case that the mud becomes a stone. But this objection confuses the medieval notion of form with the notion of shape. Form is not shape, but rather, as I explained above, the configurational state of a thing. If the whole configurational state of the matter of a stone were received naturally or materially in the matter of mud, it would produce a stone; otherwise the matter of the mud would not have the form of the stone with natural or material reception. For the same reason, even a cleverly made styrofoam replica of a stone in some museum display would not count as having the configuration of the stone. It may have some of the shape and coloring of the stone, but the configuration of the matter of the stone does not consist in just the stone's shape and color.

32 *In DA* II.14.418.

33 See, e.g., *ST* Ia.84.1.

34 *In DA* II.24.553.

35 Aquinas tends to use 'immaterial', 'intentional', and 'spiritual' roughly synonymously to refer to this kind of change or reception of form.

36 *ST* Ia.78.3.

37 *In DA* II.14.418.

38 See, e.g., S. M. Cohen, "St. Thomas Aquinas on the Immaterial Reception of Sensible Forms", *The Philosophical Review* 91 (1982): 193–209; John J. Haldane, "Aquinas on Sense-Perception", *The Philosophical Review* 92 (1983): 233–239; and Paul Hoffman, "St. Thomas Aquinas on the Halfway State of Sensible Being", *The Philsophical Review* 99 (1990): 73–92.

39 *In DA* II.12.377.

40 *QDV* II.5 ad 2.

41 *In DA* II.24.555.

42 See *In DA* II.14.418, where Aquinas says that there is a spiritual change when a *species* is received in a sensory organ or *in the medium* by means of the intentional mode of reception and not by means of the natural mode of reception.

43 *In DA* II.15.432.

44 The media for sound, e.g., are discussed in *In DA* II.16.445; the media for taste and touch are discussed in the same work in II.21.502–508; and media for smelling as well as the other senses are discussed in II.23.532–544.

45 *In DA* II.21.502. Aquinas is right on this score, of course, since neurons of touch are located within and not at the outer extremity of the skin.

46 *In DA* II.20.493–495.

47 *ST* Ia.4.3; see also *QDV* 8.8 ("there is a similitude between two things insofar as there is agreement in form")

48 *QDV* 2.3 ad 9.

49 *SCG* II.46.1234.
50 *ST* Ia.12.9.
51 *ST* Ia.79.4 ad 3.
52 *ST* Ia.84.7.
53 *ST* Ia.79.4 ad 4; see also Ia.84.7 ad 2.
54 *ST* Ia.85.1 ad 3.
55 *SCG* II.59.1365.
56 *In DA* III.5.641.
57 *In DA* III.6.657.
58 *In DA* II.4.265; see also III.12.792. I am grateful to Robert Pasnau for calling this passage to my attention.
59 *In DA* III.4.632.
60 *In DA* III.6.668.
61 *In DA* III.6.656.
62 *In DA* III.5.644.
63 *In DA* III.4.633.
64 *In DA* III.5.641.
65 *In DA* III.6.664–665.
66 *ST* Ia.84.7.
67 *In DA* III.4.634.
68 *DSC* 9.
69 Owens puts a roughly similar point this way: "*Species* is taken here in the philosophical meaning of 'form'. These impressed forms determine the imagination to produce an image or representation of the thing [sensed], an image in which the thing itself is held before the percipient's internal gaze" (1992, p. 125).
70 Aristotle's understanding of phantasia has been the subject of considerable recent discussion; see, e.g., Anne Sheppard, "Phantasia and Mental Images: Neoplatonist Interpretations of *De anima*, 3.3" in Julia Annas (ed.), *Aristotle and the Later Tradition*, Oxford Studies in Ancient Philosophy, supplementary volume (Oxford: Clarendon Press, 1991), pp. 165–174, and the literature cited in Sheppard's article. Some of the suggestions made regarding Aristotle's understanding of phantasia border on the interpretation I give regarding Aquinas's notion of phantasia. In presenting Neoplatonist readings of Aristotelian phantasia, which she thinks mirror certain contemporary controversies, Sheppard discusses phantasia's "role in interpreting the data of perception" (ibid., p. 171) and phantasia's connection with mental images.
71 See, e.g., *ST* Ia.79.6 and *SCG* II.74.1528 and *QDV* 10.2.
72 See, e.g., Sacks (1985, pp. 154–157). Sacks describes a man who had an organic amnesia for a macabre murder he himself had committed but whose memories of the deed were released by a severe head injury. Sacks says, "The murder, the deed, lost to memory before, now stood before him in vivid, almost hallucinatory, detail. Uncontrollable remniscence welled up and overwhelmed him – he kept 'seeing' the murder, enacting it; again and again" (ibid., p. 155).
73 Kandell *et al.* (1991, p. 831).
74 Some confusion can be raised by Aquinas's notion of the first operation of the intellect because it sometimes looks identical to what Aquinas sees as the final product of intellect in the acquisition of *scientia*, namely, an understanding of the definition of something. For an excellent presentation of the problem and its solution, see Kretzmann (1992).
75 For a good discussion of medieval accounts of compounding and dividing, see Norman Kretzmann, "*Sensus compositus, sensus divisus*, and propositional attitudes", *Medioevo* 7 (1981): 195–229.

76 It should be said, however, that Aquinas supposes we may need to rely on examples involving concrete particulars even when we are thinking about the abstract natures which constitute science (*ST* Ia.84.7).

77 *ST* Ia.84.7 ad 3.

78 Unlike English, Latin has a verb form cognate with 'intellect'; in Aquinas's Latin, the intellect "intelligizes" things, and its objects are intellected things. I have made do in this chapter with 'understand' and its variations as a rendering of Aquinas's 'intelligize' and its forms, although on occasion, for the sake of clarity, I have translated it as 'intellectively cognize' and have used the term 'intellected' as an adjective in place of 'understood'.

79 *ST* Ia.85.2.

80 *ST* Ia.85.2.

81 *ST* Ia.85.2.

82 *ST* Ia.85.2.

83 *ST* Ia.85.5 ad 3.

84 See, e.g., *ST* Ia.85.1: "one must say that our intellect understands material things by abstracting from phantasms"; also ad 1: "And this is abstracting a universal from a particular, or an intelligible species from phantasms, namely, considering the nature of a species without consideration of the individual principles, which are represented by the phantasms."

85 See, e.g., *ST* Ia.84.6.

86 If Aquinas's view here seems odd, it might be reassuring to notice that a somewhat similar claim is made by modern neurobiology. A recent text, e.g., reports that "the occipital lobe receives input from the eyes, and hence it processes visual information." The seen object acts on the eyes to produce "input", but that input is itself acted upon by the occipital lobe, which "processes" it. And, from a neurophysiological point of view, the efficient causation exercised by extramental things underdetermines cognition: "the same information is treated in different ways in different parts of the brain ... Thus, although the kind of information sent to a network restricts what it can do, the input alone does not determine what a network computes" (Stephen Kosslyn and Oliver Koenig, *Wet Mind: The New Cognitive Neuroscience* (New York: Macmillan, 1992), p. 33).

87 In fact, it seems Aquinas was wrong about the passivity of sensory cognition. Even so simple an act of sensory cognition as registering a color turns out to require a great deal of active processing by more than one brain center. For an excellent account of color vision, see Semir Zeki, *A Vision of the Brain* (London: Blackwell Scientific Publications, 1993).

88 For an account of this theory in Averroes and the related theory in Avicenna, see Zdzislaw Kuksewicz, "The Potential and the Agent Intellect", and "Criticisms of Aristotelian Psychology and the Augustinian-Aristotelian Synthesis" in Norman Kretzmann, Anthony Kenny and Jan Pinborg (eds), assoc. editor, Eleonore Stump, *The Cambridge History of Later Medieval Philosophy* (Cambridge: Cambridge University Press, 1982), pp. 595–602 and 623–628. For an account of Aquinas's relation to the medieval tradition, including his reaction to Arabic accounts, see Edward Mahoney, "Sense, Intellect, and Imagination in Albert, Thomas, and Siger", in the same volume.

89 For an introduction to these issues, see Kuksewicz (1982).

90 See, e.g., *ST* Ia.79.4.

91 *ST* Ia.85.8.

92 See, e.g., *In DA* III.8.705–706. For a discussion of natures and their role in Aquinas's metaphysical scheme, see also Chapter 1 on Aquinas's theory of things.

93 *ST* Ia.85.1.

94 *ST* Ia.85.1 ad 1.

95 *ST* Ia.85.1 ad 2.

96 See, e.g., *In DA* III.11.746–760.

97 *QDV* 10.6 ad 6. Aquinas says very little about the mechanisms of innate cognition. But it is clear that we need not suppose that innate cognition of certain first principles requires innate possession of intelligible *species*. It might be the case that we are "hard-wired" for certain foundational beliefs, but that these beliefs are triggered in us only in certain contexts, when we have acquired the intelligible *species* in question. This is, apparently, the way in which the ability to learn language works. It is hard-wired in us, but it is activated only in certain social environments; feral children raised without the experience of language become permanently unable to learn language, although the ability to learn language is clearly an innate human cognitive capacity.

98 *ST* Ia.79.5 ad 3.

99 Although the analogy is only a rough one, since the external senses are passive and the intellect is active in the reception of *species*.

100 A very helpful account of the entire, complicated notion of intention in Aquinas's thought can be found in Robert W. Schmidt, *The Domain of Logic According to St. Thomas Aquinas* (The Hague: Martinus Nijhoff, 1966). I am also indebted to Schmidt's book for calling my attention to various texts useful for my purposes here which I might otherwise have overlooked. I am grateful to Robert Pasnau for making me aware of the relevance of this book for a study of Aquinas's account of cognition.

101 See, e.g., *ST* Ia.85.2 ad 3.

102 *SCG* I.53.443.

103 *SCG* I.53.444.

104 *SCG* IV.11.3473.

105 *SCG* IV.11.3466.

106 I say 'seem' here because, of course, it is possible that such patients have intelligible *species* but are not able to process them into intentions. In such a case, patients with severe dementia would be like agnosia patients, but unlike typical agnosia patients, they would be agnosic for all senses. Although this is possible, it does not seem to me a plausible way to think of dementia. A globally agnosic patient would nonetheless retain a good deal of what we think of as intelligence. She would be able, e.g., to think about the Pythagorean theorem; she would be able to sing to herself old songs she used to listen to; and so on. But demented patients certainly seem to have no capacities of this sort.

107 I disagree strongly, therefore, with Anthony Kenny, who says things of this sort about Aquinas's views of cognition:

> The various accounts which Aquinas gives of the physical processes of sense-perception are almost always mistaken, and need not detain us ... For explanation of the nature of sense-perception we have to look to the experimental psychologists, whose investigations have superannuated the naive and mistaken accounts which Aquinas gives of the physical processes involved.
>
> (*Aquinas on Mind*, London: Routledge, 1993, p. 34)

My evaluation of Aquinas's account of cognition differs so widely from Kenny's in large part because we interpret that account in such different ways.

108 See, e.g., John Heil, "Perceptual Experience" and Fred Dretske's response, "Perception: Heil", in Brian McLaughlin (ed.), *Dretske and His Critics* (Oxford: Blackwell, 1991), pp. 1–16 and 180–184.

109 *ST* Ia.84.7.

110 *ST* Ia.85.5.

111 See, e.g., *ST* IaIIae.90.1 ad 2, where Aquinas talks about three operations of the speculative reason. In my example Hannah is engaged in practical reasoning, but Aquinas speaks of syllogisms and arguments in practical reasoning also.

112 Of course, in the act of answering the question "What is that?", Hannah is engaged at least in the second operation of the intellect, compounding, since in the context her answer is, implicitly, "That is a cat".

113 Someone might object that there is a confusion here, since intellect is said to be able to apprehend such features of the cat as size and color, but such an objection would be mistaken. It is true that color and size and similar characteristics are received primarily by the senses. But there is an intellectual apprehension of such properties which even a person in Tom's condition, temporarily deprived of sensory powers, is able to have. Color is, of course, apprehended differently by the senses and by the intellect. The intellect apprehends the universal; the senses apprehend this particular color. This is the sort of thing Aquinas has in mind, I think, when he says, e.g., that the intellect can apprehend flesh and bones, but the senses apprehend *this* flesh and *these* bones. (*ST* Ia.85.1 ad 2.)

114 We might wonder, however, whether a human cognizer (such as Aquinas) could not cognize a material individual (say, Aristotle) with whom he had never had any sensory epistemic contact. This question is, of course, tied to the difficult question about what individuates. If, as Aquinas tends to say, matter individuates, then someone who has no epistemic contact with the matter that constitutes Aristotle also has no epistemic contact with that individual. The most that can be said in that case is that someone such as Aquinas knows about Aristotle, or knows descriptions of Aristotle; he may know who Aristotle is, but he does not know Aristotle. On the other hand, if a conglomeration of accidents individuates, then someone who knows all (or, at any rate, enough) of those accidents will know the individual, even though the accidents are all universals. Because Aquinas does not accept the view that accidents can individuate, he maintains that intellect by itself cannot know a material individual directly. (But Aquinas's views of the nature of the individuation of material objects is subtle, and I am glossing over some complexities here.) I am grateful to Norman Kretzmann for calling this problem to my attention.

115 *ST* Ia.86.1.

116 *In DA* III.8.712–713.

117 *QDV* 10.6 ad 7.

118 *QDV* 10.4.

119 *QDV* 2.5 ad 17.

120 For an example of such a conflation in an otherwise helpful book, see, e.g., François-Xavier Putallaz, *Le Sens de la Reflexion chez Thomas D'Aquin* (Paris: Librairie Philosophique J. Vrin, 1991), p. 119: "*l'intellect* dans son acte d'abstraction ou d'apprehénsion, n'atteint pas d'abord le singulier comme tel: par lui, l'homme connaît la quiddité abstraite des objets matériels donnés dans la perception." This discussion concludes with the remark: "*L'homme* jouit ainsi d'un pouvoir de connaissance indirecte et imparfaite du singulier" (p. 121; emphasis added).

121 *ST* Ia.12.9.

122 *QDV* 8.5.

123 *In DA* III.13.789.
124 *In DA* III.13.789.
125 Owens 1992, p. 114.
126 Whether this would be a good explanation or not is a matter of some controversy. See, e.g., Alvin Plantinga, "An Evolutionary Argument Against Naturalism", *Logos* 12 (1992): 27–49.
127 Those inclined to find this claim exaggerated should consult, e.g., the highly vituperative reviews by Ned Block, of Daniel Dennett's *Consciousness Explained*, and by Daniel Dennett, of John Searle's *The Rediscovery of the Mind*, both in *The Journal of Philosophy* 90 (1993): 181–204.
128 In working on this chapter, I have benefited greatly from Robert Pasnau's *Theories of Cognition in the Later Middle Ages* (Cambridge: Cambridge University Press, 1997). My views differ from those of Pasnau's in many ways, but I learned a great deal from reading his work.

9 Freedom: action, intellect and will

1 It, however, is true that some recent discussion of the will shows signs of moving in the direction of such a conception without any explicit trace of an association with (or even awareness of) Aquinas's account. See, e.g., the following seminal papers, which have generated considerable discussion in the literature: Harry Frankfurt, "Freedom of the Will and the Concept of a Person", *Journal of Philosophy* 68 (1971): 5–20; Gary Watson, "Free Agency", *Journal of Philosophy* 72 (1975): 205–220; Susan Wolf, "Asymmetric Freedom", *Journal of Philosophy* 77 (1980): 151–166. For one of the most detailed developments of this line of thought in the current literature, see John Martin Fischer and Mark Ravizza, *Responsibility and Control: A Theory of Moral Responsibility* (Cambridge: Cambridge University Press, 1998).
2 As I will discuss further in this chapter, by 'libertarians' I understand those who hold that human beings have freedom with regard to mental and bodily acts but that that freedom is incompatible with determinism.
3 Aquinas was not alone in the thirteenth century in taking such an attitude towards the will. For a discussion of thirteenth-century attitudes towards the will and its relations to intellect, see Bonnie Kent, *Virtues of the Will: The Transformation of Ethics in the Late Thirteenth Century* (Washington, DC: The Catholic University of America Press, 1995), esp. Chapters 3 and 4. I am not always in agreement with Kent's interpretation of Aquinas, but her exposition of the history of discussions of the will in the thirteenth century is helpful and interesting.
4 See, e.g., Klaus Riesenhuber, "The Bases and Meaning of Freedom in Thomas Aquinas", *Proceedings of the American Catholic Philosophical Association* 48 (1974): 99–111; Riesenhuber says, "Aquinas' later writings (after 1270), especially *De malo*, q.6 ..., contain a rather unobtrusive, but thoroughgoing rethinking and new formulation of his teaching on the freedom of the will" (p. 101).
5 In his article "Free Will and Free Choice" in the *Cambridge History of Later Medieval Philosophy* (ed. Norman Kretzmann, Anthony Kenny, Jan Pinborg, associate editor Eleonore Stump, Cambridge University Press, 1981), J. Korolec says:

> The cluster of problems concerning human freedom and action which are discussed by modern and contemporary English-speaking philosophers under the title 'freedom of the will' were discussed in the Middle Ages under the heading '*liberum arbitrium*'. But the Latin expression cannot

simply be translated by the English one, because it does not contain the Latin word for will (*voluntas*), and it is a matter of debate, among those who believed in the existence of *liberum arbitrium*, whether it was the will, or some other faculty, which was the bearer of the freedom involved in *liberum arbitrium* .... 'Freedom of choice' is probably a less misleading translation of '*liberum arbitrium*'; but here too there is the difficulty that the Latin expression does not contain the technical word for choice (*electio*).

(ibid., p .630)

See also the analogous discussion in David Gallagher, "Thomas Aquinas on the Will as Rational Appetite", *Journal of the History of Philosophy* 29 (1991): 559–584; Gallagher suggests 'free decision' as the least misleading translation (p. 570, n.26). The tendency to confuse *liberum arbitrium* in Aquinas's thought with the contemporary notion of freedom of the will has led some scholars to suppose that Aquinas changed his mind about the nature of free will by the time he wrote *QDM* 6. For a a helpful discussion of this confusion, see Daniel Westberg, "Did Aquinas Change His Mind about the Will?", *The Thomist* 58 (1994): 41–60.

6 For an interesting and helpful account relating human freedom to divine action, see David Burrell, *Freedom and Creation in Three Traditions* (Notre Dame, IN: University of Notre Dame Press, 1993). Cf. also Brian Davies, *The Thought of Thomas Aquinas* (Oxford: Clarendon Press, 1992), pp. 174–178.

7 *ST* IaIIae.10.1 and Ia.82.1.

8 The distinction between referential and attributive uses of linguistic expressions is easier to illustrate than to define. If we say "The President of the United States might have been the son of Chinese immigrants", we might be using the phrase 'the President of the United States' attributively, rather than referentially, to indicate that the position of President could have been filled by a person of Chinese ancestry. If, on the other hand, we were using the phrase referentially, we would be saying that the current president could have had different parents from the ones he had.

9 *ST* Ia.82.4.

10 *ST* Ia.59.1 obj. 3.

11 For a discussion of sensory cognition, see Chapter 8 on the mechanisms of cognition.

12 See, e.g., *ST* Ia.59.1. See also *ST* Ia.93.1; IaIIae.6.1; and *QDV* 24.1.

13 See, e.g., the reference to Aristotle in *ST* Ia.59.1 obj. 1.

14 See, e.g., *ST* Ia.19.1.

15 See *ST* IaIIae.9.1, *ST* Ia.82.4, and *ST* IaIIae.17.1.

16 To say that the will is an efficient cause of bodily motion is not to say that an act of will is sufficient by itself in any and all circumstances to produce bodily motion. Any true generalization that A's are the efficient causes of B's must include a description of a set of conditions, difficult to spell out in its entirety, which needs to hold in order for an A to bring about a B. (For an interesting recent account of causation which helps make this point clear, see Nancy Cartwright, *Nature's Capacities and Their Measurement*, Oxford: Clarendon Press, 1989.) So, e.g., blocked coronary arteries cause heart attacks, unless the heart is being artificially supplied with blood, or the collateral arteries are enlarged through exercise and can supply the heart's needs, and so on. Although the will is the efficient cause of bodily motion, then, an act of will can fail to produce bodily motion if the movement of the body is impeded by some external cause or by some defect in the body itself.

17 Although faith is divinely infused, according to Aquinas, he also seems to suppose that faith results from such an action of the will on the intellect. See, e.g., Aquinas's *QDV* where Aquinas talks of the will's commanding intellect to produce faith; *QDV* 14.3 reply, ad 2, and ad 10. For further discussion of this issue, see Chapter 13 on grace and free will.

18 See *ST* IaIIae.17.1 and IaIIae.17.6. For further discussion of Aquinas's account of the will's control over the intellect, see Chapter 11 on wisdom.

19 In this kind of case, the acts of intellect and will are likely to be tacit, rather than fully conscious. Nonetheless, if we were to ask you why you turned the page just then, your explanation, if you are a self-reflective person, is likely to produce an account of this Thomistic sort.

20 *ST* IaIIae.9.2.

21 *ST* Ia.81.3 and IaIIae.10.3.

22 *ST* Ia.81.3.

23 Cf. *ST* IaIIae.9.1.

24 Cf. *QDM* 6.1, where Aquinas says that even as regards happiness, the *exercise* of the will at a particular time is not necessary since a person can always will on a particular occasion not to think about happiness.

25 In such a case, of course, the intellect is relying on data presented by the senses, as it does in any case in which it cognizes particulars. By 'intellect' in this chapter, I understand the intellect in its full range of functions, including the use it makes of sensory data. For the way in which the intellect makes use of sensory cognition to apprehend particulars, see Chapter 8 on the mechanisms of cognition.

26 See *ST* Ia.82.2.

27 The ultimate good simpliciter is God, on Aquinas's account. Happiness, whose perfection comes in union with God, is the ultimate good for human beings. Hence, the sight of God in the beatific vision also moves the will necessarily.

28 *ST* Ia.82.1.

29 *ST* Ia.82.2.

30 *QDV* 22.12.

31 There is something misleading about talk of the intellect's cognizing or the will's willing. This sort of locution is common in contemporary neuroscience and philosophy of mind, where we read, e.g., that the hippocampus stores and reads maps. Such locutions are misleading, however, insofar as they suggest that components of the mind are homuncular and have cognitive or conative abilities of their own. Aquinas himself recognizes the danger in such locutions; see, e.g., *ST* Ia.75.2 ad 2. Having pointed out the dangers of such locutions, however, I will continue to use them for ease of exposition.

32 *ST* IaIIae.1.4, esp. obj. 3 and ad 3.

33 For a discussion of this problem for contemporary accounts and some examination of the way in which Aquinas's account avoids the problem, see Eleonore Stump, "Sanctification, Hardening of the Heart, and Frankfurt's Concept of Free Will", *Journal of Philosophy* 85 (1988): 395–420; reprinted in John Martin Fischer and Mark Ravizza (eds), *Perspectives on Moral Responsibility* (Ithaca, NY: Cornell University Press, 1993), pp. 211–234.

34 *ST* Ia.82.4; *QDV* 22.12. Cf. also *QDM* 6.1.

35 *ST* IaIIae.17.1.

36 *ST* IaIIae.50.5, IaIIae.52.1, and IaIIae.66.1.

37 Cf., e.g., *ST* IaIIae.17.2 and IaIIae.17.5 ad 1.

38 This distinction is related to the distinction between external and internal actions. For a helpful discussion of this distinction, see David Gallagher, "Aquinas on Moral Action: Interior and Exterior Acts", *Proceedings of the*

American Catholic Philosophical Association 64 (1990): 118–129. A provocative contemporary discussion of the same distinction can be found in Rogers Albritton, "Freedom of Will and Freedom of Action", *American Philosophical Association Proceedings and Addresses* 59 (1985): 239–251.

39 See, e.g., *ST* IaIIae.6.4, and *QDV* 24.1 ad 1. Cf. also *QDM* 6.1 ad 22, where Aquinas says, "he who does what he does not want [to do] does not have free action, but he can have free will."

40 *ST* IaIIae.10.3.

41 *ST* IaIIae.17.1 ad 2.

42 *ST* IaIIae.6.2 and IaIIae.17.5.

43 *ST* IaIIae.6.3 ad 3.

44 *ST* IaIIae.6.1 s.c.

45 *ST* IaIIae.6 proemium.

46 *ST* IaIIae.6.7 ad 3.

47 *ST* IaIIae.6.1.

48 *ST* IaIIae.6.2.

49 *ST* IaIIae.9.6. The exception to this claim about extrinsic principles is God, who can be an extrinsic cause without removing voluntariness since he is the extrinsic cause creating the will with its inclinations and its connections to the intellect. This is the one sort of extrinsic principle which not only does not remove voluntariness but is essential for producing it. (See, e.g., *ST* Ia.105.4 ad 2.)

50 *ST* IaIIae.6.4.

51 *ST* IaIIae.80.3.

52 I discuss the relationship of libertarianism and the ability to do otherwise at some length later in this chapter.

53 Aquinas distinguishes between *actus humanus*, which is a real human action, and *actus hominis*, which is any activity generated by a human being, in, e.g., *ST* IaIIae.1.1.

54 For a good recent analysis of Aquinas's theory of action, including helpful descriptions of the history of the topic in ancient philosophy and earlier medieval philosophy, see Daniel Westberg, *Right Practical Reason. Aristotle, Action, and Prudence in Aquinas* (Oxford: Clarendon Press, 1994). There is some controversy over exactly how many stages are to be found in Aquinas's analysis of action. An older tradition puts the number at twelve; Westberg argues for cutting the number back to eight. I am not persuaded by Westberg's arguments for reducing the number just to eight, and what follows is more in line with the traditional account.

55 *ST* IaIIae.8.3.

56 For Aquinas's distinction between simple volition of an end and the volition of the means for the sake of that end, see, e.g., *ST* IaIIae.8.3.

57 *ST* IaIIae.12.1 ad 4.

58 See, e.g., *ST* IaIIae.15.3.

59 Consider, e.g., 'Therefore choose life' (Deut.30:19), which seems a volition of an end without consideration of means; 'Choose this day whom you will serve' (Josh. 24:15) or 'I have chosen your precepts' (Psalm 119:173), which indicate intentions, acts of will directed at ends (being a servant of God's, being obedient to God's commands) considered as within the power of the willer to achieve by certain means.

60 *ST* IaIIae.15.3 ad 3.

61 And if the body is normal in normal circumstances, without external impediment, etc.

62 Cited in Gita Sereny, *Albert Speer: His Battle with Truth* (New York: Alfred A. Knopf, 1995), p. 463. Sereny gives a detailed and intriguing discussion of whether either Hanke or Speer could really have been surprised in 1944 at the fate of Jews in Auschwitz or any of the other camps.

63 Sereny (1995, p. 574).

64 Sereny (1995).

65 Speer's case is therefore different from the case of a man such as Goebbels, whose conscience was so perverted by his fanatical adherence to Hitler that, at least sometimes, he appears to have believed sincerely in the goodness of the Nazis' inflicting torments on their victims. For a discussion of erring conscience and the way in which it can be brought about by interactions of intellect and will, see Chapter 11 on wisdom.

66 *ST* Ia.83.1 obj. 2. See also *ST* Ia.83.3, where Aquinas says, "we are said to have *liberum arbitrium* when we can receive one and reject another".

67 *ST* Ia.83.3 s.c.

68 Aquinas's point here is that just as reason is a discursive ability that allows a person to move from fundamental principles to conclusions or to move from known effects to a description of their causes, so *electio* is a discursive ability of the will because it allows a person presented with alternatives to move to the selection of one of them.

69 *ST* Ia.83.4.

70 *ST* Ia.59.3 obj. 1.

71 *QDV* 24.6.

72 See also *In NE* III.5.434 where Aquinas says that the genus of *electio* is the voluntary; on his view, although "every [act of] *electio* is something voluntary, *electio* and the voluntary are not altogether the same, but the voluntary is in more [acts than *electio* is]." One reason for insisting that *electio* is not identical to the voluntary is this: [436] "Those things which we do quickly we say are voluntary, because their source is in us, but they are not said [to be done] with *electio*, because they don't arise from deliberation."

73 *ST* Ia.19.10 obj. 2.

74 *ST* Ia.83.3.

75 *ST* Ia.83.4.

76 Cf. *QDM* 16.2 where Aquinas says, "evil cannot arise in an appetite in virtue of the appetite's being discordant with the apprehension it follows".

77 It is true, as Norman Kretzmann has pointed out to me, that in such cases what intellect is presenting to will is the only suitable means, not the only possible means. But since on Aquinas's account, acts of will are dependent on preceding acts of intellect, it is not open to the will in such a case to assent to any of the alternatives rejected by the intellect as non-suitable. Nonetheless, I do not mean to suggest that in such a case there is never any alternative possibility open to an agent, since the will may selectively direct the attention of the intellect in such a way that on reconsideration the intellect reaches a different conclusion. What is important for my purposes here is just this. It may be that for a particular agent at a certain time no alternatives besides that presented by the intellect are conceivably acceptable, so that no amount of reconsideration on the intellect's part would yield any other conclusion. (Suppose, e.g., that you love your daughter extravagantly, you place very little value on a nickel, and a nickel is not a necessary means to anything you value at least as much as your daughter. If I offer you a nickel to torture your daughter to death, presumably the only alternative acceptable to you – no matter how often you reconsider my proposition – is to reject my offer.) In such a case, the fact that there is only one alternative available to the agent does not take away the agent's freedom of will

for Aquinas. That is why Aquinas can suppose that *electio* can collapse into consent without his ever suggesting that at least sometimes such a collapse destroys freedom.

78 Of course, it is possible for there to be habits of intellect and will, and these habits will make a difference to the ease with which the will and the intellect can be caught off guard. Such habits, which are moral and intellectual virtues and vices, will be discussed in Chapters 10, 11 and 12 on justice, wisdom, and faith.

79 *QDV* 24.12.

80 *QDM* 6.1.

81 God's grace does operate on the will with causal efficacy, but Aquinas's account of grace is complicated and it is not at all clear that the operations of grace constitute an exception to his claim here. See Chapter 13 on grace and free will for further discussion of this issue.

82 *QDV* 22.5; see also *QDV* 24.10 obj.5 and ad 5.

83 *QDV* 22.5 ad 3 in contrarium.

84 See, e.g., *QDM* 16.5, where Aquinas says that there is no state in which human beings lack *liberum arbitrium*. (One assumes that he means normal adults in normal states here, given what he says elsewhere about the connection between rational faculties and *liberum arbitrium*.)

85 *QDV* 22.6.

86 *ST* Ia.82 corpus and ad 1.

87 For different versions of PAP and an assessment of their strengths and weaknesses, see, e.g., Thomas Flint, "Compatibilism and the Argument from Unavoidability", *Journal of Philosophy* 84 (1987): 423–440.

88 See, e.g., Harry Frankfurt, "Alternate Possibilities and Moral Responsibility", *Journal of Philosophy* 66 (1969): 829–839.

89 See my discussion in "Intellect, Will, and Alternate Possibilities", reprinted in John Martin Fischer and Mark Ravizza (eds), *Perspectives on Moral Responsibility* (Ithaca, NY: Cornell University Press, 1993), pp. 237–262.

90 I have discussed PAP and Frankfurt-style counterexamples in various other papers, including "Sanctification, Hardening of the Heart, and Frankfurt's Concept of Free Will", *Journal of Philosophy* 85 (1988): 395–420, and "Intellect, Will, and the Principle of Alternate Possibilities", in Michael Beaty (ed.), *Christian Theism and the Problems of Philosophy* (Notre Dame, IN: University of Notre Dame Press, 1990), pp. 254–285. (Both of these papers are reprinted in Fischer and Ravizza (1993, pp. 211–262). See also my "Libertarian Freedom", in Daniel Howard-Snyder and Jeff Jordan (eds), *Faith, Freedom, and Rationality: Philosophy of Religion Today* (Rowman and Littlefield, 1996) pp. 73–88; "Persons: Identification and Freedom", *Philosophical Topics* 24 (1996): 183–214; "Alternative Possibilities and Moral Responsibility: The Flicker of Freedom", *The Journal of Ethics*, 3 (1999): 299–324; "Transfer Principles and Moral Responsibility" (with John Martin Fischer), *Philosophical Perspectives*, 14 (2000): 47–55.

91 See, e.g., David Widerker, "Libertarian Freedom and the Avoidability of Decisions", *Faith and Philosophy*, 12 (1995): 113–118, and "Libertarianism and Frankfurt's Attack on the Principle of Alternative Possibilities", *The Philosophical Review* 104 (1995): 247–261.

92 David Widerker, "Libertarian Freedom and the Avoidability of Decisions", *Faith and Philosophy* 12 (1995): 113.

93 Since Aquinas recognizes all four Aristotelian causes, it may perhaps be necessary here to point out that the only sort of causation at issue in this discussion is efficient causation.

94 I have discussed this claim and David Widerker's use of it to call in question Frankfurt-style counterexamples in "Libertarian Freedom and the Principle of Alternate Possibilities" in Daniel Howard-Snyder and Jeff Jordan (eds), *Faith, Freedom, and Rationality: Philosophy of Religion Today* (Rowman and Littlefield, 1996), pp. 73–88.

95 In this connection, see Chapter 6 on the soul.

96 For discussion of the extent to which Descartes held Cartesian dualism, see, e.g., Margaret Wilson, *Descartes* (London: Routledge and Kegan Paul, 1978), pp. 177–185, and Tad Schmaltz, "Descartes and Malebranche on Mind and Mind–Body Union", *The Philosophical Review* 101 (1992): 281–325.

97 The best-known contemporary example is Peter van Inwagen. For his defense of libertarianism, see *An Essay on Free Will* (Oxford: Clarendon Press, 1983); and for his rejection of any sort of dualism, see, e.g., "The Possibility of Resurrection", *The International Journal for Philosophy of Religion* 9 (1978): 114–121.

98 For further discussion of and argument for this claim, see my "Moral Responsibility without Alternative Possibilities", in David Widerker and Michael McKenna (eds), *Moral Responsibility and Alternative Possibilities* (Aldershot: Ashgate Press, 2002, pp. 139–158).

99 With the usual exception of God and grace.

100 See, e.g., Alan Garfinkel, "Reductionism", and Philip Kitcher, "1953 and All That: A Tale of Two Sciences", in Richard Boyd, Philip Gasper, and J.D. Trout (eds), *The Philosophy of Science* (Cambridge, MA: MIT Press, 1993), pp. 443–459 and pp. 553–570.

101 John Dupré, *The Disorder of Things. Metaphysical Foundations of the Disunity of Science* (Cambridge, MA: Harvard University Press, 1993); see especially Chapters 4–6.

102 Dupré (1993, p. 101).

103 Dupré (1993, p. 101).

104 Or some probabilistic analogue to determinism which is compatible with quantum mechanics.

105 Dupré (1993, p. 102).

106 See Chapter 1 on Aquinas's theory of things.

107 Dupré (1993, pp. 216–217).

108 Dupré (1993, pp. 215–216).

109 Here, too, the notion of grace introduces a complexity, but I am leaving it to one side in this chapter. See Chapter 13 on grace and free will.

110 See John Martin Fischer and Mark Ravizza, *Responsibility and Control. A Theory of Moral Responsibility* (Cambridge: Cambridge University Press, 1998). For an interesting recent argument to the same conclusion based on arguments about responsibility for failure to act, see Walter Glannon, "Responsibility and the Principle of Possible Action", *Journal of Philosophy* 92 (1995): 261–274.

111 See, e.g., Fred Dretske, *Explaining Behavior: Reasons in a World of Causes* (Bradford Books, 1988).

10 A representative moral virtue: justice

1 Annette Baier, "The Need for More than Justice", in Virginia Held (ed.), *Justice and Care. Essential Readings in Feminist Ethics* (Boulder, CO: Westview Press, 1995), p. 48.

2 Baier (1995, p .52).

3 Baier (1995, p. 55).

4 Baier (1995, p. 54).

5 *ST* IIaIIae.60.5 reply; see also IIaIIae.57.2.

6 *ST* IIaIIae.57.2 ad 3.

7 For some description of the complex ordering at issue here, see Chapter 11 on wisdom.

8 There is some controversy over whether Aquinas had the concept of a right, in our sense; see, e.g., Richard Tuck, *Natural Rights Theories. Their Origin and Development* (Cambridge: Cambridge University Press, 1979), p. 19 and the literature cited there. (I am grateful to James Bohman for calling Tuck's work to my attention.) I have no wish to enter this controversy. I am using the term 'right' here only in a broad sense: A has a right with regard to B only if B is obligated in the relevant respect with regard to A. To make the connection between obligations and rights clear and precise is a difficult matter and beyond the scope of this paper. There is also a considerable literature on it. I have discussed some of these issues in "God's Obligations", *Philosophical Perspectives* vol. 6, James Tomberlin (ed.) (Atascadero, CA: Ridgeview Publishing, 1992), pp. 475–492.

9 For an argument to this effect, see, e.g., Nel Noddings, "Caring", in Virginia Held (ed.), *Justice and Care. Essential Readings in Feminist Ethics* (Boulder, CO: Westview Press, 1995), pp. 7–30.

10 From "Professions for Women", quoted in Jean Hampton, "Feminist Contractarianism", in Louis Anthony and Charlotte Witt (eds), *A Mind of One's Own. Feminist Essays on Reason and Objectivity* (Boulder, CO: Westview Press, 1993), p. 231.

11 *Equality and Partiality* (Oxford: Oxford University Press, 1991), p. 3.

12 Nagel (1991, pp. 4–5).

13 Nagel (1991, p. 11).

14 Nagel (1991, p. 12).

15 Nagel (1991, p. 14).

16 Nagel (1991, p. 15).

17 Nagel 91991, pp. 170–171).

18 Nagel (1991, p. 171).

19 Nagel (1991, p. 3).

20 For an example of the way in which he proceeds to weave together all of these ethical and theological groupings, see Chapter 11 on wisdom.

21 Justice as a general virtue is perhaps roughly equivalent to what we mean by moral obligation in general. See, e.g., *ST* IIaIIae.58.5.

22 Cf., e.g., *ST* IIaIIae.58.8 s.c., where Aquinas approvingly cites Aristotle's line that justice is specially about those things that pertain to social life.

23 See, e.g., *ST* IaIIae.95.2 and IIaIIae.60.5. See Norman Kretzmann, "Lex Iniusta Non Est Lex: Laws on Trial in Aquinas' Court of Conscience", *American Journal of Jurisprudence* 33 (1988): 99–122.

24 For a discussion of natural law, see Chapter 2 on goodness.

25 *In NE* V.12, 1018–1019. Cf. also *ST* IaIIae.94.5, where Aquinas distinguishes two sorts of natural justice, one to which nature inclines us, and one which is such that nature does not incline us against it. Aquinas thus picks out the justice which he takes to be grounded in the nature of things by the inclination built in to human nature to accept it as just. (As his analogy makes clear, he also thinks that one can pick out indemonstrable first principles, whose truth is grounded in the natures of things or in God's nature, on the basis of the universal human inclination to find them true.) One might suppose that Aquinas's understanding of natural justice would commit him to the patently false belief that there is a common core to all human views about justice as well as to a very optimistic belief about the capacity of human beings to get moral

matters right. But this supposition is a mistake. Aquinas's claim is that human beings are by nature *inclined* to accept certain things as just, not that they always act on this inclination or that the inclination cannot be overridden.

26 *In NE* V.12, 1020–1023.

27 See, e.g., Paul Sigmund, "Law and Politics", in Norman Kretzmann and Eleonore Stump (eds), *The Cambridge Companion to Thomas Aquinas* (Cambridge: Cambridge University Press, 1993), p. 220. Sigmund is compelled to admit, however, that there is an "admixture of constitutional and republican elements in Aquinas's monarchism" (ibid., p. 221).

28 *DRP* 1.4.756.

29 *ST* IaIIae.96.3–4.

30 *ST* IaIIae.97.3 ad 3.

31 *DRP* 1.3.754.

32 *DRP* 1.4.756.

33 *In NE* V.11, 1010.

34 *In NE* V.11, 1011.

35 The practice of electing monarchs was found in some medieval states; in parts of Europe, such as Bohemia, it continued into the seventeenth century. I am grateful to Howard Louthan for pointing this out to me.

36 *ST* IaIIae.105.1.

37 *DRP* I.7.767.

38 See, e.g., *In II Sent* 44.2.2 ad 5; for a more nuanced view, see *DRP* I.7.768–770.

39 *ST* IIaIIae.42.2 ad 3.

40 See, e.g., *ST* IIaIIae.10.8, IIaIIae.10.11, IIaIIae.10.12.

41 *ST* IIaIIae.12.2.

42 *ST* IIaIIae.10.12. And when the child does come to the age of reason, it remains unjust for it to be brought to Christianity by any sort of compulsion.

43 Justice, e.g., has quasi-integral parts and quasi-potential parts (which are the virtues adjoined to justice). See *ST* IIaIIae.61 proemium.

44 *In NE* V.4, 928.

45 *In NE* V.6, 954.

46 *In NE* V.6, 950.

47 *In NE* V.7, 964.

48 *ST* IIaIIae.61.2. It is not entirely clear what to say about gift-giving on this view. On the one hand, giving presents clearly isn't in general a case of injustice, as Aquinas himself says (see, e.g., *ST* IIaIIae.63.1 ad 3). Giving presents can only be voluntary, of course; justice is preserved if someone chooses to sell, rather than give, his possession. So it seems as if ensuring that the parties to a transaction stand in the same relationship after the transaction as before it is sufficient for justice, although it is not always necessary for it. (It is the fact that meeting the conditions for commutative justice can still constitute an injustice when it comes to almsgiving that generates the puzzle of almsgiving discussed here.) On the other hand, it is possible for someone to choose freely to make a gift so great, so undeserved, so uncompensated that accepting it seems an injustice, and for just the sorts of reasons behind the notion of commutative justice.

49 *In NE* V.4, 927.

50 *In NE* V.4, 935.

51 *In NE* V.5, 941.

52 *In NE* V.4, 937. It is clear that Aquinas's basis for desert even in a democracy would exclude many of those living in the democracy from an equal share; the emphasis on freedom is apparently meant to exclude slaves, e.g..

53 *In NE* V.6, 953.

54 Punishments and fines might look like commutative exchanges in which the parties don't have the same at the end of the exchange as they did at the beginning, but, of course, punishments and fines are supposed to be remedies for the inequalities of earlier exchanges.
55 *ST* IIaIIae.60.4.
56 *ST* IIaIIae.68.3.
57 *ST* IIaIIae.59.1.
58 *ST* IIaIIae.57.1; see also *ST* IIaIIae.58.2.
59 *ST* IIaIIae.77.1 reply.
60 *ST* IIaIIae.77.1 s.c.
61 *ST* IIaIIae.77.2.
62 *ST* IIaIIae.77.2.
63 *ST* IIaIIae.62.2.
64 *ST* IIaIIae.78.1.
65 *DRJ* 1.728.
66 *ST* IIaIIae.77.4.
67 The reluctance can be seen in his claim that trading is the sort of thing which clerics should avoid just because of its connection with profit; *ST* IIaIIae.77.4 ad 3.
68 *ST* IIaIIae.77.4.
69 *ST* IIaIIae.71.4.
70 As long, that is, as the ruler did not suppose that keeping them was essential to salvation; *ST* IaIIae.104.3.
71 *ST* IaIIae.105.2.
72 This is Will Kymlicka's analysis of Nozick's view; see Kymlicka, *Contemporary Political Philosophy. An Introduction* (Oxford: Clarendon Press, 1990), p. 97. I am grateful to James Bohman for calling this work to my attention.
73 *ST* IaIIae.105.2. One supposes that in this case the Latin rendered 'men' would not be appropriately translated 'human beings'. I have nothing to say about Aquinas's generally unfavorable view of women, which expresses the spirit of his age.
74 *ST* IaIIae.105.2.
75 *ST* IaIIae.105.2.
76 To make this system even conceivably workable, it is clear that prices will need to vary depending on how close the Jubilee year is.
77 *ST* IIaIIae.87.1.
78 *ST* IIaIIae.32.7 ad 1.
79 *ST* IIaIIae.66.7 s.c.
80 Presumably, the need would have to be great and the taking would have to be such that it did not put the owner of the abundance into a state of need. A homely but helpful example of taking of this sort can be found in Victor Klemperer's *I Will Bear Witness: A Diary of the Nazi Years*, 2 vols., trans. Martin Chalmers (New York: Random House, 1998); originally published as *Ich will Zeugnis ablegen bis zum letzten. Tagebücher 1933–1945* (Berlin: Aufbau Verlag, 1996). He reports that when he and his wife were reduced by Nazi restrictions to a diet of potatoes, and an inadequate quantity of those, he regularly stole a spoonful of jam or a slice of bread from a neighbor who had more food than she and her family could eat.
81 *ST* IIaIIae.118.1.
82 The sort of job and position a person has in society may make a difference to what a person needs to sustain life appropriately, on Aquinas's view. So, e.g., the President of the United States may need to spend more for clothing than an assistant professor of philosophy.
83 Cf. *ST* IIaIIae.32.5.

84 *ST* IIaIIae.66.3 ad 2.

85 *ST* IIaIIae.87.1 s.c. and ad 4.

86 The obligations and rights surrounding almsgiving are complicated. As Aquinas's approving quotation of Basil shows, he thinks that the poor have a right to the sorts of things they get as alms, such as food, clothing, and shelter. It is also clear that, in his view, those who have more than they need are obligated to give alms. And yet it is not the case on his views that a particular almsgiver A is obligated to give alms to a particular needy person N, or that N has a right to property belonging to A. A might have given all he has to give before he encounters N, or A might have chosen persons other than N as the recipients of his alms. How exactly to explain the rights and obligations at issue in Aquinas's account of the obligatoriness of almsgiving is an interesting issue, but beyond the scope of this chapter.

87 *ST* IIaIIae.32.5. The connection between alms and charity is a large topic and not one which can be considered in passing here. Furthermore, Aquinas treats the giving of tithes but not the giving of alms in the treatise on justice (although he does suggest that there is a sense in which an act of almsgiving is also an act of justice; *ST* IIaIIae.32.1 ad 2.) Nonetheless, it is clear that in his view the general obligation to succor the poor is an obligation of justice, at least in the general sense of 'justice'. See, e.g., *ST* IIaIIae.122.6, where he says that justice is a matter of paying what is due to all in general; *ST* IIaIIae.117.5 ad 3, where he says that to give liberally to needy strangers belongs to justice; *ST* IIaIIae.32.3 s.c., where he cites with approval Augustine's dictum that to send the poor away empty is to ignore the claims of justice; and *ST* IIaIIae.118.3, where he says that one kind of covetousness, which is obtaining and keeping possessions which are owed to others, is opposed to justice. And, of course, one of the main purposes of giving tithes, which is a matter of justice in its special sense, is to enable the clergy to relieve the needs of the poor (*ST* IIaIIae.87.1 ad 4).

88 *ST* IIaIIae.32.5 ad 2. (I liked and therefore used the translation of the quotation of the passage from Basil given in the Dominican Fathers translation of the *ST* passage.)

89 Locke, *The Second Treatise of Government*, sec.46, ed. Peter Laslett (New York: New American Library, 1963), p. 342.

90 As one scholar, hostile to Locke's position, puts it, Locke's "whole theory of property is a justification of the natural right not only to unequal property but to unlimited individual appropriation." (C. B. MacPherson, *The Political Theory of Possessive Individualism. Hobbes to Locke*, Oxford: Clarendon Press, 1965, p. 221. I am grateful to James Bohman for calling this work to my attention.) MacPherson's views of Locke are controversial, and it may be a distortion to think of this one feature as Locke's "whole theory of property"; but MacPherson does seem to me right that Locke, unlike Aquinas, is willing to countenance unlimited acquisition as just.

91 Nothing in what I say about Aquinas's economic views, of course, has any implications regarding the ways in which the poor were *actually* treated in the Middle Ages. For an unflattering historical study of poverty in the medieval period, see, e.g., Michael Mollat, *The Poor in the Middle Ages*, trans. Arthur Goldhammer (New Haven, CT: Yale University Press, 1986).

92 It is for this reason that there is no similar puzzle about the moral acceptability of giving presents. A present is something that its recipient does not have a right to. Consequently, a person A who decided to give some object O to person B but only on the receipt from B of something of equal value to O would not violate any of B's rights or engage in any injustice towards B. There

is no obligation for A to give O to B as a *present*. (There may, of course, be all sorts of social situations in which something is given which has some of the features of a gift but is in fact a reparation for a previous wrong, an expected contribution to a social function, or something else of the sort. In such case, it may be obligatory to give what looks like, but is not really, a gift.)

93 There is certainly reason to suppose that some of Aquinas's views about the lawfulness of private property were influenced by the Franciscan controversy over poverty. For a brief review of the literature on this topic, see Tuck (1979, pp. 20 ff).

94 *ST* IIaIIae.66.2.

95 *ST* IIaIIae.66.2 ad 2.

96 *ST* IIaIIae.66.7 ad 2.

97 Aquinas makes a similar point in connection with his explanation of the Old Testament story of the spoiling of the Egyptians. See *ST* IIaIIae.66.5 ad 1.

98 *ST* IIaIIae.66.7.

99 I do not mean to suggest, and nothing in this interpretation requires one to hold, that a human person involved in such an exchange is *aware* of acting as God's agent.

100 I am assuming (1) that ensuring equality in exchange is necessary as well as sufficient for justice in commutative exchanges if neither party is voluntarily choosing to make a gift to the other of his share in the transaction, and (2) that if it were not for the precepts governing the Jubilee year, A would be unwilling to make a gift of his possession to B.

101 In arguing that it would be morally acceptable for a ruler to govern his state in accordance with Old Testament law, including the law of the Jubilee year, Aquinas is in effect claiming that the precepts of that law are in accordance with justice as a general virtue.

102 Since the obligation to give alms is an obligation of general justice, not of special justice, the puzzle would also disappear if something could be simultaneously just in accordance with general justice and unjust in accordance with commutative justice, or the other way around – unjust as regards general justice but just as regards commutative justice. But, of course, the price of this solution would be a moral system on which, in certain circumstances, a person would be in violation of a moral obligation, no matter what he did. Some ethical systems do countenance intractable moral dilemmas, but it is hard to suppose that Aquinas's is one of them. Worse yet, interpreted in this way, Aquinas's ethical system would yield such intractable dilemmas not in the rare, tragic case, but commonly, on an everyday basis.

103 Economic exchanges such as buying and selling are undoubtedly commutative exchanges for Aquinas, who tends to speak of them as 'voluntary commutations'. See, e.g., *ST* IIaIIae.77 proemium.

104 K. D. M. Snell, e.g., says that Britain in the period of enclosure was "permeated with a confusion... of moral rectitude with economic well being"; *Annals of the Laboring Poor. Social Change and Agrarian England 1160–1900*, Cambridge Studies in Population, Economy and Society in Past Time, vol. 2 (Cambridge: Cambridge University Press, 1987), p.170. See also Gertrude Himmelfarb, *The Idea of Poverty: England in the Early Industrial Age* (New York: Knopf, 1983). The distinction between the deserving and the undeserving poor is older than the Enlightenment, however. It can be found, e.g., in Martin Luther's recommendation to state authorities to provide for those poor who had *"honorably labored"* at their craft or in agriculture" (my emphasis) but who could work no longer (cited in Frances Fox Piven and Richard Cloward, *Regulating the Poor: The Function of Public Welfare* (New York: Vintage Books, 1971), p. 9.) Piven

and Cloward also provide an interesting discussion of the attempt, beginning in the Renaissance and continuing into the Enlightenment period, to shift from private and Church relief of the poor to state-regulated welfare systems, a shift prompted in part by the great growth in the numbers of the poor, which in Britain stemmed from the enclosure of the commons and the disruption of the parish system, among other factors. I am grateful to James Bohman for calling this book to my attention. Finally, something like the distinction between the deserving and the undeserving poor can be found as early as the Patristic period. Ambrose dismisses it with scorn. He says:

> You should not look to what each person deserves. Mercy is not wont to judge on the basis of merit but to meet needs, not to examine as to uprightness but to help the poor ... Since you have the means to be gracious, then, do not delay ... lest you lose the opportunity to give ... But why do I say that you should not delay your generosity? It is more a matter of not hastening to robbery, it is more a matter of not extorting what you desire, it is more a matter of not seeking someone else's property.
>
> ("On Naboth", in *Ambrose*, ed. and tran. Boniface Ramsey, O.P., London: Routledge, 1997, p. 130)

105 *ST* IIaIIae.32.5.
106 *DRJ* 1.727. By pointing out these passages in this work, I do not mean to leave the impression that, in my view, Aquinas's attitude towards the Jews is not anti-Semitic or is minimally morally acceptable. There is a great deal in this treatise and other works to show that his attitude towards the Jews is morally offensive. In this respect as in many others, the best that can be said is that he is a child of his age.
107 *In NE* V.4, 937.
108 *ST* IIaIIae.6.3 s.c.
109 *ST* IIaIIae.63 proemium. That is, Aquinas thinks of honor as one of the goods a society has to distribute, and he regards it as morally wrong to pick wealth on the basis of which to distribute this good.
110 As I pointed out above, Aquinas thinks that the Old Testament judicial precepts, of which he approves, have reducing inequality among their purposes.
111 See *ST* IIaIIae.33.1 s.c.
112 Fraternal correction as directed to the amendment of the wrongdoer is an act of justice only in the general sense of justice; as directed towards amending the effects of his wrongdoing on others, however, it is an act of justice even in the special sense of justice. See *ST* IIaIIae.33.1. Whether in this sense it is an act of commutative or distributive justice depends on the nature of the wrong being remedied.
113 Aquinas's idea that the moral obligatoriness of "fraternal correction" admits of exceptions in these circumstances seems to me to capture what is right about Hannah Arendt's oft (and correctly) criticized views about Jewish collaboration with the Nazis. And Aquinas's recognition that fraternal correction may well be inefficacious distinguishes his position from Arendt's much sterner view. For Arendt, victims of injustice, such as the Jews in Nazi Germany, are "partly responsible for [their] own position and therewith for the blot on mankind which it represented", quoted in Richard Bernstein, *Hannah Arendt and the Jewish Question* (Cambridge, MA: MIT Press, 1996), p. 37. Arendt's point, as Bernstein explains it, is that there is a duty to political action against injustice and that those victims of social injustice who have not fulfilled that duty are

therefore to a certain extent responsible (at least politically, if not morally) for the position in which they find themselves. Aquinas's position is more forgiving. He makes the duty to social dissent contingent on certain circumstances, rather than absolute; and since he also recognizes that such dissent may be inefficacious, his position avoids the conclusion that victims of social injustice are always partly responsible for their own suffering.

114 *ST* IIaIIae.33.2 ad 3. There is also a more complicated case in which failure to reprove a wrongdoer is not itself a serious moral wrong, when one is hesitant to engage in moral reproof but would certainly do it if one could see clearly that it would result in some amendment on the part of the person reproved. In such a case, failure to reprove is still morally wrong, but it is not a serious moral wrong.

115 *ST* IIaIIae.33.2 reply and ad 4.

116 See, e.g., what Aquinas says about the obligations of accusers, *ST* IIaIIae.68.3 ad 1. It isn't entirely clear whether the one being reproved must really be guilty of the sin in question; see note 127 below.

117 In fact, slander and gossip are violations of commutative justice. See, e.g., *ST* IIaIIae.64 proemium, IIaIIae.67 proemium, and IIaIIae.72 proemium.

118 *ST* IIaIIae.33.2 s.c.

119 *ST* IIaIIae.33.4.

120 *ST* IIaIIae.33.4 ad 2.

121 *ST* IIaIIae.33.7.

122 *ST* IIaIIae.33.2 ad 3.

123 *ST* IIaIIae.33.2 ad 3. In this connection, it is hard not to think of dictators, such as Hitler and Mao, and to wonder how different the fate of the societies they ruled would have been if there had been people around them who acted on the normative views Aquinas expresses here. Cf. also Adolf Eichmann's complaint that "[n]obody ... came to me and reproached me for anything in the performance of my duties" (quoted in Bernstein, 1996, p. 164).

124 Flattery is discussed in connection with the virtues annexed to justice, that is, virtues which have to do with moral obligations between individuals in a society, but which in some way do not share all the features of justice; flattery is a vice opposed to the virtues annexed to justice. Aquinas explains his complicated division of the virtues annexed to justice, and their opposite vices, including flattery, in *ST* IIaIIae.80.1.

125 Li Zhisui, *The Private Life of Chairman Mao*, trans. Tai Hung-chao (New York: Random House, 1994).

126 *ST* IIaIIae.115.2.

127 *ST* IIaIIae.73.1 ad 3 and IIaIIae.73.2 reply. It is not clear whether Aquinas thinks that the absence of any of these conditions is sufficient to make an act not an act of detraction. e.g., if A's intention is to injure B's reputation and A doesn't have good evidence for his accusation, but in fact B really is guilty of the charge, is A's accusation still an act of detraction? I am inclined to think Aquinas would say 'yes', but the texts do not seem to me decisive on this point. (There are various other unclear points in this description of detraction as well; see notes 129 and 130 below.)

128 See, e.g., *ST* IIaIIae.72 proemium, IIaIIae.64 proemium, IIaIIae.67 proemium.

129 It is not hard to think of circumstances in which slandering someone in fact does that person a great deal of good. Imagine, e.g., that B is a German guard of Jewish prisoners on a work detail shoveling snow and that B is trying to give his prisoners what help he can by allowing them to take frequent breaks in a warm shelter. Suppose that B is suspected by his superiors of being friendly towards Jews and that friendliness towards Jews on the part of a

German guard is punishable by imprisonment in a concentration camp. Then a Jewish prisoner who complained loudly in the presence of B's superiors that B treated his prisoners harshly would be slandering B, but he would be doing B a great good, which outweighs the evil of the slander.

As an illustration for Aquinas's account of detraction, my story here has at least two problems. (1) I am supposing that slander, or publicly harming someone's reputation, involves attributing objectively bad things to someone, even if some of those hearing the slander would mistakenly think those bad things good. But Aquinas's account of detraction is not clear on this point. Is it detraction if A attributes bad things to B, intending to injure B's reputation, but A's audience is entirely composed of people who only think more highly of B after hearing what A has to say about him? (2) It is not entirely clear whether Aquinas's first requirement for detraction, that the detractor intend to do a significant injury to his victim's reputation, is to be read as a requirement that the detractor intend to harm his victim or just that he intend to harm his victim's reputation. Depending on how we interpret this requirement and depending on how we fill out the story in my example here, the Jewish prisoner might or might not be guilty of detraction in denouncing his guard in the presence of the guard's superiors. (Of course, if we read Aquinas's requirement for detraction in the second way, and assume that the Jewish prisoner was trying to help his guard, then my story counts as a counterexample to Aquinas's claim that detraction is always a sin.) So neither my example nor Aquinas's account of detraction is precise in some important respects. But I mean my example only to stimulate intuitions about the ways in which being a victim of detraction can in fact do good to the victim.

130 Although here, too, Aquinas's account is imprecise. If A wants to engage in fraternal correction of B and has the right motive to do so, then is it enough for fraternal correction that A have good evidence that B is guilty of the sin in question, or does it have to be the case that A's accusation is true? If A has good evidence but in fact B is nonetheless not guilty, then is A's act no longer an act of fraternal correction? Would A have to be *certain* that B was guilty in order to fraternally correct B?

131 Here, as in the case of corporal almsgiving, nothing in what I say should be taken as implying that giving a present is incompatible with justice on Aquinas's view. If a person wants to give a free gift of himself or his resources for the sake of improving his neighbor or his state, the moral acceptability of his doing so is not in tension with commutative justice as Aquinas presents it. The puzzle arises only because Aquinas takes almsgiving to be obligatory, so that it is a mortal sin to omit fraternal correction in some circumstances.

132 *ST* IIaIIae.64 proemium.

133 *ST* IIaIIae.64.5 obj. l.

134 *ST* IIaIIae.64.5 reply and ad 1. It is not clear, of course, whether suicide can properly be considered a case of commutative injustice even if we think of it as an injustice directed against the community and God. It is also not clear in what way anything can be considered an injustice against God, who cannot sustain any sort of harm or suffer any sort of disadvantage, on Aquinas's view. I am less interested here in sorting out Aquinas's views on suicide than in showing the light his reasoning about suicide casts on his attitude towards fraternal correction.

135 *ST* IIaIIae.64.5.

136 Aquinas perhaps has in mind here the sort of bodily mutilation which Origen performed on himself as an aid to chastity. See the discussion of bodily mutilation and "eunuchs for the kingdom of God", *ST* IIaIIae.65.1 ad 3.

137 *ST* IIaIIae.65.1.

138 *ST* IaIIae.96.4; see also the similar remark in *ST* IIaIIae.64.5.

139 *ST* IIaIIae.64.5.

140 For explanation and defense of this claim, see Chapter 9 on freedom.

141 Baier (1995, p. 52).

142 Baier (1995, p. 55).

143 It is true that part of what is sought after in an ethics of care is an affective attitude of a warm sort, and one might suppose that this is missing in Aquinas's account of care for others as *obligatory*. But such a supposition would be mistaken. A full account of Aquinas's account of justice would show the way in which justice, and all other real virtues, must be connected to charity or love. This connection is one more of the many things left out here on the grounds that one cannot do everything in one chapter.

144 I put the point this way not only because corporal almsgiving looks as if it might be interpretable as at least related to distributive justice, but also because Aquinas explicitly says that fraternal correction counts as falling under commutative justice in connection with its second aim, protecting individuals or the community from the effects of someone else's wrongdoing.

145 *ST* IIaIIae.68.3.

146 Of course, there might be cases of unjust commutative exchange in which the one treated unjustly is willing to be treated in this way. I am not suggesting that the injustice of unjust commutative exchanges is solely a function of the fact that the person who gets less than his share suffers unwillingly. Rather, the point here is just that voluntariness is necessary for almsgiving.

147 A related question, of course, is whether anyone has a right to such submissiveness on Ophelia's part. But this question can be conveniently subsumed under the question whether Ophelia is obligated to be submissive, since the answer to this latter question is 'no'. It is very difficult to imagine a case in which P has a right to certain treatment at O's hands, but O has no obligation to treat P in that way. So if Ophelia has no obligation to be submissive towards Polonius, then Polonius has no right to such submissiveness on Ophelia's part. Of course, if we were to answer the question about Ophelia's obligations in the affirmative, we might still be left with an open question about Polonius's rights. Unless rights and obligations are invariably correlative, and I do not think that they are (see Stump, 1992), then it does seem possible that some person O could have obligations to treat some person P in a certain way, but that P not have a right to that treatment at O's hands.

148 A differently worrisome sort of case arises if we imagine that no one person made exploitative or unjust demands on Ophelia, but that many, many persons each made a small and reasonable demand. If Ophelia tries to meet all these small and reasonable demands, she will be destroyed as surely as if she is the victim of one person's exploitation. One response to this sort of case consists in remembering that for Aquinas, God's purposes include the flourishing of all human beings. Ophelia is included in this group. To the extent to which her crazy attempt to meet very many small demands is destructive for her, her compliance will contravene God's purposes. I owe the objection and the solution to John Greco.

149 I think the question also underestimates the power moral goodness has to make human beings flourish even in abysmal circumstances. For a moving example of human grandeur and flourishing in horrendous circumstances, see Klemperer (1996/1998).

150 See Robert Ericksen, *Theologians under Hitler* (New Haven, CT: Yale University Press, 1985), pp. 28–29.

151 Gita Sereny, *Into That Darkness* (New York: Vintage Books, 1983), p. 364.
152 See note 27.

11 A representative intellectual virtue: wisdom

1 When wisdom is a virtue in our sense of 'virtue', Aquinas thinks of it as a gift of the Holy Spirit. The subsequent discussion will help clarify the terminology.

2 Virtue epistemology, of course, is the subject of much contemporary discussion; but the cognitive virtues of virtue epistemology are not explicitly presented or discussed as involving both a cognitive excellence and an excellence of will. (The extent to which virtue epistemology may be implicitly committed to a role for will in believing is not clear.) For a good recent discussion of virtue epistemology, see, e.g., John Greco, "Virtues and Vices of Virtue Epistemology", *Canadian Journal of Philosophy*, 23 (1993): 413–432, and also Linda Trinkaus Zagzebski, *Virtues of the Mind* (Cambridge: Cambridge University Press, 1996).

3 Muriel Deutsch Lezak, *Neuropsychological Assessment*, 2nd edn (Oxford: Oxford University Press, 1983), p. 21.

4 Some psychologists point out the "inadvisability of drawing inferences about neuropsychological status" from a consideration of scores on these tests; see, e.g., Lezak (1983, p. 242). The same author says, "Both Verbal and Performance Scale IQ scores ... are based on the averages of some quite dissimilar functions that have relatively low intercorrelations and bear no regular neuroanatomical or neuropsychological relationship to one another", and "it is impossible to predict specific disabilities and areas of intellectual competency or dysfunction from the averaged ability test scores" (ibid., pp. 242, 243).

5 Michael Gazzaniga, *Nature's Mind: The Biological Roots of Thinking, Emotions, Sexuality, Language, and Intelligence* (New York: Basic Books, 1992), pp. 98–99.

6 Gazzaniga (1992, p. 104).

7 'Scientia' is often translated as 'knowledge', but in my view this is a misleading translation; see Chapter 7 on the foundations of knowledge. (For a somewhat different approach to Aquinas's account of *scientia*, see Scott MacDonald, "Theory of Knowledge", in Norman Kretzmann and Eleonore Stump (eds), *The Cambridge Companion to Aquinas* (Cambridge: Cambridge University Press, 1993), pp. 160–195.) In order to avoid adjudicating complex issues with a translation, I will leave the word '*scientia*' untranslated. In my view, the least misleading way to translate '*scientia*' is as 'science', where it is understood that science can encompass, e.g., metaphysics.

8 *ST* Ia.82.4.

9 Aquinas seems to suppose that faith results from such an action of the will on the intellect. See, e.g., *QDV* where he talks of the will's commanding intellect to produce faith; *QDV* 14.3 reply, ad 2, and ad 10. For further discussion of Aquinas's views of faith, see Chapter 12 on faith.

10 See *ST* IaIIae.17.1 and IaIIae.17.6.

11 *ST* Ia.82.4.

12 *ST* IaIIae. 9.2.

13 *ST* Ia.81.3 and IaIIae.10.3.

14 *ST* IaIIae.9.1. The relation between the will and the sensitive powers of the soul is outside the scope of this chapter, but it is not hard to see that the will has at least some indirect control over the sensitive powers since, e.g., one can will to direct one's gaze or will to close one's eyes and thereby control what one sees.

15 *ST* Ia.82.4. See also *ST* IaIIae.9.1. There is no suggestion in Aquinas that the direction of the will towards the good in general somehow naturally results in

the will's governance of the other powers; this line of his may just be intended to explain why God gave the will the governance it has.

16 I take the notion of a design plan of cognitive faculties, and associated notions, from Alvin Plantinga's *Warrant and Proper Function* (Oxford: Oxford University Press, 1993).

17 Of course, on Aquinas's account of the relations between the intellect and the will, an act of will is dependent on some act of intellect (whether tacit or explicit) apprehending something as good. What is not clear is whether Aquinas thinks that the intellect's apprehension is the only constraint on the will in its relations to the other powers it can command, or whether he recognizes as well what seems clearly to be the case, namely, that acts of will are also constrained by the nature of the power or faculty or body part being commanded. Since the latter point is not only true but also commonsensical and reasonably obvious, I will assume that it is part of what Aquinas has in mind here.

18 *ST* IaIIae.17.6.

19 In his article, "What Ought We to Believe? or The Ethics of Belief Revisited" (*American Philosophical Quarterly* 17 (1980): 15–24), Jack Meiland makes a similar point about this tradition in epistemology, although he assigns a slightly different reason for it.

20 Roderick M. Chisholm, "Lewis' Ethics of Belief", in Paul Arthur Schilpp (ed.), *The Philosophy of C.I. Lewis* (London: Cambridge University Press, 1968), p. 224.

21 See, e.g., "Concepts of Epistemic Justification" and "The Deontological Conception of Epistemic Justification", reprinted in *Epistemic Justification. Essays in the Theory of Knowledge* (Ithaca, NY: Cornell University Press, 1989), pp. 81–152.

22 See, e.g., *Warrant: The Current Debate* (Oxford: Oxford University Press, 1993). Unlike Alston, Plantinga is cautiously sympathetic to attempts to show that the will has a role in belief (see pp. 148–161), because he sees some merit in Bas van Fraassen's argument for the claim that "Belief is a matter of the will" ["Belief and the Will", *The Journal of Philosophy* 81 (1984): 256]. In that paper, van Fraassen says little about the nature of the interaction between the will and the intellect, and so I will not discuss his views here.

23 One caveat at the outset may be helpful. It is widely agreed that desire can influence belief. Double-blind experiments in science, e.g., have as their purpose minimizing the role of desire in belief. But it is not clear what the relation of desire to volition is. Harry Frankfurt defines a volition as an effective desire. That is, on his view, a desire which eventuates in action (if there are no external impediments) is just a volition. So if Frankfurt is right, then when desires for beliefs result in the mental action of belief formation, those desires are volitions; in that case, any instance of a belief's resulting from desire will count as an instance of the will's producing belief (whether directly or indirectly). Because the connection between desire and volition is a large and controversial issue, however, I will set aside cases of beliefs resulting from desire and not consider them here.

For Frankfurt's view on volition as effective desire, see his "Freedom of the Will and the Concept of a Person", *The Journal of Philosophy* 68 (1971): 5–20; reprinted in *The Importance of What We Care About* (Cambridge: Cambridge University Press, 1988), see esp. p. 14. It is perhaps worth noting that thinkers in other periods have held similar views. Jonathan Edwards, e.g., says:

> In every act of the will for, or towards something not present, the soul is in some degree inclined to that thing; and that inclination, if in a considerable degree, is the very same with the affection of desire. The will, and the affec-

tions of the soul, are not two faculties; the affections are not essentially distinct from the will, nor do they differ from the mere actings of the will and inclination, but only in the liveliness and sensibility of exercise.

(*A Treatise Concerning Religious Affections*, pt. 1, section 1)

(I am grateful to Alvin Plantinga for calling my attention to this work.)

24 "Deciding to Believe", in Bernard Williams, *Problems of the Self* (New York: Cambridge, 1973), pp. 136–151.

25 Barbara Winters, "Willing to Believe", *The Journal of Philosophy* 76 (1979): 243–256. See also Jonathan Bennett, "Why is Belief Involuntary?", *Analysis* 50 (1990): 87–107; Bennett also criticizes Williams's position, but for my purposes here Winters's objections are more interesting.

26 Winters (1979, p. 243).

27 The case of enlisting the help of a therapist to rid one of a belief is, clearly, itself a case in which the will has an effect on belief; but since the will's control of belief in this case is very indirect, this case will perhaps be uncontroversial. It should perhaps be added that the process of ridding oneself of a belief one thinks has no appropriate connection with truth may involve processes that have little or nothing to do with the will's control over belief.

28 Winters (1979, p. 244).

29 She gives as a special case of her principle "it is impossible for me to believe of a particular belief *b* that *b* is a present belief of mine and sustained at will". (Winters, 1979, p. 256).

30 The conditions she gives also seem presupposed by others who argue against voluntary control over belief; see, e.g., Williams (1973), and Alston (1989).

31 Alston (1989, pp. 244–245).

32 In fact, I do not think that (1)–(3) do capture what it is to believe at will or that their analogues capture what it is to move at will. A habitual hummer, e.g., who hums without realizing that she is doing so, nonetheless seems to me to hum at will.

33 Although we sometimes think of such episodes as involuntary, in fact it is clear that the muscles are not moving by themselves in such cases; they are still under the control of the will.

34 *ST* Ia.82.4. For further discussion of this topic, see Chapter 7 on the foundations of knowledge.

35 In order to operate in accordance with the design plan of what it commands, of course, the will does not require any recognition on the part of the intellect that it is doing so or any apprehension of the nature of the design plan on the part of the intellect. The will can command the head to turn without the intellect's apprehending the nature of the musculature of the head.

36 *ST* IaIIae.9.1.

37 And this point holds whether the will tries to command the intellect to believe something which is evidently false or whether the will tries to command the intellect to believe something when the truth-value of the belief is utterly unapparent. In the latter cases, we might act as if we assented to the belief, but the will could not successfully command the intellect to adopt it.

38 Alston (1989, p. 122).

39 Alston (1989, p. 123).

40 Although it is not entirely clear on this point, the novel suggests that in the end, even if only briefly, Winston succeeds in altering his perceptual beliefs about what he in fact sees. If Orwell thought it is possible for a man who sees

four fingers in front of him to will successfully to believe that there are five fingers in front of him, then in my view Orwell is mistaken.

41 This very phenomenon, of course, is an example of the way in which desire (if not volition) can influence perceptual beliefs.

42 Nothing in this example suggests that a person will always be successful when the will issues a command of this sort; it is not the case either that any person who can sometimes, in one free basic action, touch his toes will always be able to do so when the will commands it. For some discussion of the cases involving perception, see, e.g., Irvin Rock, *The Logic of Perception* (Cambridge, MA: MIT Press, Bradford Books, 1987), esp. Chapter 3. Rock sees a role for the will in the formation of perceptual beliefs also. He puts the point this way:

> Consistent with my suggestion about figure-ground organization, I would like to suggest that grouping on the basis of factors such as proximity, similarity, ... is the result of a decision to describe the stimulus array in one way rather than other possible ways ... a particular grouping is linked to a particular description and therefore is of the nature of a decision rather than of a spontaneous interaction.
>
> (p.75)

(I myself think that Rock's use of 'decision' here is infelicitous, suggesting an implausible degree of awareness or even deliberation. The claim that the will has a role in perception is a weaker claim.) A recent neurobiology text, speaking of a different sort of figure/ground discrimination, says, "The exact shape is ambiguous ... *With some conscious effort* one can mentally shift the light source ... and change the apparent curvature of the object" (emphasis mine). See Eric Kandel, James Schwartz, and Thomas Jessell (eds), *Principles of Neural Science*, 3rd edn (New York: Elsevier, 1991), p. 444.

43 Someone might suppose that this is a case in which the will influences perceptual belief only indirectly, and that this case is analogous to one in which the will, e.g., commands the head to turn so that the eyes can see what is behind the willer, with the result that new perceptual beliefs are formed as an indirect result of the act of the will. In the case I have described, of course, there is no intermediary of voluntary muscle movement between the will's command and the new perceptual belief. But someone might still object that there is nonetheless an intermediary between the command of the will and the perceptual belief, namely, the new perception. If this objection were right, any instance of perception occurring between a command of the will and the resulting perceptual belief would be enough by itself to make the will's control of the belief indirect; and it would consequently be impossible for true perceptual beliefs to be the direct result of a command of the will. In that case, the will's control over perceptual belief could be only indirect. But put this way, the objection relies on the view that perception can be cleanly dissociated from perceptual belief. But even those who accept this view should grant this much: if the perceptual belief in question is the spontaneous and unavoidable concomitant of the perception (as it is in the case involving the ambiguous figure discussed in the text), then in virtue of being able to produce the perception directly by an act of will, the willer also has direct voluntary control over the perceptual belief, since he controls his having that perceptual belief by an act of will alone, without the intermediary of muscle movement or other intervening acts of will. I am grateful to Peter van Inwagen, whose objections helped me to think through the issues involved here.

44 e.g., you find yourself afflicted with a memory of a colleague's contumelious treatment of you, and you can feel your anger growing out of all bounds as the images of the wretched occasion recur repeatedly to your mind. "Forget it," you say to yourself sternly, "put it out of your mind." And in virtue of that act of will (perhaps repeated more than once), you succeed in moving the images of the event out of short-term memory and into dispositional memory, so that the memory beliefs become dispositional rather than occurrent. There is also considerable evidence that if the events are awful enough and if the will to erase the memory is strong enough, it is possible to move the images of the event not only out of short-term memory but out of consciously accessible long-term memory as well, so that they are repressed and entirely forgotten. Inaccessible to consciousness and not available for retrieval at the initiative of the agent, the images of such awful events remain just in some sort of cognitive deep storage, where they can be jogged loose by blows to the head or equally jarring psychological shocks or probing psychotherapy. Repression of traumatic childhood events, such as violent sexual abuse, has been widely discussed. In addition to the mechanisms for the release of such previously repressed memories, there is also in some cases a little understood spontaneous release of memories. For a case in which a blow to the head releases previously repressed traumatic memories, see Oliver Sacks, *The Man Who Mistook His Wife for a Hat* (New York: Harper Perennial, 1985), pp.161–165. It seems, then, that the will has some control over memory, too.

These cases of will's influence on memory are apparently not ones in which the will is acting in accordance with the design plan of the cognitive faculties, since the will here has a role in suppressing information which would otherwise have been available to the cognitive faculties. But some cognitive modules, or some cognitive modules in some circumstances, have something other than the cognition of truth as part of their design plan. In these cases of memory repression, we might say that the primary design plan of the memory module – namely, the storage of information about past experience – is overridden in favor of a secondary design plan aimed at psychic survival. When the primary design plan would store information destructive to the psyche, the secondary design plan overrides it and represses the memory. Considered in this way, the will is acting in accordance with the design plan of memory even in bringing about the repression of memories.

Finally, in some cases, there is also voluntary control, of a limited sort, over occurrent memory beliefs. e.g., the will can command memory to retain certain information in such a way as to form occurrent memory beliefs. You make an appointment to see the Dean tomorrow, but you have a lamentable tendency to forget appointments, in spite of your best efforts, and you are worried that this one will skip your mind, too. So you issue repeated commands to memory: "Don't forget! You have an appointment with the Dean at three tomorrow." And the result is that you do remember this appointment, unlike the others you characteristically forget. (That it takes effort, time, and repeated trying for the will to be successful in these cases does not show that the acts in question are not free basic actions. A person who was out of condition might find that it took him effort, time, and three or four tries to touch his toes, but his act of touching his toes would still be a free basic action.) Or you are being tested on digit span by an educational tester who has, unprofessionally enough, explained to you that your colleague who works in mathematical logic was able to hold in memory a span of ten digits. Eaten with envy, you will to remember at least twelve, and as a result of the determination of the will you do so.

45 This is not to say, of course, that we have voluntary control of any sort over all our beliefs, that we are morally responsible for having the beliefs we do, that we are morally culpable for any morally wrong beliefs we have, and so on. My claim here is only the limited one stated in the text.

46 Once we understand the way in which the will can govern the faculties or modules or body parts it commands, it is not difficult to find examples not only of direct voluntary control of belief, such as those above, but also of indirect voluntary control, where the will governs the intellect by directing attention. There are cases, e.g., of what Alston calls immediate (although indirect) control, that is, cases in which "the agent is able to carry out the intention 'right away', in one uninterrupted intentional act, without having to return to the attempt a number of times after having been occupied with other matters" (Alston, 1989, p. 129). You have a difficult and quarrelsome colleague who is also afflicted with a brain deficit which leaves him unable to express emotion in facial expression or the pitch of spoken speech. When he greets you in the morning, you find yourself believing spontaneously that he is angry at you. But just as your intellect is thinking up a nasty response, your will commands your intellect to review the evidence available to you, including your understanding of his brain deficit. On that basis, you bite back the unpleasant remark you were framing; you reject the belief that he is angry at you and chalk your original reaction up to a mistaken assessment of his facial expression. Or it turns out that the chief event at the party your best friend has arranged for you consists of plane rides in sporty little two-seater planes. You are generally unable to believe that flying is a safe and acceptable way to travel, but you want very badly not to disappoint your friend. So when your friend asks you to get in the plane, your will instructs your intellect to review quickly all the evidence available to you relevant to this instance of flying. As a result, you form the belief that this one plane ride will be acceptably safe, and you get in the plane. In the first of these two cases, someone might suppose that intellect is looking for "evidence to decide an unresolved issue", but in the second case it is clear that "the search for evidence was undertaken with the intention of taking up a certain attitude toward a particular proposition" (Alston, 1989, p. 130), which is what Alston thinks we need for a genuine case of voluntary control of belief. Here, too, for immediate indirect control of belief, a ready formula for finding examples that show the will's role in belief is to look for cases in which the cognitive faculties are beginning to go wrong, either in virtue of reacting inappropriately to something misleading in the cognitive environment (as in the case of the brain-damaged colleague) or in virtue of being swayed by the pull of a passion (as in the case of the fear of flying) or for some other reason. In such cases, the will works together with the design plan of the cognitive faculties to counteract the localized cognitive problem.

47 Or perhaps the thing to say here is that in these cases the design plan of what the will commands is being satisfied, if we take 'design plan' in a narrow sense, while it is being violated if we take 'design plan' is quite a broad sense. A keyboard operator's fingers are being used in accordance with their design plan when she types; and when she wills to type, the will is commanding the relevant body parts in accordance with their design plan. Carpal tunnel syndrome, however, develops in some people who regularly type many hours a day; the design plan of the fingers, taken in a larger sense, is not suited to endless repetitions of the same movements without substantial and frequent intervals of rest. So there is a sense in which operating a keyboard continuously is not in accordance with the design plan of the fingers even if any individual movement of the fingers at the keyboard is in accordance with the design plan of the body

parts used. It may be helpful here to invoke Plantinga's distinction between a snapshot design plan, which specifies how the thing works now, and a maximum design plan, which specifies how the thing will change its workings over time in different circumstances. See Plantinga (1993, pp. 22ff.).

48 Because I explicate wisdom by focusing on folly and because in folly the will exercises only immediate indirect control over the intellect, someone might suppose that for his account of wisdom Aquinas needs only the weaker claim, that the will has such indirect control, and not also the stronger claim, that the will has direct control over intellect. But this is a misimpression generated by my explication of wisdom in terms of its opposed vice, folly. The process by which the will corrupts intellect does require only indirect control over intellect on the part of the will. But the process by which the will and the intellect function together to produce wisdom has as an essential ingredient direct control by the will over the intellect. Wisdom is an outgrowth of charity, which in turn depends on faith; and faith is a case in which the will exercises direct control over the intellect, on Aquinas's view. If there were space here to explicate Aquinas's entire account of wisdom, it would, consequently, be clear that the stronger claim is necessary.

49 See, e.g., *QDV* 14.3 obj. 2 and reply; also *ST* IaIIae.55.1 and IaIIae.57.1. In the case of intellectual virtues, from Aquinas's point of view, the will also has a role to play because of the interconnectedness of the intellect and the will on his view. The role of the will in virtue for Aquinas is brought out as well by his complete definition of virtue, which is more complicated than we can deal with here: a virtue is a good quality of the mind, by which we live righteously, of which no one can make bad use, which God works in us without us; see *ST* IaIIae.55.4.

50 See, e.g., *ST* IaIIae.57.2 and IaIIae.57.4.

51 Prudence has to do with reasoning about things that are to be done in order to obtain human good; art has to do with reasoning about things that are to be made in order to obtain human good. *ST* IaIIae.57.2.

52 See, e.g., *ST* IaIIae.66.5; also *In PA* II.20.15, *In NE* VI.6.1190 and 1193, and *QDP* 1.4.

53 As Aquinas of course understood, some of what is included in Aristotelian metaphysics is what we now would think of as philosophical theology. See, e.g., *ST* IIaIIae.19.7.

54 The discussion of Aristotle here and in the next sections should not obscure the fact that Aquinas's views of intellectual excellence in general and wisdom in particular have an Augustinian root as well. For some discussion of the way in which Aquinas and Augustine are related here, see, e.g., Mark Jordan, *Ordering Wisdom: The Hierarchy of Philosophical Discourses in Aquinas* (Notre Dame, IN: University of Notre Dame Press, 1986), pp. 122ff.

55 Nothing in this claim implies anything about the way in which knowledge of God's nature and actions is acquired. It might be acquired even by the simple and unlearned in consequence of being told parts of God's revelation in Scripture.

56 See *ST* IaIIae.68.1.

57 See, e.g., *ST* IIaIIae.45.1 ad 2. See also *ST* IaIIae.68.1; there Aquinas summarizes the details of the distinction between virtues in general and gifts by saying that the virtues make a person apt to follow reason, and the gifts make a person apt to follow the promptings of the Holy Spirit. See also *In Sent* III.35.2.1.1 ad 1.

58 See *ST* IaIIae.61.2 and IaIIae.62.3.

59 These are distinguished into acquired and infused, but this is a distinction which need not concern us here.

60 See, e.g., *ST* IaIIae.84.4. It is easy for us to misunderstand the items on this list. e.g., we naturally tend to think of sloth as laziness. But laziness is not an interesting or important sin for the medievals, and sloth is much more like garden-variety, non-clinical depression than it is like laziness. A person who thinks everybody hates him, nobody likes him, and he might as well eat worms has sloth, on the medieval view, and the medievals saw this attitude as a sin (perhaps at least in part on the grounds that it is not morally acceptable to treat any of God's creatures in a demeaning or degrading way, even when the creature in question is oneself). It may also be helpful to note that the medievals grouped the last three of the deadly sins – avarice, gluttony, and lust – together as the carnal sins. (Avarice has an ambiguous character, sometimes counting as a carnal sin and sometimes as a spiritual sin. See *ST* IaIIae.72.2, esp. ad 4.) The carnal sins as a group are understood by the medievals to be significantly less serious than the other sins in the list.

61 *ST* IaIIae.70.3. Although the Latin translated 'chastity' ('*castitas*') can be taken as narrowly as the English 'chastity', by '*castitas*' in such contexts is often meant something broader than restraint with respect to sexual desire. In the broader sense, the word refers to self-discipline with regard to desires for earthly things when those desires are morally unacceptable. Controlling yourself and not kicking your dog at the end of an exasperating day is thus an example of *castitas* since the desire to take out your frustrations by kicking the dog is a desire which it is never acceptable to act on. The Latin for the opposite of chastity – '*luxuria*' – is typically translated 'lust', but it can range as broadly as '*castitas*', to pick out any lack of self-discipline with regard to morally unacceptable desires.

62 *ST* IaIIae.69.3.

63 *ST* IIaIIae.8 and IIaIIae.9.

64 *ST* IIaIIae.15.

65 See, e.g., *QDV* 14.8 ad 10. I am grateful to Norman Kretzmann for calling this passage to my attention.

66 *ST* IIaIIae.28.4 and IIaIIae.29.4.

67 *ST* IIaIIae.45.6.

68 *ST* IIaIIae.46.3. See also note 61 above.

69 *ST* IIaIIae.45.1 and IaIIae.57.2.

70 *ST* IIaIIae.45.3. It is therefore distinct from prudence, which is a virtue of the practical intellect alone. Aquinas holds that wisdom directs human actions, as prudence does, too, but wisdom directs them in light of its understanding of God and true goodness, which is God's. And so he says, "Prudence is wisdom in human affairs, but not wisdom unconditionally, because it is not about the unconditionally highest cause, for it is about human good, but human beings are not the best of the things there are" (*ST* IIaIIae.47.2 ad 1).

71 In *ST* IIaIIae.45.4, Aquinas says that although wisdom which is an intellectual virtue can be in a person guilty of mortal sin, wisdom which is a gift cannot. Wisdom in this sense presupposes charity, and charity cannot occur together with mortal sin. (It is because charity can occur together with venial sin that venial sin does not preclude wisdom.) In that same question, IIaIIae.45.6 ad 3, Aquinas says that because wisdom not only contemplates divine things but also regulates human acts, it requires distancing oneself from evil, which is incompatible with wisdom. That is why fear of God is the beginning of wisdom, because fear initiates the distancing from evils.

72 *ST* IIaIIae.46.1.

73 *ST* IIaIIae.46.1.

74 Perhaps the paradigm cases of shame are those in which a person shares with a selected set of the public around him a correct morally low opinion of himself.

In that case, he both is shamed and also feels ashamed. But while it seems necessary for shame that the low opinion be correct, it is not necessary that the shamed person should understand the low opinion to be correct. Ike Turner is shamed, even if he cannot recognize that the low opinion people have of him is right. Some people might suppose that the requirement that the low opinion be correct is similarly unnecessary. But this view does not seem right. Socrates was not shamed at his trial even though many people there apparently held a morally low opinion of him, just because their low opinion was incorrect. In cases where a person shares with others a low opinion of himself which he and they erroneously suppose to be correct, it seems to me better to describe such a person as humiliated, rather than as shamed. It is a consequence of this way of thinking about shame that a person can be mistaken in thinking that he is shamed. Finally, if we suppose that there are cases in which a person has a correct low opinion of himself and there is no one else (not even God) who shares it with him, it seems to me better to speak of low self-esteem or maybe humility, rather than shame.

75 His diary is available in English translation in Jadwiga Bezwinska and Danuta Czech, *KL Auschwitz Seen by the SS Hoess, Broad, Kremer* (New York: Howard Fertig, 1984).

76 Johann Paul Kremer, previously an anatomy professor at the University of Muenster, came to Auschwitz in August 1942. After the war, he was tried in Poland and sentenced to death, but because of his age the sentence was commuted to ten years. On his release, he returned to Münster, where he created a stir by trying to portray himself as a martyr to the German cause. The upshot was that he was tried in Münster and convicted a second time. See Bezwinska and Czech (1984, p. 8).

77 Gita Sereny, *Into That Darkness. An Examination of Conscience* (New York: First Vintage Books Edition, 1983). Also helpful in this connection is Robert Jay Lifton, *The Nazi Doctors* (New York: Basic Books, 1986), esp. the pages on socialization, pp. 193–213.

78 Sereny (1983, pp. 48ff.).

79 I am not trying to argue that the only way in which to interpret Stangl's case is in terms of Aquinas's theory of wisdom and folly. My point is only that Stangl's story is a good illustration for Aquinas's theory and that Aquinas's theory provides a helpful elucidation of Stangl's story. For a detailed study of Aquinas's moral psychology and the cases of Franz Stangl and Albert Speer, see Ian Boyd, "Self-Deception", dissertation, St. Louis University, 2001.

80 That is, *luxuria*, in the broad medieval sense described above; see note 61.

81 Sereny (1983, p. 55).

82 See, e.g., *ST* IaIIae.19.3, where Aquinas explains that the will's object is always proposed to it by intellect, so that understood good (as distinct from what is really good) is what the will wants. See also *ST* IaIIae.15.3 where Aquinas explains the progression towards action in this way: intellect's apprehension of the end, the desire of the end, counsel about the means, and the desire of the means. Also *ST* IaIIae.74.7 ad 1, ad 2, and ad 3, where Aquinas says that consent to sin is an act of the appetitive power in consequence of an act of reason, so that reason's approving as good something which is in fact not good precedes sinful acts. Finally, in *ST* IaIIae.75.2 he explains that the cause of sin is some apparent good, and therefore both intellect and will play a role in sinning.

83 Sereny (1983, p. 58).

84 Sereny documents the part religious authorities played in both condoning and condemning the Nazi euthanasia program, and the degree to which Germans, Stangl included, were aware of church attitudes towards euthanasia. e.g., she

quotes Frau Stangl's claim that she discussed with her husband a widely publicized sermon by the Bishop of Münster condemning euthanasia (ibid., p. 59).

85 It helps, of course, in this process that the Nazis were so careful with language. The higher-up who assigned Stangl to the euthanasia institute spoke to him in abstract and high-flown language, and Stangl records his distress at subsequently having to deal with a different superior who did not observe such linguistic conventions:

> My heart sank when I met him ... [he had] this awful verbal crudity; when he spoke about the necessity for this euthanasia operation, he wasn't speaking in humane or scientific terms, the way Dr. Werner had described it to me. ... He spoke of 'doing away with useless mouths' and said that 'sentimental slobber' about such people made him 'puke'.
>
> (Sereny, 1983, p. 54)

Clearly, the Nazi gift for Orwellian misdescription made it easier to misprogram the intellect in the way Aquinas thinks necessary for moral evil. In this connection, see also Lifton (1986, pp.202–203 and 445–446).

86 Sereny (1983, p. 114).

87 Sereny (1983, p. 157).

88 Sereny (1983, p. 164). Stangl sometimes suggests that cooperating with the Nazis was the only way he could live in a different sense; failure to cooperate, in his view, would have cost him not only his position but even his life. But here Stangl is unduly melodramatic. The historical record is full of people who declined Stangl's sort of cooperation and received virtually no punishment of any sort. But even if Stangl seriously believed that his life would have been forfeit if he had not agreed to participate in the torture and mass murder of Jewish men, women, and children, his decision to save his life at such cost itself shows a monumental failure of speculative and practical intellect.

89 I do not mean to imply that this interaction between intellect and will is all there is to say about the descent into evil. For some excellent discussion of associated factors, see Lifton (1986, pp. 418–465).

90 In *Pilgrim's Progress* Bunyan has a vivid image for this process. As he illustrates it in his allegory, the soul that strays from the right path has to walk every step of the way back; there are no short-cuts.

91 *ST* IIaIIae.45.6.

92 See Harry Frankfurt, "Freedom of the Will and the Concept of a Person", *Journal of Philosophy* 68 (1971): 5–20; reprinted in Harry Frankfurt, *The Importance of What We Care About* (Cambridge: Cambridge University Press, 1988), pp. 11–25. A large literature has been generated by this original paper of Frankfurt's. For use of his work in connection with issues of grace and free will, see my "Sanctification, Hardening of the Heart, and Frankfurt's Concept of Free Will", *Journal of Philosophy* 85 (1988): 395–420; reprinted in John Martin Fischer and Mark Ravizza (eds), *Perspectives on Moral Responsibility* (Ithaca, NY: Cornell University Press, 1993), pp. 211–234, and "Augustine on Free Will", in Eleonore Stump and Norman Kretzmann (eds), *The Cambridge Companion to Augustine* (Cambridge: Cambridge University Press, 2001); see also Chapter 13 on grace and free will.

93 It is not hard to understand why this claim is true with respect to subjective moral evil, but Aquinas also means it to hold for objective moral evil, for the reasons given in the rest of this section.

94 For an excellent study of Arendt's views on this and other matters, see Richard Bernstein, *Hannah Arendt and the Jewish Question* (Cambridge, MA: MIT Press, 1996).

12 A representative theological virtue: faith

1 Aquinas's views of the interrelations of intellect and will are crucial to his account of faith; but because I have discussed those views of his extensively in the earlier chapters on freedom and wisdom, I will only summarize them briefly in this chapter, supplementing just a little where the specialized discussion of faith requires it.

2 See *ST* IIaIIae.2.1; *QDV* 14.1.

3 *ST* IIaIIae.1.4.

4 For some discussion of the ways in which will can influence intellect, see Chapters 9 and 11 on freedom and on wisdom.

5 For a presentation and discussion of the variety of such cases and a defense of the role of will in the production of intellectual assent in them, see Chapter 11 on wisdom.

6 For a review of these cases and an examination of Aquinas's position with regard to them, see Chapter 11 on wisdom.

7 See, e.g., *ST* IIaIIae.5.2; cf. also *QDV* 14.1.

8 We might suppose that this is just a case in which Dorothea is weighing evidence, the evidence of what she has seen against the evidence of her knowledge of Ladislaw's character, and coming down on the side of the evidence based on her knowledge of his character. If this were a correct analysis of the case, then it would not constitute an example of the will's effecting assent to a belief. But, in fact, I think this analysis is not true to the phenomena in more than one way. In the first place, Dorothea does not deliberate or weigh evidence. Although she reflects on what she has seen, her tendency from the outset is to exonerate Ladislaw. Furthermore, this analysis by itself cannot account for Dorothea's standing by Ladislaw. The evidence of the scene she sees is sufficient to outweigh her past experience of him. It is not psychologically possible for her in the immediate aftermath of that scene to think of an innocuous explanation of his conduct, and she is aware of the sad truth that no one, however splendid his character has been, is immune from a moral fall.

9 *ST* IIaIIae.1.2.

10 For present purposes, I will take 'the propositions of faith' broadly to mean all those propositions that are appropriately believed in faith, including those propositions, such as 'God exists,' that in Aquinas's view some persons can know by natural reason and therefore do not need to hold only by faith.

11 Some propositions of faith, such as the proposition that God is one substance but three persons, might seem to some people sufficient to move the will to dissent from them. For considerations of space I leave such propositions of faith and their problems to one side. But for an example of what can be done even in such cases to disarm the claim that some propositions of faith are repugnant to reason, see Peter van Inwagen, "And Yet They Are Not Three Gods But One God", in Thomas V. Morris (ed.), *Philosophy and the Christian Faith* (South Bend, IN: The University of Notre Dame Press, 1988), pp. 241–278.

12 What Aquinas means by 'certainty' in this connection I will consider in a later section.

13 *ST* IIaIIae.1.4, IIaIIae.2.1–2.

14 Cf. *ST* IIaIIae.4.1; *QDV* 14.1–2.

15 Cf. *ST* IaIIae.113.4, where it is clear that the faith in question is the faith of religious believers.
16 The generally cited biblical text in this connection is James 2:19.
17 See *ST* IIaIIae.4.3–4; cf. also *ST* IIaIIae.6.2.
18 *ST* IIaIIae.5.2.
19 Cf. in this connection Aquinas's discussion in *ST* IIaIIae.6.1 ad 2 of the deformity in faith when the will of the believer is not informed by charity.
20 *ST* IIaIIae.5.2 ad 3.
21 *ST* IIaIIae.5.2.
22 *ST* IIaIIae.4.1, 4, 5; IIaIIae.7.1; *QDV* 14.2, 5, and 6.
23 Somewhat different analyses of Aquinas's account of faith are given in the following works: Terence Penelhum, "The Analysis of Faith in St. Thomas Aquinas", *Religious Studies* 13 (1977): 133–151; Louis Pojman, *Religious Belief and the Will* (London: Routledge and Kegan Paul, 1986), esp. pp. 32–40; Timothy Potts, "Aquinas on Belief and Faith", in James F. Ross (ed.), *Inquiries in Medieval Philosophy: A Collection in Honor of Francis P. Clark* (Westport, CT: Greenwood, 1971), pp. 3–22; James Ross, "Aquinas on Belief and Knowledge", in William Frank and Girard Etzkorn (eds), *Essays Honoring Allan B. Wolter* (Saint Bonaventure, NY: Franciscan Institute, 1985), pp. 245–269, and "Believing for Profit", in Gerald McCarthy (ed.), *The Ethics of Belief Debate* (Atlanta, GA: Scholars Press, 1986), pp. 221–235. My objections to the interpretations of Aquinas in the work of Penelhum and Potts are given in effect in my own analysis above; and the problems they raise for Aquinas's account in my view either are solved or do not arise in the first place on the interpretation of Aquinas presented here. Although there are some superficial differences between my interpretation of Aquinas and that argued for by Ross, my account is in many respects similar to his, and I am indebted to his papers for stimulating my interest in Aquinas's views of faith.
24 Nothing in this chapter requires one account of justification rather than another, but of the currently discussed accounts, the one I am inclined to find most plausible is that of William Alston. See, e.g., William P. Alston, "Concepts of Epistemic Justification", *The Monist* 68 (1985): 57–89; reprinted in his *Epistemic Justification: Essays in the Theory of Knowledge* (Ithaca, NY: Cornell University Press 1989). On Alston's view, to be justified in believing that p is to believe that p in such a way as to be in a strong position to believe something true.
25 See Chapter 7 on the foundations of knowledge.
26 Consider, e.g., the belief that Christ rose from the dead. We would have to add to Aquinas's metaphysics of goodness some considerations either of other metaphysical attributes of God and their relation to the divine goodness or of the perfectly good will of God, and these additional considerations will be the basis of an explanation of the justification of belief in the resurrection.
27 *ST* Ia.5.1; *QDV* 21.1–2. Aquinas's meta-ethics is discussed in detail in the chapter on goodness above; see also Jan Aertsen, *Nature and Creature: Thomas Aquinas's Way of Thought* (Leiden: E. J. Brill , 1988). See also Scott MacDonald (ed.), *Being and Goodness: The Concept of the Good in Metaphysics and Philosophical Theology* (Ithaca, NY: Cornell University Press, 1991).
28 For Aquinas, perfect being is being that is whole and complete, without defect or limit. But to be entirely whole and without defect, on Aquinas's view, is to be without any unactualized potentiality. Perfect being, then, is altogether actual. Anything that is altogether actual, however, must have its existence included within its essence; otherwise, according to Aquinas, there would be in it the potential for non-existence. But if perfect being has its existence as part of its essence, if it has no potential for non-existence, then it is necessarily existent.

See, e.g., *ST* Ia.3.4. Considerations of this sort lie behind his view that perfect being necessarily exists. For further discussion of these claims, see Chapter 3 on God's simplicity.

29 Since Aquinas identifies perfect being with God, someone might object at this point that if we accept his reasoning from perfect goodness to perfect being, we have an argument for the existence of God, a peculiar variation on the ontological argument But this line of thought is confused. The premises of such a putative argument could be accepted only by someone who already accepted Aquinas's sort of classical theism, so that the argument would be blatantly question-begging.

30 See, e.g., William P. Alston, "Level Confusions in Epistemology", in Peter A. French, Theodore E. Uehling, Jr. and Howard K. Wettstein (eds), *Midwest Studies in Philosophy*, vol. 5 (Minneapolis: University of Minnesota Press, 1980), pp. 135–150; reprinted in his *Epistemic Justification*.

31 See Chapter 9 on freedom.

32 See *ST* IIaIIae.4.8.

33 *ST* IIaIIae.4.8.

34 Someone might object that anyone who believes God to be both omnipotent and perfectly good will also believe that in allying himself with perfect goodness he is putting himself on the side of power and that therefore it is not possible to decouple the desire for goodness from the desire for power in the case of believers. The objector's premise seems to me fundamentally correct, but the conclusion he seeks to draw from it does not follow. Someone who believes in an omnipotent, perfectly good God will believe that in following goodness he is also associating himself with power. But as long as it is not overwhelmingly obvious to a believer that there is a being who is both omnipotent and perfectly good, it will not be overwhelmingly obvious that in following what seems to him good he is allying himself with power. e.g., in the case of someone such as Mother Teresa, although it is clear that she has dedicated herself to goodness, it is not equally obvious, to believers observing her and even (one supposes) to her herself, that she is on the side of power. In such a case it is possible for the desire for goodness and the desire for power to pull a person in different directions, in spite of her belief in an omnipotent, perfectly good God; and so it is possible to decouple the desire for goodness from a desire for power when it is not overwhelmingly obvious that there is an omnipotent, perfectly good God. For a sensitive and penetrating portrayal of this point, see the representation of the temptations of Christ in Milton's *Paradise Regained*. I am grateful to Steve Maitzen for calling my attention to this objection.

35 It also helps explain what anecdotal evidence suggests, namely, that most conversions to faith are not prompted by philosophical or theological arguments. Rather, they are initiated by something's moving the will, in consequence of which the will in turn moves the intellect to assent to the propositions of faith.

36 For a fuller treatment of issues connected with Aquinas's views of the doctrine of the atonement, see Chapter 15 on the atonement.

37 *ST* IaIIae.113.6.

38 *ST* IaIIae.113.1.

39 *ST* IaIIae.113.2 ad 2.

40 *ST* IaIIae.111.2 ad 4.

41 For some philosophical explanation of cooperating grace and the way in which it is compatible even with libertarian freedom, see my "Augustine on Free Will", in Eleonore Stump and Norman Kretzmann (eds), *The Cambridge Companion to Augustine* (Cambridge: Cambridge University Press, 2001).

42 *Sermo* 169.11.13.
43 *ST* IaIIae.111.2 ad 2.
44 *ST* IaIIae.113.7.
45 *ST* IaIIae.113.8.
46 In this connection, see also Chapter 5 on God's knowledge.
47 *ST* IaIIae.111.2 ad 1.
48 *ST* IaIIae.113.3.
49 *SCG* III.148; cf. also III.149–150.
50 *ST* IaIIae.113.5; cf. also IaIIae.113.6–7. A person does not have to remember and detest each sin he has ever committed in order to be justified, Aquinas says; rather, he has to detest those sins of which he is conscious and be disposed to detest any other sin of his if he should remember it.
51 *ST* IaIIae.111.2 reply.
52 *ST* IaIIae.113, esp. article 7, reply.
53 When the faith which Paul is adopting in this act of will becomes habitual and eventuates in other physical and mental acts, it becomes a virtue; as such, it is nurtured by cooperating grace and is a source of merit.
54 I do not mean to suggest that Paul's assent may not also be praiseworthy in a certain respect. A child who, after all the cajoling, bribing, and threatening his ingenious mother can think of, finally opens his mouth and lets her spoon in his hated vegetables hardly seems to have acquired merit by the mere failure to keep his mouth clamped shut. But his mother, who has done all the work of getting him to eat his vegetables, may nonetheless correctly praise him for having assented to her feeding him. Similarly, Paul's assent may be praiseworthy in a certain respect without counting as a good act on Paul's part. For further discussion of this issue, see Chapter 13 on grace and free will.
55 *ST* IaIIae.113.5.
56 For a discussion of hierarchy in the will, see Chapter 11 on wisdom. Harry Frankfurt has written many papers pertinent to this subject; his classic paper on the subject is "Freedom of the Will and the Concept of a Person", *Journal of Philosophy* 68 (1971): 5–20.
57 There is something at least mildly puzzling about the initial description of the act of will at issue as the believer's volition that God bring him to righteousness since the proper objects of our volitions are only those things which are in our power to do. Lydgate in Eliot's *Middlemarch* may wish or desire that Bulstrode make up his mind to lend him money; but it would be odd to say Lydgate *wills* that Bulstrode give him a loan, because what Bulstrode chooses to do can be an object only of Bulstrode's will and not of Lydgate's. Furthermore, this way of describing the second-order volition seems to violate the definition of a second-order volition, as the will's commanding itself. But there are occasions when it does seem appropriate to say something somewhat similar to 'Lydgate wills that Bulstrode lend him money', and reflections on these help to solve both problems. To take just one sort of example, if Lydgate needed medical attention (rather than money) and at last consented to an operation, we might be inclined to describe his situation by saying that Lydgate wills the doctor to operate on him. But what we are describing here is not a situation in which the doctor's action is the object of Lydgate's volition. In this example, the doctor is urging medical treatment which Lydgate is reluctant to undergo. In saying that Lydgate wills the doctor to operate, we mean that Lydgate has both ceased to offer resistance to the doctor's proposal and made up his mind to consent to the operation. The object of Lydgate's volition, then, is not an action on the doctor's part, but rather his own first-order volitions. In willing the doctor to operate, he

wills not to have a will that resists the doctor's urging and to have instead a will that permits the operation; that is, he wills to have a will that wills all those things necessary on his part before the doctor is able (legally and morally) to operate.

58 See Chapter 9 on Aquinas's account of freedom above. Cf. also, e.g., *SCG* III.148 and *ST* IaIIae.111.2 ad 1, in which Aquinas says that grace operates on the will in the manner of a formal cause, rather than in the manner of an efficient cause. See Chapter 13 on grace and free will for further discussion.

59 Cf. my "Augustine on Free Will", in Eleonore Stump and Norman Kretzmann (eds), *The Cambridge Companion to Augustine* (Cambridge: Cambridge University Press, 2001), which gives detailed argument for a similar position held by Augustine.

60 I do not mean to suggest that the changes occurring in the process of justification will take place only in the will on Aquinas's views. Insofar as the intellect and the will are connected as Aquinas takes them to be, changes in one faculty or power will result in changes in the other as well. My focus here, however, is on justification and atonement, and so Aquinas's views of changes in the will are more important for my purposes.

61 Cf. Aquinas's discussion of Pelagianism in *ST* IIaIIae.6.1.

62 A metaphor somewhat similar to the one used in my example of Aaron can be found in Luther's commentary on Romans 4:7. See Wilhelm Pauck (ed.) *Luther: Lectures on Romans*, Library of Christian Classics (Philadelphia: Westminster Press, 1961), p. 127.

63 1 Timothy 2:4.

64 See, e.g., Luther, *Lectures on Romans*, op. cit., p. 127.

65 For Aquinas, the sin in question cannot be an act of mortal sin, because mortal sin is incompatible with charity; and without charity formed faith becomes unformed or lifeless faith. Cf. in this connection *ST* IIaIIae.4.4, where Aquinas makes clear that formed faith is lost through mortal sin. Nonetheless, sinful inclinations, habits and dispositions are compatible with even formed faith.

66 Rom. 4:17.

67 Rom. 3:26.

68 *ST* IaIIae.113.1.

69 Cf. Gal. 3:7.

70 Rom. 4:11–18.

71 Gal. 3:8.

72 Cf. Aquinas, *In Gal* 3.3, and *In Rom*, esp. 4.3, where Aquinas discusses a variety of implications of the Pauline passages involving Abraham.

73 *ST* IIaIIae.2.5–7.

74 *ST* IIaIIae.2.7 ad 3. Aquinas's thought here is illustrated vividly by an incident related in Colin Turnbull's study of Pygmies. The Pygmy serving as Turnbull's aid and guide was introduced to a Catholic priest, Father Longo, who took the opportunity to try to evangelize him. According to Turnbull, the Pygmies have a religion of their own; without much in the way of theology or established religious institutions, they believe in a god of the forest in which they live and whose children they hold themselves to be. On an occasion after the encounter with the priest, when the Pygmy was specially moved by the natural beauty of his surroundings, he exclaimed, "The Pere Longo was right, this God must be the same as our God in the forest." (Colin Turnbull, *The Forest People* (1961; reprint, New York: Simon and Schuster, 1968), p. 258.)

75 It should be understood at the outset that the atonement has several functions in the plan of salvation, according to Aquinas, and that its role in the process of justification by faith is only one of them. Aquinas in fact lists five major effects

of Christ's passion and death, including liberation from punishment and reconciliation with God. Here my focus is solely on the atonement in its relationship to justifying faith. For detailed discussion of Aquinas's account of the atonement, see Chapter 15 on the atonement.

76 For a good representative of an interpreter of Aquinas who understands Aquinas's view differently from the interpretation I am arguing for in this section, see R. Garrigou-Lagrange, *God, His Existence and Nature*, 5th edn, trans. Dom Bede Rose (St. Louis, MO: Herder, 1955), p. 546. My reasons for thinking Garrigou-Lagrange's position mistaken are found throughout this book, but see especially the discussion in Chapter 3 on God's simplicity of Garrigou-Lagrange's view that God is always determining and never determined.

77 I have described the will's state in such a case as if it consisted in ceasing to do an action, rather than as performing the action of ceasing, both because the description of the will as passive seems to me truer to the phenomena and because Aquinas's philosophical psychology allows for this possibility, which is the basis for the position I am arguing for. For further discussion of this issue, see Chapter 13 on grace and free will.

78 I have discussed the way in which God might bring about such a volition in the case of a person whose religious beliefs I described as vaguely theistic. We could, however, tell a similar story, although one bound to be longer and more complicated, about the way in which God might bring an atheist to the same sort of volition.

13 Grace and free will

1 *ST* Ia.82.1.
2 *SCG* III.88.
3 *QDV* 22.5 reply.
4 *ST* IaIIae.113.3. The rest of the passage contains the other side of Aquinas's position, namely, that this act of free will is produced by God.
5 *SCG* III.148.
6 *QDV* 22.8.
7 *QDV* 22.8 reply.
8 *QDV* 22.8 ad 9.
9 *QDV* 27.1 ad 3.
10 *QDV* 28.7 ad 5.
11 *QDV* 28.9 reply.
12 See, e.g., *QDV* 28.7 reply.
13 See, e.g., *ST* IaIIae.9.1.
14 See, e.g.., *ST* IaIIae.10.2.
15 See also my "Augustine on Free Will", in Eleonore Stump and Norman Kretzmann (eds), *The Cambridge Companion to Augustine* (Cambridge: Cambridge University Press), pp. 124–147.
16 The difference between willed inattention, on the one hand, and simple or distracted inattention, on the other, is analogous to a distinction between kinds of omission. One kind of omission is a result of a decision to omit, as when one omits to send a birthday present because one is angry with the person having the birthday; the other kind is a simple failure to act, as when one omits to send a birthday present because one does not know that the person in question is having a birthday. Cf., e.g., Harry G. Frankfurt, "An Alleged Asymmetry Between Actions and Omissions", *Ethics*, 104 (3) (1994): 620–623, and John Martin Fischer, "Responsibility, Control, and Omissions", *Journal of Ethics*, 1 (1) (1997): 45–64.

17 I am grateful to both Timothy O'Connor and Derk Pereboom for calling to my attention the need to consider this sort of case.

18 For more discussion of the nature of second-order desires and volitions and the possibilities for division in the will, see Chapter 11 on wisdom.

19 There is some reason for supposing that in Augustine's case in the garden, the conflict in the intellect had to do with second-order acts of will, and the higher-order desire in question was a third-order desire. For some discussion of the rare cases in which third-order desires and volitions play a role, see my "Sanctification, Hardening of the Heart, and Frankfurt's Concept of Free Will", *Journal of Philosophy* 85 (1988): 395–420; reprinted in John Martin Fischer and Mark Ravizza (eds), *Perspectives on Moral Responsibility* (Ithaca, NY: Cornell University Press, 1993), pp. 211–234.

20 Children and adult human beings in non-normal conditions pose special problems which complicate the case, and so I am simply leaving those cases to one side here.

21 I am presenting this position as one which allows Aquinas to have both the apparently incompatible claims he wants, but I am not proposing this position as problem free.

22 I will have it pointed out to me that in the chapter following the one from which I am quoting, Aquinas qualifies his position by saying that after a person has once sinned, it is not in his power to fail to provide an impediment for grace unless he is first helped to do so by grace. Nonetheless, in that very chapter (*SCG* III.160), Aquinas also says this:

> although it is not possible for those who are in sin to avoid, by their own power, providing an impediment to grace ... unless they are first helped by grace, nonetheless this is imputed to them as fault, because this defect is left in them as a result of the preceding fault ... Furthermore, although the person who is in sin does not have it in his power to avoid sin altogether, he nonetheless has it in his power now to avoid this or that sin, and so whatever he commits, he commits voluntarily.

The position Aquinas is concerned to rule out here is the position of the Pelagians, that a sinful person can do good without grace (see his discussion of the Pelagians in this same chapter, *SCG* III.161). But the will's ceasing to act is not itself an act of will of any kind; *a fortiori*, the will's quiescing is not a good act of will.

23 *SCG* III.159.

14 The metaphysics of the incarnation

1 So, e.g., I disagree with much of Richard Cross's otherwise excellent analysis of Aquinas's account of the incarnation because I understand the underlying metaphysics differently from the way in which he does; see Richard Cross, "Aquinas on Nature, Hypostasis, and the Metaphysics of the Incarnation", *The Thomist* 60 (1996): 171–202. In this chapter, I will be relying on Chapter 1 on Aquinas's theory of things, and although in some places in a note I direct the reader's attention to that chapter, I do not do so in every case in which it would be helpful to have read that chapter before this one.

2 There is some ambiguity in the notion of person in the case of Christ, as Aquinas himself recognizes; cf. *ST* IIIa.2.4. Because Christ is one and just one person, and a person is a substance of a particular sort, there is just one substance in Christ. That substance is composite. It includes a human soul and

body and the divine nature. So Christ is one composite person. On the other hand, the second person of the Trinity, who is identical with his divine nature, is a constituent of the composite Christ. So in the case of Christ 'person' can refer either to the substance which Christ is, or to the second person of the Trinity in his incarnate state. I will use the expression 'the person of Christ' to refer to the incarnate second person of the Trinity; to refer to the composite person which the incarnate Christ is, I will use the expression 'the person Christ'. Although there is this ambiguity in the notion of person when it comes to Christ, it does not follow that there are two persons or two substances in Christ. The human nature, body and soul, are assumed by the second person of the Trinity and united to him in a union of person. Consequently, the new composite is the same person as before the incarnation. For some intuitive explanation of this claim, see the science fiction story below. For some discussion of the metaphysical difficulties of this claim, see the discussion below regarding the notion of a union in person in the incarnation. Finally, it is worth noticing here that this ambiguity does not mean that the term 'person' is equivocal. In either of its ambiguous uses as regards Christ, the medieval definition of a person as *individual substance of a rational nature* applies. On the one hand, Christ in his divine nature cognizes reasons, and the deity is one thing; so the medieval definition of person fits the second person of the Trinity, too (as long as we are careful not to define the terms in that definition in such a way as to make them incapable of applying to what is simple). On the other hand, when the second person of the Trinity assumes a human nature, it does so in a union of person, so that the resulting composite is still only one supposit. Since this supposit is an individual substance and one which is rational, the composite incarnate Christ is also an individual substance of a rational nature.

3 See, e.g., *ST* III.2.3–4 and III.17.1; *De unione verbi incarnati* 4.

4 See, e.g., *ST* III.2.4.

5 The doctrine of simplicity makes it illegitimate to say that the deity *has* any characteristics, because this formulation makes a distinction between the deity and the characteristics the deity has; but on the doctrine of simplicity there are no such distinctions in a simple God.

6 See, e.g., *ST* III.2.8.

7 *SCG* IV.43 (3807).

8 Cf. *ST* III.2.6 ad 2; *ST* III.16.2 ad 3 and III.16.3 ad 2; *SCG* IV.49 (3838).

9 For help in understanding how both the claims about the assumption in time and the claims about the assumption in eternity are compatible, see Chapter 4 on God's eternity.

10 For an explanation of these claims about substantial forms and matter, as well as for other basic metaphysical claims in this chapter, the reader should consult Chapter 1 on Aquinas's theory of things.

11 *ST* III.2.5 and *CT* I c.209 (402–404).

12 *De unione verbi incarnati* 5.

13 *ST* III.9.11.

14 *ST* III.18.1.

15 Strictly speaking, this locution is inaccurate. The divine nature is simple, and so it is not accurate to speak of a divine person as having an intellect and a will. But the locutions needed to try to speak accurately in accordance with the doctrine of divine simplicity are so clumsy that Aquinas himself does not always avoid the simpler but inaccurate locutions. Having noted the constraints of divine simplicity, in the rest of the chapter I will avail myself of the simpler locutions such as that used here, which describes the person of Christ as having an intellect and will.

16 See, e.g., *QDVC* 20.1 and 20.4.
17 *ST* III.18.4.
18 *ST* III.16.5, but see the qualification in the following 16.6.
19 Cf. *ST* III.15.4–6.
20 For the notions of unity of nature and unity of person, or hypostatic union, see also Chapter 1 on Aquinas's theory of things.
21 *ST* III.2.3 ad 2.
22 Cf. *De unione verbi incarnati* 1 ad 6.
23 *SCG* IV.36 (3740).
24 For further discussion of this in Aquinas's metaphysics, see Chapter 1 on Aquinas's theory of things.
25 *ST* III.2.3 ad 1.
26 *SCG* IV.49 (3837).
27 *SCG* IV.41 (3792) and 49 (3846).
28 In correspondence, Brian Leftow has asked whether it is possible to avoid attributing a conjunctive nature to Christ. If Christ is human and divine, then it seems as if he has one nature, namely, the nature of being human-and-divine. I think, however, that Aquinas's metaphysics rule out such a conjunctive nature, and I also think that Aquinas is concerned to spell out his views in such a way that they do not conflate natures in Christ. On Aquinas's views, a nature is something conferred by a substantial form (or a form which is a substance in the case of immaterial things). If there were only one nature in Christ, then there would be only one substantial form, or one form which is a substance. But the substantial form of a human being does not configure all the components of the incarnate Christ, because it does not configure the second person of the deity; the substantial form of a human being configures matter. The form which is the second person of the Trinity does not configure all of the components of the incarnate Christ either, however, because the second person is not a form configuring matter. So there is not one substantial form (or one form which is a substance) which configures all the components in the incarnate Christ; rather there are two such forms. Consequently, there are two natures, not one. It is for this very reason that Aquinas has so much difficulty in explaining what the kind of union of the components is in the incarnate Christ, as I explain below.
29 For an example of a contemporary interpretation of the Chalcedonian formula which suffers this sort of defect, see Thomas Morris, *The Logic of God Incarnate* (Ithaca, NY: Cornell University Press, 1986). Morris attempts to keep the two natures of Christ separate, but the way in which he tries to do so makes it seem as if he has in fact conflated the natures. So, Peter van Inwagen, commenting on Morris's interpretation, says, "One might wonder whether it is not a form of monophysitism" ("Incarnation and Christology", *The Routledge Encyclopedia of Philosophy*, London: Routledge: 1999) See also my review of Morris's book, *Faith and Philosophy* 6 (1989): 218–223.
30 Aquinas uses or discusses the reduplicative strategy in many places. See, e.g., *ST* III.16.10–12; cf. also *CT* I c.210 (407), c.229, and c.232.
31 Cf. *ST* III.13.1.
32 Morris 1986, p.48.
33 See van Inwagen 1999 for a helpful and succinct expression of the challenge to the reduplicative strategy, which he calls 'a predicative solution'. Van Inwagen says:

> A satisfactory predicative solution must supplement the abstract theses ... [which give a reduplicative form to statements predicating attributes of Christ] with some sort of reply to the following challenge: Where *F* and *G*

are incompatible properties, and *K1* and *K2* are 'kinds', what does it mean to say of something that it is *F qua K1* but *G qua K2*? – or that it is *F qua K1* but is not *F qua K2*? And can any more or less uncontroversial examples of such pairs of statements be found?

This section of the chapter is an attempt to show that Aquinas's metaphysics has the resources to respond to this challenge, and the example of the borrowed properties of C/EBP, discussed just below in the text, is an attempt to provide a more ordinary and less controversial case of such pairs of statements.

34 A different and elegant solution to the problem of the apparent logical incoherence of the doctrine of the incarnation can be found in Peter van Inwagen, "Not by Confusion of Substance, but by Unity of Person", in A.G. Padgett (ed.), *Reason and the Christian Religion: Essays in Honour of Richard Swinburne* (Oxford: Clarendon Press, 1994). In this paper, van Inwagen provides an analysis of reduplicative propositions in terms of relative identity. On this interpretation, God is the same person as the human being Jesus of Nazareth, but not the same substance or being. Aquinas considers a solution at least very similar to this one (see *ST* III.2.3 and *De unione verbi incarnati* 2), but he rejects it, as he has to do. On his metaphysics, a person is an individual substance of a rational nature, and so for any individuals *x* and y, *x* is the same person as *y* only if *x* is the same substance as *y*.

35 For Aquinas's account of constitution and the notion of borrowed or derivative properties, see Chapter 1 on Aquinas's theory of things.

36 For further discussion of this example in the context of Aquinas's metaphysics, see Chapter 1 on his theory of things.

37 Cf., e.g., Steven Lanier McKnight, "Molecular Zippers in Gene Regulation", *Scientific American* 264 (1991): 54–64.

38 See Lynne Rudder Baker, "Unity Without Identity: A New Look at Material Constitution", in *Midwest Studies in Philosophy* 23 (1999): 151–160.

39 Someone might suppose that we should simply re-identify the characteristics which are being attributed to the whole. Someone might hold, that is, that C/EBP has the properties *being coiled with respect to its alpha helix constituents* and *not being coiled with respect to its Y-shaped constituent*. On this way of understanding the characteristics in question, it is easier to see that the simultaneous predication of these attributes does not violate any laws of logic, and this feature of this way of specifying C/EBP's characteristics is no doubt an advantage. On the other hand, this formulation may make it seem as if the characteristics in question – *being coiled* and *not being coiled* – are in fact just characteristics of the constituents of the molecule and not characteristics of the whole molecule; and that is a significant disadvantage of this formulation. Some theological claims central to Christianity require attributing to the whole composite that is Christ properties had in their own right only by a constituent of the composite. So, e.g., a central Christian claim is that Christ died on the cross. Here the property of dying on the cross is attributed to the whole. It is, however, not possible that immutable, eternal deity die. Human beings can die; God cannot. Therefore, it is true that Christ dies only in case a property had in its own right by a constituent of Christ, the human body and soul, is also properly attributed to the whole. For this reason, as well as for the metaphysical reasons given earlier, it seems to me better to say that a whole borrows properties of its parts, so that the whole can be said to be coiled, e.g., in virtue of having a part that is coiled. I am grateful to Scott MacDonald and Brian Leftow for calling my attention to the need to address this alternative.

40 In correspondence, Brian Leftow has suggested that some of Christ's divine properties, such as the property of being omnipotent, should be considered properties had in their own right by the whole Christ; on this view, a property such as being omnipotent is not a borrowed property for Christ. Leftow argues that a being having both a fast and a slow body would have the property *being fast* in its own right, because "one is fast if one can run fast on some occasions (e.g., when using the right body)". Analogous reasoning suggests that *being omnipotent* is a property the whole has in its own right also. My purpose in this chapter is only to show the way in which Aquinas's metaphysics supports the reduplicative strategy, and so it does not matter for my purposes exactly which properties of Christ's are borrowed and which are had by the whole Christ in their own right. But I am inclined to think that whether or not a property such as *being fast* is equivalent to a property had by a whole in its own right or to a borrowed property depends on the reasons for the ability in question. C/EBP has the property *able to reconfigure DNA on some occasions* in virtue of the shape of the molecule as a whole, and so the property in question is appropriately considered a property the whole has in its own right. But it has the property *being able to uncoil* only in virtue of the fact that it has a coiled part, and so this property is borrowed from a part. Because running fast for normal human beings requires a coordination of the whole body, from brain to toes, the property *being fast* does seem to be a property had in its own right by a whole human being. But in the case of Christ, who is a composite of one person and two natures, the property of being unlimited in power is a property had by the whole only in virtue of the fact that one constituent of the whole, the divine nature, has this property. Furthermore, if all the constituents of Christ other than the divine nature were removed, what remained would still be omnipotent. By contrast, it is not the case that we could remove all but one constituent of a human body and still have a fast human being. For these reasons, it seems to me that *being fast* is disanalogous to *being omnipotent*, so that *being omnipotent* is a borrowed property of Christ's, even if *being fast* is not a borrowed property for a human being.

41 See, e.g., *ST* Ia.75.2 ad 2.

42 *ST* III.10.1.

43 *SCG* IV.33 (3691); *ST* III.15.8.

44 The bond and the inability are thus relative to an act of will; or, in Aquinas's terms, the bond and the inability are secundum quid, not simpliciter. The case is analogous to the case of an alcoholic who takes a pill that makes him violently ill if he tries to ingest alcohol. While he takes the pills, he is really unable to drink, and the pills are a bond or a constraint on what he can do. But whether or not he takes the pills is up to him.

45 Aquinas himself discusses analogous cases involving different modes of ordinary human perception. See, e.g., *De rationibus fidei* 6 (992); *De unione verbi incarnati* 1 ad 16; and *SCG* IV.36 (3745); and *De unione verbi incarnati* 5; see also *ST* III.19.1, where Aquinas conveys an analogous point by comparing a person's abilities to operate through different parts of the body.

46 For a detailed discussion of cases of agnosia in a different context, see Chapter 5 on God's knowledge. Cf., e.g., Martha J. Farah, *Visual Agnosia* (Cambridge, MA: MIT Press, 1990).

47 Cf. *ST* III.4.2–3 and III.5.3–4.

48 See also *De unione verbi incarnati* 2 ad 10, where Aquinas goes so far as to say that if the human nature were separated from Christ, it would then be a person in its own right; but as long as it is part of the larger composite in Christ, it is not a person.

49 See, e.g., *De unione verbi incarnati* 1.

50 There are other modes of union for things which are artifacts or heaps, but these are not relevant to the case of Christ.
51 *ST* III.2.1; see also *ST* III.4.2.
52 See, e.g., *ST* III.2.6.
53 *ST* III.2.1.
54 Cf. *SCG* I.23 and I.27.
55 *SCG* IV.32 (3678).
56 *SCG* IV.41 (3800).
57 *SCG* IV.41 (3796).
58 See, e.g., *De unione verbi incarnati* 1.
59 Cf. *De unione verbi incarnati* 2.
60 *SCG* IV.41 (3795).
61 *ST* III, prologue.
62 For a translation of the relevant document, see Norman P. Tanner (ed.), *Decrees of the Ecumenical Councils*, vol. 1 (London: Sheed & Weed; Washington, DC: Georgetown University Press, 1990).

15 Atonement

1 In *ST* III.48, Aquinas says Christ's passion operated as a source of merit, as a sacrifice, as a mode of redemption, and as satisfaction making atonement for human sins.
2 See, e.g., *CT* 226–230. Robert Adams has suggested to me that alcoholism may be a bad example to illustrate the problem of future sin because we tend to think of alcoholism as a disease involving physical addiction, and perhaps his suggestion is right, although it seems to me that the cure of alcoholism typically includes a painful and difficult moral struggle which is illustrative of the problem of future sin. We could, however, readily replace the example involving alcoholism with other examples of habitual evil such as chronic marital infidelity.
3 See, e.g., *CT* 227.
4 *CT* 227. Cf. also *ST* III.46.1 and *SCG* IV.55.
5 *ST* III.22.3.
6 *ST* III.46.2.
7 ST III.46.2 ad 3.
8 *ST* III.46.3. In conversation with me, Thomas Tracy raised a problem for this part of Aquinas's account and also helpfully suggested a solution. According to Tracy, it might occur to someone to wonder whether God would be justified in allowing the innocent Christ to suffer if his suffering was not necessary for salvation, as Aquinas claims it is not. In terms of my analogy (yet to come in the text), we might wonder whether Anna was morally justified in allowing Aaron to suffer in the process of restoring the garden if his suffering was not necessary to bring about a change of heart in Nathan. Tracy's solution is to suggest that Aquinas's account requires a traditional Christology. In the case of Anna, we might very well be inclined to deny that she is justified in allowing the unnecessary suffering. But if we add traditional Christology to Aquinas's account of the atonement, then the one who suffers unnecessarily is both truly man and truly God. Thus God does not allow the unnecessary suffering of some third party but rather himself endures it as a means of redemption. And just as we would have no moral qualms about the case if Anna herself chose to endure some unnecessary suffering to rescue her son, so there seems no basis for objecting to God's undergoing unnecessary suffering as a means to human

redemption. So although Aquinas does not hold that the passion and death of Christ are necessary for salvation, once God has chosen to save people in that way it is necessary that God be the one suffering. I have some sympathy for Tracy's solution.

9 *ST* III.1.2. Cf. also *ST* III.46.1.
10 *ST* III.46.1 ad 3.
11 *ST* III.90.2.
12 *ST* III.84.5.
13 *ST* III.85.1.
14 *ST* III.85.3 and IIIa.86.2.
15 *ST* IaIIae.113.2.
16 *ST* IaIIae.113.2.
17 *SCG* IV.55.
18 *SCG* IV.55.
19 *ST* III.90.4.
20 *SCG* III.158.
21 *ST* IaIIae.86.2.
22 *ST* IaIIae.87.8.
23 *ST* III.48.2.
24 *ST* IaIIae.87.7.
25 *ST* III.46.3.
26 *ST* III.46.3.
27 I am grateful to Philip Quinn for raising this question in his comments on an earlier draft.
28 *ST* III.46.2–3.
29 *ST* III.48.2.
30 *ST* IaIIae.86.2.
31 *ST* IaIIae.89.1.
32 See, e.g., *In Sent* III.19.1.4.
33 *ST* III.46.3 ad 2; cf. *SCG* IV.55.
34 *ST* III.48.2.
35 *ST* III.49.4.
36 *ST* III.49.1 ad 5.
37 *ST* III.49.1 ad 5.
38 *ST* III.49.1 and III.49.3 ad 1; cf. also *ST* IIIa.62.5 ad 2 and *SCG* IV.72.
39 Cf., e.g., *SCG* III.158.
40 See, e.g., *ST* IaIIae.82.3.
41 *ST* III.46.3.
42 *ST* III.49.1.
43 As for those who lived before Christ, Aquinas holds that all persons in hell were visited by Christ in the period between his crucifixion and resurrection; see, e.g., *ST* III.52. Aquinas interprets the doctrine of Christ's harrowing of hell in a traditionally stern fashion; those whom Christ takes out of hell with him are only those who had some foreknowledge of him and were united to him in faith and love, namely, the righteous among the Jews who were awaiting him as Messiah.
44 *ST* III.49.2 ad 3.
45 *CT* 227.
46 *ST* III.49.1 and III.49.3.
47 Cf. *QDV* 27.3 ad 6 and *QDV* 29.4.
48 *ST* III.8.3.
49 *ST* III.8.1.
50 *ST* III.8.1.

51 See, e.g., *ST* III.8.5. See also *QDV* 29.6–7.
52 *ST* III.8.6 and III.48.1.
53 See, e.g., *In Sent* III.18, divisio textus.
54 *In Sent* III.18.1.2.
55 *ST* IaIIae.114.4.
56 *ST* IIaIIae.23.1.
57 For an exposition and defense of the Thomistic doctrine of simplicity, on which this claim is based, see Chapter 3 on God's simplicity.
58 *ST* IIaIIae.23.7.
59 *ST* IIaIIae.23.8.
60 *In Sent* III.18.1.5.
61 *ST* III.46.6.
62 *SCG* IV.55.
63 For explanation of the different philosophical and theological problems posed by operating grace and cooperating grace, together with some attempt to find a Thomistic solution to these problems, see Chapter 12 on faith.
64 *QDV* 27.1.
65 *QDV* 27.3.
66 See, e.g., *ST* IaIIae.108.1 and IaIIae.109.4.
67 *CT* 143.
68 *ST* IIaIIae.7.12.
69 *ST* IIaIIae.23.2.
70 For Aquinas's views of free will, see Chapter 9 on freedom. For detailed discussion about the way in which the bestowal of grace can be taken to be compatible with free will, see Chapter 13 on grace and free will.
71 *ST* IIaIIae.23.2.
72 *ST* IaIIae.111.2.
73 *ST* IaIIae.113.7.
74 *ST* III.89.2.
75 Cf. *QDV* 28.3 where Aquinas says that no one having the use of free will can be justified without the use of the free will he has at the time of his justification.
76 *QDV* 28.3.
77 *ST* IaIIae.113.3. See also the discussion of justification in *QDV* 28.3, where Aquinas says:
Justification is a certain change of the will. Now 'will' refers both to a certain power and to an act of [that] power. But an act of the power [that is] the will cannot be changed unless the will itself cooperates, for if [the act] were not in [the will], it would not be an act of the will ... And so for the justification of adults an act of free will is required.
Cf. also *QDV* 28.4–5.
78 *SCG* IV.70.
79 See, e.g., *CT* 144; *ST* IaIIae.112.3 ad 2 and IaIIae.113.2; and *SCG* III.159. For some discussion of Aquinas's notion of an obstacle to grace and the role of the will in producing such an obstacle, see Chapter 12 on faith.
80 *ST* IaIIae.110.3.
81 *ST* IaIIae.109.3–4.
82 *In Sent* II.26.4.
83 *ST* IaIIae.110.3.
84 *ST* IaIIae.111.3.
85 *QDV* 27.4.; see also *QDV* 27.7.
86 *QDV* 28.2.
87 See, e.g., *ST* III.73.3.

88 *ST* III.62.5.
89 *ST* III.73.3 ad 3.
90 *QDV* 27.4.
91 *ST* III.49.3.
92 *SCG* IV.58.
93 *SCG* IV.61.
94 *ST* III.79.1.
95 *ST* III.79.1 ad 1.
96 *ST* III.75.1 and III.76.4–5.
97 *ST* III.73.3 ad 2.
98 In fact, Aquinas goes so far as to say that faith and love are efficacious without the Eucharist if a person has an implicit desire for the Eucharist but is somehow prevented from acting on that desire; see, e.g., *ST* III.73.3.
99 *ST* III.62.5 ad 2.
100 *In Sent* III.19.1.1.2. Cf. also *ST* III.1.2, where Aquinas is discussing the benefits of the incarnation and points especially to charity in human beings, which (he says) "is stimulated to the highest degree by this".
101 *ST* III.49.1.
102 *ST* III.49.1.
103 *ST* III.73.3 and IIIa.80.2.
104 *ST* III.79.1.
105 *ST* III.79.4 and IIIa.79.6.
106 *ST* III.79.1 ad 2.
107 *ST* IaIIae.113.6.
108 Cf. *QDV* 28.1, where Aquinas says that justification is the movement whereby sin is removed and righteousness is acquired.
109 'Likely' is a necessary qualifier here, because grace is not efficacious without an act of free will. It is possible for David to react to the Eucharist with perversity or hardness of heart.
110 The grace at issue in my example is cooperative grace; for an example illustrating the relationship of the atonement to operative grace, see Chapter 12 on faith. For a more detailed discussion of operative grace, see Chapter 13 on grace and free will.
111 Cf., e.g., *ST* IaIIae.111.2.
112 Compare, e.g., Augustine's struggle for continence and his agonized prayer that God give him chastity – "but not yet;" *Confessions*, tran. Edward Pusey (New York: Macmillan Publishing Co., 1961), Book VIII, p. 125.
113 In telling this story of David, of course, I have picked an example of a person whose sense of himself makes him naturally likely to receive the Eucharist in a way favorable to Aquinas's interpretation of the atonement, and it might occur to someone to wonder whether so unusual a story as that of David could be generalized to ordinary cases, involving people (with Thomistic Christian views) who come to the Eucharist with relatively untroubled consciences. I know of no way to prove that the Eucharist would have similar effects on such participants in the rite. But it does occur to me to point out that Aquinas, who was reputed never to have confessed a deadly sin, was apparently deeply moved by the Eucharist, as the poem about the Eucharist *Adoro devote* (which has been generally attributed to him) shows. For those interested, I include here a translation of that poem.

I venerate you with devotion, hidden truth,
who lie beneath these forms, truly hidden.
My whole heart gives itself to you

because, contemplating you, it is wholly undone.
Sight, touch, taste are deceived in you;
hearing alone is safely believed.
Whatever the son of God has said I do believe;
nothing is more true than this word of truth.
Only deity was hidden on the cross;
humanity as well lies hidden here.
And I, believing and confessing both,
seek from you what the thief sought, repenting.
Like Thomas, I do not see your wounds,
and yet I confess you as my God.
Make me always increase in belief in you,
in hope in you, in love of you.
O memorial of the death of the Lord,
bread providing true life to man,
provide for my mind to live from you,
to know always the sweet taste of you.
Pelican of pietas, Jesus Lord,
cleanse my unclean self in your blood;
one small drop of it could cleanse
the whole world, from every evil saved.
Veiled Jesus, whom I now look upon,
when will what I so desire come to be?
When will I see your face, unveiled,
and in the vision of your glory blessed be?

114 *ST* IaIIae.112.1; cf. *ST* Ia.38.2.
115 *ST* IaIIae.86.
116 Nothing in Aquinas's theory of the incarnation rules this idea out. It is true, of
course, that in his divine nature Christ could not have any "stains", and it is
also true that for Aquinas Christ cannot have anything sinful even in his
human nature. But a stain, understood in the way I have explained here, is not
by itself a sin, and it is therefore possible, consonant with the other things
Aquinas wants to say about the incarnation, for Christ to have stains on the
soul in his human nature.

16 Providence and suffering

1 Norman Kretzmann has discussed some of the issues raised in Aquinas's
commentary on Romans; see his "Warring against the Law of My Mind:
Aquinas on Romans 7", in Thomas Morris (ed.), *Philosophy and the Christian
Faith* (Notre Dame, IN: University of Notre Dame Press, 1988), pp. 172–195.
2 This commentary, *Expositio super Job ad litteram*, is available in the Leonine
edition of Aquinas's works, vol. 26, and in an English translation: *Thomas
Aquinas, the Literal Exposition on Job: A Scriptural Commentary Concerning
Providence*, trans. Anthony Damico and Martin Yaffe, The American Academy
of Religion Classics in Religious Studies (Atlanta, GA: Scholars Press, 1989).
The commentary was probably written while Aquinas was at Orvieto, in the
period 1261/2–1264. See James Weisheipl, *Friar Thomas D'Aquino: His Life,
Thought, and Works*, 2d edn (Washington, DC: Catholic University of America
Press, 1983), p. 153; see also Simon Tugwell (ed.), *Albert and Thomas: Selected*

Writings, Classics of Western Spirituality (Mahwah, NJ: Paulist Press, 1988), p. 223.

3 The commentaries on the Pauline epistles were probably written during Aquinas's second Parisian regency, 1269–1272, and during his subsequent stay in Naples. See Tugwell (1988, p. 248); Weisheipl (1983, p. 373).

4 For discussion of the doctrine of simplicity and the connection between the simple being of God and the nature of goodness, see Chapter 3 on God's simplicity.

5 *ST* Ia.22.1.

6 Cf. *ST* Ia.103.4.

7 Cf. *ST* Ia.19.6.

8 The objections of the second group are concerned with two main points: (1) the manner of divine governance, that is, whether God's providence directly produces all human actions and events stemming from secondary causes and (2) the implications of divine governance, that is, whether divine providence can be exercised over human persons without destroying their freedom of will.

9 In comments on an earlier draft of this chapter, Tom Flint raised a worry about the mechanism by which providence is exercised given the way human lives are intertwined. Since one and the same evil can have radically different effects on different people, how are we to suppose God's providence can manage to govern the world in a way that ensures maximum benefit to all people? Flint's worry, which raises important questions, is a difficulty not only for any robust account of God's providence, but even for accounts of God's benevolence. If the farmers in some area are desperately praying for rain and a commune of sculptors building a large outdoor clay sculpture are praying, with equal urgency, for dry weather, how are we to explain the way in which a benevolent God will satisfy all those who trust in him for help? Though these are good questions, they lie outside the scope of this chapter. Flint himself supposes that we must ascribe middle knowledge to God in order to have an acceptable notion of divine providence, but my own sympathies lie rather with Aquinas's views, which are not hospitable to middle knowledge. But see Flint's *Divine Providence: The Molinist Account* (Ithaca, NY: Cornell University Press, 1998).

10 See *ST* Ia.19.6, Ia.22.2, Ia.103.8.

11 *ST* Ia.19.6 ad 3.

12 Cf. *In Sent* I.46.1.1.

13 Aquinas himself tends to attribute the distinction to Damascene; see, e.g., *QDV* 23.2.

14 Cf. *QDV* 23.2 ad 8, where Aquinas explicitly rules out such an interpretation of the distinction.

15 In human beings it is often the case that an antecedent volition temporally precedes a consequent one, because it not infrequently happens that a person forms a volition and then learns about some circumstance which inclines him to will differently. For the same sort of reason, a human person's consequent will is often an expression of the frustration of a previously framed antecedent will. But neither circumstance can hold for an eternal, omniscient being.

16 *QDV* 23.2.

17 See, e.g., *ST* Ia.19.6.

18 *QDV* 23.2.

19 That God, however, does not always will to let an evildoer accomplish what he wills is also clear in various biblical stories that Aquinas took to be authoritative; see, e.g., the story of Haman in the book of Esther.

20 In the incarnate Christ, who as human is not impassible, the antecedent will can take the form of longing (cf. Matthew 23:37 and see Chapter 14 on the incarnation); in the impassible divine nature, the antecedent will consists in a determination that the object of the antecedent will would be the good to be pursued if the circumstances did not have to be taken into account.

21 *SCG* III.71.

22 See, e.g., *SCG* III.71.

23 *QDV* 5.4.

24 See, e.g., *ST* Ia.19.9.

25 For discussion of the relation between God and contingency in the world, see Norman Kretzmann, "Goodness, Knowledge, and Indeterminacy in the Philosophy of Thomas Aquinas", *Journal of Philosophy* 80 (1983): 631–649. See also Chapter 5 on God's knowledge.

26 See *ST* Ia.22.2, Ia.103.1, Ia.116.1.

27 For further discussion of the compatibility of contingency and God's nature and acts, see Chapter 3 on God's simplicity.

28 See *ST* Ia.19.8.

29 *ST* Ia.19.9, Ia.22.4, Ia.103.7 IaIIae.10.4.

30 *Expositio super Job* 7.1–4, Damico and Yaffe, p.145. Although I have preferred to give my own translations, I have found the Damico and Yaffe translation helpful, and I will give references to this commentary both to the Latin and to the Damico and Yaffe translation.

31 See, e.g., *In Rom* 12.2.

32 See, e.g., Marilyn Adams, "Redemptive Suffering: A Christian Solution to the Problem of Evil", in Robert Audi and William Wainwright (eds), *Rationality, Religious Belief and Moral Commitment: New Essays in the Philosophy of Religion* (Ithaca, NY: Cornell University Press, 1986), 248–67; and *Horrendous Evils and the Goodness of God* (Ithaca, NY: Cornell University Press, 1999).

33 See, e.g., William Rowe, "The Empirical Argument from Evil", in Robert Audi and William Wainwright (eds), *Rationality, Religious Belief and Moral Commitment: New Essays in the Philosophy of Religion* (Ithaca, NY: Cornell University Press, 1986).

34 *In Rom* 8.6.

35 *SCG* III.112. See also *Expositio super Job* 7.10–18; Damico and Yaffe, 151, 153.

36 *In Rom* 8.6; see also *In II Cor* 12.3, where Aquinas explicitly includes mortal sins in the list of things that work for the good to those who love God.

37 *In Rom* 8.6.

38 *SCG* III.30.

39 *SCG* III.32.

40 *SCG* III.28.

41 *SCG* III.48.

42 *In Heb* 12.2.

43 *Expositio super* Job 9.24–30; Damico and Yaffe, p. 179.

44 For an annotated translation of the text, see Nicholas Ayo, *The Sermon-Conferences of St. Thomas Aquinas on the Apostles' Creed* (Notre Dame, IN: University of Notre Dame Press, 1988). Although I have preferred to use my own translation, I found Ayo's helpful, and for this work I give citations both to the Latin and to Ayo's translation. Thomas Aquinas, *Collationes Credo in Deum*, sec. III; Ayo, pp. 40–42. For some argument that Aquinas's approach to the problem of evil is right, see my papers "The Problem of Evil", *Faith and Philosophy* 2 (1985): 392–424, and "Providence and the Problem of Evil", in Thomas Flint (ed.), *Christian Philosophy* (Notre Dame, IN: University of Notre Dame Press, 1990), pp. 51–91. (See also my "Saadya Gaon and the Problem of Evil", *Faith and*

Philosophy 14 (1997): 523–549.) In those papers I discuss reasons for supposing that a good God would create a world in which human beings have such a cancer of the soul, that suffering is the best available means to cure the cancer in the soul, and that God can justifiably allow suffering even though it sometimes eventuates in the opposite of moral goodness or love of God.

45 There is a translation of this commentary: *Commentary on Saint Paul's First Letter to the Thessalonians and the Letter to the Philippians by St. Thomas Aquinas*, trans. F. R. Larcher and Michael Duffy (Albany, NY: Magi Books, 1969). Although I have preferred to use my own translations, I found the Larcher and Duffy translation helpful, and I will give citations for this work and for the commentary on Philippians both to the Latin and to this translation., *In I Thess*, prologue; Larcher and Duffy, p. 3.

46 *In Heb* 12.1.

47 *In Heb* 2.

48 *In Heb* 2.

49 *Expositio super Job* 1.20–21; Damico and Yaffe, p. 89.

50 *Expositio super Job* 9.15–21; Damico and Yaffe, p. 174.

51 Only one of the two metaphors is in the text translated in the Revised Standard Version, the King James, and the Anchor Bible.

52 *Expositio super Job* 7.1; Damico and Yaffe, p. 146. The idea here seems to be that there are degrees of glory or degrees of reward in heaven, and those persons who are better are given more suffering for the sake of the concomitant greater glory. Presumably, part of what makes such persons better is that they would be willing to accept greater suffering for the sake of greater glory; see the section on martyrs in my "Providence and the Problem of Evil", op. cit. Someone might suppose that Aquinas ought to say not that better people suffer more but rather that worse people, who need more suffering, suffer more. But here I think an analogy with chemotherapy is helpful. Sometimes the most effective kinds of chemotherapy cannot be used on those who need it most because their systems are too weak to bear the treatments, and so the strongest kinds of treatment tend to be reserved for those who are not too weak or too advanced in the disease or too riddled with secondary complications – in other words, for those who are (aside from the particular cancer) strong and robust.

53 *In I Thess* 4.2; Larcher and Duffy, p. 39.

54 *In Phil* 3.2; Larcher and Daffy, p. 102.

55 *In Rom* 5.1.

56 Plato, *Gorgias* 481C.

57 There is a nineteenth-century translation of the whole work: *Morals on the Book of Job by Gregory the Great, the First Pope of That Name* (Oxford, 1844). Although I have preferred to use my own translations, I give the reference both to the Latin and to this translation: Gregory the Great, *Moralia in Job*, book 5, introduction; *Morals*, pp. 241–242. (A contemporary translation of part of the work by James O'Donnell is also available online.) The line taken by Gregory has the result that if we come across saintly people who do not suffer much, we should be inclined to wonder whether they really are as saintly as they seem.

58 One should not misunderstand this claim and suppose Aquinas to be claiming that human beings can earn their way to heaven by the merit badges of suffering. Aquinas is quite explicit that salvation is through Christ only. Aquinas's claim here is not about what merits salvation for us but only about what is useful in the process of salvation. It would take us too far afield here to consider Aquinas's view of the relation between Christ's work of redemption and the role of human suffering in that process (but see Chapters 12 and 15 on faith and on the atonement). What is important for my purposes is just to see that on

Aquinas's account suffering is an indispensable element in the course of human salvation, merited by Christ.

59 See, e.g., *Expositio super Job*, Chapter 7, sec. 1, Damico and Yaffe, p. 145; and Chapter 19, 23–29, Damico and Yaffe, pp. 268–71, where Aquinas makes these points clear and maintains that Job was already among the redeemed awaiting the resurrection and union with God. Someone might wonder whether it is possible to maintain this approach to suffering when the suffering consists in madness, mental retardation, or some form of dementia. This doubt is based on the unreflective assumption that those suffering from these afflictions have lost all the mental faculties needed for moral or spiritual development. For some suggestions to the contrary, see the sensitive and insightful discussion of retarded and autistic patients in Oliver Sacks, *The Man Who Mistook His Wife for a Hat* (New York: Summit Books, 1985).

60 For a vigorous response of this sort to all kinds of theodicy, see Terrence W. Tilley, *The Evils of Theodicy* (Washington, DC: Georgetown University Press, 1991).

61 As late as the end of the nineteenth century, even *Scientific American* was publishing diatribes against anesthetics (see the quotation in *Scientific American*, August 1991, p. 14), and the lamentable nineteenth-century animus against anesthetics, particularly in connection with childbirth, often had a religious basis. For a detailed discussion of nineteenth-century attitudes toward anesthetics, see Martin S. Pernick, *A Calculus of Suffering: Pain, Professionalism, and Anesthesia in Nineteenth Century America* (New York: Columbia University Press, 1985).

62 *In I Cor* 15.2.

63 See, e.g., the description in the relevant article in David Hugh Farmer, *The Oxford Dictionary of Saints* (Oxford: Oxford University Press, 1988).

64 Clearly sometimes we do know or at least have a pretty good idea, as when loving parents deliberately inflict some suffering on their children in response to intolerable behavior on the children's part.

65 For some explanation of the *ceteris paribus* clause, see the section on fraternal correction in Chapter 10 on justice.

66 Job 31. In supporting Aquinas's line here, I am assuming that sins of thought and deed are worse than the analogous sins of thought alone. That is, I am assuming that someone who is murderous but who is prevented by his friends from acting on his intentions is morally better off than he would have been if he had been allowed to go ahead and commit murder. This assumption is widely, though not universally, shared.

67 See also *ST* IIaIIae.32.5–6, where Aquinas argues that not giving alms, or keeping for oneself more than one needs, can be punished with damnation. (See also Chapter 10 on justice.)

68 Two caveats are perhaps necessary here. (1) Nothing in these remarks should be taken as denigrating asceticism as a whole. Rigorous training, of body or mind, does take self-discipline and, by implication, self-denial. But it is possible to become obsessed with the self-denial itself, so that it effaces the goal for which it was originally intended as a means. There is a difference between anorexia and dieting, and one can see the problems in anorexia without thereby eschewing discipline as regards eating. (2) By saying that Simeon sought suffering for its own sake, I do not mean to deny that he might have believed that the purpose of the ascetic suffering he engaged in was spiritual progress. It seems nonetheless true that many of his actions focus just on inflicting suffering on himself, rather than focusing on the goal to which the suffering was supposed to be a means. It certainly appears as if he lost sight of the professed goal of spiritual

well-being in his fixation on mortifying the flesh. I am grateful to Marilyn Adams for comments on this point.

69 1 Cor. 15:19.
70 *In I Cor* 15.2.
71 I have discussed ways in which this sort of approach to the problem of evil might be applied to those who are not adults or to those who are not Christian in "The Problem of Evil", op. cit.
72 *Collationes Credo in Deum* 11; Ayo, pp. 116–118.
73 *Collationes Credo in Deum* 1.2; Larcher and Duffy, p. 63; also, 1.2; Larcher and Duffy, p. 68.
74 See, e.g., *In Rom* 5.1.
75 There is an English translation of this work: *Commentary on Saint Paul's Epistle to the Galatians by St. Thomas Aquinas*, trans. F. R. Larcher and Richard Murphy (Albany, NY: Magi Books, 1966). Although I have preferred to use my own translations, I found the Larcher and Murphy translation helpful, and I will give citations for this work both to the Latin and to the Larcher and Murphy translation. *In Gal* 5.6; Larcher and Murphy, pp. 179–180.
76 *In Phil* 4.1; Larcher and Duffy, p. 113.
77 Someone might suppose that this statement is false, on the grounds that sometimes pain or sickness makes us just irritable and unable to find any joy or even relief in the presence of a person we love. The mistake in this view can be seen by considering cases of childbirth. In the painful, humiliating, or embarrassing circumstances which sometimes arise in childbirth, a woman may get irritable enough at the father of her child to lash out at him, verbally or even physically. That she wants him there anyway, that his presence is a great comfort to her underneath and around the irritation, is made manifest by the fact that she still wants him in the delivery room, that she would find his leaving intolerable. Being irritable under pain in the presence of someone you love is compatible with finding great comfort in his presence at another level. It should perhaps also be said, as an additional consideration in this connection, that the degree of joy or comfort one person has at the presence of another will be proportional to the intensity of the love between them.
78 *In Gal* 5.6; Larcher and Murphy, p. 180. Also, *In Gal* 5.6; Larcher and Murphy, p. 179; and *In Heb* 12.2.
79 *Expositio super Job* 9.15–21; Damico and Yaffe, p. 174.
80 Job 42:5.
81 See, e.g., Aquinas, *Collationes Credo in Deum* 6; Ayo, p. 69, p. 73.
82 Aquinas therefore supposes that Job's later return to worldly prosperity is at least in part a divine concession to the fact that Job is part of a pre-Christian culture.

> And [Job's return to prosperity] was appropriate to the time, because of the position of the Old Testament in which temporal goods are promised, so that in this way by the prosperity which he recovered an example was given to others, to turn them to God.
> (*Expositio super Job* 42.10–16; Damico and Yaffe, p. 472)

It should also be said that nothing in Aquinas's position requires him to hold that all Christian adults experience divine consolation in their suffering. For some people, the point of the suffering might be to bring them to the stage where they are able to experience consolation; and even for those people who are well advanced in spiritual or moral progress, consolation can always be warded off by a spirit which refuses it.

83 *In II Cor* 1.2.
84 *In II Cor* 1.2. See also *In Rom* 8.7.
85 *In Phil* 4.1; Larcher and Daffy, p. 112.
86 *Expositio super Job* 1.6–7; Damico and Yaffe, p. 79.
87 *Expositio super Job* 17.2–9: Damico and Yaffe, p. 252.
88 *Devotio Moderna: Basic Writings*, trans. John van Engen (New York: Paulist Press, 1988), p. 151. I am grateful to John van Engen for calling my attention to the intriguing material in this book.
89 Tilley, *The Evils of Theodicy*, p. 219.
90 For further discussion of Aquinas's sort of theodicy in contemporary philosophical theory, see my *Wandering in Darkness: Narrative and the Problem of Suffering* (forthcoming).

SELECT BIBLIOGRAPHY

The secondary literature on Aquinas is voluminous, and it is not possible to cite all or even the very best of it here. For a fuller bibliography, the reader should consult the major Thomistic bibliographies by Miethe and Bourke and by Ingardia listed below. The relevant contemporary philosophical literature on the topics treated in Aquinas's thought is similarly vast, and an analogous point applies to it: only a small portion of the interesting and helpful literature is cited here. Finally, strictly scientific literature is cited only in the notes and is not listed here.

Adams, Marilyn McCord (1986) "Redemptive Suffering: A Christian Solution to the Problem of Evil", in Robert Audi and William Wainwright (eds), *Rationality, Religious Belief and Moral Commitment: New Essays in the Philosophy of Religion* (Ithaca, NY: Cornell University Press), pp. 248–267.

Adams, Robert Merrihew (1971) "Has It Been Proved that All Real Existence is Contingent?", *American Philosophical Quarterly* 8: 284–291.

—— (1973) "A Modified Divine Command Theory of Ethical Wrongness", in Gene Outka and John P. Reeder Jr. (eds), *Religion and Morality* (Garden City, NY: Doubleday Anchor), pp. 318–347.

—— (1979) "Divine Command Metaethics Modified Again", *Journal of Religious Ethics* 7 (Spring): 66–79.

—— (1983) "Divine Necessity", *Journal of Philosophy* 80: 741–752.

—— (1987) "Divine Commands and the Social Nature of Obligation", *Faith and Philosophy* 4: 262–275.

—— (1999) *Finite and Infinite Goods: A Framework for Ethics* (New York: Oxford University Press).

Aertsen, Jan (1988) *Nature and Creature: Thomas Aquinas's Way of Thought* (Leiden: E. J. Brill).

—— (1993) "Aquinas' Philosophy in its Historical Setting", in N. Kretzmann and E. Stump (eds), *The Cambridge Companion to Aquinas* (Cambridge: Cambridge University Press), pp. 12–37.

—— (1996) *Medieval Philosophy and the Transcendentals: The Case of Thomas Aquinas* (Leiden: E. J. Brill).

Albritton, Rogers (1985) "Freedom of Will and Freedom of Action", *American Philosophical Association Proceedings and Addresses* 59: 239–251.

Alston, William (1988) "The Deontological Conception of Epistemic Justification", in J.E. Tomberlin (ed.), *Philosophical Perspectives 2 Epistemology* (Atascadero, CA: Ridgeview Publishing Co.), pp. 257–299; reprinted in *Epistemic Justification: Essays in the Theory of Knowledge* (Ithaca, NY: Cornell University Press, 1989), pp. 115–152.

—— (1989) "Concepts of Epistemic Justification", *The Monist* 68 (1985), 57–89; reprinted in *Epistemic Justification. Essays in the Theory of Knowledge* (Ithaca, NY: Cornell University Press), pp. 81–114.

—— (1993) "Aquinas on Theological Predication: A Look Backward and a Look Forward," in Eleonore Stump (ed.), *Reasoned Faith* (Ithaca, NY: Cornell University Press), pp. 145–178.

Ameno, Romano (1950) "Probabile fonte della nozione boeziana di eternità", *Filosofia* I: 365–373.

Anderson, James F. (1953) *An Introduction to the Metaphysics of St. Thomas Aquinas* (Chicago: Henry Regnery Co.).

Armstrong, Arthur Hilary (ed.) (1967) *Plotinus*, vol. 3. (London and Cambridge, MA: Harvard University Press).

Ashworth, Earline Jennifer (1991) "Signification and Modes of Signifying in Thirteenth-Century Logic: A Preface to Aquinas on Analogy", *Medieval Philosophy and Theology* 1: 39–67.

Audi, Robert (1993) "The Dimensions of Faith and the Demands of Reason", in Eleonore Stump (ed.), *Reasoned Faith* (Ithaca, NY: Cornell University Press), pp. 70–92.

Ayo, Nicholas (1988) *The Sermon-Conferences of St. Thomas Aquinas on the Apostles' Creed* (Notre Dame, IN: University of Notre Dame Press).

Baker, Lynne Rudder (1997) "Why Constitution is Not Identity", *Journal of Philosophy* 94: 599–621.

—— (1999) "Unity Without Identity: A New Look at Material Constitution", *Midwest Studies in Philosophy* 23: 144–165.

—— (2000) *Persons and Bodies. A Constitution View* (Cambridge: Cambridge University Press).

Barnes, Jonathan (1975) "Aristotle's Theory of Demonstration", in Jonathan Barnes, Malcolm Schofield, and Richard Sorabji (eds), *Articles on Aristotle* (London: Duckworth), pp. 65–87.

Beierwaltes, Werner (1967) *Plotin über Ewigkeit und Zeit* (Enneade iii 7) (Frankfurt am Main: Klostermann).

Bennett, Daniel (1969) "The Divine Simplicity", *Journal of Philosophy* 66: 628–637.

Bennett, Jonathan (1990) "Why is Belief Involuntary?", *Analysis* 50: 87–107.

Bernstein, Richard (1996) *Hannah Arendt and the Jewish Question* (Cambridge, MA: MIT Press).

Bezwinska, Jadwiga and Czech, Danuta (1984) *KL Auschwitz Seen by the SS: Hoess, Broad, Kremer* (New York: Howard Fertig).

Bigongiari, Dino (ed.) (1953) *The Political Ideas of St. Thomas Aquinas* (New York: Hafner).

Blandino, G. and Molinaro, A. (eds) (1989) *The Critical Problem of Knowledge* (Rome: Herder – Pontifical University of Lateran).

Boethius (1973) *The Consolation of Philosophy*, in H. F. Stewart, E. K. Rand, and S. J. Tester, *Boethius: The Theological Tractates and The Consolation of Philosophy* (London and Cambridge, MA: Harvard University Press).

Boyd, Richard (1980) "Materialism without Reductionism: What Physicalism Does Not Entail", in Ned Block (ed.), *Readings in Philosophy of Psychology*, vol. 1 (Cambridge, MA: Harvard University Press).

Bracken, W. Jerome (1978) "Why Suffering in Redemption? A New Interpretation of the Theology of the Passion in the Summa Theologica, 3, 46–49, by Thomas Aquinas", PhD dissertation, Fordham University.

Bradley, Denis (1997) *Aquinas on the Twofold Human Good: Reason and Human Happiness in Aquinas's Moral Science* (Washington, DC: Catholic University of America Press).

Brady, Ignatius (1974) "John Pecham and the Background of Aquinas' *De Aeternitate Mundi*", in A.A. Maurer (ed.), *St. Thomas Aquinas 1274–1974: Commemorative Studies* (Toronto: Pontifical Institute of Mediaeval Studies), vol. II, pp. 141–178.

Braine, David (1988) *The Reality of Time and the Existence of God: The Project of Proving God's Existence* (Oxford: Oxford University Press).

—— (1992) *The Human Person: Animal and Spirit* (Notre Dame, IN: University of Notre Dame Press).

Brezik, Victor B. (ed.) (1981) *One Hundred Years of Thomism* (Houston, TX: Center for Thomistic Studies).

Brock, Stephen Louis (1998) *Action and Conduct: Thomas Aquinas and the Theory of Action* (Edinburgh: T&T Clark).

Brown, Oscar James (1981) *Natural Rectitude and Divine Law in Aquinas* (Toronto: Pontifical Institute of Medieval Studies).

Burrell, David (1979) *Aquinas: God and Action* (Notre Dame, IN: University of Notre Dame Press).

—— (1986) *Knowing the Unknowable God: Ibn Sina, Maimonides, Aquinas* (Notre Dame, IN: University of Notre Dame Press).

—— (1992) "Review of Christopher Hughes's A Complex Theory of a Simple God", *The Journal of Religion* 72: 120–121.

—— (1993a) *Freedom and Creation in Three Traditions* (Notre Dame, IN: University of Notre Dame Press).

—— (1993b) "Aquinas and Islamic and Jewish Thinkers", in N. Kretzmann and E. Stump (eds), *The Cambridge Companion to Aquinas* (Cambridge: Cambridge University Press), pp. 60–84.

Busa, Roberto (1974–80) *Index Thomisticus: Sanci Thomae Aquinatis operum omnium indices et concordantiae in quibus verborum omnium et singulorum formae et lemmata cum suis frequentiis et contextibus variis modis* (Stuttgart-Bad Cannstatt: Frommann-Holzboog).

Campodonico, Angelo (1986) *Alla Scoperta dell'Essere: Saggio sul pensiero di Tommaso d'Aquino* (Milan: Jaca Book).

—— (1996) *Integritas metafisica ed etica in San Tommaso* (Fiesole: Nardini).

Cartwright, Nancy (1989) *Nature's Capacities and Their Measurement* (Oxford: Clarendon Press).

Catan, John R. (ed.) (1980) *St. Thomas Aquinas on the Existence of God: Collected Papers of Joseph Owens* (Albany NY: State University of New York Press).

Chenu, Marie-Dominique (1964) *Toward Understanding St. Thomas* (Chicago: Regnery).

—— (2002) *Aquinas and His Role in Theology*, trans. Paul Philibert (Wilmington, DE: Michael Glazier Books).

Chisholm, Roderick (1968) "Lewis' Ethics of Belief", in Paul Arthur Schilpp (ed.), *The Philosophy of C.I. Lewis* (London: Cambridge University Press).

—— (1991) "On the Simplicity of the Soul", in James Tomberlin (ed.), *Philosophical Perspectives*, vol. 5 (Atascadero, CA: Ridgeview Publishing Co.).

Churchland, Patricia (1990) *Neurophilosophy. Toward a Unified Science of the Mind/Brain* (Cambridge, MA: MIT Press).

Cohen, Sheldon M. (1982) "St. Thomas Aquinas on the Immaterial Reception of Sensible Forms", *The Philosophical Review* 91: 193–209.

Copleston, Frederick Charles (1955) *Aquinas* (Baltimore, MD: Penguin Press).

Craig, William Lane (1979) "God, Time and Eternity", *Religious Studies* 29: 165–170.

—— (1985) "Was Thomas Aquinas a B-Theorist of Time?" *New Scholasticism* 59: 473–483.

—— (1990) "God and Real Time", *Religious Studies* 26: 335–347.

—— (1991) "Time and Infinity", *International Philosophical Quarterly* 31: 387–401.

—— (1996) "Timelessness and Creation", *Australasian Journal of Philosophy* 74: 646–656.

—— (1997) "Divine Timelessness and Necessary Existence", *International Philosophical Quarterly* 37: 217–224.

—— (1998a) "The Tensed vs. Tenseless Theory of Time: A Watershed for the Conception of Divine Eternity", in R. LePoidevin (ed.), *Questions of Time and Tense* (Oxford: Oxford University Press), pp. 221–250.

—— (1998b) "Divine Timelessness and Personhood", *International Journal for Philosophy of Religion* 43: 109–124.

—— (2000a) "Timelessness and Omnitemporality", *Philosophia Christi* 2: 29–33.

—— (2000b) "Omniscience, Tensed Facts, and Divine Eternity", *Faith and Philosophy* 17: 225–241.

—— (2001a) *Time and Eternity: Exploring God's Relationship to Time* (Wheaton, IL: Crossway).

—— (2001b) *God, Time and Eternity* (Dordrecht: Kluwer Academic Publishers).

Crotty, Nicholas (1962) "The Redemptive Role of Christ's Resurrection", *The Thomist* 25: 54–106.

Cross, Richard (1996) "Aquinas on Nature, Hypostasis, and the Metaphysics of the Incarnation", *The Thomist* 60: 171–202.

—— (2002) *The Metaphysics of the Incarnation: Thomas Aquinas to Duns Scotus* (Oxford: Oxford University Press).

Daly, Mary (1971) "The Notion of Justification in the Commentary of St. Thomas Aquinas on the Epistle to the Romans", PhD dissertation, Marquette University, Milwaukee.

Davies, Brian (1992) *The Thought of Thomas Aquinas* (Oxford: Clarendon Press).

Deferrari, Roy J. and Barry, M. Inviolata (1948) *A Complete Index of the Summa Theologica of St. Thomas Aquinas* (Washington, DC: Catholic University of America Press).

De la Trinité, Philippe (1961) *What is Redemption?*, trans. Anthony Armstrong (New York: Hawthorn Books).

Dennett, Daniel (1991) *Consciousness Explained* (Boston: Little, Brown and Co.).

Descartes, René (1984) *The Philosophical Writings of Descartes*, vol. II. trans. John Cottingham, Robert Stoothoff, and Dugald Murdoch (Cambridge: Cambridge University Press).

De Tocco, Guillaume (1323) *Ystoria sancti Thome de Aquino de Guillaume de Tocco*, edited, with introduction and notes, by Claire Le Brun-Gouanvic (Toronto: Pontifical Insitute of Medieval Studies, 1996).

Dienstag, Jacob I. (ed.) (1975) *Studies in Maimonides and St. Thomas Aquinas* (New York: KTAV Publishing House, Inc.).

Dittoe, John T. (1946) "Sacramental Incorporation into the Mystical Body", *The Thomist* 9: 469–514.

Dobbs-Weinstein, Idit (1995) *Maimonides and St. Thomas on the Limits of Reason* (Albany, NY: State University of New York Press).

Doig, James (1972) *Aquinas on Metaphysics: A Historico-Doctrinal Study of the Commentary on the Metaphysics* (The Hague: Martinus Nijhoff).

Donagan, Alan (1977) *The Theory of Morality* (Chicago: University of Chicago Press).

—— (1982) "Thomas Aquinas on Human Action", in N. Kretzmann, A. Kenny and J. Pinborg (eds), *The Cambridge History of Later Medieval Philosophy* (Cambridge: Cambridge University Press), pp. 642–654.

—— (1985) *Human Ends and Human Actions: An Exploration in St. Thomas's Treatment* (Milwaukee: Marquette University Press).

Dretske, Fred (1988) *Explaining Behavior: Reasons in a World of Causes* (Cambridge, MA: MIT Press).

—— (1991) "Perception: Heil", in Brian McLaughlin (ed.), *Dretske and His Critics* (Oxford: Blackwell), pp. 180–184.

Dummett, Michael (1964) "Bringing About the Past", *Philosophical Review* 73: 338–359.

Dupré, John (1993) *The Disorder of Things. Metaphysical Foundations of the Disunity of Science* (Cambridge, MA: Harvard University Press).

Eco, Umberto (1988) *Problema Estetico in Tommaso d'Aquino* (Cambridge, MA: Harvard University Press).

Edwards, Jonathan (1961) *A Treatise Concerning Religious Affections* (Edinburgh: Banner of Truth Trust).

Elders, Leo (1990a) *The Philosophical Theology of St. Thomas Aquinas*, Studien und Texte zur Geistesgeschichte des Mittelalters (New York: E. J. Brill).

—— (ed.) (1990b) "La doctrine de la revelation divine de saint Thomas d'Aquin", *Studi Tomistici* 37. (Rome: Pontificia Accademia di S. Tommaso: Libreria Editrice Vaticana).

Eschmann, Ignatius (1997) *The Ethics of Saint Thomas Aquinas* (Toronto: Pontifical Institute of Medieval Studies).

Fabro, Cornelio (1961) *Participation et causalité selon Saint Thomas d'Aquin* (Participation and Causality in the Work of Saint Thomas Aquinas) (Louvain: Publications Universitaires de Louvain).

Fine, Kit (1999) "Things and Their Parts", *Midwest Studies in Philosophy* 23: 61–74.

Finnis, John (1980) *Natural Law and Natural Rights* (New York: Oxford University Press).

—— (1998) *Aquinas. Moral, Political, and Legal Theory* (Oxford: Oxford University Press).

Fischer, John Martin and Ravizza, Mark (1998) *Responsibility and Control. A Theory of Moral Responsibility* (Cambridge: Cambridge University Press).

Flint, Thomas (1987) "Compatibilism and the Argument from Unavoidability", *Journal of Philosophy* 84: 423–440.

Flint, Thomas P. and Freddoso, Alfred J. (1983) "Maximal Power", in Alfred J. Freddoso (ed.), *The Existence and Nature of God* (Notre Dame, IN: University of Notre Dame Press), pp. 81–113.

Foley, John (1994) *Creativity and the Roots of Liturgy* (Portland, OR: Pastoral Press).

Foster, Kenelm (1959) *The Life of Saint Thomas Aquinas, Biographical Documents* (London: Longmans, Green).

Frankfurt, Harry (1969) "Alternate Possibilities and Moral Responsibility", *Journal of Philosophy* 66: 829–839.

—— (1971) "Freedom of the Will and the Concept of a Person", *The Journal of Philosophy* 68: 5–20; reprinted in *The Importance of What We Care About* (Cambridge: Cambridge University Press, 1988).

Gallagher, David M. (1988) "Thomas Aquinas on the Causes of Human Choice", Dissertation. Catholic University of America, 1988.

—— (1990) "Aquinas on Moral Action: Interior and Exterior Acts", *Proceedings of the American Catholic Philosophical Association* 64: 118–129.

—— (1991) "Thomas Aquinas on the Will as Rational Appetite", *Journal of the History of Philosophy* 29: 559–584.

—— (1994) *Thomas Aquinas and His Legacy*, Studies in Philosophy and the History of Philosophy, vol. 28 (Washington, DC: Catholic University of America Press).

Garfinkel, Alan (1993) "Reductionism", in Richard Boyd, Philip Gasper, and J.D. Trout (eds), *The Philosophy of Science* (Cambridge, MA: MIT Press), pp. 443–459.

Garrigou-Lagrange, Reginald (1943) *The One God* (St.Louis and London: B. Herder Book Co.).

—— (1950) *Christ the Savior: A Commentary on the Third Part of St. Thomas' Theological Summa* (St.Louis and London: B. Herder Book Co.).

—— (1955) *God: His Existence and His Nature: A Thomistic Solution of Certain Agnostic Antinomies*, vol. 2, trans. Dom Bede Rose (St. Louis and London: B. Herder Book Co.).

Gauthier, René Antoine (1961) "Introduction", in *Saint Thomas d'Aquin: Contra Gentiles*, Livre premier (Lyons: P. Lethielleux).

—— (1993) *Saint Thomas d'Aquin: Somme contre les gentils: Introduction*, Collection Philosophie Européane, dirigée par H. Hude (Paris: Editions Universitaires).

Geach, Peter (1969) *God and the Soul* (London: Routledge & K. Paul).

—— (1977) *Providence and Evil* (Cambridge: Cambridge University Press).

Gellman, Jerome (1977) "Omnipotence and Impeccability", *The New Scholasticism* 51: 21–37.

Gilby, Thomas (1955) *The Political Thought of Thomas Aquinas* (Chicago: University of Chicago Press).

Gilson, Etienne (1956) *The Christian Philosophy of St. Thomas Aquinas*, trans. L.K. Shook (New York: Random House).

—— (1960) *Elements of Christian Philosophy* (New York: New American Library).

Glannon, Walter (1955) "Responsibility and the Principle of Possible Action", *Journal of Philosophy* 92: 261–274.

Greco, John (1993) "Virtues and Vices of Virtue Epistemology", *Canadian Journal of Philosophy*, 23: 413–432.

Grene, Marjorie (1972) "Aristotle and Modern Biology", *Journal of the History of Ideas* 33: 395–424.

Griffin, David Ray (1976) *God, Power, and Evil: A Process Theodicy* (Philadelphia, PA: Westminster Press).

Haldane, John J. (1983) "Aquinas on Sense-Perception", *The Philosophical Review* 92: 233–239.

Hankey, W. J. (1987) *God in Himself: Aquinas' Doctrine of God as Expounded in the Summa Theologiae* (Oxford: Oxford University Press).

Heil, John (1991) "Perceptual Experience", in Brian McLaughlin (ed.), *Dretske and His Critics* (Oxford: Blackwell), pp. 1–16.

Henle, Robert John (1956) *Saint Thomas and Platonism* (The Hague: Martinus Nijhoff).

Hoffman, Joshua (1979) "Can God Do Evil?", *Southern Journal of Philosophy* 17: 213–220.

Hoffman, Joshua and Rosencrantz, Gary (1991) "Are Souls Unintelligible?", in James Tomberlin (ed.), *Philosophical Perspectives*, vol. 5 (Atascadero, CA: Ridgeview Publishing Co.).

Hoffman, Paul (1990) "St. Thomas Aquinas on the Halfway State of Sensible Being", *The Philosophical Review* 99: 73–92.

Hood, John (1995) *Aquinas and the Jews* (Philadelphia, PA: University of Pennsylvania Press).

Hughes, Christopher (1989) *A Complex Theory of a Simple God* (Ithaca, NY: Cornell University Press).

Ingardia, Richard (1993) *Thomas Aquinas: International Bibliography 1977–1990* (Bowling Green, KY: The Philosophy Documentation Center).

Irwin, Terence H. (1984) 'The Metaphysical and Psychological Basis of Aristotle's Ethics,' in Amélie Rorty (ed.), *Essays on Aristotle's Ethics* (Berkeley, CA: University of California Press).

—— (1988) *Aristotle's First Principles* (Oxford: Clarendon Press).

—— (1992) "Who Discovered the Will?", in J.E. Tomberlin (ed.), *Philosophical Perspectives 6: Ethics* (Atascadero, CA: Ridgeview Publishing Co.).

Jaffa, Harry V. (1952) *Thomism and Aristotelianism* (Chicago: University of Chicago Press).

Jenkins, John (1997) *Knowledge and Faith in Thomas Aquinas* (Cambridge: Cambridge University Press).

Johnston, Mark (1992) "Constitution is Not Identity", *Mind* 101: 89–105

Jordan, Mark (1983) "The Names of God and the Being of Names" in Alfred J. Freddoso (ed.), *The Existence and Nature of God* (Notre Dame, IN: University of Notre Dame Press), pp. 161–190

—— (1986) *Ordering Wisdom: The Hierarchy of Philosophical Discourses in Aquinas* (Notre Dame, IN: University of Notre Dame Press).

—— (1993) "Theology and Philosophy", in Norman Kretzmann and Eleonore Stump (eds), *The Cambridge Companion to Aquinas* (Cambridge: Cambridge University Press), pp. 232–251.

Kavanaugh, John (2001) *Who Count as Persons?: Human Identity and the Ethics of Killing* (Washington, DC: Georgetown University Press).

Keenan, James F. (1992) *Goodness and Righteousness in Thomas Aquinas's Summa Theologiae* (Washington, DC: Georgetown University Press).

Kenny, Anthony (1969a) "Divine Foreknowledge and Human Freedom", in A. Kenny (ed.), *Aquinas: A Collection of Critical Essays* (Garden City, NY: Anchor Books).

—— (ed.) (1969b) *Aquinas: A Collection of Critical Essays* (Garden City, NY: Doubleday).

—— (1979) *The God of the Philosophers* (Oxford: Clarendon Press).

—— (1980a) *Aquinas* (New York: Hill & Wang).

—— (1980b) *The Five Ways: St Thomas Aquinas' Proofs of God's Existence* (Notre Dame, IN: University of Notre Dame Press).

—— (1993) *Aquinas on Mind* (London: Routledge).

Kent, Bonnie (1995) *Virtues of the Will: The Transformation of Ethics in the Late Thirteenth Century* (Washington, DC: The Catholic University of America Press).

Kim, Jaegwon (1993a) "Supervenience for Multiple Domains", reprinted in *Supervenience and Mind* (Cambridge: Cambridge University Press), pp. 109–130.

—— (1993b) "Concepts of Supervenience", reprinted in *Supervenience and Mind* (Cambridge: Cambridge University Press, 1993).

Kirn, Arthur G. (ed.) (1967) *G.B. Phelan: Selected Papers* (Toronto: Pontifical Institute of Mediaeval Studies).

Kitcher, Philip (1993) "1953 and All That: A Tale of Two Sciences", in Richard Boyd, Philip Gasper, and J.D. Trout (eds), *The Philosophy of Science* (Cambridge, MA: MIT Press), pp. 553–570.

Klee, Robert L. (1984) "Micro-determinism and Concepts of Emergence", *Philosophy of Science* 51: 44–63.

Klemperer, Victor (1996) *Ich will Zeugnis ablegen bis zum letzten: Tagebücher 1933–45* (Berlin: Aufbau Verlag).

Kneale, Martha (1968–9) "Eternity and Sempiternity", *Proceedings of the Aristotelian Society*, 69: 223–238.

Kneale, William (1960) "Time and Eternity in Theology", *Proceedings of the Aristotelian Society* 61: 87–108.

—— (1967) "Eternity", in Paul Edwards (ed.), *The Encyclopedia of Philosophy*, vol. 3 (New York: Macmillan).

Knuuttila, Simo (1993) *Modalities in Medieval Philosophy* (London: Routledge).

Korolec, J. (1981) "Free Will and Free Choice" in Norman Kretzmann, Anthony Kenny, Jan Pinborg (eds), assoc. ed. Eleonore Stump, *Cambridge History of Later Medieval Philosophy* (Cambridge: Cambridge University Press).

Kosman, L. A. (1984) "Being Properly Affected: Virtues and Feelings in Aristotle's Ethics", in Amélie Rorty (ed.), *Essays on Aristotle's Ethics* (Berkeley, CA: University of California Press).

Kremer, Klaus (1971) *Die neuplatonische Seinsphilosophie und ihre Wirkung auf Thomas von Aquin* (Neoplatonist Metaphysics and Their Effect on Thomas Aquinas) (Leiden: E. J. Brill).

Kretzmann, Norman (1976) "Time Exists – But Hardly, or Obscurely *(Physics* iv, 10; 217b29–218a33)", *Aristotelian Society Supplementary Volume* I: 91–114.

—— (1981) "*Sensus compositus, sensus divisus*, and propositional attitudes", *Medioevo* 7: 195–229.

—— (1983a) "Goodness: Knowledge, and Indeterminacy in the Philosophy of Thomas Aquinas", *Journal of Philosophy* 80: 631–649.

—— (1983b) "Abraham, Isaac, and Euthyphro: God and the Basis of Morality", in Donald Stump *et al.* (eds), *Hamartia: The Concept of Error in the Western Tradition* (New York and Toronto: The Edwin Mellen Press), pp. 27–50.

—— (1984) "Nos Ipsi Principia Sumus: Boethius and the Basis of Contingency", in Tamar Rudavsky (ed.), *Divine Omniscience and Omnipotence in Medieval Philosophy* (Dordrecht: D. Reidel), pp. 23–50.

—— (1988a) "Lex iniusta non est lex: Laws on Trial in Aquinas' Court of Conscience", *The American Journal of Jurisprudence* 33: 99–122.

—— (1988b) "Warring against the Law of My Mind: Aquinas on Romans 7", in Thomas Morris (ed.), *Philosophy and the Christian Faith* (Notre Dame, IN: University of Notre Dame Press), pp. 172–195.

—— (1988c) "God Among the Causes of Moral Evil: Hardening of Hearts and Spiritual Blinding", *Philosophical Topics* 16: 189–214.

—— (1992a) "Infallibility, Error, and Ignorance", *Canadian Journal of Philosophy*, supp. vol. 17: 159–194.

—— (1992b) "Infallibility, Error, and Ignorance", in Richard Bosley and Martin Tweedale (eds), *Aristotle and His Medieval Interpreters*, *Canadian Journal of Philosophy*, supplementary volume (Calgary: University of Calgary Press).

—— (1993) "Philosophy of Mind", in N. Kretzmann and E. Stump (eds), *The Cambridge Companion to Aquinas* (Cambridge: Cambridge University Press), pp. 128–159.

—— (1997) *The Metaphysics of Theism: Aquinas's Natural Theology in summa contra gentiles I* (Oxford: Clarendon Press).

—— (1999) *The Metaphysics of Creation: Aquinas's Natural Theology in summa contra gentiles II* (Oxford: Clarendon Press).

Kretzmann, Norman and Stump, Eleonore (eds) (1993) *The Cambridge Companion to Aquinas* (Cambridge: Cambridge University Press).

Kuksewicz, Zdzislaw (1982) "The Potential and the Agent Intellect", and "Criticisms of Aristotelian Psychology and the Augustinian-Aristotelian Synthesis", in Norman Kretzmann, Anthony Kenny, Jan Pinborg (eds), assoc. ed., Eleonore Stump. *The Cambridge History of Later Medieval Philosophy* (Cambridge: Cambridge University Press), pp. 595–602 and 623–628.

LaCroix, Richard (1977) "Augustine on the Simplicity of God", *New Scholasticism* 51: 453–469.

Lawler, Michael (1971) "Grace and Free Will in Justification: A Textual Study in Aquinas", *The Thomist* 35: 601–630.

Leftow, Brian (1989) "The Roots of Eternity", *Religious Studies* 24: 189–212.

—— (1990a) "Aquinas on Time and Eternity", *American Catholic Philosophical Quarterly* 64: 387–399.

—— (1990b) "Boethius on Eternity", *History of Philosophy Quarterly* 7: 123–142.

—— (1991a) *Time and Eternity* (Ithaca, NY: Cornell University Press).

—— (1991b) "Timelessness and Foreknowledge", *Philosophical Studies* 63: 309–325.

—— (1991c) "Eternity and Simultaneity", *Faith and Philosophy* 8: 148–179.

—— (1992) "Timelessness and Divine Experience", *Sophia* 30: 43–53.

Lehrer, Keith (1990) *Theory of Knowledge* (Boulder, CO: Westview Press).

Leibniz, Gottfried (1969) "On the Radical Origination of Things", trans. Leroy E. Loemker in *Gottfried Wilhelm Leibniz, Philosophical Papers and Letters*, 2nd edn (Dordrecht: D. Reidel), pp. 486–491.

Lewis, David (1986) "The Problem of Temporary Intrinsics", in *On the Plurality of Worlds* (Oxford: Blackwell), reprinted in Peter van Inwagen and Dean Zimmerman (eds), *Metaphysics: The Big Questions* (Malden, MA: Blackwell, 1998), pp. 204–206.

Lifton, Robert Jay (1986) *The Nazi Doctors* (New York: Basic Books).

Lisska, Anthony J. (1996) *Aquinas's Theory of Natural Law. An Analytic Reconstruction* (Oxford: Clarendon Press).

Lonergan, Bernard (1946) *Grace and Freedom: Operative Grace in the Thought of St. Thomas Aquinas*, J.P. Burns (ed.) (New York: Herder & Herder).

—— (1967) *Verbum: Word and Idea in Aquinas*, David Burrell (ed.) (Notre Dame, IN: University of Notre Dame Press)

Lynn, William D. (1962) *Christ's Redemptive Merit: The Nature of its Causality According to St. Thomas. Analecta Gregoriana* 115, Series Facultatis Theologicae (Rome: Gregorian University).

McCormack, Stephen (1944) "The Configuration of the Sacramental Character", *The Thomist* 7: 458–491.

MacDonald, Scott (1984) "The Esse/Essentia Argument in Aquinas' *De ente et essentia*", *Journal of the History of Philosophy* 22: 157–172.

—— (ed.) (1991a) *Being and Goodness: The Concept of the Good in Metaphysics and Philosophical Theology* (Ithaca, NY: Cornell University Press).

—— (1991b) "Ultimate Ends in Practical Reasoning: Aquinas' Aristotelian Moral Psychology and Anscombe's Fallacy", *The Philosophical Review* 100: 31–66.

—— (1993a) "Christian Faith", in Eleonore Stump (ed.), *Reasoned Faith* (Ithaca, NY: Cornell University Press), pp. 42–69.

—— (1993b) "Theory of Knowledge", in Norman Kretzmann and Eleonore Stump (eds), *The Cambridge Companion to Aquinas* (Cambridge: Cambridge University Press), pp. 160–195.

MacDonald, Scott and Stump, Eleonore (eds) (1999) *Aquinas's Moral Theory. Essays in Honor of Norman Kretzmann* (Ithaca, NY: Cornell University Press).

Macierowski, E. M. (1998) *Thomas Aquinas's Earliest Treatment of the Divine Essence.* (Binghamton, NY: Center for Medieval and Renaissance Studies, Binghamton University).

McInerny, Ralph (1977) *St. Thomas Aquinas* (Boston: Twayne Publishers).

—— (1981) *Rhyme and Reason: St. Thomas and Modes of Discourse* (Milwaukee: Marquette University Press).

—— (1986) *Being and Predication. Thomistic Interpretations*, Studies in Philosophy and the History of Philosophy, vol. 16 (Washington, DC: Catholic University of America Press).

—— (1990a) *Boethius and Aquinas* (Washington, DC: Catholic University of America Press).

—— (1990b) *A First Glance at St. Thomas Aquinas* (Notre Dame, IN: University of Notre Dame Press).

—— (1992) *Aquinas on Human Action* (Washington, DC: Catholic University of America Press).

—— (1993a) *Aquinas against the Averoists: On There Being Only One Intellect* (West Lafayette, IN: Purdue University Press).

—— (1993b) "Ethics", in Norman Kretzmann and Eleonore Stump (eds), *The Cambridge Companion to Aquinas* (Cambridge: Cambridge University Press), pp. 196–216.

—— (1996) *Aquinas and Analogy* (Washington, DC: Catholic University of America Press).

—— (1997) *Ethica Thomistica: The Moral Philosophy of Thomas Aquinas* (Washington, DC: Catholic University of America Press).

McLaughlin, Brian (1992) "The Rise and Fall of British Emergentism", in Ansgar Beckermann, Hans Flohr and Jaegwon Kim (eds), *Emergence or Reduction? Essays on the Prospects of Nonreductive Physicalism* (Berlin: Walter de Gruyter), pp. 49–93.

Mahoney, Edward (1982) "Sense, Intellect, and Imagination in Albert, Thomas, and Siger", in Norman Kretzmann, Anthony Kenny, Jan Pinborg (eds), assoc. ed. Eleonore Stump, *The Cambridge History of Later Medieval Philosophy* (Cambridge: Cambridge University Press).

Mann, William (1975) "The Divine Attributes", *American Philosophical Quarterly* 12: 151–159.

—— (1982) "Divine Simplicity", *Religious Studies*: 451–471.

—— (1983) "Simplicity and Immutability in God", *International Philosophical Quarterly* 23: 267–276.

Marinelli, Francesco (1977) *Segno e Realita. Studi di sacramentaria tomista* (Rome: Lateranum).

Maritain, Jacques (1942) *Saint Thomas and the Problem of Evil* (Milwaukee: Marquette University Press).

—— (1951) *Man and the State* (Chicago: University of Chicago Press).

Marrone, Steven P. (1985) *Truth and Scientific Knowledge in the Thought of Henry of Ghent* (Cambridge, MA: The Medieval Academy of America).

Martin, Christopher (ed.) (1988) *The Philosophy of Thomas Aquinas: Introductory Readings* (London: Routledge).

Meiland, Jack (1980) "What Ought We to Believe? or The Ethics of Belief Revisited", *American Philosophical Quarterly* 17: 15–24.

Miethe, T. L. and Bourke, Vernon (1980) *Thomistic Bibliography 1940–1978* (Westport, CT: Greenwood Press).

Miller, Fred (1974) "Aristotle on the Reality of Time", *Archiv für Geschichte der Philosophie* 61: 132–155.

Moore, Sebastian (1977) *The Crucified is No Stranger* (London: Darton, Longman and Todd Ltd.).

Morris, Thomas V. (1984) "The God of Abraham, Isaac, and Anselm", *Faith and Philosophy* 1: 177–187.

—— (1986) *The Logic of God Incarnate* (Ithaca, NY: Cornell University Press).

—— (1987) "The Necessity of God's Goodness", in *Anselmian Explorations: Essay in Philosophical Theology* (Notre Dame, IN: University of Notre Dame Press), pp. 42–69.

Nathan, N. M. L. (1993) "Weak Materialism", in Howard Robinson (ed.), *Objections to Physicalism* (Oxford: Clarendon Press).

Nelson, Herbert (1987) "Time(s), Eternity, and Duration", *International Journal for Philosophy of Religion* 22: 3–19.

Nussbaum, Martha C. (1992) "The Text of Aristotle's *De anima*", in Martha C. Nussbaum and Amélie O. Rorty (eds), *Essays on Aristotle's De anima* (Oxford: Clarendon Press), pp. 1–6.

O'Connor, Timothy (1994) "Emergent Properties", *American Philosophical Quarterly* 31: 91–104.

O'Leary, Joseph M (1952) *The Development of the Doctrine of St. Thomas Aquinas on the Passion and Death of Our Lord* (Chicago: J. S. Paluch Co., Inc.).

Olson, Eric (1997) *The Human Animal* (Oxford: Oxford University Press).

O'Meara, Thomas F. (1997) *Thomas Aquinas: Theologian* (Notre Dame, IN: University of Notre Dame Press).

Owen, Gwilym Ellis Lane (1966) "Plato and Parmenides on the Timeless Present", *Monist* L: 317–340.

Owens, Joseph (1980) *St. Thomas Aquinas on the Existence of God: Collected papers of Joseph Owens*, (ed.) J. Catan (Albany, NY: State University of New York Press).

—— (1986) "Aquinas' Distinction at *De ente et essentia* 4.119–123", *Mediaeval Studies* 48: 264–287.

—— (1992a) "Aristotle and Aquinas on Cognition", in Richard Bosley and Martin Tweedale (eds), *Aristotle and His Medieval Interpreters*, *Canadian Journal of Philosophy*, supplementary volume (Calgary: University of Calgary Press), pp. 103–123.

—— (1992b) *Cognition: An Epistemological Inquiry* (Houston, TX: Center for Thomistic Studies).

—— (1993) "Aristotle and Aquinas", in N. Kretzmann and E. Stump (eds), *The Cambridge Companion to Aquinas* (Cambridge: Cambridge University Press), pp. 38–59.

Parente, Pietro (1949) *De verbo incarnato*, 3rd edn (Rome: Marietti).

Pasnau, Robert (1997) *Theories of Cognition in the Later Middle Ages* (Cambridge: Cambridge University Press).

—— (2002) *Thomas Aquinas on Human Nature: A Philosophical Study of Summa theologiae 1a, 75–89* (London: Cambridge University Press).

Pegis, Anton Charles (1934) *St Thomas and the Problem of the Soul in the Thirteenth Century* (Toronto: Pontifical Institute of Mediaeval Studies).

Pernick, Martin S. (1985) *A Calculus of Suffering: Pain, Professionalism, and Anesthesia in Nineteenth Century America* (New York: Columbia University Press).

Perry, John (1979) "The Problem of the Essential Indexical", *Nous* 13: 3–21.

Peter of Spain (1972) *Tractatus*, (ed.) L.M. De Rijk (Amsterdam: Van Gorcum & Co.).

Plantinga, Alvin (1980) *Does God Have a Nature?* (Milwaukee: Marquette University Press).

—— (1983) "Reason and Belief in God", in Alvin Plantinga and Nicholas Wolterstorff (eds), *Faith and Rationality: Reason and Belief in God* (Notre Dame, IN: University of Notre Dame Press).

—— (1992) "An Evolutionary Argument Against Naturalism", *Logos* 12: 27–49.

—— (1993a) *Warrant: The Current Debate* (Oxford: Oxford University Press).

—— (1993b) *Warrant and Proper Function* (Oxford: Oxford University Press).

—— (2000) *Warranted Christian Belief* (Oxford: Oxford University Press).

Pieper, Josef (1962) *Guide to Thomas Aquinas* (Notre Dame, IN: University of Notre Dame Press).

Pike, Nelson (1969) "Omnipotence and God's Ability to Sin", *American Philosophical Quarterly* 6: 208–216.

—— (1970) *God and Timelessness* (London: Routledge and Kegan Paul).

Potts, Timothy (ed.) (1980) *Conscience in Medieval Philosophy* (Cambridge: Cambridge University Press).

Putallaz, François-Xavier (1991) *Le Sens de la Reflexion chez Thomas D'Aquin* (Paris: Librairie Philosophique J. Vrin).

Quinn, Philip (1978) *Divine Commands and Moral Requirements* (Oxford: Clarendon Press).

—— (1997) "Tiny Selves: Chisholm on the Simplicity of the Soul", in Louis E. Hahn (ed.), *Roderick M. Chisholm* (Boston: Open Court Press).

Rand, Edward Kennard (1946) *Cicero in the Courtroom of St. Thomas Aquinas* (Milwaukee: Marquette University Press).

Reith, Herman (1958) *The Metaphysics of St. Thomas Aquinas* (Milwaukee: The Bruce Publishing Company).

Riesenhuber, Klaus (1974) "The Bases and Meaning of Freedom in Thomas Aquinas", *Proceedings of the American Catholic Philosophical Association* 48: 99–111.

Rivière, Jean (1909) *The Doctrine of the Atonement: A Historical Essay*, trans. Luigi Cappadelta. (St. Louis, MO: Herder).

Robinson, Howard (ed.) (1993) *Objections to Physicalism* (Oxford: Clarendon Press).

Rock, Irvin (1987) *The Logic of Perception* (Cambridge, MA: MIT Press, Bradford Books).

Rogers, Eugene F. (1995) *Thomas Aquinas and Karl Barth: Sacred Doctrine and the Natural Knowledge of God* (Notre Dame, IN: University of Notre Dame Press).

Ross, James F. (1969) *Philosophical Theology* (Indianapolis and New York: Bobbs-Merrill).

—— (1981) *Portraying Analogy* (Cambridge: Cambridge University Press).

—— (1985) "Aquinas on Belief and Knowledge", in G. Etzkorn (ed.), *Essays Honoring Allan B. Wolter* (St. Bonaventure, NY: Franciscan Institute).

Rowe, William (1984) "Rationalistic Theology and Some Principles of Explanation", *Faith and Philosophy* 1: 357–369.

—— (1986) "The Empirical Argument from Evil", in Robert Audi and William Wainwright (eds), *Rationality, Religious Belief and Moral Commitment: New Essays in the Philosophy of Religion* (Ithaca, NY: Cornell University Press).

—— (1993) "The Problem of Divine Perfection and Freedom", in Eleonore Stump (ed.), *Reasoned Faith* (Ithaca, NY: Cornell University Press), pp. 223–233.

Salmon, Wesley C. (1975) *Space, Time, and Motion* (Encino, CA: Dickenson Publishing Company).

Schieck, Charles A. (1955) "St. Thomas on the Nature of Sacramental Grace", *The Thomist* 18: 1–30 and 242–278.

Schmaltz, Tad (1992) "Descartes and Malebranche on Mind and Mind-Body Union", *The Philosophical Review* 101: 281–325.

Schmidt, Robert W. (1966) *The Domain of Logic According to St. Thomas Aquinas* (The Hague: Martinus Nijhoff).

Schofield, Malcolm (1970) "Did Parmenides Discover Eternity?", *Archiv für Geschichte der Philosophie* 52: 113–135.

Searle, John (1992) *The Rediscovery of the Mind* (Cambridge, MA: MIT Press).

Sentis, Laurent (1992) *Saint Thomas D'Aquin et le Mal* (Paris: Beauchesne).

Sereny, Gita (1983) *Into That Darkness: An Examination of Conscience* (New York: First Vintage Books Edition).

—— (1995) *Albert Speer: His Battle with Truth* (New York: Alfred A. Knopf).

Shanley, Brian (1997) "Eternal Knowledge of the Temporal in Aquinas", *American Catholic Philosophical Quarterly* 71: 197–224.

—— (1998) "Divine Causation and Human Freedom in Aquinas", *American Catholic Philosophical Quarterly* 72: 99–122.

—— (2002) *The Thomist Tradition* (Dordrecht: Kluwer Academic Publishers).

Shoemaker, Sydney (1984) *Identity, Cause, and Mind* (Cambridge: Cambridge University Press).

Shoemaker, Sydney and Swinburne, Richard (1984) *Personal Identity* (Oxford: Basil Blackwell).

Sheppard, Anne (1991) "Phantasia and Mental Images: Neoplatonist Interpretations of *De anima*, 3.3", in Julia Annas (ed.), *Aristotle and the Later Tradition*, Oxford Studies in Ancient Philosophy, supplementary volume (Oxford: Clarendon Press), pp. 165–174.

Sigmund, P. E. (1993) "Law and Politics", in N. Kretzmann and E. Stump (eds), *The Cambridge Companion to Aquinas* (Cambridge: Cambridge University Press), pp. 217–231.

Stump, Eleonore (1979) "Petitionary Prayer", *American Philosophical Quarterly*, 16: 81–91.

—— (1983) "Hamartia in Christian Belief: Boethius on the Trinity", in Donald Stump *et al.* (eds), *Hamartia: The Concept of Error in the Western Tradition* (New York and Toronto: The Edwin Mellen Press), pp. 131–148.

—— (1985) "The Problem of Evil", *Faith and Philosophy* 2: 392–424.

—— (1988) "Sanctification, Hardening of the Heart, and Frankfurt's Concept of Free Will", *Journal of Philosophy* 85: 395–420; reprinted in John Martin Fischer and Mark Ravizza (eds), *Moral Responsibility* (Ithaca, NY: Cornell University Press, 1993), pp. 211–234.

—— (1989a) *Dialectic and Its Place in the Development of Medieval Logic* (Ithaca, NY: Cornell University Press).

—— (1989b) "Review of Thomas Morris's *The Logic of God Incarnate*", *Faith and Philosophy* 6: 218–223.

—— (1990a) "Providence and the Problem of Evil", in Thomas Flint (ed.), *Christian Philosophy* (Notre Dame, IN: University of Notre Dame Press), pp. 51–91.

—— (1990b) "Intellect, Will, and the Principle of Alternate Possibilities", in Michael Beaty (ed.), *Christian Theism and the Problems of Philosophy* (Notre Dame, IN: University of Notre Dame Press), pp. 254–285. Reprinted in John Martin Fischer and Mark Ravizza (eds), *Moral Responsibility* (Ithaca, NY: Cornell University Press, 1993), pp. 237–262.

—— (1992) "Aquinas on the Foundations of Knowledge", *Canadian Journal of Philosophy*, supp. vol. 17: 125–158.

—— (1993a) "Aquinas on the Sufferings of Job", in E. Stump (ed.) *Reasoned Faith* (Ithaca, NY: Cornell University Press), pp. 328–357.

—— (1993b) "Biblical Commentary and Philosophy", in N. Kretzmann and E. Stump (eds), *The Cambridge Companion to Aquinas* (Cambridge: Cambridge University Press), pp. 252–268.

—— (1993c) "Intellect, Will, and Alternate Possibilities", reprinted in John Martin Fischer and Mark Ravizza (eds), *Perspectives on Moral Responsibility* (Ithaca, NY: Cornell University Press), pp. 237–262.

—— (1996a) "Libertarian Freedom", in Daniel Howard-Snyder and Jeff Jordan (eds), *Faith, Freedom, and Rationality: Philosophy of Religion Today* (Lanham, MD: Rowman and Littlefield), pp. 73–88.

—— (1996b) "Persons: Identification and Freedom", *Philosophical Topics* 24: 183–214.

—— (1999a) "Ockham on Sensory Cognition", in Paul Spade (ed.), *The Cambridge Companion to Ockham* (Cambridge: Cambridge University Press), pp. 168–203.

—— (1999b) "Word and Incarnation", in Marco Olivetti (ed.), *Incarnation* (Padua: Edam), pp. 543–554.

—— (1999c) "Alternative Possibilities and Moral Responsibility: The Flicker of Freedom", *The Journal of Ethics*, 3: 299–324.

—— (2000) "Transfer Principles and Moral Responsibility" (with John Martin Fischer), *Philosophical Perspectives*, 14: 47–55.

—— (2001) "Augustine on Free Will", in Eleonore Stump and Norman Kretzmann (eds), *The Cambridge Companion to Augustine* (Cambridge: Cambridge University Press), pp. 124–147.

—— (forthcoming) "Moral Responsibility without Alternative Possibilities", in David Widerker and Michael McKenna (eds), *Moral Responsibility and Alternative Possibilities* (Aldershot: Ashgate Press).

Stump, Eleonore and Kretzmann, Norman (1988) "Being and Goodness", in T.V. Morris (ed.), *Divine and Human Action* (Ithaca, NY: Cornell University Press), pp. 281–312.

—— (1992) "Eternity, Awareness, and Action", *Faith and Philosophy* 9: 463–482.

—— (1998) "Eternity and God's Knowledge: A Reply to Shanley", *The American Catholic Philosophical Quarterly* 72: 439–445.

Stump, Eleonore and MacDonald, Scott (eds) (1998) *Aquinas's Moral Theory: Essays in Honor of Norman Kretzmann* (Ithaca, NY: Cornell University Press).

Swinburne, Richard (1979) *The Existence of God* (Oxford: Clarendon Press).

—— (1986) *The Evolution of the Soul* (Oxford: Clarendon Press).

—— (1993) "God and Time", in Eleonore Stump (ed.), *Reasoned Faith* (Ithaca, NY: Cornell University Press), pp. 204–222.

Tachau, Katharine (1982) "The Problem of the *species in medio* at Oxford in the Generation after Ockham", *Mediaeval Studies* 44: 394–443.

—— (1988) *Vision and Certitude in the Age of Ockham: Optics, Epistemology and the Foundations of Semantics 1250–1345* (Leiden: E. J. Brill).

Tilley, Terrence W. (1991) *The Evils of Theodicy* (Washington, DC: Georgetown University Press).

Tomarchio, John (1996) "The Modus Principle in the Writings of Saint Thomas Aquinas", dissertation, The Catholic University of America, Washington, DC.

Torrell, Jean-Pierre O. P. (1993) *Initiation à Saint Thomas d'Aquin: Sa Personne et son Oeuvre* (Introduction to Saint Thomas Aquinas: His Character and His Work) (Fribourg and Paris: Éditions Universitaires and Éditions du Cerf). Translated as

Saint Thomas Aquinas. The Person and his Work, vol. 1, trans. Robert Royal (Washington, DC: Catholic University of America Press).

Tugwell, Simon (1988) *Albert and Thomas: Selected Writings*, The Classics of Western Spirituality (Mahwah, NJ: Paulist Press).

Tuninetti, Luca (1996) *"Per se notum". Die logische Beschaffenheit des Selbstverständlichen im Denken des Thomas von Aquin* (Leiden: E. J. Brill).

Tweedale, Martin (1990) "Mental Representation in Later Medieval Scholasticism", in J. C. Smith (ed.), *Historical Foundations of Cognitive Science* (Dordrecht: Kluwer Academic Publishers), pp. 35–52.

Van Engen, John (1988) *Devotio Moderna: Basic Writings* (New York: Paulist Press).

Van Fraassen, Bas (1984). "Belief and the Will", *The Journal of Philosophy* 81: 235–256.

Van Inwagen, Peter (1978) "The Possibility of Resurrection", *The International Journal for Philosophy of Religion* 9: 114–121.

—— (1983) *An Essay in Free Will* (Oxford: Clarendon Press).

—— (1988) "And Yet There Are Not Three Gods But One God", in Thomas V. Morris (ed.), *Philosophy and the Christian Faith* (Notre Dame, IN: The University of Notre Dame Press), pp. 241–278.

—— (1990) *Material Beings* (Ithaca, NY: Cornell University Press).

—— (1994a) "Composition as Identity", in James Tomberlin (ed.), *Philosophical Perspectives*, vol. 8 (Atascadero, CA: Ridgeview Publishing Co.), pp. 207–219.

—— (1994b) "Not by Confusion of Substance, but by Unity of Person", in A.G. Padgett (ed.), *Reason and the Christian Religion: Essays in Honour of Richard Swinburne* (Oxford: Clarendon Press).

—— (1999) "Incarnation and Christology", *The Routledge Encyclopedia of Philosophy* (London: Routledge).

Van Riet, Georges (1965) *Thomistic Epistemology*, vols 1–2. Trans. Donald G. McCarthy and George E. Hertrich. (St. Louis: B. Herder Book Co.).

Van Steenberghen, F. (1980a) *Le problème de l'existence de Dieu dans les écrits de S. Thomas d'Aquin* (Louvain-la-Neuve: Editions de l'Institut Supérieur de Philosophie).

—— (1980b) *Thomas Aquinas and Radical Aristotelianism* (Washington, DC: Catholic University of America Press).

Velde, Roelf Arend te (1995) *Participation and Substantiality in Thomas Aquinas* (Leiden: E. J. Brill).

Watson, Gary (1975) "Free Agency", *Journal of Philosophy* 72: 205–220.

Weisheipl, James (1983) *Friar Thomas D'Aquino: His Life, Thought, and Works* (Washington, DC: Catholic University of America Press).

Westberg, Daniel (1994a) *Right Practical Reason: Aristotle, Action, and Prudence in Aquinas* (Oxford: Clarendon Press).

—— (1994b) "Did Aquinas Change His Mind about the Will?", *The Thomist* 58: 41–60.

Widerker, David (1995a) "Libertarian Freedom and the Avoidability of Decisions", *Faith and Philosophy* 12: 113–118.

—— (1995b) "Libertarianism and Frankfurt's Attack on the Principle of Alternative Possibilities", *The Philosophical Review* 104: 247–261.

Wierenga, Edward (1983) "Omnipotence Defined", *Philosophy and Phenomenological Research* 43: 363–376.

Williams, Bernard (1973) *Problems of the Self* (New York: Cambridge University Press).

Wilson, Margaret (1978) *Descartes* (London: Routledge and Kegan Paul).

Winters, Barbara (1979) "Willing to Believe", *The Journal of Philosophy* 76: 243–256.

Wippel, John F. (1984) *Metaphysical Themes in Thomas Aquinas* (Washington, DC: Catholic University of America Press).

—— (1987) "Thomas Aquinas and Participation", in J.F. Wippel (ed.) *Studies in Medieval Philosophy* (Washington, DC: Catholic University of America Press).

—— (1989) "Truth in Thomas Aquinas (part I)", *Review of Metaphysics* 43: 295–326.

—— (1990) "Truth in Thomas Aquinas (part II)", *Review of Metaphysics* 43: 543–567.

—— (1993) "Metaphysics", in N. Kretzmann and E. Stump (eds) *The Cambridge Companion to Aquinas* (Cambridge: Cambridge University Press), pp. 85–127.

—— (2000) *The Metaphysical Thought of Thomas Aquinas. From Finite Being to Uncreated Being* (Washington, DC: Catholic University of America Press).

Wolf, Susan (1980) "Asymmetric Freedom", *Journal of Philosophy* 77: 151–166.

Wolterstorff, Nicholas (1975) "God Everlasting", in Clifton J. Orlebeke and Lewis B. Smedes (eds), *God and the Good* (Grand Rapids, MI: Eerdmans), pp. 181–203.

—— (1984) *Reason Within the Bounds of Religion* (Grand Rapids, MI: Eerdmans).

—— (1986) "The Migration of the Theistic Arguments: From Natural Theology to Evidentialist Apologetics", in Robert Audi and William Wainwright (eds), *Rationality and Religious Belief* (Ithaca, NY: Cornell University Press), pp. 38–81.

—— (1991) "Divine Simplicity", in James E. Tomberlin (ed.), *Philosophical Perspectives, 5: Philosophy of Religion, 1991* (Atascadero, CA: Ridgeview Publishing Company).

—— (1992) "Divine Simplicity", in Kelly James Clark (ed.), *Our Knowledge of God: Essays in Natural and Philosophical Theology* (Dordrecht and Boston: Kluwer Academic Publishers), pp. 133–150.

Yablo, Stephen (1990) "The Real Distinction Between Mind and Body", *The Canadian Journal of Philosophy*, supplementary volume 16: 149–201.

—— (1992) "Mental Causation", *The Philosophical Review* 101: 245–280.

Zagzebski, Linda (1996) *Virtues of the Mind* (Cambridge: Cambridge University Press).

Zimmermann, Albert (1965) *Ontologie oder Metaphysik? Die Diskussion über den Gegenstand der Metaphysik im 13. und 14. Jahrhundert* (Ontology or Metaphysics? The Discussion of the Object of Metaphysics in the Thirteenth and Fourteenth Centuries) (Leiden: E. J. Brill).

Zimmerman, Dean (1998) "Temporary Intrinsics and Presentism", in Peter van Inwagen and Dean Zimmerman (eds), *Metaphysics: The Big Questions* (Malden, MA: Blackwell), pp. 206–219.

INDEX